SOURCEBOOK ON THE ENGLISH LEGAL SYSTEM

Second Edition

Gary Slapper, LLB, LLM, PhD, PGCE (Law)
Director of the Law Programme, The Open University

David Kelly, BA, BA(Law), PhD
Principal Lecturer in Law, Staffordshire University

Cavendish
Publishing
Limited

London • Sydney

Second edition first published in Great Britain 2001 by Cavendish Publishing Limited, The Glass House, Wharton Street, London WC1X 9PX, United Kingdom

Telephone: +44 (0)20 7278 8000   Facsimile: +44 (0)20 7278 8080

Email: info@cavendishpublishing.com

Website: www.cavendishpublishing.com

British Library Cataloguing in Publication Data

Slapper, Gary
Sourcebook on English legal system – 2nd ed
1 Law – England 2 Law – Wales
I Title II Kelly, David III English legal system
347. 4'2

ISBN 1 85941 553 9

Printed and bound in Great Britain

PREFACE

A good comprehension of the English legal system requires knowledge and skill in a number of disciplines. The system itself is the result of developments in law, economy, politics, sociological change, and the theories which feed all these bodies of knowledge. A detailed knowledge of several areas of law is indispensable but students are also expected to appreciate the historical development of many legal institutions, and the social and political debates which surround legal issues.

The aim of this book is to provide a richness of diverse materials from which the structure, operation, objectives, and problems of the English legal system can be appreciated. To this end we have drawn on committee reports, Green Papers, White Papers, legislation, case decisions, academic and professional articles, and the thoughts and criticisms of all types of commentators.

It is important to understand the legal theory which is behind policies on matters as diverse as the law relating to arrest, search and seizure; the distribution of work amongst different types of court; the structure of legal services; judicial review of administrative discretion; the operation of the doctrines of precedent and statutory interpretation; plea bargaining, contingency fees and public funding. Being proficient in this subject also means being familiar with contemporary changes and proposed changes. This text, therefore, includes such materials.

During the last five years the legal system has undergone major and comprehensive changes. The Access to Justice Act 1999 has led to the establishment of the Legal Services Commission and the Community Legal Service, and has re-drawn the legal landscape. The 1998 Civil Procedure Rules came into force in 1999 and have been amended and updated 21 times since – the rules revolutionise the way that people make civil claims and the way in which the courts deal with them.

The Human Rights Act 1998 came into force in October 2000, and has already begun to ramify into virtually all aspects of law, and thus how the legal system operates. To prepare for it, the judiciary underwent the most comprehensive and detailed formal training in its entire thousand-year history.

Other changes abound: the Auld Committee has undertaken a root and branch review of the criminal justice system. The Crown Prosecution Service has been re-organised, the nature of judicial impartiality has been authoritatively defined, the role of the jury has been exposed to intense public and legal debate, liability of advocates for courtroom negligence has been established, the appeals system has been altered, alternative dispute resolution has become a major feature of British life, and European law has continued to widen and deepen its application.

The second edition of this text incorporates all of these changes. In the selection of materials, our aim has been to provide literature not just of official, declaratory and expository sorts, but also that which helps in the understanding of law in its social, economic and philosophic contexts.

Gary Slapper
David Kelly
September 2001

ACKNOWLEDGMENTS

Grateful acknowledgment is made for permission to reproduce the following:

Burnett-Hitchcock, J, 'Class action' (1995) *Law Society Gazette*, 22 November

The Guardian: Lord Donaldson, 'Beware this abuse', 4 April 1995; H Young, 'Justice being seen to be done', 7 May 1996; H Young, 'Choosing a chief for the judges', 9 May 1996

Floyer Acland, A, 'Simply negotiation with knobs on', Legal Action, November 1995

Gillard, M, 'Why fraud juries need help' (1994) *The Observer*, 30 October

Hayek, FA, *Road to Serfdom*, 1962, London: Routledge

Thompson, EP, 'The rule of law', in *Whigs and Hunters*, 1977, London: Penguin

Jackson, B, *Making Sense in Law: Linguistic, Psychological and Semiotic Perspectives*, 1995, Liverpool: Deborah Charles

Sir Stephen Sedley, 'The future of advocacy', the Lord Morris Memorial Lecture, Cardiff University, 28 September 1999

'What is mediation?', produced by the registered charity Mediation UK

Robins, J, 'What is the real price of justice' (2001)*The Independent*, 9 January

Young, R and Saunders, A, *Criminal Justice*, London: Butterworths

Kairys, D, *The Politics of Law: A Progressive Critique*, 1982, New York: Pantheon

T StJ Bates, 'The contemporary use of legislative history in the United Kingdom' (1995) 54(1) CLJ 127

Grateful acknowledgment is also made to the Controller of Her Majesty's Stationery Office for permission to reproduce Crown Copyright materials; to the Lord Chancellor's Department and the Law Commission for various materials; to Butterworths for permission to reproduce extracts from the *New Law Journal* and *Counsel*; to Sweet & Maxwell for permission to reproduce extracts from the *Criminal Law Review*, *Public Law* and the *Law Quarterly Review*; to Blackwell Publishers for permission to reproduce extracts from *Journal of Law and Society*, *The Howard Journal of Criminal Justice* and *Ratio Juris*; to *Solicitors Journal*; and to the Incorporated Council of Law Reporting for England and Wales for permission to reproduce extracts from the *Law Reports* and *Weekly Law Reports*.

Every effort has been made to trace all the copyright holders but if any have been inadvertently overlooked the publishers will be pleased to make the necessary arrangement at the first opportunity.

Once again we are indebted to the patience of encouragement of Suzanne, Jane, Hannah, Emily, Charlotte and Michael. Great thanks are due to Jo Reddy, Sonny Leong, Cara Annett, Jon Lloyd and Ruth Massey at Cavendish. In various ways their ideas, encouragement and skill have contributed substantially to this book. Thanks also to Frances Gibb, Legal Editor at *The Times*, for her constant critical elucidation of the legal system. A great debt also to Doreen and Ivor Slapper, David and Julie Whight, Matthew Weait, Raie Schwartz, Alison Morris and Hugh McLaughlan.

CONTENTS

TABLE OF CASES

TABLE OF STATUTES

TABLE OF STATUTORY INSTRUMENTS

CHAPTER 1

LAW, THE LEGAL SYSTEM AND THE RULE OF LAW

INTRODUCTION

This book is concerned with the institutions and procedures, both civil and criminal, through which law operates to ensure a particular form of social order. It starts from the clear premise that law is inherently a political institution and must be studied in that light. Law and, indeed, social order are not given, although we sometimes take them for granted. Social order has to be continuously created and recreated and law is one mechanism through which social order is established. The point behind this contention is the fact that law is a social construct; as such, it is challengeable and open to change: it is not an unchangeable given or an immutable system. Law is then about choice, but this raises the question as to who makes the choices that are embodied in law and, further, who or what gives those who make the choices the right to do so and to what extent are they accountable for those decisions.

As stated in G Slapper and D Kelly, *The English Legal System*, 5th edn, 2001, London: Cavendish Publishing, Chapter 1:

> Law is a formal mechanism of social control and as such it is essential that the student of law be fully aware of the nature of that formal structure. There are, however, other aspects to law that are less immediately apparent but of no less importance such as the inescapable political nature of law. Some textbooks focus more on this particular aspect of law than others and these differences become evident in the particular approach adopted by the authors. The approach favoured by the authors of this book is to recognise that studying the English legal system is not just about learning legal rules but is also about considering a social institution of fundamental importance.

The cases and materials that have been selected for consideration have been chosen with the above objects in mind.

LEGAL LANGUAGE

Common law refers to the substantive law and procedural rules that have been created by the judiciary through the decisions in the cases they have heard. Statute law refers to law that has been created by Parliament in the form of legislation. There has been a significant increase in statute law in the 20th century which continues into the present century, but the courts still have an important role to play in creating and operating law. Judges retain the power to develop the common law to fit new situations in line with contemporary social attitudes and practices, but, equally, they have the power to create law through determining the meaning and operation of legislation. How these aspects of judicial creativity work in practice will be considered in detail in Chapter 2, below, but for the moment it is necessary to focus attention on a difficulty that is shared by both common law and statute law and which permits scope for such judicial creativity.

Legal sources, whether previous cases or statutes, do not simply speak for themselves. They have to be actively created through interpretation. A key attribute of language is its essential fluidity; words can have more than one meaning and the particular meaning to be attributed to a word depends on the context in which it is used. Law suffers from the general difficulties inherent in making sense of any linguistic communication, but it also suffers from the particular problem of what some have described as deliberate obscurantism and poor drafting. In Chapter 4 of Bernard Jackson's *Making Sense in Law* (footnotes omitted), he considers the problems that arise in relation to legal language.

Bernard Jackson, *Making Sense in Law*, 1995, Liverpool: Deborah Charles

Dimensions of legal languages

Where law is expressed in writing, we must expect it to display the characteristics of the written word (as opposed to speech) in addition to features particular to legal writing. It will not be constrained by the limits of memory in processing speech, and so will tolerate more lists than would speech. It will be more 'autoglottic' and less dependent for its meaning upon the context in which it is known to have originated. Because of the possibility of 'backward scanning', greater complexity and precision may be sought than is possible in speech, or at least in a more concise form than is possible in intelligible speech.

Written legal language may be considered a particular register of the 'grapholect': it shares the grammar of the 'standard' form of the language and is capable of utilising any part of its lexicon – a lexicon far more extensive than that normally used in speech. Nevertheless, law's adherence to the grapholect places constraints upon it, since the grapholect includes rules regarding the appropriateness of language: some words permissible in speech may not be used in writing.

Writing can, of course, be used for a huge variety of purposes, ranging from intimate, personal communication (in private correspondence), to the heights of aesthetics (poetry, etc), to the publication of scientific research and the archiving of official knowledge. Legal writing is capable of a similar range – correspondence between solicitors and clients (and between the opposing solicitors) regarding a case; briefs to counsel; counsel's opinions; court orders; judgments; student textbooks; professional manuals; research articles; private legal documents (themselves serving a variety of purposes: wills, settlements, contracts, conveyances, leases, etc); primary legislation (Act of Parliament); secondary legislation (statutory instruments, local authority byelaws, etc). We lack detailed comparisons of these various forms of legal writing, but many of them would assuredly emerge as sufficiently distinctive to merit being regarded as a 'genre' (s 1).

In so far as linguists have analysed written legal documents, they have tended to concentrate upon primary legislation and private legal documents (particularly contracts). It was in this latter context that Crystal and Davy strikingly remarked:

> To speak of legal language as communicating meaning is in itself rather misleading. Of all the uses of language it is perhaps the least communicative, in that it is designed not so much to enlighten language-users at large as to allow one expert to register information for scrutiny by another.

In other words, much legal writing of this kind is 'archival': to put certain information (here normative information, consisting in the rights and obligations of the parties to the contract) 'on the record' as having been agreed, in case it should ever need to be retrieved and used in the future. The object of this type of legal document thus goes far beyond the provision of information required for immediate use. It seeks rather to register in advance what should occur in all types of future contingency, however unlikely they may be. Unlike literary writing, where meanings may frequently be 'deferred' (left to be negotiated in the future), it is a characteristic of the private legal document that it claims to be able now to register the future as existing information.

Where legal writing is used for archival purposes it will frequently be at the price of immediate intelligibility. Yet the characteristics of legal writing are not definitive of sense construction in law. Morison and Leith have made a powerful case for the 'oral nature of law'. Despite the fact that the rules are committed to writing, they argue, the law in practice consists in the ways in which lawyers talk about it, and negotiate its meanings through such talk. Perhaps consideration of the features of written law has a rather restricted importance, as describing no more than the symbolic form in which the law seeks to describe itself and present itself to the public? The matter, however, is more complicated than this. We have considered the view of Ong that 'writing restructures consciousness', including the claim that even in literate cultures, there remains an 'oral residue'. If writing does indeed restructure consciousness, then it must also have an effect upon forms of speech: those whose consciousness has been sufficiently restructured by writing will tend to talk as they write, rather than write as they talk. To the extent, therefore, that lawyers are trained to use a particular genre of written legal language their conversation cannot fail but to be influenced also. It will not, of course, become merely a spoken version of legalese, but it may be sufficiently affected to impede communication with those who still write as they talk, rather than talk as they write.

The archival character of what is often taken to be typical legal language is not the only source of its unintelligibility. In s 1.3, we noted a number of characteristics of legal semantics: the use of foreign, uncommon, and archaic words; the presence of common words with uncommon meanings; the organisation of meanings by 'hyponymy' rather than opposition. We should not assume that these characteristics are found equally within all genres of legal language. There remains, however, an underlying problem which is common: only the expert user of the language will know when terms are used in a monosomic, exclusively legal way, or when the attribution of a meaning from ordinary language (or, at least, the grapholect) is permissible.

Observers of the style of legal documents do not find only legalese. While they note, in general, that the style of legal documents tends towards the explicit, the comprehensive, the impersonal (the use of the third person: 'whoever', 'a person who ...'), the use of traditional forms, and even to the complete absence of colour and humanity, some have also found elements of poetisation, such as the use of assonance (repetition of vowel patterns), alliteration (repetition of initial consonantal patterns), rhyme, rhythm, phonetic contrast, and end-weight. The witness oath currently in use in English courts may serve as an example: 'I swear by Almighty God that the evidence I shall give shall be the truth, the whole truth and nothing but the truth.' Such rhetorical devices function, it is argued, as forms of closure, providing a psychologically gratifying sense of completion and coherence (we may compare the 'peroration' of a speech, or the climax or coda of a symphony). Why, we may ask, should this be psychologically satisfying? Danet answers in terms of what she calls the 'magic flute' syndrome:

> Ordered sound (or signs) provides a temporary ordering of experience, with lasting consequences for the ordering of behaviour and the perception of order in experience. Thus the ordering of what can be controlled is substituted for the ordering of what cannot.

In the context of legislation, a well-structured statute serves to create the illusion of control over a form of behaviour that cannot be ordered. One might interpret such features as structure and poetisation as ideological devices, designed to create a false impression of control. Danet, however, rejects any conspiracy theory. Though poetisation has the effect of *'thickening'* the language thus increasing the sense of its importance and power, it is an *intuitive* mobilisation of the resources of language a form of what was described above) as 'natural rhetoric'.

The 'Plain English' movement

Interest in those features of legal language which inhibit its intelligibility to the general public (and, it should be said, sometimes to lawyers themselves) does not (unsurprisingly) derive primarily from the concerns of lawyers themselves or from the interests of legal scholars. It has arisen largely from the concerns of the consumer movement, aided by the research of sociolinguists and psycholinguists. It seeks, in particular, to combat those features of legal language which psycholinguistic research has shown to be associated with difficulties of comprehension. Why psycholinguists? Because comprehension is a cognitive, and not merely a linguistic problem. As Lloyd-Bostock puts it: 'Comprehension is closely linked to perception and memory. Anything that slows down these processes by adding extra cognitive work (such as unfamiliar words) makes language more difficult to understand.'

For the consumer movement, the client is a customer who has rights in respect of the legal services being purchased. Those rights include a 'right to understand'. Despite this clear goal, some have complained that there are no clear criteria for what is Plain English. Redish defines it as '... writing that is straightforward, that reads as if it were spoken. It means writing that is unadorned with archaic, multisyllabic words and majestic turns of phrase ... Plain English is clear, direct and simple'.

If Plain English must, indeed, read as if it were spoken, then one may wonder, on the argument advanced in the last section, whether lawyers are capable of writing it. As for other criteria, they are either negative (what Plain English should not be) or vague. Nevertheless, tests of rewriting legal documents into Plain English have shown considerable degrees of improvement in comprehension. A particularly elaborate experiment was conducted by the Charrows in the United States. Potential jurors were asked to paraphrase each of 14 standard civil jury instructions. The instruction was presented in each case on audio tape, played twice, and the paraphrase was also requested orally, and taped. The jury instructions were then rewritten to eliminate those items and constructions which had appeared to present problems of comprehension, and the paraphrase task was repeated on the rewritten instructions with new subjects. Significant overall improvement was found for the modified instructions and, in the process, those specific linguistic features of jury instructions which interfered with the layperson's understanding of legal language were identified. The Charrows claim that some, at least, of these features are recurring elements also in other genres of legal language.

The Plain English movement has attracted notable institutional support in a number of countries, especially Australia and the United States. President Carter issued two executive orders calling for Plain English in Federal Regulations, and the Document Design Center in Washington offers workshops in Plain English to federal agencies. A number of States have legislation requiring the use of Plain English in certain types of consumer transactions. Responding to consumer pressure, American businesses have, increasingly, been seeking the services of professional document designers: Plain English has come to be seen as 'good business' (though, in Britain, the Plain English Campaign has commented that 'Unfortunately, lawyers are rarely asked to write Plain English by the people who pay their bills'). The first insurance policy in Plain English was issued in Australia in 1976 and most Australian insurance companies have followed suit. In Britain, the National Consumer Council supported the establishment in 1979 of a Plain English Campaign and, in 1986, the Campaign published a history and guide to the use of Plain English. Some government departments and public utilities in the United Kingdom now appear more responsive to Plain English and, on 1 July 1995, the Unfair Terms in Consumer Contracts Regulations 1994 (implementing a European Commission directive) came into force, requiring that: 'A seller or supplier shall ensure that any written term of a contract is expressed in plain, intelligible language.' However, as Bhatia observes, though the Plain English movement has had 'tremendous' achievements in respect of commercial and administrative documents, including insurance policies, residential leases, tax return forms and social benefit claim forms, it has not been able to soften the attitude of parliamentary draftsmen in respect of legislative provisions.

It is not difficult to understand why legislation has been resistant. Plain English is premised on a claim that the object of the document is indeed to communicate to the layperson; if it is not, the sender can hardly be expected to comply. Legislation is pre-eminently a genre of legal document designed to allow one expert (in this instance, the parliamentary draftsman) to register information for scrutiny by other experts (lawyers, judges). Also, there is a fear of compromising legal certainty and the rights which go with it. In the United Kingdom, the Renton Committee on the Preparation of Legislation commented:

> Ordinary language relies upon the good offices of the reader to fill in omissions and give the sense intended to words or expressions capable of more than one meaning. It can afford to do this. In legal writing, on the other hand, not least in statutory writing, a primary objective is certainty of legal effect, and the United Kingdom legislature tends to prize this objective exceptionally highly.

A further fear, rarely as directly articulated, relates to the perceived authority of the law. Reduction in the formality of its language – including those features described by Danet as poetisation – might compromise the 'majesty' of law. Bhatia puts much the same argument in terms of genre: after simplification, he argues, '... the resulting text tends either to obscure or even lose the generic integrity of the original'. For legislation, at least, he prefers a two document solution. A final argument which, if correct, would affect all Plain English activities is that what impedes comprehension is not the language, but the legal concepts expressed by the language. The Charrows report a widespread belief to this affect amongst lawyers, but their own research indicated that the greater the apparent conceptual difficulty, the greater the improvement when the instruction was rewritten.

The particular problem of legislation

We have observed already the greater resistance of statutory language to Plain English than private legal documents. Not all lawyers have been complacent about the problem. The Renton Committee on the Preparation of Legislation observed: 'To the ordinary citizen the provisions of the statute book might sometimes as well be written in a foreign language for all the help he may expect to obtain there as to his rights and duties under the law.'

Yet, linguists have shown both understanding of the problems and appreciation of the results. In the common law tradition, at least, legislation seeks '... to attain if possible to a degree of precision which a person reading in bad faith cannot misunderstand. It is all the better if he cannot pretend to misunderstand it'.

As Hoey argues, the statute is written with awareness of potential court room contexts about its meaning, and with a concern to avoid such litigation. Its writer has to assume an 'unco-operative' reader:

> The point being made here is that the apparently convoluted syntax of legislative language is a product of the uncooperative reading it will encounter. Whereas normally a reader will supply the omissions in what an author has written, in a statute the writer has to supply all the omissions for him or herself, since not only will the reader not supply them but he or she will actively seek to capitalise on their existence.

Though the Gricean 'co-operative principle' was formulated in respect of face to face conversations, it is also useful for the analysis of written language. One aspect of it says, '... do not make your contribution more informative than is required'. But 'than is required' requires us to consider the particular purpose of the communication. The statute writer may argue that this form of drafting is, indeed, no more informative than is required, given the manner in which the drafting is likely to be used in court. It would be quite different if reliance could be placed, in the words of the Renton Committee, on 'the good offices of the reader' – if, that is, the reader were assumed to be 'co-operative', endowed with knowledge of the purpose of the legislation, and desirous of complying with its spirit.

Contemporary drafting makes no such assumption. In order to combat 'the age-old human capacity to wriggle out of obligations and to stretch rights to unexpected limits', it becomes necessary for legislation to cover every possible contingency, but this goal of 'all-inclusiveness', as Bhatia argues, is almost incompatible with clarity and even precision. Nevertheless, the linguist Bowers concludes his study of Canadian legislation with a very positive evaluation:

> ... as a particularly important instance of public composition, statutory expression should, and generally did, in its language and form, maintain and promote the standard written form of English as an instrument of broad expressiveness and wide accessibility.

> Statutes written since the middle of the nineteenth century have largely avoided excessive pomposity, tedious cataloguing, and private jargon, maintaining a style that is formal enough for the serious purpose of a public Act yet not remote from the ordinary written usage of standard English.

Underlying these remarks, there appears to lurk a normative conception of the grapholect: standard written English is taken to be widely accessible because it ought generally to be understood. Perhaps this begs the question of whose English standard English is conceived to be. Bowers may be correct to claim that much statutory language ought, with just a bit of effort, to be accessible to the well- (university?-) educated. But the linguistic community whose conduct is regulated by legislation extends far more widely than this.

Any judgment that statutory language is 'not remote from the ordinary written usage of standard English' would appear, at least as regards UK legislation, to ignore many of the features discussed above and, particularly, those relating to style. There is no unique and exclusive way of achieving the aims of legislative drafting, but, in seeking to do, so any legal system is likely to develop a particular drafting tradition. As Bhatia puts it:

> ... the concern of the specialist community for clarity, precision, unambiguity and all-inclusiveness has been taken rather too far in some cases. Legislative writing has generated its own tradition and the style of legal documents has become firmly standardised. Legal draftsmen thus become 'comfortable' with tried, tested and time-honoured linguistic expressions and style of writing over a period of time. Each subsequent generation of parliamentary draftsmen is trained by the preceding one while on the job.

In short, a self-perpetuating sense of familiarity develops within the cadre of draftsmen, such that the familiar style is sensed as 'the' right and appropriate one. This tradition is perceived by the non-specialist in very different terms:

> ... to the non-specialist this is a mere ploy to promote solidarity between members of the specialist community, and to keep non-specialists at a respectable distance. It is, therefore, regarded by them as linguistic nonsense that is pompous, verbose, flabby and circumlocutory.

Do such perceptions, one might wonder, derive solely from the sense of the language, or do they reflect also popular images of the users of the language (as pompous, verbose and flabby)? Bhatia, for one, sees the truth as lying somewhere in between the internal and external views. He proposes two strategies. The first entails moderate reform of the nature of statutory language (he calls it 'easification' rather than 'simplification'): reduction in proviso-clauses and syntactic discontinuities, more frequent inclusion of statements of purpose (as proposed by the Renton Committee), the addition of (non-formative) illustrations and shorter sentences linked by more cross-references. The second may be described as the 'two document solution'. We should recognise that there are two distinct and irreconcilable audiences for legislation '... each of whom has a very different background knowledge and different motivations for reading and understanding the document. The two versions, therefore, represent two different genres'. We should, therefore, seek to produce popular (non-normative) versions in plain language for the lay audience, as has been attempted by the Law Reform Commission of Victoria.

Bhatia compares the practices of scientific publication, where, '... there is a fairly well-established tradition to produce two different versions of scientific reports, one for fellow scientists and the other for popular consumption by science enthusiasts'. But, this only throws the problem into relief. The object in the statutory context is hardly to produce a version for 'popular consumption by law enthusiasts', but rather for people whose lives will be affected by the accuracy of their understanding of the law. The problem of the ideological pretensions of the Rule of Law will not go away by production of documents stating the 'gist' of legislation. The popular audience which relies on such documents is no less engaged in a game whose rules it does not know than when it relies on lawyers and *ex post facto* court judgments.

Presentational issues

The sense of the written word is a function of two separate elements, the language used and the printed appearance of the language. Most of the discussion of legal documents focuses upon the former. But the latter, too, has a not inconsiderable importance. Legal tradition has developed conventions as much for the style of print as for the language used in it. Plain English campaigns against the use of 'small print' even when the language is clear. But the size of print is not the only design feature which can influence intelligibility.

Psychologists have found, for example, that readers find it easier to read print that is set with equal, rather than variable, spacing between words.

Punctuation itself is said to have originated as a guide to the oral reading of written documents (such as proclamations). Until recently, statutes were not punctuated and, even now, the courts are reluctant to attach significance to punctuation. The legal tradition has been one of unadorned, linear text. Such visual aids to presentation as indentation (for example, to highlight the logical structure of paragraphs) are relatively recent innovations. Bhatia indicates that we can go much further in the use of non-linear alternatives to prose, such as logical trees or flow-charts, list structures and tabulated presentations.

The use of such techniques deploys the resources of the vertical as well as the horizontal dimension of the printed page. But the written document remains restricted to those two dimensions. With the aid of modern information technology, we are now able to add a third dimension, that of the 'depth' (layers of text) present with 'hypertext' documents. Hypertext software has been marketed as a means to deliver alternative versions of text, each designed for a different audience (for example, business presentations with levels both for the generalist and the expert). In principle, this type of technique may be just what is needed in order to solve the problem of the two audiences for legislation. Not only is it capable of delivering different versions for the different audiences; it can do so in an integrated form, so that it is possible to move from one to the other and see exactly how they are related. This may prove as useful for the legal expert as for the layperson: the former has access to the manner in which the public is likely to understand the legislation; the latter is able to see the legal basis from which the popular version is derived and exercise an independent (but here guided) judgment on its accuracy. As well as hypertext, information technology can provide further aids to intelligibility – expert system assistance, voice annotations and multi-media presentations.

THE NATURE OF JUDICIAL INTERPRETATION

Taking up the idea that judicial interpretation of statutes and cases is an active process, Lawrence M Friedman raises the possibility that legal interpretation is not concerned with what a text really means, in any literal sense; and standards for judging legal interpretation are different from the standards of judging other forms of communication, such as literature. Indeed, he points out that a judge can be considered great precisely because of his creative acts of misinterpretation. Friedman maintains that from an external, sociological point of view 'interpretation', in its normal juristic sense, is primarily a process in which decision makers with secondary legitimacy link their decisions to authority of primary legitimacy. He goes on to suggest that the type of legitimacy which is dominant within the legal system greatly influences the style of interpretation.

The actual practice of judicial interpretation will be considered in detail in Chapter 2, below.

Lawrence M Friedman, 'On the interpretation of laws' (1988) *Ratio Juris*, pp 252–62

Law is in many ways an interpretive discipline. In one very literal sense, major actors within the legal system are engaged on a daily basis with the task of interpreting texts – judges and jurists, very notably, try to extract meaning from the words of statutes or other forms of 'authority'. In many modern legal systems, a code or codes of law occupy the centre stage in writings about law and legal systems. Codes are, of course, written documents, often difficult, ambiguous or incomplete. And somebody must necessarily 'interpret' the codes, so as to make them fit particular instances.

In most European systems of law, the work of the judge, in traditional legal theory, consists of interpretation and nothing more. In theory, enacted law – the codes – are the only legitimate source of legal doctrine. In common law systems, the theory has always been somewhat more complicated. The 'law' is composed, in part, of statutes, which must be 'interpreted', just as in France or Italy. But there is also the so-called 'unwritten' or common law (it is in fact anything but unwritten). Here, however, theory treats the principles of common law as a kind of rambling, scattered text, which evolves at a somewhat sluggish pace. The judges 'interpret' this text, in the course of deciding concrete cases. Curiously enough, this rather archaic view of the common law can be dressed up today in the latest and most fashionable hermeneutic language. It has become commonplace to say that 'adjudication is interpretation', and that the acts of judges, in common law countries, are essentially and unavoidably interpretive.

Of course, the word 'interpretation' has many meanings and many scholars use the word in an expanded sense. There is a sense in which interpretation is much more than a task for lawyers and judges. It is part of everyday life to interpret: to discover a meaning in words, acts, and attitudes of others. In this sense, all social behaviour is interpretive, legal life and legal action no less than any other. In the realm of living law, however, interpretation goes on constantly in a much more literal sense. Everybody 'interprets' law, even when 'law' is as simple a matter as a speed limit, or a sign in a public place that forbids smoking. No action is possible without some interpretive screen, some filter in the mind of the observer.

There are, no doubt, important insights here for those who study legal processes. But I think it is important to try to limit the meaning of 'interpretation' to a less gaudy and expansive sense. Otherwise, it is too easy to reduce interpretation to total subjectivity; to a purely psychological phenomenon; or to a purely normative phenomenon. There is, in fact, an enormous literature on legal interpretation, or the interpretation of statutes and the like that is overwhelmingly written as it were, from the inside of the legal system, that is, normatively – in search of 'correct' ways to interpret, and 'correct' meanings of text .

My aim here is to examine 'interpretation' in a limited sense; and from the outside, as it were, as a socio-legal phenomenon. I will confine myself to a discussion of what jurists have in mind when they write about legal reasoning, or about the interpretation of legal texts; but I will use criteria which jurists themselves would not use. The subject, then, is 'interpretation' in its conventional sense. It refers primarily to formal, written statements of reasons – explicit interpretation of law, as these appear either in the opinions of judges, or in the treatises of scholars and jurists.

This kind of legal interpretation – in any event as it is usually described – is a rather forbidding and highly stylised form. Judges do not write in colloquial language, or even in ordinary literary language. Thus, one of the most obvious traits of legal interpretation is the language in which it is cast. This language is the language of legalism; opinions present themselves as logical arguments, cold, neutral, passionless, deductive. Except in rare cases, they avoid all hint of emotion. There are other peculiarities as well; legal reasoning, in many systems, is not at all the same as common sense reasoning, or as formal reasoning of a type not used or as in other areas of life. Many legal systems have special rules, canons, guidelines, and principles of interpretation. Jurists in their texts, and judges when they prepare written opinions, tend to follow these rules quite scrupulously.

When a judge writes an opinion, in modern legal systems, he takes care to cast his opinion in proper legal form. This does not, of course, correspond with what actually happens in his mind – his conscious thought processes. An opinion, in other words, is carefully *composed*, just as a person might compose a letter applying for a job, to make sure the latter is in proper and effective form. Legal reasoning is not true reasoning, in short. Indeed, it is hard to imagine a mind so grotesque that it indulges in legal reasoning when it goes to work.

There is, of course, no way to enter the mind of a judge. There is no way to tell whether a judge 'really' means what she says, when she says it. Perhaps she first made up her mind, and then cast about for proper 'legal' reasons. Perhaps legal arguments actually persuaded her. Or perhaps some other facts or factors, quite external to 'legal' facts or factors, determined the outcome. A judge who takes bribes can construct a good, logical, workmanlike opinion as easily as a judge who sincerely tries to determine 'the law', and apply it to the case at hand. Thus an interpretive opinion is not the written reverberation or recounting of inner mental processes. Rather, legal interpretation follows traditional forms, manners, and styles. But what is the source of these forms?

To understand them, we can begin by asking what purposes legal reasoning serves. A judicial opinion is, first of all, a mode of communication – a message; and second, a mode of excusing, justifying, legitimating, or explaining what the judge is doing, wants to do, or proposes to do. The message is a prediction or warning about the way this judge, and perhaps others as well, will probably behave in similar cases. Of course, the decision itself carries a message but this message can be incomplete or ambiguous. Plaintiff or defendant can win for many different reasons. The interpretative part of the opinion makes the message understandable in context. It tells the reader how far it is safe or plausible to think of the decision in general terms. When one company sues another company over misdelivery of a shipload of TV sets, the decision tells us who wins, and the damages, if any; only the *opinion* tells us why. The why will not comfort the loser, nor perhaps even interest him; but it is more helpful than the naked *decision* to the lawyers, judges, and jurists in general – and, in some cases, to ordinary people as well. It is the opinion that gives clues to the future behaviour of this judge, other judges, and perhaps some members of the public.

The message is delivered mainly to judges and lawyers, and speaks their language. Why is their language so technical? There are good, common sense reasons for using technical language; but legal language goes beyond these. This brings us to the second vital function of interpretative reasoning: It *justifies* the decision. Not every legal actor, law maker, jurist, or judge has to use formal reasoning, or 'interpret' existing law. A legislature, for example, does not 'interpret' anything; it simply makes new law, or changes old law. Statutes come into the world as naked fiat. They consist of propositions, sentences, and premises; but they rarely explain what they do. Some statutes have explanatory preambles; this is the exception, not the rule. For reasons, one has to look outside the text. If the legislation fixes the top income tax rate at 55%, or establishes a maximum of 20 years in prison as the penalty for burglary, the statute will not explain where these words and numbers came from, and why. Nothing in any statute will explain why 'good faith' is implied in the terms of a contract, why plumbers cannot work without a license, or any of the thousand other things the people's representatives decree.

In short, it is mostly judges of high courts who are obligated to explain, through reasoned arguments, why they decide as they do. They are required to justify their actions. Legislatures, of course, are concerned above all with general rules; judges work on a case-by-case basis, although they decide, or seem to decide, on the strength of broad principle. In any event, they write 'opinions', and they use reasoning to link their decisions, their fact-situations, their problems to something of higher authority – a code provision, or some pre-existing legal doctrine.

This simple fact tells us why some actors in the legal system give formal reasons for what they do, while others do not. The difference lies in the legal culture, specifically in social theories of *legitimacy*. What concepts of legitimacy, in a given society support the behaviour of specific legal actors?

We can distinguish between two kinds of legitimacy: primary and secondary. Primary legitimacy is authority that is, for whatever reason, treated as legitimate in itself, and not derived from some higher authority. In every society there is some institution or person with primary legitimacy. This may be a king, a pope, a chief, an elder, a parliament, a political party, 'the people', or a sacred book. In theocratic systems, primary authority may reside theoretically in God, transferred perhaps to a priestly caste or class, or enshrined in the text of some holy scripture. The locus of primary legitimacy differs from society to society. Its place and scope may or may not be clear-cut; these may themselves be matters for interpretation.

In any society, all authority which is not primary is secondary; that is, its rightness must derive from something else. It must justify itself, must link itself to some primary authority. This helps us to locate, sociologically speaking, the role of reasoning or interpretation within a legal system. Reasoning and interpretation constitute the process through which secondary authority links its decisions and acts to authority of unquestioned or primary legitimacy. For example, in a parliamentary democracy, theory insists that Parliament, as the representative of the people, has ultimate and primary law-making authority. Thus the legislature need not and does not give formal reasons for its act. But a judge who decides a case has only secondary legitimacy, as far as the law is concerned. Consequently, the judge must link his decision to duly enacted law. In a common law country, too, the judge must link his decision to higher authority – either a statute or, failing that, to principles or precedents of the common law, which already possess legitimacy or recognition.

Styles of legal reasoning differ greatly over time and place. The variations are by no means accidental. They reflect legal culture; they reflect the scholarly legal tradition (if there is one); above all, they reflect the particular structure of authority and legitimacy within the society. We can distinguish, for example, between closed and open legal systems. In a closed legal system, judges and other decision-makers lack primary authority, and, moreover, can only reason from a fixed, finite set of legal premises or propositions. In an open system, there is no single, fixed set of premises. Probably no real-world legal system is completely closed in the sense the term is used here. But a number of systems, past and present, do approximate it.

Imagine, for example, a theocratic society, with a single holy book or text, which is revered as the only true source of law; and which cannot be altered in any way. In such an ultra-conservative book-religion, decision-makers are trapped within the confines of the holy text. Except for the rare case of fresh revelation, no judge can go beyond the text; all decisions take the form of 'interpretation'.

As years and centuries roll by, the sacred texts gets more and more out of date, in the quite ordinary, literal sense that questions come up which the book does not and cannot answer in any obvious way. Imagine trying to squeeze decisions about income tax law, test-tube babies, drug addiction, or bankruptcy preferences out of the Torah or Koran – or a code drafted in the 18th century. But if all decisions must rest on some holy text, or an unchangeable text, if judges cannot deviate, and cannot legitimately add to the stock of premises, then 'interpretation' will become necessarily, distorted. A luxuriant crop of legalism, casuistry, and legal fictions will spring up, and a wild efflorescence of reasoning by analogy. In theory, everything is in the sacred text; only it is harder and harder to get that everything out. Caught in the middle, decision-makers resort to 'non-literal' interpretation, in various shapes and kinds.

Many legal systems show at least some resemblance to our ideal type; classical Jewish law, for example. In Jewish law, modes and patterns of 'interpretation' grew extravagantly, partly in order to correct for the fixed, unchanging stock of premises – just as the Chinese language needs *tones* to expand on the tiny number of acceptable syllables. The sages of the Talmud carefully listed rules for squeezing meaning out of sacred texts. The texts were, after all, divine; there was no limit to the store of *hidden* meanings; it was only a question of uncovering them. Some rules of 'interpretation' were rules of common sense or lay logic; others were far removed from popular reasoning. To take one example: Hebrew letters also serve as numbers, starting with aleph, which stands for one. Thus every Hebrew word has a numerical value, as well as a lexical meaning. Through a process called *gematria*, the sages drew inferences from the numbers each word in the Bible implied. This kind of 'reasoning' is likely to be allowed, or used, only in a closed or almost-closed system.

Sacred-law systems are, in a way, the extreme case; but processes of interpretation deviate from common sense reasoning, or even from rules of logic in many legal systems. This is never mere accident; and to ascribe it to 'tradition' merely invites a further question as to why the tradition persists. On the contrary, rules of interpretation reflect the essential structure of the legal system. The common law system, for example, in its classic form had traits comparable to those of a closed system. To be sure, the common law had no sacred text – indeed, no text at all in the literal sense. But the system, on the whole, was very bashful about admitting new premises and new propositions of law. Judges honoured the idea of *stare decisis*: and, in general, wrote opinions as if somewhere, in the body of common law decisions, there was a closed, fixed set of premises. These were the 'principles' of common law. Changes occurred frequently. In fact, the whole common law was in constant process of change. But changes were disguised as non-changes; as explanations or interpretations of old, received, time-honoured principles and texts. Other changes took the form of legal fictions. This was because no theory legitimated the making of new law by judges. The authority of judges was derivative; hence it was necessary for judges to reason *as if* their primary task was interpretation.

A similar point can be made about civil law judges. In the continental code-systems – the legal systems of Western Europe and Latin America – judges had no power to make law; under older, conventional theories of legitimacy, they had authority only to interpret. This led and still leads to an exuberant burst of 'interpretation'. The relative fixity of the codes makes this necessary.

In short, the structure, goals, and surrounding social facts in a particular legal system either determine or greatly influence the style and manner of 'interpretation' within that legal system. These do so in a number of ways, one of which is through their impact on the internal theory of legal legitimacy. It follows, therefore, that there is no single method of interpretation. Interpretation is not a science, and cannot be. Neither is it, exactly, an art. It is, rather, a socially-determined technology. From the sociological standpoint at least, it makes no sense to talk about 'correct' or 'incorrect' interpretation of a text. Some interpretations are more in harmony with the basic genius of the system than others; and some are viewed internally (that is, by other jurists) as correct. But what would be a valid, or correct, or even brilliant stroke of interpretation for a Talmudist might be considered fanciful or absurd in a different legal system.

Hence an outside observer watches with bemused detachment the endless debate about the right way or wrong way to interpret; about the rights and wrongs of 'literal' interpretation, and so on. Sociologically, one cannot talk about improvement or progress in modes of interpretation. Interpretation does not get better or worse, or more precise and accurate, or less so. It is a mistake to imagine that there are problems of interpretation that can be solved once and for all. Nobody can assert that the German pandectists were worse (or better) at interpreting the law than jurists in the classical Roman period, or today for that matter. One cannot sensibly talk about interpretation of legal texts in the abstract. Rather, interpretation can only be considered in the context of a particular legal system – Roman Law, or modern Islamic law, or common law – and it can be judged only in terms of the criteria of that system; or explained externally, that is, sociologically.

One cannot, therefore, speak about this or that jurist as a great interpreter – not, at least, in the way one can call Newton or Einstein a great scientist, or Beethoven a great composer. There are of course good judges and bad judges; weak judges and strong judges; great judges and ordinary judges. These terms usually refer to the technical skill, elegance, or power with which the judge structures or writes an opinion. Similarly of good or bad jurists and expositors of law. Such judges as

Benjamin Cardozo, or Lord Mansfield, are called 'great' within the common law tradition for a number of quite different reasons. Some 'great' judges have been brilliant stylists. Some have been exceptionally self-aware, and handled legal materials with unusual insight and scepticism; they were not prisoners of the webs of technicality, but rather masters. Some were outstanding because they had a social vision, and managed to translate this vision into legal terms, often through cunning manipulation of standard legal texts. But the greater the judge, the less likely to be described as an 'interpreter' of laws, in any conventional sense.

In other words, legal interpretation is not, and never has been, concerned primarily with what a text 'really' means. Of course, this can be said about other fields, too. In literature and philosophy, there are schools of thought which assert that we never know what a text really means; that there is no such thing as correct meaning. But most people outside the rarefied worlds of literary criticism and philosophy feel otherwise. They believe there is something that the author, playwright, composer, or artist must be aiming toward; and that with the proper historical tools, plus intelligence and intuition, an interpreter can ferret this out.

The jurist or judge, however, does not excel by virtue of power to shed light on the 'true meaning' of some law. The great judge or jurist does not pursue the 'original understanding', that is, what the draftsmen of the French Civil Code actually had in mind; or the framers of the American constitution. Indeed, the greater the jurist or judge, the more likely he is to obfuscate, twist, extend, or manipulate the text. It is the mediocre, unimaginative judge or jurist who looks 'woodenly' to the literal or original meaning of texts. What is creative in a judge is not the power of interpreting, but, on the contrary, the power of *misinterpreting*, in a useful or clever way.

There are many ways to approach a text; different situations call for different approaches. For one thing, 'interpretation' is inevitably policy-driven. This is true of interpretation of statutes, and also of contracts, wills, and so on. The same judge who 'narrowly' interprets the printed language of an insurance contract, or the text of a criminal statute, will look at other documents and statutes much more 'broadly'. The reasons are often quite obvious and are inevitably to be sought in considerations of policy. Thus commercial documents which must be standardised and uniform, in the interests of efficiency, tend to be read most 'narrowly' of all.

To be sure that 'interpretation' *can* mean the honest search for historical meaning. That is the scholar's approach. The preacher, using a Biblical text as the basis for a sermon, is performing quite a different operation. He is not searching for historical meaning; rather he uses his text as a springboard, a stimulus; he anchors his thoughts in the text, but in a metaphorical, extended, didactic or moralising manner. In literary interpretation, there is a whole rainbow of modes for approaching a text – including the search for historical meaning, at least as one option; at times, the sermonising attitude; and many others.

Legal interpretation, it seems to me, is quite different from most forms of literary interpretation; and quite distinct from the popular conception of interpretation. It is sometimes akin to the preacher's mode of interpretation; but it is rarely the scholar's search for historical meaning. The judge's power to 'interpret' is more radical than the power of (say) a symphony conductor to 'interpret' Mozart. The judge or jurist can turn the text upside down and inside out; this can be taken as a sign of greatness, if, in the judgment of history or the peers, considerations of craft or social consequence demand the boldness and innovation that the judge or jurist exhibits.

The scientific form of interpretation, of course, *can* be applied to legal texts as well as to any others. A historian might use this approach, or a social scientist. What a historian looks for in trying to decipher the meaning of the Twelve Tables, or the Institutes, is not the same as what the Roman Jurist, or the civil law dogmatist, were looking for. An American historian will try to understand the Constitution of 1787 as a document, but in a way that has little or nothing to do with contemporary decisions of the United States Supreme Court, even though these decisions are cast in the form of 'interpretations' of the text. The historian, or social scientist, is concerned with a kind of concrete historical truth; with the 'intent' of the draftsmen, the people who wrote down the actual words. Oceans of ink have been spilled over whether these 'facts' can be discovered in any meaningful way. But ordinary historians, social scientists – and just plain people – act as if the questions have answers, or at least approximations to answers.

And surely they do, on some level. Legal scholars sneer at the concept of 'intent'. In many ways, they are quite right to do so, and to expose the *political* meaning and consequences of the search for 'original intent'. Yet an expert in 18th century language can provide interesting and meaningful insights about the American Constitution, shedding light on what particular words meant to the people who wrote them in the 18th century. There is no need to throw out the idea of meaning altogether, merely because part of it is always beyond our grasp. Otherwise no one could every carry on a conversation with another living soul. But meaning in the literal or historical sense is not what jurists are after; and should not be.

Their search for meaning is of a different nature. In many societies *theory* insists that the process is the same. Nineteenth century jurists, in particular, argued this way. The duty of the judge was to find the meaning of the text, apply it and do nothing more. A judge who went beyond this overstepped his legitimate role. This theory has been derided and refuted repeatedly; but it has amazing survival power. It persisted in European systems for generations; and it is, in some ways, the theory of theories in American constitutional law. It is important too, with regard to interpretation of statutes, principles of the common law, wills, and contractual instruments.

The persistence of the theory makes clear that its value is separate from whether it accurately describes what judges do; its value, as we have suggested, comes from its position within the system of legitimacy; and every society has *some* system of legitimacy. Similarly, the *decline* of the theory signals a change in theories of legitimacy; we may, if we wish, indulge in the pleasant daydream that jurists today are simply more sophisticated than 19th century jurists; but it is more realistic to ascribe change to shifting standards of legitimation.

What these changes consist of, and what brought them about, goes beyond the scope of this paper. It is clear, however, that an enormous body of law exists, in every modern system, which is judge-made, and cannot conceivably be deduced, logically or otherwise, from the words of the relevant texts. Judges have invented this body of law, in one way or another, and have attached it or linked it, through a chain of arguments, to some particular hook in the language of statutes or constitutions, or to some prior 'principle'.

In the United States, the problem of the legitimacy of judge-made law is most acute with regard to the Constitution, because the Constitution most closely approximates a sacred text. It is a document of primary legitimacy. It can be amended, but this is a slow and difficult process. To all intents and purposes, the Constitution is a closed book. Judges cannot add to its premises. If they limited themselves to interpretative orthodoxy, as the years went by, the Constitution would shrink in value, and become impotent and useless. The justices have, in fact, decisively rejected this approach. They have adopted the path of growth, of change; and this strategy has been basically ratified by the political leadership of the country, and the population at large. Hence, out of the Constitution's slim store of lapidary phases a whole jungle of concepts, decisions, tendencies and principles has sprung up – bold thrusts into the legal unknown. Some of it – the arcane lore on 'levels of scrutiny' is as exogenous to common-sense reading as the rules of Talmudic interpretation; and sociologically quite similar. Much of the substantive development is of course highly controversial. Moreover, civil law judges have been almost as creative, in many areas of law building huge structures of doctrine out of a few meagre sections of their codes.

How can this behaviour of judges be justified within democratic societies? Thoughtful jurists have racked their brains over the problem. They have produced a mountainous body of literature. Some part of the public also seem troubled by this issue; in the United States, they argue that the Justices of the Supreme Court have gone too far – in decisions about the rights of criminal defendants, for example; or in crafting rights of 'privacy'. Mostly, the problem comes from what the justices do, rather than what they say, and the attack on their authority for saying it in some particular manner is something of a convenient afterthought. But the terms of the debate bear witness to the strength of the old ideology. Justices are not supposed to make law, only to find it or interpret it. The judges themselves pay lip service to this notion. Defenders of the court, in turn, argue, however implausibly, that the decisions are in fact anchored in the text.

The political behaviour of the Supreme Court poses a number of distinct sociological issues. We have to explain, first, the style and rhetoric; and second, the actual behaviour – what the court does, and the substance of its decisions. Our concern here, of course, has been with style. The external analysis of that style is hardly very far advanced. We have, however, mentioned one factor; the influence of theories of legitimacy; and whether or not judges are constrained to reason within a closed system of premises. Is a judge allowed to add new concepts, based on 'external' criteria, or is he or she confined to existing premises? Generally speaking, the answer is no to new premises; but the contemporary no is a much more tentative no than the 19th century no. Legal realism in its various forms has had an impact on interpretative behaviour; it is legitimate to treat the system as *somewhat* more open than before. Whether this affects style alone, or also the substance as well, is another rationality (as opposed to the more conceptual formal rationality) which is more evident in the opinions of judges than would have been true in the 19th century.

One point has to be clearly asserted. The rise of substantive rationality, and the weakening of the 'closed' canon of premises does not mean that judges or jurists are free to make up any legal result they wish; that they can say or do whatever comes into their heads. The judge or jurist will always use styles and approaches which have been justified or legitimate, within her circle of peers, or within the concrete society. The materials can be moulded and reworked – this is the sign of the creative jurist – but there are both linguistic and cultural limits.

It is also important not to overplay the sheer stylistic element in interpretation. The actual results must somehow fit, culturally and socially. An interpreter will feel the need to satisfy himself, and his social audience. The interpretation offered must *seem* sound, just, and correct. The decision should usually strike an observer as a sensible way to approach the text. But sometimes, paradoxically, almost the opposite is true: that is, the *results* are socially satisfying, but attached to the text by a very slim thread, or none at all. In mass societies, after all, few members of the general public actually read the opinions of jurists or judges. If the decision is important – reported in newspapers, for example – readers will focus almost exclusively on the results, rather than what leads to that result. What legitimates the decision, then, is general confidence in the decision-maker; and the congruence of *results* with current, cultural demands. But even within the circle of jurists, an interpretation will seem 'right' or 'wrong' for reasons which vary from time to time and place to place; and the reactions cannot be explained, either in terms of a 'science' of interpretation, or in any terms internal to the legal order at all.

—·—·—·—·—·—·—·—·—·—·—·—·—·—·—·—

THE JUDICIAL PROCESS: THEORY AND PRACTICE

The popular perception of the judicial process is described by David Kairys as government by law, not people; together with the understanding that law is separate from, and superior to, politics, economics, culture and the values and preferences of judges. This ruling perception is based on particular attributes of the decision making process itself, which Kairys suggests comprises, amongst other things; the judicial recognition of their subservient role in constitutional theory, their passive role in the operation of the doctrine of precedent, their subordinant role in the determination and interpretation of legislation and the '... *quasi-scientific*, objective nature of legal analysis, and technical expertise of judges and lawyers'. To the extent that law is generally portrayed as quasi-scientific, the operation of objective, technical and, hence, supposedly neutral rules, to that degree are the actual decisions that judges make accepted as legitimate by the public.

**David Kairys, *The Politics of Law: A Progressive Critique*,
1982, New York: Pantheon, pp 5–7**

We Americans turn over more of our society's disputes, decisions and concerns to courts and lawyers than any other nation. Yet, in a society that places considerable value on democracy, courts would seem to have a peculiarly difficult problem justifying their power and maintaining their legitimacy. The judiciary is a non-majoritarian institution, whose guiding lights are neither popularly chosen nor even expected to express or implement the will of the people. Rather, its legitimacy rests on notions of honesty and fairness and, most importantly, on popular perceptions of the judicial decision-making process.

Basic to the popular perception of the judicial process is the notion of government by law, not people. Law is depicted as separate from – and above – politics, economics, culture or the values or preferences of judges. This separation is supposedly accomplished and ensured by a number of perceived attributes of the decision-making process, including judicial subservience to a Constitution, statutes and precedent; the quasi-scientific, objective nature of legal analysis, and the technical expertise of judges and lawyers.

Together, these attributes constitute a decision-making process in which (1) the law on a particular issue is pre-existing, clear, predictable and available to anyone with reasonable legal skills; (2) the facts relevant to disposition of a case are ascertained by objective hearing and evidentiary rules that reasonably ensure that the truth will emerge; (3) the result in a particular case is determined by a rather routine application of the law to the facts; and (4) except for the occasional bad judge, any reasonably competent and fair judge will reach the 'correct' decision.

Of course, there are significant segments of the Bar and trends in legal scholarship that repudiate this idealised model. The school of jurisprudence known as legal realism long ago exposed its falsity; and later jurisprudential developments, such as theories rating the legitimacy of law on the existence of widely shared values, at least implicitly recognise the social and political content of law. Moreover, concepts like public policy and social utility, while limited to certain notions of the public good, are generally acknowledged as appropriate considerations for judges, and it is commonly known that the particular judge assigned to a case has a significant bearing on the outcome.

But most of this thinking is either limited to law journals or compartmentalised, existing alongside and often presented as part of the idealised process. For example, balancing tests, where judges decide which of two or more conflicting policies or interests will predominate, are presented and applied as if there were objective and neutral answers, as if it were possible to perform such a balance independent of political, social and personal values which vary among our people and (to a lesser extent) among our judges.

Despite the various scholarly trends and the open consideration of social policy and utility, legal decisions are expressed and justified, and the courts (as well as their decisions) are depicted and discussed throughout society, in terms of the idealised process. The public perception – the crucial perception from the standpoint of legitimacy – is generally limited to the idealised model. One will often hear cynical views about the law, such as 'the system is fixed', but even such observations are usually meant to describe departures from, rather than characteristics of, the legal process. While this perception of the idealised model is not monolithic or static (at various times substantial segments of society have come to question the model), it has fairly consistently had more currency in the United States than in any other country.

Indeed, public debate over judicial decisions usually focuses on whether courts have deviated from the idealised model rather than on the substance of decisions or the nature and social significance of judicial power. Perceived deviations undermine the legitimacy and power of the courts, and are usually greeted with a variety of institutional and public challenges, including attacks by politicians and the press, proposals for statutory or constitutional change and, occasionally, threats or attempts to impeach judges.

While there is presently considerable dissatisfaction with the courts and their decisions from a variety of political perspectives, it is usually expressed in terms of this notion of deviation from the idealised model. Thus, the conservative criticism that the courts have over-stepped their bounds – going beyond or outside legal reasoning and the idealised process – is now commonplace, as is the accompanying plea for judicial restraint to allow our 'democratic processes' to function.

The authors of this book are also dissatisfied, however, the content and implications of our critique are very different. At this early stage there appear to be four basic elements of our evolving legal theory.

First, we reject the idealised model and the notion that a distinctly legal mode of reasoning or analysis characterises the legal process or even exists. The problem is not that courts deviate from legal reasoning. There is no legal reasoning in the sense of a legal methodology or process for reaching particular, correct results. There is a distinctly legal and quite elaborate system of discourse and body of knowledge, replete with its own language and conventions of argumentation, logic and even manners. In some ways these aspects of the law are so distinct and all-embracing as to amount to a separate culture, and for many lawyers the court house, the law firm, the language and the style become a way of life.

But in terms of a method or process for decision-making – for determining correct rules, facts or results – the law provides only a wide and conflicting variety of stylised rationalisations from which courts pick and choose. Social and political judgments about the substance, parties and context of a case guide such choices, even when they are not the explicit or conscious basis of decision.

Judges are the often unknowing objects, as well as among the staunchest supporters, of the myth of legal reasoning. Decisions are predicated upon a complex mixture of social, political, institutional, experiential and personal factors; however, they are expressed and justified, and largely perceived by judges themselves, in terms of 'facts' that have been objectively determined and 'law' that has been objectively and rationally found and applied. One result is a judicial schizophrenia which permeates decisions, arguments, and banter among lawyers.

Second, we place fundamental importance on democracy, by which we mean popular participation in the decisions that shape our society and affect our lives. While there is a very real sense of powerlessness that pervades contemporary society, to blame this solely or even principally on the courts misses the point.

Those democratic processes that the courts are supposedly invading in the conservative view consist essentially of the right to vote and freedom of speech and association. Our society allows no democracy outside this public sphere of our lives. For example, the economic decisions that most crucially shape our society and affect our lives, on basic social issues such as the use of our resources, investment, the energy problem, and the work of our people, are regarded as private and are not made democratically or even by the government officials elected in the public sphere. The public/private split ideologically legitimises private – mainly corporate – dominance, masks the lack of real participation or democracy, and personalises the powerlessness it breeds.

The law plays a crucial role in this: the idealised model, the notion of technical expertise, and the notion of the law as neutral, objective and quasi-scientific lend legitimacy to the judicial process, which in turn lends a broader legitimacy to the social and power relations and ideology that are reflected, articulated and enforced by the courts. However, existing democratic processes do not provide meaningful choices or constitute meaningful mechanisms for popular control or input, which is perhaps why half our people do not vote. These processes – and the law – provide a false legitimacy to existing social and power relations.

The current and seemingly endless debate over judicial restraint or activism also misses the point. There is no coherent framework or principled resolution of this debate within the legal system, just as and because there is no legal reasoning. Rather, with very few exceptions, the pleas for judicial restraint and activism, sometimes unintentionally or unconsciously, mask a political direction and are wholly dependent on the historical and social contexts. If one favoured social security and restriction of child labour over maximisation of profits during the New Deal, one was for judicial restraint; if one favoured racial equality and justice over maintenance of white privilege and the historical oppression of black people in the 1960s, one was for judicial activism; if one favoured prohibition of abortions by choice in the 1980s, one was for judicial restraint. There is afoot these days a conservative brand of 'democracy' using, in part, the fashionable label of judicial restraint, that allows little or no room for popular participation or scrutiny. In this view, powerful (largely corporate) interests, the patriarchal, authoritarian family and, in selected areas, government officials are not to be interfered with, by the courts or by the people.

Third, we reject the common characterisation of the law and the state as neutral, value-free arbiters, independent of and unaffected by social and economic relations, political forces and cultural phenomena. Traditional jurisprudence largely ignores social and historical reality, and marks the existence of social conflict and oppression with ideological myths about objectivity and neutrality. The dominant system of values has been declared value free; it then follows that all others suffer from bias and can be thoughtlessly dismissed.

Left thinking about the law and the state has long recognised this political content and lack of neutrality. However, there has been a tendency to oversimplify with analyses that often seek an almost mystical, linear, causal chain that translates economics into law. For example, a common orthodox Marxist explanation is that law is a superstructural phenomenon that is mysteriously governed and determined by an underlying base of economic relations and/or instrumentally controlled by the ruling elite or class. But the law is not simply an armed receptacle for values and priorities determined elsewhere; it is part of a complex social totality in which it constitutes as well as is constituted, shapes as well as is shaped. Moreover, such analyses lose sight of the fact that the law consists of people-made decisions and doctrines, and the thought processes and modes of reconciling conflicting considerations of these people (judges) are not mystical, inevitable or very different from the rest of us. It is often difficult to resist dehumanisation of one's opponents and a blanket rejection of all people and institutions which constitute and symbolise a system one deeply wishes to transform.

However, judges are not robots that are – or need to be – mysteriously or conspiratorially controlled. Rather, they, like the rest of us, form values and prioritise conflicting considerations based on their experience, socialisation, political perspectives, self-perceptions, hopes, fears and a variety of other factors.

The results are not, however, random. Their particular backgrounds, socialisation and experiences – in which law schools and the practice of largely commercial firms of law play an important role – result in a patterning, a consistency, in the ways they categorise, approach and resolve social and political conflicts. This is a great source of the law's power; it enforces, reflects, constitutes and legitimises dominant social and power relations without a need for or the appearance of control from outside and by means of social actors who largely believe in their own neutrality and the myth of legal reasoning.

Fourth, while the law has many important functions, the legitimation function is crucial to an understanding of its doctrines, rationalisations, results and social role. The law's ultimate mechanism for control and enforcement is institutional violence, but it protects the dominant system of social and power relations against political and ideological as well as physical challenges. The law is a major vehicle for the maintenance of existing social and power relations by the consent or acquiescence of the lower and middle classes. The law's perceived legitimacy confers a broader legitimacy on a social system and ideology that, despite their claims to kinship with nature, science or God, are most fairly characterised by domination by a very small, mainly corporatised elite. This perceived legitimacy of the law is primarily based on notions of technical expertise and objectivity and the idealised model of the legal process – in short, as described above, on the distorted notion of government by law, not people. But it is also greatly enhanced by the reality, often ignored in orthodox left thinking, that the law is, on some occasions, just and sometimes serves to restrain the exercise of power.

A realistic, understandable approach to the law that explains its operation and social role must acknowledge the fundamental conflicts in society; the class, race and sex base of these conflicts; and the dominance of an ideology that is not natural, scientifically determined, or objective. The discretionary nature of court decisions, the importance of social and political judgments, and the dominance of the ideology of advanced capitalism characterise our judicial process far better than any notions of objectivity, expertise or science.

THE ROLE OF THE JUDGE IN DECIDING CASES

The Kairys piece raises the fundamental question of the appropriate constitutional role of the judges, and reveals judicial interpretation and decision making as an overtly political process. Within this political context, the doctrine of the separation of powers is posited on the existence of three distinct functions of government; the legislative, executive and judicial functions, and the conviction that these functions should be kept apart in order to prevent the centralisation of too much power. Establishing the appropriate relationship between the actions of the State and the legal control over those actions crucially involves a consideration of whether any absolute limit can be placed on the authority of the democratically elected government of the day. This, inevitably, raises the question as to the extent to which the unelected and, therefore, unaccountable judiciary legitimately can oppose the wishes of the Government expressed in the form of legislation, or the extent to which it can interfere with the pursuit of those wishes.

Until now it has been a commonplace of political thought that although the United Kingdom *might* not have a written constitution *its unwritten constitution* was *nonetheless* based on fundamental principles. Amongst these principles were the sovereignty of Parliament and the Rule of Law.

The centrality within the United Kingdom constitution of the doctrine of Parliamentary sovereignty has traditionally meant that Parliament can make such law as it determines, but the validity of such an interpretation has been questioned by some. The justifications for such challenges to absolute Parliamentary sovereignty are based on the United Kingdom's membership of both the European Union and the Council of Europe with the implications of higher authorities than Parliament, in the former's legislation and the latter's endorsement of inalienable individual rights.

As for the Rule of Law, although it is a notoriously amorphous concept, it has provided the courts with scope for challenging the actions of the executive and, indeed, to a more limited degree, the legislature. The mechanism through which the courts have previously exercised their burgeoning constitutional and, by definition, political role is judicial review by means of which they have asserted the right to subject the actions and operations of the executive to the gaze and control of the law in such a way as to prevent the executive from abusing its power. However, such power has been greatly extended by the enactment of the Human Rights Act (HRA) 1998. The Act only came into effect in October 2000 so the question remains as to how the courts will use the powers given to them under that Act. The remaining articles in this chapter will consider the wider political context within which the judiciary operate as well as focusing on the Rule of Law and the HRA 1998.

In an article 'Law and democracy', published in the Spring 1995 edition of *Public Law*, Sir John Laws, Justice of the High Court, Queen's Bench Division, considered the appropriate role of judges within the constitution from the perspective of the judge (footnotes omitted).

Sir John Laws, 'Law and democracy' [1995] *Public Law*, Spring, pp 72–93

In 406 BC, towards the end of the Peloponnesian War, the Athenians were victorious in a sea battle at Arginusea, to the south of Lesbos. But 24 Athenian ships had been lost, with their crews. A north wind, of the kind that still today blows very strong in those beautiful but unpredictable waters, had hindered any rescue. In Athens, still governed by its direct democracy, the eight commanders were blamed. In their turn they blamed the trierarchs, the captains of individual ships. Proceedings were brought against the generals. The Council of the Athenians, which prepared the case for trial before the Assembly of the people, had yielded to public anger and decided that they would all be tried together, on a single motion. That was unfair and contrary to the law: each should have been entitled to have his separate case judged on its merits. A motion was brought to challenge the procedure as invalid. The presiding committee had to decide whether to accept this motion, or to allow an immediate vote on a resolution to try all the generals together. They were intimidated by the people, the democratic voice. There were threats of impeachment and arrest. The presiding committee gave way. The eight generals were tried together on a single vote. They were condemned to death. Six were executed: they included the son of the great statesman, Pericles. The other two, as the historian Bury coyly puts it, 'had prudently kept out of the way'. But the presiding committee had not been unanimous. Unanimity was not required for their ruling. One member, the philosopher Socrates, had stood out against the illegal and unjust procedure for which the people bayed, although in vain. Afterwards the Athenians repented. They knew that what had been done was illegal. Socrates had been right, though when, seven years later, he reminded his own accusers of the fact, it did not save him from sentence of death. Democrats, no doubt, do not like to be reminded of democracy's failings.

In this article, ... I shall be saying that a democratic constitution is in the end undemocratic if it gives all power to its elected government; at the same time democratic institutions are a necessary – though not sufficient – condition for the establishment of fundamental freedoms. We should not forget, not least in the welter of present-day accusations against the modern Greek state, that the Athenians invented democracy.

'The ideal of law' is no doubt a grand phrase, and I do not intend to embark on a philosophical discussion of the nature of law. What I am concerned with is the difference between those interests in a decent society whose service and protection is distinctly the function of the law, especially our public law, and those which distinctly lie within the province of the democratically elected legislature and government; and with the relationship between the two. This is a large canvas, and it is impossible to do it comprehensive justice within the compass of a single article of reasonable length; but I hope, at least, that what I have to say may provoke further thought by others who, like myself, are concerned with the service delivered to the people by our unwritten constitution at a time when many of its facets are increasingly subject to critical scrutiny.

Judges and politics

The template for this article was the annual Public Law Project lecture which I gave in the summer of 1994 with the title 'Law and Politics – No-go Areas for Judges?'. The title is apt for the first part of my present discussion, which concerns the notion that judges should not enter into political issues. This is a proposition which needs to be addressed, since it may too easily be regarded as a mantra which inhibits dynamic evolution of our constitutional law.

I should at the outset make it clear that I am not concerned with what the English judges are or ought to be entitled to say out of court. As regards that, the strictness of the earlier position, established by what were known as the Kilmuir rules, has of course been much relaxed by the present Lord Chancellor, and judges are by and large expected to make sensible decisions for themselves about whether and in what terms to talk to the media or otherwise express their views out of court. It is by no means my purpose here to engage in the degree of effrontery to my colleagues on the bench, and for that matter to others also, which would be implicit in my pontificating about how judges generally should approach such questions. What I am concerned with is the present and future state of the law.

Next, it is necessary to dispose of the confusion and loose thinking that lies behind the proposition that the judges are not concerned with political questions. It seems to me that there has been very little rigorous reasoning as to what is meant by this. At one level it is an obvious truth: no judge should decide a question before him according to his own party political opinion; but that means only this, that he should not favour a particular resolution of a case because it would be convenient or helpful to the party for which, at election time, he proposed to vote in the privacy of the ballot-box. This is no more than a jejune truth; if a judge were seen to favour a particular party as such he would of course lose all claim to impartiality. It is no more than an instance of the rule against bias. Even outside court, a judge should no doubt appear to favour no political party, lest his extra-curial opinions be perceived to infect his decisions in court.

But this has nothing to do with the deeper question, whether good judicial decisions are themselves fuelled by ideals which are not morally neutral, but which represent ethical principles about how the state should be run, and in that sense may be said to be political principles. The difficulty is that the term 'politics' and its cognates are ambiguous; they may be taken to refer only to party politics, or to broader issues. If one accepts for present purposes the more limited sense of the term, then it is of course uncontentious that no judge is concerned with political questions. But as I have said this establishes only that the judge should entertain no bias on personal grounds. This obvious fact has nothing to do with what I have to say.

Let me next identify a sense in which it is manifestly false that the judges do not, or should not, engage in issues which are at least concerned with political questions. It arises within the territory of modern judicial review: within that jurisdiction the judges do, and must, adjudicate in cases which involve questions of acute political controversy. The ban on *viva voce* broadcasts by terrorist sympathizers; the rights of persons claiming refugee status; local government finance; a local authority's ban on hunting across its land; grant maintained schools; the disposal of nuclear waste; the government's decision to ratify the Maastricht Treaty: you cannot construct a litany of the subject-matter of modern judicial review without being struck by the fact that time and again it engages questions upon whose merits the politicians (and others) are in rancorous disagreement.

There is no question, as once there certainly might have been, of the judges standing aloof from such cases, or at least some of them, on the footing of the controversial nature of their subject-matter renders them unfit for judicial determination. Such a consideration is, first, irrelevant to the reach of the judge's jurisdiction. We now possess a jurisdiction in which every public body is in principle subject to the supervision of the court as regards every decision it makes. The only true exception, in the present state of law, is the Queen in Parliament, exercising the function of enacting primary legislation, and this exception is now constrained so as not to apply where the legislation on its face is credibly asserted to be inconsistent with the law of the European Union. I shall have more to say about it. All other exceptions are apparent, not real: the *dicta* in CCSU about national security, diplomatic relations with foreign sovereign states, and so forth, only describe cases where it is thought (rightly or wrongly) that an intrusive jurisdiction cannot sensibly be exercised, not cases where there is no jurisdiction at all.

The question left open in CCSU whether judicial review might go to the direct exercise of the Royal prerogative has been concluded at Divisional Court level by *Ex p Bentley* (1994) in favour of the existence of such a jurisdiction.

Other exceptions might be thought to consist in those cases where statute has apparently excluded the jurisdiction of the court, as for example by a 'no *certiorari*' provision. The most celebrated instance is the landmark case of *Anisminic* (1969); but there the House of Lords found the means to uphold the court's jurisdiction and thus the rule of law despite the terms of the provision in question (s 4(4) of the Foreign Compensation Act 1950). It is, as it happens, a striking feature of the law's evolution that since *Anisminic* Parliament has made but modest use of 'no *certiorari*' provisions; but the point of principle is that such cases do not, and cannot, mark any systematic limitation of the court's jurisdiction so as to amount to an axiom of the constitution, a rule which is logically prior to the court's power and thus in part at least defines that power. Whenever the bite of an exclusory provision is challenged, the issue will always be one of statutory construction, and the construction of statutes is always and entirely within the keeping of the courts. This is true even of Article 9 of the Bill of Rights 1688: '... the freedom of speech and debates or proceedings in Parliament ought not to be impeached or questioned in any court or place out of Parliament.'

In *Pepper v Hart* (1993) Lord Browne-Wilkinson offered a construction of Article 9 en route to his conclusion that there was no legal inhibition upon the courts, in a proper case from looking at *Hansard* as an aid to the construction of main legislation. The Bill of Rights was treated as a statute like any other. It has no primordial force. No doubt the preservation of free speech in Parliament without the risk of civil or criminal penalty is so vital a constitutional necessity that the courts – in contrast to the House's decision in *Anisminic* – will continue hereafter to construe Article 9 so as to accord the widest latitude to what Parliamentarians may say in the execution of their office. But the reach of Article 9, like that of any other statute, is for the courts to decide.

Thus, save as regards the Queen in Parliament, there is in principle always jurisdiction in the court to review the decisions of public bodies.

So the subject-matter of a putative judicial review cannot be consigned outside the court's jurisdiction on the footing that the merits of the decision under challenge are politically controversial. Not only that, however: the political nature of the case is no more a ground for refusing relief as a matter of *discretion* than it is for denying the court's *jurisdiction*. In the national security context (and some others) it is of course true that the judges still decline to go into the issues with the intrusive rigour that they would apply in other areas. They do so partly out of a perception that in the security cases the very exercise would publicise what must not be publicised; partly because these are fields where delicate decisions have to be made on a basis often of deep specialisation or of pure judgment rather than fact-finding, on whose merits the search-lights of judicial review can, so it is thought, illuminate little or nothing. There is certainly no judicial self-restraint on the ground only that the subject-matter is politically controversial.

We may see, then, that a judge may readily arrive at a decision, and grant relief accordingly, which, though not taken on the basis of any party political preference entertained by him, may in the result amount to a blessing or a can of worms to the party in government; and judges frequently do so.

So the *subject-matter* of a case offers no inhibition to legal adjudication on grounds of its political content. It will of course be said, however, that the actual decisions made by the courts in such cases cannot themselves be described as political decisions; this is because of what is a received axiom in our public law, that a judicial review challenge will not engage the judge in a trial of the merits of the decision impugned.

There is an exception, which I propose for present purposes to leave out of account but which I should identify; it arises where the statute authorising the action which is challenged requires some precedent condition to be established before the action can be taken; then, the judge must find as a fact whether the condition is met. A well-known example concerns the Secretary of State's power to remove illegal immigrants under Schedule 2 to the Immigration Act 1971: where a proposed removal is challenged, the Secretary of State must prove to the satisfaction of the judicial review court that the person in question falls within the definition of 'illegal entrant' in the statute.

But most instances of discretionary power conferred by statute are not subject to such prior conditions. In those cases, the judge cannot review the merits of what is done or proposed to be done. He is confined to an examination of the legality of the decision, which in turn will generally depend upon whether or not the decision-maker has transgressed one or more of Lord Diplock's trilogy of rules in CCSU: illegality, irrationality and procedural propriety. These are however no longer exhaustive, if they ever were: for my part I consider that proportionality ought not to be regarded as a separate head of challenge. But, strictly for this part of my argument, the three traditional categories suffice to indicate the broad nature of a conventional judicial review exercise.

It is no coincidence, no happenstance (as the Americans might say), that the public law jurisdiction draws a line in principle between review on these three grounds and the business of decision-making on the merits, as I shall seek to show; and the difference between the two, although regarded as elementary by public law practitioners, is not always clearly understood.

The difference has nothing to do with the extent to which the reviewed body's decision is controversial, whether in political terms or otherwise. It arises as a matter of definition from the very nature of the public power respectively lying in the hands of the courts and those whom they review. The paradigm of a public body subject to the public law jurisdiction is one whose power is conferred by statute. The statute is logically prior to it; and by the constitution it is for the courts to police the statute. But they do not act under the statute. They are altogether outside it. Their power is not derived from it; nor, ultimately, from any Act of Parliament. This state of affairs has two consequences. First, the judges have to see that the power given by the statute is not transgressed by its donee, second, they have no business themselves to exercise powers conferred by it, precisely because they are not the donee. Hence the essence of the judicial review jurisdiction. It vindicates the rule of law not only by confining statutory power within the four corners of the Act, but also by ensuring that the statute is not usurped by anyone – including the courts themselves.

So far this may appear no more than a standard account of the public law court's functions. My purpose in giving it is first to demonstrate that the well-known limits upon the jurisdiction have nothing whatever to do with problems about the judges embarking upon political disputes. They are simply a function of the rule of law: the judges are no more than anyone else entitled to exercise power which legally belongs to another. It would be idle and misleading to describe this state of affairs in terms of any judicial avoidance of political controversy.

Judicial creativity and political ideals

The next path I am to take is a little less clearly mapped. Lord Diplock's judicial review criterion of illegality is plain enough: no subordinate body may exceed the express bounds of its statutory power: that is, the power which on its proper construction the Act confers. But what of the other heads of review, *Wednesbury* unreasonableness and procedural unfairness? They are not as elementary as illegality. In the elaboration of these principles the courts have imposed and enforced judicially created standards of public behaviour. But the civilised imperative of their existence cannot be derived from the simple requirement that public bodies must be kept to the limits of their authority given by Parliament. Neither deductive logic nor the canons of ordinary language, which are the basic tools of statutory construction, can attribute them to that ideal, since although their application may be qualified by the words of any particular statute, in principle their roots have grown from another seed altogether. In some formulations, it is true, they have purportedly been justified by the attribution of an intention to the legislature that statutory decision-makers should act reasonably and fairly; but this is largely fictitious. In recent times, before *Ridge v Baldwin* it was not generally thought (to put it crudely) that administrative, non-judicial bodies owed such duties as to hear the other side. Before *Padfield* it was not generally thought that it was an enforceable function of every statute conferring public power that it only justified action to promote the distinct purposes of the Act, even though the Act did not state them. Before the concept of legitimate expectation assumed the status of a substantive legal principle (whose precise date may be nicely debated), it was not generally thought that decision-makers should be prevented from departing from previous assurances as to their actions without giving those affected an opportunity to make representations. *Wednesbury* itself reaches back to older law; but its fruition and its maturity came 20 years and more after it was decided. It cannot be suggested that all these principles, which represent much of the bedrock of modern administrative law, were suddenly interwoven into the legislature's intentions in the 1960s and 1970s and onwards, in which period they have been articulated and enforced by the courts. They are, categorically, judicial creations. They owe neither their existence nor their acceptance to the will of the legislature. They have nothing to do with the intention of Parliament, save as a fig-leaf to cover their true origins. We do not need the fig-leaf any more.

But my purpose with them is first to ask this question: judicial creations as they are, should they be regarded as political ideals? In one sense they are certainly nothing less. They are not morally neutral; they are, as the philosopher RM Hare would say, prescriptive; they are about how powerful people ought to behave. Much of politics in any ordinary sense of the term is about how powerful people ought to behave. It is not on the face of it easy to see why this class of standards, created by the judges, should be categorised as wholly apolitical while other classes, also concerned with the quality of public decision-making, should be roundly and unarguably regarded as well within the political sphere.

One thing is quite clear: if these public law rules may be described as political in nature, there is no question of the judges repenting them on such grounds; no question, either, of anyone else doing so – unless there are a few diehards who think that public bodies should be allowed to be unreasonable and unfair, perhaps on the grounds that many of them, including of course the government, are democratically elected. But in fact and in substance, these principles are accepted across the party political divide as an uncontentious and necessary element in the conduct of public life in England. There are many who say they do not go far enough. If the sinews of proportionality grow as strong in the law as the other principles, I believe it will command a like acceptance.

Let us now try to gather and express more tightly the effect of these reflections, as a prelude to the endeavour to penetrate the relationships between the ideals of democracy and law. We have these following propositions:

(i) The substantive principles of judicial review are judge-made, owing neither their content nor their authority as law to the legislature.

(ii) Yet they confine the scope within which discretionary decisions may be taken under statute, even though on a bare reading of the Act the power conferred would have a greater reach.

(iii) These principles are not morally colourless – far from it. They constitute ethical ideals as to the virtuous conduct of the state's affairs. It is essential to the theme (and anyway important) to recognise the moral force of the basis on which control of public power is effected by the unelected judges.

(iv) The established limits of the jurisdiction are in essence set by the very same ideal which has fuelled its growth: that all public bodies should keep within the power which the law accords to them. Neither these limits, nor any other aspect of our public law as it presently stands, can usefully be explained by reference to lines of demarcation drawn on political grounds.

Distinctions between judicial and elective power

I may now pose directly the question whether these judicial ideals ought to be described as in their nature political, though only to reformulate it, or to embark on a different and more important enquiry. However, first, the more direct question: are they political ideals, is apt to promote conceptual confusion. The adjective 'political' is what some philosophers used to call a portmanteau word – rather like 'good'. You may have a good book, a good man, or (as Tom Stoppard said) a good bacon sandwich; all the word's uses share (at least) the idea of commendation, but things are good in different senses. The notion which is central to issues or ideas which we might as a matter of language call political is, I think, that in one way or the other they all concern the way in which the state is to be run, the people are to be governed. In that sense the principles of judicial review are undoubtedly political. But this tells us close to nothing. What in reality I am in search of is a rigorous appraisal of the true distinctions between judicial and elective power. Since, as I believe, the present reach of judicial review is not now considered, in most quarters at least, to present or to threaten any unacceptable encroachments upon the legitimate authority of governments or other elected bodies, this exercise would very largely be of academic interest only, were the public law jurisdiction to remain static. The true differences between judicial and elective power are of the greatest importance if we are to entertain a respectable theory as to the basis on which judicial review may hereafter develop – as is hoped – towards offering an explicit and systematic protection of constitutional rights. Might the judges in the future, if they claim a greater jurisdiction to establish and insist upon fundamental rights, affront the imperative of democracy? Might they stake a claim, however well-intentioned, which transgresses the proper bounds of their unelected power? What would be the position if they sought to review main legislation?

The true distinctions between judicial and elective power cannot be arrived at by a merely factual account of what the judges do and what governments or Parliaments (or local authorities) do. This is so because of the logical nature of an unwritten constitution. Though there are of course established constitutional norms, some of considerable antiquity, the absence of what I will call a sovereign text means that the legal distribution of public power consists ultimately in a dynamic settlement, acceptable to the people, between the different arms of government. It is not written in stone; it is not even written in paper. It cannot therefore be ascertained by reference to the pages of a book whose authority is unquestioned scriptural. The settlement is dynamic because, as our long history shows, it can change; and in the last 300 years has done so without revolution. In the end, it is not a matter of what is, but of what ought to be. The journey to find it is a search for principle, not the unfolding of a rule book.

Democracy and fundamental rights

As a matter of fundamental principle, it is my opinion that the survival and flourishing of a democracy in which basic rights (of which freedom of expression may be taken as a paradigm) are not only respected but enshrined requires that those who exercise democratic, political power must have limits set to what they may do: limits which they are not allowed to overstep. If this is right, it is a function of democratic power itself that it be not absolute.

I will begin the task of justifying and explaining this position by saying a little about fundamental rights. This is fortunately a subject much in vogue nowadays; though pleas to incorporate the ECHR are of course far from new. While, along with many others, we would welcome incorporation, the concern of this article is not merely to add our name to the call; it has repeatedly been made by voices with much greater authority, and there is of course much literature on the subject. The idea of incorporation is beset by conceptual difficulties so long as we adhere to what we believe to be the outdated, or perhaps misunderstood, notion of the sovereignty of Parliament. What I am to address is not the maze of conundrums through which the incorporators have to find a path, but rather the extent to which the concepts of fundamental rights ought in principle to affect the reach and length of democratic power – incorporation or no. I will do it by reference to freedom of expression. Other rights, which in the compass of this lecture I will not discuss, would call for analogous, but adapted, arguments.

I will start with the notion of extremism. Generally, I would say that an extremist opinion is one which admits of no exceptions. Its hallmark is the claim to a monopoly of the truth. In the party political sphere, extremism is thought to be the province of the far left and the far right. But it cannot be defined in such terms; extreme liberalism may lay as dead a hand on freedom as the others. Its danger is that it may make intolerance and cowardice respectable. A heartfelt conviction, for example, of the evils of racial or sexual prejudice may all too easily lead to a call for the suppression of voices thought to extol them. It leads to the neo-fascist corruption of the language exemplified in what is called 'politically correct' speech. I should here make two connected points. The first is, I take it, as obvious as it is unoriginal: the vice of such prejudices (or any other, for that matter) is no less a vice only because its adherents are free to commend it; and it may be as roundly and rightly condemned by one who would not think of silencing its supporters as by another who only approves the expression of opinions he finds congenial. The second, no less obvious, is to notice the important distinction between the substance of an opinion held, which may be thoroughly justified, and its putative imposition on others, which is generally unjustified. I do not mean to say that one should not, with all the energy at one's command, seek to persuade the holder of barbarous views to recant; but to entertain the notion that he can or should be compelled to do so is to treat him as a slave.

Extremism may be found in the substance of a base opinion; but it may consist as surely in a preparedness to suppress views at variance with an opinion which itself is essentially decent. In both, the claim to a monopoly of the truth is urged. The latter case, however, carries the seeds of an insidious danger: it is that the very merits of the opinion being promoted may serve to blow the trumpet of suppression louder, and to weaken the resolve of any who insist that the holder of a vile view is entitled to have his say. All this, of course, takes for granted the value to be attributed to free speech, about which I shall have more to say. But the distinction between the two forms of extremism to which I have pointed uncovers a deeper question, which engages the role of government and therefore of the law. An individual citizen has little power to suppress the opinions of others. He may be a petty tyrant in his home or at his work, but his spurious writ can never run very far. A government, however, is a legally established hegemony; its very function is to rule; and though it may exhort and encourage; it rules in the end by force of compulsory law.

Yet however pressing the force of law may be, it cannot, short of vindicating a process we would recognise and condemn as brain-washing, itself exact a change of mind in any man. Government may persuade, but the attempt to do so is a right it shares with the citizen, not a prerogative it enjoys alone. It cannot enforce good opinions, save by obviously unacceptable means. It cannot therefore be its legitimate task to try. It follows that in the exercise of its true prerogative, which is the use of legal power, it is ineluctably committed to the primacy of pluralism. Its power is circumscribed by the very fact that the citizen's will is free ...

The separation of powers in the British constitution

Professor Robert Stevens, in his recent book *The Independence of the Judiciary: The View from the Lord Chancellor's Office*, says:

> Nothing underlines the atheoretical nature of the British Constitution more than the casualness with which it approaches the separation of powers.

Sedley J, in his review of the book, ascribes to this what he calls 'a hint of transatlantic self-satisfaction'. But it represents an important truth about the nature of state power in Britain. It is characteristic of the intellectual insouciance which marks our unwritten constitution that though higher-order law is an imperative required for the establishment of institutions to govern a free people, not only is it nowhere to be found, but its emphatic denial, in the shape of the absolute sovereignty of Parliament, is actually represented by our traditional writers such as Dicey as a constitutional cornerstone.

I have so far used the term 'government' indifferently as between the Legislature and the Executive. On the face of it that is a solecism which no first-year constitutional law student would be likely to commit. Everyone knows that the Executive is subject to the Legislature, and only the latter is taken to be sovereign. However, the fact that Parliament often, perhaps generally, lacks sufficient systematic control over the Executive government has become a melancholy truism of our day. These are well recognised concerns, and I will not lengthen this paper by anything amounting to a systematic description of the difficulties, which are undoubtedly sensed by many Parliamentarians themselves. Like everything else I have said, they have nothing to do with any party political divide. The power of the House of Lords is in the last resort only to delay measures which have been passed by the Commons, and the Monarch may be taken, in any presently foreseeable circumstances to be obliged to give Her assent to whatever legislation has passed, through both Houses. The real power of Parliament rests in the House of Commons, which, for most of the time, is manned by a majority which will support the governing party – the Executive – on major issues.

Clearly, however, Parliament is far from being a dead letter. The force of debate may cause the government to think again: it may win the vote but lose the argument, and the press will justifiably trumpet the fact. Ministers – especially the Prime Minister – must answer questions in the House; their weaknesses and strengths are thus exposed. Parliamentary committees do work of enormous value. There may be serious revolts by backbenchers, threatening the government majority. Despite its limited powers, and quite apart from s 2(1) of the Parliament Act 1911, the House of Lords may impose important defeats on the government, or may in debate express authoritative disagreement with what the Commons puts to it, and policy may be revised as a result. But in the end, for most of the time, the Executive can bend Parliament to its will.

There is a certain irony in this state of affairs. The result of the constitutional settlement of the 17th century, whatever the logic of the matter, was to establish the supremacy of Parliament over the King; of the Legislature over the Executive. When the government was in the possession of the Monarch personally, the ideal of Parliamentary sovereignty amounted to a claim that the ultimate political power should rest in the hands of the people's elected representatives, not those of an unelected autocrat. But the function of Executive government has passed from the Sovereign to Her ministers, who are members of Parliament; and the very convention that requires command of a majority in the House of Commons as a condition of the right to rule has, in fact though not in name, given back the final power to the Crown, at least for most of the time; though it is exercised not by the Monarch but by others in Her name.

However the same convention means of course that the sovereign power in the state is effectively in the hands of an elected body. Those old battles have long ago been won. They have, however, been won at a certain cost, namely the suppression to a considerable degree of the power of Parliament as a body independent of the Executive. What has in crude terms happened since the 17th century is that there has been a trade-off between two ideals: one is the notion that Parliament should be sovereign; the other is that the Executive government should be democratically accountable. It has been done by clothing the Executive, previously autocratic and unaccountable, with the legitimacy of Parliament.

The power which is generally enjoyed by the Executive over the Legislature is so great that it loosens the ties between the people and their rulers. The benign force of democracy is diminished. While it rules, the Executive enjoys great autocratic power which is only indirectly vouchsafed by the elective process. But – and this is the emphasis of my position – even if Parliament enjoyed a true hegemony over the Executive, still its rule should not in the last resort be absolute: still a higher-order law would be needed for the entrenchment of constitutional rights and the protection of democracy itself.

Conclusion

We may now come full circle, and after this long discussion I can identify what seems to me to be the essence of the difference between judicial and elective power. The latter consists in the authority to make decisions of policy within the remit given by the electorate; this is a great power, with which neither the judges nor anyone else have any business to interfere. This is the place held by democracy in our constitution. It is the place of government. Within it, Parliament, even given its present unsatisfactory relationship with the Executive, is truly and totally supreme. It possesses what we may indeed call a political sovereignty. It is a sovereignty which cannot be objected to, save at the price of assaulting democracy itself. But it is not a constitutional sovereignty; it does not have the status of what earlier I called a sovereign text, of the kind found in states with written constitutions. Ultimate sovereignty rests, in every civilised constitution, not with those who wield governmental power, but in the conditions under which they are permitted to do so. The constitution, not the Parliament, is in this sense sovereign. In Britain these conditions should now be recognised as consisting in a framework of fundamental principles which include the imperative of democracy itself and those other rights, prime among them freedom of thought and expression, which cannot be denied save by a plea of guilty to totalitarianism.

For its part judicial power in the last resort rests in the guarantee that this framework will be vindicated. It consists in the assurance that, however great the democratic margin of appreciation (to use Strasbourg's language) that must be accorded to the elected arm of the state, the bedrock of pluralism will be maintained. We have no other choice. The dynamic settlement between the powers of the state requires, in the absence of a constitutional scripture, just such a distribution of authority. The judges are rightly and necessarily constrained not only by a prohibition against intrusion into what is Parliament's proper sphere, but by the requirement, and the truth, that they have in their duty no party political bias. Their interest and obligation in the context of this discussion is to protect values which no democratic politician could honestly contest: values which, therefore, may be described as apolitical, since they stand altogether above the rancorous but vital dissensions of party politicians. The judges are constrained also, and rightly, by the fact that their role is reactive; they cannot initiate; all they can do is to apply principle to what is brought before them by others. Nothing could be more distinct from the duty of political creativity owed to us by Members of Parliament.

Though our constitution is unwritten, it can and must be articulated. Though it changes, the principles by which it goes can and must be elaborated. They are not silent; they represent the aspirations of a free people. They must be spoken and explained and, indeed, argued over. Politicians, lawyers, scholars, and many others have to do this. Constitutional theory has, perhaps, occupied too modest a place here in Britain, so that the colour and reach of public power has not been exposed to a glare that is fierce enough. But the importance of these matters is so great that, whatever the merits or demerits of what I have had to say, we cannot turn our backs on the arguments. We cannot risk the future growth without challenge of new, perhaps darker, philosophies. We cannot fail to give principled answers to those who ask of the nature of state power by what legal alchemy, in any situation critical to the protection of our freedoms, the constitution measures the claims of the ruler and the ruled. The imperatives of democracy and fundamental rights do not only demand acceptance; they demand a vindication that survives any test of intellectual rigour. There must always be voices to speak for them, in and out of the law. By their very nature, these imperatives require also that their enemies by given full rein to express their views. It means that the defence of these values cannot be assumed, but must always be asserted. There is no point at which there is nothing more to say; there is no moment at which they are indefensible, no imaginable circumstances in which to consign them to silence, like the oracle at Delphi when Julian the Apostate sent to it in the 4th century AD:

> Tell ye the King, the carven hall is fallen in decay;
> Apollo hath no chapel left, no prophesying bay,
> No talking spring. The stream is dry, and had so much to say.

You will forgive, I hope, this Grecian flourish at the end.

— · — · — · — · — · — · — · — · — · — · — · — · — · — · —

THE RULE OF LAW

The previous article explicitly set out the links and tensions between the doctrine of the Rule of Law and the relationship of the courts and the executive, and the implications for the use of judicial review as a means of controlling the exercise of executive power. This naturally leads on to a consideration of what is actually meant by the Rule of Law.

The Rule of Law represents a symbolic ideal against which proponents of widely divergent political persuasions measure and criticise the shortcomings of contemporary State practice. Its lack of a clear precise core definition allows commentators apparently from the extreme ends of the political spectrum to harness it in the pursuit of their divergent political goals. The first extract in this part is taken from *The Road to Serfdom* by FA Hayek, the proponent of free market philosophy and economics. The second is taken from *Whigs and Hunters* by the Marxist historian EP Thompson. Both Thompson and Hayek are distrustful of the encroachments of the modern State into the day to day lives of its citizens. From Thompson's perspective, however, the problem arises not so much from the fact that the State is undermining the operation of the market economy, but from the way in which the State has used its control over the legislative process to undermine civil liberties. The question that has to be asked is whether such incompatible understandings as held by Hayek and Thompson render the concept of the Rule of Law utterly without meaning, or whether there is, in fact, any core meaning that can be preserved and used positively.

FA Hayek, *The Road to Serfdom*, 1962, London: Routledge and Kegan Paul

[Chapter VI] Planning and the Rule of Law

Nothing distinguishes more clearly conditions in a free country from those in a country under arbitrary government than the observance in the former of the great principles known as the Rule of Law. Stripped of all technicalities this means that government in all its actions is bound by rules fixed and announced beforehand – rules which make it possible to foresee with fair certainty how the authority will use its coercive powers in given circumstances, and to plan one's individual affairs on the basis of this knowledge. Though this ideal can never be perfectly achieved, since legislators as well as those to whom the administration of the law is entrusted are fallible men, the essential point, that the discretion left to the executive organs wielding coercive power should be reduced as much as possible, is clear enough. While every law restricts individual freedom to some extent by altering the means which people may use in the pursuit of their aims, under the Rule of Law the government is prevented from stultifying individual efforts by *ad hoc* action. Within the known rules of the game the individual is free to pursue his personal ends and desires, certain that the powers of government will not be used deliberately to frustrate his efforts.

The distinction we have drawn before between the creation of a permanent framework of laws within which the productive activity is guided by individual decisions, and the direction of economic activity by a central authority, is thus really a particular case of the more general distinction between the Rule of Law and arbitrary government. Under the first the government confines itself to fixing rules determining the conditions under which the available resources may be used, leaving to the individuals the decision for what ends they are to be used. Under the second the government directs the use of the means of production to particular ends. The first type of rules can be made in advance, in the shape of formal rules which do not aim at the wants and needs of particular people. They are intended to be merely instrumental in the pursuit of people's various individual ends. And they are, or ought to be, intended for such long periods that it is impossible to know whether they will assist particular people more than others. They could almost be described as a kind of instrument of production, helping people to predict the behaviour of those with whom they must collaborate, rather than as efforts towards the satisfaction of particular needs.

Economic planning of the collectivist kind necessarily involves the very opposite of this. The planning authority cannot confine itself to providing opportunities for unknown people to make whatever use of them they like. It cannot tie itself down in advance to general and formal rules which prevent arbitrariness. It must provide for the actual needs of people as they arise and then choose deliberately between them. It must constantly decide questions which cannot be answered by formal principles only, and in making these decisions it must set up distinctions of merit between the needs of different people. When the government has to decide how many pigs are to be reared or how many buses are to be run, which coal mines are to operate, or at what prices boots are to be sold, these decisions cannot be deduced from formal principles, or settled for long periods in advance. They depend inevitably on the circumstances of the moment, and in making such decisions it will always be necessary to balance one against the other the interests of various persons and groups. In the end somebody's views will have to decide whose interests are more important; and these views must become part of the law of the land, a new distinction of rank which the coercive apparatus of government imposes upon the people.

The distinction we have just used between formal law or justice and substantive rules is very important and at the same time most difficult to draw precisely in practice. Yet the general principle involves is simple enough. The difference between the two kinds of rules is the same as that between laying down a Rule of the Road, as in the Highway Code, and ordering people where to go; or, better still, between providing signposts and commanding people which road to take. The formal rules tell people in advance what action the state will take in certain types of situations, defined in general terms, without reference to time and place or particular people. They refer to typical situations into which anyone may get and in which the existence of such rules will be useful for a great variety of individual purposes. The knowledge that in such situations the state will act in a definite way, or require people to behave in a certain manner, is provided as a means for people to use in making their own plans. Formal rules are thus merely instrumental in the sense that they are expected to be useful to yet unknown people, for purposes for which these people will decide to use them, and in circumstances which cannot be foreseen in detail. In fact, that we do now know their concrete effect, that we do not what particular ends these rules will further, or which particular people they will assist, that they are merely given the form most likely on the whole to benefit all the people affected by them, is the most important criterion of formal rules in the sense in which we here use this term. They do not involve a choice between particular ends or particular people, because we just cannot know beforehand by whom and in what way they will be used.

In our age, with its passion for conscious control of everything, it may appear paradoxical to claim as a virtue that under one system we shall know less about the particular effect of the measures the state takes than would be true under most other systems and that a method of social control should be deemed superior because of our ignorance of its precise results. Yet this consideration is in fact the rationale of the great liberal principle of the Rule of Law. And the apparent paradox dissolves rapidly when we follow the argument a little further.

This argument is two-fold; the first is economic and can here only briefly be stated. The state should confine itself to establishing rules applying to general types of situations, and should allow the individuals freedom in everything which depends on the circumstances of time and place, because only the individuals concerned in each instance can fully know these circumstances and adapt their actions to them. If the individuals are to be able to use their knowledge effectively in making plans, they must be able to predict actions of the state which may affect these plans. But if the actions of the state are to be predictable, they must be determined by rules fixed independently of the concrete circumstances which can neither be foreseen nor taken into account beforehand: and the particular effects of such actions will be unpredictable. If, on the other hand, the state were to direct the individual's actions so as to achieve particular ends, its action would have to be decided on the basis of the full circumstances of the moment and would therefore be unpredictable. Hence the familiar fact that the more the stage 'plans' the more difficult planning becomes for the individual.

The second, moral or political argument is even more directly relevant to the point under discussion. If the state if precisely to foresee the incidence of its actions, it means that it can leave those affected no choice. Wherever the state can exactly foresee the effects on particular people of alternative courses of action, it is also the state which chooses between the different ends. If we want to create new opportunities open to all, to offer chances of which people can make what use they like, the precise results cannot be foreseen. General rules, genuine laws as distinguished from specific orders, must therefore be intended to operate in circumstances which cannot be foreseen in detail, and, therefore, their effect on particular ends or particular people cannot be known beforehand. It is in this sense alone that it is at all possible for the legislature to be impartial. To be impartial means to have no answer to certain questions – to the kind of questions which, if we have to decide them, we decide by tossing a coin. In a world where everything was precisely foreseen, the state could hardly do anything and remain impartial. But where the precise effects of government policy on particular people are known, where the government aims directly at such particular effects, it cannot help knowing these effects, and therefore it cannot be impartial. It must, of necessity, take sides, impose its valuations upon people and, instead of assisting them in the advancement of their own ends, choose the ends for them. As soon as the particular effects are foreseen at the time a law is made, it ceases to be a mere instrument to be used by the people and becomes instead an instrument used by the law-giver upon the people and for his ends. The state ceases to be a piece of utilitarian machinery intended to help individuals in the fullest development of their individual personality and becomes a 'moral' institution – where 'moral' is not used in contrast to immoral, but describes an institution which imposes on its members its views on all moral questions, whether these views be moral or highly immoral. In this sense the Nazi or any other collectivist state is 'moral', while the liberal state is not.

Perhaps it will be said that all this raises no serious problem because in the kind of questions which the economic planner would have to decide he need not and should not be guided by his individual prejudices, but could rely on the general conviction of what is fair and reasonable. This contention usually receives support from those who have experience of planning in a particular industry and who find that there is no insuperable difficulty about arriving at a decision which all those immediately interested will accept as fair. The reason why this experience proves nothing is, of course, the selection of the 'interests' concerned when planning is confined to a particular industry. Those most immediately interested in a particular issue are not necessarily the best judges of the interests of society as a whole. To take only the most characteristic case: when capital and labour in an industry agree on some policy of restriction and thus exploit the consumers, there is usually no difficulty about the division of the spoils in proportion to former earnings or on some similar principle. The loss which is divided between thousands or millions is usually either simply disregarded or quite inadequately considered. If we want to test the usefulness of the principle of 'fairness' in deciding the kind of issues which arise in economic planning, we must apply it to some question where the gains and the losses are seen equally clearly. In such instances it is readily recognised that no general principle such as fairness can provide an answer. When we have to choose between higher wages for nurses or doctors and more extensive services for the sick, more milk for children and better wages for agricultural workers, or between employment for the unemployed or better wages for those already employed, nothing short of a complete system of values in which every want of every person or group has a definite place is necessary to provide an answer.

In fact, as planning becomes more and more extensive, it becomes regularly necessary to qualify legal provisions increasingly by reference to what is 'fair' or 'reasonable'; this means that it becomes necessary to leave the decision of the concrete case more and more to the discretion of the judge or authority in question. One could write a history of the decline of the Rule of Law, the disappearance of the Rechtsstaat, in terms of the progressive introduction of these vague formulae into legislation and jurisdiction, and of the increasing arbitrariness and uncertainty of, and the consequent disrespect for, the law and the judicature, which in these circumstances could not but become an instrument of policy. It is important to point out once more in this connection that this process of the decline of the Rule of Law had been going on steadily in Germany for some time before Hitler came into power, and that a policy well advanced towards totalitarian planning had already done a great deal of the work which Hitler completed.

There can be no doubt that planning necessarily involves deliberate discrimination between particular needs of different people, and allowing one man to do what another must be prevented from doing. It must lay down by a legal rule how well off particular people shall be and what different people are to be allowed to have and do. It means in effect a return to the rule of status, a reversal of the 'movement of progressive societies' which, in the famous phrase of Sir Henry Maine, 'has hitherto been a movement from status to contract'. Indeed, the Rule of Law, more than the rule of contract, should probably be regarded as the true opposite of the rule of status. It is the Rule of Law, in the sense of the rule of formal law, the absence of legal privileges of particular people designated by authority, which safeguards that equality before the law which is the opposite of arbitrary government.

A necessary, and only apparently paradoxical, result of this is that formal equality before the law is in conflict, and in fact incompatible, with any activity of the government deliberately aiming at material or substantive equality of different people, and that any policy aiming at a substantive ideal of distributive justice must lead to the destruction of the Rule of Law. To produce the same result for different people it is necessary to treat them differently. To give different people the same objective opportunities is not to give them the same subjective chance. It cannot be denied that the Rule of Law produces economic inequality – all that can be claimed for it is that this inequality is not designed to affect particular people in a particular way. It is very significant and characteristic that socialists (and Nazis) have always protested against 'merely' formal justice, that they have always objected to a law which had no views on how well off particular people ought to be, and that they have always demanded a 'socialisation of the law', attacked the independence of judges, and at the same time, given their support to all such movements as the *Freirechtsschule* which undermined the Rule of Law.

It may even be said that for the Rule of Law to be effective it is more important that there should be a rule applied always without exceptions, than what this rule is. Often the content of the rule is indeed of minor importance, provided the same rule is universally enforced. To revert to a former example: it does not matter whether we all drive on the left or on the right hand side of the road so long as we all do the same. The important thing is that the rule enables us to predict other people's behaviour correctly, and this requires that it should apply to all cases – even if in a particular instance we feel it to be unjust.

The conflict between formal justice and formal equality before the law on the one hand, and the attempts to realise various ideals of substantive justice and equality on the other, also accounts for the widespread confusion about the concept of 'privilege' and its consequent abuse. To mention only the most important instance of this abuse – the application of the term privilege to property as such. It would indeed be privilege if, for example, as has sometimes been the case in the past, landed property were reserved to members of the nobility. And it is privilege if, as is true in our time, the right to produce or sell particular things is reserved to particular people designated by authority. But to call private property as such, which all can acquire under the same rules, a privilege, because only some succeed in acquiring it, is depriving the word privilege of its meaning.

The unpredictability of the particular effects, which is the distinguishing characteristic of the formal laws of a liberal system, is also important because it helps us to clear up another confusion about the nature of this system: the belief that its characteristic attitude is inaction of the state. The question whether the state should or should not 'act' or 'interfere' poses an altogether false alternative, and the term *laissez-faire* is a highly ambiguous and misleading description of the principles on which a liberal policy is based. Of course, every state must act and every action of the state interferes with something or other. But that is not the point. The important question is whether the individual can foresee the action of the state and make use of this knowledge as a datum in forming his own plans, with the result that the state cannot control the use made of its machinery, and that the individual knows precisely how far he will be protected against interference from others, or whether the state is in a position to frustrate individual efforts. The state controlling weights and measures (or preventing fraud and deception in any other way) is certainly acting, while the state permitting the use of violence, for example, by strike pickets, is inactive. Yet it is in the first case that the state observes liberal principles and in the second that it does not. Similarly with respect to most of the general and permanent rules which the state may establish with regard to production, such as building regulations or factory laws: these may be wise or unwise in the particular instance, but they do not conflict with liberal principles so long as they are intended to be permanent and are not used to favour or harm particular people.

It is true that in these instances there will, apart from the long-run effects which cannot be predicted, also be short-run effects on particular people which may be clearly known. But with this kind of laws the short-run effects are in general not (or at least ought not to be) the guiding consideration. As these immediate and predictable effects become more important compared with the long-run effects, we approach the border-line where the distinction however, clear in principle, becomes blurred in practice ...

The Rule of Law was consciously evolved only during the liberal age and is one of its greatest achievements, not only as a safeguard but as the legal embodiment of freedom. As Immanuel Kant put it (and Voltaire expressed it before him in very much the same terms), 'Man is free if he needs to obey no person but solely the laws'. As a vague ideal it has, however, existed at least since Roman times, and during the last few centuries it has never been as seriously threatened as it is today. The idea that there is no limit to the powers of the legislator is in part a result of popular sovereignty and democratic government. It has been strengthened by the belief that so long as all actions of the state are duly authorised by legislation, the Rule of Law will be preserved. But this is completely to misconceive the meaning of the Rule of Law. This rule has little to do with the question whether all actions of government are legal in the juridical sense. They may well be and yet not conform to the Rule of Law. The fact that somebody has full legal authority to act in the way he does gives no answer to the question whether the law gives it power to act arbitrarily or whether the law prescribes unequivocally how he has to act. It may well be that Hitler has obtained his unlimited powers in a strictly constitutional manner and that whatever he does is therefore legal in the juridical sense. But who would suggest for that reason that the Rule of Law still prevails in Germany?

To say that in a planned society the Rule of Law cannot hold is, therefore, not to say that the actions of the government will not be legal or that such a society will necessarily be lawless. It means only that the use of the government's coercive powers will no longer be limited and determined by pre-established rules. The law can, and to make a central direction of economic activity possible must, legalise what to all intents and purposes remains arbitrary action. If the law says that such a Board or Authority may do what it pleases, anything that Board or Authority does is legal – but its actions are certainly not subject to the Rule of Law. By giving the government unlimited powers the most arbitrary rule can be made legal: and in this way a democracy may set up the most complete despotism imaginable.

If, however, the law is to enable authorities to direct economic life, it must give them powers to make and enforce decisions in circumstances which cannot be foreseen and on principles which cannot be stated in generic form. The consequence is that as planning extends, the delegation of legislative powers to diverse Boards and Authorities becomes increasingly common. When before the last war, in a case to which the late Lord Hewart has recently drawn attention, Mr Justice Darling said 'that Parliament had enacted only last year that the Board of Agriculture in acting as they did should be no more impeachable than Parliament itself', this was still a rare thing. It has since become an almost daily occurrence. Constantly the broadest powers are conferred on new authorities which, without being found by fixed rules, have almost unlimited discretion in regulating this or that activity of the people.

The Rule of Law thus implies limits to the scope of legislation: it restricts it to the kind of general rules known as formal law, and excludes legislation either directly aimed at particular people, or at enabling anybody to use the coercive power of the state for the purpose of such discrimination. It means, not that everything is regulated by law, but, on the contrary, that the coercive power of the state can be used only in cases defined in advance by the law and in such a way that it can be foreseen how it will be used. A particular enactment can thus infringe the Rule of Law. Anyone ready to deny this would have to contend that whether the Rule of Law prevails today in Germany, Italy, or Russia, depends on whether the dictators have obtained their absolute power by constitutional means ...

─ ·─ ·─ ·─ ·─ ·─ ·─ ·─ ·─ ·─ ·─ ·─ ·─ ·─

EP Thompson, 'The rule of law', in *Whigs and Hunters*, 1977, Harmondsworth: Penguin

... We might be wise to end here. But since readers of this study may be provoked to some general reflections upon the law and upon British traditions, perhaps we may allow ourselves the same indulgence.

From a certain traditional middle ground of national historiography the interest of this theme (the Black Act and its evolution) may be evident. But this middle ground is now being eroded, from at least two directions. On one hand the perspective within which British political and social historians have been accustomed to view their own history is, quite properly, coming under challenge. As the last imperial illusions of the twentieth century fade, so preoccupation with the history and culture of a small island off the coast of Europe becomes open to the charge of narcissism. The culture of constitutionalism which flowered here, under favoured conditions, is an episode too exceptional to carry any universal significance. If we judge it in terms of its own self-sufficient values we are imprisoned within its own parochialism.

Alternative perspectives must diminish the complacency of national historical preoccupation. If we see Britain within the perspective of the expansion of European capitalism, then the contest over interior rights and laws will be dwarfed when set beside the exterior record of slavetrading, of the East India Company, or commercial and military imperialism. Or, to take up a bright new conservative perspective, the story of a few lost common rights and of a few deer-stealers strung from the gallows is a paltry affair when set beside the accounts of mass repression of almost any day in the day-book of the twentieth century. Did a few foresters get a rough handling from partisan laws? What is that beside the norms of the Third Reich? Did the villagers of Winkfield lose access to the peat within Swinley Rails? What is that beside the liquidation of the kulaks? What is remarkable (we are reminded) is not that the laws were bent but the fact that there was, anywhere in the eighteenth century, a rule of law at all. To ask for greater justice than that is to display mere sentimentalism. In any event, we should adjust our sense of proportion; against the handfuls carried off on the cart to Tyburn (and smaller handfuls than have been carried off in Tudor times) we must see whole legions carried off by plague or death.

From these perspectives concern with the rights and wrongs of law of a few men in 1723 is concern with trivia. And the same conclusion may be reached through a different adjustment of perspective, which may coexist with some of the same arguments. This flourishes in the form of a sophisticated, but (ultimately) highly schematic Marxism which, to our surprise, seems to spring up in the footsteps of those of us in an older Marxist tradition. From this standpoint, the law is, perhaps more clearly than any other cultural or institutional artifact, by definition a part of a 'superstructure' adapting itself to the necessities of an infrastructure of productive forces and productive relations. As such, it is clearly an instrument of the *de facto* ruling class: it both defines and defends these rulers' claims upon resources and labour-power – it says what shall be property and what shall be crime – and it mediates class relations with a set of appropriate rules and sanctions, all of which, ultimately, confirm and consolidate existing class power. Hence the rule of law is only another mask for the rule of a class. The revolutionary can have no interest in law, unless as a phenomenon of ruling-class power and hypocrisy; it should be his aim simply to overthrow it. And so, once again, to express surprise at the Black Act or at partial judges is unless as confirmation and illustration of theories which might easily be demonstrated without all this labour – simply to expose one's own naivety.

So the old middle ground of historiography is crumbling on both sides. I stand on a very narrow ledge, watching the tides come up. Or, to be more explicit, I sit here in my study, at the age of fifty, the desk and the floor piled high with five years of notes, xeroxes, rejected drafts, the clock once again moving into the small hours, and see myself, in a lucid instant, as an anachronism. Why have I spent these years in trying to find out what could, in essential structures, have been known without any investigation at all? And does it matter a damn who gave Parson Power his instructions; which forms brought 'Vulcan' Gates to the gallows; or how an obscure Richmond publican managed to evade a death sentence already determined upon by the Law Officers, the First Minister and the King?

I am disposed to think that it does matter; I have a vested interest (in five years of labour) to think it may. But to show this must involve evacuating received assumptions – that narrowing ledge of traditional middle ground – and moving out onto an even narrower theoretical ledge. This would accept, as it must, some part of the Marxist-structural critique; indeed, some parts of this study have confirmed the class-bound and mystifying functions of the law. But it would rejects its ulterior reductionism and would modify its typology of superior and inferior (but determining) structures.

First, analysis of the eighteenth century (and perhaps of other centuries) calls in question the validity of separating off the law as a whole and placing it in some typological superstructure. The law when considered as institution (the courts, with their class theatre and class procedures) or as personnel (the judges, the lawyers, the Justices of the Peace) may very easily be assimilated to those of the ruling class. But all that is entailed in 'the law' is not subsumed in these institutions. The law may also be seen as ideology, or as particular rules and sanctions which stand in a definite and active relationship (often a field of conflict) to social norms; and finally, it may be seen simply in terms of its own logic, rules and procedures – that is, simply as law. And it is not possible to conceive of any complex society without law.

We must labour this point, since some theorists today are unable to see the law except in terms of 'the fuzz' setting about inoffensive demonstrators or cannabis-smokers. I am no authority on the twentieth century, but in the eighteenth century matters were more complex than that. To be sure I have tried to show, in the evolution of the Black Act, an expression of the ascendancy of a Whig oligarchy, which created new laws and bent old legal forms in order legitimize its own property and status; this oligarchy employed the law, both instrumentally and ideologically, very much as a modern structural Marxist should expect it to do. But this is not the same thing as to say that the rulers had need of law, in order to oppress the ruled, while those who were ruled had need of none. What was often at issue was not property, supported by law, against no-property; it was alterative definitions of property-rights; for the landowner, enclosure – for the cottager, common rights: for the forest officialdom, 'preserved grounds' for the deer; for the foresters, the right to take turfs. For as long as it remained possible, the ruled – if they could find a purse and a lawyer – would actually fight for their rights by means of law; occasionally the copyholders, resting upon the precedents of sixteenth century law, could actually win a case. When it ceased to be possible to continue the fight at law, men still felt a sense of legal wrong: the propertied had obtained their power by illegitimate means.

Moreover, if we look closely into such an agrarian context, the distinction between law, on the one hand, conceived of as an element of 'superstructure', and the actualities of productive forces and relations on the other hand, becomes more and more untenable. For law was often a definition of actual agrarian practice, as it had been pursued 'time out of mind'. How can we distinguish between the activity of farming or of quarrying and the rights to this strip of land or to that quarry? The farmer or forester in his daily occupation was moving within visible or invisible structures of law: this mere stone which marked the division between strips; that ancient oak – visited by processional on each Rogation Day – which marked the limits of the parish grazing; those other invisible (but potent and sometimes legally enforceable) memories as to which parishes had the right to take turfs in this waste and which parishes had not; this written or unwritten customal which decided how many stints on the common land and for whom – for copyholders and freeholders only, or for all inhabitants?

Hence 'law' was deeply imbricated within the very basis of productive relations, which would have been inoperable without this law. And, in the second place, this law, as definition or as rules (imperfectly enforceable through institutional legal forms), was endorsed by norms, tenaciously transmitted through the community. There were alternative norms; that is a matter of course; this was a place, not of consensus, but of conflict. But we cannot, then, simply separate off all law as ideology, and assimilate this also to the state apparatus of a ruling class. On the contrary, the norms of foresters might reveal themselves as passionately supported values, impelling them upon a course of action which would lead them into bitter conflict – with 'the law'.

So we are back, once again, with *that* law: the institutionalised procedures of the ruling class. This, no doubt, is worth no more of our theoretical attention; we can see it as an instrument of class power *tout court*. But we must take even this formulation, and see whether its crystalline clarity will survive immersion in scepticism. To be sure, we can stand no longer on that traditional ground of liberal academicism, which offers the eighteenth century as a society of consensus, ruled within the parameters of paternalism and deference, and governed by a 'rule of law' which attained (however imperfectly) towards impartiality. That is not the society which we have been examining: we have not observed a society of consensus; and we have seen the law being devised and employed, directly and instrumentally, in the imposition of class power. Nor can we accept a sociological refinement of the old view, which stresses the imperfections and partiality of the law, and its subordination to the functional requirements of socio-economic interest groups. For what we have observed is something more than the law as a pliant medium to be twisted this way and that by whichever interests already possess effective power. Eighteenth century law was more substantial than that. Over and above its pliant, instrumental functions it existed in its own right, as ideology; as an ideology which not only served, in most respects, but which also legitimised class power. The hegemony of the eighteenth-century gentry and aristocracy was expressed, above all, not in military force, not in the mystifications of a priesthood or of the press, not even in economic coercion, but in the rituals of the study of the Justices of the Peace, in the quarter-sessions, in the pomp of Assizes and in the theatre of Tyburn.

Thus the law (we agree) may be seen instrumentally as mediating and reinforcing existent class relations and, ideologically, as offering to these a legitimation. But we must press our definitions a little further. For if we say that existent class relations were mediated by the law, this is not the same thing as saying that the law was no more than those relations translated into other terms, which masked or mystified the reality. This may, quite often, be true but it is not the whole truth. For class relations were expressed, not in any way one likes, but through the forms of law; and the law, like other institutions which from time to time can be seen as mediating (and masking) existent class relations (such as the Church or the media of communication), has its own characteristics, its own independent history and logic of evolution.

Moreover, people are not as stupid as some structuralist philosophers suppose them to be. They will not be mystified by the first man who puts on a wig. It is inherent in the especial character of law, as a body of rules and procedures, that it shall apply logical criteria with reference to standards of universality and equality. It is true that certain categories of person may be excluded from this logic (as children or slaves), that other categories may be debarred from access to parts of the logic (as women or, for many forms of eighteenth century law, those without certain kinds of property), and that the poor may often be excluded, through penury, from the law's costly procedures. All this, and more, is true. but if too much of this is true, then the consequences are plainly counterproductive. Most men have a strong sense of justice, at least with regard to their own interests. If the law is evidently partial and unjust, then it will mask nothing, legitimise nothing, contribute nothing to any class's hegemony. The essential precondition for the effectiveness of law, in its function as ideology, is that it shall display an independence from gross manipulation and shall seem to be just. It cannot seem to be so without upholding its own logic and criteria of equity; indeed, on occasion, by actually being just. And furthermore it is not often the case that a ruling ideology can be dismissed as a mere hypocrisy; even rulers find a need to legitimise their power, to moralise their functions, to feel themselves to be useful and just. In the case of an ancient historical formation like the law, a discipline which requires years of exacting study to master, there will always be some men who actively believe in their own procedures and in the logic of justice. The lay may be rhetoric, but it need not be empty rhetoric. Blackstone's *Commentaries* represent an intellectual exercise far more rigorous than could have come from an apologist's pen.

I do not know what transcultural validity these reflections may have. But they are certainly applicable to England in the eighteenth century. Douglas Hay, in a significant essay in *Albion's Fatal Tree*, has argued that the law assumed unusual pre-eminence in that century, as the central legitimizing ideology, displacing the religious authority and sanctions of previous centuries. It gave way, in its turn, to economic sanctions and to the ideology of the free market and of political liberalism in the nineteenth. Turn where you will, the rhetoric of eighteenth century England is saturated with the notion of law. Royal absolution was placed behind a high hedge of law; landed estates were tied together with entails and marriage settlements made up of elaborate tissues of law; authority and property punctuated their power by regular 'examples' made upon the public gallows. More than this, immense efforts were made (and Hay has explored the forms of these) to project the image of a ruling class which was itself subject to the rule of law, and whose legitimacy rested upon the equity and universality of those legal forms. And the rulers were, in serious senses, whether willingly or unwillingly, the prisoners of their own rhetoric; they played the games of power according to rules which suited them, but they could not break those rules or the whole game would be thrown away. And, finally, so far from the ruled shrugging off this rhetoric as a hypocrisy, some part of it at least was taken over as part of the rhetoric of the plebeian crowd, of the 'free-born Englishman' with his inviolable privacy, his habeas corpus, his equality before the law. If this rhetoric was a mask, it was a mask which John Wilkes was to borrow, at the head of ten thousand masked supporters.

So that in this island and in that century above all one must resist any slide into structural reductionism. What this overlooks, among other things, is the immense capital of human struggle over the previous two centuries against royal absolutism, inherited, in the forms and traditions of the law, by the eighteenth century gentry. For in the sixteenth and seventeenth centuries the law had been less an instrument of class power than a central arena of conflict. In the course of conflict the law itself had been changed; inherited by the eighteenth century gentry, this changed law was, literally, central to their whole purchase upon power and upon the means of life. Take law away, and the royal prerogative, or the presumption of the aristocracy, might flood back upon their properties and lives; take law away and the string which tied together their lands and marriages would fall apart. But it was inherent in the very nature of the medium which they had selected for their own self-defence that it could not be reserved for the exclusive use only of their own class. The law, in its forms and traditions, entailed principles of equity and universality which, perforce, had to be extended to all sorts and degrees of men. And since this was of necessity so, ideology could turn necessity to advantage. What had been devised by men of property as a defence against arbitrary power could be turned into service as an apologia for property in the face of the propertyless. And the apologia was serviceable up to a point: for these 'propertyless', as we have seen, comprised multitudes of men and women who themselves enjoyed, in fact, petty property rights or agrarian use-rights whose definition was inconceivable without the forms of law. Hence the ideology of the great struck root in a soil, however shallow, of actuality. And the courts gave substance to the ideology by the scrupulous care with which, on occasion they adjudged petty rights, and, on all occasions, preserved proprieties and forms.

We reach, then, not a simple conclusion (law = class power) but a complex and contradictory one. On the one hand, it is true that the law did mediate existent class relations to the advantage of the rulers; not only is this so, but as the century advanced the law became a superb instrument by which these rulers were able to impose new definitions of property to their even greater advantage, as in the extinction by law of indefinite agrarian use-rights and in the furtherance of enclosure. On the other hand, the law mediated these class relations through legal forms, which imposed, again and again, inhibitions upon the actions of the rulers. For there is a very large difference, which twentieth-century experience ought to have made clear even to the most exalted thinker, between arbitrary extra-legal power and the rule of law. And not only were the rulers (indeed, the ruling class as a whole) inhibited by their own rules of law against the exercise of direct unmediated force (arbitrary imprisonment, the unemployment of troops against the crowd, torture, and those other conveniences of power with which we are all conversant), but they also believed enough in these rules, and in their accompanying ideological rhetoric, to allow, in certain limited areas, the law itself to be a genuine forum within which certain kinds of class conflict were fought out. There were even occasions (one recalls John Wilkes and several of the trials of the 1790s) when the Government itself retired from the courts defeated. Such occasions served, paradoxically, to consolidate power, to enhance its legitimacy, and to inhibit revolutionary movements. But, to turn the paradox around, these same occasions served to bring power even further within constitutional controls.

The rhetoric and the rules of a society are something a great deal more than sham. In the same moment they may modify, in profound ways, the behaviour of the powerful, and mystify the powerless. They may disguise the true realities of power, but, at the same time, they may curb that power and check its intrusions. And it is often from within that very rhetoric that a radical critique of the practice of the society is developed: the reformers of the 1790s appeared, first of all, clothed in the rhetoric of Locke and of Blackstone.

These reflections lead me on to conclusions which may be different from those which some readers expect. I have shown in this study a political oligarchy inventing callous and oppressive laws to serve its own interests. I have shown judges who, no less than bishops, were subject to political influence, whose sense of justice was humbug, and whose interpretation of the laws served only to enlarge their inherent class bias. Indeed, I think that this study has shown that for many of England's governing elite the rules of law were a nuisance, to be manipulated and bent in what ways they could; and that the allegiance of such men as Walpole, Hardwicke or Paxton to the rhetoric of law was largely humbug. But I do not conclude from this that the rule of law itself was humbug. On the contrary, the inhibitions upon power imposed by law seem to me a legacy as substantial as any handed down from the struggles of the seventeenth century to the eighteenth, and a true and important cultural achievement of the agrarian and mercantile bourgeoisie, and of their supporting yeomen and artisans.

More than this, the notion of the regulation and reconciliation of conflicts through the rule of law – and the elaboration of rules and procedures which, on occasion, made some approximate approach towards the ideal – seems to me a cultural achievement of universal significance. I do not lay any claim as to the abstract, extra-historical impartiality of these rules. In a context of gross class inequalities, the equity of the law must always be in some part sham. Transplanted as it was to even more inequitable contexts, this law could become an instrument of imperialism. For this law has found its way to a good many parts of the globe. But even here the rules and the rhetoric have imposed some inhibitions upon the imperial power. If the rhetoric was a mask, it was a mask which Ghandi and Nehru were to borrow, at the head of a million masked supporters.

I am not starry-eyed about this at all. This has not been a star-struck book. I am insisting only upon the obvious point, which some modern Marxists have overlooked, that there is a difference between arbitrary power and the rule of law. We ought to expose the shams and inequities which may be concealed beneath this law. But the rule of law itself, the imposing of effective inhibitions upon power and the defence of the citizen from power's all-intrusive claims, seems to me to be an unqualified human good. To deny or belittle this good is, in this dangerous century when the resources and pretensions of power continue to enlarge, a desperate error of intellectual abstraction. More than this, it is a self-fulfilling error, which encourages us to give up the struggle against bad laws and class-bound procedures, and to disarm ourselves before power. It is to throw away a whole inheritance of struggle about law, and within the forms of law, whose continuity can never be fractured without bringing men and women into immediate danger.

In all of this I may be wrong. I am told that, just beyond the horizon, new forms of working-class power are about to arise which, being founded upon egalitarian productive relations, will require no inhibition and can dispense with the negative restrictions of bourgeois legalism. A historian is unqualified to pronounce on such utopian projections; all that he knows is that he can bring in support of them no historical evidence whatsoever. His advice might be: watch this new power for a century or two before you cut your hedges down.

I therefore crawl out onto my own precarious ledge. It is true that in history the law can be seen to mediate and to legitimize existence class relations. Its forms and procedures may crystallise those relations and mask ulterior injustice. But this mediation, through the forms of law, is something quite distinct from the exercise of unmediated force. The forms and rhetoric of law acquire a distinct identity which may, on occasion, inhibit power and afford some protection to the powerless. Only to the degree that this is seen to be so can law be of service in its other aspect, as ideology. Moreover, the law in both its aspects, as formal rules and procedures and as idealogy, cannot usefully be analyzed in the metaphorical terms of a superstructure distinct from an infrastructure. While this comprises a large and self-evident part of the truth, the rules and categories of law penetrate every level of society, effect vertical as well as horizontal definitions of men's rights and status, and contribute to men's self-definition or sense of identity. As such law has not only been imposed upon men from above: it has also been a medium within which other social conflicts have been fought out. Productive relations themselves are in part only meaningful in terms of their definitions at law: the serf, the free labourer; the cottager with common rights, the inhabitant without; the un-free proletarian, the picket conscious of his rights; the landless labourer who may still sue his employer for assault. And if the actuality of the law's operation in class-divided societies has, again and again, fallen short of its own rhetoric of equity, yet the notion of the rule of law is itself an unqualified good.

This cultural achievement – the attainment towards a universal value – found one origin in Roman jurisprudence. The uncodified English common law offered an alternative notation of law, in some ways more flexible and unprincipled – and therefore more pliant to the 'common sense' of the ruling class – in other ways more available as a medium through which social conflict could find expression, especially where the sense of 'natural justice' of the jury could make itself felt. Since this tradition came to its maturity in eighteenth century England, its claims should command the historian's interest. And since some part of the inheritance from this cultural moment may still be found, within greatly changed contexts, within the United States or India or certain African countries, it is important to re-examine the pretensions of the imperialist donor.

This is to argue the need for a general revaluation of eighteenth century law, of which this study offers only a fragment. This study has been centred upon a bad law, drawn by bad legislators, and enlarged by the interpretations of bad judges. No defence, in terms of natural justice can be offered for anything in the history of the Black Act. But even this study does not prove that all law as such is bad. Even this law bound the rulers to act only in the ways which its forms permitted; they had difficulties with these forms; they could not always override the sense of natural justice of the jurors; and we may imagine how Walpole would have acted, against Jacobites or against disturbers of Richmond Park, if he had been subject to no forms of law at all.

If we suppose that law is no more than a mystifying and pompous way in which class power is registered and executed, then we need not waste our labour in studying its history and forms. One Act would be much the same as another, and all, from the standpoint of the ruled, would be Black. It is because law matters that we have bothered with this story at all. And this is also an answer to those universal thinkers, impatient of all except the *longue durée*, who cannot be bothered with cartloads of victims at Tyburn when they set these beside the indices of infant mortality. The victims of smallpox testify only to their own poverty and to the infancy of medical science; the victims of the gallows are exemplars of a conscious and elaborated code, justified in the name of a universal human value. Since we hold this value to be a human good, and one whose usefulness the world has not yet outgrown, the operation of this code deserves our most scrupulous attention. It is only when we follow through the intricacies of its operation that we can show what it was worth, how it was bent, how its proclaimed values were falsified in practice. When we note Walpole harrying John Huntridge, Judge Page handing down his death sentences, Lord Hardwicke wrenching the clauses of his Act from their context and Lord Mansfield compounding his manipulations, we feel contempt for men whose practice belied the resounding rhetoric of the age. But we feel contempt not because we are contemptuous of the notion of a just and equitable law but because this notion has been betrayed by its own professors. The modern sensibility which views this only within the perspectives of our own archipelagos of *gulags* and of *stalags*, for whose architects the very notion of the rule of law would be a criminal heresy, will find my responses over-fussy. The plebs of eighteenth century England were provided with a rule of law of some sort, and they ought to have considered themselves lucky. What more could they expect?

In fact, some of them had the impertinence, and the imperfect sense of historical perspective, to expect justice. On the gallows men would actually complain, in their 'last dying words' if they felt that in some particular the due forms of law had not been undergone. (We remember Vulcan Gates complaining that since he was illiterate he could not read his own notice of proclamation; and performing his allotted role at Tyburn only when he had seen the Sheriff's dangling chain.) For the trouble about law and justice, as ideal aspirations, is that they must pretend to absolute validity or they do not exist at all. If I judge the Black Act to be atrocious, this is not only from some standpoint of those whom the Act oppressed, but also according to some ideal notion of the standards to which 'the law' as regulator of human conflicts of interest, ought to attain. For 'the law', as a logic of equity, must always seek to transcend the inequalities of class power which, instrumentally, it is harnessed to serve. And 'the law' as ideology, which pretends to reconcile the interests of all degrees of men, must always come into conflict with the ideological partisanship of class.

We face, then, a paradox. The work of sixteenth and seventeenth century jurists, supported by the practical struggles of such men as Hampden and Lilburne, was passed down as a legacy to the eighteenth century, where it gave rise to a vision, in the minds of some men, of an ideal aspiration towards universal values of law. One thinks of Swift or of Goldsmith, or, with more qualifications, of Sir William Blackstone or Sir Michael Foster. If we today have ideal notions of what law might be, we derive them in some part from that cultural moment. It is, in part, in terms of that age's own aspiration that we judge the Black Act and find it deficient. But at the same time this same century, governed as it was by the forms of law, provides a text-book illustration of the employment of law, as instrument and as idealogy, in serving the interests of the ruling class. The oligarchs and the great gentry were content to be subject to the rule of law only because this law was serviceable and afforded to their hegemony the rhetoric of legitimacy. This paradox has been at the heart of this study. It was also at the heart of eighteenth century society. But it was also a paradox which that society could not in the end transcend, for the paradox was held in equipoise upon an ulterior equilibrium of class forces. When the struggles of 1790–1832 signalled that this equilibrium had changed, the rulers of England were faced with alarming alternatives. They could either dispense with the rule of law, dismantle their elaborate constitutional structures, countermand their own rhetoric and exercise power by force; or they should submit to their own rules and surrender their hegemony. In the campaign against Paine and the printers, in the *Two Acts* (1795), the *Combination Acts* (1799–1800), the repression of Peterloo (1819) and the *Six Acts* (1820) they took halting steps in the first direction. But in the end, rather than shatter their own self-image and repudiate 150 years of constitutional legality, they surrendered to the law. In this surrender they threw retrospective light back on the history of their class, and retrieved for it something of its honour; despite Walpole, despite Paxton, despite Page and Hardwicke, that rhetoric had not been altogether sham.

THE HUMAN RIGHTS ACT 1998

The enactment of the Human Rights Act (HRA) 1998 marked a watershed in United Kingdom law. The incorporation of the European Convention on Human Rights and Fundamental Freedoms into domestic law marked a shift towards a new rights based jurisprudence. For the moment at least, lip-service remains paid to Parliamentary sovereignty, but the Act has the potential for judicial creativity, no to say expansionism, which could lead to the development of a constitutional court on similar lines to the Supreme Court in the United States of America. As yet it is too early to predict how the courts will use their new powers, although Helen Fenwick's second article demonstrates how the courts can use their new powers to develop the common law. The introduction of the HRA 1998 has major implications for the operation of the criminal justice system and these will be considered in Chapters 7 and 8.

Human Rights Act 1998 Chapter 42

[9th November 1998]

BE IT ENACTED by the Queen's most Excellent Majesty, by and with the advice and consent of the Lords Spiritual and Temporal, and Commons, in this present Parliament assembled, and by the authority of the same, as follows:–

Introduction

The Convention Rights

1. –(1) In this Act 'the Convention rights' means the rights and fundamental freedoms set out in–

   (a)   Articles 2 to 12 and 14 of the Convention,

   (b)   Articles 1 to 3 of the First Protocol, and

   (c)   Articles 1 and 2 of the Sixth Protocol,

   as read with Articles 16 to 18 of the Convention.

   (2)   Those Articles are to have effect for the purposes of this Act subject to any designated derogation or reservation (as to which see sections 14 and 15).

   (3)   The Articles are set out in Schedule 1.

   (4)   The Secretary of State may by order make such amendments to this Act as he considers appropriate to reflect the effect, in relation to the United Kingdom, of a protocol.

   (5)   In subsection (4) 'protocol' means a protocol to the Convention–

   (a)   which the United Kingdom has ratified; or

   (b)   which the United Kingdom has signed with a view to ratification.

   (6)   No amendment may be made by an order under subsection (4) so as to come into force before the protocol concerned is in force in relation to the United Kingdom.

Interpretation of Convention rights

2. –(1) A court or tribunal determining a question which has arisen in connection with a Convention right must take into account any–

   (a)   judgment, decision, declaration or advisory opinion of the European Court of Human Rights,

   (b)   opinion of the Commission given in a report adopted under Article 31 of the Convention,

   (c)   decision of the Commission in connection with Article 26 or 27(2) of the Convention, or

   (d)   decision of the Committee of Ministers taken under Article 46 of the Convention, whenever made or given, so far as, in the opinion of the court or tribunal, it is relevant to the proceedings in which that question has arisen.

(2) Evidence of any judgment, decision, declaration or opinion of which account may have to be taken under this section is to be given in proceedings before any court or tribunal in such manner as may be provided by rules.

(3) In this section 'rules' means rules of court or, in the case of proceedings before a tribunal, rules made for the purposes of this section–

(a) by the Lord Chancellor or the Secretary of State, in relation to any proceedings outside Scotland;

(b) by the Secretary of State, in relation to proceedings in Scotland; or

(c) by a Northern Ireland department, in relation to proceedings before a tribunal in Northern Ireland–

(i) which deals with transferred matters; and

(ii) for which no rules made under paragraph (a) are in force.

Legislation

Interpretation of Legislation

3. – (1) So far as it is possible to do so, primary legislation and subordinate legislation must be read and given effect in a way which is compatible with the Convention rights.

(2) This section–

(a) applies to primary legislation and subordinate legislation whenever enacted;

(b) does not affect the validity, continuing operation or enforcement of any incompatible primary legislation; and

(c) does not affect the validity, continuing operation or enforcement of any incompatible subordinate legislation if (disregarding any possibility of revocation) primary legislation prevents removal of the incompatibility.

Declaration of incompatibility

4. – (1) Subsection (2) applies in any proceedings in which a court determines whether a provision of primary legislation is compatible with a Convention right.

(2) If the court is satisfied that the provision is incompatible with a Convention right, it may make a declaration of that incompatibility.

(3) Subsection (4) applies in any proceedings in which a court determines whether a provision of subordinate legislation, made in the exercise of a power conferred by primary legislation, is compatible with a Convention right.

(4) If the court is satisfied–

(a) that the provision is incompatible with a Convention right, and

(b) that (disregarding any possibility of revocation) the primary legislation concerned prevents removal of the incompatibility, it may make a declaration of that incompatibility.

(5) In this section 'court' means–

    (a) the House of Lords;

    (b) the Judicial Committee of the Privy Council;

    (c) the Courts-Martial Appeal Court;

    (d) in Scotland, the High Court of Justiciary sitting otherwise than as a trial court or the Court of Session;

    (e) in England and Wales or Northern Ireland, the High Court or the Court of Appeal.

(6) A declaration under this section ('a declaration of incompatibility')–

    (a) does not affect the validity, continuing operation or enforcement of the provision in respect of which it is given; and

    (b) is not binding on the parties to the proceedings in which it is made.

Right of Crown to intervene

5. –(1) Where a court is considering whether to make a declaration of incompatibility, the Crown is entitled to notice in accordance with rules of court.

(2) In any case to which subsection(1) applies–

    (a) a Minister of the Crown (or a person nominated by him),

    (b) a member of the Scottish Executive,

    (c) a Northern Ireland Minister,

    (d) a Northern Ireland department, is entitled, on giving notice in accordance with rules of court, to be joined as a party to the proceedings.

(3) Notice under subsection (2) may be given at any time during the proceedings.

(4) A person who has been made a party to criminal proceedings (other than in Scotland) as the result of a notice under subsection (2) may, with leave, appeal to the House of Lords against any declaration of incompatibility made in the proceedings.

(5) In subsection (4)–

'criminal proceedings' includes all proceedings before the Courts-Martial Appeal Court; and

'leave' means leave granted by the court making the declaration of incompatibility or by the House of Lords.

Public authorities

Acts of public authorities

6. –(1) It is unlawful for a public authority to act in a way which is incompatible with a Convention right.

(2) Subsection (1) does not apply to an act if–

    (a) as the result of one or more provisions of primary legislation, the authority could not have acted differently; or

    (b) in the case of one or more provisions of, or made under, primary legislation which cannot be read or given effect in a way which is compatible with the Convention rights, the authority was acting so as to give effect to or enforce those provisions.

(3) In this section 'public authority' includes–

(a) a court or tribunal, and

(b) any person certain of whose functions are functions of a public nature,

but does not include either House of Parliament or a person exercising functions in connection with proceedings in Parliament.

(4) In subsection (3) 'Parliament' does not include the House of Lords in its judicial capacity.

(5) In relation to a particular act, a person is not a public authority by virtue only of subsection (3)(b) if the nature of the act is private.

(6) 'An act' includes a failure to act but does not include a failure to–

(a) introduce in, or lay before, Parliament a proposal for legislation; or

(b) make any primary legislation or remedial order.

Proceedings

7. – (1) A person who claims that a public authority has acted (or proposes to act) in a way which is made unlawful by section 6(1) may–

(a) bring proceedings against the authority under this Act in the appropriate court or tribunal, or

(b) rely on the Convention right or rights concerned in any legal proceedings,

but only if he is (or would be) a victim of the unlawful act.

(2) In subsection (1)(a) 'appropriate court or tribunal' means such court or tribunal as may be determined in accordance with rules; and proceedings against an authority include a counterclaim or similar proceeding.

(3) If the proceedings are brought on an application for judicial review, the applicant is to be taken to have a sufficient interest in relation to the unlawful act only if he is, or would be, a victim of that act.

(4) If the proceedings are made by way of a petition for judicial review in Scotland, the applicant shall be taken to have title and interest to sue in relation to the unlawful act only if he is, or would be, a victim of that act.

(5) Proceedings under subsection (1)(a) must be brought before the end of–

(a) the period of one year beginning with the date on which the act complained of took place; or

(b) such longer period as the court or tribunal considers equitable having regard to all the circumstances,

but that is subject to any rule imposing a stricter time limit in relation to the procedure in question.

(6) In subsection (1)(b) 'legal proceedings' includes–

(a) proceedings brought by or at the instigation of a public authority; and

(b) an appeal against the decision of a court or tribunal.

(7) For the purposes of this section, a person is a victim of an unlawful act only if he would be a victim for the purposes of Article 34 of the Convention if proceedings were brought in the European Court of Human Rights in respect of that act.

(8) Nothing in this Act creates a criminal offence.

(9) In this section 'rules' means–

    (a) in relation to proceedings before a court or tribunal outside Scotland, rules made by the Lord Chancellor or the Secretary of State for the purposes of this section or rules of court,

    (b) in relation to proceedings before a court or tribunal in Scotland, rules made by the Secretary of State for those purposes,

    (c) in relation to proceedings before a tribunal in Northern Ireland–

        (i) which deals with transferred matters; and

        (ii) or which no rules made under paragraph (a) are in force,

    rules made by a Northern Ireland department for those purposes,

and includes provision made by order under section 1 of the Courts and Legal Services Act 1990.

(10) In making rules, regard must be had to section 9.

(11) The Minister who has power to make rules in relation to a particular tribunal may, to the extent he considers it necessary to ensure that the tribunal can provide an appropriate remedy in relation to an act (or proposed act) of a public authority which is (or would be) unlawful as a result of section 6(1), by order add to–

    (a) the relief or remedies which the tribunal may grant; or

    (b) the grounds on which it may grant any of them.

(12) An order made under subsection (11) may contain such incidental, supplemental, consequential or transitional provision as the Minister making it considers appropriate.

(13) 'The Minister' includes the Northern Ireland department concerned.

Judicial remedies

8. – (1) In relation to any act (or proposed act) of a public authority which the court finds is (or would be) unlawful, it may grant such relief or remedy, or make such order, within its powers as it considers just and appropriate.

    (2) But damages may be awarded only by a court which has power to award damages, or to order the payment of compensation, in civil proceedings.

    (3) No award of damages is to be made unless, taking account of all the circumstances of the case, including–

    (a) any other relief or remedy granted, or order made, in relation to the act in question (by that or any other court), and

    (b) the consequences of any decision (of that or any other court) in respect of that act,

the court is satisfied that the award is necessary to afford just satisfaction to the person in whose favour it is made.

(4) In determining–

    (a)   whether to award damages, or

    (b)   the amount of an award,

the court must take into account the principles applied by the European Court of Human Rights in relation to the award of compensation under Article 41 of the Convention.

(5) A public authority against which damages are awarded is to be treated–

    (a)   in Scotland, for the purposes of section 3 of the Law Reform (Miscellaneous Provisions) (Scotland) Act 1940 as if the award were made in an action of damages in which the authority has been found liable in respect of loss or damage to the person to whom the award is made;

    (b)   for the purposes of the Civil Liability (Contribution) Act 1978 as liable in respect of damage suffered by the person to whom the award is made.

(6) In this section–

'court' includes a tribunal;

'damages' means damages for an unlawful act of a public authority; and

'unlawful' means unlawful under section 6(1).

Judicial acts

9. –(1) Proceedings under section 7(1)(a) in respect of a judicial act may be brought only–

    (a)   by exercising a right of appeal;

    (b)   on an application (in Scotland a petition) for judicial review; or

    (c)   in such other forum as may be prescribed by rules.

(2) That does not affect any rule of law which prevents a court from being the subject of judicial review.

(3) In proceedings under this Act in respect of a judicial act done in good faith, damages may not be awarded otherwise than to compensate a person to the extent required by Article 5(5) of the Convention.

(4) An award of damages permitted by subsection (3) is to be made against the Crown; but no award may be made unless the appropriate person, if not a party to the proceedings, is joined.

(5) In this section–

'appropriate person' means the Minister responsible for the court concerned, or a person or government department nominated by him;

'court' includes a tribunal;

'judge' includes a member of a tribunal, a justice of the peace and a clerk or other officer entitled to exercise the jurisdiction of a court;

'judicial act' means a judicial act of a court and includes an act done on the instructions, or on behalf, of a judge; and

'rules' has the same meaning as in section 7(9).

Remedial action

Power to take remedial action

10. –(1) This section applies if–

  (a) a provision of legislation has been declared under section 4 to be incompatible with a Convention right and, if an appeal lies–

    (i) all persons who may appeal have stated in writing that they do not intend to do so;

    (ii) the time for bringing an appeal has expired and no appeal has been brought within that time; or

    (iii) an appeal brought within that time has been determined or abandoned; or

  (b) it appears to a Minister of the Crown or Her Majesty in Council that, having regard to a finding of the European Court of Human Rights made after the coming into force of this section in proceedings against the United Kingdom, a provision of legislation is incompatible with an obligation of the United Kingdom arising from the Convention.

  (2) If a Minister of the Crown considers that there are compelling reasons for proceeding under this section, he may by order make such amendments to the legislation as he considers necessary to remove the incompatibility.

  (3) If, in the case of subordinate legislation, a Minister of the Crown considers–

  (a) that it is necessary to amend the primary legislation under which the subordinate legislation in question was made, in order to enable the incompatibility to be removed, and

  (b) that there are compelling reasons for proceeding under this section, he may by order make such amendments to the primary legislation as he considers necessary.

  (4) This section also applies where the provision in question is in subordinate legislation and has been quashed, or declared invalid, by reason of incompatibility with a Convention right and the Minister proposes to proceed under paragraph 2(b) of Schedule 2.

  (5) If the legislation is an Order in Council, the power conferred by subsection (2) or (3) is exercisable by Her Majesty in Council.

  (6) In this section 'legislation' does not include a Measure of the Church Assembly or of the General Synod of the Church of England.

  (7) Schedule 2 makes further provision about remedial orders.

Other rights and proceedings

Safeguard for existing human rights

11. A person's reliance on a Convention right does not restrict–

  (a) any other right or freedom conferred on him by or under any law having effect in any part of the United Kingdom; or

  (b) his right to make any claim or bring any proceedings which he could make or bring apart from sections 7 to 9.

Freedom of expression

12. –(1) This section applies if a court is considering whether to grant any relief which, if granted, might affect the exercise of the Convention right to freedom of expression.

    (2) If the person against whom the application for relief is made ('the respondent') is neither present nor represented, no such relief is to be granted unless the court is satisfied–

    (a) that the applicant has taken all practicable steps to notify the respondent; or

    (b) that there are compelling reasons why the respondent should not be notified.

    (3) No such relief is to be granted so as to restrain publication before trial unless the court is satisfied that the applicant is likely to establish that publication should not be allowed.

    (4) The court must have particular regard to the importance of the Convention right to freedom of expression and, where the proceedings relate to material which the respondent claims, or which appears to the court, to be journalistic, literary or artistic material (or to conduct connected with such material), to–

    (a) the extent to which–

    (i) the material has, or is about to, become available to the public; or

    (ii) it is, or would be, in the public interest for the material to be published;

    (b) any relevant privacy code.

    (5) In this section–

    'court' includes a tribunal; and

    'relief' includes any remedy or order (other than in criminal proceedings).

Freedom of thought, conscience and religion.

13. –(1) If a court's determination of any question arising under this Act might affect the exercise by a religious organisation (itself or its members collectively) of the Convention right to freedom of thought, conscience and religion, it must have particular regard to the importance of that right.

    (2) In this section 'court' includes a tribunal.

Derogations and reservations

Derogations

14. –(1) In this Act 'designated derogation' means–

    (a) the United Kingdom's derogation from Article 5(3) of the Convention; and

    (b) any derogation by the United Kingdom from an Article of the Convention, or of any protocol to the Convention, which is designated for the purposes of this Act in an order made by the Secretary of State.

    (2) The derogation referred to in subsection (1)(a) is set out in Part I of Schedule 3.

    (3) If a designated derogation is amended or replaced it ceases to be a designated derogation.

(4) But subsection (3) does not prevent the Secretary of State from exercising his power under subsection (1)(b) to make a fresh designation order in respect of the Article concerned.

(5) The Secretary of State must by order make such amendments to Schedule 3 as he considers appropriate to reflect–

(a) any designation order; or

(b) the effect of subsection (3).

(6) A designation order may be made in anticipation of the making by the United Kingdom of a proposed derogation.

Reservations

15. –(1) In this Act 'designated reservation' means–

(a) the United Kingdom's reservation to Article 2 of the First Protocol to the Convention; and

(b) any other reservation by the United Kingdom to an Article of the Convention, or of any protocol to the Convention, which is designated for the purposes of this Act in an order made by the Secretary of State.

(2) The text of the reservation referred to in subsection (1)(a) is set out in Part II of Schedule 3.

(3) If a designated reservation is withdrawn wholly or in part it ceases to be a designated reservation.

(4) But subsection (3) does not prevent the Secretary of State from exercising his power under subsection (1)(b) to make a fresh designation order in respect of the Article concerned.

(5) The Secretary of State must by order make such amendments to this Act as he considers appropriate to reflect–

(a) any designation order; or

(b) the effect of subsection (3).

Period for which designated derogations have effect

16. –(1) If it has not already been withdrawn by the United Kingdom, a designated derogation ceases to have effect for the purposes of this Act–

(a) in the case of the derogation referred to in section 14(1)(a), at the end of the period of five years beginning with the date on which section 1(2) came into force;

(b) in the case of any other derogation, at the end of the period of five years beginning with the date on which the order designating it was made.

(2) At any time before the period–

(a) fixed by subsection (1)(a) or (b), or

(b) extended by an order under this subsection,

comes to an end, the Secretary of State may by order extend it by a further period of five years.

(3) An order under section 14(1)(b) ceases to have effect at the end of the period for consideration, unless a resolution has been passed by each House approving the order.

(4) Subsection (3) does not affect–

    (a) anything done in reliance on the order; or

    (b) the power to make a fresh order under section 14(1)(b).

(5) In subsection (3) 'period for consideration' means the period of forty days beginning with the day on which the order was made.

(6) In calculating the period for consideration, no account is to be taken of any time during which–

    (a) Parliament is dissolved or prorogued; or

    (b) both Houses are adjourned for more than four days.

(7) If a designated derogation is withdrawn by the United Kingdom, the Secretary of State must by order make such amendments to this Act as he considers are required to reflect that withdrawal.

Periodic review of designated reservations

17. –(1) The appropriate Minister must review the designated reservation referred to in section 15(1)(a)–

    (a) before the end of the period of five years beginning with the date on which section 1(2) came into force; and

    (b) if that designation is still in force, before the end of the period of five years beginning with the date on which the last report relating to it was laid under subsection (3).

(2) The appropriate Minister must review each of the other designated reservations (if any)–

    (a) before the end of the period of five years beginning with the date on which the order designating the reservation first came into force; and

    (b) if the designation is still in force, before the end of the period of five years beginning with the date on which the last report relating to it was laid under subsection (3).

(3) The Minister conducting a review under this section must prepare a report on the result of the review and lay a copy of it before each House of Parliament.

Judges of the European Court of Human Rights

Appointment to European Court of Human Rights

18. –(1) In this section 'judicial office' means the office of–

    (a) Lord Justice of Appeal, Justice of the High Court or Circuit judge, in England and Wales;

    (b) judge of the Court of Session or sheriff, in Scotland;

    (c) Lord Justice of Appeal, judge of the High Court or county court judge, in Northern Ireland.

(2) The holder of a judicial office may become a judge of the European Court of Human Rights ('the Court') without being required to relinquish his office.

(3) But he is not required to perform the duties of his judicial office while he is a judge of the Court.

(4) In respect of any period during which he is a judge of the Court–

    (a) a Lord Justice of Appeal or Justice of the High Court is not to count as a judge of the relevant court for the purposes of section 2(1) or 4(1) of the Supreme Court Act 1981 (maximum number of judges) nor as a judge of the Supreme Court for the purposes of section 12(1) to (6) of that Act (salaries etc);

    (b) a judge of the Court of Session is not to count as a judge of that court for the purposes of section 1(1) of the Court of Session Act 1988 (maximum number of judges) or of section 9(1)(c) of the Administration of Justice Act 1973 ('the 1973 Act') (salaries etc);

    (c) a Lord Justice of Appeal or judge of the High Court in Northern Ireland is not to count as a judge of the relevant court for the purposes of section 2(1) or 3(1) of the Judicature (Northern Ireland) Act 1978 (maximum number of judges) nor as a judge of the Supreme Court of Northern Ireland for the purposes of section 9(1)(d) of the 1973 Act (salaries etc);

    (d) a Circuit judge is not to count as such for the purposes of section 18 of the Courts Act 1971 (salaries etc);

    (e) a sheriff is not to count as such for the purposes of section 14 of the Sheriff Courts (Scotland) Act 1907 (salaries etc);

    (f) a county court judge of Northern Ireland is not to count as such for the purposes of section 106 of the County Courts Act Northern Ireland) 1959 (salaries etc).

(5) If a sheriff principal is appointed a judge of the Court, section 11(1) of the Sheriff Courts (Scotland) Act 1971 (temporary appointment of sheriff principal) applies, while he holds that appointment, as if his office is vacant.

(6) Schedule 4 makes provision about judicial pensions in relation to the holder of a judicial office who serves as a judge of the Court.

(7) The Lord Chancellor or the Secretary of State may by order make such transitional provision (including, in particular, provision for a temporary increase in the maximum number of judges) as he considers appropriate in relation to any holder of a judicial office who has completed his service as a judge of the Court.

Parliamentary procedure

Statements of compatibility

19. –(1) A Minister of the Crown in charge of a Bill in either House of Parliament must, before Second Reading of the Bill–

    (a) make a statement to the effect that in his view the provisions of the Bill are compatible with the Convention rights ('a statement of compatibility'); or

    (b) make a statement to the effect that although he is unable to make a statement of compatibility the government nevertheless wishes the House to proceed with the Bill.

(2) The statement must be in writing and be published in such manner as the Minister making it considers appropriate.

Supplemental Orders etc under this Act

20. –(1) Any power of a Minister of the Crown to make an order under this Act is exercisable by statutory instrument.

(2) The power of the Lord Chancellor or the Secretary of State to make rules (other than rules of court) under section 2(3) or 7(9) is exercisable by statutory instrument.

(3) Any statutory instrument made under section 14, 15 or 16(7) must be laid before Parliament.

(4) No order may be made by the Lord Chancellor or the Secretary of State under section 1(4), 7(11) or 16(2) unless a draft of the order has been laid before, and approved by, each House of Parliament.

(5) Any statutory instrument made under section 18(7) or Schedule 4, or to which subsection (2) applies, shall be subject to annulment in pursuance of a resolution of either House of Parliament.

(6) The power of a Northern Ireland department to make–

(a) rules under section 2(3)(c) or 7(9)(c), or

(b) an order under section 7(11), is exercisable by statutory rule for the purposes of the Statutory Rules (Northern Ireland) Order 1979.

(7) Any rules made under section 2(3)(c) or 7(9)(c) shall be subject to negative resolution; and section 41(6) of the Interpretation Act (Northern Ireland) 1954 (meaning of 'subject to negative resolution') shall apply as if the power to make the rules were conferred by an Act of the Northern Ireland Assembly.

(8) No order may be made by a Northern Ireland department under section 7(11) unless a draft of the order has been laid before, and approved by, the Northern Ireland Assembly.

Interpretation, etc

21. –(1) In this Act–

'amend' includes repeal and apply (with or without modifications);

'the appropriate Minister' means the Minister of the Crown having charge of the appropriate authorised government department (within the meaning of the Crown Proceedings Act 1947);

'the Commission' means the European Commission of Human Rights;

'the Convention' means the Convention for the Protection of Human Rights and Fundamental Freedoms, agreed by the Council of Europe at Rome on 4th November 1950 as it has effect for the time being in relation to the United Kingdom;

'declaration of incompatibility' means a declaration under section 4;

'Minister of the Crown' has the same meaning as in the Ministers of the Crown Act 1975;

'Northern Ireland Minister' includes the First Minister and the deputy First Minister in Northern Ireland;

'primary legislation' means any–

(a)   public general Act;

(b)   local and personal Act;

(c)   private Act;

(d)   Measure of the Church Assembly;

(e)   Measure of the General Synod of the Church of England;

(f)   Order in Council–

   (i)   made in exercise of Her Majesty's Royal Prerogative;

   (ii)   made under section 38(1)(a) of the Northern Ireland Constitution Act 1973 or the corresponding provision of the Northern Ireland Act 1998; or

   (iii)   amending an Act of a kind mentioned in paragraph (a), (b) or (c);

   and includes an order or other instrument made under primary legislation (otherwise than by the National Assembly for Wales, a member of the Scottish Executive, a Northern Ireland Minister or a Northern Ireland department) to the extent to which it operates to bring one or more provisions of that legislation into force or amends any primary legislation;

'the First Protocol' means the protocol to the Convention agreed at Paris on 20th March 1952;

'the Sixth Protocol' means the protocol to the Convention agreed at Strasbourg on 28th April 1983;

'the Eleventh Protocol' means the protocol to the Convention (restructuring the control machinery established by the Convention) agreed at Strasbourg on 11th May 1994;

'remedial order' means an order under section 10;

'subordinate legislation' means any–

   (a)   Order in Council other than one–

      (i)   made in exercise of Her Majesty's Royal Prerogative;

      (ii)   made under section 38(1)(a) of the Northern Ireland Constitution Act 1973 or the corresponding provision of the Northern Ireland Act 1998; or

      (iii)   amending an Act of a kind mentioned in the definition of primary legislation;

   (b)   Act of the Scottish Parliament;

   (c)   Act of the Parliament of Northern Ireland;

   (d)   Measure of the Assembly established under section 1 of the Northern Ireland Assembly Act 1973;

   (e)   Act of the Northern Ireland Assembly;

   (f)   order, rules, regulations, scheme, warrant, byelaw or other instrument made under primary legislation (except to the extent to which it operates to bring one or more provisions of that legislation into force or amends any primary legislation);

(g)   order, rules, regulations, scheme, warrant, byelaw or other instrument made under legislation mentioned in paragraph (b), (c), (d) or (e) or made under an Order in Council applying only to Northern Ireland;

(h)   order, rules, regulations, scheme, warrant, byelaw or other instrument made by a member of the Scottish Executive, a Northern Ireland Minister or a Northern Ireland department in exercise of prerogative or other executive functions of Her Majesty which are exercisable by such a person on behalf of Her Majesty;

'transferred matters' has the same meaning as in the Northern Ireland Act 1998; and

'tribunal' means any tribunal in which legal proceedings may be brought.

(2)   The references in paragraphs (b) and (c) of section 2(1) to Articles are to Articles of the Convention as they had effect immediately before the coming into force of the Eleventh Protocol.

(3)   The reference in paragraph (d) of section 2(1) to Article 46 includes a reference to Articles 32 and 54 of the Convention as they had effect immediately before the coming into force of the Eleventh Protocol.

(4)   The references in section 2(1) to a report or decision of the Commission or a decision of the Committee of Ministers include references to a report or decision made as provided by paragraphs 3, 4 and 6 of Article 5 of the Eleventh Protocol (transitional provisions).

(5)   Any liability under the Army Act 1955, the Air Force Act 1955 or the Naval Discipline Act 1957 to suffer death for an offence is replaced by a liability to imprisonment for life or any less punishment authorised by those Acts; and those Acts shall accordingly have effect with the necessary modifications.

Short title, commencement, application and extent

22. –(1) This Act may be cited as the Human Rights Act 1998.

(2)   Sections 18, 20 and 21(5) and this section come into force on the passing of this Act.

(3)   The other provisions of this Act come into force on such day as the Secretary of State may by order appoint; and different days may be appointed for different purposes.

(4)   Paragraph (b) of subsection (1) of section 7 applies to proceedings brought by or at the instigation of a public authority whenever the act in question took place; but otherwise that subsection does not apply to an act taking place before the coming into force of that section.

(5)   This Act binds the Crown.

(6)   This Act extends to Northern Ireland.

(7)   Section 21(5), so far as it relates to any provision contained in the Army Act 1955, the Air Force Act 1955 or the Naval Discipline Act 1957, extends to any place to which that provision extends.

SCHEDULE 1

The Articles

Part I

The Convention Rights and Freedoms

Article 2: Right to Life

1   Everyone's right to life shall be protected by law. No one shall be deprived of his life intentionally save in the execution of a sentence of a court following his conviction of a crime for which this penalty is provided by law.

2   Deprivation of life shall not be regarded as inflicted in contravention of this Article when it results from the use of force which is no more than absolutely necessary:

    (a)   in defence of any person from unlawful violence;

    (b)   in order to effect a lawful arrest or to prevent the escape of a person lawfully detained;

    (c)   in action lawfully taken for the purpose of quelling a riot or insurrection.

Article 3: Prohibition of Torture

No one shall be subjected to torture or to inhuman or degrading treatment or punishment.

Article 4: Prohibition of Slavery and Forced Labour

1   No one shall be held in slavery or servitude.

2   No one shall be required to perform forced or compulsory labour.

3   For the purpose of this Article the term 'forced or compulsory labour' shall not include:

    (a)   any work required to be done in the ordinary course of detention imposed according to the provisions of Article 5 of this Convention or during conditional release from such detention;

    (b)   any service of a military character or, in case of conscientious objectors in countries where they are recognised, service exacted instead of compulsory military service;

    (c)   any service exacted in case of an emergency or calamity threatening the life or well-being of the community;

    (d)   any work or service which forms part of normal civic obligations.

Article 5: Right to Liberty and Security

1   Everyone has the right to liberty and security of person. No one shall be deprived of his liberty save in the following cases and in accordance with a procedure prescribed by law:

    (a)   the lawful detention of a person after conviction by a competent court;

(b)   the lawful arrest or detention of a person for non-compliance with the lawful order of a court or in order to secure the fulfilment of any obligation prescribed by law;

(c)   the lawful arrest or detention of a person effected for the purpose of bringing him before the competent legal authority on reasonable suspicion of having committed an offence or when it is reasonably considered necessary to prevent his committing an offence or fleeing after having done so;

(d)   the detention of a minor by lawful order for the purpose of educational supervision or his lawful detention for the purpose of bringing him before the competent legal authority;

(e)   the lawful detention of persons for the prevention of the spreading of infectious diseases, of persons of unsound mind, alcoholics or drug addicts or vagrants;

(f)   the lawful arrest or detention of a person to prevent his effecting an unauthorised entry into the country or of a person against whom action is being taken with a view to deportation or extradition.

2   Everyone who is arrested shall be informed promptly, in a language which he understands, of the reasons for his arrest and of any charge against him.

3   Everyone arrested or detained in accordance with the provisions of paragraph 1(c) of this Article shall be brought promptly before a judge or other officer authorised by law to exercise judicial power and shall be entitled to trial within a reasonable time or to release pending trial. Release may be conditioned by guarantees to appear for trial.

4   Everyone who is deprived of his liberty by arrest or detention shall be entitled to take proceedings by which the lawfulness of his detention shall be decided speedily by a court and his release ordered if the detention is not lawful.

5   Everyone who has been the victim of arrest or detention in contravention of the provisions of this Article shall have an enforceable right to compensation.

Article 6: Right to a Fair Trial

1   In the determination of his civil rights and obligations or of any criminal charge against him, everyone is entitled to a fair and public hearing within a reasonable time by an independent and impartial tribunal established by law. Judgment shall be pronounced publicly but the press and public may be excluded from all or part of the trial in the interest of morals, public order or national security in a democratic society, where the interests of juveniles or the protection of the private life of the parties so require, or to the extent strictly necessary in the opinion of the court in special circumstances where publicity would prejudice the interests of justice.

2   Everyone charged with a criminal offence shall be presumed innocent until proved guilty according to law.

3   Everyone charged with a criminal offence has the following minimum rights:

(a)   to be informed promptly, in a language which he understands and in detail, of the nature and cause of the accusation against him;

(b)   to have adequate time and facilities for the preparation of his defence;

(c)   to defend himself in person or through legal assistance of his own choosing or, if he has not sufficient means to pay for legal assistance, to be given it free when the interests of justice so require;

(d)   to examine or have examined witnesses against him and to obtain the attendance and examination of witnesses on his behalf under the same conditions as witnesses against him;

(e)   to have the free assistance of an interpreter if he cannot understand or speak the language used in court.

Article 7: No Punishment without Law

1   No one shall be held guilty of any criminal offence on account of any act or omission which did not constitute a criminal offence under national or international law at the time when it was committed. Nor shall a heavier penalty be imposed than the one that was applicable at the time the criminal offence was committed.

2   This Article shall not prejudice the trial and punishment of any person for any act or omission which, at the time when it was committed, was criminal according to the general principles of law recognised by civilised nations.

Article 8: Right to Respect for Private and Family Life

1   Everyone has the right to respect for his private and family life, his home and his correspondence.

2   There shall be no interference by a public authority with the exercise of this right except such as is in accordance with the law and is necessary in a democratic society in the interests of national security, public safety or the economic well-being of the country, for the prevention of disorder or crime, for the protection of health or morals, or for the protection of the rights and freedoms of others.

Article 9: Freedom of Thought, Conscience and Religion

1   Everyone has the right to freedom of thought, conscience and religion; this right includes freedom to change his religion or belief and freedom, either alone or in community with others and in public or private, to manifest his religion or belief, in worship, teaching, practice and observance.

2   Freedom to manifest one's religion or beliefs shall be subject only to such limitations as are prescribed by law and are necessary in a democratic society in the interests of public safety, for the protection of public order, health or morals, or for the protection of the rights and freedoms of others.

Article 10: Freedom of Expression

1   Everyone has the right to freedom of expression. This right shall include freedom to hold opinions and to receive and impart information and ideas without interference by public authority and regardless of frontiers. This Article shall not prevent States from requiring the licensing of broadcasting, television or cinema enterprises.

2   The exercise of these freedoms, since it carries with it duties and responsibilities, may be subject to such formalities, conditions, restrictions or penalties as are prescribed by law and are necessary in a democratic society, in the interests of national security, territorial integrity or public safety, for the prevention of disorder or crime, for the protection of health or morals, for the protection of the reputation or rights of others, for preventing the disclosure of information received in confidence, or for maintaining the authority and impartiality of the judiciary.

Article 11: Freedom of Assembly and Association
1   Everyone has the right to freedom of peaceful assembly and to freedom of association with others, including the right to form and to join trade unions for the protection of his interests.

2   No restrictions shall be placed on the exercise of these rights other than such as are prescribed by law and are necessary in a democratic society in the interests of national security or public safety, for the prevention of disorder or crime, for the protection of health or morals or for the protection of the rights and freedoms of others. This Article shall not prevent the imposition of lawful restrictions on the exercise of these rights by members of the armed forces, of the police or of the administration of the State.

Article 12: Right to Marry
Men and women of marriageable age have the right to marry and to found a family, according to the national laws governing the exercise of this right.

Article 14: Prohibition of Discrimination
The enjoyment of the rights and freedoms set forth in this Convention shall be secured without discrimination on any ground such as sex, race, colour, language, religion, political or other opinion, national or social origin, association with a national minority, property, birth or other status.

Article 16: Restrictions on Political Activity of Aliens
Nothing in Articles 10, 11 and 14 shall be regarded as preventing the High Contracting Parties from imposing restrictions on the political activity of aliens.

Article 17: Prohibition of Abuse of Rights
Nothing in this Convention may be interpreted as implying for any State, group or person any right to engage in any activity or perform any act aimed at the destruction of any of the rights and freedoms set forth herein or at their limitation to a greater extent than is provided for in the Convention.

Article 18: Limitation on Use of Restriction of Rights
The restrictions permitted under this Convention to the said rights and freedoms shall not be applied for any purpose other than those for which they have been prescribed.

SCHEDULE 2

Remedial Orders

Orders

1 – (1) A remedial order may–

    (a) contain such incidental, supplemental, consequential or transitional provision as the person making it considers appropriate;

    (b) be made so as to have effect from a date earlier than that on which it is made;

    (c) make provision for the delegation of specific functions;

    (d) make different provision for different cases.

  (2) The power conferred by sub-paragraph (1)(a) includes–

    (a) power to amend primary legislation (including primary legislation other than that which contains the incompatible provision); and

    (b) power to amend or revoke subordinate legislation (including subordinate legislation other than that which contains the incompatible provision).

  (3) A remedial order may be made so as to have the same extent as the legislation which it affects.

  (4) No person is to be guilty of an offence solely as a result of the retrospective effect of a remedial order.

Procedure

2 – No remedial order may be made unless–

  (a) a draft of the order has been approved by a resolution of each House of Parliament made after the end of the period of 60 days beginning with the day on which the draft was laid; or

  (b) it is declared in the order that it appears to the person making it that, because of the urgency of the matter, it is necessary to make the order without a draft being so approved.

Orders laid in draft

3 – (1) No draft may be laid under paragraph 2(a) unless–

    (a) the person proposing to make the order has laid before Parliament a document which contains a draft of the proposed order and the required information; and

    (b) the period of 60 days, beginning with the day on which the document required by this sub-paragraph was laid, has ended.

  (2) If representations have been made during that period, the draft laid under paragraph 2(a) must be accompanied by a statement containing–

    (a) a summary of the representations; and

    (b) if, as a result of the representations, the proposed order has been changed, details of the changes.

Urgent cases

4 – (1) If a remedial order ('the original order') is made without being approved in draft, the person making it must lay it before Parliament, accompanied by the required information, after it is made.

(2) If representations have been made during the period of 60 days beginning with the day on which the original order was made, the person making it must (after the end of that period) lay before Parliament a statement containing–

(a) a summary of the representations; and

(b) if, as a result of the representations, he considers it appropriate to make changes to the original order, details of the changes.

(3) If sub-paragraph (2)(b) applies, the person making the statement must–

(a) make a further remedial order replacing the original order; and

(b) lay the replacement order before Parliament.

(4) If, at the end of the period of 120 days beginning with the day on which the original order was made, a resolution has not been passed by each House approving the original or replacement order, the order ceases to have effect (but without that affecting anything previously done under either order or the power to make a fresh remedial order).

Definitions

5 In this Schedule–

'representations' means representations about a remedial order (or proposed remedial order) made to the person making (or proposing to make) it and includes any relevant Parliamentary report or resolution; and

'required information' means–

(a) an explanation of the incompatibility which the order (or proposed order) seeks to remove, including particulars of the relevant declaration, finding or order; and

(b) a statement of the reasons for proceeding under section 10 and for making an order in those terms.

Calculating periods

6 In calculating any period for the purposes of this Schedule, no account is to be taken of any time during which–

(a) Parliament is dissolved or prorogued; or

(b) both Houses are adjourned for more than four days.

– · – · – · – · – · – · – · – · – · – · – · – · –

The implications of introducing the European Convention into United Kingdom law were pointed out by the Lord Chancellor in the following speech.

**The Tom Sargant Memorial Lecture: The Development Of Human Rights
In Britain Under An Incorporated Convention On Human Rights,[1]
Lord Irvine of Lairg, The Lord Chancellor**

On 23rd October I introduced the Human Rights Bill into Parliament. It will incorporate into the domestic law of the United Kingdom the rights and liberties guaranteed by the European Convention on Human Rights. It will mean that our citizens can secure their rights from our own UK courts. They will not have to take the long slow road to the Court in Strasbourg. It is one of the major constitutional changes which this Government is making.

I am sure Tom Sargant, in whose memory this Lecture is given, would have approved. Tom Sargant was not a lawyer. Nor even had he gone to University. His family's financial difficulties stood in his way. So he did not take up the scholarship he had won at Cambridge. His memorial is Justice, which he made the conscience of the legal profession. He was the first Secretary of Justice, for 25 years from its creation in 1957. It was he who took up – contrary to instructions – the cases of prisoners complaining of wrongful convictions. So began Justice's proud and successful tradition of case work. Tom Sargant demonstrated throughout his life a strong and firm belief in a just society. He always stood up for ordinary people. He would have applauded, I believe, the commitment to stand up for ordinary people, their rights and liberties, which the Government demonstrates in making the Human Rights Bill one of its first acts of legislation.

I want to speak this evening about the significance the Human Rights Bill has for individuals; but also to go beyond the extensive area in which the Act will bite and to consider how the Human Rights Bill will influence and mould the process of law making and the content of the law in other and wider areas. It will be a constitutional change of major significance: protecting the individual citizen against erosion of liberties, either deliberate or gradual. It will also help develop a process of justice based on the promotion of positive rights.

I start with a little history.

Today we talk readily of Human Rights law. There is now a corpus of law, international and national, recognising fundamental freedoms. It is called International Human Rights law. Fifty years ago it would not have been possible to talk of such a body of law.

Until then very few issues would have been regarded in any way as the province of international law. Piracy and slavery were the major exceptions. For many years the existence of internationally recognised norms of human rights was simply inconsistent with central propositions of international law, the positivist doctrines of State sovereignty and domestic jurisdiction.

This view was particularly expounded by John Austin in his Lectures on Jurisprudence, delivered at the newly founded University College London between 1828 and 1832. He brought together many of the ideas scattered through Bentham's own voluminous works.[2] Law, according to Austin's definition, was a body of rules fixed and enforced by a sovereign political authority. There could be

---

1   I am indebted to Peter Goldsmith QC for the great assistance he has given me in the preparation of this Lecture.

2   See Sabine, *A History of Political Theory*, 3rd ed, Harrap, p 684.

no such thing as international law, it followed, since there was no sovereign political authority over the individual sovereign States themselves to set or enforce any rules of conduct. It also followed that under the doctrine of State sovereignty, individuals received no protection under international law. Their protection had to come in courts of purely domestic jurisdiction. It was a breach of international law for one State to intervene in another State's sphere of exclusive domestic jurisdiction, unless authorised by permissive rules to the contrary.[3]

The idea of State sovereignty was not new. The Dutch lawyer, Hugo Grotius, usually, but not universally,[4] recognised as the father of contemporary international law, had in his great work on the Law of War and Peace[5] accepted the sovereign State as the basic unit of international law over 200 years before. Yet the exaggerated importance Austin was to attach to the theory of sovereignty was easily exploitable by despots to justify resisting outside 'interference' in their oppressive domestic conduct towards their own peoples. It can be powerfully argued that the acceptance by lawyers of this view of State sovereignty did much to hold back the development of international norms of human rights.[6]

It took the horrors of the Second World War and the Holocaust to start a decisive transformation in international law. The United Nations Charter recognised specifically an international obligation to secure human rights. Its Preamble identifies one of the United Nations' own primary purposes as '*Promoting and encouraging respect for human rights and for fundamental freedoms for all without distinction as to race, sex, language or religion'*.[7] The enlightened draftsmen of the Charter, determined to do all in their power to remove the threat of a return to conflict and genocide, saw the need for these fundamental freedoms not only as common justice but also as part of the process of guaranteeing peace. And so Article 55 of the Charter placed on the United Nations an obligation to promote '*Universal respect for, and observance of, human rights and fundamental freedoms for all without distinction as to race, sex, language, or religion';*[8] and to do so, in the words of the Charter '*With a view to the creation of conditions of stability and well being which are necessary for peaceful and friendly nations based on respect for the principle of equal rights and determination of peoples'*. The members themselves pledged co-operation with the United Nations and to take joint and separate action to achieve those purposes.[9]

In the five years that followed the agreement of the Charter, international law moved in a decisive new direction. The Genocide Convention,[10] the Geneva Conventions for the Protection of Victims of War,[11] relative to the Protection of

---

3 Schwarzenberger, p 65.

4 See for example Schwarzenberger, *A Manual of International Law*, 5th ed, Stevens, p 19.

5 *De Jure Bellis ac Pacis* (1625).

6 For example by FS Nariman, Chairman of the Executive Committee of the International Commission of Jurists in an address to the International Bar Association given at the United Nations, New York in June 1977.

7 Charter of the United Nations preamble 3; UNTS xvi; UKTS 67 (1946) Cmd 7015.

8 Articles 55 and 56 *ibid*.

9 Article 56 *ibid*.

10 Convention on the Prevention and Punishment of the Crime of Genocide 1948 78 UNTS 277; Cmnd 2904.

11 Geneva III, (1949) 75 UNTS 31.

Civilian Persons in Time of War[12] and in relation to Condition of Wounded Servicemen[13] were all promulgated and agreed during this fertile legislative period. So also was the Universal Declaration of Human Rights itself.[14] It celebrates its half centenary in 1998.

Two other important events occurred in the same period.

First, the judgement at the Nuremberg Trials, presided over by Lord Justice Lawrence, gave concrete evidence that victims of crimes against humanity committed even by their own Governments were entitled to the protection of international criminal law.[15] The significance of those trials cannot be underestimated. Yet the decision to stage them had not been lightly reached. Churchill, for one, had been against them. But the Allies had committed themselves in the Declarations of St James of 1942 and the Moscow Declarations of November 1943.[16] The United Kingdom has been a strong supporter of the successors to that first international war crimes tribunal, now sitting to deal with events in the former Yugoslavia and Rwanda. The present Government showed our own strong commitment to this process when earlier this year British soldiers were involved in the arrest of suspected war criminals.

It was during the same fertile period that the Council of Europe, established as part of the Allies' programme to rebuild Europe, produced the European Convention on Human Rights. As the White Paper introducing the Human Rights Bill records, the simple power of the language of its articles led Sir Edward Gardner QC, the Conservative MP, to say in 1987, when introducing an earlier attempt to incorporate the Convention:

> It is language which echoes down the corridors of history. It goes deep into our history and as far back as the Magna Carta.[17]

The history of the United Kingdom's quickness to ratify the Convention but slowness to adopt the jurisdiction of the Court of Human Rights for individual petition, and even greater slowness to incorporate its provision into domestic law, have been chronicled by Lord Lester of Herne Hill QC. I pay tribute to his long campaign to see the Convention given greater effect in the UK.

So, spurred by the urgent need to reconstruct civilisation after the winter of World War II, in this short period legal innovation had turned the individual citizen into a subject of international law. In 1950 the distinguished international lawyer, Hersch Lauterpacht, later Judge of the International Court of Justice, was able to assert that 'The individual has now acquired a status and a stature which have transformed him from an object of international compassion into a subject of international right'.[18]

---

12 Geneva IV (1949) 75 UNTS 31, Cmnd 550.

13 Convention for the Amelioration of the Condition of Wounded and Sick in Armed Forces in the Field (1949); Convention for the Amelioration of the Condition of Wounded and Sick and Shipwrecked Members of Armed Forces at Sea (1949) Geneva II.

14 General Assembly Resolution 217A(III), UN Doc A/810 at 71 (1948).

15 See generally Davies, *Europe, A History*, Pimlico, 1997.

16 *Rights Brought Home: The Human Rights Bill* Ch 3872.

17 Hansard, 6 February 1987, col 1224.

18 Lauterpacht, *International Law and Human Rights* (1950).

I have dealt with this background because it is right to remind ourselves of our history and of the roots of the Convention. It is right to remind ourselves that these rights are part of the bedrock laid down after 1945 for a safe and just society. It is also right to remind ourselves of the strong justification for recognising in domestic law international human rights obligations.

A Rights Based System

Against this background, I turn to the Human Rights Bill and its effects.

A major change which the Act will bring flows from the shift to a rights based system. Under this system a citizen's right is asserted as a positive entitlement expressed in clear and principled terms. For example, under Article 5 of the Convention 'Everyone has the right to liberty and security of person.' Whilst there are reservations to that right, the reservations take effect as explicit exceptions and derogations which must be justified according to the terms of the Article. They represent exceptions which, in the public interest, are justified and reasonable. For example, the basic right in Article 5 is qualified by a list of the defined and circumscribed cases where a person may be deprived of his liberty. So, where a national authority wants to justify a detention, it will need to show how the facts fit into one of those defined categories and how it has met other requirements of the Convention; for example, the fair trial guarantees in Article 6.

This approach contrasts with the traditional common law approach to the protection of individual liberties. The common law approach, described by the great constitutional lawyer, Albert Venn Dicey, Vinerian Professor, in his *Introduction to the Study of Law of the Constitution*[19] first published in 1885, treats liberty only as a 'negative' right. As explained by Lord Donaldson MR in one of the Spycatcher cases[20] this negative approach means that 'the starting point of our domestic law is that every citizen has a right to do what he likes, unless restrained by the common law or by Statute.' The liberty of the subject is therefore the 'negative' right of what is left over when all the prohibitions have limited the area of lawful conduct. There are numerous examples of prohibitions either by the common law (for instance, the law of libel limiting the extent of free speech to prohibit defamatory statements or the law of nuisance limiting the activities in which a person may engage on his own land) or by Statute (of which the examples are too obvious to merit illustration).

Dicey saw merit in this negative approach. He believed that the absence of writing lent the common law a flexibility to develop to meet changing conditions. But the approach has disadvantages which are greater. By proposing this law the Government has decisively demonstrated its view that the more serious threat to liberty is an absence of written guarantees of freedom. For the negative approach offers little protection against a creeping erosion of freedom by a legislature willing to countenance infringement of liberty or simply blind to the effect of an otherwise well intentioned piece of law. As Professor Dworkin, Professor of Jurisprudence at the University of Oxford argued in an important article in 1988, the challenge to liberty is not only from despots. A Government may show 'a more mundane but still corrupting insensitivity to liberty, a failure to grasp its force and

---

19   10th ed, Macmillan, 1959.
20   *AG v Guardian Newspapers (No 2)* [1990] 1 AC 109.

place in democratic ideals.'[21] The Human Rights Bill is our bulwark against that danger.

When he was Prime Minister John Major used to say:

We have no need of a Bill of Rights because we have freedom.

What that demonstrated was an enervating insularity. The traditional freedom of the individual under an unwritten constitution to do himself that which is not prohibited by law gives no protection from misuse of power by the State, nor any protection from acts or omissions by public bodies which harm individuals in a way that is incompatible with their human rights under the Convention.

Our legal system has been unable to protect people in the 50 cases in which the European Court has found a violation of the Convention by the United Kingdom. The proposition that because we have liberty we have no need of human rights must be rejected.

The Implications of the Change

What then are the practical implications of this change to a rights based system within the field of civil liberties?

First, the Act will give to the courts the tools to uphold freedoms at the very time their infringement is threatened. Until now, the only remedy where a freedom guaranteed by the Convention is infringed and domestic law is deficient, has been expensive and slow proceedings in Strasbourg. They could not even be commenced until after all the domestic avenues of complaint and appeal had been exhausted. The courts will now have the power to give effect to the Convention rights in the course of proceedings when they arise in this country and to grant relief against an unlawful act of a public authority (a necessarily widely drawn concept). The courts will not be able to strike down primary legislation. But they will be able to make a declaration of incompatibility where a piece of primary legislation conflicts with a Convention right. This will trigger the ability to use in Parliament a special fast-track procedure to bring the law into line with the Convention.

This innovative technique will provide the right balance between the judiciary and Parliament. Parliament is the democratically elected representative of the people and must remain sovereign. The judiciary will be able to exercise to the full the power to scrutinise legislation rigorously against the fundamental freedoms guaranteed by the Convention but without becoming politicised. The ultimate decision to amend legislation to bring it into line with the Convention, however, will rest with Parliament. The ultimate responsibility for compliance with the Convention must be Parliament's alone.

That point illustrates the second important effect of our new approach. If there are to be differences or departures from the principles of the Convention they should be conscious and reasoned departures, and not the product of rashness, muddle or ignorance. This will be guaranteed both by the powers given to the courts but also by other provisions which will be enacted. In particular, Ministers and administrators will be obliged to do all their work keeping clearly and directly in

---

21 I cited this in a speech in the House of Lords on 23 May 1990.

mind its impact on human rights, as expressed in the Convention and the jurisprudence which attaches to it. For, where any Bill is introduced in either House, the Minister of the Crown, in whose charge it is, will be required to make a written statement that, either, in his view, the provisions of the Bill are compatible with the Convention rights; or that he cannot make that statement but the Government nonetheless wishes the House to proceed with the Bill. In the latter case the Bill would inevitably be subject to close and critical scrutiny by Parliament. Human rights will not be a matter of fudge. The responsible Minister will have to ensure that the legislation does not infringe guaranteed freedoms, or be prepared to justify his decision openly and in the full glare of Parliamentary and public opinion.

That will be particularly important whenever there comes under consideration those articles of the Convention which lay down what I call principled rights, subject to possible limitation. I have in mind Articles 8–11, dealing with respect for private life; freedom of religion; freedom of expression; and freedom of assembly and association; which confer those freedoms subject to possible limitations, such as, for instance in the case of Article 10 (freedom of expression):

> are prescribed by law and are necessary in a democratic society in the interests of national security, territorial integrity or public safety, for the prevention of disorder or crime, for the protection of health or morals, for the protection of the reputation or rights of others, for preventing the disclosure of information received in confidence, or for maintaining the authority and impartiality of the judiciary.

In such cases, administrators and legislators, will have to think clearly about whether what they propose really is necessary in a democratic society and for what object it is necessary. Quite apart from the concentration on the Convention and its jurisprudence this will require, the process should produce better thought-out, clearer and more transparent administration.

The important requirements of transparency on Convention issues that will accompany the introduction of all future legislation will ensure that Parliament knows exactly what it is doing in a human rights context. I regard this improvement in both the efficiency and the openness of our legislative process as one of the main benefits produced by incorporation of the Convention.

Substantive Rights

Thirdly, the Convention will enable the Courts to reach results in cases which give full effect to the substantive rights guaranteed by the Convention. It would not be appropriate for me to deal with individual aspects of the law which may come up for decision in the Courts in future, but some general observations are possible.

The Courts have not ignored the Convention rights. As long ago as 1972 in *Broome v Cassell* Lord Kilbrandon referred to the Convention as supporting the existence of '*A constitutional right to free speech*' when warning against holding the profit motive to be sufficient to justify punitive damages for defamation.

But the courts have only had limited ability to give effect to those rights. Lord Bingham of Cornhill, in his maiden speech in the House of Lords on taking the office of Lord Chief Justice, enumerated six ways in which the Courts have been able to take the Convention rights into account.[22] Of these, the first and the most important has been as an aid to construction. *'Where'*, as Lord Bingham explained, *'a United Kingdom statute is capable of two interpretations, one consistent with the Convention and one inconsistent, then the courts will presume that Parliament did not intend to legislate in violation of international law.'* A further instance is in developing the common law where it is uncertain, unclear or incomplete.[23]

But the Courts are not enforcing the Convention when they act in this way. They are enforcing statutory or common law. It follows – and it is emphasised in all the authorities – that recourse cannot be had to the terms of he Convention unless the terms of the Statute, or the content of the common law[24] is uncertain or ambiguous.

If Parliament has spoken with sufficient certainty, in terms that exclude or contradict the Convention, the latter has no place. The decision of the House of Lords in *ex parte Brind*[25] is a case in point. That concerned a challenge by a group of broadcasters to the restrictions then imposed preventing the broadcast of the voices of members of proscribed organisations, notably Sinn Fein. The Secretary of State had acted under a power broadly drawn in the Broadcasting Act 1981[26] empowering him to prohibit the broadcast of 'any matter or classes of matter specified in the notice.' The Applicants tried, unsuccessfully, to persuade the Court to impose a limitation on those words to make them consistent with the right of freedom of expression in Article 10 of the Convention. The House of Lords could find no ambiguity allowing them to read in such words of limitation.

It is moreover likely – although individual cases will be for the Courts to determine and I should not attempt to prejudge them- that the position will in at least some cases be different from what it would have been under the pre-incorporation practice. The reason for this lies in the techniques to be followed once the Act is in force. Unlike the old Diceyan approach where the Court would go straight to what restriction had been imposed, the focus will first be on the positive right and then on the justifiability of the exception. Moreover, the Act will require the Courts to read and give effect to the legislation in a way compatible with the Convention rights 'so far as it is possible to do so.'[27] This, as the White Paper makes clear, goes far beyond the present rule. It will not be necessary to find an ambiguity. On the contrary the Courts will be required to interpret legislation so as to uphold the Convention rights unless the legislation itself is so clearly incompatible with the Convention that it is impossible to do so. Moreover, it should be clear from the Parliamentary history, and in particular the Ministerial statement of compatibility which will be required by the Act, that Parliament did not intend to cut across a Convention right. Ministerial statements of compatibility

---

22 3 July 1996, Hansard, col 1465.

23 See eg the Court of Appeal in *R v Secretary of State for the Home Department ex p Brind* [1991] 1 AC 696.

24 'Courts in the United Kingdom should have regard to the provisions of the [Convention] ... where our domestic law is not firmly settled' *AG v BBC* [1981] AC 303 at p 352 *per* Lord Fraser.

25 *R v Home Secretary ex p Brind* [1991] 1 AC 696.

26 Section 29(3).

27 Clause 3(1).

will inevitably be a strong spur to the courts to find means of construing statutes' compatibly with the Convention.

Whilst this particular approach is innovative, there are some precedents which will assist the Courts. In cases involving European Community law, decisions of our Courts already show that interpretative techniques may be used to make the domestic legislation comply with the Community law, even where this requires straining the meaning of words or reading in words which are not there. An illustrative case is *Litster* concerning the construction of the Transfer of Undertakings Regulations. The issue was whether protection in the Regulations, limited to those employed in the business 'Immediately before' the time of the transfer, extended to employees unfairly dismissed very shortly before the transfer. The applicants had clearly not been employed in the business immediately before the transfer as those words would normally be interpreted. Nor were the words ambiguous. Yet the House of Lords interpreted the Regulations (so as to accord with the European Court's existing interpretation of the underlying Community obligation which the Regulations were intended to implement) by implying additional words 'or would have been so employed if they had not been unfairly dismissed [by reason of the transfer]'.

This implication of appropriate language into an apparently unambiguous provision is the sort of tool which could have led to a different result in a case like Brind. It shows the strong interpretative techniques that can be expected in Convention cases.

Guidance may also be found in the jurisprudence of the New Zealand Courts. Under the New Zealand Bill of Rights[28] a meaning consistent with the rights and freedoms contained in the Bill of Rights is to be given in preference to any other meaning 'wherever an enactment can be given [such] a meaning.' The existing New Zealand decisions seem to show that the only cases where the legislation will not be interpreted consistently with the protected rights is where a statutory provision contains a clear limitation of fundamental rights.[29] The difference from the approach until now applied by the English courts will be this. The Court will interpret as consistent with the Convention not only those provisions which are ambiguous in the sense that the *language* used is capable of two different meanings but also those provisions where there is *no* ambiguity in that sense, unless a *clear* limitation is expressed. In the latter category of case it will be 'possible' (to use the statutory language) to read the legislation in a conforming sense because there will be no clear indication that a limitation on the protected rights was intended so as to make it 'impossible' to read it as conforming.

The Morality of Decisions

The fourth point may be shortly stated but is of immense importance. The Courts' decisions will be based on a more overtly principled, indeed moral, basis. The Court will look at the positive right. It will only accept an interference with that right where a justification, allowed under the Convention, is made out. The scrutiny will not be limited to seeing if the *words* of an exception can be satisfied. The Court will need to be satisfied that the *spirit* of this exception is made out. It

---

28 New Zealand Statute 1990 no 109.
29 See especially *R v Laugalis* (1993) 10 CRNZ; and also *Ministry of Transport v Noort* [1992] 3 NZLR 260; *R v Rangi* [1992] 1 NZLR 385.

will need to be satisfied that the interference with the protected right is justified in the public interests in a free democratic society. Moreover, the Courts will in this area have to apply the Convention principle of proportionality. This means the Court will be looking *substantively* at that question. It will not be limited to a secondary review of the decision making process but at the primary question of the merits of the decision itself.

In reaching its judgment, therefore, the Court will need to expand and explain its own view of whether the conduct is legitimate. It will produce in short a decision on the *morality* of the conduct and not simply its compliance with the bare letter of the law.

The Influence on Other Areas of Law

I believe, moreover, that the effects of the incorporation of the Convention will be felt way beyond the sphere of the application of the rights guaranteed by the Convention alone. As we move from the traditional Diceyan model of the common law to a rights based system, the effects will be felt throughout the common law and in the very process of judicial decision-making. This will be a healthy and dynamic development in our law.

There is good precedent for this sort of influence on the common law in the effect which European Community law has already produced. Under the European Communities Act, the precedence accorded to European law can lead to legislation being suspended[30] or disapplied[31] or declared to be unlawful.[32] As I pointed out in a Lecture I delivered in October 1995[33] British Courts are as a result now required to perform a number of tasks which would have been unthinkable even 20 years ago.

Although the legislative technique adopted under the Human Rights Bill is different from that under the European Communities Act, the effect on the general process of deciding cases will, I believe, be as influential. Courts will, from time to time be required to determine if primary or secondary legislation is incompatible with the Convention rights.[34] They will decide if the acts of public authorities are unlawful through contravention, perhaps even conscious contravention, of those rights.[35] They may have to award damages as a result.[36]

These are all new remedies for our courts to apply and, as they begin to develop the tools and techniques to apply them, an influence on other areas of law and judicial decision making is, I believe, inevitable.

This spillover effect has been seen already from the application here of European Community law. Cases may be seen where the very exposure of practitioners and judges to a new body of law presents new solutions even for purely domestic problems. A good example, was the reliance by Lord Goff of Chieveley on

---

30 *K v Secretary of State for Transport ex p Factortame Ltd (No 2)* [1991] 1 AC 603.

31 For example *Marshall v Southampton and South West Area Health Authority (No 2)* [1994] 2 WLR 292.

32 *R v Secretary of State for Employment ex p Equal Opportunities Commission* [1995] 1 AC 1.

33 The 1995 Administrative Law Bar Association lecture published in [1996] Public Law 59 under the title *Judges and Decision-makers – The Theory and Practice of Wednesbury Review*.

34 Under Clause 4.

35 Under Clause 6.

36 Under Clause 8(2).

principles of German law in deciding in the House of Lords the question of the responsibility to the disappointed beneficiary of an English solicitor who failed to draw up a will before the demise of the would-be testators.[37] Another example is *Woolwich Equitable Building Society v Inland Revenue Commissioners*.[38] The House of Lords had to decide whether the Inland Revenue was liable to pay interest when it returned tax originally paid by the tax payer under regulations held to be invalid. This was a purely domestic question and no issue of Community law arose. Classic common law principles suggested interest would only be payable where the tax had been paid under compulsion or mistake of fact and not (as here) through a payment made voluntarily through a mistake of law. Yet the majority of the House concluded that interest was payable by the Revenue by extending the categories of obligation to repay money to cases where money was paid pursuant to an unlawful demand by a public authority. A comparison with community law seems to have played a part in this decision to change the common law of England.

Lord Goff of Chieveley noted in terms that the European Court of Justice had held[39] that a person who pays charges levied by a Member State contrary to community rules is entitled to repayment of the charge. He went on to say:

> ... at a time when Community law is becoming increasingly important, it would be strange if the right of the citizen to recover overpaid charges were to be more restricted under domestic law than it is under European law.[40]

The spillover influence of Community law in the field of procedure and judicial decision making is as marked. In *Pepper v Hart*[41] the long established convention that the courts do not look at Hansard to discover the parliamentary intention behind legislation was reversed. It is strongly arguable that this was a consequence of the influence of Community law where it is common to look for the purpose of a law in order to interpret that law and to look for that purpose in the legislative history. That Community influence can be seen when examining how *Pepper v Hart* came to be decided. Its direct precursor was the earlier decision in *Pickstone v Freemans*.[42] That was a Community law case. There the House of Lords referred to passages in Hansard to understand national regulations made by the UK Parliament to give effect to Community law. The justification for that unusual approach was the special position of Community law. Yet the very basis of allowing that exceptional approach in *Pickstone* was discarded in *Pepper v Hart* as being 'logically indistinguishable from the similar exercise of statutory interpretation of purely national legislation'.[43]

So too it is becoming increasingly hard not explicitly to recognise in English administrative law the Community law doctrine of proportionality.

That doctrine, drawn from German Administrative law principles, is a tool for judging the lawfulness of administrative action. It amounts to this. Excessive

---

37 *White v Jones* [1995] 1 All ER 691.

38 *Woolwich Equitable Building Society v IRC* [1993] AC 70.

39 In Case 199/82 *Amministrazione delle Finanze dello Stato v SpA San Giorgio* [1983] ECR 3595.

40 *Woolwich Equitable Building Society v IRC* [1993] AC 70 at p 177.

41 [1993] AC 593.

42 *Pickstone v Freemans plc* [1989] AC 66.

43 *Pepper v Hart* [1993] AC 593 at p 635 *per* Lord Browne-Wilkinson.

means are not to be used to attain permissible objects. Or, as it was more pithily put by Lord Diplock, 'a steam hammer should not be used to crack a nut'.[44] There has been much argument whether this principle now forms a part of the criteria for review of public decisions generally since Lord Diplock opened that door in 1985.[45] It seemed to have been slammed shut in Brind in 1991. This is not the occasion to trace those developments. Yet, by whatever name, it seems undeniable that the traditional common law concepts converge with their continental cousins. This is but another example of the inevitable incremental effects of introducing another system of law to be applied alongside traditional common law principles.

One other example will illustrate the point. In *M v Home Office*[46] a contempt application was made against the Secretary of State for failure to procure the return of an applicant for political asylum. The Court had to consider the extent of its powers over the Executive. In purely domestic cases these were traditionally narrow. But in cases where Community law obligations were at issue it had been shown that the powers were wider. They extend to granting interlocutory injunctions against the Crown as shown in the *Factortame* case.[47] This distinction troubled the Court. Although both the Court of Appeal (and ultimately the House of Lords)[48] found a way round the concerns, Lord Donaldson MR was driven to condemn as 'anomalous and ... wrong in principle' distinctions in the powers of the court to hold the ring by interlocutory injunctions which depended on the identity of the defendant. And even more anomalous that the extent of those powers over central government should depend on whether the obligation in question arose under Community law or purely domestic law.

This illustrates the difficulty of maintaining a rigid distinction between two differing sets of principles of law, co-existing side by side.[49] Nor would I want in all cases to maintain rigid distinctions. The greatness of the common law lies in its flexibility and ability to adapt to changing economic and social conditions. It is enriched by drawing on the principles and solutions found in other developed legal systems.

The Emergence of a New Approach

I have referred to the effect the introduction of European Community law has had on the development of our own domestic law. I believe that incorporating into our own law the Convention rights will have an equally healthy effect.

Any court or tribunal determining any question relating to a Convention Right will be obliged to take into account the body of jurisprudence of the Court and Commission of Human rights and of the Council of Ministers.[50] This is obviously right; it gives British courts both the benefit of 50 years' careful analysis of the Convention rights and ensures British Courts interpret the Convention consistently with Strasbourg. The British courts will therefore need to apply the

---

44   In *R v Goldstein* [1983] 1 WLR 151 at 155.

45   In *Council of Civil Services Unions v Minister for the Civil Service* [1985] AC 374.

46   *M v Home Office* [1992] QB 270.

47   *Op cit.*

48   *M v Home Office* 3 WLR 433.

49   See further on this topic the valuable discussion in O'Neill, *Decisions of the European Court of Justice and their Constitutional Implications*, 1994, Butterworths, Chapter 5.

50   See Clause 2.

same techniques of interpretation and decision-making as the Strasbourg bodies. I have already mentioned recourse to Parliamentary materials such as Hansard – where we are now closer in line with our continental colleagues. I will mention three more aspects. As I do so, it should be remembered that the courts which will be applying these techniques will be the ordinary courts of the land; we have not considered it right to create some special human rights court alongside the ordinary system; the Convention rights must pervade all law and all the courts' systems. Our courts will therefore learn these techniques and inevitably will consider their utility in deciding other non-Convention cases.

First there is the approach to statutory interpretation. The tools of construction in use in mainland Europe are known to be different from those the English courts have traditionally used. I will refer to just one: the so-called teleological approach which is concerned with giving the instrument its presumed legislative intent. It is less concerned with the textual analysis usual to the common law tradition of interpretation.[51] It is a process of moulding the law to what the Court believes the law should be trying to achieve.[52] It is undoubtedly the case that our own domestic approach to interpretation of statutes has become more purposive. Lord Diplock had already identified this trend 20 years ago when he noted that:

> If one looks back to the actual decisions of the [House of Lords] on questions of statutory construction over the last 30 years one cannot fail to be struck by the evidence of a trend away from the purely literal towards the purposive construction of statutory provisions.[53]

This trend has not diminished since then, although there are cases where the Courts have declined to adopt what was in one case described as an 'over purposive' approach.[54]

Yet as the Courts, through familiarity with the Convention jurisprudence, become more exposed to methods of interpretation which pay more heed to the purpose, and less to whether the words were felicitously chosen to achieve that end, the balance is likely to swing more firmly yet in the direction of the purposive approach.

Secondly, there is the doctrine of proportionality, to which I have already referred. This doctrine is applied by the European Court of Human Rights.[55] Its application is to ensure that a measure imposes no greater restriction upon a Convention right than is absolutely necessary to achieve its objectives. Although not identical to the principle as applied in Luxembourg, it shares the feature that it raises questions foreign to the traditional *Wednesbury*[56] approach to judicial review. Under the *Wednesbury* doctrine an administrative decision will only be struck down if it is so bad that no reasonable decision-maker could have taken it.

---

51 The Court of Human Rights also adopts a dynamic approach which enables it to take account of changing social conditions.

52 See Lord Denning's description in *James Buchanan v Babco* [1977] 2 WLR 107 at 112.

53 *Carter v Bradbeer* [1975] 1 WLR 1204 at 1206–07.

54 By Dillon LJ in *R v Poplar Coroner ex p Thomas* [1993] 2 All ER 381 at 387; and see the criticism by Bennion in The All England Reports Annual Review 1996 of the House of Lords decision in *R v Preddy* [1996] 3 All ER 481.

55 See eg *Soering v UK* (1989) Series A, vol 161.

56 *Associated Provincial Picture Houses v Wednesbury Corporation* [1948] 1 KB 223.

Closely allied with the doctrine of proportionality is the concept of the margin of appreciation. The Court of Human Rights has developed this doctrine which permits national courts a discretion in the application of the requirements of the Convention to their own national conditions. This discretion is not absolute, since the Court of Human Rights reserves the power to review any act of a national authority or court; and the discretion is more likely to be recognised in the application of those articles of the Convention which expressly include generally stated conditions or exceptions, such as Articles 8–11, rather than in the area of obligations which in any civilised society should be absolute, such as the rights to life, freedom from torture and freedom from slavery and forced labour that are provided by Articles 2–4.

This 'margin of appreciation', was first developed by the Court in a British case, *Handyside v UK*.[57] It concerned whether a conviction for possessing an obscene article could be justified under Article 10(2) of the Convention as a limitation upon freedom of expression that was necessary for the 'protection of morals'. The court said:

> By reason of their direct and continuous contact with the vital forces of their countries, state authorities are in principle in a better position than the international judge to give an opinion on the exact content of those requirements [of morals] as well as on the 'necessity' of a 'restriction' or 'penalty' intended to meet them ... [58]

Although there is some encouragement in British decisions for the view that the margin of appreciation under the Convention is simply the *Wednesbury* test under another guise[59] statements by the Court of Human Rights seem to draw a significant distinction. The Court of Human Rights has said in terms that its review is not limited to checking that the national authority 'exercised its discretion reasonably, carefully and in good faith'. It has to go further. It has to satisfy itself that the decision was based on an 'acceptable assessment of the relevant facts' and that the interference was no more than reasonably necessary to achieve the legitimate aim pursued.[60]

That approach shows that there is a profound difference between the Convention margin of appreciation and the common law test of rationality. The latter would be satisfied by an exercise of discretion done 'reasonably, carefully and in good faith' although the passage I have cited indicates that the Court of Human Rights' review of action is not so restricted. In these cases a more rigorous scrutiny than traditional judicial review will be required. An illustration of the difference may be found in the speech of Simon Brown LJ in *ex p Smith* (the armed forces homosexual policy case):

> If the Convention for the Protection of Human Rights and Fundamental Freedoms were part of our law and we were accordingly entitled to ask whether the policy answers a pressing social need and whether the restriction on human rights involved can be shown proportionate to its benefits, then

---

57   (1976) Series A, vol 24.

58   *Ibid*, paras [48]–[49].

59   See eg *R v Home Secretary ex p Patel* [1995] Imm AR 223; *R v Home Secretary ex p Mbatube* [1996] Imm AR 184.

60   *Vogt v Germany* (1996) Series A, No 323, para 52; (1996) 21 EHRR 205, 235.

clearly the primary judgement (subject only to a limited 'margin of appreciation') would be for us and not for others; the constitutional balance would shift. But that is not the position. In exercising merely a secondary judgement, this court is bound, even though adjudicating in a human rights context, to act with some reticence.

The question I pose is how long the courts will restrict their review to a narrow *Wednesbury* approach in non-Convention cases, if used to inquiring more deeply in Convention cases? There will remain distinctions of importance between the two categories of case which should be respected. But some blurring of line may be inevitable.

I have expressed my views in my Administrative Law Bar Association Lecture in 1995 on how the Courts ought properly to regard the dividing line between their function and that of Parliament. But the process is not one way. British influence or the application of the Convention rights is likely to increase. British officials were closely involved in the drafting of the Convention. When our British courts make their own pronouncements on the Convention, their views will be studied in other Convention countries and in Strasbourg itself with great respect. I am sure that British judges' influence for the good of the Convention will be considerable. They will bring to the application of the Convention their great skills of analysis and interpretation. But they will also bring to it our proud British traditions of liberty.

The Shift from Form to Substance

So there is room to predict some decisive and far reaching changes in future judicial decision making. The major shift may be away from a concern with form to a concern with substance. Let me summarise the reasons.

In the field of review by judges of administrative action, the courts' decisions to date have been largely based on something akin to the application of a set of rules. If the rules are broken, the conduct will be condemned. But if the rules are obeyed, (the right factors are taken into account, no irrelevant factors taken into account, no misdirection of law and no out and out irrationality) the decision will be upheld, usually irrespective of the overall objective merits of the policy. In some cases much may turn – or at least appear to turn – on the form in which a decision is expressed rather than its substance. Does the decision as expressed show that the right reasons have been taken into account? Does it disclose potentially irrational reasoning? Might the court's review be different if the reasoning were expressed differently so as to avoid the court's *Wednesbury* scrutiny?

Now, in areas where the Convention applies, the Court will be less concerned whether there has been a failure in this sense but will inquire more closely into the merits of the decision to see for example that necessity justified the limitation of a positive right, and that it was no more a of a limitation than was needed.[61] There is a discernible shift which may be seen in essence as a shift from form to substance. If, as I have suggested, there is a spillover into other areas of law, then that shift from form to substance will become more marked.

This may be seen as a progression of an existing and now long standing trend. In modern times, the emphasis on identifying the true substance at issue has been seen in diverse areas: in tax where new techniques have developed to view the

---

61 Albeit within the margin of appreciation left to the public authority.

substance of a transaction overall rather than to be mesmerised by the form of an isolated step, or in the areas of statutory control of leases, where the Courts are astute to prevent form being used to obscure the reality of the underlying transaction. In what may seem at first blush a very different area, that of interpretation of contracts, recent decisions also emphasise the need to cast away the baggage of older years where literal and semantic analysis was allowed to override the real intent of the parties.[62]

In a very broad sense we can see here a similarity of approach: to get to the substance of the issue and not be distracted by the form.

These are trends already well developed but I believe they will gain impetus from incorporation of the Convention. In addition the Courts will be making decisions founded more explicitly and frequently on considerations of morality and justifiability.

This Bill will therefore create a more explicitly moral approach to decisions and decision making; will promote both a culture where positive rights and liberties become the focus and concern of legislators, administrators and judges alike; and a culture in judicial decision making where there will be a greater concentration on substance rather than form.

If that is so, we will more readily be able to refute TS Eliot's sardonic version of the lawyers' motto cited by one of my predecessors:

The spirit killeth, the letter giveth life.[63]

— ·· — ·· — ·· — ·· — ·· — ·· — ·· — ·· — ·· — ·· — ·· —

The way in which the Human Rights Act would impact on the United Kingdom legal system was explained in the following article.

Helen Fenwick, 'The European Convention on Human Rights and the Human Rights Act 1998' (1999) 27 SLR 13–16

The Human Rights Act 1998, which will implement the European Convention on Human Rights in domestic law, will provide the UK with something very close to a modern Bill of Rights, for the first time. It is one of the dominant constitutional matters at the present time and, therefore, in Summer 1999, Constitutional Law exam papers are almost bound to contain questions on it.

Its key provisions, which will allow the European Convention on Human Rights to be relied on directly in domestic courts, is not expected to come into force until November 1999, or, as is becoming increasingly likely, until 1 January 2000.

The model chosen in order to give the Convention further effect in domestic law has some rather odd and complex features: the intention is not simply to incorporate it into domestic law so that the Convention becomes in effect a statute. The Strasbourg jurisprudence surrounding the Convention itself has led to the development of a number of 'Strasbourg concepts' of some complexity. Below, certain key features of the Act and Convention are considered.

---

62 See *Mannai v Eagle Star Life Assurance Co Ltd* [1997] 2 WLR 945 and *Investors Compensation Scheme v West Bromwich Building Society* 24 June 1997 (as yet unreported).

63 The British Legal System Today (1983 Hamlyn Lectures) p 49.

'Public authorities' and individual citizens

The provisions of the Act regarding the relationship between citizens and 'public authorities' are central to the operation of the Human Rights Act and the impact it is likely to have. The Act allows a person who is (or would be) the victim of a breach of a Convention right by a public authority to bring proceedings against the authority (s 7) and, if successful, to receive 'such relief or remedy or ... order ... as [the court] considers just and appropriate' (s 8).

Under s 6, Convention guarantees are binding only against public authorities. These are defined as bodies which have a partly public function. The definition is therefore quite wide. Under s 6(3)(b), 'public authority' includes 'any person certain of whose functions are functions of a public nature'. Under s 6(5), 'in relation to a particular act, a person is not a public authority by virtue only of s 6(3)(b) if the nature of the act is private'. Not only is this definition non-exhaustive, it also leaves open room for much debate on the meaning of 'functions of a public nature'. On the face of it, this means that private bodies which cannot be brought within the definition can violate Convention rights with impunity (in so far as domestic statutes or other legal rules allow when interpreted to be compatible with the Convention). Liability between public bodies and citizens is often referred to as 'vertical'.

Private bodies and individual citizens

If liability between public bodies and citizens is referred to as 'vertical', liability between private bodies and individual citizens or between two citizens may be referred to as 'horizontal'. What scope is there in the Act for the creation of horizontal effects?

A citizen wishing to sue a private body under the Human Rights Act, alleging breach of a Convention right could:

(a) Identify a statute affecting the matter in question and then invoke s 3 (see below).

(b) Argue that the court, as a public body, must afford a remedy itself for the breach. This is problematic. To begin with, the litigant would have to find a cause of action in order to get into court at all. Even if this was possible (for example, a very weak claim in reliance on an uncertain area of the common law), the court might not accept that Parliament could have intended to allow the distinction between private and public bodies under s 6 to be destroyed by this means. Even if the court was prepared to find a breach of the Convention, it appears that it would be unable to afford a remedy to the litigant under s 9(3).

(c) Argue that the court as a public body is under a duty to interpret the common law so as to render it compatible with the Convention. A court is already under a duty to do this where the common law is unclear, but the litigant could argue that there is a common law obligation which resembles that under s 3 in respect of legislation.

The interpretative obligation under s 3

Under s 3 of the Human Rights Act, primary and subordinate legislation must be given effect in a manner which makes it compatible with the Convention rights;

the judiciary will be placed under an obligation to ensure such compatibility 'so far as it is possible to do so'. This goes well beyond resolving ambiguity in statutory provisions by adopting the Convention based interpretation, which is, of course, already occurring in the pre-Human Rights Act era. Section 3 appears to place the judiciary under an obligation to render legislation compatible with the Convention if there is any loop-hole at all allowing them to do so, even if this means twisting the natural meaning of the statutory words.

Section 3 also provides that this interpretative obligation does not affect the validity, continuing operation or enforcement of any incompatible primary legislation. Thus, the Convention cannot be used to strike down any part of an existing statute as unconstitutional. This is clearly an important limitation. In practice, the judiciary are likely to find that compatibility can generally be ensured. The Convention rights are open ended and the interpretation of them in the European Court and Commission of Human Rights has not always been rigorous, because Member States have been afforded a margin of appreciation (a degree of leeway) in determining what is necessary to protect the rights in their national legal systems. This is discussed below. It is likely that courts will strive to construe legislation so as to conform with the Convention, since, otherwise, the plaintiff or defendant would have to suffer a breach of Convention rights, possibly for a considerable period of time.

A declaration of incompatibility

Under s 6(2), if a court cannot render a statutory provision compatible with a particular Convention right, it must simply apply the domestic legislation. However, if the case reaches certain higher courts, they may be prepared to make a declaration under s 4 that it is not possible to construe the legislation in question to harmonise with the Convention. This procedure is itself problematic, since the potential victim of the breach of the right will normally have no interest in obtaining the declaration.

This difficulty may particularly arise in respect of criminal procedure. An example may be illustrative. Article 6(1) speaks of a 'criminal charge'. At Strasbourg, the fact that national law classifies an act as non-criminal is relevant but not conclusive.

In *Benham v UK* (1996) 22 EHRR 293, the leading case on 'criminal charge', the Court found that, although the legislation in question (s 41 of the Community Charge (Administration and Enforcement) Regulations) clearly did not create a criminal offence in UK law, it should be accounted criminal for Art 6(1) purposes.

The proceedings against the applicant (in respect of default on payment of the community charge or poll tax) were brought by the public authorities; the proceedings had some punitive elements and the bringing of them implied fault on the part of the applicant. Further, the penalty was severe (committal to prison for up to three months). The magistrates could only exercise their power of committal on a finding of wilful refusal to pay or culpable neglect (para 56 of the Judgment). A national court will be placed in a difficulty where there is classification of an act as non-criminal, but Art 6 suggests that it is criminal. Sections 1 and 2 of the Crime and Disorder Act 1998 allow for the making of anti-social behaviour orders and sex offender orders. According to the 1998 Magistrates' Courts Rules applicable to these orders, they will be made on the civil standard of proof, no legal aid is available, and there is the possibility of five years' imprisonment if the order is breached.

If a defendant in the magistrates' court raised the issue of the compatibility of the 1998 Act with Art 6, but the magistrates found – in the defence view, wrongly – that no incompatibility arose and made the Order, the issue could not be dealt with until the proceedings were over. Theoretically, the issue could then be dealt with on an appeal to the High Court by way of case stated. The High Court can make a declaration of incompatibility under s 4. But, the defendant would gain nothing from obtaining the declaration since the Order would still stand. Indeed, if the appeal alleged incompatibility it would appear to disclose no ground on which the Order could be overturned.

The defendant would have to appeal on the basis that, properly interpreted, the two could be rendered compatible but that the resolution of the issue of compatibility by the magistrates had led to an error of law. The defendant would have to hope that, properly interpreted, compatibility could be found in a manner which led to the overturning of the Order.

As a further example, if a lower court (a court outside the meaning of 'court' within s 4(5)) finds in criminal proceedings that the police have bugged a person's home in accordance with the Police Act 1997 but possibly contrary to Art 8 (providing a right to respect for privacy) of the Convention, the court may be unable to exclude the evidence derived from the bug since that would probably be contrary to the 1997 Act. The court cannot make a declaration of incompatibility and the defendant would have no interest in appealing to a higher court in order to obtain such a declaration, since it would provide him or her with no personal benefit. No damages could be awarded due to the provisions of s 6(2). Thus, change to particular parts of the law in order to ensure compatibility with the Convention rights may be slow in coming.

The courts may seek to address these difficulties in two ways. First, the lower courts may come to be very reluctant to find that UK law is incompatible with the Convention. Given the broad and open ended wording of the Convention, it will often be easy to find that compatibility exists. In the example given above, the lower court could seek to twist the wording of the Crime and Disorder Act 1998 to ensure compliance with Art 6 in order to avoid making the Order. Alternatively, it could find that Art 6 did not require such avoidance. The danger in this approach is that instead of 'levelling up', that is, bringing UK law up to the level of the Convention standards, UK courts may level down – adopt the interpretation of the Convention which gives the lowest possible level of protection.

Thus, this procedure places aspects of Convention rights in a doubtful and precarious position, and this is especially a matter of concern where criminal proceedings are in question due to the implications for the defendant while the matter of compatibility is being resolved.

The fast track procedure

If a declaration is made s 10 will apply, which means that a Minister may make amendments to the offending legislation by means of the so called fast track procedure. In other words, the amendment can be made outside the full Parliamentary process which would be required for primary legislation. However, the Minister is under no obligation to make the amendment(s) and may only do so if there are 'compelling reasons' to do so. In other words, the fact that a declaration of incompatibility has been made is not in itself a compelling reason.

It would be politically embarrassing for a Minister to refuse to make the amendment and, therefore, it would probably be made eventually. But, during the period before the making of the amendment, the plaintiff or defendant (the victim of the breach) would continue to suffer from the breach. The consequences of so doing could include uncertainty and loss of liberty or considerable financial loss. Most commentators appear to agree that this procedure constitutes a flaw in the Act, since it is not likely to encourage litigants to seek a declaration and, therefore, bring about a change in the law. Thus, there may be periods of uncertainty during which citizens cannot rely on aspects of their Convention rights.

Statements of compatibility

When legislation is introduced into Parliament once the Act is fully in force, s 19 will apply. Under s 19, when a Minister introduces a Bill into either House of Parliament, he or she must make and publish a written statement to the effect either that in his/her view the provisions of the Bill are compatible with the Convention rights, or that although he/she is unable to make such a statement, the Government nevertheless wishes to proceed with the Bill.

If the latter statement is made, it can be presumed that the judiciary will allow the provisions of the legislation to override the Convention, just as they would if a clause was included in it stating: 'this statute is to be given effect notwithstanding the provisions of the Human Rights Act 1998, Art X'. But this would be bound to cause political embarrassment and, almost certainly, successful applications to Strasbourg. It is, therefore, likely to be a very rare occurrence.

Strasbourg jurisprudence in domestic courts

Under s 2 of the Human Rights Act, the domestic judiciary 'must take into account' any relevant Strasbourg jurisprudence, although they are not bound by it. The term exhaustively covers: any 'judgment, decision, declaration or advisory opinion of the Court'; any 'opinion of the Commission given in a report adopted under Art 31'; any 'decision of the Commission in connection with Art 26 or 27(2)'; or any 'decision of the Committee of Ministers taken under Art 46'. This is quite a weak obligation, since it is open to the judiciary to consider but disapply a particular decision.

Strasbourg concepts 1: the margin of appreciation

Limitations on the scope and impact in practice of the Convention rights flow from the operation of the doctrine of the margin of appreciation. The doctrine was first adopted in respect of emergency situations but it has gradually permeated all the Articles. It has a particular application with respect to para 2 of Arts 8–11 but it can affect all the guarantees. In different instances, a wider or a narrower margin may be allowed. If it is narrow, a very full and detailed review of the interference with the guarantee in question will be conducted.

This occurred in the *Sunday Times* case ((1980) 2 EHRR 245); it was found that Strasbourg review is not limited to asking whether the State had exercised its discretion reasonably, carefully, and in good faith: its conduct must also be examined in Strasbourg to see whether it is compatible with the Convention. If a broader margin is allowed, Strasbourg review will be highly circumscribed. For example, the minority in the *Sunday Times* case (nine judges) wanted to confine the role of Strasbourg to asking only whether the discretion in question was exercised in good faith and carefully and whether the measure was reasonable in the circumstances.

It is hard to predict when each approach will be taken, but it seems to depend on a number of identifiable factors. The Court and Commission consider that in certain matters, most notably national security (see *Leander v Sweden*, Series A 116 para 67 (1987)), but also the protection of morals (see *Handyside v UK*, Series A 24 para 48 (1976)), States are best placed to determine what is needed within their own particular domestic situation. In *Civil Service Unions v UK* ((1988) 10 EHRR 269), the European Commission, in declaring the Unions' application inadmissible, found that national security interests should prevail over freedom of association even though the national security interest was weak while the infringement of the primary right was very clear: an absolute ban on joining a trade union had been imposed.

The high (or low) point of deference was perhaps reached in *Brannigan and McBride v UK*, Series A, 258-B (1993), in which the European Court of Human Rights upheld a derogation entered by the UK after the decision in the case of *Brogan and Others v UK* (judgment of 29 November 1988, (1989) A145; (1989) 11 ECHR 117). The European Court of Human Rights had found in *Brogan and Others v UK* that powers under the Prevention of Terrorism (Temporary Provisions) Act allowing detention of terrorist suspects without charge for up to seven days, violated Art 5 which protects liberty. At the time of the violation, there was no derogation in force in respect of Art 5 because the UK had withdrawn its derogation. This suggested either that there was no need for it or that the UK had failed to derogate despite the gravity of the situation which would have justified so doing.

However, after *Brogan*, the UK entered the derogation stating that an emergency situation was in being at the time. This was challenged unsuccessfully in *Brannigan* as an invalid derogation. The Court found that 'a wide margin of appreciation [on the question] of the presence of an emergency ... and on the nature and scope of derogations necessary to avert it [should be allowed]' (para 207). One of the government contentions uncritically accepted by the Court was that, in the particular situation, the judiciary should not be permitted a role in protecting the liberty of detainees. As Judge Walsh pointed out in his dissenting opinion, this was a role which the public would expect a judge to have (see *Handyside v UK*, Series A 24 para 48 (1976)).

Otto-Preminger Institut v Austria (1994) 19 EHRR 34 concerned the seizure of a film satirising aspects of Christianity. In considering whether the seizure and forfeiture of the film was 'necessary in a democratic society', in order to protect the rights of others to respect for their religious views, the European Court of Human Rights took into account the lack of a uniform conception within the Member States of the significance of religion in society and therefore considered that the national authorities should have a wide margin of appreciation in assessing what was necessary to protect religious feeling. In ordering the seizure of the film, the Austrian authorities had taken its artistic value into account but had not found that it outweighed its offensive features. The Court found that the national authorities had not overstepped their margin of appreciation and therefore decided that no breach of Art 10 had occurred. This decision left a very wide discretion to the Member State, a discretion which the dissenting judges considered to be too wide.

Similarly, in *Wingrove v UK* (1997) 24 EHRR 1, the European Court of Human Rights found that the English common law offence of blasphemy was sufficiently clear and precise. The Court further found that 'there is as yet not sufficient common ground in the legal and social orders of the Member States of the Council of Europe to conclude that a system whereby a State can impose restrictions on the propagation of material on the basis that it is blasphemous is in itself unnecessary in a democratic society and incompatible with the Convention' (para 57).

As these decisions suggest, the margin of appreciation doctrine may tend to undermine the Convention; its growth has therefore attracted criticism. Van Dijk and Van Hoof have written of it as 'a spreading disease. Not only has the scope of its application been broadened to the point where in principle none of the Convention rights or freedoms are excluded, but also has the illness been intensified in that wider versions of the doctrine have been added to the original concept' (Van Dijk and Van Hoof, *Theory and Practice of the European Convention on Human Rights*, p 604).

The doctrine of the margin of appreciation is an international law doctrine, based on the need to respect the decision making of individual States. Therefore, it would not appear to have any application in national law. As Sir John Laws put it ([1998] PL 254, p 258):

> The margin of appreciation doctrine as it has been developed at Strasbourg will necessarily be inapt to the administration of the Convention in the domestic courts for the very reason that they are domestic; they will not be subject to an objective inhibition generated by any cultural distance between themselves and the State organs whose decisions are impleaded before them.

The result is that the domestic judiciary will be faced with difficulties in interpreting the Convention. If they disapply decisions at Strasbourg which have been influenced by the doctrine, they will be left with little guidance as to the application of the Convention rights.

Strasbourg concepts 2 – justifying interferences with rights: proportionality

To be justified, State interference with Arts 8–11 guarantees must be prescribed by law, have a legitimate aim, be necessary in a democratic society and be applied in a non-discriminatory fashion. Strasbourg's main concern has been with the 'necessary in a democratic society' requirement; the notion of 'prescribed by law' has been focused upon to some extent, but usually with the result that it has been found to be satisfied. The 'legitimate aim' requirement will normally be readily satisfied; as Harris, O'Boyle and Warbrick point out, the grounds for interference are so wide that 'the State can usually make a plausible case that it did have a good reason for interfering with the right' (*Law of the European Convention on Human Rights*, Butterworths, 1995, p 290). The provision against non-discrimination arises under Art 14.

The Court has interpreted 'necessary in a democratic society' as meaning that: '... an interference corresponds to a pressing social need and, in particular, that it is proportionate to the legitimate aim pursued' (*Olsson v Sweden*, A 130 para 67

(1988)). The doctrine of proportionality is strongly linked to the principle of the margin of appreciation: the Court has found, 'the margin of appreciation extends in particular to the choice of the reasonable and appropriate means to be used by the authority to ensure that lawful manifestations can take place peacefully' (*Chorherr v Austria*, Series A 266-B, para 31 (1993)). In *Markt intern Verlag v FRG* (Series A 165 para 47 (1989)), the Court found: '... the European Court of Human Rights should not substitute its own evaluation for that of the national courts in the instant case, where those courts, on reasonable grounds, had considered the restrictions to be necessary.'

Thus, in considering the doctrine of proportionality, the domestic judiciary may find guidance in the principles enunciated at Strasbourg, but not in the outcome of particular decisions, in which particular forms of interference have been found to be proportionate to the legitimate aim in view, such as the prevention of disorder, or the 'rights of others'.

The following article describes how even at an early stage the judges took the opportunity to extend the protection offered by the HRA 1998 beyond merely public bodies and, in so doing, to develop a right of privacy previously unrecognised at common law.

Helen Fenwick, 'Privacy rights under the Human Rights Act' (2001) 33 SLR 2–8

Until recently, it was unclear whether legal protection for key privacy rights existed. No tort of invasion of privacy in respect of the non-consensual disclosure of personal information was available.

The Law Commission has remarked that 'It is a glaring inadequacy of the present law that ... the confidentiality of information improperly obtained ... may be unprotected' (*Breach of Confidence*, Law Com No 110, para 5.5). The Court of Appeal in the notorious case of *Kaye v Robertson* severely criticised the plaintiff's lack of a privacy remedy, while decrying their inability to develop the common law so as to furnish him with one. More recently, *dicta* in a decision of the House of Lords ([1991] FSR 62 CA) remarked upon 'the continuing, widespread concern at the apparent failure of the law to give individuals a reasonable degree of protection from unwarranted intrusion in many situations' (*per* Lord Nicholls).

In a recent speech to a conference on the press and human rights (*Human Rights, Privacy and the Media*, organised by the Constitution Unit and The Centre for Communication and Information Law, held at UCL on 8 January 1999), Alan Russbridge, Editor of *The Guardian*, listed a string of examples from the previous few months in which elements of the print media had perpetrated the most gross invasions of privacy by publishing surreptitiously obtained details about the personal lives of celebrities with either no or the flimsiest of 'public interest' justifications. The submission of Victim Support to the Calcutt Committee (see Cm 1102 (1990)) included a large number of case histories in which ordinary victims of crime and their families had had their suffering markedly exacerbated by intrusive and insensitive publication of the details of their plight in local and national newspapers. Many had suffered intense emotional distress, usually from the publication of quite needless details.

In effect, all the weapons of the secret police could be deployed by reporters – the use of very sophisticated surveillance devices, informers and contacts with State agents, with the probable effect of creating an intensive and relentless invasion of privacy which would then be exacerbated when the information received mass publicity. The weapons available to agents of the State may themselves be literally involved; without going into this area in any depth, what real assurance is there under the Interception of Communications Act (to be replaced by the Regulation of Investigatory Powers Act 2000) or any other instrument, that information obtained by telephone or email tapping might not eventually find its way into the hands of the media, including freelance journalists?

In contrast to media coverage, State use of the information gained, assuming that the subject is unconcerned in criminal activity or espionage, may involve a less vicious and gross invasion of privacy since it will be retained rather than exposed to the popular gaze. Publication of personal details in the media is done, in the main, for no good end but usually merely to maximise profit, and often very arbitrarily. Arbitrariness arises in, for example, the following instance. A well known and greatly respected actor has always chosen not to reveal his homosexuality. He lives quietly with his partner and attracts little media attention other than what is proper and expected. Suddenly, due to a mark of recognition which is awarded to him, he receives a great deal of extremely intrusive and sensationalist media attention. The fact that he is a homosexual is abruptly revealed without his consent and details of his private life are exposed in lurid and misleading terms. An occasion that should be a time of national honour is transformed, from his point of view, and from the viewpoint of other UK citizens, into a moment of national shame. When the State invades privacy it is subject to certain controls (it is not suggested that these are necessarily effective) and it uses them, at least ostensibly, for ends many would have some sympathy with, such as the protection of national security or the prevention of crime.

In contrast to the position in the US, and in virtually every other Western democracy, the injury created when private information is reported in newspapers in lurid terms had no remedy in a privacy law in this country. How far, if at all, will the Human Rights Act 1998 (HRA) allow this situation to be remedied through its introduction into UK law of Art 8 of the European Convention on Human Rights (the term 'introduction' is used since there is considerable doubt as to the accuracy of speaking of 'incorporating' the rights under the ECHR. For discussion, see Marshall, A, 'Patriating rights: with reservations', in Hare and Forsyth (eds), *Constitutional Reform in the United Kingdom: Practice and Principles*, 1998, Oxford: Hart, p 75) providing a right to respect for private life? (Article 8 of the Convention provides: 'Everyone has the right to respect for his private and family life, his home and his correspondence,' and then specifies a number of grounds permitting interference 'by a public authority' with this right.)

Media coverage of the introduction into Parliament of the Human Rights Bill focused overwhelmingly upon just this subject. Much of the debate was ill-informed and sensationalist, as one would expect. Discussion tended to focus around fears that the Act would introduce a right to privacy against the press 'through the back door', due either to judicial development of the common law in the post-HRA era, or to the probable status of the Press Complaints Commission as a public authority, itself bound to act compatibly with the Convention under s 6 of the HRA. Sometimes, the basic point was missed that the Convention rights will not directly bind newspapers since they are not public authorities. (The definition of 'public authority' appears in s 6(1), (3)(b) and (5) of the Act, discussed HL Deb vol 582 cols 1277, 1293–94 and 1309–10, 3 November 1997, and vol 583 cols 771–811, 24 November 1997.) In other words, s 6 prevents the creation of full, direct 'horizontal' effect, that is, legal effects between private parties (for example, citizens, newspapers); it seeks to create only 'vertical' effect, that is, legal effects between private parties and public authorities.

Where a public authority has arguably breached a Convention right, the victim of the breach can bring an action against it relying on s 7(1)(a) of the HRA (allowing for the bringing of proceedings against public authorities who have breached s 6 or are about to do so). If the victim cannot use s 7(1)(a) since the other party is not a public authority, he or she must identify an existing cause of action in order to bring proceedings. If ss 6 and 7 had made no distinction between private and public bodies, the HRA would have had full direct horizontal effect. (It may be noted that s 3 of the HRA clearly does create a form of horizontal effect, since all statutes are affected. However, no statute, apart from the Data Protection Act 1998, which has limited impact in this area as indicated below, clearly covers the area under consideration.)

The aim of this article is to comment on the specific issue of the impact of the HRA on interference with personal information by the media by examining two recent key cases in which this was the central concern. Now that these two decisions are available, it is possible to say that there is a right to privacy in UK law which will affect newspapers and the print media in general, even thought they are not directly bound by the Convention rights under s 6 of the HRA.

Michael Douglas, Catherine Zeta-Jones, Northern and Shell plc v Hello! Ltd (2000) 21 December, CA, www.courtservice.gov.uk

Facts

The magazine *OK!* secured an agreement with Mr Douglas and Ms Zeta-Jones eight days before their wedding, under which it agreed to pay a very large sum of money to them in respect of rights to publish exclusive photographs of the wedding and an article about it. The couple trusted *OK!* to project only the images they wanted projected to the public. They also retained rights of approval in relation to anything that was to be published. Mr Douglas and Ms Zeta-Jones undertook to use their best efforts to ensure that:

> ... no other media (including but not limited to photographers, television crews or journalists) shall be permitted access to the Wedding, and that no guests or anyone else present at the Wedding (including staff at the venues) shall be allowed to take photographs.

The rival magazine *Hello!* had tendered for the rights but had failed. *Hello!* clearly knew that exclusive rights were to be granted for coverage of the wedding, and that it had not secured them. However, the security operation at the wedding failed to prevent some unauthorised photos from being taken and *Hello!* obtained them. The couple were informed after the wedding that copies of *Hello!* were already in the UK with a photo of the wedding on the front cover and that they would be distributed very shortly. They rapidly obtained an *ex parte* injunction restraining publication.

The issues before the court

The court had to decide whether an injunction restraining this publication should be continued in force until trial, thereby effectively 'killing' this issue of *Hello!*. The key issues were: (a) the applicability of the law of confidence; (b) the relevance of the HRA 1998; (c) whether the injunction should be continued until the trial of the action or whether the claimants should be left to seek to obtain damages at the trial.

Findings

(a) The applicability of the law of confidence

The doctrine of confidence originally arose from the exercise of the equitable jurisdiction to restrain freedom of speech in circumstances in which it would be unconscionable to publish private material. If information was accepted on the basis that it would be kept secret, the recipient's conscience would be bound by that confidence, and it would be unconscionable for him to break his duty of confidence by publishing the information to others (*Stephens v Avery* [1988] Ch 449, p 456). In *Argyll v Argyll* [1967] Ch 302, pp 329f–330b, it was said: 'It ... seems to me that the policy of the law, so far from indicating that communication between husband and wife should be excluded from protection against breaches of confidence given by the court in accordance with *Prince Albert v Strange* ((1849) 2 De Gex & Sm 652; on appeal 1 Mac & G 25), strongly favours its inclusion.' In *Michael Barrymore v News Group Newspapers Ltd* [1997] FSR 600, Jacob J followed these principles in a case in which a newspaper sought to publish information concerning an intimate homosexual relationship.

Thus, the law of confidence has developed to the point at which it can provide a right to privacy, in so far as a privacy right may be viewed as covering matters which are distinct from those which confidence has come to be viewed as capable of covering. (Arguably, it might have reached this point even independently of the HRA.) In particular, it is arguable that confidence does not cover surreptitious takings of personal information by someone whose conscience cannot be said to be bound to maintain confidence – a 'stranger' – and that such takings are more readily covered by a right to privacy, albeit originating from confidence. (The point appears to be that, although such takings could be covered by confidence: see *Francome v MGM* [1984] 1 WLR 892 and *dicta* in *AG v Guardian Newspapers (No 2)* [1990] 1 AC 109, p 281, the notion of an implied obligation to maintain confidence might be viewed as artificial, depending on the circumstances.) In this instance, the photographs may have been taken by a guest (who would come under an obligation of confidence), in which case it would be immaterial whether the cause of action was called confidence or privacy. A cause of action would be available. In *Hellewell v Chief Constable of Derbyshire* [1995] 1 WLR 804, Laws LJ said:

> I entertain no doubt that disclosure of a photograph may, in some circumstances, be actionable as a breach of confidence ... If someone with a telephoto lens were to take from a distance and with no authority a picture of another engaged in some private act, his subsequent disclosure of the photograph would, in my judgment, as surely amount to a breach of confidence as if he had found or stolen a letter or diary in which the act was recounted and proceeded to publish it. In such a case the law would protect

what might reasonably be called a right of privacy, although the name accorded to the cause of action would be breach of confidence.

If the photos in the instant case were taken by a 'stranger', the cause of action would arguably be termed a right to privacy, and the HRA aids this conclusion.

(b) The relevance of the Human Rights Act

The Act gives a force to the above argument – that confidence has developed in such a way as to provide a right to privacy – which it might not otherwise have.

Sedley LJ found: *'We have reached a point at which it can be said with confidence that the law recognises and will appropriately protect a right of personal privacy.'*

He based this finding in part on the coming into force of the HRA since it requires the courts of this country – as public authorities under s 6 of the HRA – to give effect to the right to respect for private and family life set out in Art 8 of the European Convention on Human Rights. He said that the jurisprudence of the Court and the common law 'now run in a single channel because, by virtue of s 2 and s 6 of the Act, the courts of this country must not only take into account jurisprudence of both the Commission and the European Court of Human Rights which points to a positive institutional obligation to respect privacy; they must themselves act compatibly with that and the other Convention rights. This, for reasons I now turn to, arguably gives the final impetus to the recognition of a right of privacy in English law'.

His key point in relation to a possible difference between confidence and privacy was: '... a concept of privacy does ... accord recognition to the fact that the law has to protect not only those people whose trust has been abused but those who simply find themselves subjected to an unwanted intrusion into their personal lives. The law no longer needs to construct an artificial relationship of confidentiality between intruder and victim: it can recognise privacy itself as a legal principle drawn from the fundamental value of personal autonomy.'

Article 8(1) of the Convention creates a right to respect for private and family life. But Art 8(2) of the Convention, and ss 6, 7 and 8 of the HRA, make it clear that these rights are enforceable only against public authorities. However, the European Court of Human Rights has relied on the positive duty imposed on the Member States by Art 1 of the Convention (see the judgment of the court in *A v UK* 27 EHRR 61). Therefore, Art 8 does recognise the applicability of its guarantee as between private parties.

However, in an action between private parties, how can it be said that the defendant is bound by the Convention since it is not a public authority under s 6 of the HRA? Sedley LJ found that the court as itself a public authority under s 6, is obliged to give some effect to Art 8, among other provisions of the Convention. Its duty appears to allow it to 'take the step from confidentiality to privacy' (an argument supported by M Hunt, in 'The "horizontal effect" of the Human Rights Act' [1998] PL 423). In so far as there is doubt as to the scope of the duty of the court under s 6, s 12(4) makes the matter crystal clear where interference with the right to freedom of expression is in issue. Section 12(4) requires the Court to have particular regard to the right to freedom of expression under Art 10.

Therefore, it is clear that Art 10 is directly applicable as between one private party to litigation and another; in other words, it has horizontal effect. However, Art 10(2) is qualified in respect of the reputation and rights of others and the protection of information received in confidence. Therefore, in having particular regard to Art 10 it is also necessary to have such regard to the other Convention rights, including Art 8. Section 12(4) does not therefore merely give freedom of expression priority over the other rights. In weighing up the competing claims, the court also had to take the Code policed by the Press Complaints Commission into account under s 12(4)(b); it did not appear that the photographer had complied with the provision of cl 3 (which provides, in part, that 'A publication will be expected to justify intrusions into any individual's private life without consent ... The use of long lens photography to take pictures of people in private places without their consent is unacceptable'). This clause is qualified by the exceptions where a public interest can be demonstrated to apply. That was not the case in this instance.

The court found that the claimants had an arguable case that they had suffered a breach of their privacy; this claim was based on the law of confidence, interpreted compatibly with Art 8, due to the requirements of s 12(4).

(c) The injunction

Section 12(3) provides that prior restraint on expression should not be granted except where the court considers that the claimant is 'likely' to establish at trial that publication should not be allowed. Under s 3 of the HRA, the court has a duty to construe all legislation, which must include the HRA itself, compatibly with the Convention rights 'so far as it is possible to do so'. Therefore, clearly, both sub-sections must be read in such a way as to ensure that all the rights are given full weight; s 2(3) must not accord more weight to Art 10 than to the other rights. The outcome in any particular instance will be determined principally by considerations of proportionality. Sedley LJ said that the court has to 'look ahead to the ultimate stage and to be satisfied that the scales are likely to come down in the applicant's favour. That does not conflict with the Convention, since it is merely requiring the court to apply its mind to how one right is to be balanced, on the merits against another right, without building in additional weight on one side'.

Taking into account the fact that the claimants had in a sense already 'sold' their privacy, Sedley LJ found that their rights to privacy were outweighed by the right of publication and considered that they should be left to a claim for damages at the trial of the action.

But the court also had to consider the effects of leaving the claimants to a damages claim. In *American Cyanamid Co v Ethicon Ltd* [1975] AC 396, it was found that a judge must weigh the respective risks that injustice may result from his deciding one way or the other at the interim stage. If an injunction is refused but the claimant does succeed in establishing his legal right at the trial which he sought to protect by means of the injunction, he might in the meantime suffer harm which cannot adequately be compensated for by an award of money. On the other hand, there is the risk that if the injunction is granted but the claimant fails at the trial, the defendant in the meantime may have suffered harm which is also irrecompensable. This weighing up is sometimes termed 'the balance of convenience'. Lord Justice Brooke found that the balance of convenience appeared to favour leaving *OK!* to assert its legal rights at the trial of what he said was 'essentially a commercial dispute between two magazine enterprises'.

Therefore, although the court found that the claim might succeed at trial and result in an award of compensation, it also found that the injunction should be discharged. Thus, *Hello!* could publish the issue which contained the wedding photographs.

Jon Venables, Robert Thompson v News Group Newspapers Ltd, Associated Newspapers Ltd, MGM Ltd (2001) 8 January, QBD, www.courtservice.gov.uk

Facts

Jon Venables and Robert Thompson were claimants in proceedings for injunctions. In 1993 they had murdered a boy of two, James Bulger, when they were 10 years old. The murder was particularly shocking and distressing and the facts were widely publicised in the media. They were sentenced to be detained during Her Majesty's pleasure under s 53(1) of the Children and Young Persons Act 1933 (CYPA), and they were placed in separate secure units. At the conclusion of their trial, the judge granted comprehensive injunctions restricting publication of further information about the two boys, with no limit of time, based under both s 39 of the CYPA and the inherent jurisdiction of the High Court to deal with children.

The claimants reached 18 and wanted the injunctions to continue. The injunctions were principally designed to protect their new identities when they were released into the community.

Issues before the court

The court had to decide whether there was jurisdiction to grant an injunction in respect of an adult to protect his identity and other relevant information. That issue raised the question of the effect of the implementation of the HRA 1998 and, in particular, the applicability of the Convention since the proceedings were private ones.

The case in favour of the newspapers

The speech of Lord Steyn in *R v Secretary of State for the Home Department ex p Simms* [1999] 3 WLR 328, p 337, supported the presumption in favour of freedom of expression. The speech of Lord Templeman in *AG v Guardian Newspapers* (1987) 1 WLR 1248, p 1297, the judgment of Hoffman LJ in *R v Central Television* (1994) Fam 192, pp 203E, 204C, and the judgment of Munby J in *Kelly v BBC* [2000] 3 FCR 509, p 525, also provided support. It was not a question of a balancing exercise by the court since freedom of expression had presumptive priority.

Further, if either of the claimants was discovered by a journalist, it should be left to the judgment of the editor whether or not to publish the information. Instances could be found where the press was asked by the court not to publish and did not do so (see *Broadmoor Hospital Authority and Another v R* [2000] 2 All ER 727).

Also, if injunctions were granted, they would become a precedent for the future. An example would arise if Myra Hindley were ever released. The Court of Appeal in *R v Chief Constable of the North Wales Police* [1999] QB 396 refused to grant injunctions to prevent the Chief Constable from revealing to the owner of a caravan site the past convictions of two paedophiles living on the site.

There was a positive obligation on a public authority to ensure proper protection of rights under the Convention, including the right to freedom of expression.

The case for injunctions

The key issue concerned the grave danger to the claimants if their new identities and whereabouts became known since threats against them had frequently been made, including threats to their lives. They were also likely to suffer serious and relentless invasions of privacy.

Findings

The court found that, in the light of the judgments in the *Michael Douglas* case regarding the effect of s 12(4) of the HRA, it was clear that Art 10 had to be applied directly. The injunctions were granted on the basis of the inherent jurisdiction of the Family Division of the High Court to protect minors, and on the statutory provisions in s 39 of the CYPA. That basis no longer existed but the court considered that the injunction could be based upon the law of confidence, taking into account the implementation of the HRA.

The newspapers could not be said to be public authorities under s 6 of the HRA and, therefore, the Convention rights were not directly applicable to them. But the tort of breach of confidence is an established cause of action. Therefore, since a case based on confidence might be made out, the court had to look at s 12. As indicated above, the court would then have to consider Art 10 and also the other Convention rights by virtue of the protection of the rights of others under Art 10(2).

Megarry J in *Coco v Clark* [1969] RPC 41, p 47, identified three essentials of the tort of breach of confidence: the information must have 'the necessary quality of confidence about it'. It 'must have been imparted in circumstances importing an obligation of confidence'. There must be an 'unauthorised use of the information to the detriment of the party communicating it'. In *AG v Guardian Newspapers (No 2)* [1990] 1 AC 109, Lord Goff of Chieveley said, p 281:

> I start with the broad principle (which I do not in any way intend to be definitive) that a duty of confidence arises when confidential information comes to the knowledge of a person (the confidant) in circumstances where he has notice, or is held to have agreed, that the information is confidential, with the effect that it would be just in all the circumstances that he should be precluded from disclosing the information to others ... in the vast majority of cases ... the duty of confidence will arise from a transaction or relationship between the parties ... but it is well settled that a duty of confidence may arise in equity independently of such cases.

The public interest in preserving confidence could be outweighed by some other countervailing public interest favouring disclosure. Therefore, the court had to carry out a balancing operation, weighing the public interest in maintaining confidence against the interest in disclosure. However, s 12 of the HRA and Art 10(1) of the Convention give an enhanced importance to freedom of expression and so to the right of the press to publish. Therefore, under the HRA, a balancing exercise is no longer appropriate. On the facts, a duty to maintain confidence was found to arise, partly on the ground of the threat to the lives of the claimants.

The court went on to find that the freedom of the media to publish could only be restricted if the need for those restrictions could be shown to fall within the exceptions set out in Art 10(2). In considering the limits to the law of confidence, and whether a remedy is available to the claimants within those limits, it was found that the exceptions must be narrowly interpreted. The claimants' right under Art 2 (right to life), Art 3 (right to freedom from torture and inhuman and degrading treatment) and Art 8 (right to respect for private life) were in issue. The rights under Arts 2 and 3 are not capable of derogation. In *Osman v UK* [1999] 1 FLR 193, the European Court held that the provisions of Art 2 enjoined a positive obligation upon Contracting States to take measures to secure the right to life. The case concerned the failure of the police to act to protect a family from criminal acts, including murder. The Court said, paras 115–16: 'The court notes that the first sentence of Art 2(1) enjoins the State not only to refrain from the intentional and unlawful taking of life, but also to take appropriate steps to safeguard the lives of those within its jurisdiction ... it must be established that the authorities knew or ought to have known at the time of the existence of a real and immediate risk to life of an identified individual or individuals from the criminal acts of a third party and that they failed to take measures within the scope of their powers which, judged reasonably, might have been expected to avoid that risk.'

Since in the instant case the court found that there was a real possibility that the claimants might be the objects of vigilante or revenge attacks, the potential breaches of Arts 2, 3 and 8 had to be scrupulously evaluated. Further, since a restriction on freedom of expression was in issue, all the criteria in Art 10(2), narrowly interpreted, had to be met. The court was satisfied that confidence could extend to cover the injunctions sought and that therefore, the restrictions proposed were in accordance with the law. It was found that the common law continues to evolve and was given 'considerable impetus' to do so by the implementation of the Convention into domestic law.

Also it was a strong probability that on the release of the claimants there would be great efforts to find them and some of those seeking to do so would be determined upon revenge. The requirement in the Convention that there can be no derogation from the rights under Arts 2 and 3 provided strong support for the very pressing social need that their confidentiality should be protected. The provision of injunctions to achieve the object sought also had to be proportionate to the legitimate aims they pursued. The aim was to protect the claimants from serious and possibly irreparable harm. The court noted that Lord Woolf said in *R v Lord Saville of Newdigate ex p A* [2000] 1 WLR 1885, p 1857: '... when a fundamental right such as the right to life is involved, the options open to the reasonable decision-maker are curtailed. They are curtailed because it is unreasonable to reach a decision which contravenes or could contravene human rights unless there are sufficiently significant countervailing considerations. In other words it is not open to the decision-maker to risk interfering with fundamental rights in the absence of compelling justification ...'

Bearing that finding in mind, it appeared that the appropriate measures to be taken were to grant the injunctions, since they would substantially reduce the risk to each of the claimants. It was not thought that this extension of the law of confidence would lead to the granting of general restrictions on the media in cases where anonymity would be desirable, since under the strict application of Art 10(2) it would only be appropriate to grant injunctions to restrain the media where it could be convincingly demonstrated, within those exceptions, that it is strictly necessary. The court left open the question whether it would be appropriate to grant injunctions to restrict the press in this case if only Art 8, as opposed to Arts 2 and 3, had been likely to be breached. Although the breach of the claimants' right to respect for family life and privacy would have been likely to be serious, it might not have been sufficient to meet the importance of the preservation of the freedom of expression in Art 10(1).

In any event, the court was satisfied that there was a real and serious risk to the rights of the claimants under Arts 2 and 3 and it was found that, in principle, jurisdiction to grant the injunctions to protect the claimants was present.

The court went on to assess the strength of the evidence relating to those risks; finding that a real risk existed and that the protection represented by the injunctions was proportionate to the need for confidentiality, the injunctions were granted. The injunctions are intended to last for their whole lives.

Conclusions

It can now be said, then, with a certainty that was not previously appropriate, that the law recognises and will protect a right of personal privacy. That right finds its roots in an existing cause of action, the doctrine of confidence. The HRA has, as commentators predicted, given the courts the impetus to develop confidence to this point.

It is important to understand how this stage was reached. The *Michael Douglas* decision did not rely on the creation of so called direct horizontal effect in the sense of the creation of a new free-standing cause of action: the HRA precludes an action directly against newspapers based on Art 8, since newspapers are not public authorities within the meaning of s 6 of the HRA. But, once the claimants were in court presenting an arguable case for an injunction on grounds of confidence, the court had a duty, under s 12(4) of the HRA (if not under s 6 as a public authority), to develop that action by reference to Art 10, which meant also giving full weight to Art 8 as a right recognised under Art 10(2). In taking Art 8 into account, the domestic courts have also now have accepted that, as interpreted at Strasbourg, its guarantees clearly affect the relations between private parties.

Where prior restraint is in question s 12(3) requires consideration of the merits of the privacy right and of expression in the particular circumstances. Also, as the *Venables* case made clear, such prior restraint must be justified by a strict application of the tests under Art 10(2), in particular those of necessity and proportionality. The so called 'public interest defence' under the doctrine of confidence can no longer lead to a balancing of such interest against maintaining confidentiality: the tests under Art 10(2) have taken its place.

The new privacy right is of great significance, as the introduction to this article made clear. However, it has limits due to its origins: it is clear that physical intrusion by information seekers cannot be directly addressed even under the new style law of privacy deriving from confidence. Possibly the Data Protection Act 1998 (which, while arguably likely to prove ineffective in many circumstances in relation to journalists, due, *inter alia*, to the provision of s 32(4), can also provide a potential alternative remedy in relation to the non-consensual disclosure of personal information) or the Protection from Harassment Act 1997 might be applicable. Their provisions will, of course, have to be interpreted compatibly with the Convention rights, including those under Art 8, under s 3 of the HRA.

The new right to privacy will affect the print media most significantly as the worst offenders, although it will have an application to all media forms, including electronic ones, which rely at least partially on the invasion of personal privacy. The new right could be used against the BBC and Channel 4, but they will (clearly in the case of the BBC and probably in the case of Channel 4) fall also within the definition of 'public authority' under s 6 of the HRA and so will be bound directly by the Convention. The new right is unlikely to have much impact in relation to the complex and controversial issue of invasion of privacy by State bodies. Such bodies are public authorities and are therefore directly bound by Art 8. Therefore, an action could be brought against them either relying on confidence or on s 7(1)(a) of the HRA (allowing for the bringing of proceedings against public authorities who have breached s 6 or are about to do so). But the secrecy of State invasion of privacy and the provisions preventing or curbing consideration of such invasion in court (see, for example, s 17 of the Regulation of Investigatory Powers Act 2000) means that actions in reliance on Art 8 brought by either route are unlikely.

CHAPTER 2

SOURCES OF LAW

INTRODUCTION

Although the material in this chapter deals with both statute law and common law the focus will be on the role played by the judiciary in relation to both of those sources. As the previous chapter demonstrated, neither legislation nor cases speak for themselves and their meaning is a product of active interpretation. That places the judges in a central role with regard to legislation as well as more obviously in relation to common law.

COMMON LAW

The common law is the creation of the judges operating through the creation and following of precedents in earlier cases. It is dependent on the hierarchical structure of the courts and the part of the decision that is binding on later courts is the *ratio decidendi*, anything else is merely *obiter dicta* and not binding. Problems arise in deciding what exactly constitutes *ratio* as opposed to *obiter* statements. Also, the fact that the *ratio* in any case depends upon the particular facts of that case, allows later judges to distinguish the immediate case from the precedent. These possibilities allow scope for judicial creativity and reform of the common law as may be seen in the case extracts below.

THE HIERARCHY OF THE COURTS

The House of Lords

The House of Lords stands at the summit of the English court structure and its decisions are binding on all courts below it in the hierarchy. As regards its own previous decisions, until 1966 the House of Lords regarded itself as bound by its previous decisions. In a Practice Statement of that year, however, Lord Gardiner indicated that the House of Lords would, in future, regard itself as free to depart from its previous decisions where it appeared right to do so.

Practice Statement (Judicial Precedent), 83 Cr App R 191, 73 Cr App R 266, 26 July 1966

Lord Gardiner LC: Their Lordships regard the use of precedent as an indispensable foundation upon which to decide what is the law and its application to individual cases. It provides at least some degree of certainty upon which individuals can rely in the conduct of their affairs, as well as a basis for orderly development of legal rules.

Their lordships nevertheless recognise that too rigid adherence to precedent may lead to injustice in a particular case and also unduly restrict the proper development of the law. They propose, therefore, to modify their present practice and, while treating former decisions of this House as normally binding, to depart from a previous decision when it appears right to do so.

In this connection they will bear in mind the danger of disturbing retrospectively the basis on which contracts, settlements of property and fiscal arrangements have been entered into and also the especial need for certainty as to the criminal law.

This announcement is not intended to affect the use of precedent elsewhere than in this House.

Operation of Practice Statement

Given the potentially destabilising effect on existing legal practice based on previous decisions of the House of Lords, this is not a discretion that the House of Lords exercises lightly. There have been a number of cases, however, in which the House of Lords has overruled or amended its own earlier decisions. One example is *Miliangos v George Frank (Textiles) Ltd*.

Miliangos v George Frank (Textiles) Ltd [1975] 3 All ER 801

By an agreement made in May 1971 the plaintiff, a national of Switzerland, agreed to sell, and the defendants, an English company, agreed to buy, a quantity of polyester yarn. The defendants did not pay any part of the price. On 20 April 1972, the plaintiff issued a writ claiming payment of the sterling equivalent of the contract price at the date when payment should have been made. Between that date and the date of the hearing of the action sterling fell in value against the Swiss franc with the result that, at the date of the hearing, the contract price in Swiss francs was equivalent to a much larger sterling sum than it had been in 1971. At the hearing the plaintiff obtained leave to amend the statement of claim so as to claim the amount due to him in Swiss francs. The defendants contended that the plaintiff was not in law entitled to judgment for a sum of money expressed in a foreign currency.

> **Lord Wilberforce:** ... On 26 November 1974 the Court of Appeal (Lord Denning MR, Lawton LJ and Foster J) announced their decision in a case involving a claim in German currency: *Schorsch Meier GmbH v Hennin*.
>
> Although they were faced with a unanimous decision of this House in *Re United Railways of the Havana and Regla Warehouses Ltd* that, on a foreign currency claim, judgment can only be given in sterling, to which the foreign currency must be converted as at the date when the debt became due, the court held by a majority that an English court could give a money judgment in a foreign currency, when that currency was the currency of the contract. Lawton LJ, dissenting, considered that he was bound by the *Havana Railways* case ...
>
> This decision was naturally welcomed by the respondent [in the *Milangos* case]. So when this action came on for hearing on 2 December 1974 he applied to amend his

statement of claim so as to claim the amount due to him in Swiss francs. This amendment was allowed by Bristow J so that the claim became one for 415,522.45 Swiss francs for the price plus 621.75 the cost of protesting the two bills, making together 416,144.20 Swiss francs.

Since, between the date in 1971 when payment was due and the date of the hearing, sterling had fallen in value as against the Swiss franc from 9.90 to 6.00 Swiss francs approximately to the pound, this meant that if the respondent could obtain judgment in Swiss francs he could recover in sterling terms some £60,000, whereas if he had to accept the sterling equivalent at the 1971 rate he could recover only some £42,000.

This amendment having been made, the action came on for trial. The learned judge found himself in a difficult position. On the one hand there was the decision of this House in the *Havana Railways* case which clearly precluded him from giving judgment in Swiss francs or from awarding the sterling equivalent of the sum due converted at any other date than the date when the sum claimed was due. On the other hand there was the decision of the Court of Appeal in *Schorsch Meier* which had declined to apply the *Havana Railways* decision. In these circumstances he decided that he ought to follow the decision of this House and that the decision in *Schorsch Meier* was given *per incuriam*.

An appeal was brought to the Court of Appeal and was heard in February 1975 by Lord Denning MR, Stephenson and Geoffrey Lane LJJ. It was submitted that the court, on indistinguishable facts, was bound by and should follow the *Havana Railways* case, but the court declined to do so. It held that the majority decision in *Schorsch Meier* was not given *per incuriam* and that it was binding on the court. It therefore varied the judgment of Bristow J so as to give judgment for the respondent for the sum claimed in Swiss francs. From this judgment appeal has come to this House ... It has to be reaffirmed that the only judicial means by which decisions of this House can be reviewed is by this House itself, under the declaration of 1966. Whether it can or should do so is a difficult enough question, which I shall now examine.

... the standing authority on the question now at issue ... is that procedurally an action cannot be brought here for recovery or payment of a sum expressed in foreign currency, and that, in effect, it can only be brought for a sum expressed in sterling, recoverable by way of damages.

I now have to ask, what is the position at the present time? Have any fresh considerations of any substance emerged which should induce your Lordships to follow a different rule?

... if I am faced with the alternative of forcing commercial circles to fall in with a legal doctrine which has nothing but precedent to commend it or altering the doctrine so as to confirm with what commercial experience has worked out, I know where my choice lies. The law should be responsive as well as, at times, enunciatory, and good doctrine can seldom be divorced from sound practice.

... Courts are bound by their own procedural law and must obey it, if imperative, though to do so may seem unjust. But if means exist for giving effect to the substance of a foreign obligation, conformably with the rules of private international law, procedure should not unnecessarily stand in the way ...

The ... considerations and the circumstances I have set forth, when related to the arguments which moved their Lordships in the *Havana Railways* case, lead me to the conclusion that, if these circumstances had been shown to exist in 1960, some at least of their Lordships, assuming always that the interests of justice in the particular case so required, would have been led, as one of them very notably has been led, to take a different view.

This brings me to the declaration made by this House in 1966. Under it, the House affirmed its power to depart from a previous decision when it appears right to do so, recognising that too rigid adherence to precedent might lead to injustice in a particular case and unduly restrict the proper development of the law. My Lords, on the assumption that to depart from the *Havana Railways* case would not involve undue practical difficulties, that a new and more satisfactory rule is capable of being stated, I am of opinion that the present case falls within the terms of the declaration. To change the rule would, for the reasons already explained, avoid injustice in the present case. To change it would enable the law to keep in step with commercial needs and with the majority of other countries facing similar problems ...

... My Lords, in conclusion I would say that, difficult as this whole matter undoubtedly is, if once a clear conclusion is reached as to what the law ought now to be, declaration of it by this House is appropriate. The law on this topic is judge made; it has been built up over the years from case to case. It is entirely within this House's duty, in the course of administering justice, to give the law a new direction in a particular case where, on principle and in reason, it appears right to do so. I cannot accept the suggestion that because a rule is long established only legislation can change it – that may be so when the rule is so deeply entrenched that it has infected the whole legal system, or the choice of a new rule involves more far-reaching research than courts can carry out ... [F]rom some experience in the matter, I am led to doubt whether legislative reform, at least prompt and comprehensive reform, in this field of foreign currency obligation, is practicable. Questions as to the recovery of debts or of damages depend so much on individual mixtures of facts and merits as to make them more suitable for progressive solutions in the courts. I think that we have an opportunity to reach such a solution here.

The Court of Appeal

The Court of Appeal generally is bound by its own previous decisions in civil cases. There are, however, a number of exceptions to this general rule. Lord Greene MR listed these exceptions in *Young v Bristol Aeroplane Co Ltd* (1944).

Young v Bristol Aeroplane Co Ltd [1944] 2 All ER 293

Lord Greene MR: ... It is surprising that so fundamental a matter should at this date still remain in doubt. To anyone unacquainted with the rare cases in which it has been suggested or asserted that this court is not bound to follow its own decisions or those of a court of co-ordinate jurisdiction the question would, we think, appear to be beyond controversy.

Cases in which this court has expressed its regret at finding itself bound by previous decisions of its own and has stated in the clearest terms that the only remedy of the unsuccessful party is to appeal to the House of Lords are within the recollection of all of us and numerous examples are to be found in the reports. When in such cases the matter has been carried to the House of Lords it has never, so far as we know, been suggested by the House that this view was wrong and that this court could itself have done justice by declining to follow a previous decision of its own which it considered to be erroneous.

On the contrary, the House has, so far as we are aware, invariably assumed and in many cases expressly stated that this court was bound by its own previous decision to act as it did ...

It is true that ... [the] cases [in which] the court held itself to be bound by previous decisions consisted of three members only. But we can find no warrant for the argument that what is conveniently but inaccurately called the Full Court has any greater power in this respect than a division of the court consisting of three members only.

The Court of Appeal is a creature of statute and its powers are statutory. It is one court though it usually sits in two or three divisions; each division has co-ordinate jurisdiction, but the full court has no greater powers or jurisdiction than any division of the court. Its jurisdiction is mainly appellate, but it has some original jurisdiction.

To some extent its decisions are final (for example, in appeals in bankruptcy and from the county courts), but in the majority of cases there is an appeal from its decisions to the House of Lords either with the leave of the Court of Appeal or of the House of Lords. Neither in the statute itself nor (save in two cases mentioned hereafter) in decided cases is there any suggestion that the powers of the Court of Appeal sitting with six or nine or more members are greater than those which it possesses when sitting as a division with three members.

In this respect, although we are unable to agree with certain views expressed by Greer LJ as will presently appear, we think that he was right in saying that what can be done by a full court can equally well be done by a division of the court. The corollary of this is, we think, clearly true, namely, that what cannot be done by a division of the court cannot be done by the full court.

In considering the question whether or not this court is bound by its previous decisions and those of courts of co-ordinate jurisdiction, it is necessary to distinguish four classes of case.

The first is that with which we are now concerned, namely, cases where this court finds itself confronted with one or more decisions of its own or of a court of co-ordinate jurisdiction which cover the question before it, and there is no conflicting decision of this court or of a court of co-ordinate jurisdiction. The second is where there is such a conflicting decision. The third is where this court comes to the conclusion that a previous decision, although not expressly overruled, cannot stand with a subsequent decision of the House of Lords. The fourth (a special case) is where this court comes to the conclusion that a previous decision was given *per incuriam*.

In the second and third classes of case it is beyond question that the previous decision is open to examination. In the second class, the court is unquestionably entitled to choose between the two conflicting decisions. In the third class of case the court is merely giving effect to what it considers to have been a decision of the House of Lords by which it is bound. The fourth class requires more detailed examination and we will refer to it again later in this judgment.

For the moment it is the first class which we have to consider. Although the language both of decision and of *dictum* as well as the constant practice of the court appears to us clearly to negative the suggested power, there are to be found *dicta* and, indeed, decisions the other way. So far as *dicta* are concerned, we are, of course, not bound to follow them. In the case of decisions we are entitled to choose between those which assert and those which deny the existence of the power. On a careful examination of the whole matter we have come to the clear conclusion that this court is bound to follow previous decisions of its own as well as those of courts of co-ordinate jurisdiction. The only exceptions to this rule (two of them apparent only) are those already mentioned which for convenience we here summarise:

(i) The court is entitled and bound to decide which of two conflicting decisions of its own it will follow.

(ii) The court is bound to refuse to follow a decision of its own which, though not expressly overruled, cannot in its opinion stand with a decision of the House of Lords.

(iii) The court is not bound to follow a decision of its own if it is satisfied that the decision was given *per incuriam*.

— · — · — · — · — · — · — · — · — · — · — · — · — · — · —

As was seen in relation to *Schorsch Meier GmbH v Hennin*, mentioned in *Miliangos v George Frank (Textiles) Ltd* considered above, Lord Denning had already shown his willingness to disregard previous decisions of the Court of Appeal in the pursuit of what he considered to be a just decision. He elucidated his approach to precedent in relation to the Court of Appeal in *Davis v Johnson*.

Davis v Johnson [1979] AC 264, CA and HL

Lord Denning: On principle, it seems to me that, whilst this court should regard itself as normally bound by a previous decision of the court, nevertheless it should be at liberty to depart from it if it is convinced that the previous decision was wrong. What is the argument to the contrary?

It is said that, if an error has been made, this court has no option but to continue the error and leave it to be corrected by the House of Lords.

The answer is this: the House of Lords may never have an opportunity to correct the error; and thus it may be perpetuated indefinitely, perhaps for ever. That often happened in the old days when there was no legal aid. A poor person had to accept the decision of this court because he had not the means to take it to the House of Lords ... Apart from monetary considerations, there have been many instances where cases have been settled pending an appeal to the House of Lords; or, for one reason or another, not taken there, especially with claims against insurance companies or big employers. When such a body has obtained a decision of this court in its favour, it will buy off an appeal to the House of Lords by paying ample compensation to the appellant. By so doing, it will have a legal precedent on its side which it can use with effect in later cases ... By such means an erroneous decision on a point of law can again be perpetuated forever. Even if all those objections are put on one side and there is an appeal to the House of Lords, it usually takes 12 months or more for the House to reach its decision. What then is the position of the lower courts meanwhile? They are in a dilemma. Either they have to apply the erroneous decision of the Court of Appeal, or they have to adjourn all fresh cases to await the decision of the House of Lords. That has often happened. So justice is delayed, and often denied, by the lapse of time before the error is corrected.

The present case is a crying instance. If it took the ordinary course of appeals to the House, it would take some months before it was decided. Meanwhile many women would be denied the protection which Parliament intended they should have. They would be subjected to violence without redress; because the county court judges would have to say to them: 'We are sorry but the Court of Appeal says we have no jurisdiction to help you. We were told that, in this very case, because of the urgency, the House might take special measures to hear it before Christmas. But, even so, I doubt whether they would be able to give their decision until well on in the New Year. In order to avoid all the delay, and the injustice consequent on it, it seems to me that this court, being convinced that the two previous decisions were wrong, should have the power to correct them and give these women the protection which Parliament intended they should have.'

It was suggested that, if we did this, the county court judges would be in a dilemma. They would not know whether to follow the two previous decisions or the later decision of this court. There would be no such dilemma. They should follow this later decision. Such a position always arises whenever the House of Lords corrects an error made by a previous decision. The lower courts, of course, follow the latest decision. The general rule is that, where there are conflicting decisions of courts of co-ordinate jurisdiction, the later decision is to be preferred, if it is reached after full consideration of the earlier decision.

So much for principle. But what about our precedents? What about *Young v Bristol Aeroplane Co Ltd*?

The position before 1944

The Court of Appeal in its present form was established in 1873. It was then the final court of appeal. Appeals to the House of Lords were abolished by that Act and only restored a year or two later.

The Court of Appeal inherited the jurisdiction of the previous courts of appeal such as the Court of Exchequer Chamber and the Court of Appeal in Chancery. Those earlier courts had always had power to reconsider and renew the law as laid down in previous decisions; and, if that law was found to be wrong, to correct it; but without disturbing the actual decision. This is taken from the statements of eminent judges of those days who knew the position. In particular in 1852 Lord St Leonards LC in *Bright v Hutton*, said in the House of Lords: '... you are not bound by any rule of law which you may lay down, if upon a subsequent occasion, you should find reason to differ from that rule; that is, like every Court of Justice, possesses an inherent power to correct an error into which it may have fallen.'

In *Young v Bristol Aeroplane Co Ltd* the court overruled the practice of a century. Lord Greene MR, sitting with a court of five, laid down that this court is bound to follow its previous decision as well as those of co-ordinate jurisdiction, subject to only three exceptions:

(i)   where there are two conflicting decisions;

(ii) where a previous decision cannot stand with a decision of the House of Lords;

(iii) if a previous decision was given *per incuriam*. Even as the judges in *Young v Bristol Aeroplane Co Ltd* thought fit to discard the practice of a century and declare a new practice or usage, so we in 1977 can discard the guidelines of 1944 and set up new guidelines of our own or revert to the old practice ... Nothing said in the House of Lords, before or since, can stop us from doing so. Anything said about it there must needs be *obiter dicta* ...

The new guidelines

So we suggest that new guidelines are entitled to be laid down. To my mind, this court should apply similar guidelines to those adopted by the House of Lords in 1966. Whenever it appears to this court that a previous decision was wrong, we should be at liberty to depart from it if we think it right to do so. Normally, in nearly every case of course, we would adhere to it. But in an exceptional case we are at liberty to depart from it.

Alternatively, in my opinion, we should extend the exceptions in *Young v Bristol Aeroplane Co Ltd* when it appears to be a proper case to do so ...

When *Davis v Johnson* eventually got to the House of Lords they did not resist the opportunity to reaffirm their disapproval of Lord Denning's attempts to free the Court of Appeal from the strictures of *stare decisis* as it had previously been understood to operate in relation to that court and to reassert the orthodoxy as stated in *Young v Bristol Aeroplane Co Ltd*.

Lord Diplock: ... So far as civil matters are concerned the law on this question is now clear and unassailable. It has been so for more than 30 years. I do not find it necessary to trace the origin and development of the doctrine of *stare decisis* before the present structure of the courts was created in 1875. In that structure the Court of Appeal in civil actions has always played, save in a few exceptional matters, an intermediate and not a final appellate role. The application of the doctrine of *stare decisis* to decisions of the Court of Appeal was the subject of close examination by a Court of Appeal composed of six of its eight regular members in *Young v Bristol Aeroplane Co Ltd*.

... The rule as expounded in the *Bristol Aeroplane* case was not new in 1944. It had been acted on numerous occasions and had, as recently as the previous year, received the express confirmation in this House. Although prior to 1944 there had been an occasional deviation from the rule, which was why a court of six was brought together to consider it, there has been none since. It has been uniformly acted on by the Court of Appeal and re-affirmed, notably in a judgment of a Court of Appeal of five, of which Lord Denning MR as Denning LJ was a member, in *Morelle Ltd v Wakeling*. This judgment emphasised the limited scope of the *per incuriam* exception to the general rule that the Court of Appeal is bound by its own previous decisions.

The rule has also been uniformly accepted by this House as being correct. Because until recently it has never been questioned the acceptance of the rule has generally been tacit in the course of recounting the circumstances which have rendered necessary an appeal to your Lordships' House; but occasionally the rule has been expressly referred to, as by Viscount Simon in the *Bristol Aeroplane* case itself and by Lord Morton of Henryton and Lord Porter in *Bonsor v Musicians' Union*.

Furthermore, the provisions of the Administration of Justice Act 1969 which authorise 'leap frog' appeals in civil cases direct from the High Court to this House are based on the tacit assumption that the rule as stated in the *Bristol Aeroplane* case is correct. One of the two grounds on which a High Court judge may authorise a 'leap frog' appeal is if he is satisfied that a point of law of general importance involved in his decision (s 12(3)(b)):

> is one in respect of which the judge is bound by a decision of the Court of Appeal or of the House of Lords in previous proceedings, and was fully considered in the judgments given by the Court of Appeal or the House of Lords (as the case may be) in those previous proceedings.

The justification for by-passing the Court of Appeal when the decision by which the judge is bound is one given by the Court of Appeal itself in previous proceedings is because that court also is bound by the decision, if the point of law was fully considered and not passed over *per incuriam*.

So the rule as it had been laid down in the *Bristol Aeroplane* case had never been questioned thereafter until, following on the announcement by Lord Gardiner LC in 1966 that the House of Lords would feel free in exceptional cases to depart from a previous decision of its own, Lord Denning MR conducted what may be described, I hope without offence, as a one-man crusade with the object of freeing the Court of Appeal from the shackles which the doctrine of *stare decisis* imposed on its liberty of decision by the application of the rule laid down in the *Bristol Aeroplane* case to its previous decisions; or, for that matter, by any decisions of this House itself of which the Court of Appeal disapproved ...

In an appellate court of last resort a balance must be struck between the need on the one side for the legal certainty resulting from the binding effect of previous decisions and on the other side the avoidance of undue restriction on the proper development of the law.

In the case of an intermediate appellate court, however, the second desideratum can be taken care of by appeal to a superior appellate court, if reasonable means of access to it are available; while the risk to the first desideratum, legal certainty, if the court is not bound by its own previous decisions grows ever greater with increasing membership and the number of three-judge divisions in which it sits, as the arithmetic which I have earlier mentioned shows. So the balance does not lie in the same place as in the case of a court of last resort. That is why Lord Gardiner LC's announcement about the future attitude towards precedent of the House of Lords in its judicial capacity concluded with the words: 'This announcement is not intended to affect the use of precedent elsewhere than in this House.'

Much has been said in the instant case about the delay and expense which would have been involved if the Court of Appeal had treated itself as bound by its previous decisions in *B v B* and *Cantliff v Jenkins*, so as to make it necessary for the respondent to come to this House to argue that those decisions should be overruled. But a similar reasoning could also be used to justify any High Court or county court judge in refusing to follow a decision of the Court of Appeal which he thought was wrong. It is true that since the appeal in the instant case was from the county court, not the High Court, the 'leap-frog' procedure was not available, but since it was conceded that the instant case was indistinguishable from *Cantliff v Jenkins*, there was no need for anything but the briefest of hearings in the Court of Appeal. The appeal to this House could in that event have been heard before Christmas instead of in January; and at less cost. The decision could have been announced at once and the reasons given later.

... In my opinion, this House should take this occasion to re-affirm expressly, unequivocally and unanimously that the rule laid down in the *Bristol Aeroplane* case as to *stare decisis* is still binding on the Court of Appeal.

_ ._ ._ ._ ._ ._ ._ ._ ._ ._ ._ ._ ._ ._ ._ ._ —

Question

• What does the House of Lords provide that the Court of Appeal does not? Did Lord Denning's attempts to save time and money achieve their stated ends?

_ ._ ._ ._ ._ ._ ._ ._ ._ ._ ._ ._ ._ ._ ._ ._ —

CASE STUDIES IN THE OPERATION OF JUDICIAL PRECEDENT

The following are two important case studies that provide grounds for the examination of the way in which courts, and particularly the House of Lords, view with circumspection the necessity of changing long established legal principles. Extensive coverage of the cases has been provided in order to allow a consideration of the way in which, in each case, the Court of Appeal suggested, and justified, a radical alteration of a long standing legal presumption, and the way in which the House of Lords either accepted or rejected the alteration.

In *R v R*, the courts decided that what had previously been the understanding, that a husband could not be guilty of the offence of rape against his wife, was no longer to be accepted as part of the law. Such a decision was justified on the basis that it was not the creation of a new offence, but merely the 'removal of a common law fiction which has become anachronistic and offensive'. The case also involved the court in interpreting the meaning of the word 'unlawful' in the context of the Sexual Offences (Amendment) Act 1976. And, somewhat surprisingly, it was decided that it didn't really mean anything in that context.

In *Curry v DPP*, the Court of Appeal attempted to remove the previous presumption that children between the ages of 10 and 14, charged with a criminal offence, did not know that what they did was seriously wrong and that the prosecution had to provide evidence to rebut that presumption. Mann LJ justified reversing the presumption by stating that, although it had often been assumed to be the law, it had never actually been specifically considered by earlier courts. On such reasoning he felt justified in departing from previous decisions of the Court of Appeal which otherwise would have bound him. The House of Lords subsequently restored the previous presumption, stating that, although they recognised the problem, they thought it was a matter for Parliamentary action rather than judicial intervention.

R v R (1991), Court of Appeal and House of Lords

The defendant married his wife in 1984. In 1989 the wife left the matrimonial home and returned to live with her parents, informing the defendant of her intention to petition for divorce. While the wife was staying at her parents' house, the defendant forced his way in, attempted to have sexual intercourse with her, and assaulted her. He was charged on indictment with attempted rape and assault occasioning actual bodily harm and found guilty on both charges.

He later appealed against his conviction for attempted rape.

Court of Appeal [1991] 2 WLR 1065

Lord Lane CJ: The question which the judge had to decide was whether in those circumstances, despite her refusal in fact to consent to sexual intercourse, the wife must be deemed by the fact of marriage to have consented. The argument before us has ranged over a wider field and has raised the question whether there is any basis for the principle, long supposed to be part of the common law, that a wife does by the fact of marriage give any implied consent in advance for the husband to have sexual intercourse with her; and secondly, the question whether, assuming that principle at one time existed, it still represents the law in either a qualified or unqualified form.

Any consideration of this branch of the law must start with the pronouncement by Sir Matthew Hale which appears in his *History of the Pleas of the Crown* (1736), Vol 1, Chap 58, p 629: 'But the husband cannot be guilty of a rape committed by himself upon his lawful wife, for by their mutual matrimonial consent and contract the wife hath given up herself in this kind unto her husband which she cannot retract.'

That was published in 1736, although Hale had died 60 years earlier in 1676. He held the office of Chief Justice for five years, and there can be little doubt that what he wrote was an accurate expression of the common law as it then stood, despite the fact that it was contained in a part of the work that his revision had not yet reached.

It is of interest to note that immediately before the passage cited, Hale says that the wider defence based on cohabitation stated by Bracton was no longer the law. Hale explained the change in the law on the basis that though 'unlawful cohabitation' might be evidence of consent, 'it is not necessary that it should be so, for the woman may forsake that unlawful course of life.'

It seems clear from the passage cited and from a later passage in the same chapter where Hale wrote, at p 629, 'in marriage [the wife] hath given up her body to her husband,' that he founded the proposition that a husband could not be guilty of rape upon his lawful wife on the grounds: (a) that on marriage a wife 'gave' up her body to her husband; and (b) that on marriage she gave her irrevocable consent to sexual intercourse. These two grounds are similar, though not identical.

The theory that on marriage a wife gave her body to her husband was accepted in matrimonial cases decided in the Ecclesiastical Courts. Thus in *Popkin v Popkin* (1794) 1 Hag Ecc 765, Lord Stowell, in a suit by a wife for divorce *a mensa et thoro*, stated, at p 767: 'The husband has a right to the person of his wife,' though he added the important qualification, 'but not if her health is endangered.'

These concepts of the relationship between husband and wife appear to have persisted for a long time and may help to explain why Hale's statement that a husband could not be guilty of rape on his wife was accepted as an enduring principle of the common law.

The first edition of Archbold, *A Summary of the Law Relative to Pleading and Evidence in Criminal Cases* 1822, at p 259, stated simply: 'A husband also cannot be guilty of a rape upon his wife.'

However, in *R v Clarence* (1888) 22 QBD 23, there was no unanimity among the judges of a full court of Crown Cases Reserved on the effect of Hale's proposition. Wills J said, at p 33: 'If intercourse under the circumstances now in question constitute an assault on the part of the man, it must constitute rape, unless, indeed, as between married persons rape is impossible, a proposition to which I certainly am not prepared to assent, and for which there seems to me to be no sufficient authority.'

Field J in the course of his judgment said, at p 57: 'But it is argued that here there is no offence, because the wife of the prisoner consented to the act, and I entertain no doubt that, if that was so, there was neither assault nor unlawful infliction of harm. Then, did the wife of the prisoner consent? The ground for holding that she did so, put forward in argument, was the consent to marital intercourse which is imposed upon every wife by the marriage contract, and a passage from *Hale's Pleas of the Crown*, Vol 1, p 629, was cited, in which it is said that a husband cannot be guilty of rape upon his wife, "for by their mutual matrimonial consent and contract the wife hath given up herself in this kind to her husband, which she cannot retract".

The authority of Hale CJ on such a matter is undoubtedly as high as any can be, but no other authority is cited by him for this proposition, and I should hesitate before I adopted it. There may, I think, be many cases in which a wife may lawfully refuse intercourse, and in which, if the husband imposed it by violence, he might be held guilty of a crime.'

Apart from those *dicta* in *R v Clarence* no one seems to have questioned Hale's proposition until Byrne J in *R v Clarke* [1949] 2 All ER 448 held that the husband's immunity was lost where the justices had made an order providing that the wife should no longer be bound to cohabit with the defendant. In the course of his ruling Byrne J said, at p 448: 'As a general proposition it can be stated that a husband cannot be guilty of rape on his wife. No doubt, the reason for that is that on marriage the wife consents to the husband's exercising the marital right of intercourse during such time as the ordinary relations created by the marriage contract subsist between them.'

However, in *R v Miller* [1954] 2 QB 282, Lynskey J, having examined the authorities, ruled Hale's proposition as correct and that the husband had no case to answer on a charge of rape although the wife had before the act of intercourse presented a petition for divorce, which had not reached the stage of a decree nisi. In *R v O'Brien* [1974] 3 All ER 663, 665 Park J ruled that a decree nisi effectively terminated a marriage and upon its pronouncement the consent to marital intercourse given by a wife at the time of marriage was revoked.

Park J: Between the pronouncement of a decree nisi and the obtaining of a decree absolute a marriage subsists as a mere technicality. There can be no question that by a decree nisi a wife's implied consent to marital intercourse is revoked. Accordingly, a husband commits the offence of rape if he has sexual intercourse with her thereafter without her consent.

In *R v Steele* (1976) 65 Cr App R 22, this court held that where a husband and wife are living apart and there is in existence an undertaking given by the husband to the court not to molest the wife, that is in effect equivalent to the granting of an injunction and eliminates the wife's implied consent to sexual intercourse. In the course of delivering the judgment of that court, having referred to the cases already mentioned here, I said, at p 25:

> Here there has been no decree of the court, here there has been no direct order of the court compelling the husband to stay away from his wife. There has been an undertaking by the husband not to molest his wife. The question which the court has to decide is this. Have the parties made it clear, by agreement between themselves, or has the court made it clear by an order or something equivalent to an order, that the wife's consent to sexual intercourse with her husband implicit in the act of marriage,no longer exists?

I then went on to set out, *obiter*, a number of matters which would not be sufficient to remove the husband's immunity, having the judgment of Lynskey J in *R v Miller* [1954] 2 QB 282 in mind. *R v Roberts* [1986] Crim LR 188 was another decision of this court. The husband had been restrained from molesting or going near to his wife for two months; an ouster order was made ordering him out of the matrimonial home. On the same day a formal deed of separation was entered into; there was no non-cohabitation or non-molestation clause. The trial judge had rejected a submission that the wife's implied consent to intercourse with her husband revived when the injunction ran out in August 1984. It was held that the lack of a non-molestation clause in the deed of separation could not possibly have operated to revive the consent of the wife which had been terminated. It is against that brief historical background that we turn to consider the submissions of the appellant advanced by Mr Buchanan in a carefully researched argument that the husband's immunity was not lost by what had happened between his wife and himself and that accordingly he was not liable to be tried or convicted for rape. In the course of his ruling upon the submission, Owen J, having set out the authorities, reached a conclusion in the following terms [1991] 1All ER 747, 754:

> What, in law, will suffice to revoke that consent which the wife gives to sexual intercourse upon marriage and which the law implies from the facts of marriage? ... It must be sufficient for there to be an agreement of the parties. Of course, an agreement of the parties means what it says. It does not mean something which is done unilaterally ... As it seems to me, from his action in telephoning her and saying that he intended to see about a divorce and thereby to accede to what she was doing, there is sufficient here to indicate that there was an implied agreement to a separation and to a withdrawal of that consent to sexual intercourse, which the law, I will assume and accept, implies. The next question is whether a third set of circumstances maybe sufficient to revoke that implicit consent. Mr Milmo argues that the withdrawal of either party from cohabitation is sufficient for that consent to be revoked ... I accept that it is not for me to make the law. However, it is for me to state the common law as I believe it to be. If that requires me to indicate a set of circumstances

which have not so far been considered as sufficient to negative consent as in fact so doing, then I must do so. I cannot believe that it is a part of the common law of this country that where there has been withdrawal of either party from cohabitation, accompanied by a clear indication that consent to sexual intercourse has been terminated, that does not amount to a revocation of that implicit consent. In those circumstances, it seems to me that there is ample here, both on the second exception and the third exception, which would enable the prosecution to prove a charge of rape or attempted rape against this husband.

Since that ruling in July 1990 there have been two other decisions at first instance to which reference must be made. The first was on 5 October 1990, when Simon Brown J in the Crown Court at Sheffield was asked to rule upon a similar question in *R v C (Rape: Marital Exemption)* [1991] 1 All ER 755. The judge examined in detail the pros and cons of the various suggested solutions to the problem and came to the conclusion that Hale's proposition was no longer the law. He said, at p 758:

> Were it not for the deeply unsatisfactory consequences of reaching any other conclusion upon the point, I would shrink, if sadly, from adopting this radical view of the true position in law. But adopt it I do. Logically, I regard it as the only defensible stance, certainly now as the law has developed and arrived in the late 20th century. In my judgment, the position in law today is, as already declared in Scotland, that there is no marital exemption to the law of rape. That is the ruling I give.

The mention of Scottish law by Simon Brown J is a reference to the decision of the High Court of Justiciary in *S v HM Advocate*, 1989 SLT 469 delivered by the Lord Justice-General, Lord Emslie. The proposition which had governed courts in Scotland for very many years in the same way as Hale's proposition had operated in England, emanated from Baron Hume, *Commentaries on the Law of Scotland, Respective Crimes* 1797, Vol 1, Chap 7, and contained the following passage, at p 306: 'This is true without exception even of the husband of the woman, who though he cannot himself commit a rape on his own wife, who has surrendered her person to him in that sort, may, however, be accessory to that crime ... committed upon her by another.'

In the course of his opinion, Lord Emslie said, at p 473:

> the soundness of Hume's view, and its application in the late 20th Century, depends entirely upon the reason which is said to justify it. Our first observation is that if what Hume meant was that by marriage a wife expressly or impliedly consented to sexual intercourse with her husband as a normal incident of marriage, the reason given affords no justification for his statement of the law because rape has always been essentially a crime of violence and indeed no more than an aggravated assault ... If ... Hume meant that by marriage a wife consented to intercourse against her will and obtained by force, we take leave to doubt whether this was ever contemplated by the common law, which was derived from the canon law, regulating the relationship of husband and wife.

The final decision to which we must refer is a ruling of Rougier J in *R v J (Rape: Marital Exemption)* [1991] 1 All ER 759. The argument in that case proceeded upon different lines from those adopted in *R v C (Rape: Marital Exemption)* [1991] 1 All ER 755. The submission addressed on behalf of the prosecution to Rougier J was based on the wording of the Sexual Offences (Amendment) Act 1976, s 1(1) of which provides: 'For the purposes of section 1 of the Sexual Offences Act 1956 (which relates to rape) a man commits rape if – (a) he has unlawful sexual intercourse with a woman who at the time of the intercourse does not consent to it ...'

Section 1(1) of the Sexual Offences Act 1956 provided: 'It is felony for a man to rape a woman.' The contention was that the Act of 1976 for the first time provided a statutory definition of rape; that the only possible meaning which can be ascribed to the word 'unlawful' is 'illicit', that is to say outside the bounds of matrimony, and that accordingly Parliament's intention must have been to preserve the husband's immunity. This argument was reinforced by reference to the decision of this Court in *R v Chapman* [1959] 1 QB 100, which gave that interpretation to the use of the word 'unlawful' in the Act of 1956, which of course was dealing with the same type of offence. Moreover, it was pointed out that if the word in s 1 of the 1976 Act is mere surplusage, this would, it is said, be the only place in the Act where that is so. The judge rejected the contentions of the prosecution and ruled that the intervention of the Act of 1976 has, as he put it, 'precluded any up-to-date declaration of the state of the common law on this subject. The matter has become one of statutory interpretation and remains so'. The judge also rejected the subsidiary argument addressed to him by the prosecution, namely that the wording of the Act still left it open to the court to enlarge the number of exceptions to the husband's immunity and did so in the following terms, at p 767:

> Once Parliament has transferred the offence from the realm of common law to that of statute and, as I believe, had defined the common law position as it stood at the time of the passing of the Act, then I have very grave doubt whether it is open to judges to continue to discover exceptions to the general rule of marital immunity by purporting to extend the common law any further. The position is crystallised as at the making of the Act and only Parliament can alter it.

Those three recent decisions, including that of Owen J in the instant case, neatly exemplify the possible solutions, each with its concomitant drawbacks with which we are confronted. They may be summarised as follows:

(i) The literal solution. The Act of 1976 by defining rape as it did and including the word 'unlawful' made it clear that the husband's immunity is preserved, there being no other meaning for the word except 'outside the bounds of matrimony'. It is not legitimate to treat the word as surplusage when there is a proper meaning which can be ascribed to it.

(ii) The compromise solution. The word 'unlawful' is to be construed in such a way as to leave intact the exceptions to the husband's immunity which have been engrafted on to Hale's proposition from the decision in *R v Clarke*[1] onwards and is also to be construed so as to allow further exceptions as the occasion may arise.

(iii) The radical solution. Hale's proposition is based on a fiction and moreover a fiction which is inconsistent with the proper relationship between husband and wife today. For the reasons expressed by Lord Emslie in *S v HM Advocate*,[2]

---

1   [1949] 2 All ER 448.
2   1989 SLT 469.

it is repugnant and illogical in that it permits a husband to be punished for treating his wife with violence in the course of rape but not for the rape itself which is an aggravated and vicious form of violence. The court should take the same attitude to this situation as did Lord Halsbury LC, albeit in different circumstances, in *R v Jackson*:[3] 'I confess to regarding with something like indignation the statement of the facts of this case, and the absence of a due sense of the delicacy and respect due to a wife whom the husband has sworn to cherish and protect.'

The drawbacks are these. The first solution requires the word 'unlawful' to be given what is said to be its true effect. That would mean that the husband's immunity would remain unimpaired so long as the marriage subsisted. The effect would be to overrule the decisions in *R v Clarke*;[4] *R v O'Brien (Edward)*;[5] and *R v Steele*;[6] and all the other cases which have engrafted exceptions on to Hale's proposition. It is hard to believe that Parliament intended that result. If it was intended to preserve the exceptions which existed at the time the Act of 1976 came into force, it would have been easy to say so. The second or compromise solution adopts what is, so to speak, the open-ended interpretation of the Act of 1976 and would permit further exceptions to be engrafted on to Hale's proposition. In particular, an exception in circumstances such as those in the instant case where the wife has withdrawn from cohabitation so as to make it clear that she wishes to bring to an end matrimonial relationships. There would be formidable difficulties of definition and interpretation. How, one asks,would it be possible accurately to define 'withdrawal from cohabitation?' It is not every wife who can, as the wife here could, go to live with her parents or indeed has anywhere else other than the matrimonial home in which to live. It may be thought that a total abolition of the immunity would be a preferable solution, as has been the experience in some other common law jurisdictions, Canada, Victoria, New South Wales, Western Australia, Queensland, Tasmania and notably in New Zealand, where the compromise solution was found to be unworkable. The third or radical solution is said to disregard the statutory provisions of the Act of 1976 and, even if it does not do that, it is said that it goes beyond the legitimate bounds of judge-made law and trespasses on the province of Parliament. In other words the abolition of a rule of such long standing, despite its emasculation by later decisions, is a task for the legislature and not the courts. There are social considerations to be taken into account, the privacy of marriage to be preserved and questions of potential reconciliation to be weighed which make it an inappropriate area for judicial intervention. It can be seen that there are formidable objections, and others no doubt exist, to each of the possible solutions.

What should be the answer? Ever since the decision of Byrne J in *R v Clarke* courts have been paying lip service to the Hale proposition, whilst at the same time increasing the number of exceptions, the number of situations to which it does not apply. This is a legitimate use of the flexibility of the common law which can and should adapt itself to changing social attitudes. There comes a time when the changes are so great that it is no longer enough to create further exceptions

---

3   [1891] 1 QB 671, at 681.
4   [1949] 2 All ER 448.
5   [1974] 3 All ER 663.
6   (1976) 65 Cr App R 22.

restricting the effect of the proposition, a time when the proposition itself requires examination to see whether its terms are in accord with what is generally regarded today as acceptable behaviour. For the reasons already adumbrated, and in particular those advanced by the Lord Justice-General in *S v HM Advocate*, with which we respectfully agree, the idea that a wife by marriage consents in advance to her husband having sexual intercourse with her whatever her state of health or however proper her objections (if that is what Hale meant), is no longer acceptable. It can never have been other than a fiction, and fiction is a poor basis for the criminal law. The extent to which events have overtaken Hale's proposition is well illustrated by his last four words, 'which she cannot retract'. It seems to us that where the common law rule no longer even remotely represents what is the true position of a wife in present day society, the duty of the court is to take steps to alter the rule if it can legitimately do so in the light of any relevant Parliamentary enactment. That in the end comes down to consideration of the word 'unlawful' in the Act of 1976. It is at the best, perhaps a strange word to have used if the draftsman meant by it 'outside marriage'. However sexual intercourse outside marriage may be described, it is not 'unlawful' if one gives to the word its ordinary meaning of 'contrary to law'. We have not overlooked the decision in *R v Chapman* to which we have already referred, but if the word is to be construed as 'illicit' or 'outside marriage', then it seemingly admits of no exception. The husband who is the subject of an injunction or undertaking to the court or in respect of whose marriage a decree nisi has been pronounced or is a party to a formal separation agreement would be nevertheless immune from prosecution for raping his wife. This would apply equally to a husband who is the subject of a family protection order, a situation which was the subject of a judgment by Swinton Thomas J in the Crown Court at Stafford in *R v S* (unreported), 15 January 1991. The alternative to that unwelcome conclusion would be to interpret the word as including the various exceptions to the husband's immunity which we have examined earlier in this judgment. If so, one asks whether the situation crystallises at the date the Act came into force. If that is the case, then all the decisions since the time when the Act of 1976 came into force which have narrowed the husband's immunity would have been wrongly decided. It may be on the other hand that the draftsman intended to leave it open to the common law to develop as it has done since 1976. The only realistic explanations seem to us to be that the draftsman either intended to leave the matter open for the common law to develop in that way or, perhaps more likely, that no satisfactory meaning at all can be ascribed to the word and that it is indeed surplusage. In either event, we do not consider that we are inhibited by the Act of 1976 from declaring that the husband's immunity as expounded by Hale no longer exists. We take the view that the time has now arrived when the law should declare that a rapist remains a rapist subject to the criminal law, irrespective of his relationship with his victim. The remaining and no less difficult question is whether, despite that view, this is an area where the court should step aside to leave the matter to the Parliamentary process. This is not the creation of a new offence, it is the removal of a common law fiction which has become anachronistic and offensive and we consider that it is our duty having reached that conclusion to act upon it.

In *R v R* in the House of Lords, Lord Keith delivered the leading judgment with which all the other Law Lords agreed.

House of Lords [1991] 4 All ER 481

Lord Keith of Kinkel: For over 150 years after the publication of Hale's work there appears to have been no reported case in which judicial consideration was given to his proposition ... It may be taken that the proposition was generally regarded as an accurate statement of the common law of England. The common law is, however, capable of evolving in the light of changing social, economic and cultural developments. Hale's proposition reflected the state of affairs in these respects at the time it was enunciated. Since then the status of women, and particularly of married women, has changed out of all recognition in various ways which are very familiar and upon which it is unnecessary to go into detail. Apart from property matters and the availability of matrimonial remedies, one of the most important changes is that marriage is in modern times regarded as a partnership of equals, and no longer one in which the wife must be the subservient chattel of the husband. Hale's proposition involves that by marriage a wife gives her irrevocable consent to sexual intercourse with her husband under all circumstances and irrespective of the state of her health or how she happens to be feeling at the time. In modern times any reasonable person must regard that conception as quite unacceptable.

... [In] all the decisions in the field prior to the ruling by Owen J in the present case ... lip service, at least, was paid to Hale's proposition. Since then there have been three further decisions by single judges. The first of them is *R v C (Rape: Marital Exemption)* [1991] 1 All ER 755. There were nine counts in an indictment against a husband and a co-accused charging various offences of a sexual nature against an estranged wife.

One of these was of rape as a principal. Simon Brown J followed the decision in *S v HM Advocate* 1989 SLT 469 and held that the whole concept of a marital exemption in rape was misconceived. He said (at 758):

> Were it not for the deeply unsatisfactory consequences of reaching any other conclusion on the point, I would shrink, if sadly, from adopting this radical view of true position in law. But adopt it I do. Logically, I regard it as the only defensible stance, certainly now as the law has developed and arrived in the late 20th century. In my judgment, the position in law today is, as already declared in Scotland, that there is no marital exemption to the law of rape. That is the ruling I give. Count seven accordingly remains and will be left to the jury without any specific direction founded on the concept of marital exemption.

A different view was taken in the other two cases, by reason principally of the terms in which rape is defined in s 1(1) of the Sexual Offences (Amendment) Act 1976, namely:

> For the purposes of section 1 of the Sexual Offences Act 1956 (which relates to rape) a man commits rape if (a) he has unlawful sexual intercourse with a woman who at the time of the intercourse does not consent to it; and (b) at the time he knows that she does not consent to the intercourse or he is reckless as to whether she consents to it ...

In *R v J (Rape: Marital Exemption)* [1991] 1 All ER 759 a husband was charged with having raped his wife, from whom he was living apart at the time. Rougier J ruled that the charge was bad, holding that the effect of s 1(1)(a) of the 1976 Act was that the marital exemption embodied in Hale's proposition was preserved, subject to those exceptions established by cases decided before the Act was passed. He took the view that the word 'unlawful' in the subsection meant 'illicit', ie outside marriage, that being the meaning which in *R v Chapman* [1958] 3 All ER 143, [1959] 1 QB 100 it had been held to bear in s 19 of the Sexual Offences Act 1956. Then in *R v S* (15 January 1991, unreported), Swinton Thomas J followed Rougier J in holding that s 1(1) of the 1976 Act preserved the marital exemption subject to the established common law exceptions. Differing, however, from Rougier J, he took the view that it remained open to judges to define further exceptions. In the case before him the wife had obtained a family protection order in similar terms to that in *R v Sharples* [1990] Crim LR 198. Differing from Judge Fawcus in that case, Swinton Thomas J held that the existence of the family protection order created an exception to the marital exemption. It is noteworthy that both Rougier and Swinton Thomas JJ expressed themselves as being regretful that s 1(1) of the 1976 Act precluded them from taking the same line as Simon Brown J in *R v C (Rape: Marital Exemption)* [1991] 1 All ER 755.

The position then is that part of Hale's proposition which asserts that a wife cannot retract the consent to sexual intercourse which she gives on marriage has been departed from in a series of decided cases. On grounds of principle there is no good reason why the whole proposition should not be held inapplicable in modern times.

The only question is whether s 1(1) of the 1976 Act presents an insuperable obstacle to that sensible course. The argument is that 'unlawful' in the subsection means outside the bond of marriage. That is not the most natural meaning of the word, which normally describes something which is contrary to some law or enactment or is done without lawful justification or excuse. Certainly in modern times sexual intercourse outside marriage would not ordinarily be described as unlawful. If the subsection proceeds on the basis that a woman on marriage gives a general consent to sexual intercourse, there can never be any question of intercourse with her by her husband being without her consent. There would thus be no point in enacting that only intercourse without consent outside marriage is to constitute rape ... Sexual intercourse in any of the cases covered by the exceptions still takes place within the bond of marriage. So if 'unlawful' in the subsection means 'outside the bond of marriage' it follows that sexual intercourse in a case which falls within the exceptions is not covered by the definition of rape, notwithstanding that it is not consented to by the wife. That involves that the exceptions have been impliedly abolished. If the intention of Parliament was to abolish the exceptions it would have been expected to do so expressly, and it is in fact inconceivable that Parliament should have had such an intention. In order that the exceptions might be preserved, it would be necessary to construe 'unlawfully' as meaning 'outside marriage or within marriage in a situation covered by one of the exceptions to the marital exemption'. Some slight support for that construction is perhaps to be gathered from the presence of the words 'who at the time of the intercourse does not consent to it', considering that a woman in a case covered by one of the exceptions is treated as having withdrawn the general consent to intercourse given on marriage but may nevertheless have given her consent to it on the particular occasion. However, the gloss which the suggested construction would place on the word 'unlawfully' would give it a meaning unique to this particular subsection, and if the mind of the draftsman had been directed to the existence of the exceptions he would surely have dealt with them specifically and not in such an oblique fashion ...

The fact is that it is clearly unlawful to have sexual intercourse with any woman without her consent, and that the use of the word in the subsection adds nothing. In my opinion there are no rational grounds for putting the suggested gloss on the word, and it should be treated as being mere surplusage in this enactment ... I am therefore of the opinion that s 1(1) of the 1976 Act presents no obstacle to this House declaring that in modern times the supposed marital exception in rape forms no part of the law of England.

In an article in the *New Law Journal*, entitled 'Retrospective crime', Ralph Beddard raised the question of retrospective criminalisation with respect to previous decisions.

Ralph Beddard, 'Retrospective crime' (1995) 145 NLJ 663

Article 7 of the *European Convention on Human Rights* protects the individual from retrospective criminal legislation; it provides that no one may be held guilty of any criminal offence on account of any act or omission which did not constitute a criminal offence under national or international law at the time when it was committed ... difficult problems arise in the case of the Common Law and these have recently been the subject of consideration by the Commission in the cases of CR and SW against the United Kingdom. (Applications 20190/92 and 20166/92.) The question raised by these cases relates to the difficulties of determining the initiation of a law under the case law system of the Common Law ... The two cases under consideration by the Court in which retrospective criminal legislation was alleged concern rape and attempted rape by a husband against his wife ... Was the conviction of the applicant in each of these two cases flawed because at the time when he committed the acts his behaviour was not against the accepted law or were the decisions of the High Court and the House of Lords within a margin of interpretation necessary to ensure that the law is kept in line with changing circumstances? ... The Criminal Law Revision Committee reporting in 1984 was, by a small majority, of the view that there should be no change in the basic principle of marital immunity and whilst its members were in favour of extending the exceptions where co-habitation had ceased, they saw difficulties of definition and problems of uncertainty. The Law Commission in its Working Paper Rape within Marriage published in September 1990, after the Crown Court conviction in *R v R* but before the appeal, was of the view that the implied agreement to separate or a unilateral decision not to co-habit, accepted by the trial judge as revoking the marital immunity, was difficult to reconcile with previous authorities and that it appeared substantially to extend what had previously been thought to be the law. The Law Commission proposed that the present marital immunity should be abolished. Necessarily, the Law Commission's proposal was that it should be abolished by legislation but in view of its opinion of the extent of the change, it may well be argued that the matter was not open for change by the House of Lords. Similarly no legislation by Parliament had followed the Criminal Law Revision Committee's report. The majority of the European Commission of Human Rights, in holding that there had not been a violation, commented on the progressive development of the law by the courts and felt that the implied agreement to seek a divorce in CR and the unilateral withdrawal of cohabitation by the wife would indicate in contemporary society an anticipation that a court might embark upon the legitimate adaptation of the ingredients of the crime and that this was reasonably foreseeable by the applicant. The Commission was of the view that it was inconceivable that the applicant when he embarked on the course of conduct could have held any genuine belief that it was lawful. The minorities in each report, while not hesitating to state that in their view the marital immunity was in need of reform, were not prepared to accept the correctness of reform by the courts. The dissenting opinion(s) in CR state:

> ... as a result of the above judgment (R v R), the law as regards one of the existing elements of the offence of rape, that is consent, has been fundamentally changed to the applicant's detriment. It was neither a clarification of the existing elements of the offence in question, nor an adaptation of such elements to new circumstances which could reasonably be brought under the original concept of the offence ... A change through the case-law of the courts could not have been reasonably foreseeable to the applicant even with the assistance of legal advice ...

The minority in SW was greater and picked up the point that the conviction was based almost wholly on the abolition of the marital rape immunity and hardly on the extension of the exception thereto. In that case the couple were still co-habiting and there was no agreement to separate or divorce, but only the unilateral statement of the wife that she intended to leave the husband ... The cases have been referred to the European Court of Human Rights which will hold a hearing in the summer. In many ways it seems unfortunate that the questions appertaining to retrospective criminal law-making by the UK courts should be tested in relation to the sensitive subject-matter of marital rape where the anachronisms of the earlier law are well recognised and where strong desire for legal change is indicated by everyone except the accused. Nevertheless, the basic question which should be posed is whether the accused's treatment was more detrimental than it would have been at the time when the activity took place. In the implausible event of R taking legal advice before attempting to have sexual intercourse with his wife, it is almost certain that he would have been told that although there was a groundswell reaction to the immunity it was still valid under the Common Law and, more importantly, the advice given by the Criminal Law Revision Committee in 1984 had been that there should be no change. S too would have been counselled that the Law Commission was of the view that legislation was necessary to change the law. The Common Law fits uneasily, at times, within the European Convention pattern. The system of case law as it exists within the Common Law system is rightly hailed as a sensitive means of adaptation which can respond to changing ideas. It must not, however, go beyond the boundaries of interpretation.

European Court of Human Rights

In November 1995 the ECHR unanimously held that the English courts decisions in both SW and CR did not amount to a breach of Article 7.1 of the Convention. In the course of its judgment the ECHR *observed that* a crucial issue in the judgment of the Court of Appeal in R v R related to the definition of rape in section 1(1)(a) of the 1976 Act: 'unlawful sexual intercourse with a woman who at the time of the intercourse does not consent to it'. The question was whether removal of the marital immunity would conflict with the statutory definition of rape, in particular whether it would be prevented by the word 'unlawful'. The Court of Appeal carefully examined various strands of interpretation of the provision in the case law, including the argument that the term 'unlawful' excluded intercourse within marriage from the definition of rape. In that connection, the Court recalled that it was in the first place for the national authorities, notably the courts, to interpret and apply national law: see, for instance, *Kemnache v France (No 3)* of 24 November 1994 (Series A No 296–C, pp 86–87, paragraph 37). It saw no reason to disagree with the Court of Appeal's conclusion, which was subsequently upheld by the House of Lords, that the word 'unlawful' in the definition of rape was merely surplusage and did not inhibit them from 'removing a common law fiction which had become anachronistic and offensive' and from declaring that 'a rapist remains a rapist subject to the criminal law, irrespective of his relationship with his victim'.

The decisions of the Court of Appeal and then the House of Lords did no more than continue a perceptible line of case law development dismantling the immunity of a husband from prosecution for rape upon his wife. There was no doubt under the law as it stood on 18 September 1990 and on 12 November 1989, respectively, that a husband who forcibly had sexual intercourse with his wife could, in various circumstances, be found guilty of rape. Moreover, there was an evident evolution, which was consistent with the very essence of the offence, of the criminal law through judicial interpretation towards treating such conduct generally as within the scope of the offence of rape. That evolution had reached a stage where judicial recognition of the absence of immunity had become a reasonably foreseeable development of the law.

The essentially debasing character of rape was so manifest that the result of the decisions of the Court of Appeal and the House of Lords, that the applicants could be convicted of rape and attempted rape, irrespective of their relationship with the victims, could not be said to be at variance with the object and purpose of article 7, namely to ensure that no one should be subjected to arbitrary prosecution, conviction or punishment, fundamental objectives of the Convention, the very essence of which was respect for human dignity and human freedom. Consequently, in the case of SW, by following the Court of Appeal's ruling in *R v R* in the applicant's case, Mr Justice Rose did not render a decision permitting a finding of guilt incompatible with article 7.

Having reached that conclusion, the Court did not find it necessary to inquire into whether the facts in the applicants' cases were covered by the exceptions to the immunity rule already made by the English courts before 18 September 1990 or 12 November 1989. In short, the Court, like the Government and the Commission, found unanimously, in both cases, that the national courts' decisions that the applicants could not invoke immunity to escape conviction and sentence for rape and attempted rape upon their wives did not give rise to a violation of their rights under article 7.1.

––·––·––·––·––·––·––·––·––·––·––·––·––·––·––

C (A Minor) v Director of Public Prosecutions (1994–95)
Court of Appeal and House of Lords

The defendant, who was aged 12, was seen by police officers to be holding the handlebars of a motor cycle while another boy was attempting to force the chain and padlock which secured it with a crowbar. When the police officers approached, the two boys ran off, leaving the crowbar in the chain. The defendant was charged with interfering with a motor cycle with the intention that an offence of theft should be committed, contrary to s 9(1) of the Criminal Attempts Act 1981. On the basis of the facts found the justices drew the inference that the defendant had known that what he had done was seriously wrong and found that there was sufficient evidence to rebut the presumption that, since he was only 12 years old, he was incapable of committing a crime and they convicted him.

Court of Appeal [1994] 3 WLR 888

Laws J: ... The defendant was 12 years old at the time of the incident. It was accordingly submitted to the justices, as it has been submitted to us, that the law presumed him to be *doli incapax*. Such a presumption applies, it is said, in any case where a defendant to a criminal charge is between the ages of 10 and 14 at the time of the alleged offence. Below the age of 10, of course, there is an absolute presumption that a child is incapable of committing a crime. Thereafter until he is 14, so the submission goes, there is a rebuttable presumption that he does not know that his act is 'seriously wrong' as opposed to 'merely naughty'. The presumption must be rebutted by positive proof adduced by the prosecution that in fact he knew full well that what he did was seriously wrong. In the present case it was argued before the justices that the prosecution had adduced no such proof. ... The requirement of specific evidence to rebut the presumption, which is generally supported in the cases, is consistent with Blackstone's treatment of the issue in *Blackstone's Commentaries on the Laws of England*, Book IV, 1st edn, 1769, pp 23–4:

> But by the law, as it now stands, and has stood at least ever since the time of Edward the third, the capacity of doing ill, or contracting guilt, is not so much measured by years and days, as by the strength of the delinquent's understanding and judgment. For one lad of eleven years old may have as much cunning as another of fourteen; and in these cases our maxim is, that *'malitia supplet aetatem'* ... under fourteen, though an infant shall be *prima facie* adjudged to be *doli incapax*; yet if it appear to the court and jury, that he was *doli capax*, and could discern between good and evil, he may be convicted and suffer death ... But, in all such cases, the evidence of that malice, which is to supply age, ought to be strong and clear beyond all doubt or contradiction.

In my view the cases demonstrate that, if this presumption is to be rebutted, there must be clear positive evidence that the defendant knew his act was seriously wrong, not consisting merely in the evidence of the acts amounting to the offence itself. On that basis, there having been no such evidence here, this appeal must succeed if the presumption together with the manner of its application through the authorities remains part of our law.

Whatever may have been the position in an earlier age, when there was no system of universal compulsory education and when, perhaps, children did not grow up as quickly as they do nowadays, this presumption at the present time is a serious disservice to our law. It means that a child over 10 who commits an act of obvious dishonesty, or even grave violence, is to be acquitted unless the prosecution specifically prove by discrete evidence that he understands the obliquity of what he is doing. It is unreal and contrary to common sense; and it is no surprise to find that modern judges have looked upon the rule with increasing unease and perhaps rank disapproval. Aside from anything else, there will be cases in which in purely practical terms, evidence of the kind required simply cannot be obtained. The child defendant may have answered no questions at the police station, as is his right. He may decline to give evidence in court. That is his right also. He and his parents, or perhaps his schoolteachers, may well not co-operate with any prosecution attempt to obtain factual material about his background which may be adverse to him. But, quite apart from such pragmatic considerations, the presumption is in principle objectionable. It is no part of the general law that a defendant should be proved to appreciate that his act is 'seriously wrong'. He may even think his crime to be justified; in the ordinary way no such consideration can be prayed in aid in his favour. Yet in a case where the presumption applies, an additional requirement, not insisted upon in the case of an adult, is imposed as a condition of guilt, namely a specific understanding in the mind of the child that his act is seriously wrong. This is out of step with the general law. The requirement is also conceptually obscure. What is meant by 'seriously wrong?' It cannot mean 'against the law' – there is no trace in the authorities that the presumption is intended to displace the general rule that ignorance of the law affords no defence. One would suppose, therefore, that what must be proved is that the child appreciated the moral obliquity of what he was doing. Yet in *JM (A Minor) v Runeckles* (1984) 79 Cr App R 255, 260, Robert Goff LJ said: 'I do not however feel able to accept the submission that the criterion in cases of this kind is one of morality ... the prosecution has to prove that the child knew that what he or she was doing was seriously wrong. The point is that it is not enough that the child realised that what he or she was doing was naughty or mischievous.'

But if 'seriously wrong' means neither 'legally wrong' nor 'morally wrong', what other yardstick remains? But that is by no means the end of the disturbing, even nonsensical, implications of this presumption. The cases indicate that the presumption may be rebutted by proof that the child was of normal mental capacity for his age. If that is right, the underlying premise is that a child of average or normal development is in fact taken to be *doli capax*, but the effect of the presumption is then that a defendant under 14 is assumed to possess a subnormal mental capacity, and for that reason to be *doli incapax*. There can be no respectable justification for such a bizarre state of affairs. It means that what is by definition the exception is presumed to be the rule. It means that the law presumes nothing as regards a child between 10 and 14 except that he lacks the understanding of all his average peers. If that is the state of the law, we should be ashamed of it. Not only this: the presumption's application may also give rise to the risk of injustice. In *R v B* [1979] 1 WLR 1185, to which I have already referred, the Court of Appeal held that a child's previous convictions may in principle be admitted in evidence to rebut the presumption. If that were to happen before a jury, in a case where the child defendant disputed the primary facts, the prejudicial consequences can only too readily be imagined. It is no answer to say that the judge would possess a discretion to exclude such evidence. So he would; but the case might be one where there was no other evidence available to counter the presumption's application, and the judge would then be faced with an impossible choice between doing rank injustice to the defendant and doing rank injustice to the prosecution. No doubt that would be an extreme case. But it illustrates the needlessly distortive effect which this rule produces in the execution of criminal justice.

Even that is not the end of it. The rule is divisive and perverse: divisive, because it tends to attach criminal consequences to the acts of children coming from what used to be called good homes more readily than to the acts of others; perverse, because it tends to absolve from criminal responsibility the very children most likely to commit criminal acts. It must surely nowadays be regarded as obvious that, where a morally impoverished upbringing may have led a teenager into crime, the facts of his background should go not to his guilt, but to his mitigation; the very emphasis placed in modern penal policy upon the desirability of non-custodial disposals designed to be remedial rather than retributive – especially in the case of young offenders – offers powerful support for the view that delinquents under the age of 14, who may know no better than to commit antisocial and sometimes dangerous crimes, should not be held immune from the criminal justice system, but sensibly managed within it. Otherwise they are left outside the law, free to commit further crime, perhaps of increasing gravity, unchecked by the courts whose very duty it is to bring them to book. It is precisely the youngster whose understanding of the difference between right and wrong is fragile or non-existent who is most likely to get involved in criminal activity. Yet this outdated and unprincipled presumption is, no less precisely, tailored to secure his acquittal if he is brought before the court. The prosecution are in effect required to prove, as a condition of his guilt, that he is morally responsible: But it is because he is morally irresponsible that he has committed the crime in the first place.

It is not surprising that this presumption took root in an earlier era, when the criminal law was altogether more draconian. When Blackstone wrote, young children along with adults suffered capital punishment, and for offences much less grave than homicide. Blackstone gives an instance (Book IV, at p 24) of a boy of eight hanged for firing two barns. Little wonder that at a time when criminal guilt led to such ferocious retribution, the law developed a means by which mercy was exceptionally extended to child defendants. But the philosophy of criminal punishment has, very obviously, changed out of all recognition since those days. This presumption has no utility whatever in the present era. It ought to go. The question is, therefore, whether this court has the authority to abolish it. Three arguments might be advanced to persuade the court that it ought not, or cannot, abolish the rule.

(i) The court's decision would have retroactive effect, since our law has not yet developed a practice of prospective rulings. Accordingly, by holding that this presumption is no longer part of our criminal jurisprudence we should be changing the legal rules effective at the time of the defendant's actual or putative crime, and doing so retrospectively. In many cases this argument is a powerful inhibition upon the extent to which the common law courts may with justice alter the scope of the criminal law. Very obviously, there would be manifest injustice were the court to extend the ambit of a criminal offence beyond its earlier limits and so pronounce a defendant guilty whose relevant actions were taken at a time when the definition of the offence in question did not touch them. But this is not such a case. The question is whether abolition of the presumption would visit injustice upon this defendant. He can hardly have said to himself, 'I may pinch this motor bike and not be punished for it, because the law will assume I am not capable of crime.' If he did, that would be firm evidence that he was indeed *doli capax*. There is no conceivable injustice to him if we consign this presumption to legal history.

(ii) The presumption is of such long standing in our law that it should only be changed by Parliament, or at least by a decision of the House of Lords. But antiquity of itself confers no virtue upon the legal *status quo*. If it did, that would assault one of the most valued features of the common law, which is its capacity to adapt to changing conditions. The common law is not a system of rigid rules, but of principles, whose application may alter over time, and which themselves may be modified. It may, and should, be renewed by succeeding generations of judges, and so meet the needs of a society that is itself subject to change. In the present case the conditions under which this presumption was developed in the earlier law now have no application. It is our duty to get rid of it, if we properly can.

(iii) We are bound by the doctrine of precedent to adhere to the presumption. This is the most important argument, because the rules as to *stare decisis* provide a crucial counterpoint to the law's capacity for change: apparently established principles are not to be altered save through the measured deliberation of a hierarchical system. First instance courts do not, on the whole, effect root and branch changes to legal principle, since if they were permitted to do so legal certainty, which is at least as important as legal adaptability, would be hopelessly undermined. But the Divisional Court is in a peculiar position. In point of hierarchy, it is a first instance court, an arm of the Queen's Bench Division. But it is also an appellate court for cases like the present; and in such cases there is no appeal from its decisions save to the House of Lords. All the cases cited to us were decided either in the Divisional Court or at trial at first instance, save two: *R v B* [1979] 1 WLR 1185 and *R v Coulbourn* (1988) 87 Cr App R 309, which were decisions of the Court of Appeal (Criminal Division). It is clear on authority that the Divisional Court has the power to depart from its own previous decisions: *R v Greater Manchester Coroner, ex p Tal* [1985] QB 67. The rule is that the court will follow a decision of a court of equal jurisdiction unless persuaded that it is clearly wrong. It is, perhaps, not plain what is added by the adverb 'clearly': it can mean no more in my view than that judicial comity and the obvious need for conformity in decisions of the higher courts create a legitimate pressure in favour of consistent results at the Divisional Court level; and this would apply also to the decisions of single judges sitting in the Crown Office List. So understood, *Tal's* case does not establish a rule of *stare decisis*, since such a rule entails the proposition that the second court has not the legal authority to depart from what the first court said.

In the present case, all the earlier decisions proceeded upon the unargued premise that the presumption now in question was undoubtedly part of the fabric of English criminal law. To discard it, therefore, does not involve any disagreement with the express reasoning in the cases. I would hold that there is not the least impediment upon our departing from the earlier Divisional Court authorities so far as, by implication, they upheld the existence of this presumption (as they plainly did): to do so is no affront to any principle of judicial comity, far less the doctrine of precedent.

The two cases in the Court of Appeal proceeded upon the same unargued premise. The presumption was simply assumed to apply. No doubt in general this court is bound by decisions of the Court of Appeal (Criminal Division). But the question whether this presumption is or should remain part of our law has never, so far as has been ascertained, fallen for distinct argument as an issue requiring that court's specific determination. That being so, in my view this court is entitled to depart from the premise which lay behind the Court of Appeal's two decisions; to do so does not involve a departure from any adjudication which that court was required to make upon an issue in dispute before it. In those circumstances, I would hold that the presumption relied on by the defendant is no longer part of the law of England.

On appeal in the House of Lords, the leading speech with which all the other Law Lords agreed was delivered by Lord Lowry.

House of Lords [1995] 2 WLR 383

Lord Lowry: My Lords, the point of this appeal is: 'Whether there continues to be a presumption that a child between the ages of 10 and 14 is *doli incapax* and, if so, whether that presumption can only be rebutted by clear positive evidence that he knew that his act was seriously wrong, such evidence not consisting merely in the evidence of the acts amounting to the offence itself.'

... The presumption has been discussed in many Official Reports and has been the background of legislation concerning the age of criminal responsibility. In 1927 the Report of the Molony Committee on the Treatment of Young Offenders (Cmnd 2831) stated, at p 21: 'As the law stands at present no act done by any person under seven years of age is a crime and no act done by any person over seven and under 14 is a crime unless it be shown affirmatively that such person had sufficient capacity to know that the act was wrong. The age of seven was adopted hundreds of years ago and the whole attitude of society towards offences committed by children has since been revolutionised. We think the time has come for raising the age of criminal responsibility, and we think it could safely be placed at eight. For children over this age courts should bear in mind the requirement referred to above.' (The last sentence here was a reference to the importance of reformation of children as distinct from punishment.) In consequence, no doubt, of that Report the minimum age of criminal responsibility was raised to eight years by s 50 of the Children and Young Persons Act 1933. In 1960 the Report of the Ingleby Committee on Children and Young Persons (Cmnd 1191) recommended raising the age of criminal responsibility to 12, with the possibility of its becoming 13 or 14; instead of criminal proceedings that committee contemplated that children under the given age would be brought before a court as being in need of care, protection, discipline or control. It can therefore be seen that the proposal, when fully implemented, would have meant that there was no criminal responsibility up to the age to which the presumption applied and still applies. By s 16 of the Children and Young Persons Act 1963 the minimum age of criminal responsibility was raised to 10 years but, failing any express enactment on the point, the common law upper limit stayed at 14 for the purpose of the presumption. In 1965, the Government having changed, a White Paper, *The Child, the Family and the Young Offender* (Cmnd 2742) proposed the extinction of the *doli incapax* rule by raising the minimum age of criminal responsibility to 16. This reform was to be accompanied by the abolition of the Juvenile Court. Another point of view, which was also more in harmony with the Ingleby Report appeared in s 4 of the Children and Young Persons Act 1969, which provided that a person should not be charged with an offence except homicide by reason of anything done or omitted while he was a child, that is, under 14. Sections 34 and 73 of the Act enabled the minimum age of criminal responsibility to be increased gradually from 10 to 14 by Order, but a day was never appointed for s 4 to come into effect. Meanwhile, in 1985, there was laid before Parliament a draft Bill codifying the criminal law, which had been prepared under the auspices of the Law Commission by a committee of distinguished academic lawyers under the chairmanship of Professor JC Smith CBE, QC (Law Com No 143). Draft clause 36 reads: 'A child is not guilty of an offence by reason of anything he does when under ten years of age.' The committee's commentary is significant:

> 11.21 Child under 10. This clause restates the present law – without expressing the matter, as the present law does, in terms of a conclusive presumption of incapacity.

> 11.22 Child over 10 but under 14. The law at present is that such a child can be guilty of an offence but only if, in addition to doing the prohibited act with such fault as is required in the case of an adult, he knows that what he is doing is 'seriously wrong'. It is presumed at his trial that he did not have such knowledge, and the prosecution must rebut this presumption by proof beyond reasonable doubt. The presumption, it has been said, 'reflects an outworn mode of thought' and 'is steeped in absurdity;' and it has long been recognised as operating capriciously. Its abolition was proposed in 1960 by the Ingleby Committee on Children and Young Persons. We believe that there is no case for its survival in the Code.

> 11.23 The Children and Young Persons Act 1969, s 4 provides: 'A person shall not be charged with an offence, except homicide, by reason of anything done or committed while he was a child' (that is, under 14). The intention of the government of the day was that the minimum age for prosecution should in fact be raised to 14 by stages; and the Act contains provisions enabling this to be done. No government, however, has acted to bring s 4 into force; it appears to be a dead letter. It ought no doubt to be repealed with the enactment of the Code (if not before). It is not, however, strictly speaking inconsistent with the present clause. The clause specifies the lowest age at which a person can commit an offence, while s 4 specifies an age below which, although committing an offence, a person does not thereby render himself liable to prosecution.

The intended effect of the draft was, therefore, to get rid of the presumption and to let a child pass from complete criminal irresponsibility to full responsibility without any intermediate zone.

... The sequence was completed by s 72 of the Criminal Justice Act 1991, which repealed s 4 of the Children and Young Persons Act 1969.

The material which Mr Robertson put before your Lordships convinces me that the presumption is still universally recognised as an effective doctrine which the Government has recently reaffirmed to be, in the Government's view, part of the criminal law. The imperfections which have been attributed to that doctrine cannot, in my view, provide a justification for saying that the presumption is no longer part of our law. To sweep it away under the doubtful auspices of judicial legislation is to my mind, quite impracticable ...

It is hard, when discussing the propriety of judicial law-making, to reason conclusively from one situation to another, but ... I believe, however, that one can find in the authorities some aids to navigation across an uncertainly charted sea.

(1) If the solution is doubtful, the judges should beware of imposing their own remedy.

(2) Caution should prevail if Parliament has rejected opportunities of clearing up a known difficulty or has legislated, while leaving the difficulty untouched.

(3) Disputed matters of social policy are less suitable areas for judicial intervention than purely legal problems.

(4) Fundamental legal doctrines should not be lightly set aside.

(5) Judges should not make a change unless they can achieve finality and certainty.

I consider that all these aids, in varying degrees, point away from the solution proposed in the court below.

... It is quite clear that, as the law stands, the Crown must, as part of the prosecution's case, show that a child defendant is *doli capax* before that child can have a case to meet. To call the proposed innovation a merely procedural change greatly understates, in my view, its radical nature, which would not be disguised by continuing to impose the persuasive burden of proof upon the prosecution. The change would not merely alter the trial procedure but would in effect get rid of the presumption of *doli incapax* which must now be rebutted before a child defendant can be called for his defence and the existence of which will in practice often prevent a charge from even being brought. This reflection must be enough to discourage any thought of 'judicial legislation' on the lines proposed. In the course of his argument Mr Henriques invited your Lordships to take courage from the decision in *R v R* [1992] 1 AC 599, whereby your Lordships' House disposed of Hale's proposition that a man could not be guilty of rape upon his wife. That case dealt with a situation in which the wife had left home and thus was similar in its facts to a number of cases in which the Hale principle had already been departed from. It must, however, be acknowledged that the decision (since given statutory effect by s 142 of the Criminal Justice and Public Order Act 1994) was quite general in its terms and thus contemplated that a husband living with his wife could, if he forced himself upon her, have been charged with rape, contrary, it could be argued, to the non-retrospective principle of law reform. But, apart from this feature, what was done in *R v R* seems to me very different from what the respondent asks your Lordships to do in the present case. *R v R* dealt, in the first place, with a specific act and not with a general principle governing criminal liability. It was based on a very widely accepted modern view of marital rape and it derived support from a group of up-to-date decisions. The principle rejected in *R v R* stood on a dubious legal foundation. And, in contrast to the present case, a definite solution could be, and was, achieved. Moreover, unlike the presumption here, Hale's doctrine had not been given the stamp of legislative, judicial, governmental and academic recognition. Certainly the abolition of the presumption could never in the present case be described as 'the removal of a common law fiction'. Clearly then, in my view, the presumption, for better or worse, applies to cases like the present.

... The wisdom of protecting young children against the full rigour of the criminal law is beyond argument. The difficulty lies in determining when and under what circumstances that protection should be removed. The distinction between the treatment and the punishment of child 'offenders' has popular and political overtones, a fact which shows that we have been discussing not so much a legal as a social problem, with a dash of politics thrown in, and emphasises that it should be within the exclusive remit of Parliament. There is need to study other systems, including that which holds sway in Scotland, a task for which the courts are not equipped. Whatever change is made, it should come only after collating and considering the evidence and after taking account of the effect which a change would have on the whole law relating to children's anti-social behaviour. This is a classic case for parliamentary investigation, deliberation and legislation. I believe, my Lords, that we have reached the stage when the author of a lengthy judgment (or a lengthy argument) needs an excuse for his prolixity. My excuse is that, reviewing a bold and imaginative judgment, I have deemed it not only courteous but also necessary to demonstrate my reasons for saying that the presumption is still part of our law, and not just to assert the fact. Secondly, without suggesting the answer, which I am not qualified to give, I hope that my survey may help to provide the incentive for a much-needed new look at an undoubted problem.

_ . _ . _ . _ . _ . _ . _ . _ . _ . _ . _ . _ . _ . _ . _ . _ . _

The old doctrine of *doli incapax* was eventually removed by s 34 of the Crime and Disorder Act 1998. The age of criminal responsibility in England and Wales is now simply set at 10.

Questions

- What distinguishes the principle of *doli incapax* from the marital exception to rape? Why should one be open to judicial reform and not the other?
- Critically examine the claim that changes in the common law might have the effect of retrospectively criminalising previously lawful behaviour.
- Are the courts the appropriate body to reform law and are they competent to do so?

LEGISLATION

Under United Kingdom constitutional law, it is recognised that Parliament has the power to enact, revoke or alter such, and any, law as it sees fit. But, as has been stated previously, legislation has to be interpreted in order to give it meaning and effect. Such interpretation is the function of the judiciary. However, before considering statutory interpretation, some consideration must be given to the part played by the Law Commission in the generation of legislation.

LAW COMMISSION

Annex A to the Law Commission's Annual Report for the year 2000 provides a short explanation of its functions.

Law Commission, *Annual Report*, Annex A, 2000

The Law Commission's Role and Methods

The Law Commission has now been in operation for 35 years. It was established by the Law Commissions Act 1965 to review the law of England and Wales with a view to its systematic development and reform. A number of specific types of reform were mentioned:

- codification
- removal of anomalies
- repeal of obsolete and unnecessary enactments
- consolidation
- generally the simplification and modernisation of the law.

Law reform projects may be included in a programme of work submitted to the Lord Chancellor, or be referred to the Commission usually by a Government department. The current programme of work is the Seventh Programme, approved in 1999. The Commission initiates or accepts a law reform project according to its assessment of the relevant considerations, the most significant of which are the importance of the issues, the availability of resources in terms of both expertise and funding and the suitability of the issues to be dealt with by the Commission. The Commission's general aims for law reform are to make the law simpler, fairer, more modern and cheaper to use.

The Commission's work is based on thorough research and analysis of case law, legislation, academic and other writing, law reports and other relevant sources of information both in the United Kingdom and overseas. It takes full account both of the European Convention on Human Rights and of other European law. It acts in consultation with the Scottish Law Commission. It normally publishes a consultation paper inviting views before it finalises its recommendations. The consultation paper describes the present law and its shortcomings and sets out possible options for reform. The views expressed in response by consultees are analysed and considered very carefully.

The Commission's final recommendations are set out in a report which contains a draft Bill where the recommendations involve primary legislation. The report is laid before Parliament. It is then for the Government to decide whether it accepts the recommendations and to introduce any necessary Bill in Parliament, unless a Private Member or Peer does so. After publication of a report the Commission often gives further assistance to Government Ministers and departments, so as to ensure that the best value is obtained from the effort and resources devoted to the project by the Commission and others.

The Commission also has the task of consolidating statute law, substituting one Act, or a small group of Acts, for all the existing statutory provisions in several different Acts. In addition, the Commission prepares legislation to repeal statutes which are obsolete or unnecessary.

The following extracts are taken from the Law Commission's consideration of involuntary manslaughter.

Item 11 of the Sixth Programme of Law Reform: Criminal Law, *Legislating the Criminal Code: Involuntary Manslaughter*

To the Right Honourable the Lord Mackay of Clashfern, Lord High Chancellor of Great Britain

Part I

Introduction – The scope and structure of this report

1.1 This report is concerned with the criminal liability of those who kill when they do not intend to cause death or serious injury. There are two conflicting schools of thought about the way in which the law should deal with such people. Some argue that society should always punish a person who causes terrible consequences to occur. Professor Hart puts the opposite view in these terms:

> All civilised penal systems make liability to punishment for at any rate serious crime dependent not merely on the fact that the person to be punished has done the outward act of a crime, but on his having done it in a certain state or frame of mind or will.

In this report we consider what 'frame of mind or will' ought to be required if criminal liability is to be imposed for unintentional killing.

1.2 There are only two general homicide offences under the present law. The more serious of these, murder, requires proof of intention to kill or to cause serious injury, and the absence of such mitigating circumstances as the fact that the killer was provoked, or acted under diminished responsibility, or was the survivor of a suicide pact. Every other case of unlawful killing is included within the second homicide offence, manslaughter. This offence is, therefore, extremely broad. It 'ranges in its gravity from the borders of murder right down to those of accidental death'.

1.3 Although it is a single offence, manslaughter is commonly divided by lawyers into two separate categories, 'voluntary' and 'involuntary' manslaughter. The first of these describes cases where the accused intended to cause death or serious injury, but is excused liability for murder because some mitigating factor may be present. In the present project we are concerned only with the second type, 'involuntary' manslaughter. This expression covers cases where there was no intention to kill or to cause serious injury, but where the law considers that the person who caused death was blameworthy in some other way.

1.4 Under the law as it stands at present, a person who unintentionally causes death is treated as sufficiently blameworthy to attract serious criminal sanctions in two cases. The first, known as 'unlawful act manslaughter', arises where the person who causes death was engaged in a criminal act which carried with it a risk of causing some, perhaps slight, injury to another person. The second type of involuntary manslaughter, 'gross-negligence manslaughter', is harder to define. To put it very simply, the offence is committed by those who cause death through extreme carelessness.

1.5 In Part II we summarise the present law relating to both types of involuntary manslaughter, and in Part III we examine the contemporary problems they create. There are a number of minor problems in the form of uncertainties arising from the way in which the law has been formulated in particular cases. In addition to these uncertainties, however, there are two major problems. The first is that the present offence of manslaughter is too wide. This can cause problems both for judges on sentencing and for the public, who have difficulty in understanding the sentencing dilemma that faces a judge when an offence is so wide. It is in any event inappropriate that the same label should apply both to conduct on the borders of murder and to conduct on the borders of mere carelessness.

The second major problem relates to unlawful act manslaughter: we consider that it is wrong in principle that a person should be convicted for causing death when the gravest risk apparently inherent in his conduct was the risk of causing some injury. This is a matter which we consider thoroughly in Part IV.

1.6 That Part is devoted to an exploration of the distinction between punishing a person for the consequences of his acts and punishing him for the state of mind in which he acted. The extent to which a person is responsible for the unintended consequences of his actions is, as we say there, one which has troubled philosophers for many years. There is no easy answer. However, it was important for us to come to a decision on this issue because we believe very strongly that the criminal law should rest, so far as is possible, on consistent, logical and principled foundations.

1.7 We were greatly assisted by the very helpful comments sent to us on consultation, and by the advice of our consultant Professor Andrew Ashworth of King's College, London. We have eventually concluded that a person ought to be criminally liable for causing death only where he was aware that his conduct created a risk of causing death or serious injury to another, or where he was seriously at fault in failing to be aware of this risk. We believe that someone should only be blamed for failing to advert to such a risk if it would have been obvious to a reasonable person in his position, and he was himself capable of appreciating it at the material time.

1.8 In Part V we set out our detailed recommendations for a modern, codified law of involuntary manslaughter. In brief, we recommend the creation of two new offences in order to resolve the problems caused by the width of the present law. The more serious of the two offences, with a maximum penalty of life imprisonment, is called 'reckless killing'. It would be committed by a person who unreasonably and consciously decides to run a risk of causing death or serious injury. The second new offence is called 'killing by gross carelessness'. This would require proof of three matters. First, that the defendant's conduct involved an obvious risk of causing death or serious injury, of which he need not actually have been aware, as long as he was capable of appreciating it. Secondly, that his conduct fell far below what could be expected of him in all the circumstances, or that he intended to cause some unlawful injury to another or was reckless whether he did so. And, thirdly, that he caused death. We make no recommendation as to the maximum sentence for this offence, and if our recommendations are implemented it will be for others to determine what maximum is appropriate; but we have no reason to suppose that the maximum would be set at such a figure as to affect the levels of sentence currently imposed by the courts.

1.9 If our recommendations were implemented, English law would then possess, in effect, four degrees of general criminal homicide: murder, (voluntary) manslaughter, reckless killing and killing by gross carelessness. There would also be, as now, certain homicide offences aimed at specific situations, such as causing death by dangerous driving, infanticide and aiding and abetting suicide.

Part IX

Summary of our recommendations

Individual manslaughter

1. We recommend the creation of two different offences of unintentional killing, based on differing fault elements, rather than one single, broad offence.

Reckless killing

2. We recommend the creation of a new offence of reckless killing, which would be committed if:

    (1) a person by his or her conduct causes the death of another;

    (2) he or she is aware of a risk that his or her conduct will cause death or serious injury; and

    (3) it is unreasonable for him or her to take that risk, having regard to the circumstances as he or she knows or believes them to be.

Unlawful act manslaughter

3. We recommend the abolition of unlawful act manslaughter in its present form.

Killing by gross carelessness

4. We recommend the creation of a new offence of killing by gross carelessness, which would be committed if:

    (1) a person by his or her conduct causes the death of another;

    (2) a risk that his or her conduct will cause death or serious injury would be obvious to a reasonable person in his or her position;

    (3) he or she is capable of appreciating that risk at the material time; and

    (4) *either*

        (a) his or her conduct falls far below what can reasonably be expected of him or her in the circumstances, or

        (b) he or she intends by his or her conduct to cause some injury, or is aware of, and unreasonably takes, the risk that it may do so, and the conduct causing (or intended to cause) the injury constitutes an offence.

Omissions

5. We recommend that the duty to act continue to be governed by the common law for the purposes of involuntary manslaughter for the time being.

Alternative verdicts

6. We recommend that both of the new homicide offences should be available as alternative verdicts to murder.

7. We recommend that the long established practice, that where there is a possibility on a count of murder of the jury returning a verdict of manslaughter, a separate count of manslaughter is not added to the indictment, be abandoned.

8. We recommend that the question whether any other offence may constitute an alternative on a charge of reckless killing or killing by gross carelessness should be governed by the general provisions of s 6(3) of the Criminal Law Act 1967.

9. We recommend that killing by gross carelessness should be an alternative to a charge of reckless killing.

Motor manslaughter

10. We recommend that no change should be made to the existing offences of causing death by bad driving, and that it should also be possible, where appropriate, to prosecute such cases as reckless killing or killing by gross carelessness.

Corporate manslaughter

11. We recommend

    (1) that there should be a special offence of corporate killing, broadly corresponding to the individual offence of killing by gross carelessness;

    (2) that (like the individual offence) the corporate offence should be committed only where the defendant's conduct in causing the death falls far below what could reasonably be expected;

    (3) that (unlike the individual offence) the corporate offence should not require that the risk be obvious, or that the defendant be capable of appreciating the risk; and

    (4) that, for the purposes of the corporate offence, a death should be regarded as having been caused by the conduct of a corporation if it is caused by a failure, in the way in which the corporation's activities are managed or organised, to ensure the health and safety of persons employed in or affected by those activities.

Causation

12. We recommend that, for the purposes of the corporate offence, it should be possible for a management failure on the part of a corporation to be a cause of a person's death even if the immediate cause is the act or omission of an individual.

Potential defendants

13. We recommend that the offence of corporate killing should be capable of commission by any corporation, however and wherever incorporated, other than a corporation sole.

14. We recommend that the offence or corporate killing should not be capable of commission by an unincorporated body.

15. We recommend that the offence of corporate killing should not be capable of commission by an individual, even as a secondary party.

Territorial jurisdiction

16. We recommend that there should be liability for the corporate offence only if the injury that results in the death is sustained in such a place that the English courts would have had jurisdiction over the offence had it been committed by an individual other than a British subject.

Consents

17. We recommend that there should be no requirement of consent to the bringing of private prosecutions for the corporate offence.

Mode of trial

18. We recommend that the offence of corporate killing should be triable only on indictment.

Alternative verdicts

19. We recommend that, where the jury finds a defendant not guilty of any of the offences we recommend, it should be possible (subject to the overall discretion of the judge) for the jury to convict the defendant of an offence under section 2 or 3 of the Health and Safety at Work etc Act 1974.

Remedial action

20. We recommend that

    (1) a court before which a corporation is convicted or corporate killing should have power to order the corporation to take such steps, within such time, as the order specifies for remedying the failure in question and any matter which appears to the court to have resulted from the failure and been the cause or one of the causes of the death;

    (2) the power to make such an order should arise only on an application by the prosecution (or the Health and Safety Executive or any other body or person designated for this purpose by the Secretary of State, either generally or in relation to the case in question) specifying the terms of the proposed order; and

    (3) any such order should be on such terms (whether those proposed or others) as the court considers appropriate having regard to any representations made, and any evidence adduced, by the prosecution (or any other body or person applying for such an order) or on behalf of the corporation.

Corporate liability for the individual offences

21. We recommend that the ordinary principles of corporate liability should apply to the individual offences that we propose.

The Law Commission Report included a draft Bill.

Involuntary Homicide Bill

Arrangement of clauses

Clause

Schedule:

Consequential amendments.

Draft of a Bill to:

> AD 1995. Create new offences of reckless killing, killing by gross carelessness and corporate killing to replace the offence of manslaughter in cases where death is caused without the intention of causing death or serious injury.

Be it enacted by the Queen's most Excellent Majesty, by and with the advice and consent of the Lords Spiritual and Temporal, and Commons, in this present Parliament assembled, and by the authority of the same, as follows:

Reckless killing

1. – (1) A person who by his conduct causes the death of another is guilty of reckless killing if–

    (a) he is aware of a risk that his conduct will cause death or serious injury; and

    (b) it is unreasonable for him to take that risk having regard to the circumstances as he knows or believes them to be.

  (2) A person guilty of reckless killing is liable on conviction on indictment to imprisonment for life.

Killing by

2. – (1) A person who by his conduct causes the death of another gross carelessness is guilty of killing by gross carelessness if–

    (a) a risk that his conduct will cause death or serous injury would be obvious to a reasonable person in his position;

    (b) he is capable of appreciating that risk at the material time; and

(c)   either–

(i)   his conduct falls far below what can reasonably be expected of him in the circumstances; or

(ii)   he intends by his conduct to cause some injury or is aware of, and unreasonably takes, the risk that it may do so.

(2)   There shall be attributed to the person referred to in subsection (1)(a) above–

(a)   knowledge of any relevant facts which the accused is shown to have at the material time; and

(b)   any skill or experience professed by him.

(3)   In determining for the purposes of subsection (1)(c)(i) above what can reasonably be expected of the accused regard shall be had to the circumstances of which he can be expected to be aware, to any circumstances shown to be within his knowledge and to any other matter relevant for assessing his conduct at the material time.

(4)   Subsection (1)(c)(ii) above applies only if the conduct causing, or intended to cause, the injury constitutes an offence.

(5)   A person guilty of killing by gross carelessness is liable on conviction on indictment to imprisonment for a term not exceeding [ ] years.

Omissions

3.   A person is not guilty of an offence under sections 1 or 2 above causing death by reason of an omission unless the omission is in breach of a duty at common law.

Corporate killing

4. – (1) A corporation is guilty of corporate killing if–

(a)   a management failure by the corporation is the cause or one of the causes of a person's death; and

(b)   that failure constitutes conduct falling far below what can reasonably be expected of the corporation in the circumstances.

(2)   For the purposes of subsection (1) above–

(a)   there is a management failure by a corporation if the way in which its activities are managed or organised fails to ensure the health and safety of persons employed in or affected by those activities; and

(b)   such a failure may be regarded as a cause of a person's death notwithstanding that the immediate cause is the act or omission of an individual.

(3)   A corporation guilty of an offence under this section is liable on conviction on indictment to a fine.

(4)   No individual shall be convicted of aiding, abetting, counselling or procuring an offence under this section but without prejudice to an individual being guilty of any other offence in respect of the death in question.

(5)   This section does not preclude a corporation being guilty of an offence under section 1 or 2 above.

(6)   This section applies if the injury resulting in death is sustained in England and Wales or–

(a)   within the seaward limits of the territorial sea adjacent to the United Kingdom;

(b)   on a British ship or vessel;

(c)   on a British controlled aircraft as defined in section 92 of the Civil Aviation Act 1982; or

(d)   in any place to which an Order in Council under section 22(1) of the Oil and Gas (Enterprise) Act 1982 applies (criminal jurisdiction in relation to offshore activities).

(7)   For the purposes of subsection (6)(b) and (c) above an injury sustained on a ship, vessel or aircraft shall be treated as including an injury sustained by a person who is then no longer on board, and who sustains the injury, in consequence of the wrecking of, or of some other mishap affecting, the ship, vessel or aircraft.

(8)   In this section 'a corporation' does not include a corporation sole but includes any body corporate wherever incorporated.

—·—·—·—·—·—·—·—·—·—·—·—·—·—·—·—·—

The Government is now proposing to legislate on this matter. It accepts some but not all of the Law Commission's draft Bill.

Home Office, 'The Law Commission's Draft Involuntary Homicide Bill and Government comments on it', *Reforming the Law on Involuntary Manslaughter: The Government's proposals,* **CC NO 77828, May 2000, pp 30–36**

The Government has set out below some (but not all) of the proposed changes to the Law Commissions draft Involuntary Homicide Bill, reprinted opposite. Most of these result from those issues identified earlier in this Paper where the Government takes a different view from the Law Commission. For the sake of consistency the Government has determined that on all the issues where the same words are used in its own draft Offences Against the Person (OATP) Bill and the draft Law Commission's Involuntary Homicide Bill, such as the definition of 'injury', we will ensure that the same meaning/definitions are applied to those terms for both OATP and Involuntary Homicide.

Clause I: Reckless killing

This clause of the Law Commission's Bill shares almost the same subjective definition of recklessness as the Government's draft OATP Bill. We are satisfied that this subjective definition is appropriate (relating to the risk and the circumstances as the defendant knew or believed them to be) rather than an objective standard, such as is applied in the Criminal Damage Act.

Neither Bill defines what is meant by serious injury. The Law Commission has argued that it is for the courts to decide when an injury is serious. The Government has accepted this view in the OATP context, and it would he consistent to apply the same conclusion to the Involuntary Homicide Bill.

Clause 2: Killing by gross carelessness [no suggested changes]

Clause 3: Omissions causing death

The clause refers to a person not being guilty under sections 1 or 2 by reason of an omission unless the omission is in breach of a duty at common law. The Law Commission have made it clear that they wanted to ensure that all those duties, including statutory duties, which apply at present to involuntary manslaughter should continue to apply to the new offences. The Government intends to amend clause 3 to give effect to this intention.

Clause 4: Corporate killing

The Government considers that there is no good reason why an individual should not be convicted for aiding, abetting, counselling or procuring an offence of corporate killing and therefore proposes that clause 4(4) of the Law Commission's draft Bill should be removed.

Clause 5: Remedial orders against convicted corporations [no suggested changes]

Clause 6: Alternative verdicts

The principle of alternative verdicts – of being able to substitute a lesser offence when the more serious offence that is charged is not sufficiently proved – is well established. The proposals in the Governments OATP Bill extend the provisions to the magistrates' court; alternative verdicts have been available in the Crown Court since the Criminal Law Act 1967. The Government therefore accepts the proposed set of alternative verdicts for manslaughter proposed by the Law Commission.

Clause 7: Abolition of involuntary manslaughter [no suggested changes]

Clause 8: Supplementary provisions

Both the Law Commission Bill and the Government's draft Bill on OATP preserve existing common law defences, lawful authority, justification or excuse for an act or omission. On intoxication the Government proposes that clause 19 of its draft OATP Bill, dealing with intoxication, should also apply to the involuntary homicide offences. The Law Commission's draft Bill will be amended accordingly.

Once again the Law Commission's annual report for the year 2000 provides some interesting statistics.

— · — · — · — · — · — · — · — · — · — · — · — · — · —

Law Commission Law Reform Reports Awaiting Implementation

Of all the Law Commission's 162 law reform reports, the 21 listed below remain outstanding. Nine of these, marked *, have been accepted by the Government in full or in part, subject to Parliamentary time being available.

Date	Law Com No	Title
1991	194	*Distress for Rent*
1992	208*	*Business Tenancies: Landlord and Tenant Act 1954, Part II*
1993	218*	*Legislating the Criminal Code: Offences Against the Person and General Principles*
1994	222	*Binding Over*
	226	*Judicial Review and Statutory Appeals*
1995	229	*Intoxication and Criminal Liability*
	231*	*Mental Incapacity*
1996	237*	*Involuntary Manslaughter*
	238	*Landlord and Tenant: Responsibility for State and Condition of Property*
1997	245*	*Evidence in Criminal Proceedings: Hearsay and Related Topics*
	246	*Shareholder Remedies*
	247*	*Aggravated, Exemplary and Restitutionary Damages*
1998	248*	*Legislating the Criminal Code: Corruption*
	249	*Liability for Psychiatric Illness*
	251	*The Rules Against Perpetuities and Excessive Accumulations*
	253*	*The Execution of Deeds and Documents by or on behalf of Bodies Corporate*
	255*	*Consents to Prosecution*
1999	257	*Damages for Personal Injury: Non-Pecuniary Loss*
	261	*Company Directors: Regulating Conflicts of Interests and Formulating a Statement of Duties*
	262	*Damages for Personal Injury: Medical, Nursing and other Expenses; Collateral Benefits*
	263	*Claims for Wrongful Death*

APPROACHES TO STATUTORY INTERPRETATION

There are essentially two contrasting views as to how judges should go about determining the meaning of a statute: the restrictive, literal approach and the more permissive, purposive one. The literal approach holds that the judge should look primarily to the words of the legislation in order to construe its meaning. The purposive approach, on the other hand, allows the judge the power to look beyond the words of the statute, to determine the reason for its enactment.

Rules of interpretation

The three rules of statutory interpretation are as follows:

(i) *The literal rule* – under this rule the judge is required to consider what the legislation actually says rather than considering what it might mean.

(ii) *The golden rule* – this rule is applied in circumstances where the application of the literal rule is likely to result in, what appears to the court, to be an obviously absurd result.

(iii) *The mischief rule* – is clearly the most flexible rule of interpretation, but in its traditional expression it is limited by being restricted to using previous common law rules in order to decide the operation of contemporary legislation (*Heydon's Case* (1584)).

The selective deployment of the various approaches to statutory interpretation has already been seen in *R v R* above, but the following cases allow further critical study of the procedure used and clearly reveal the purpositive, political understandings that lie behind the choice of which rule to implement.

Royal College of Nursing of the United Kingdom v Department of Health and Social Security [1981] 1 All ER 545

This case involved the interpretation of the Abortion Act 1967 s 1(1) of which provided that: '... a person shall not be guilty of an offence under the law relating to abortion when a pregnancy is terminated by a registered medical practitioner ...'

Section 1(3) that: '... any treatment for the termination of pregnancy must be carried out in a hospital ... or a place for the time being approved ... by ... the Secretary of State.' And s 1(4) that: 'Subsection (3) of this section ... shall not apply to the termination of a pregnancy by a registered medical practitioner where he is of the opinion ... that the termination is immediately necessary to save the life ... of the pregnant woman.'

In a letter dated 21 February 1980 sent to regional and area medical officers and regional, area and district nursing officers, the Department of Health and Social Security purported to explain the law relating to abortion in connection with the termination of pregnancy by medical induction. The department's advice was that termination by medical induction using the extra-amniotic method could properly be said to be termination by a registered medical practitioner provided it was decided on and initiated by him [*sic*] and provided he remained throughout responsible for its overall conduct and control in the sense that acts needed to bring it to its conclusion were done by appropriately skilled staff acting on his specific instructions, but not necessarily in his presence. The department stated that the first stage of the procedure, insertion of an extra-amniotic catheter and an intravenous infusion cannula, must be carried out by a registered medical practitioner, but that the second stage, connection of infusions of the abortifacient drugs to the catheter and, if appropriate, to the cannula, and regulation of the infusions, could be carried out by an appropriately skilled nurse or midwife acting in accordance with precise instructions given by the registered medical practitioner. The Royal College of Nursing sought a declaration that the circular was wrong in law.

Woolf J refused the declaration, and granted the department a declaration that their advice did not involve the performance of any unlawful act by members of the college.

The Court of Appeal reversed his decision but on further appeal the House of Lords, Lord Wilberforce and Lord Edmund-Davies dissenting, reinstated the decision of Woolf J.

In the Court of Appeal Lord Denning MR delivered the following judgment (emphasis added):

> **Lord Denning MR**: Abortion is a controversial subject. The question for us today is this: when a pregnancy is terminated by medical induction, who should do the actual act of termination? Should it be done by a doctor? Or can he leave it to the nurses? The Royal College of Nursing say that the doctor should do the actual act himself and not leave it to the nurses. The Department of Health and Social Security take a different view. They say that a doctor can initiate the process and then go off and do other things, so long as he is 'on call'. The controversy is so acute that it has come before us for decision. *Throughout the discussion I am going to speak of the unborn child.* The old common lawyers spoke of a child *en ventre sa mere*. Doctors speak of it as the foetus. In simple English it is an unborn child inside the mother's womb. Such a child was protected by the criminal law almost to the same extent as a new-born baby. If anyone terminated the pregnancy – and thus destroyed the unborn child – he or she was guilty of a felony and was liable to be kept in penal servitude for life (see s 58 of the Offences Against the Person Act 1861) unless it was done to save the life of the mother: see *R v Bourne* [1939] 1 KB 687. Likewise anyone who assisted or participated in the abortion was guilty, including the mother herself. I have tried several cases of 'back-street abortions' – where the mother died or was made seriously ill. I have passed severe sentences of imprisonment for the offence.

> *The Abortion Act 1967*

> The approach to the subject was revolutionised by the Abortion Act 1967. It legalised abortion if it was done so as to avoid risk to the mother's health, physical or mental. *This has been interpreted by some medical practitioners so loosely that abortion has become obtainable virtually on demand.* Whenever a woman has an unwanted pregnancy, there are doctors who will say it involves a risk to her mental health. But the Act contains some safeguards. It provides that, in order for the abortion to be lawful, it is subject to three conditions: (1) the woman has to get two doctors to give a certificate; (2) the abortion has to be done in hospital; and (3) the pregnancy has to be 'terminated by a registered medical practitioner'. It is this last condition which comes up for consideration today. It arises because of the advance in medical science. The material words of the Act of 1967 are: '… a person shall not be guilty of an offence under the law relating to abortion when a pregnancy is terminated by a registered medical practitioner …'

At the time that the Act was passed – and for five years afterwards – there was no difficulty of interpretation. All abortions then – at any rate when the mother was three months pregnant or more – were done by surgical methods. *The knife with the cutting edge was operated by a registered medical practitioner. He used it to remove the unborn child.* The knife was never handled by a nurse. She was not a registered medical practitioner.

Medical induction

Since 1972 a new method has been used. It is called medical induction. It does not involve a knife. It started quite simply in ordinary full-time births – so as to induce labour a few hours early – to save the mother the stress of waiting – or for the convenience of doctors and staff. But it is now becoming much used to effect abortions – when the mother is pregnant for three months or more. It is done by pumping a chemical fluid into the mother's womb. It is called prostaglandin. This fluid so affects the muscles and shape of the mother's inside that it forces her into labour prematurely – so *that the unborn child is expelled from the body – usually dead, but sometimes at the point of death.*

There are two distinct stages in this process. The first stage is done by a doctor – a registered medical practitioner. The mother is taken from the ward to the operating theatre. She is given a general anaesthetic. The doctor inserts a fine catheter into her body so as to reach a particular part of her womb. But no fluid is pumped into her at that stage. She is then taken back to the ward. She is left there until she recovers from the anaesthetic. *The doctor writes out a few notes telling the nurse what to do. He then goes off, saying: 'Give me a call if there is any difficulty.'*

The second stage is done by the nurses. When the mother comes round from the anaesthetic, *they get a flexible tube and connect up the catheter with a pump which is electrically driven, or with a dripping device. They then get the special fluid called prostaglandin.* They have to see that it is of the right concentration. They have it in a bottle, and pump the fluid into the woman's body. They have to regulate the dose and control the intake – by speed and amount – as occasion requires. If need be, they have to get another bottle. They have to watch the woman and note her reactions, and take such steps as occasion requires. Labour is induced. The unborn child is expelled from the woman's body. The process may take 18 hours, or even up to 30 hours. If the unborn child is not expelled by that time, the process is stopped. The child is allowed to live on – to await normal delivery later.

Here I would stop for a moment to point out that the first stage (done by the doctor) does nothing to terminate the pregnancy. The insertion of the catheter is only a preparatory act. It is the second stage (done by the nurses) which terminates the pregnancy. There is an agreed statement of fact which shows that the causative factor is the administration of prostaglandin. This is the way in which it is put:

> It will be appreciated that in the medical induction process the causative factor in inducing the labour and hence the termination of pregnancy is the effect of the administration of prostaglandin and/or oxytocin and not any mechanical effect from the insertion of the catheter or cannula. In that the nurse does, on the instructions of the doctor, commence or augment the flow of prostaglandin or oxytocin, and even sometimes effect the connection between the already inserted catheter and the prostin pump and the already intravenous cannula and the oxytocin infusion, her role in the process does include acts which have, and are intended to have, an abortifacient effect.

To take a parallel from the removal of an appendix, the anaesthetist makes all the preparations, but the removal is done by the surgeon himself. So here, the doctor makes the preparations – inserting the catheter – but the pregnancy is terminated by the act – the continuous act – done by the nurses, from the moment that they start the pump or the drip to the moment the baby is expelled.

The Royal College objection

I can quite understand that many nurses dislike having anything to do with these abortions. It is a soul-destroying task. The nurses are young women who are dedicated by their profession and training to do all they can to preserve life. Yet here they are called upon to destroy it. It is true that the statute gives them an escape clause. They can refuse to participate in any treatment to which they have a 'conscientious objection': see s 4 of the Act of 1967. But the Report of the Committee on the Working of the Abortion Act (1974) (Cmnd 5579), the Lane Report, shows that *many nurses do not take advantage of this 'escape clause'. Because it means that other nurses will have to do this heart-rending task. And they feel it may be held against them by their superiors. So they take part in it – much against their will,* see para 321–74 of the Lane Report.

It is against this background that the Royal College of Nursing ask the question: is it lawful for nurses to be called upon to terminate pregnancy in this way? The Royal College says 'No. It is not lawful. It is not a nurse's job to terminate a pregnancy.' The Department of Health say 'Yes. It is lawful.' They have issued a circular in which they presume to lay down the law for the whole of the medical profession. They say that it is no offence if the pregnancy is terminated by a suitably qualified person in accordance with the written instructions of a registered medical practitioner. This is the wording of the circular:

> However, the Secretary of State is advised that the termination can properly be said to have been termination by the registered medical practitioner provided it is decided upon by him, initiated by him, and that he remains throughout responsible for its overall conduct and control in the sense that any actions needed to bring it to conclusion are done by appropriately skilled staff acting on his specific instructions but *not necessarily in his presence*.

Note those words 'not necessarily in his presence'. They are crucial.

The interpretation of the Abortion Act 1967

The lawfulness depends on the true interpretation of the statute: but, before going into it, I would say a word or two about the approach to it.

(i) Abortion is a subject on which many people feel strongly. In both directions. Many are for it. Many against it. Some object to it as the destruction of life. Others favour it as the right of the woman. Emotions run so high on both sides that I feel that we as judges must go by the very words of the statute – without stretching it one way or the other – and writing nothing in which is not there.

(ii) Another thing to remember is that the statute is directed to the medical profession – to the doctors and nurses who have to implement it. It is they who have to read it and to act upon it. They will read it – not as lawyers – but as laymen. So we should interpret it as they would.

(iii) If there should ever be a case in the courts, the decision would ultimately be that of a jury. Suppose that during the process the mother died or became seriously ill – owing to the nurse's negligence in administering the wrong chemical fluid – and the nurse was prosecuted under the Offences against the Person Act 1861 for unlawfully administering her a noxious thing or using other means with intent to procure her miscarriage. The nurse would have no defence unless the pregnancy was 'terminated by a registered medical practitioner'. Those are simple English words which should be left to a jury to apply – without the judge attempting to put his own gloss upon them: see *Cozens v Brutus* [1973] AC 861. I should expect the jury to say that the pregnancy was not terminated by a registered medical practitioner, but by a nurse.

(iv) If in such as case there were a claim for damages, the nurse might not be covered by insurance because she would not be engaged in 'nursing professional services accepted by the Royal College of Nursing'.

(v) Statutes can be divided into two categories. In the first category Parliament has expressly said 'by a registered medical practitioner or by a person acting in accordance with the directions of any such practitioner,' or words to that effect: see the Radioactive Substances Act 1948, s 3(1)(a); Therapeutic Substances Act 1956, s 9(1)(a); Drugs (Prevention of Misuse) Act 1964, s 1(2)(g); Medicines Act 1968, s 58(2)(b); Tattooing of Minors Act 1969, s 1. In the second category Parliament has deliberately confined it, 'by a fully registered medical practitioner', omitting any such words as 'or by his direction': see the Human Tissues Act 1961, s 1(4). This statute is in the second category.

Woolf J tested the statute by supposing that a registered medical practitioner performed an abortion operation upon a woman whom he believed to be pregnant but who was not so in fact. The Act of 1967 would give him no defence to a charge under the Act of 1861. That is such a fanciful instance that I do not think it throws any light on the true construction of this statute.

(vi) The Solicitor-General emphasised the word 'treatment' in ss 1(3), 3(1)(a) and (c) and 4(1). He suggested that s 1(1) should be read as if it said that a person should not be guilty of an offence 'when the treatment (for termination of a pregnancy) is by a registered medical practitioner'. He submitted that whenever the registered medical practitioner did what the Department of Health advised it satisfied the statute, because the treatment, being initiated by him and done under his instructions, was 'by' him. I cannot accept this interpretation. I think the word 'treatment' in those sections means 'the actual act of terminating the pregnancy'. When the medical induction method is used, this means the continuous act of administering prostaglandin from the moment it is started until the unborn child is expelled from the mother's body. This continuous act must be done by the doctor personally. It is not sufficient that it is done by a nurse when he is not present.

Conclusion

Stress was laid by the Solicitor-General on the effect of this ruling. The process of medical induction can take from 18 to 30 hours. No doctor can be expected to be present all that time. He must leave it to the nurses: or not use the method at all. If he is not allowed to leave it to the nurses, the result will be either that there will be fewer abortions or that the doctor will have to use the surgical method with its extra hazards. This may be so. But I do not think this warrants us departing from the statute. The Royal College of Nursing have advised their nurses that under the statute they should not themselves terminate a pregnancy. *If the doctor advises it, he should do it himself, and not call upon the nurses to do it.*

I think that the Royal College are quite right. If the Department of Health want the nurses to terminate a pregnancy, the Minister should go to Parliament and get the statute altered. He should ask them to amend it by adding the words 'or by a suitably qualified person in accordance with the written instructions of a registered medical practitioner'. I doubt whether Parliament would accept the amendment. It is too controversial. At any rate, that is the way to amend the law: and not by means of a departmental circular.

Brightman LJ: ... There was discussion as to whether s 1 of the Act should receive a broad construction or a narrow construction. Emphasis was placed on the fact that the section only exempts from criminality an occasion when a pregnancy 'is terminated', and therefore would not exempt from criminality the 2% of cases where an abortion is attempted but fails; or the case where an abortion is attempted but no pregnancy is terminated because it turns out, as may happen, that the woman is not pregnant. It was pointed out that although the opening words of s 1 use the formula 'a pregnancy is terminated', sub-s (3), as also s 3(1)(a), refer to 'the treatment' for termination of the pregnancy, and s 4(1) refers to 'treatment authorised by this Act'. Such a construction does not in my opinion involve adding any words at all to the statute. I think it is what the section means on its true construction in the context in which the words are found. It is a construction which removes the apparent absurdity which would arise if, for example, the operation did not succeed in terminating the pregnancy; or if the woman proved not to be with child; or if the operation were carried out under the constant, immediate and whole time supervision of the doctor who allowed a nurse to do some of the 'mechanical' acts in his presence and under his immediate eye.

Having attempted to construe the Act, I hope correctly, I must apply such construction to the facts supposed in Annex B on the basis of 'maximum nurse participation'. It will be recalled that in the case supposed the doctor inserts the catheter into the womb and also inserts the cannula into the vein but is then free to leave, and does leave, the operating theatre or ward before any infusions are administered, and he does not necessarily return unless specifically recalled. In my opinion it would be a misuse of language to describe such a termination of a pregnancy as done 'by' a registered medical practitioner; or to describe such a treatment for termination of a pregnancy as 'carried out by' a registered medical practitioner – however detailed and precise the written instructions given by the registered medical practitioner to the nurse. It would not be far removed from the nurse carrying out the operation from detailed instructions in a text book. The true analysis is that the doctor has provided the nurse with the means to terminate the pregnancy, not that the doctor has terminated the pregnancy.

Sir George Baker: ... In my opinion there is nothing in the Act or Regulations to indicate that the intention of Parliament was other than that clearly expressed in the simple words 'when a pregnancy is terminated by a registered medical practitioner'. They are words which have to be understood by ordinary mortals in legislation on a topic which can arouse great emotions: see *Paton v British Pregnancy Advisory Services Trustees* [1979] QB 276, 278. Maybe Parliament never had in mind abortions by medical induction which, as the Ministry letter indicates, has been employed in the past 10 years; maybe a decision that it can be done only by a registered medical practitioner and not by a nurse on doctor's orders in any causative respect will result in a safe and easy method being less used with consequent hardship or even greater danger to pregnant women, I do not know. Even if so, it is not for judges 'to read words into an Act of Parliament unless clear reason for it is to be found within the four corners of the Act itself,' *per* Lord Loreburn LC in *Vickers, Sons & Maxim Ltd v Evans* [1910] AC 444, 445, cited by Viscount Dilhorne in *Stock v Frank Jones (Tipton) Ltd* [1978] 1 WLR 231, 235A. Nor is a judge entitled to read an Act differently from what it says simply because he thinks Parliament would have so provided had the situation been envisaged at that time. In the words of Lord Simon of Glaisdale in *Stock's* case, at p 237: '... in a society living under the rule of law citizens are entitled to regulate their conduct according to what a statute has said, rather than by what it was meant to say or by what it would have otherwise said if a newly considered situation had been envisaged ...'

There is no manifest absurdity; on the contrary the provision is clear and understandable. If the intention had been to make lawful the acts of persons participating in or carrying out the termination of a pregnancy on doctors' orders that could have been expressly stated either as the department suggest the section should be read, or by some other appropriate words. The Abortion Act 1967 requires the termination to be by the operative acts of the registered medical practitioner himself; his orders are not enough. I, too, would allow the appeal.

— · — · — · — · — · — · — · — · — · — · — · — · — · — · — · — · —

The majority in the House of Lords adopted a different interpretation of the statute.

Lord Wilberforce: ... In interpreting an Act of Parliament it is proper, and indeed necessary, to have regard to the state of affairs existing, and known by Parliament to be existing, at the time. It is a fair presumption that Parliament's policy or intention is directed to that state of affairs. Leaving aside cases of omission by inadvertence, this being not such a case, when a new state of affairs, or a fresh set of facts bearing on policy, comes into existence, the courts have to consider whether they fall within the Parliamentary intention. They may be held to do so, if they fall within the same genus of facts as those to which the expressed policy has been formulated. They may also be held to do so if there can be detected a clear purpose in the legislation which can only be fulfilled if the extension is made. How liberally these principles may be applied must depend upon the nature of the enactment, and the strictness or otherwise of the words in which it has been expressed. The courts should be less willing to extend expressed meanings if it is clear that the Act in question was designed to be restrictive or circumscribed in its operation rather than liberal or permissive. They will be much less willing to do so where the subject-matter is different in kind or dimension from that for which the legislation was passed. In any event there is one course which the courts cannot take, under the law of this country; they cannot fill gaps; they cannot by asking the question 'What would Parliament have done in this current case – not being one in contemplation – if the facts had been before it?' attempt themselves to supply the answer, if the answer is not to be found in the terms of the Act itself.

In my opinion this Act should be construed with caution. It is dealing with a controversial subject involving moral and social judgments on which opinions strongly differ. It is, if ever an Act was, one for interpreting in the spirit that only that which Parliament has authorised on a fair reading of the relevant sections should be held to be within it. The new (post-1967) method of medical induction is clearly not just a fresh species or example of something already authorised. The Act is not for 'purposive' or 'liberal' or 'equitable' construction. This is a case where the courts must hold that anything beyond the legislature's fairly expressed authority should be left for Parliament's fresh consideration.

Lord Diplock: ...The Abortion Act 1967 which it falls to this House to construe is described in its long title as 'An Act to amend and clarify the law relating to termination of pregnancy by registered medical practitioners' ... Whatever may be the technical imperfections of its draftsmanship, however, its purpose in my view becomes clear if one starts by considering what was the state of the law relating to abortion before the passing of the Act, what was the mischief that required amendment, and in what respect was the existing law unclear ... My Lords, the wording and structure of the section are far from elegant, but the policy of the Act, it seems to me, is clear. There are two aspects to it: the first is to broaden the grounds upon which abortions may be lawfully obtained; the second is to ensure that the abortion is carried out with all proper skill and in hygienic conditions ... I have spoken of the requirements of the Act as to the way in which 'treatment for the termination of the pregnancy' is to be carried out rather than using the word 'termination' or 'terminated' by itself, for the draftsman appears to use the longer and the shorter expressions indiscriminately, as is shown by a comparison between sub-ss (1) and (3) of s 1, and by the reference in the conscience clause to 'treatment authorised by this Act.' Furthermore if 'termination' or 'terminated' meant only the event of miscarriage and not the whole treatment undertaken with that object in mind, lack of success, which apparently occurs in 1–2% of cases, would make all who had taken part in the unsuccessful treatment guilty of an offence under s 58 or 59 of the Offences against the Person Act 1861. This cannot have been the intention of Parliament.

The requirement of the Act as to the way in which the treatment is to be carried out, which in my view throws most light upon the second aspect of its policy and the true construction of the phrase in subsection (1) of section 1 which lies at the root of the dispute between the parties to this appeal, is the requirement in subsection (3) that, except in cases of dire emergency, the treatment must be carried out in a National Health Service hospital (or private clinic specially approved for that purpose by the minister). It is in my view evident that in providing that treatment for termination of pregnancies should take place in ordinary hospitals, Parliament contemplated that (conscientious objections apart) like other hospital treatment, it would be undertaken as a team effort in which, acting on the instructions of the doctor in charge of the treatment, junior doctors, nurses, para-medical and other members of the hospital staff would each do those things forming part of the whole treatment, which it would be in accordance with accepted medical practice to entrust to a member of the staff possessed of their respective qualifications and experience.

Subsection (1) although it is expressed to apply only 'when a pregnancy is terminated by a registered medical practitioner' (the subordinate clause that although introduced by 'when' is another protasis and has caused the differences of judicial opinion in the instant case) also appears to contemplate treatment that is in the nature of a team effort and to extend its protection to all those who play a part in it. The exoneration from guilt is not confined to the registered medical practitioner by whom a pregnancy is terminated, it extends to any person who takes part in the treatment for its termination.

What limitation on this exoneration is imposed by the qualifying phrase: 'when a pregnancy is terminated by a registered medical practitioner'? In my opinion in the context of the Act, what it requires is that a registered medical practitioner, whom I will refer to as a doctor, should accept responsibility for all stages of the treatment for the termination of the pregnancy. The particular method to be used should be decided by the doctor in charge of the treatment for termination of the pregnancy; he should carry out any physical acts, forming part of the treatment, that in accordance with accepted medical practice are done only by qualified medical practitioners, and should give specific instructions as to the carrying out of such parts of the treatment as in accordance with accepted medical practice are carried out by nurses or other members of the hospital staff without medical qualifications. To each of them, the doctor, or his substitute, should be available to be consulted or called on for assistance from beginning to end of the treatment. In other words, the doctor need not do everything with his own hands; the requirements of the subsection are satisfied when the treatment for termination of a pregnancy is one prescribed by a registered medical practitioner carried out in accordance with his directions and of which a registered medical practitioner remains in charge throughout.

Lord Edmund-Davies: ... My Lords, the opening words of s 1(1) are clear and simple, clear to understand and simple to apply to the only abortive methods professionally accepted in 1967 when the Act was passed. Save in grave emergency, only a qualified doctor or surgeon could then lawfully perform the orthodox surgical acts, and the statute could have had no other person in mind. Then should s 1 be interpreted differently now that abortive methods undreamt of in 1967 have since been discovered and become widely applied? The answer must be that its simple words must not be distorted in order to bring under the statutory umbrella medical procedures to which they cannot properly be applied however desirable such an extension may be thought to be ... In my judgment, it is impossible to regard an abortion resulting from such procedure as one 'terminated by a registered medical practitioner', for the acts indispensable to termination are in many such cases performed not by the doctor but by the nurses over a long period of hours after the doctor last saw the pregnant woman. And, despite the claims of the Solicitor-General that he sought simply to give the statutory words 'their plain and ordinary meaning', he substantially departed from that approach by submitting that they should be read as meaning 'terminated by treatment for the termination of pregnancy carried out by a registered medical practitioner in accordance with recognised medical practice'. My Lords, this is redrafting with a vengeance ... My Lords, at the end of the day the appellants were driven to rely on a submission that, were s 1(1) given its literal meaning, such absurd consequences would follow that a liberal construction is unavoidable if the Act of 1967 is to serve a useful purpose. In the foreground was the submission that, were a termination of pregnancy embarked upon when (as it turned out) the woman was not pregnant, the Act would afford no defence to a doctor prosecuted under the Act of 1861. And it was secondly urged that he would be equally defenceless even where he personally treated a pregnant woman throughout if, for some reason, the procedure was interrupted and the pregnancy not terminated. I have respectfully to say that in my judgment it is these objections which are themselves absurd ... there is no reason for not giving the specific words of s 1 of the Act their plain and ordinary meaning. Doing just that, the prostaglandin treatment presently adopted requires the nursing staff to participate unlawfully in procedures necessitating their personally performing over a period of several hours a series of acts calculated to bring about a termination of pregnancy. This they cannot lawfully do ... If it is sought to render such medical induction lawful, the task must be performed by Parliament. But under the present law it is a registered medical practitioner who must terminate pregnancy.

Lord Keith of Kinkel: ... In my opinion this argument involves placing an unduly restricted and unintended meaning on the words 'when a pregnancy is terminated'. It seems to me that these words, in their context, are not referring to the mere physical occurrence of termination. The sidenote to s 1 is 'Medical termination of pregnancy'. 'Termination of pregnancy' is an expression commonly used, perhaps rather more by medical people than by laymen, to describe in neutral and unemotive terms the bringing about of an abortion. So used, it is capable of covering the whole process designed to lead to that result, and in my view it does so in the present context ... This conclusion is the more satisfactory as it appears to me to be fully in accordance with that part of the policy and purpose of the Act which was directed to securing that socially acceptable abortions should be carried out under the safest conditions attainable.

Lord Roskill: ... My Lords, the long title of the Abortion Act 1967 is 'An Act to amend and clarify the law relating to the termination of pregnancy by registered medical practitioners'. The respondents accepted before your Lordships' House that the Act of 1967 had a social purpose, namely the making of abortions available more freely and without infringement of the criminal law but subject always to the conditions of that Act being satisfied ... My Lords, I have read and re-read the Act of 1967 to see if I can discern in its provisions any consistent pattern in the use of the phrase 'a pregnancy is terminated' or 'termination of a pregnancy' on the one hand and 'treatment for the termination of a pregnancy' on the other hand. One finds the former phrase in s 1(1) and (1)(a), the latter in s 1(3), the former in s 1(4), the latter in s 2(1)(b), and again in s 3(1)(a) and (c). Most important to my mind is s 4 which is the conscientious objection section. This section in two places refers to 'participate in treatment' in the context of conscientious objection. If one construes s 4 in conjunction with s 1(1), as surely one should do in order to determine to what it is that conscientious objection is permitted, it seems to me that s 4 strongly supports the wider construction of s 1(1). It was suggested that acceptance of the appellants' submission involved re-writing that subsection so as to add words which are not to be found in the language of the subsection. My Lords, with great respect to that submission, I do not agree. If one construes the words 'when a pregnancy is terminated by a registered medical practitioner' in s 1(1) as embracing the case where the 'treatment for the termination of a pregnancy is carried out under the control of a doctor in accordance with ordinary current medical practice' I think one is reading 'termination of pregnancy' and 'treatment for termination of pregnancy' as virtually synonymous and as I think Parliament must have intended they should be read. Such a construction avoids a number of anomalies as, for example, where there is no pregnancy or where the extra-amniotic process fails to achieve its objective within the normal limits of time set for its operation. This is, I think, the view which appealed to Woolf J and to Brightman LJ and I find myself in respectful agreement with that view. But with respect I am unable to share the learned Lord Justice's view on the facts. I think that the successive steps taken by a nurse in carrying out the extra-amniotic process are fully protected provided that the entirety of the treatment for the termination of the pregnancy and her participation in it is at all times under the control of the doctor even though the doctor is not present throughout the entirety of the treatment.

My Lords, I have reached this conclusion simply as a matter of construction of the 1967 Act.

Questions

- Consider the highlighted passages in Lord Denning's judgment. Is this really the language of disinterested judicial interpretation?
- Which judges restrict themselves to a literal interpretation of the statute and which adopt a purposive approach and more importantly why do they differ?
- Is 'treatment for termination' synonymous with 'the act of termination' and why is any distinction important in interpreting the section?

  Section 58 of the Offences Against the Person Act provides:

  '... whosoever, with intent to procure the miscarriage of any woman, whether she be or be not with child, shall unlawfully administer to her or cause to be taken by her any poison or other noxious thing, or shall unlawfully use any instrument or other means whatsoever with like intent, shall be guilty of felony ...'

- Does a literal interpretation of s 1(1) of the Abortion Act provide an exception to this offence if:

  (i) the woman in question is pregnant?

  (ii) the woman in question is not pregnant?

- Did Lord Roskill reach his conclusion 'simply as a matter of construction of the 1967 Act'? Did any of the judges?

AG's Ref (No 1 of 1988) [1989] 2 All ER 1

This is of interest not just as an example of the use of s 36 of the Criminal Justice Act 1972 but it also shows the courts interpreting and differing over the interpretation of a common word within a statute.

The appellant contemplated making a take over offer for a publicly quoted company and had discussions with the company's merchant bankers. Shortly afterwards, the company's chairman agreed to the company being taken over by another company. The merchant bankers informed the appellant of the proposed take-over and told him that a public announcement would be made shortly but that until then the information was sensitive and highly confidential. The appellant promptly purchased 6,000 shares in the company and, following the announcement of the take over, made a substantial profit. He was charged with two offences of dealing in the securities of a company as a prohibited person, contrary to s 1(3) and (4)(a) of the Company Securities (Insider Dealing) Act 1985 (subsequently replaced by Criminal Justice Act 1993, Pt V). The trial judge directed the jury to acquit the appellant on the ground that there was no evidence that he had 'obtained' the information, for the purposes of s 1(3), since it had been given to him unsolicited. The Attorney General then referred to the Court of Appeal for its opinion the question of the meaning of 'obtained' in s 1(3) of the 1985 Act. The Court of Appeal held that a person obtained information for the purposes of s 1(3) and (4)(a) of the 1985 Act, even if he came by it without any positive action on his part. On the appellant's application the Court of Appeal referred the point to the House of Lords.

> **Lord Lowry**: My Lords, this appeal is concerned with the meaning of the word 'obtained' in s 1(3) of the Company Securities (Insider Dealing) Act 1985, which, with sub-s (4)(a), provides:
>
> > (3) The next subsection applies where – (a) an individual has information which he knowingly obtained (directly or indirectly) from another individual who – (i) is connected with a particular company, or was at any time in the six months preceding the obtaining of the information so connected, and (ii) the former individual knows or has reasonable cause to believe held the information by virtue of being so connected, and (b) the former individual knows or has reasonable cause to believe that, because of the latter's connection and position, it would be reasonable to expect him not to disclose the information except for proper performance of the functions attaching to that position.
> >
> > (4) Subject to section 3, the former individual in that case – (a) shall not himself deal on a recognised stock exchange in securities of that company if he knows that the information is unpublished price sensitive information in relation to those securities ...
>
> ... The answer depends on the meaning in context of the word 'obtained'. The first meaning in the *Oxford English Dictionary* is:
>
> > To come into the possession or enjoyment of (something) by one's own effort, or by request to procure or gain, as the result of purpose and effort: hence, generally, to acquire, get.
>
> The primary meaning of 'obtain', which stems from the Latin, is consistent, and consistent only, with the appellant's case but the words following the colon and commencing 'hence, generally' clearly denote a general meaning derived from the primary meaning: the words 'acquire' and 'get', unaccompanied by any adverb or adverbial phrase, are wide enough to cover both the primary meaning and the secondary meaning of coming into possession of a thing without effort on one's own part ... The next step is to decide whether Parliament must have intended the

word 'obtained' to convey and include its secondary or general meaning. If so, the offence is made out; if, however, one cannot be satisfied of that, then the ambiguity remains and ... compels your Lordships to adopt the primary or narrow meaning.

The following points assist the Crown.

(1) The offence is dealing on a stock exchange in securities of a company in defined circumstances. It can be committed by a primary insider or by a secondary insider who has knowingly obtained information (directly or indirectly) from a primary insider. Whether the secondary insider solicited the information or merely received it does not increase or diminish the undesirability of his making use of it or the ultimate effect on the other party to his dealing.

(2) It is permissible to look at circumstances preceding the legislation in order to see what was considered to be the mischief in need of a remedy: see *Black-Clawson International Ltd v Papierwerke Waldhof-Aschaffenburg AG* [1975] 1 All ER 810 at 814, 842–45, [1975] AC 591 at 614, 645–58 *per* Lord Reid and Lord Simon. I draw attention to para 22 of the White Paper entitled *The Conduct of Company Directors* (Cmnd 7037 (1977)):

'Insider dealing is understood broadly to cover situations where a person buys or sells securities when he, but not the other party to the transaction, is in possession of confidential information which affects the value to be placed on those securities. Furthermore the confidential information in question will generally be in his possession because of some connection which he has with the company whose securities are to be dealt in (eg he may be a director, employee or professional adviser of that company) or because someone in such a position has provided him, directly or indirectly, with the information. Public confidence in directors and others closely associated with companies requires that such people should not use insider information to further their own interests. Furthermore, if they were to do so, they would frequently be in breach of their obligations to the companies, and could be held to be taking an unfair advantage of the people with whom they were dealing.'

This tends to show that the mischief consists of dealing in securities while in possession of the confidential information. The words above, 'because someone ... has provided him, directly or indirectly, with the information', cannot of course be used as a guide to the meaning of the word 'obtained' in the legislation which followed, but they look to the possession of the crucial information and not to the method of its acquisition. The same White Paper, having dealt with the position of primary insiders, goes on to say in para 28: 'However, in addition to the specific list of persons who are to be treated as insiders, the Government proposes that anyone who receives information which he knows to be price sensitive and not generally available and which he realises has come directly or indirectly from an insider should also refrain from dealing.'

The majority view and, as I accept, the preferable view in the *Black-Clawson* case was that an observation like this cannot be used as a guide to the meaning of the word 'obtained' in the subsequent legislation, but para 28 still confirms that the use of sensitive information by a secondary insider was regarded as one of the evils to be dealt with. (A further White Paper, *Changes in Company Law* (Cmnd 7291 (1978)), incorporated a draft Bill. This was the basis for sections of the Companies Act 1980 which were consolidated in the 1985 Act.)

(3) A primary insider is forbidden to use any information of the specified description. One may properly ask why a secondary insider should be prohibited only from using part of the information which may come to his hands, namely that which he has procured by his own efforts: the procurement is not the guilty act. In this connection, ss 1(8), 2(1)(a) and 5(1) are worthy of consideration.

(4) The object of the legislation must be partially defeated if the narrow meaning of 'obtained' is adopted.

(5) That meaning would create a need to make fine distinctions, which will not arise if the wider meaning prevails.

At first I thought that the word 'knowingly' might further support the Crown's interpretation, but I accept as correct the explanation of counsel for the appellant that its use in ss 1(3)(a) and 2(1)(a) denotes that, to be guilty, the user of the confidential information has to know from whom he has obtained it.

Against these points the appellant advanced arguments which it is necessary to take account of before reaching a conclusion. They were as follows.

(1) 'Obtain' is used in its primary sense in the statutory provisions which were considered in cases like *Fisher v Raven* [1963] 2 All ER 389, [1964] AC 210 and *R v Hayat* (1976) 63 Cr App R 181 and also in s 15 of the Theft Act 1968. It is easy to see why this is so, because the examples given can only arise from situations in which the active procurement of a thing constitutes the guilty act. More potent, though less specific, is counsel's observation that, whenever a criminal statute uses the word 'obtain', it uses that word in the primary sense. The reason for this, however, is not hard to understand.

(2) Relying on what he called a family relationship between the 1985 Act and the Insolvency Act 1986, counsel pointed to the word 'obtains' used in its primary meaning in s 360 of the 1986 Act which, as s 155 of the Bankruptcy Act 1914, was considered in *Fisher v Raven* [1963] 2 All ER 389, [1964] AC 210. But the words 'obtains' and 'obtained' are used in different contexts with a difference, I would suggest, in meaning which the 'relationship' is powerless to annul.

(3) By reference to Lord Diplock's test in *Black-Clawson*'s case [1975] 1 All ER 810 at 836, [1975] AC 591 at 638 of 'what the words of the statute would be reasonably understood to mean by those whose conduct it regulates', it was suggested that someone in the position of a secondary insider would (particularly if he consulted a dictionary) feel safe in using confidential information which he had acquired unsolicited from the forbidden source. With respect, I feel that it could as easily be asserted that someone in that position would feel far from safe, particularly if his dictionary contained the words 'hence, generally, to acquire, get'.

(4) It was further submitted that words ought to be given their natural and ordinary meaning, and *Spillers Ltd v Cardiff (Borough) Assessment Committee* [1931] 2 KB 21, [1931] All ER 524 was strongly relied on for the proposition that words must be construed in their ordinary and proper sense and not in their loose sense. But ... in this case the choice is between the primary meaning and the secondary but correct and acceptable meaning ...

(6) Finally, by reference to the change of wording from 'information which ... he holds' in s 1(1) and (2) to 'information which he knowingly obtained' in s 1(3),

it has been submitted that, unless the word 'obtained' connotes effort on the part of the individual concerned, it adds nothing to the requirement of having or holding information which applies in the case of the earlier subsections. I cannot accept this reasoning the addition of the relative clause ('which he knowingly obtained' etc) in s 1(3) is due to the need to describe the forbidden source from which a secondary insider must have obtained the information. The grammatical construction of s 1(3)(a) is equally consistent with both meanings of the word 'obtained'. Therefore this argument does not help the appellant.

Having carefully weighed the points on either side, and not forgetting that we are dealing with a penal statute, I am, in the words of Lord Reid in *DPP v Ottewell* [1968] 3 All ER 153 at 157, [1970] AC 642 at 649, satisfied that the wider meaning is the meaning which Parliament must have intended the word 'obtained' to have in this Act and that, accordingly, there is no room for the kind of ambiguity on which the appellant has attempted to rely. Therefore I would answer the questions posed by the reference in the same way as the Court of Appeal.

Lord Templeman: ... The argument is that, according to the dictionary, information is not 'obtained' if the information is volunteered. The object of the 1985 Act was to prevent insider dealing. The appellant became an insider when he learnt of the take-over agreement and he became an insider dealer when he bought 6,000 shares. Parliament cannot have intended that a man who asks for information which he then misuses should be convicted of an offence while a man who, without asking, learns the same information which he also misuses should be acquitted ... My Lords, without troubling any dictionary, I am satisfied that the appellant obtained information which he made no effort to obtain and that his subsequent misuse of that information was in breach of the 1985 Act.

Questions

- Compare the approaches of Lords Lowry and Templeman. Which rule of interpretation did Lord Lowry use and what sources did he rely on to determine the meaning of 'obtain'?
- Was reference to a dictionary necessary to reach the conclusion?
- In *Davis v Johnson*, Lord Denning, apparently without irony, delivered the following clear statement of the literal approach to statutory interpretation:

'... when the words of the statute are plain, then it is not open to any decision of any court to contradict the statute; because the statute is the final authority on what the law is. No court can depart from the plain words of a statute'.

Consider the assumptions that such a claim makes.

Aids to construction

In addition to the three main rules of interpretation there are a number of secondary aids to construction. These can be categorised as either intrinsic or extrinsic in nature.

- Intrinsic assistance is derived from the statute which is the object of interpretation; the judge using the full statute to understand the meaning of a particular part of it.

- Extrinsic assistance, that is, reference to sources outside the Act itself, may, on occasion, be resorted to in determining the meaning of legislation; but which sources? Some external sources are unproblematic. For example, judges have always been entitled to refer to dictionaries in order to find the meaning of non-legal words (see *AG's Reference (No 1 of 1988)* above). They also have been able to look into textbooks for guidance in relation to particular points of law; and, in using the mischief rule, they have been able to refer to earlier statutes to determine the precise mischief at which the statute they are trying to construe is aimed.

The historically restrictive approach has been gradually relaxed to the extent that judges were allowed to use extrinsic sources to determine the mischief at which particular legislation was aimed, and in *Pepper v Hart* the House of Lords decided to overturn the previous exclusionary rule. In a majority decision, it was held that, where the precise meaning of legislation was uncertain or ambiguous or where the literal meaning of an Act would lead to a manifest absurdity, the courts could refer to *Hansard*'s reports of Parliamentary debates and proceedings as an aid to construing the meaning of the legislation.

Pepper (Inspector of Taxes) v Hart [1992] 3 WLR 1032

On appeal by taxpayers, the Appellate Committee having heard the appeal but before judgment referred it to an enlarged Appellate Committee to determine the question whether the existing exclusionary rule relating to the construction of statutes should be relaxed so as to enable *Hansard* to be consulted as an aid to construction.

Allowing the appeal, the majority, Lord Mackay dissenting, held that, subject to any question of Parliamentary privilege, the rule excluding reference to Parliamentary material as an aid to statutory construction should be relaxed so as to permit such reference where: (a) legislation was ambiguous or obscure or led to absurdity; (b) the material relied upon consisted of one or more statements by a minister or other promoter of the Bill together, if necessary, with such other Parliamentary material as was necessary to understand such statements and their effect; and (c) the statements relied upon were clear.

Lord Mackay: ... Much wider issues than the construction of the Finance Act 1976 have been raised in these appeals and for the first time this House has been asked to consider a detailed argument upon the extent to which reference can properly be made before a court of law in the United Kingdom to proceedings in Parliament recorded in *Hansard*.

For the appellant Mr Lester submits that it should now be appropriate for the courts to look at *Hansard* in order to ascertain the intention of the legislators as expressed in the proceedings on the Bill which has then been enacted in the statutory words requiring to be construed. This submission appears to me to suggest a way of making more effective proceedings in Parliament by allowing the court to consider what has been said in Parliament as an aid to resolving an ambiguity which may well have become apparent only as a result of the attempt to apply the enacted words to a particular case. It does not seem to me that this can involve any impeachment, or questioning of the freedom of speech and debates or proceedings in Parliament, accordingly I do not see how such a use of *Hansard* can possibly be thought to infringe Article 9 of the Bill of Rights and I agree with my noble and learned friend's more detailed consideration of that matter.

The principal difficulty I have on this aspect of the case is that in Mr Lester's submission reference to Parliamentary material as an aid to interpretation of a statutory provision should be allowed only with leave of the court and where the court is satisfied that such a reference is justifiable: (a) to confirm the meaning of a provision as conveyed by the text, its object and purpose; (b) to determine a meaning where the provision is ambiguous or obscure; or (c) to determine the meaning where the ordinary meaning is manifestly absurd or unreasonable. I believe that practically every question of statutory construction that comes before the courts will involve an argument that the case falls under one or more of these three heads. It follows that the parties' legal advisors will require to study *Hansard* in practically every such case to see whether or not there is any help to be gained from it. I believe this is an objection of real substance. It is a practical objection not one of principle ... Such an approach appears to me to involve the possibility at least of an immense increase in the cost of litigation in which statutory construction is involved. It is of course easy to overestimate such cost but it is I fear equally easy to underestimate ... Your Lordships are well aware that the costs of litigation are a subject of general public concern and I personally would not wish to be a party to changing a well established rule which could have a substantial effect in increasing these costs against the advice of the Law Commissions and the Renton Committee unless and until a new inquiry demonstrated that that advice was no longer valid ... Reference to proceedings in Parliament has already been allowed in *Pickstone v Freemans Plc* [1989] AC 66 without, I think, any argument upon whether or not it was permissible for, ascertaining the purpose of subordinate legislation and also in other cases for ascertaining the purpose for which a power to make subordinate legislation was used. I believe that such statements are likely to be readily identified in Parliamentary proceedings and the cases in which they are relevant will be determined by the nature of the subject-matter. Allowing reference to *Hansard* in such cases does not have the large practical consequences to which I have referred. If reference to Parliamentary material is permitted as an aid to the construction of legislation which is ambiguous, or obscure or the literal meaning of which leads to an absurdity, I believe as I have said that in practically every case it will be incumbent on those preparing the argument to examine the whole proceedings on the Bill in question in both Houses of Parliament. Questions of construction may be involved on what is said in Parliament and I cannot see how if the rule is modified in this way the parties' legal advisers could properly come to court without having looked to see whether there was anything in the *Hansard* Report on the Bill which could assist their case. If they found a passage which they thought had a bearing on the issue in this case, that passage would have to be construed in the light of the proceedings as a whole.

Lord Browne-Wilkinson delivered the leading judgment in the majority.

Lord Browne-Wilkinson: Should the rule prohibiting references to Parliamentary material be relaxed?

Under present law, there is a general rule that references to Parliamentary material as an aid to statutory construction is not permissible ('the exclusionary rule') ... This rule has now been relaxed so as to permit reports of commissioners, including law commissioners, and white papers to be looked at for the purpose solely of ascertaining the mischief which the statute is intended to cure but not for the purpose of discovering the meaning of the words used by Parliament to effect such cure ... Although courts' attitude to reports leading to legislation has varied, until recently there was no modern case in which the court had looked at parliamentary debates as an aid to construction. However, in *Pickstone v Freemans Plc* [1989] AC 66 this House, in construing a statutory instrument, did have regard to what was said by the Minister who initiated the debate on the regulations ...

Mr Lester, for the taxpayers, did not urge us to abandon the exclusionary rule completely. His submission was that where the words of a statute were ambiguous or obscure or were capable of giving rise to an absurd conclusion it should be legitimate to look at the Parliamentary history, including the debates in Parliament, for the purpose of identifying the intention of Parliament in using the words it did use. He accepted that the function of the court was to construe the actual words enacted by Parliament so that in no circumstances could the court attach to words a meaning that they were incapable of bearing. He further accepted that the court should only attach importance to clear statements showing the intention of the promoter of the Bill, whether a minister or private member: there could be no dredging through conflicting statements of intention with a view to discovering the true intention of Parliament in using the statutory words ...

The reasons put forward for the present rule are first, that it preserves the constitutional proprieties leaving Parliament to legislate in words and the courts (not Parliamentary speakers) to construe the meaning of the words finally enacted; second, the practical difficulty of the expense of researching Parliamentary material which would arise if the material could be looked at; third, the need for the citizen to have access to a known defined text which regulates his legal rights; fourth, the improbability of finding helpful guidance from *Hansard*. The Law Commissions of England and Scotland in their joint Report on the Interpretation of Statutes in 1969 and the Renton Committee on the Preparation of Legislation both recognised that there was much to be said in principle for relaxing the rule but advised against a relaxation at present on the same practical grounds as are reflected in the authorities. However, both bodies recommended changes in the form of legislation which would, if implemented, have assisted the court in its search for the true Parliamentary intention in using the statutory words ...

My Lords, I have come to the conclusion that, as a matter of law, there are sound reasons for making a limited modification to the existing rule (subject to strict safeguards) unless there are constitutional or practical reasons which outweigh them. In my judgment, subject to the questions of the privileges of the House of Commons, reference to Parliamentary material should be permitted as an aid to the construction of legislation which is ambiguous or obscure or the literal meaning of which leads to an absurdity. Even in such cases references in court to Parliamentary material should only be permitted where such material clearly discloses the mischief aimed at or the legislative intention lying behind the ambiguous or obscure words. In the case of statements made in Parliament, as at present advised I cannot foresee that any statement other than the statement of the minister or other promoter of the Bill is likely to meet these criteria.

... My main reason for reaching this conclusion is based on principle. Statute law consists of the words that Parliament has enacted. It is for the courts to construe those words and it is the court's duty in so doing to give effect to the intention of Parliament in using those words. It is an inescapable fact that, despite all the care taken in passing legislation, some statutory provisions when applied to the circumstances under consideration in any specific case are found to be ambiguous. One of the reasons for such ambiguity is that the members of the legislature in enacting the statutory provision may have been told what result those words are intended to achieve. Faced with a given set of words which are capable of conveying that meaning it is not surprising if the words are accepted as having that meaning. Parliament never intends to enact an ambiguity. Contrast with that the position of the courts. The courts are faced simply with a set of words which are in fact capable of bearing two meanings. The courts are ignorant of the underlying Parliamentary purpose. Unless something in other parts of the legislation discloses such purpose, the courts are forced to adopt one of the two possible meanings using highly technical rules of construction. In many, I suspect most, cases references to Parliamentary materials will not throw any light on the matter. But in a few cases it may emerge that the very question was considered by Parliament in passing the legislation. Why in such a case should the courts blind themselves to a clear indication of what Parliament intended in using those words? The court cannot attach a meaning to words which they cannot bear, but if the words are capable of bearing more than one meaning why should not Parliament's true intention be enforced rather than thwarted?

A number of other factors support this view. As I have said, the courts can now look at white papers and official reports for the purpose of finding the 'mischief' sought to be corrected, although not at draft clauses or proposals for the remedying of such mischief. A ministerial statement made in Parliament is an equally authoritative source of such information: why should the courts be cut off from this source of information as to the mischief aimed at? In any event, the distinction between looking at reports to identify the mischief aimed at but not to find the intention of Parliament in enacting the legislation is highly artificial. Take the normal Law Commission Report which analyses the problem and then annexes a draft Bill to remedy it. It is permissible to look at the report to find the mischief and at the draft Bill to see that a provision in the draft was not included in the legislation enacted: see the *Factortame* case [1990] 2 AC 85. There can be no logical distinction between that case and looking at the draft Bill to see that the statute as enacted reproduced, often in the same words, the provision in the Law Commissions's draft. Given the purposive approach to construction now adopted by the courts in order to give effect to the true intentions of the legislature, the fine distinctions between looking for the mischief and looking for the intention in using words to provide the remedy are technical and inappropriate. Clear and unambiguous statements made by Ministers in Parliament are as much the background to the enactment of legislation as white papers and Parliamentary reports.

The decision in *Pickstone v Freemans Plc* [1989] AC 66 which authorises the court to look at ministerial statements made in introducing regulations which could not be amended by Parliament is logically indistinguishable from such statements made in introducing a statutory provision which, though capable of amendment, was not in fact amended.

... a number of distinguished judges have admitted to breaching the exclusionary rule and looking at *Hansard* in order to seek the intention of Parliament. When this happens, the parties do not know and have no opportunity to address the judge on the matter. A vivid example of this occurred in the *Hadmor* case [1983] 1 AC 191 where Lord Denning in the Court of Appeal relied on his own researches into *Hansard* in reaching his conclusions: in the House of Lords, counsel protested that there were other passages to which he would have wished to draw the court's attention had he known that Lord Denning was looking at *Hansard*: see the *Hadmor* case at p 233. It cannot be right for such information to be available, by a sidewind, for the court but the parties be prevented from presenting their arguments on such material.

Against these considerations, there have to be weighed the practical and constitutional matters urged by the Attorney General many of which have been relied on in the past in the courts in upholding the exclusionary rule. I will first consider the practical difficulties. It is said that Parliamentary materials are not readily available to, and understandable by, the citizen and his lawyers who should be entitled to rely on the words of Parliament alone to discover his position. It is undoubtedly true that *Hansard* and particularly records of Committee debates are not widely held by libraries outside London and that the lack of satisfactory indexing of Committee stages makes it difficult to trace the passage of a clause after it is redrafted or renumbered. But such practical difficulties can easily be overstated. It is possible to obtain Parliamentary materials and it is possible to trace the history. The problem is one of expense and effort in doing so, not the availability of the material. In considering the right of the individual to know the law by simply looking at legislation, it is a fallacy to start from the position that all legislation is available in a readily understandable form in any event: the very large number of statutory instruments made every year are not available in an indexed form for well over a year after they have been passed. Yet, the practitioner manages to deal with the problem albeit at considerable expense. Moreover, experience in New Zealand and Australia (where the strict rule has been relaxed for some years) has not shown that the non-availability of materials has raised these practical problems. Next, it is said that lawyers and judges are not familiar with Parliamentary procedures and will therefore have difficulty in giving proper weight to the Parliamentary materials. Although, of course, lawyers do not have the same experience of these matters as members of the legislature, they are not wholly ignorant of them. If, as I think, significance should only be attached to the clear statements made by a minister or other promoter of the Bill, the difficulty of knowing what weight to attach to such statements is not overwhelming ...

Then it is said that court time will be taken up by considering a mass of Parliamentary material and long arguments about its significance, thereby increasing the expense of litigation. In my judgment, though the introduction of further admissible material will inevitably involve some increase in the use of time, this will not be significant as long as courts insist that Parliamentary material should only be introduced in the limited cases I have mentioned and where such material contains a clear indication from the minister of the mischief aimed at, or the nature of the cure intended, by the legislation. Attempts to introduce material which does not satisfy those tests should be met by orders for costs made against those who have improperly introduced the material. Experience in the United States of America, where legislative history has for many years been much more generally admissible than I am now suggesting, shows how important it is to maintain strict control over the use of such material. That position is to be contrasted with what has happened in New Zealand and Australia (which have relaxed the rule to approximately the extent that I favour): there is no evidence of any complaints of this nature coming from those countries.

There is one further practical objection which, in my view, has real substance. If the rule is relaxed legal advisers faced with an ambiguous statutory provision may feel that they have to research the materials to see whether they yield the crock of gold, ie, a clear indication of Parliament's intentions. In very many cases the crock of gold will not be discovered and the expenditure on the research wasted. This is a real objection to changing the rule. However again it is easy to overestimate the cost of such research: if a reading of *Hansard* shows that there is nothing of significance said by the minister in relation to the clause in question, further research will become pointless. In sum, I do not think that the practical difficulties arising from a limited relaxation of the rule are sufficient to outweigh the basic need for the courts to give effect to the words enacted by Parliament in the sense that they were intended by Parliament to bear. Courts are frequently criticised for their failure to do that. This failure is due not to cussedness but to ignorance of what Parliament intended by the obscure words of the legislation. The courts should not deny themselves the light which Parliamentary materials may shed on the meaning of the words Parliament has used and thereby risk subjecting the individual to a law which Parliament never intended to enact.

Is there, then, any constitutional objection to a relaxation of the rule? The main constitutional ground urged by the Attorney General is that the use of such material will infringe Article 9 of the Bill of Rights as being a questioning in any court of freedom of speech and debates in Parliament. As I understood the submission, the Attorney General was not contending that the use of Parliamentary material by the courts for the purposes of construction would constitute an 'impeachment' of freedom of speech since impeachment is limited to cases where a Member of Parliament is sought to be made liable, either in criminal or civil proceeding, for what he has said in Parliament, eg by criminal prosecution, by action for libel or by seeking to prove malice on the basis of such words. The submission was that the use of *Hansard* for the purpose of construing an Act would constitute a 'questioning' of the freedom of speech or debate. The process, it is said, would involve an investigation of what the Minister meant by the words he used and would inhibit the Minister in what he says by attaching legislative effect to his words. This, it was submitted, constituted 'questioning' the freedom of speech or debate. Article 9 is a provision of the highest constitutional importance and should not be narrowly construed. It ensures the ability of democratically elected Members of Parliament to discuss what they will (freedom of debate) and to say what they will (freedom of speech). But even given a generous approach to this construction, I find it impossible to attach the breadth of meaning to the word 'question' which the Attorney General urges ... Relaxation of the rule will not involve the courts in criticising what is said in Parliament. The purpose of looking at *Hansard* will not be to construe the words used by the minister but to give effect to the words used so long as they are clear. Far from questioning the independence of Parliament and its debates, the courts would be giving effect to what is said and done there ... Accordingly in my judgment the use of clear ministerial statements by the court as a guide to the construction of ambiguous legislation would not contravene Article 9 ...

The Attorney General raised a further constitutional point, namely, that for the court to use Parliamentary material in construing legislation would be to confuse the respective roles of Parliament as the maker of law and the courts as the interpreter. I am not impressed by this argument. The law, as I have said, is to be found in the words in which Parliament has enacted. It is for the courts to interpret those words so as to give effect to that purpose. The question is whether, in addition to other aids to the construction of statutory words, the courts should have regard to a further source ...

I therefore reach the conclusion, subject to any question of Parliamentary privilege, that the exclusionary rule should be relaxed so as to permit reference to Parliamentary materials where: (a) legislation is ambiguous or obscure, or leads to an absurdity; (b) the material relied upon consists of one or more statements by a minister or other promoter of the Bill together if necessary with such other Parliamentary material as is necessary to understand such statements and their effect; (c) the statements relied upon are clear. Further than this, I would not at present go.

... For the reasons I have given, as a matter of pure law this House should look at *Hansard* and give effect to the Parliamentary intention it discloses in deciding the appeal ... I trust when the House of Commons comes to consider the decision in this case, it will be appreciated that there is no desire to impeach its privileges in any way. Your Lordships are motivated by a desire to carry out the intentions of Parliament in enacting legislation and have no intention or desire to question the processes by which such legislation was enacted or of criticising anything said by anyone in Parliament in the course of enacting it. The purpose is to give effect to, not thwart, the intentions of Parliament.

In an article published in the *Cambridge Law Journal*, T St J N Bates considered the subsequent use of the relaxation in *Pepper v Hart*.

T St J N Bates, 'The contemporary use of legislative history in the United Kingdom' [1995] 54(1) CLJ 127

... The principle of excluding parliamentary history, as an element of the parol evidence rule, emerged in the eighteenth century. However, even in *Millar v Taylor* (1769) which is regarded as the first English judicial expression of the exclusionary rule in its absolute form, Wiles J having stated the rule then departed from it, as did Ashton J sitting with him. The late 19th century and early 20th century perhaps marked the high point of the application of the exclusionary rule, but even in that period examples of judicial departure from the rule are to be found. More recently there has been a cautious and limited judicial retreat from the full rigour of the exclusionary rule. Parliamentary material was, for instance, admitted to establish legislative purpose rather than for statutory interpretation, a distinction perhaps drawn with more care than conviction. *Hansard* was admitted as an aid to the construction of delegated legislation; a Law Commission report was admitted for the purpose of drawing an inference as to parliamentary intention from the fact that Parliament had not expressly implemented one of the Law Commission's recommendations. So, by 1992, there were firm judicial pronouncements of the highest authority excluding parliamentary material as an aid to statutory interpretation but there were numerous exceptions, some more clearly defined than others.

The House of Lords decision in *Pepper (Inspector of Taxes) v Hart* provided a further significant shift in judicial approach by creating a general, though circumscribed, exception to the exclusionary rule. An important aspect of this aspect of this exception was that it effectively recognised the Executive dominance of Parliament. One commentator observed that in future, when an Act is unclear, the intention of Parliament is apparently to be equated with the policy of the government or with what a minister chose to say about that policy in the House of Commons; an approach which he described as 'rather chilling'. Whatever the temperature *Pepper v Hart* had important implications for those concerned with the enactment and application of legislation. As the case provided a broad and rather imprecise indication of the circumstances in which legislative history would be admissible, the nature and scope of these implications depended on the judicial response to *Pepper v Hart*.

... from the subsequent reported cases which have considered it, the application of this relaxation of the exclusionary rule is uncertain. Furthermore, having relaxed the exclusionary rule, *Pepper v Hart* gave no guidance as to the relationship between reference to parliamentary material as an aid to statutory construction and other aids to construction. It entered a judicial *mélange* of canons of construction to which unregulated weight may be given. So, for example, it offered no guidance on the weight to be given to an admissible ministerial statement that a situation was not covered by one clause but was covered by another, where that statement was in conflict with a construction based on a textual examination of the legislation as a whole. Similar difficulties could arise where an admissible ministerial statement on a provision would lead to one result and a construction based on prior or subsequent legislative provisions, or, say on the punctuation of the provision, would lead to another. Neither was it clear what effect *Pepper v Hart* would have on rebuttable judicial presumptions on the intention of Parliament; for example, that Parliament cannot have intended to oust the jurisdiction of the courts or the presumption that Parliament does not intend to legislate in breach of international or European Union law.

... One implication of the requirement that statements should be clear is that only positive statements are admissible; and unlike some other jurisdictions, submissions based on analysis of parliamentary material which reveal no reference to a particular statutory construction would be inadmissible. It may prove difficult for the courts to maintain this position where, for example, they are faced with submissions that parliamentary material reveals a clear parliamentary intention that construction (A) is intended, which are supported by argument that there is no reference in the parliamentary material to alternative construction (B).

... The guidelines in *Pepper v Hart* on the admissibility of legislative history are, at least in modern times, an innovation in the United Kingdom. At one level, they may be characterised as a technique for more effective judicial regulation of Executive action, which recognises that the Legislature is more commonly the forum for, rather than the fount of, legislation. The guidelines do, however, bring with them the imprecision and indiscipline which is so often a feature of the common law. The judicial application of the guidelines has not, to date, proved comforting, it has been at best somewhat haphazard ... In the two years following *Pepper v Hart*, there have been over 70 cases reported, or otherwise available on LEXIS in which the *Pepper v Hart* guidelines were applied. These cases, in many fields of both public and private law, have raised a number of issues which were not specifically addressed in *Pepper v Hart*, and have also disclosed some inconsistencies of approach in the application of the guidelines ...

CHAPTER 3

THE CIVIL COURT STRUCTURE

Like almost all other aspects of the English legal system, the courts are undergoing a re-structuring. A good overview of the work of the civil courts is provided in the following extract.

Office for National Statistics, *The Official Yearbook of Britain, 2000*, London: HMSO, pp 226–27

Civil Justice System

Jurisdiction in civil matters is split between the High Court and the county courts. Some 90% of all cases are dealt with by the county courts, but most civil disputes do not go to court at all. Many are dealt with through statutory or voluntary complaints mechanisms, or through mediation and negotiation. Arbitration is a common form of adjudication in commercial and building disputes. Ombudsmen have the power to determine complaints in the public sector, and, on a voluntary basis, in some private sector activities (for example, banking, insurance and pensions).

A large number of tribunals exist to determine disputes. About 80 different types of tribunal are supervised by a statutory supervisory body, the Council on Tribunals, and deal with disputes such as liability for tax (Commissioners for Income Tax), eligibility for social benefit (Social Security Appeals Tribunals) and the compulsory treatment of an Individual for mental health problems (Mental Health Review Tribunals).

Courts

The High Court is divided into three Divisions.

- The Queen's Bench Division deals with disputes relating to contracts, general commercial matters (in a specialist Commercial Court), and liability in tort (general civil wrongs, such as accidents caused by negligence, or defamation of character). A Queen's Bench Divisional Court has special responsibility for dealing with applications for judicial review of the actions of public bodies, and has the power to declare the action of a public individual, department or body unlawful.

- The Chancery Division deals with disputes relating to land, wills, companies and insolvency.

- The Family Division deals with matters relating to divorce and the welfare of children.

The county courts deal with claims in contract and in tort, with family matters (including divorce and the welfare of children) and a wide range of statutory matters. Magistrates' courts have limited civil jurisdiction, in family matters (when they sit as a Family Proceedings Court) and in miscellaneous civil orders.

Appeals in civil cases in the county courts or High Court generally go to the Court of Appeal (Civil Division). Appeals from magistrates' courts in civil matters go to the High Court, on matters of law, or to the Crown Court, if the case is to be re-heard. A further appeal on points of law of public importance goes to the House of Lords. The Access to Justice Act 1999 will reform the jurisdiction of the courts to hear appeals in civil and family cases, and the constitution of the Civil Division of the Court of Appeal.

REFORM OF THE CIVIL JUSTICE SYSTEM

The Government has stated its intention to modernise and simplify court procedures, wherever possible, and reduce delay. Following a thorough review of the civil justice system, the first phase of reform was implemented in April 1999. The key elements are the introduction of:

(a) a unified code of procedural rules, written in plain English, and replacing separate sets of High Court and county court rules. The main objective of the new rules is to enable the courts to deal with cases more appropriately. This includes the court taking a more active case management role than before, to ensure that cases are dealt with in a way which is proportionate to their value, complexity and importance;

(b) pre-action protocols (for clinical negligence and personal injury cases) setting standards and timetables for the conduct of cases before court proceedings are started. This will require more exchange of information and fuller investigation of claims at an earlier stage. People should therefore be in a better position to make a realistic assessment of the merits of a case, far earlier than before, encouraging them to settle disputes without recourse to litigation. Where litigation is unavoidable, cases coming to court should be better prepared than before. Judges are expected to apply the protocols strictly, and impose sanctions on those breaching them; and

(c) a system of three tracks to which disputed claims will be assigned by a judge according to the value and complexity of the case. These are:

- the small claims track, which will deal with cases worth less than £5,000 at an informal hearing by a district judge;

- the fast track, which will deal with cases worth from £5,000 to £15,000 and set a fixed timetable from allocation to trial; and

- the multitrack, for cases worth over £15,000 or of unusual complexity, which will be supervised by a judge and given timetables tailored to each case.

The great majority of civil cases, other than small claims, will be run under the fast track procedure. Judges have a key role in ensuring that the new procedures deliver the objectives of reducing cost, delay and complexity, by managing cases to ensure that litigants and their representatives keep to the timetable, and undertake only necessary work. As part of the reform programme, the Court Service is introducing further information technology to support the work of judges and staff in civil courts.

The Access to Justice Act 1999 will reform the workings of the appeals system according to the principles of proportionality and efficiency that underpin the civil justice reforms generally. The objectives of proportionality and efficiency will be achieved by:

(a) diverting from the Court of Appeal those cases which, by their nature, do not require the attention of the most senior judges; and

(b) making various changes to the working methods and constitution of the Court, which will enable it to deploy its resources more effectively.

The Civil Justice Council

The inaugural meeting of the Civil Justice Council was held on 20 March 1998.

Hailing the meeting as a milestone event in the history of civil justice in England and Wales, its Chairman, Lord Woolf, said:

> The Civil Justice Council is the first body of its kind. Never before has a body been set up, comprising members with such a wide range of interest in all parts of the civil justice system, to advise the Lord Chancellor on ensuring that the system is fair, accessible and efficient. This presents an unprecedented opportunity to safeguard the future of civil justice and ensure that it meets the needs of the public into the twenty-first century.

The Civil Justice Council was established under the Civil Procedure Act 1997. The Council's remit is to:

(a) keep the civil justice system under review;

(b) consider how to make the civil justice system more accessible, fair and efficient;

(c) advise the Lord Chancellor and the judiciary on the development of the civil justice system;

(d) refer proposals for changes in the civil justice system to the Lord Chancellor and the Civil Procedure Rule Committee; and

(e) make proposals for research.

Civil Procedure Act 1997

... Civil Justice Council

6 – (1) The Lord Chancellor is to establish and maintain an advisory body, to be known as the Civil Justice Council.

(2) The Council must include–

    (a) members of the judiciary,

    (b) members of the legal professions,

    (c) civil servants concerned with the administration of the courts,

    (d) persons with experience in and knowledge of consumer affairs,

    (e) persons with experience in and knowledge of the lay advice sector, and

    (f) persons able to represent the interests of particular kinds of litigants (for example, businesses or employees).

(3) The functions of the Council are to include–

   (a) keeping the civil justice system under review,

   (b) considering how to make the civil justice system more accessible, fair and efficient,

   (c) advising the Lord Chancellor and the judiciary on the development of the civil justice system,

   (d) referring proposals for changes in the civil justice system to the Lord Chancellor and the Civil Procedure Rule Committee, and

   (e) making proposals for research.

(4) The Lord Chancellor may reimburse the members of the Council their travelling and out-of-pocket expenses.

_._

The civil court system is still organised according to a division between the High Court and the county courts. This division has its historical roots in the nineteenth century, and there are those who have questioned this structure The following article explains the case for change.

Richard Harrison, 'Why have two types of civil court?' (1999) 149 NLJ, 15 January, p 65

A review of the new draft civil justice forms provoked Richard Harrison to put the case for abolishing the distinction between the High Court and the County Court.

Sample draft forms for the new civil procedure rules are now available from the Court Service web site. The 'Notes for claimant on completing the claim form' has obviously been drafted to assist the average litigant in person. Whether or not this approach to court forms will succeed in avoiding confusion at that level, is unlikely to assist the average commercial litigator who will need to manage and control a large amount of irrelevant material. However, in reading:

> You must fill in the heading of the form to indicate whether you want the claim to be issued in a county court or in the High Court (The High Court means either a District Registry (attached to a county court) (*sic*) or the Royal Courts of Justice in London). There are restrictions on claims which may be issued in the High Court (see 'Value' overleaf) the form filler's mind may well be provoked to ask the question: 'why?'

With unified rules and forms (and, it is to be hoped, common enforcement and appeal procedures), the distinction between the High Court and county court is now irrelevant and probably indefensible. The next logical development is to get rid of it altogether. Is this feasible?

The Woolf Reports which inspired the new rules were so radical in parts that we must revert to them to see why, in the midst of so much revolution, a historical distinction was preserved. The matter is primarily dealt with in chapter 12 of Lord Woolf's interim report. Lord Woolf recognises that an additional step in reducing the complexity of the system would involve producing a single vertically integrated court. He nevertheless accepts that much the same result would be achieved by continuing the movement towards aligning jurisdiction and extending powers of circuit judges.

He then states that 'there are difficulties in amalgamating the High Court and the County Court which go beyond my remit' and therefore does not recommend unification. He concludes that the advantages of unity will flow from his other recommendations.

His principal reasons for not recommending amalgamation appear to be:

- the need to preserve the special status of the High Court judges;
- the existence of inherently specialist jurisdictions in each Court;
- the problem with rights of audience.

These can be examined in turn to see whether they are really valid. They are best dealt with in reverse order.

Rights of audience

Lord Woolf referred to this as being subject to a separate statutory regime and as being one of the particular difficulties of amalgamation.

The Access to Justice Bill currently before Parliament makes it clear that rights of audience will depend in future on fitness and qualification, not on whether one is a barrister or solicitor or practising in the High Court or the county court. In these circumstances, it does not appear that this will present any problem for a unified Court.

Specialist jurisdictions

The point is made that the power to hear small claims should not be extended to High Court judges and the High Court should not be asked to exercise the various statutory jurisdictions of the county court. Equally, the county court should not be given general jurisdiction over judicial review.

Yet this is not a particularly strong argument. It would not be intended that High Court judges (or judges of equivalent status) should be asked to hear small claims arbitrations or that district judges should hear the Crown Office list. There are obviously specialist lists and these will continue to be heard by specialist judges if appropriate.

It is undeniable that High Court cases of great magnitude and complexity are heard by Deputy Judges for the convenience of the Court, if sometimes to the great inconvenience of litigants (*Heffer v Tiffin, The Times*, (1998) December 28, where, following a Deputy's apparent failure to find facts, identify issues and evaluate evidence a re-trial of a complex professional negligence action was ordered by the Court of Appeal).

It would appear that the case management function which allocates cases to tracks and trial venues can also cope with matching cases to judicial specialism. It is not the value of a case which determines its complexity and it is not the complexity of a case which determines the type of judge who hears it at present. It seems to me that a unified court system will be able to perform the allocation function far more efficiently than a dual system which has to deal with an outdated and inconvenient level of complexity.

The status of the judges

Lord Woolf states that High Court judges and only High Court judges should deal with the most demanding cases in the system. He also records an acceptance that

'... for constitutional reasons it is essential that the separate status of the High Court judge is maintained and not undermined in any way'.

The constitutional distinction between the courts appears to that of 'superior' and 'inferior' courts (see *Halsbury's Law's of England*, 4th edition, para 713–14 for some distinctions). Parallel streams of statutory development going back to the original County Courts Act 1846 and the Judicature Reforms of the 1870s have led to the County Courts Act 1984 and the Supreme Court Act 1981 and the strange distinction continues. Nevertheless, Lord Woolf has proposed uniformity in practice and procedure and the Civil Procedure Act 1997 has paved the way.

The constitutional status of the High Court judge is of course steeped in history but presently derives only from the Supreme Court Act 1981. There is a definite cultural distinction between 'Her Majesty's judges' who are in theory the fount of the Common Law and the lesser cohorts of Circuit and District judges who have always been the creatures of statute. The criminal defendant sees a difference between a 'red judge' and a 'purple judge'. The High Court judge has a knighthood or a damehood to confer prestige. More importantly, his or her tenure is under letters patent and removal is only (theoretically) possible under an address from both Houses of Parliament. In the absence of a formal legal or actual doctrine of separation of powers, 'constitutional' might be putting it a hit too high.

To a certain extent, this objection can be dealt with in the same way as the previous one: in a unified system, cases are more likely to be allocated to a judge at the right level. I do not think that it is possible to argue sensibly that there should not be a distinction between levels of the judiciary with increased prestige. Respect and remuneration being afforded to an elite band (whatever they are called).

Difficulties in providing for unification

There is obviously a need for pragmatism in the development of the law and, for many, the new procedures will be radical enough change for many years to come. Reforming legislation is difficult enough and to follow through the full logic of my arguments would require the repeal and consolidated replacement of both the Supreme Court Act 1981 and the County Courts Act 1984 and their replacement. I nevertheless maintain that this should be the ultimate aim of the Court Service.

An interim practical solution

Assuming however that the functions, status and even title of High Court judge can be preserved, there is no reason not to aim for a logical and unified civil justice system as early as possible, even without root-and-branch statutory reform. So, given that the Civil Procedure Act points the way, why cannot the distinction be ignored in procedural terms? Litigants could be denied the confusing choice: cases could simply be headed 'Before the Civil Courts' or something similar. The labelling process would be hidden from litigants and case management decisions on allocation would then be made in accordance with the spirit of the Woolf reforms by the procedural judge teams charged with the task.

The new procedures would then be far less cumbersome and generally simpler. The forms and action headings would self evidently form a break with a discredited past. Rather than worrying about status or venue or other historical baggage, litigants and their solicitors might then be in better mental shape to respond to the new managed system and prepare cases for the prompt and effective disposal which is in everyone's interest.

Richard Harrison is a litigation partner at Laytons.

— - — - — - — - — - — - — - — - — - — - — - —

CIVIL APPEALS

The case of *Tanfern v Cameron McDonald and Another* [2000] 2 All ER 801 made important comment upon the new system of civil appeals. The following piece examines the significance of recent changes in the law governing appeals.

Mark Davies, '"Revolution" restricts rights of appeal' (2001) *Law Gazette*, 19 January

Mark Davies considers the new Civil Appeal Rules which came into effect on 2 May 2000, as part of the on-going 'revolution' brought about by the Civil Procedure Rules 1998.

For most litigators, 26 April 1999 will forever be etched on the memory as 'Woolf day'. But as yet, no name has been coined for 2 May 2000, that being the date when the new Civil Appeal Rules came into effect. Perhaps the central aims of the rules in pt 52 of the Civil Procedure Rules (CPR) has been to introduce a uniform system of appeals and to weed out and to deter unmeritorious appeals. Several months on, how are these changes working in practice, and are they to be welcomed? The most important lesson for practitioners is that it is more vital than ever to get things right and be properly prepared at the initial hearing, as the opportunity to appeal against the decision is now more restricted. Permission will be needed to pursue an appeal in virtually all cases, obtained either from the lower court or appellate court. This is a radical departure from the previous rules where a party had an automatic right of appeal on interlocutory orders and in most cases on final orders.

Permission will only be granted where the appellant can show a real prospect of success or some other compelling reason. The appeal court's decision on this is final and there is no further right of appeal, which was a point hammered home by the House of Lords in *R v Secretary of State for Trade and Industry, ex p Eastaway* (*The Times*, 8 November 2000).

There has also been a notable shift in the court's approach in hearing the appeal, as all appeals will now be limited to a review of the lower court's decision and the appeal will only be allowed if the court considers the lower court's decision was wrong or unjust due to a serious procedural or other irregularity. The new test imposes a tough hurdle on appellants and a complete re-hearing, such as an appeal on a summary judgment application, is a thing of the past.

The rule now is that there should only be one appeal and second or subsequent appeals are to be referred to the Court of Appeal. The Court of Appeal will only allow such appeals where they raise (i) an important point of principle or practice; or (ii) there is some other compelling reason.

The end result is that there is a much more limited right of appeal from a decision of the High Court or county court. Where the lower courts have been given discretion under the CPRs, any appeal court will only interfere with the lower court's decision in quite limited circumstances, which was a point emphasised by the Court of Appeal in *Tanfern v Cameron McDonald and Another* [2000] 2 All ER 801, which remains the leading case on pt 52 to date.

Coupled with this, the route of appeal has been altered and the general rule is that the appeal is now made to the next level of the judiciary (that is, District Judge to County Court Judge to High Court Judge – but this is subject to exceptions). The overall effect of pt 52 has been to devolve power down the judiciary. Whether these changes are to be welcomed really depends upon a party's perspective. An appellant is probably less likely to be able to overturn a lower court's decision. As with other parts of the CPRs, the effect of pt 52 has also been to front-load costs with additional burdens being imposed on appellants at an early stage in the appeal process, and it is debatable as to how far this really assists the court. More cynically minded readers may consider this to be a useful way of deterring appeals. There is likely to be more inconsistency in the judicial process with greater divergence in judicial decisions, as lower courts' judgments are less likely to be overturned on appeal, and fewer cases will end up before the Court of Appeal. In light of this, the rules have caused surprisingly little debate, and it may be that many practitioners welcome the greater discretion which has been handed down to their local courts. At the moment it appears the rules have had no discernable impact on the Court of Appeal's workload. However, if they do lead to less delay, then this is surely to be welcomed, particularly as the Court of Appeal is likely soon to be heavily involved in dealing with Human Rights Act issues. Anyone dealing with an appeal under Pt 52 for the first time would be advised to read Lord Justice Brooke's judgment in *Tanfern* for guidance.

Mark Davies is a solicitor at City-based Paisner & Co.

© *Law Gazette* 2000.

Patterns of litigation and the nature of court business can be deduced from studying the relevant part of *Judicial Statistics*, an annual document produced by the Lord Chancellor's Department. The following extracts from *Judicial Statistics 1999*, provide useful pictures of the work of the High Court Queen's Bench Division (and its associated courts like the Admiralty Court), and the work of the county courts.

Lord Chancellor's Department, *Judicial Statistics 1999,* **2000**

High Court – Queen's Bench Division

The Queen's Bench Division deals mainly with civil actions in contract and tort (civil wrongs) and also hears more specialist matters, such as applications for judicial review.

At the end of 1999 the Queen's Bench Division comprised the Lord Chief Justice (its President) and 68 High Court judges. It contains within it the Commercial Court and the Admiralty Court (dealing with shipping matters such as collision and damage to cargo) and administers the Technology and Construction Court (formerly the Official Referees Court) which hear cases involving prolonged examination of technical issues, such as construction disputes. Judges of the Queen's Bench Division also hear the most important criminal cases in the Crown Court (Chapters 6 and 9) and they also sit in the Restrictive Practices Court (Chapter 8) and Employment Appeals Tribunal (Chapter 7). Queen's Bench

Division work is dealt with at the Royal Courts of Justice in London and at district registries of the High Court, located at many of the county courts throughout England and Wales. Each registry covers a defined district consisting of one or more county court districts.

During 1999

- total claims and originating summonses issued fell 37% to 72,161;

- disposal of actions set down for trial fell nearly 19% from 3,530 in 1998 to 2,853 in 1999;

- 76% of disposals were cases settled, struck out or withdrawn before the hearing;

- 44% of court judgments related to personal injury cases, 47% of which were for sums in excess of £50,000;

- the average waiting time from issue of claim to start of trial dropped by 2% to 174 weeks ...

Queen's Bench

The Queen's Bench Division deals with common law business, that is, actions relating to contract (except those specifically allocated to the Chancery Division – see Chapter 2) and tort. Examples of contract cases dealt with in the Queen's Bench Division are failure to pay for goods and services and breach of contract. There are several types of tort (civil wrongs) including wrongs against persons only (eg defamation of character, libel) wrongs against property only (eg trespass) and wrongs which may be against persons or property (eg negligence or nuisance). Some matters may involve both contract and tort, eg personal injury cases which show negligence and breach of a contractual duty of care. Others may be crimes as well as torts, for example assault. Actions are normally started by way of a claim or an originating summons. A claim is the most common method and is used, for example, when a claim is based on an allegation of fraud or tort; it informs defendants what is claimed against them. An originating summons is used in certain cases, such as applications under specific Acts; it outlines the nature of the case. The hearing of an originating summons is usually before a master or district judge (for descriptions of masters and district judges see Chapter 2). If a defendant fails to respond to a claim a claimant may be entitled to a judgment in default. If a defendant responds any of the following may result–

(a) the claimant discontinues the action

(b) the parties settle (ie reach agreement)

(c) the court decides that the defendant has no real defence to the action and gives summary judgment under order 14 of the Rules of the Supreme Court

(d) a trial

There is a right of trial by jury for fraud, libel, slander, malicious prosecution or false imprisonment cases. In all other cases the judge has a discretion to allow trial by jury but it is only used exceptionally. A trial may result in an award of damages or a non-pecuniary remedy such as an injunction (an order to do or not do something). In jury trials the jury decides the amount of damages to be awarded. Judgments may be enforced in many ways, the following being the most frequently used–

(a) a writ of *fieri facias* (*fi-fa*) directing the sheriff (the equivalent of the bailiff in the county courts) by his officers to seize and if necessary sell the debtor's goods to raise money to pay off the debt

(b) a writ of possession of land (eviction takes place if necessary to ensure that possession of property or land is recovered)

(c) a writ of delivery of goods which is an order to hand over specific goods

(d) a charging order on land, securities or funds in court (usually on land – this has the same effect as a mortgage, so that if the property is sold the amount of the charge (debt) must be paid out of the proceeds of the sale)

(e) a garnishee order, which orders that a third party, normally a bank, holding money for the judgment debtor pay it to the judgment creditor direct

(f) appointment of a receiver who will manage the judgment debtor's property or part of it in such a way as to protect the judgment creditor's interest in it.

Oral examination is a procedure used in connection with enforcement. The debtor is required to attend court to give details of his earnings, expenses, savings, etc, so that the creditor can decide how best to enforce the judgment. Often the debtor will pay before he can be questioned (orally examined). Alternatively, a High Court judgment for money may be enforced in a county court as if it was a judgment of that court.

During 1999, 72,161 claims and originating summonses were issued, 37% less than in 1998 (114,984) ...

During 1999, 2,756 cases were set down for trial (18% less than in 1998). There were 2,853 disposals in 1999, down 677 cases on 1998. Of these, just over 23% were determined after a trial. 51% of cases disposed were struck out (eg where a case is considered to be frivolous) or withdrawn before hearing. Just over half of disposals were personal injury cases. Around 87% of claimants in cases disposed of were individuals or groups of individuals whereas around 62% of defendants were firm(s) or corporation(s).

Legal Aid was granted in 39% of cases – in most cases to the claimant only ...

There were 1,290 judgments in 1999 18% more than in 1998. 65% of judgments were in favour of the claimant only; awards in excess of £10,000 were made in most judgments. In 1999, around 42% (540) of judgments related to claims for personal injury; 47% of these judgments were for sums in excess of £50,000 ...

Although Queen's Bench Division cases are only tried at the Royal Courts of Justice and first tier centres outside London, interlocutory proceedings (applications preparatory or incidental to the main proceedings) are dealt with at all district registries and at the Royal Courts of Justice. This area of work continued to decrease in 1999 – applications for masters in London fell over 46% to 11,651. The court determines what, if anything, must be done before a case can be set down for trial, gives directions as to when this is to be done and where the trial is to take place. If either party is dissatisfied with an order of a master, an appeal may be made to a judge in chambers (a private hearing). There were 379 such appeals in 1999 ...

Admiralty Court

The Admiralty Court deals with shipping matters. The two most common matters dealt with are collision of ships and damage to cargo. Most cases are dealt with at the Royal Courts of Justice in London but some are disposed of in county courts with appropriate jurisdiction. During 1999, there were 382 Admiralty actions started in the Royal Courts of Justice, 0.5% more than in 1998 (380). Of the claims issued in London, 133 (35%) related to damaged cargo and 40 (10%) were collision cases ...

Commercial Court

The Commercial Court also deals with shipping matters but is largely concerned with matters regarding contracts related to ships, insurance, carriage of cargo and the construction and performance of mercantile contracts. Other matters dealt with involve banking, international credit, contracts relating to aircraft, the purchase and sale of commodities and the practice of arbitration and questions arising from arbitrations.

During 1999, 60% of the 1,205 claims were unliquidated. The majority of these (54%) were for breach of contract. Of the 220 judgments made during the year, 94% were in excess of £20,000. In 1998, only 23 judgments were made after a trial.

Technology and Construction Court

The Technology and Construction Court, as the name implies, deals with building and engineering disputes and computer litigation. Other matters dealt with include sale of goods, valuation disputes, landlord and tenant (especially dilapidations), torts relating to the occupation of land and questions arising from arbitrations in building and engineering disputes.

The business of the court also includes any cases in the Chancery or the Queen's Bench Divisions which involve issues or questions which are technically complex or for which trial by such judges is for any reason desirable.

There are seven full time circuit judges based in London assigned to the Supreme Court Group. They are nominated by the Lord Chancellor, and presided over by a resident High Court judge. Outside London, nominated circuit judges sit on each of the circuits with further full time designated judges at Birmingham, Manchester and Liverpool.

County Court

Around 230 county courts in England and Wales hear civil proceedings which can be commenced in either county courts or the High Court.

County courts also handle family proceedings such as divorce, domestic violence and matters affecting children. Generally the High Court handles the more substantial, important and complex cases.

During 1999 –

- claims fell by 11%
- there was a increase of nearly 4% in the number of mortgage possession orders made
- 88,389 claims were disposed of by way of small claims
- The average waiting period for a trial was 79 weeks
- creditors' and debtors' bankruptcy petitions rose by 5%
- company winding-up petitions dropped from 976 to 808 ...

Since 1 July 1991 county courts can deal with all contract and tort cases and recovery of land actions, regardless of value. In addition, all county courts deal with the following types of proceedings –

(a) certain equity and contested probate actions (for example, actions concerning an alleged breach of trust obligation by a trustee or questions concerning the administration of a will) where the value of the trust, fund or estate does not exceed £30,000

(b) any action which all parties agree to have heard in a county court (eg defamation cases) except cases on certain aspects of trust, family and admiralty law.

Some courts also hear –

(a) divorce matters

(b) bankruptcy and insolvency matters

(c) matters under the Race Relations Act 1976

Each county court is assigned at least one circuit judge and one district judge. Circuit judges generally hear the higher claims and matters of greater importance or complexity. District judges generally deal with uncontested matters and hear mortgage repossession claims and claims under £5,000 in value. In addition, district judges deal with some preliminary matters in cases which go for trial by a circuit judge.

Claims and miscellaneous hearings

The normal method of taking someone to court is for the person doing so (the claimant) to complete a claim form and issue it at a county court. The claim can be issued in any county court. On receipt of the claim form the court allocates a claim number and enters the details into the court's records. A response pack is attached to the claim form which is then sent to (served on) the person being sued (the defendant). The defendant has a specific time in which to reply to the claim. A defendant can then either pay the claim, dispute it (defend it), admit the claim and ask for time to pay it or ignore it. If the claim is defended, a judge will allocate the claim to one of three tracks for case management purposes: –

(a) the small claims track – for cases with a value up to £5,000

(b) the fast track – for cases with a value over £5,000 but less than £15,000

(c) the multi-track – cases with a value in excess of £15,000.

Each track involves a different degree of judicial involvement. Procedures in the small claims track are the most informal. If a defendant does not reply to the claim, the claimant can ask the court to enter judgment, that is to make an order that the defendant pay the claim. If the defendant has admitted the claim and asks for time to pay and the claimant accepts the offer, a request for judgment can similarly be made.

The Claims Production Centre

The Claims Production Centre (CPC) was set up in January 1990 to process claims requests received on magnetic media from major claimants – ie claimants who generally issue more than 1,000 annually. Issue and dispatch of claims is guaranteed within 24–48 hours. The CPC has customers such as banks, credit/storecard issuers, mail order catalogues and utilities. It issued 925,861 claims representing 54% of the total default claims issued. Although located in Northampton, the CPC is deemed to be part of the court in whose name the claim is issued and once the claim is issued and served, that court will deal with the case in the usual way.

The 1999 figure of 2,000,337 claims entered represented a decrease of 11% on the 1998 figure. Claims issued represented 86% of the total. The remainder were fixed date actions, 79% of which were actions for the recovery of land, mostly relating to residential premises.

Should the judgment not be paid as the court has ordered it is open to the claimant to issue enforcement proceedings to obtain payment.

CHAPTER 4

THE CRIMINAL COURT STRUCTURE

As crime has escalated, both in the number of recorded offences (there are, annually, 10 times as many offences committed today as there were each year in the 1950s) and in terms of the variety and temperature of political debates it generates, the work of the criminal law courts has enlarged accordingly. The following extract from *Britain 2000*, the *Official Yearbook of the United Kingdom*, gives a clear overview of the workings of the criminal court system.

Office for National Statistics, *Britain 2000*: *The Official Yearbook of the United Kingdom*, 2000, HMSO: London, pp 223–26

Criminal Courts

Criminal offences are divided into: *summary* offences, which are the least serious and are triable only in a magistrates' court; and indictable ones, which are subdivided into '*indictable-only*' offences (such as murder, manslaughter or robbery) which must be tried on indictment at the Crown Court by judge and jury, and *either-way* offences, which may be tried either summarily or on indictment. Either-way offences, such as theft and burglary, can vary greatly in seriousness. A magistrates' court decides whether an either-way case is serious enough to warrant trial in the Crown Court, but if the magistrates decide in favour of summary trial, the accused person can elect to have trial by jury in the Crown Court (although this right would be abolished under government proposals announced in May 1999).

Magistrates' courts deal with about 97% of criminal offence prosecutions in England and Wales.

Where a case is to be tried on indictment the magistrates court must be satisfied that there is a case to answer. In most cases this is accepted by the defence and the magistrates do not need to consider the evidence. If the defence challenges the case, the magistrates consider the documentary evidence: no witnesses are called to give evidence. If there is a case to be answered, the accused is committed for trial.

A magistrates' court usually comprises three lay magistrates … known as justices of the peace (JPs), who sit with a court clerk to advise them on law and procedure. The court clerk will be qualified to act as such, although not always a qualified lawyer. In some areas a stipendiary (paid professional) magistrate sits instead of the JPs. Stipendiary magistrates are becoming increasingly common, although most cases are still dealt with by lay magistrates.

An indictment is a written accusation against a person, charging him or her with serious crime triable by jury.

New rules came into force in January 1999 to provide for all new court clerks to be professionally qualified as a barrister or solicitor.

Responsibility for running the magistrates' courts service locally rests with magistrates' courts committees (MCCs), made up of lay magistrates selected by their colleagues. The number of MCCs is being reduced, and their areas increased, to improve efficiency and to bring their boundaries to closer alignment with those of other criminal justice agencies, such as the police and the CPS.

Youth courts are specialist magistrates' courts, which sit separately from those dealing with adults. They deal with all but the most serious charges against people aged at least ten (the age of criminal responsibility) and under 18. JPs who have been specially trained sit in youth courts. Proceedings are held in private.

The Crown Court sits at about 90 venues, in six regional areas called circuits, and is presided over by High Court judges, circuit judges and part-time recorders. The type of judge who will preside over a case, with a jury of 12 members of the public, will depend on which Crown Court the case is being heard in: not all Crown Courts deal with cases of the same level of seriousness.

Trial

Criminal trials have two parties: the prosecution and the defence. The law presumes the innocence of an accused person until guilt has been proved beyond reasonable doubt by the prosecution.

Pre-trial Procedure

Accused people have a right at all stages to remain silent; however, an adverse inference may be drawn from their failure to mention facts when questioned which they later rely upon in their defence. The prosecution discloses to the defence the material which it proposes to rely on at the trial. In addition, the law requires the prosecution to disclose to the defence material in its possession that it does not intend to use in the trial:

Primary disclosure – The prosecution must disclose material which might undermine the prosecution case.

Defence disclosure – In Crown Court cases the defence must give a statement outlining in general terms the nature of the defence, including details of any alibis. This statement is voluntary in cases tried in magistrates' courts.

Secondary disclosure – The prosecution must disclose any unused material not previously disclosed which might reasonably be expected to assist the defence as disclosed in the defence statement.

The prosecution may apply for sensitive material not to be disclosed; the defence may apply for disclosure where it considers that material which should have been disclosed has not been provided by the prosecution.

In a case to be tried on indictment, a judge may hold a preliminary hearing, where pleas of guilty or not guilty are taken. If the defendant pleads guilty the judge will proceed to sentence. In contested cases, the prosecution and defence are expected to assist the judge in identifying key issues, and to provide any additional information required for the proper and efficient trial of the case.

Trial Procedure

Criminal trials normally take place in open court. The burden of proof is on the prosecution, and strict rules of evidence govern how matters may be proved. Certain types of evidence may be excluded because of their prejudicial effect, or because of their unreliability. Documentary statements by witnesses are allowed with the consent of the other party or in limited circumstances at the discretion of the court. Otherwise evidence is taken from witnesses testifying orally on oath.

Child witnesses may testify without taking the oath and their evidence must be received by the court unless the child is incapable of giving intelligible testimony. A child in some circumstances can testify through a live TV link, and the court may consider a video-recorded interview as the evidence of the child, subject to the defence having the right to question the child in cross-examination. Further measures to help both child witnesses and adult vulnerable or intimidated witnesses to give their best evidence in court are being introduced under the Youth and Criminal Evidence Act 1999.

The Jury

In jury trials the judge decides questions of law, sums up the case to the jury, and discharges or sentences the accused. The jury is responsible for deciding questions of fact. The jury verdict may be 'guilty' or 'not guilty', the latter resulting in acquittal. Juries may, subject to certain conditions, reach a verdict by a majority of at least 10 to 2.

If an accused is acquitted, there is no right of prosecution appeal, and the accused cannot be tried again for that same offence. However, an acquittal may be set aside and a retrial ordered if the acquittal has been tainted by a conviction for interfering with or intimidating a juror.

A jury is independent of the judiciary and any attempt to interfere with its members is a criminal offence. People aged between 18 and 70 whose names appear on the electoral register are, with certain exceptions, liable for jury service; their names are chosen at random.

Sentencing

The court will sentence the offender after considering all the relevant information, which may include a pre-sentence report and any other necessary specialist report, and a plea in mitigation by a defence advocate. The powers of the magistrates' court in respect of sentence are limited to a maximum period of 12 months' imprisonment. The offender may be sent to the Crown Court for sentence if the magistrates feel their powers of sentence are insufficient.

A custodial sentence can be imposed only where the offence is so serious that a custodial sentence alone is justified. A term of up to two years' imprisonment may be suspended. A second serious violent or sexual offence requires a court to impose a life sentence unless there are exceptional circumstances. Life imprisonment is the mandatory sentence for murder, and is available for certain other serious offences.

For offences not so serious as to require a custodial sentence, community sentences may be imposed. These can include probation orders (involving supervision in the community), combination orders (a mixture of probation and community service), and curfew orders (requiring the offender to remain at a specified place for specified periods, monitored by electronic tagging). A fine is the most common punishment, with most offenders fined for summary offences. A court may also impose compensation orders, which require the offender to pay compensation for personal injury, loss or damage resulting from an offence; or impose a conditional discharge, whereby the offender may be resentenced for the original offence if the discharge is broken by reoffending. In January 1999 the Government announced the introduction of three-year minimum sentences for those convicted of a third offence of domestic burglary. This came into effect from December 1999.

Young Offenders

Offenders aged 10 to 17 years come within the jurisdiction of youth courts, but may also be tried in an adult magistrates' court or in a Crown Court, depending on the nature of the offence. Existing non-custodial penalties include: conditional discharge; fines and compensation orders (where the parents of offenders may be ordered to pay); supervision orders (where the offender would have to comply with certain requirements, which might possibly include a stay in local authority accommodation); and attendance centre orders; 16- and 17-year-olds may also be given the same probation, community service, combination and curfew orders as older offenders.

Custodial sentences are available to the courts where no alternative is considered appropriate. The main custodial sentence for those aged 15 and over is currently detention in a young offender institution. Remission of part of the sentence for good behaviour, release on parole and supervision on release are available. A secure training order may be given to those persistent offenders aged 12 to 14 who fulfil certain strict criteria.

A number of measures have been taken under the Crime and Disorder Act 1998 to prevent offending and reoffending by young people. Local authorities are required to produce annual youth justice plans detailing how youth justice services in their areas will be provided and funded. They are also having to establish one or more youth offending teams whose membership will be drawn from the police, social services, the probation service, health and education authorities and, if considered appropriate locally, the voluntary sector. As well as supervising existing community sentences, these teams will provide and supervise a range of new orders and powers under the Act (see below).

The Act introduces a statutory final warning scheme to replace the practice of repeat cautioning by the police. The scheme is intended to provide a swift response to early incidences of criminal behaviour, and a final warning will also trigger referral to a youth offending team to draw up a rehabilitation programme to address the factors which led the young person into offending.

New orders include: a *reparation order*, which will require young offenders to make non-financial reparation to the victim(s) of their offence or to the community which they have harmed; and an *action plan order*, which will require them to comply with an individually tailored action plan intended to address their offending behaviour. These new orders, together with the final warning scheme, are being piloted in certain specified areas for 18 months from the end of September 1998. There will also be a *detention and training order*, which will combine custody and community supervision; this is to be implemented in April 2000.

The new criminal orders will be complemented by a range of other powers. These include *parenting orders*, which will require a parent or guardian to attend counselling and guidance sessions, and may direct them to comply with specified requirements; and *child safety orders*, which place a child under ten who is at risk of becoming involved in crime or is behaving in an anti-social manner under the supervision of a specified, responsible officer.

The Youth Justice Board for England and Wales, established under the Crime and Disorder Act 1998, began operation in September 1998 to monitor the youth justice system, promote good practice and advise the Home Secretary on the operation of the system and the setting of national standards.

A new sentence of referral to a youth offender panel is being introduced under the Youth Justice and Criminal Evidence Act 1999. It will be available for young people pleading guilty who are convicted for a first time, and its primary aim is to prevent reoffending. The panel will work to establish a programme of behaviour for the young offender. This will include making restoration to the victim, taking responsibility for the consequences of his or her actions, and achieving reintegration into the law-abiding community.

Appeals

A person convicted by a magistrates' court may appeal to the High Court, on points of law, and to the Crown Court, by way of rehearing. Appeals from the Crown Court go to the Court of Appeal (Criminal Division). A further appeal can be made to the House of Lords on points of law of public importance. A prosecutor cannot appeal against an acquittal, but mechanisms exist to review over-lenient sentences and rulings of law. Alleged miscarriages of justice in England, Wales and Northern Ireland are reviewed by the Criminal Cases Review Commission, which is independent of both government and the courts. Referral of a case requires some new argument or evidence not previously raised at the trial or on appeal.

Coroners' Courts

The coroner (usually a senior lawyer or doctor) must hold an inquest if the deceased died violently, unnaturally, suddenly, if the cause is unknown, in prison or in certain specified circumstances. The coroner's court establishes how, when and where the deceased died. A coroner may sit alone or, in certain circumstances, with a jury.

— · — · — · — · — · — · — · — · — · — · — · — · — · —

Most serious crime is tried in the Crown Court. The work of this court, and the pattern of recent trends in its cases is well documented in the annual document *Judicial Statistics*, produced by the Lord Chancellor's Department. The following extract illustrates the work of the court.

Lord Chancellor's Department, *Judicial Statistics 1999*, 2000, Chapter 6

The Crown Court

The Crown Court, which sits at around 90 locations in England and Wales, deals with criminal matters including –

- cases committed/transferred for trial by magistrates' courts in respect of 'indictable only' offences (ie those which can *only* be heard by the Crown Court)
- 'either way' offences (ie those which can be heard in either a magistrates' court or the Crown Court)
- defendants committed from magistrates' courts for sentence
- appeals against decisions of magistrates' courts

During 1999

– total receipts for committals for trial fell 2% to 74,232 and disposals over 5% to 73,539

– cases dealt with where a plea of guilty was recorded fell by almost 10% (41,872 in 1998 to 37,883 in 1999)

– the average waiting time for defendants on bail was 15.1 weeks and 9.6 weeks for those held in custody (14.4 and 9.4 weeks respectively in 1998)

– receipts of committals for sentence rose 4% to 31,034, while appeals fell by over 5% to 15,413 ...

The Crown Court is the only court which has jurisdiction to hear criminal trials on indictment and it also exercises the appellate and other jurisdictions which had been exercised, prior to its establishment in 1972, by Quarter Sessions. It is a unitary court but currently sits in around 90 centres throughout England and Wales. Court centres are of three kinds. First-tier centres are those visited by High Court judges for Crown Court work, and also for High Court civil business. Second-tier centres are those visited by High Court judges for Crown Court business, but not for civil business. Third-tier centres are those not normally visited by High Court judges at all. Circuit judges, recorders and assistant recorders may sit at all three classes of centre to deal with Crown Court cases.

Criminal Courts Review

Lord Justice Auld is conducting a year long review of the Criminal Courts System.

The review includes, but is not limited to –

• the structure and organisation of, and distribution of work between, courts;

• their composition, including the use of juries and of lay and stipendiary magistrates;

• case management, procedure and evidence (including the use of information technology);

• service to and treatment of all those who use or have to attend courts or who are the subject of their proceedings;

• liaison between the courts and agencies involved in the criminal justice system;

• management and funding of the system.

Committals for Trial

For the purpose of trial in the Crown Court, offences are divided into four classes of seriousness according to directions given by the Lord Chief Justice, with the concurrence of the Lord Chancellor –

Class 1 These are the most serious offences and are generally to be tried by a High Court judge unless a particular case is released on the authority of a Presiding judge to a circuit judge. The offences include treason and murder

Class 2 These offences are generally also to be tried by a High Court judge unless a particular case is released on the authority of a Presiding judge to a circuit judge or other judge. The offences include manslaughter and rape

Class 3 These may be listed for trial by a High Court judge, but may be tried by a circuit judge or recorder if the listing officer, acting under the directions of a judge, so decides. Class 3 offences include all offences triable only on indictment other than those specifically assigned to classes 1, 2 and 4, for example, affray, aggravated burglary, kidnapping and causing death by dangerous driving

Class 4 These offences are normally tried by a circuit judge, recorder or assistant recorder, although they may be tried by a High Court judge. They include grievous bodily harm, robbery and conspiracy, and all 'either way' offences – those which may be tried either on indictment at the Crown Court or summarily ie at magistrates' courts. Either way offences may be committed by the magistrates' courts to the Crown Court for trial. The magistrates are required to ask defendants to indicate their plea to the charge. Where a guilty plea is indicated, the summary trial procedure is deemed to have been complied with and the defendant is deemed to have pleaded guilty under it. Where a defendant indicates a not guilty plea or gives no indication on his plea, the court, having had regard to various factors, including representations by the prosecution and the defence, indicates whether it considers the offence more suitable for summary trial on indictment. However, a court may only proceed to summary trial with the consent of the defendant.

Appeals

In criminal matters the Crown Court deals mainly with appeals by persons against their conviction and/or sentence or part of a sentence eg a compensation order or driving disqualification. The Crown Court may, if it considers it appropriate, vary all or any part of the sentence. There are also rights of appeal from other orders of magistrates' courts (for example by persons ordered to enter into a recognisance to keep the peace).

In addition to appeals in criminal matters the Crown Court also deals with a comparatively small number of appeals in certain non-criminal matters. The most important of these are –

(a) appeals from the decisions of justices in licensing matters

(b) appeals against decisions of Chief Officers of Police in firearm or shotgun certificate cases

Appeals are usually heard by a circuit judge sitting with two lay magistrates. Sometimes one magistrate is acceptable whereas for certain types (eg licensing matters) four magistrates may be required.

Receipts, Disposals and Results

During 1999, 74,232 cases were received for trial at the Crown Court, a decrease of 2% on the 1998 total. Committals for trial disposed of during 1999 totalled 73,539, a decrease of over 5%. As receipts exceeded disposals the number of cases outstanding rose 3% to 24,624 compared with 23,853 at the end of 1998. Where a defendant indicates a not guilty plea or gives no indication on his plea, the court, having had regard to various factors, including representations by the prosecution and the defence, indicates whether it considers the offence more suitable for summary trial than on indictment. However, a court may only proceed to summary trial with the consent of the defendant.

Committals for Sentence

Provisions in the Magistrates' Courts Act 1980 allow magistrates to commit defendants who have been summarily convicted of an either way offence to the Crown Court for sentence. The magistrates must be of the opinion that the offence or the combination of the offence and one or more offences associated with it is so serious that a greater punishment should be inflicted than they have power to impose or, in the case of a violent or sexual offence, that a sentence of imprisonment for a longer term than they have power to impose is necessary to protect the public from serious harm. Committals may also arise from breaches of the terms of, for example, probation orders or of suspended sentences of imprisonment ...

Defendants are committed to a fixed plea and directions hearing (PDH) in the Crown Court – within four weeks if the defendant is in custody and six weeks if the defendant is on bail. At the PDH directions are given to enable contested cases to be made ready for listing. Defendants who plead guilty are, wherever possible, dealt with immediately whilst for those pleading not guilty the earliest possible hearing dates are arranged to take place after the case is ready for trial.

A 'cracked' trial is a case that is listed at the Crown Court for a contested trial by jury but on the day of the trial, for one of a number of reasons, it is disposed of in some other way. The largest percentage of cracked trials occur when the defendant pleads guilty on the trial date (60.4% in 1999).

Other main reasons for cracking include where the prosecution accepts a plea of guilty to an alternative charge (15.7%), the prosecution offer no evidence (20.2%) and the defendant being bound over in a sum of money to keep the peace for a specified period (3.6%). The percentage of cracked trials as a proportion of all cases disposed of remained the same at 22.4%.

... cases and defendants committed for trial are dealt with, according to plea. A guilty plea is recorded when a defendant –

(a) pleads guilty to all counts

(b) pleads guilty to some counts and not guilty to others and no jury is sworn in respect of the not guilty counts

(c) pleads not guilty to some or all counts but offers a guilty plea to alternatives which are accepted (providing no jury is sworn in respect of other counts)

A case is treated as a guilty plea only if pleas of guilty are recorded in respect of all defendants.

In 1999 the number of not guilty plea cases was 2% fewer than in 1998, and the number of guilty plea cases showed a decrease of almost 10%. The guilty plea rate was 58.8% (60.6% in 1998).

... During 1999, 65% of the defendants who pleaded not guilty to all counts were acquitted representing 19% of the total 90,151 dealt with. Of these, 52% were discharged by the judge, 15% were acquitted on the direction of the judge and 33% were acquitted by a jury.

Of the 10,157 defendants convicted in 1999 after a plea of not guilty to some or all counts, 21% were convicted on a majority verdict by a jury (20% in 1998), the remainder being convicted unanimously.

... In 1999 the number of committals for sentence received at the Crown Court rose 4% to 31,034, whilst disposals rose nearly 9% from 28,224 in 1998 to 30,641 in 1999. The number outstanding at the end of 1999 rose nearly 3% to 4,837 (4,701 in 1998).

... Appeals received in 1999 fell over 5% compared with 1998 (15,413 and 16,278 respectively) whilst disposals fell nearly 7% (from 16,473 in 1998 to 15,381 in 1999). As receipts exceeded disposals the number of appeals outstanding rose slightly to 2,313.

Of the appellants dealt with in 1999, 6,670 (43%) had their appeals allowed or their sentence varied. Of the remainder, 4,826 (31%) were dismissed and 3,885 (26%) were abandoned or otherwise disposed.

... Waiting times of defendants tend to vary according to the plea entered and whether the defendant is on bail or in custody. On average, defendants who pleaded guilty during 1999 waited 10.2 weeks whilst those who pleaded not guilty waited 18.6 weeks.

Defendants committed on bail waited an average of 15.1 weeks in 1999 and for those committed in custody the average was 9.6 weeks. Waiting times also vary by circuit; in 1999 the shortest average waiting time was in the Wales and Chester circuit – 9.9 weeks – while the longest was 15.8 weeks in the Northern circuit.

— · — · — · — · — · — · — · — · — · — · — · —

Worries about the expedition with which criminal cases were being dealt with by the courts led the Government to introduce a new 'fast track' route for certain types of case. This is how the news was reported by Frances Gibb, legal editor of *The Times* in an article in July 2000.

Frances Gibb (2000) *The Times*, 14 July

The most serious criminal cases will be fast-tracked to the Crown Court within weeks of a defendant being charged, under Home Office plans announced yesterday. From January, committal proceedings in England and Wales will be abolished for all the 20,000 worst offences a year – those which can only be tried at the Crown Court. The offences include murder, rape, and the worst assaults. There will be one magistrates' court hearing to look at bail and legal aid, and then the cases will go swiftly to the Crown Court for a new preliminary hearing. That will take place within eight days if a defendant is in custody. The initiative, expected to save £15.7 million, is intended to reduce delays in the criminal justice system. The average time taken from charge to a plea hearing will be cut by more than a third – an average reduction of seven weeks.

Many more defendants are expected to plead guilty earlier, with the resulting one-third discount in sentence, reducing the number of occasions when defendants change their plea just before trial. Charles Clarke, a Home Office minister, said that pilot projects had shown wide support for the move. 'This is part of the Government's drive to modernise the criminal justice system and it is always good news when we can remove unnecessary delay and improve the quality of justice for victims and witnesses,' he said.

— · — · — · — · — · — · — · — · — · — · — · —

The move was welcomed by David Calvert-Smith QC, Director of Public Prosecutions, in the following article.

David Calvert-Smith QC, 'Quicker judgment for Solomon' (2001) NLJ 8

Solomon Grundy was caught on Monday, in custody on Tuesday, attended a bail hearing on Wednesday and ended up in the Crown Court the following Thursday.

I mangle a popular nursery rhyme and my apologies to the author, but it catches in a few lines the changes to the criminal justice system, which will lead to serious crimes being dealt with faster. For those who have ever been involved in a serious criminal case, the process can sometimes seem to go on forever. But this long drawn out process will soon be a thing of the past for more serious cases or indictable-only – those that must be heard in the Crown Court.

New measures, which start on January 15 this year, will reduce unnecessary delay for victims and witnesses, and save time and money in the courts without endangering the quality of criminal justice. The most serious criminal cases will be fast-tracked to the Crown Court, which should cut a month off the time taken to deal with a case. People who might have had to attend five hearings at magistrates' courts before being seen by a judge will now have to attend the lower court only once.

The changes will abolish committal proceedings for about 20,000 cases a year including murder, rape and the worst assaults. This will mean that there will be one magistrates' court hearing to look at bail and legal aid and then the case will go to the Crown Court for a new preliminary hearing and, if the defendant is in custody, it will take place within eight days. Undoubtedly, this will remove a significant amount of work from magistrates' courts and enable the judge in the Crown Court to take on management of the case at a very early stage.

These new procedures I have outlined will vary slightly when dealing with youths; defendants aged up to 18. Those charged with an indictable-only offence are not liable to be sent to the Crown Court in their own right. But where the youths have been jointly charged with an adult with any indictable offence and the adult has committed an indictable offence and is sent to the Crown Court for that, the magistrates may send the juvenile with the adult.

The magistrates would do this if they consider it is in the interests of justice for the youth to be tried jointly with the adult. You will rightly ask what will this mean for me in Kent, Sussex, Cumbria or any other part of England and Wales. Well, if you have ever been involved in the Criminal Justice System as either a witness or a defendant you will know that any delay is costly and emotionally draining for everyone. Also the guilty have their punishment put off and the innocent face an anxious wait to clear their name. Neither can be right.

Months can be spent on the preparation of cases in the expectation of a trial, which eventually result in a guilty plea when defendants first appear in Crown Court. Giving them the chance to plead at an earlier stage reduces unnecessary delay for everyone.

Recent pilots for these changes, trialed in England and Wales in 1999, showed that this new system could deliver swifter punishment and justice at a reduced cost. The sites were chosen to provide a representative cross-section of the police forces,

CPS Areas and magistrates' courts – ranging from the largest and busiest to the most rural. The areas selected were Tyneside, Blackburn and Burnley, Northamptonshire, North Staffordshire, North Wales and Croydon. On the whole, the majority of those involved in the pilots, magistrates' courts, CPS lawyers, the judiciary and the Bar, supported the changes. Defence solicitors were generally more neutral towards the proposals.

The pilots managed to cut by 15 per cent the average time taken to deal with offenders on bail from charge to case conclusion. Similarly, there was a 38 per cent reduction in the average time between charge and plea and directions hearing. Custody cases were reduced by an average of 30 per cent. Saving time also meant saving money and pilots showed that the likely annual savings to the Criminal Justice System as a whole were just under £16 million.

The CPS played a significant part in making the pilot a success. A single CPS lawyer took ownership of the case that previously had been managed by several lawyers, which improved continuity and handling. After the pilots finished we began an intensive round of training for all our lawyers and caseworkers.

All of those involved in the Criminal Justice System are committed to reducing delays within it. These changes will help us reach this important goal.

—··—··—··—··—··—··—··—··—··—··—··—··—

The detail of these changes, and their impact upon the criminal justice system, is examined in the next extract from an article by Stephen O'Doherty, of the Casework Directorate of the Crown Prosecution Service,

**Stephen O'Doherty, 'Indictable only offences – the new approach',
(2000) 150 NLJ 1891**

When the previous Government was in power, delays between the commission of an offence and the sentencing of the offender were a matter of concern. As a result, Martin Narey (now the head of the Prison Service) was given the task of finding ways to reduce delay. He came up with a series of observations, one of which was that cases which were inevitably going to end in the Crown Court – ie indictable only cases – were spending a large proportion of their time in the magistrates' court. He proposed that cases should be sent to the Crown Court as quickly as possible, thereby reducing the 'wasted' time spent in the magistrates' court. This recommendation was accepted in principle and found its way onto the statute book by way of s 51 of the Crime and Disorder Act 1998. After pilots designed to evaluate the new provision, it will be implemented nationally on January 15, 2001. How will the change affect that section of work which currently spends a large proportion of its time in the magistrates' court before being tried at the Crown Court?

Current practice

Until 1987, cases reached the Crown Court by one of two procedures. The most common was a committal under s 6 of the Magistrates' Courts Act 1980. A rarely used provision (which remains) was the use of a voluntary bill of indictment under s 2(2)(b) of the Administration of Justice (Miscellaneous Provisions) Act 1933. In 1987, in certain fraud cases, the case could be 'transferred' directly to the

Crown Court avoiding prolonged committal proceedings. In 1991, specified types of cases involving child witnesses could also be transferred directly to the Crown Court under the mechanism provided in the Criminal Justice Act 1991. Section 51, which deals solely with indictable only cases, is different. No longer will defendants be committed or transferred to the Crown Court; instead they will be 'sent' there. The new provision, therefore, leaves four or arguably five distinct methods of ensuring that a case is presented to the Crown Court for hearing. Under both the 1987 and 1991 Acts, there were special provisions which applied if the transfer procedure was used. Provision has been made in Sch 8 of the 1998 Act to preserve those special provisions, but only for either-way cases. If, for example, a child is raped then cases must be sent under s 51.

Speed

The pilots for s 51 commenced on January 4, 1999 and with effect from that date, all indictable only cases still in the magistrates' court immediately became subject to the new provisions. As can be imagined, this instant change to the status of some cases caused a degree of confusion. The same mistake has not been repeated for the national implementation. On the operative date, cases which have already appeared before the magistrates, will not be subject to the new provisions; only those cases which first appear on or after January 15, 2001 will be affected by the change. At present, any indictable only case, other than those affected by the voluntary bill procedure, starts life in the magistrates' court and remains within the control of that court while the prosecution puts together a committal file, a copy of which is served on the defence and the magistrates' court. If the defendant is in custody, he may make applications for bail either to the magistrates or to the Crown Court, but even if he is on bail, it is not uncommon for there to be a number of adjournments before both the prosecution and the defence are satisfied that everything is in order. The defendant is committed or transferred to the Crown Court by the magistrates on the papers, often many weeks and several adjournments after his initial appearance ...

Scope of the section

It needs to be understood that the section applies not only to cases which are, by definition, indictable only, but also to charges which are to be treated as such if the conditions are applicable, such as a defendant who has been charged with trafficking in a Class 'A' drug and who already has two previous convictions. This is because of the mandatory sentence to be imposed under s 110 of the Powers of Criminal Courts (Sentencing) Act 2000, which has replaced s 3 of the Crime (Sentences) Act 1997.

One of the advantages will be the power of the Crown Court to hear purely summary charges with indictable only matters. This overcomes the problem identified in *R v Miall* [1992] 3 All ER 153, whereby s 41 of the Criminal Justice Act 1988 only permitted summary only matters to be dealt with if they were linked to an either-way charge and not, curiously enough, an indictable only offence. The procedure for the Crown Court to deal with a summary only matter where the defendant has been sent for trial is set out in Sch 3 para 6 and follows the procedure in s 41 of the CJA 1988. If the indictable only matter no longer remains, provided the accused has not been arraigned, the Crown Court will deal with the remaining either-way matters on the same basis as the magistrates would have done, by going through the plea before venue procedure and, if necessary Mode of Trial – Sch 3 paras 6-11.

It is interesting to note that s 52(3) states that the court 'shall treat as an indictable offence for the purposes of section 51 ...' offences where the value is relevant to mode of trial, unless it is clear that the value does not exceed the prescribed sum. This is not as helpful as it might seem as it appears to suggest that criminal damage is not an indictable offence. That it is can be seen from *R v Fennell* 164 JP 386, where the Court of Appeal decided that s 22 of the MCA 1980 did not make small value criminal damage summary only, it merely provided that the court must proceed 'as if the offence were triable only summarily'. Section 52(3), therefore, only confirms what was already the position.

Other offences and defendants

Where a defendant appears before the magistrates on an indictable only charge and an either-way or summary only matter, if the 'requisite conditions' are fulfilled, the magistrates are required to send him for trial not only for the indictable matter but also for the related offence (s 51(1)). The 'requisite conditions' are that the offence could either be joined in the same indictment as the indictable only offence or, in the case of a summary only offence is punishable with imprisonment or disqualification, thereby overcoming the problem identified above in *Miall*. If a defendant has already been sent for trial and he later appears on charges which fulfill the requisite conditions, the magistrates then have a discretion to send him to the Crown Court (s 51(2)). Similar situations arise in relation to co-defendants. If the co-defendant is jointly charged with an either-way offence which is related to the indictable only matter and he appears at the magistrates' court on the same occasion as the principal defendant, the magistrates shall send the co-accused to the Crown Court forthwith. If the co-accused appears on a different occasion, again the magistrates have a discretion whether to send him or retain jurisdiction, subject to any election by the accused. If the co-defendant is sent for trial, then any other offences which fulfill the requisite conditions shall also be sent to the Crown Court.

Where the co-defendant is a child or young person who is jointly charged with an indictable offence, if the adult is sent for trial, either on that or a previous occasion, the magistrates shall send him for trial as well but only if they think it is necessary in the interests of justice (s 52(5)).

Venue for trial

Under s 7 of the Magistrates' Courts Act 1980, 'a magistrates' court committing a person for trial shall specify the place at which he is to be tried.' When sending the defendant for trial, s 51 uses similar language and requires the magistrates to 'specify ... the place at which (the defendant) is to be tried'. If the Crown Court did not have the power to alter the venue of the trial, there would be occasions where some Crown Courts would be busy with long delays and others would be relatively quiet. Section 76(1) of the Supreme Court Act 1981, when it was originally enacted, therefore gave the Crown Court the power to alter the place of trial on indictment 'by varying the decision of the magistrates' court under s 7 ... '. However, s 7 only deals with committals and not with cases 'sent' for trial. When transfers to the Crown Court were first introduced for serious fraud cases, s 76 was amended by adding the words 'or by substituting some other place for the place specified in a notice under s 4 (CJA 1987)'. This would suggest that it was accepted that s 76 in its original form only applied to cases committed. When transfers were later introduced for child witnesses in the Criminal Justice Act 1991, there was no corresponding amendment to s 76 although the point does not seem to have been taken when such cases were moved from one Crown Court centre to another. However during the pilot phase, the point was taken, but in *R v Croydon Crown Court, ex p Britton The Times* October 10, 2000, the Divisional Court held that s 76 was wide enough to permit a change in the place of trial without an amendment to cater for cases sent for trial by the magistrates. This would seem to be the end of the argument, although if this is correct then it does somewhat beg the question why s 76 needed to be amended in 1987. At least the issue has now been settled and it does give the Crown Court more flexibility over allocation of work. Section 51(10) sets out the criteria which should be used in deciding where trials should be heard and if the subsections are interpreted to be a priority list, then the convenience of the parties to the trial and the witnesses will take priority over the Lord Chancellor's desire to reduce delays in listing ...

Consequential changes

There are a number of alterations to practice and procedure as a result of s 51. For example, r 27 of the Crown Court Rules 1982 has been modified by the 1998 Rules to allow the preliminary hearing to take place in chambers but a Practice Direction has also been issued so that this hearing should normally be in the court which should be open to the public. Because this hearing is in chambers, the prosecution may be represented by Crown Prosecutors and the defence by a solicitor. Robes need not be worn. The prosecution case will need to be served within six weeks of the case being sent although this is extendable by the judge. One reason for extension may be where the consent is required, for example that of the Attorney-General, or for complex cases such as some fraud offences. There have been alterations to the legal aid to cater for the new proceedings to give the magistrates the power to grant legal aid for the Crown Court hearings. Once the case has been sent, the power is then only available to the Crown Court. Finally the Custody Time Limit Regulations have had to be amended. These provide for an overall time limit of 182 days, less any period during which the defendant had been in custody at the magistrates' court.

According to the evaluation report, s 51 appears to have proved popular with those involved in the pilots. It is achieving its aim of reducing delay and with it the wasted expense of tying up those involved in the administration of justice. Reference has already been made to a problem where the prosecution might consider that an either-way charge is more suitable than the indictable one preferred. Perhaps a more significant one is that the sheer speed may give insufficient time to the police to complete their inquiries. These are going to be the most serious cases and where there is a single incident, the inquiries may be completed without difficulty. However, if the initial investigation or charge then identifies a number of further lines of investigation or where numerous witnesses must be interviewed, there may be pressure to proceed to trial although the investigation is far from complete. It is to be hoped that in such circumstances the judge will manage the case in a way which is fair to all parties and to victims.

CHAPTER 5

THE CIVIL PROCESS

Since 1999, the civil process has undergone major change. The new Civil Procedure Rules (CPR) 1998, the most fundamental changes in civil process for over a century, have radically altered the operation of civil justice. Part of the rationale of the new rules was to expedite the way cases were dealt with and to allow more cases to be settled early through negotiation between the parties or alternative dispute resolution. In this respect, there is some evidence of success.

The overriding objective of the new CPR is to enable the court to deal justly with cases. The first Rule reads:

> 1.1(1) These Rules are a new procedural code with the overriding objective of enabling the court to deal with cases justly.

This objective will include ensuring that the parties are on an equal footing, and saving expense. When exercising any discretion given by the CPR, the court must, according to r 1.2, have regard to the overriding objective and a checklist of factors, including the amount of money involved, the complexity of the issue, the parties' financial positions, how the case can be dealt with expeditiously and by allotting an appropriate share of the court's resources while taking into account the needs of others.

The introduction of such a revolutionary change was the cause of a great deal of fierce controversy about both the desirability of the reforms and their practicability. The rules have been subject to continuing amendment and refinement in the light of some initial problems in their implementation and operation. The Civil Procedure (Amendment No 2) Rules 2001 SI 2001/1388, containing the latest changes, were introduced in May 2001.

In the first part of this chapter we present parts of the CPR (1, 2, and 3) which raise key issues for the legal system, the philosophy underlying its operation, and social policy (Part 27 of the CPR, on small claims, appears in Chapter 6). There then follow a number of articles that seek to evaluate the CPR as a whole or critically judge aspects of them.

The Civil Procedure Rules (updated to June 2001), www.lcd.gov.uk

Part 1

Overriding Objective

Contents of this Part

The Overriding Objective

1.1(1) These Rules are a new procedural code with the overriding objective of enabling the court to deal with cases justly.

(2) Dealing with a case justly includes, so far as is practicable–

   (a) ensuring that the parties are on an equal footing;

   (b) saving expense;

   (c) dealing with the case in ways which are proportionate–

      (i) to the amount of money involved;

      (ii) to the importance of the case;

      (iii) to the complexity of the issues; and

      (iv) to the financial position of each party;

   (d) ensuring that it is dealt with expeditiously and fairly; and

   (e) allotting to it an appropriate share of the court's resources, while taking into account the need to allot resources to other cases.

Application by the Court of the Overriding Objective

1.2 The court must seek to give effect to the overriding objective when it–

   (a) exercises any power given to it by the Rules; or

   (b) interprets any rule.

Duty of the Parties

1.3 The parties are required to help the court to further the overriding objective.

Court's Duty to Manage Cases

1.4 (1) The court must further the overriding objective by actively managing cases.

(2) Active case management includes–

   (a) encouraging the parties to co-operate with each other in the conduct of the proceedings;

   (b) identifying the issues at an early stage;

   (c) deciding promptly which issues need full investigation and trial and accordingly disposing summarily of the others;

   (d) deciding the order in which issues are to be resolved;

   (e) encouraging the parties to use an alternative dispute resolution(GL) procedure if the court considers that appropriate and facilitating the use of such procedure;

   (f) helping the parties to settle the whole or part of the case;

   (g) fixing timetables or otherwise controlling the progress of the case;

   (h) considering whether the likely benefits of taking a particular step justify the cost of taking it;

   (i) dealing with as many aspects of the case as it can on the same occasion;

   (j) dealing with the case without the parties needing to attend at court;

   (k) making use of technology; and

   (l) giving directions to ensure that the trial of a case proceeds quickly and efficiently.

Part 2

Application and Interpretation of the Rules

Contents of this Part

Application of the Rules

2.1 (1) Subject to paragraph (2), these Rules apply to all proceedings in–

   (a) county courts;

   (b) the High Court; and

   (c) the Civil Division of the Court of Appeal.

   (2) These Rules do not apply to proceedings of the kinds specified in the first column of the following table (proceedings for which rules may be made under the enactments specified in the second column) except to the extent that they are applied to those proceedings by another enactment–

Proceedings	Enactments
1. Insolvency proceedings	Insolvency Act 1986(1), ss.411 and 412
2. Non-contentious or common form probate proceedings	Supreme Court Act 1981(2), s.127
3. Proceedings in the High Court when acting as a Prize Court	Prize Courts Act 1894(3), s.3
4. Proceedings before the judge within the meaning of Part VII of the Mental Health Act 1983(4)	Mental Health Act 1983, s.106
5. Family proceedings	Matrimonial and Family Proceedings Act 1984(5), s.40
6. Adoption proceedings	Adoption Act 1976, s.66

The Glossary

2.2 (1)   The glossary at the end of these Rules is a guide to the meaning of certain legal expressions used in the Rules, but is not to be taken as giving those expressions any meaning in the Rules which they do not have in the law generally.

(2)   Subject to paragraph (3), words in these Rules which are included in the glossary are followed by (GL).

(3)   The words 'counterclaim', 'damages', 'practice form' and 'service', which appear frequently in the Rules, are included in the glossary but are not followed by (GL).

Interpretation

2.3 (1)   In these Rules–

'child' has the meaning given by rule 21.1(2);

'claim for personal injuries' means proceedings in which there is a claim for damages in respect of personal injuries to the claimant or any other person or in respect of a person's death, and 'personal injuries' includes any disease and any impairment of a person's physical or mental condition;

'claimant' means a person who makes a claim;

'CCR' is to be interpreted in accordance with Part 50;

'court officer' means a member of the court staff;

'defendant' means a person against whom a claim is made;

'defendant's home court' means–

(a)   if the claim is proceeding in a county court, the county court for the district in which the defendant resides or carries on business; and

(b)   if the claim is proceeding in the High Court, the district registry for the district in which the defendant resides or carries on business or, where there is no such district registry, the Royal Courts of Justice;

(Rule 6.5 provides for a party to give an address for service)

'filing', in relation to a document, means delivering it, by post or otherwise, to the court office;

'judge' means, unless the context otherwise requires, a judge, Master or district judge or a person authorised to act as such;

'jurisdiction' means, unless the context requires otherwise, England and Wales and any part of the territorial waters of the United Kingdom adjoining England and Wales;

'legal representative' means a barrister or a solicitor, solicitor's employee or other authorised litigator (as defined in the Courts and Legal Services Act 1990(7)) who has been instructed to act for a party in relation to a claim.

'litigation friend' has the meaning given by Part 21;

'patient' has the meaning given by rule 21.1(2);

'RSC' is to be interpreted in accordance with Part 50;

'statement of case'–

(a)   means a claim form, particulars of claim where these are not included in a claim form, defence, Part 20 claim, or reply to defence; and

(b)   includes any further information given in relation to them voluntarily or by court order under rule 18.1;

'statement of value' is to be interpreted in accordance with rule 16.3;

'summary judgment' is to be interpreted in accordance with Part 24.

(2)   A reference to a 'specialist list' is a reference to a list$^{(GL)}$ that has been designated as such by a relevant practice direction.

(3)   Where the context requires, a reference to 'the court' means a reference to a particular county court, a district registry, or the Royal Courts of Justice.

Power of Judge, Master or District Judge to Perform Functions of the Court

2.4 Where these Rules provide for the court to perform any act then, except where an enactment, rule or practice direction provides otherwise, that act may be performed–

(a)   in relation to proceedings in the High Court, by any judge, Master or district judge of that Court; and

(b)   in relation to proceedings in a county court, by any judge or district judge.

Court Staff

2.5 (1)   Where these Rules require or permit the court to perform an act of a formal or administrative character, that act may be performed by a court officer.

(2)   A requirement that a court officer carry out any act at the request of a party is subject to the payment of any fee required by a fees order for the carrying out of that act.

(Rule 3.2 allows a court officer to refer to a judge before taking any step)

Court Documents to be Sealed

2.6 (1)   The court must seal$^{(GL)}$ the following documents on issue–

(a)   the claim form; and

(b)   any other document which a rule or practice direction requires it to seal.

(2)   The court may place the seal$^{(GL)}$ on the document–

(a)   by hand; or

(b)   by printing a facsimile of the seal on the document whether electronically or otherwise.

(3)   A document purporting to bear the court's seal$^{(GL)}$ shall be admissible in evidence without further proof.

Court's Discretion as to Where it Deals with Cases

2.7 The court may deal with a case at any place that it considers appropriate.

Time

2.8 (1)   This rule shows how to calculate any period of time for doing any act which is specified–

(a)   by these Rules;

(b)   by a practice direction; or

(c)   by a judgment or order of the court.

(2) A period of time expressed as a number of days shall be computed as clear days.

(3) In this rule 'clear days' means that in computing the number of days –

    (a) the day on which the period begins; and

    (b) if the end of the period is defined by reference to an event, the day on which that event occurs are not included.

Examples

    (i) Notice of an application must be served at least 3 days before the hearing. An application is to be heard on Friday 20 October. The last date for service is Monday 16 October.

    (ii) The court is to fix a date for a hearing. The hearing must be at least 28 days after the date of notice. If the court gives notice of the date of the hearing on 1 October, the earliest date for the hearing is 30 October.

    (iii) Particulars of claim must be served within 14 days of service of the claim form. The claim form is served on 2 October. The last day for service of the particulars of claim is 16 October.

(4) Where the specified period–

    (a) is 5 days or less; and

    (b) includes–

        (i) a Saturday or Sunday; or

        (ii) a Bank Holiday, Christmas Day or Good Friday,

that day does not count.

Example

Notice of an application must be served at least 3 days before the hearing. An application is to be heard on Monday 20 October. The last date for service is Tuesday 14 October.

(5) When the period specified–

    (a) by these Rules or a practice direction; or

    (b) by any judgment or court order,

for doing any act at the court office ends on a day on which the office is closed, that act shall be in time if done on the next day on which the court office is open.

Dates for Compliance to be Calendar Dates and to Include Time of Day

2.9 (1) Where the court gives a judgment, order or direction which imposes a time limit for doing any act, the last date for compliance must, wherever practicable–

    (a) be expressed as a calendar date; and

    (b) include the time of day by which the act must be done.

(2) Where the date by which an act must be done is inserted in any document, the date must, wherever practicable, be expressed as a calendar date.

Meaning of 'Month' in Judgments, etc

2.10 Where 'month' occurs in any judgment, order, direction or other document, it means a calendar month.

Time Limits may be Varied by Parties

2.11   Unless these Rules or a practice direction provide otherwise or the court orders otherwise, the time specified by a rule or by the court for a person to do any act may be varied by the written agreement of the parties.

(Rules 3.8 (sanctions have effect unless defaulting party obtains relief), 28.4 (variation of case management timetable – fast track), 29.5 (variation of case management timetable – multi-track) and RSC O.59 r.2C (appeals to the Court of Appeal) in Schedule 1, provide for time limits that cannot be varied by agreement between the parties).

(1)   1986 c.45.

(2)   1981 c.54.

(3)   1894 c.39

(4)   1983 c.20.

(5)   1984 c.42. Section 40 was amended by the Courts and Legal Services Act 1990 (c.41), Schedule 18, paragraph 50.

(6)   1976 c.36.

Part 3

The Court's Case Management Powers

Contents of this Part

The Court's General Power of Management

3.1 (1)   The list of powers in this rule is in addition to any powers given to the court by any other rule or practice direction or by any other enactment or any powers it may otherwise have.

(2)   Except where these Rules provide otherwise, the court may–

     (a)   extend or shorten the time for compliance with any rule, practice direction or court order (even if an application for extension is made after the time for compliance has expired);

     (b)   adjourn or bring forward a hearing;

     (c)   require a party or a party's legal representative to attend the court;

(d)   hold a hearing and receive evidence by telephone or by using any other method of direct oral communication;

(e)   direct that part of any proceedings (such as a counterclaim) be dealt with as separate proceedings;

(f)   stay$^{(GL)}$ the whole or part of any proceedings or judgment either generally or until a specified date or event;

(g)   consolidate proceedings;

(h)   try two or more claims on the same occasion;

(i)   direct a separate trial of any issue;

(j)   decide the order in which issues are to be tried;

(k)   exclude an issue from consideration;

(l)   dismiss or give judgment on a claim after a decision on a preliminary issue;

(m) take any other step or make any other order for the purpose of managing the case and furthering the overriding objective.

(3)   When the court makes an order, it may–

    (a)   make it subject to conditions, including a condition to pay a sum of money into court; and

    (b)   specify the consequence of failure to comply with the order or a condition.

(4)   Where the court gives directions it may take into account whether or not a party has complied with any relevant pre-action protocol$^{(GL)}$.

(5)   The court may order a party to pay a sum of money into court if that party has, without good reason, failed to comply with a rule, practice direction or a relevant pre-action protocol.

(6)   When exercising its power under paragraph (5) the court must have regard to–

    (a)   the amount in dispute; and

    (b)   the costs which the parties have incurred or which they may incur.

(6A) Where a party pays money into court following an order under paragraph (3) or (5), the money shall be security for any sum payable by that party to any other party in the proceedings, subject to the right of a defendant under rule 37.2 to treat all or part of any money paid into court as a Part 36 payment.

    (Rule 36.2 explains what is meant by a Part 36 payment)

(7)   A power of the court under these Rules to make an order includes a power to vary or revoke the order.

Court Officer's Power to Refer to a Judge

3.2 Where a step is to be taken by a court officer–

    (a)   the court officer may consult a judge before taking that step;

    (b)   the step may be taken by a judge instead of the court officer.

Court's Power to Make Order of its Own Initiative

3.3 (1) Except where a rule or some other enactment provides otherwise, the court may exercise its powers on an application or of its own initiative.

(Part 23 sets out the procedure for making an application)

(2) Where the court proposes to make an order of its own initiative–

   (a)   it may give any person likely to be affected by the order an opportunity to make representations; and

   (b)   where it does so it must specify the time by and the manner in which the representations must be made.

(3) Where the court proposes–

   (a)   to make an order of its own initiative; and

   (b)   to hold a hearing to decide whether to make the order,

   it must give each party likely to be affected by the order at least 3 days' notice of the hearing.

(4) The court may make an order of its own initiative, without hearing the parties or giving them an opportunity to make representations.

(5) Where the court has made an order under paragraph (4)–

   (a)   a party affected by the order may apply to have it set aside$^{(GL)}$, varied or stayed$^{(GL)}$; and

   (b)   the order must contain a statement of the right to make such an application.

(6) An application under paragraph (5)(a) must be made–

   (a)   within such period as may be specified by the court; or

   (b)   if the court does not specify a period, not more than 7 days after the date on which the order was served on the party making the application.

   (CCR O.42, in Schedule 2, sets out the circumstances when the court may not make an order of its own initiative against the Crown)

Power to Strike Out a Statement of Case

3.4 (1) In this rule and rule 3.5, reference to a statement of case includes reference to part of a statement of case.

(2) The court may strike out$^{(GL)}$ a statement of case if it appears to the court–

   (a)   that the statement of case discloses no reasonable grounds for bringing or defending the claim;

   (b)   that the statement of case is an abuse of the court's process or is otherwise likely to obstruct the just disposal of the proceedings; or

   (c)   that there has been a failure to comply with a rule, practice direction or court order.

(3) When the court strikes out a statement of case it may make any consequential order it considers appropriate.

(4) Where–

   (a)   the court has struck out a claimant's statement of case;

   (b)   the claimant has been ordered to pay costs to the defendant; and

   (c)   before the claimant pays those costs, he starts another claim against the same defendant, arising out of facts which are the same or substantially the same as those relating to the claim in which the statement of case was struck out, the court may, on the application of the defendant, stay$^{(GL)}$ that other claim until the costs of the first claim have been paid.

(5) Paragraph (2) does not limit any other power of the court to strike out$^{(GL)}$ a statement of case.

Judgment Without Trial after Striking Out

3.5 (1) This rule applies where–

(a) the court makes an order which includes a term that the statement of case of a party shall be struck out if the party does not comply with the order; and

(b) the party against whom the order was made does not comply with it.

(2) A party may obtain judgment with costs by filing a request for judgment if–

(a) the order referred to in paragraph (1)(a) relates to the whole of a statement of case; and

(b) where the party wishing to obtain judgment is the claimant, the claim is for–

(i) a specified amount of money;

(ii) an amount of money to be decided by the court;

(iii) delivery of goods where the claim form gives the defendant the alternative of paying their value; or

(iv) any combination of these remedies.

(3) Where judgment is obtained under this rule in a case which paragraph (2)(b)(iii) applies, it will be judgment requiring the defendant to deliver goods, or (if he does not do so) pay the value of the goods as decided by the court (less any payments made).

(4) The request must state that the right to enter judgment has arisen because the court's order has not been complied with.

(5) A party must make an application in accordance with Part 23 if he wishes to obtain judgment under this rule in a case to which paragraph (2) does not apply.

Setting Aside Judgment Entered after Striking Out

3.6 (1) A party against whom the court has entered judgment under rule 3.5 may apply to the court to set the judgment aside.

(2) An application under paragraph (1) must be made not more than 14 days after the judgment has been served on the party making the application.

(3) If the right to enter judgment had not arisen at the time when judgment was entered, the court must set aside$^{(GL)}$ the judgment.

(4) If the application to set aside$^{(GL)}$ is made for any other reason, rule 3.9 (relief from sanctions) shall apply.

Sanctions for Non-payment of Certain Fees

3.7 (1) This rule applies where–

(a) an allocation questionnaire or a listing questionnaire is filed without payment of the fee specified by the relevant Fees Order;

(b) the court dispenses with the need for an allocation questionnaire or a listing questionnaire or both;

(c) these Rules do not require an allocation questionnaire or a listing questionnaire to be filed in relation to the claim in question; or

(d) the court has made an order giving permission to proceed with a claim for judicial review.

(Rule 26.3 provides for the court to dispense with the need for an allocation questionnaire and rules 28.5 and 29.6 provide for the court to dispense with the need for a listing questionnaire)

(Rule 54.12 provides for the service of the order giving permission to proceed with a claim for judicial review)

(2) The court will serve a notice on the claimant requiring payment of the fee specified in the relevant Fees Order if, at the time the fee is due, the claimant has not paid it or made an application for exemption or remission.

(3) The notice will specify the date by which the claimant must pay the fee.

(4) If the claimant does not–

(a) pay the fee; or

(b) make an application for an exemption from or remission of the fee,

by the date specified in the notice–

(i)   the claim shall be struck out; and

(ii) the claimant shall be liable for the costs which the defendant has incurred unless the court orders otherwise.

(Rule 44.12 provides for the basis of assessment where a right to costs arises under this rule)

(5) Where an application for exemption from or remission of a fee is refused, the court will serve notice on the claimant requiring payment of the fee by the date specified in the notice.

(6) If the claimant does not pay the fee by the date specified in the notice–

(a) the claim shall be struck out; and

(b) the claimant shall be liable for the costs which the defendant has incurred unless the court orders otherwise.

(7) If–

(a) a claimant applies under rule 3.9 (relief from sanctions) to have the claim reinstated; and

(b) the court grants relief under that rule,

the relief shall be conditional on the claimant–

(i)   paying the fee; or

(ii) filing evidence of exemption from payment or remission of the fee,

within 2 days of the date of the order.

(Rule 25.11 provides for when an interim injunction shall cease to have effect when a claim is struck out under this rule)

Sanctions Have Effect Unless Defaulting Party Obtains Relief

3.8 (1) Where a party has failed to comply with a rule, practice direction or court order, any sanction for failure to comply imposed by the rule, practice direction or court order has effect unless the party in default applies for and obtains relief from the sanction.

(Rule 3.9 sets out the circumstances which the court may consider on an application to grant relief from a sanction)

(2) Where the sanction is the payment of costs, the party in default may only obtain relief by appealing against the order for costs.

(3) Where a rule, practice direction or court order–

(a) requires a party to do something within a specified time, and

(b) specifies the consequence of failure to comply,

the time for doing the act in question may not be extended by agreement between the parties.

Relief from Sanctions

3.9 (1) On an application for relief from any sanction imposed for a failure to comply with any rule, practice direction or court order the court will consider all the circumstances including–

(a) the interests of the administration of justice;

(b) whether the application for relief has been made promptly;

(c) whether the failure to comply was intentional;

(d) whether there is a good explanation for the failure;

(e) the extent to which the party in default has complied with other rules, practice directions, court orders and any relevant preaction protocol(GL);

(f) whether the failure to comply was caused by the party or his legal representative;

(g) whether the trial date or the likely trial date can still be met if relief is granted;

(h) the effect which the failure to comply had on each party; and

(i) the effect which the granting of relief would have on each party.

(2) An application for relief must be supported by evidence.

General Power of the Court to Rectify Matters Where There Has Been an Error of Procedure

3.10 Where there has been an error of procedure such as a failure to comply with a rule or practice direction–

(a) the error does not invalidate any step taken in the proceedings unless the court so orders; and

(b) the court may make an order to remedy the error.

In the first four articles below, we present a range of assessments of the Woolf Reforms, published in 2000 after the first year of the reforms in operation.

**John Leslie, Queen's Bench Master, 'The Woolf reforms –
An end of year report' (2000)** *Counsel* **32**

Prior to April 1999, an intelligent, articulate and unobsessed litigant in person appeared before me at the hearing of his Summons for Directions. The opposing solicitor said that the defendant was ready neither to proceed with the hearing of the summons, nor to comply with any of the usual directions which I was being invited to give.

The litigant in person looked utterly bewildered and not a little wounded. He pointed out that Order 25 rule 1 of the Rules of the Supreme Court obliged him to issue his Summons for Directions within one month of the close of pleadings. He had done so. He thus could not understand what the solicitor was talking about or how they could not be read. The touching naivety of his puzzlement goes to the heart of the Woolf reforms. The Rules of the Supreme Court and the County Court Rules were more honoured in the breach than in the observance.

Taking control

Under the Civil Procedure Rules, such a litigant should never be puzzled nor disappointed, nor should the opposing party be unready. The Court now takes control of the case. After a Defence is filed and served the case is allocated to a track and the Court manages the case for the parties, setting a procedural timetable and fixing dates for any interlocutory hearings considered necessary and a date for trial. There is no longer any need for the parties themselves to make applications for routine case management directions.

Beneficial results

The new rules have produced a number of beneficial results and the system appears in general to be working well. In particular, parties and their representatives are complying with the exhortations in the Practice Directions to issue applications seeking 'non-routine' directions for hearing at case management conferences, thus reducing costs.

In my experience, where a stay for attempts at settlement has been ordered, the claim is in fact settled in about 50% of cases. Moreover, I have found that the power to require the attendance of the parties at case management conferences has, on a number of occasions, had a beneficial effect in settling claims.

Settling at the bar

I am sure that one reason for cases habitually settling at the door of the Court immediately before trial, is that it is the first time that the parties and their advisers have been together. In more than one case which I have heard with the parties in attendance, they have adjourned to a wine bar local to the Royal Courts of Justice and there and then settled the case. Since hearing of these settlements, I am tempted to call a requirement under rule 3.1(2)(c) a 'Daly's Order'.

It was envisaged that the culture of 'expert evidence for everyone and everything' would be difficult to change. However, orders for single experts are much more frequently suggested by the parties than expected and in circumstances which I sometimes find surprising. In particular, I had expected that there would be much more contention arising from a suggestion that there be a single expert to deal with issues which are, in reality, only peripheral to the main issues in the case.

Spirit of co-operation

There is a new spirit of co-operation abroad. Solicitors and counsel co-operate between themselves and with the Court in proposing directions, preferably in accordance with the new Pt 52. This is, I suspect engendered, at least in part, by the Pre-action Protocols and paragraph 4 of the Practice Direction that introduces them.

In any event it is a manifestation of the concept that case management should be a partnership between the parties' lawyers and the Court. The overwhelming number of case management conferences are conducted against a background of co-operative agreement as to the routine case management directions. It then only remains for the Court to review such terms as have been agreed.

There is a certain sense of satisfaction in constructing a series of directions, some of which would have been seen as innovative only a few months ago, in order to facilitate the progress of a claim to trial.

This is not to say that contentious applications are not being made – they are. If there is a smaller number of contentious interlocutory applications, then one reason may be the introduction of summary assessments of costs. From the point of view of the lay client, this seems to have brought home the true cost of litigation.

Caught without a net

On the other hand, there are some disappointments. One of the main foundations of the introduction of Court case management was the requirement for efficient management of cases by use of Information Technology. For the judiciary, this has happened only to a limited extent.

A large number of judges have now been provided with computers, which work well. However, access from them to the internet and to a number of CDs is, for the moment at least, barred, so that there is no access to, for instance, on-line text-books and law reports. The Court staff have IT for the logging and administration of claims, but the judges' hardware has no communication with that system.

Mountains of paper

A large paper mountain is building up. Prior to April 1999, it was the proud boast of the Queen's Bench Division in the Central Office that a case-file had never been lost, since there were none to lose. We are now fearful of beginning to find out how it is done. We are in danger of running out of space to keep the files.

Moreover the requirement in the rules that the parties keep the Court informed on matters of fairly routine case management and the encouragement that such communications and even applications be in an informal manner has led to a large increase in paperwork.

The lack of direct or individual secretarial or clerical assistance for individual procedural judges makes handling, processing and responding to this paperwork difficult. It is for this reason that I let slip a wry smile when I receive a letter addressed to my secretary or my clerk. We have a hard-working and dedicated staff in the Masters Support Unit, but, more often than not, they are greatly pressed.

One year on from the introduction of the Civil Procedure Rules, Jeremy Fleming of the Law Society's *Gazette* interviewed Lord Woolf and a group of leading practitioners about the first year of the reforms.

Jeremy Fleming, 'Civil justice reforms' (2000) *Gazette*, 28 April, p 18

It is hard not to be impressed by Lord Woolf's modesty. There are few judges who, while alive at least, have given their names to major overhauls of a judicial system, yet despite this and the fresh news that he will be promoted to Lord Chief Justice in June, the current Master of the Rolls seems relaxed and unstuffy.

This month's MORI poll findings – indicating that 80% of solicitors are content with the Civil Procedure Rules – have relieved him, but he acknowledges that there are still danger zones.

On the inconsistency in applying the new rules, reported by many solicitors among the judiciary, Lord Woolf is sanguine: 'I'm afraid it's got to be expected. There are bound to be teething problems; I'm only astonished that they haven't been greater.'

The issue of front-loading of costs has been effective for settlement, but some commentators believe it can prevent access to justice by deterring potential litigants. Lord Woolf is robust. 'The commentators are wrong,' he says. Explaining that some lawyers used to issue proceedings as part of a tactical process, not because they had any real intent to proceed, he believes that if those sorts of litigants are now put off, 'that increases access to justice'. He adds: 'The courts should not be used merely as a part of the tactical equipment of a macho lawyer.'

Case management conferences (CMC) are one of the mainstays of the new regime, intended to wring out opposing sides' bugbears away from the courts. But they are controversial – some commercial lawyers believe they can be inappropriate and expensive. Lord Woolf sympathises with this perception. He says that if both sides have made sensible proposals and are agreed as to how to conduct a case, 'I don't say there should never be a CMC, but I would say that the district judge should carefully weigh up whether the costs involved in the CMC are justified by the likely benefits that will be achieved'.

He acknowledges that there are no criteria which a judge can use to decide whether it's worth having a CMC. 'What will happen, I hope, is that with experience, judges will recognise those cases where it's justified.' But he reserves some criticism for commercial lawyers: 'One must remember that lawyers also must appreciate how valuable CMCs can be; that CMCs really can transform the subsequent proceedings.' Some lawyers are resistant to this, he says, and the result is that they go to the CMC unprepared. 'CMCs only work well if the lawyers on both sides are really on top of their cases, and the judge has an opportunity to lead the parties into a sensible decision for the future of the case, based on accurate information,' he contends.

Single joint experts are another controversial aspect of the reforms, with many reports of both sides in disputes appointing their own expert behind the scenes, augmenting the cost of advice.

While he accepts that this may happen, Lord Woolf sees a strategic significance for it. In complex litigation, he believes it is reasonable – where a joint expert is agreed for the parties to employ their own experts. He explains that in a number of situations, their own experts will confirm to the parties that the single expert is right thereby resolving issues, and making their own expert effectively just a safeguard.

Where their own expert disagrees with the single expert, he believes that the party concerned will have to decide if it is worth contesting that disagreement with the single expert's report. Sometimes, parties will decide it is disproportionate to do so, meaning that the single expert will have achieved his goal. In other cases, 'they will decide to challenge, but instead of a dispute that is open-ended, it will be confined to the matter upon which the experts disagree, so overall, in the great majority of cases, there will always be a benefit'.

And if this results in more expense? He maintains that such expense is 'well worthwhile if it resolves or reduces conflicts over expert issues', adding: 'If the case goes to trial, the expense of so doing is enormous, involving expert evidence being heard sometimes for days.'

If the CPR have been successfully introduced, then lawyers are still waiting for the courts to move into the information age. The IT revolution has long been promised, but not yet delivered.

Lord Woolf is too shrewd to pin a date to a moveable feast; the big problem is that the available technology is so fast-changing. 'What I would be satisfied with today, I may not be satisfied with in six months' time,' he explains. He has recently returned from Singapore, where he was deeply impressed by the almost paperless judicial system. In such a small jurisdiction, he says, this process can be achieved rapidly, but not in as large a jurisdiction as England and Wales. But he acknowledges that there have been mistakes: 'I think we may have got into a bit of a mess on IT, insofar as we were moving too fast without thinking where we were going.'

Is there also an issue of funding the IT overhaul of the courts? He does not think so, believing the private finance initiative and IT firm EDS will guarantee its delivery. However, he says one additional 'relatively modest sums' of funding would make a big difference in some areas, such as the introduction of telephone conferencing facilities, which he himself is only now about to receive.

The judiciary has held its own through the past year's reforms; a sturdy beach-hut left standing after the spring tide.

The fear is that the introduction of the Human Rights Act 1998 in October will hit it like a tidal wave. Lord Woolf says his own court has been preparing its computers for a big influx of cases. There are also procedural changes being introduced from 2 May [2000] – certain Court of Appeal cases will be dealt with at a lower level – and this, he believes, will reduce the demands on his court. He says these measures should enable the court to provide a quick and efficient service for human rights cases 'without our having to increase the size of this court, which I think would be undesirable, except possibly marginally'.

He thinks it would be 'a great mistake to underestimate the impact initially of the Human Rights Act coming into force', adding that he has heard from other jurisdictions that 'the initial impact can be significant, but then things settled own fairly quickly, although it may be at a higher level than previously, but only moderately higher, and certainly manageable'.

He adds: 'Nothing would bring the Human Rights Act more into disrepute than if we allow it to interfere with the way the courts are able to deliver justice.'

Lord Woolf takes inspiration from the great reforming lawyers of the past: Lords Wilberforce and Reid (leading 20th century law lords); Denning (inventor of promissory estoppel); Diplock (extended the judiciary's power over the government); Mansfield (anti-slavery law lord, who said 'the air of England is too pure for any slave to breathe'). He also extols some of the current judiciary, 'but I won't embarrass them by mentioning them', he adds.

As he moves to his new position, the pundits will speculate that the eyes of reform will now focus on the criminal judiciary. Lord Woolf treads carefully in responding to this speculation. 'Well, certainly, I think it is part of the responsibility of judges to make sure that our justice system is efficient and effective, and my responsibility in this job has been almost exclusively civil law ... but one of the reasons I look forward to getting involved again in crime is that I do hope that I can make a modest contribution to building on the work of my predecessors.'

_ _._ _._ _._ _._ _._ _._ _._ _._ _._ _._ _._ _._ _._ _

'Trying Woolf' (2000) *Gazette*, 28 April, pp 19–20

The *Gazette*'s first virtual on-line round table allowed leading practitioners to discuss aspects of the Woolf reforms. Many of the points made were put to Lord Woolf in the above interview. Below are extracts from the interaction, which involved:

* **Richard Chapman**, partner at Wolverhampton firm Chapman Everatt and chairman of the Forum of Insurance Lawyers' Civil Procedure Rules special interest group;

* **Ted Greeno**, partner at City firm Herbert Smith;

* **Robin Knowles QC** of 3/4 South Square, a member of the Commercial Bar Association's executive committee;

* **David Marshall**, a partner at London firm Anthony Gold Lerman & Muirhead and treasurer of the Association of Personal Injury Lawyers; and

* **Bill Vincent**, a district judge at Evesham County Court.

Q: How effective are Part 36 offers (to settle at any stage)?

David Marshall: These are a success story. Having recently won at trial an employment case with £50,000 damages, indemnity costs, and extra interest on costs and damages, my firm (and our client) are all in favour. I doubt the penalties are anything like as extreme as those facing the claimant who fails to beat a Part 36 payment, but they should make the other side think. The most important protection is indemnity costs. This gets you away from proportionality, and I also think it is unlikely that a judge could award only part costs (because you failed on a quantum issue, for example) if a Part 36 offer is still exceeded.

Bill Vincent: While a claimant who beats his pre-action offer is entitled only to have the court take that into account, I think it will be a rare case where a defendant who has put the claimant through the mill of an action rather than take up a fair offer to settle will not be landed upon from a great height. Flexibility in the court's powers does, of course, let the court tailor a just result, where an inflexible rule may not. Lack of certainty is the price inevitably paid.

Robin Knowles: The Part 36 regime, and the sanctions available to the court, of course have an important place. But there is need for care. In litigation, where the stakes can already be very high, there is a difference between creating a climate where a disciplined and sensible approach by parties towards settlement is encouraged, and creating a climate which creates undue pressure to settle regardless of merits.

Q: How are pre-action protocols working?

David Marshall: My feeling is that they are working well in personal injury cases. There is much earlier clarification of liability, saving considerable cost and stress on the part of the claimant, who was previously faced with 'tactical' denials for months or even years. There have been some issues about choice of medical expert, but I think that the 'partisan' expert (on both sides) has had his day.

So far as non-personal injury cases are concerned, my firm's experience is more mixed. There is a front-loading of cost and rather unstructured correspondence taking the place of pleading, lists of documents and formal written evidence. If this resolves the dispute, all well and good. If not, I rather suspect it will add to cost as pre-action work will be re-done post-issue. Perhaps the answer is more formal protocols in more areas of work.

Robin Knowles: Pre-action protocols are, in concept, very important. The balanced, sensible use of pre-action procedures is to be encouraged. But an attempt at fishing that is oppressive, or an attempt at a complex dry run of litigation, are to be guarded against. Pre-action protocols can help steer an appropriate path, but they require the greatest care and consultation in formulation, and discretion in application.

Q: How are case management conferences (CMCs) working?

Richard Chapman: There is a worrying trend in several courts, which involves district judges making orders on the filing of allocation questionnaires in personal injury actions, even in multi-track cases, which bypass the CMC process, setting a timetable which is really no different to the old automatic directions. The court surely needs a case summary at least, if not representations from the parties' solicitors, in order to identify the issues and give appropriate directions for resolving them.

David Marshall: My experience has been that if the parties put forward sensible directions (preferably agreed) they will normally be made without a CMC. If both sides suggest wildly different directions, the court lists a CMC. If one side only suggests directions, then unless they are obviously one-sided, there is a good chance they will be made.

The silent party has himself to blame. If neither side bothers to suggest directions (or explain why a CMC is necessary), then I'm not surprised district judges set out proposed directions.

Robin Knowles: I suspect that it all comes down to the type of case. In the Commercial Court, case management conferences are an important opening stage in each commercial case ... It allows the opportunity for a focused discussion not only between advocates, but between judge and advocates. The discussion is informed by an agreed case memorandum, an agreed list of issues, and case management questionnaires.

Ted Greeno: My greatest concern about CMCs is that they require a considerable amount of preparation which turns out to be unnecessary. This is a result of case management, and the judge being free to make orders of his own motion ... A further aspect of this problem is that it cuts across the principle that a party should know in advance the case he has to meet.

There are too many instances on judges imposing inappropriately tight timetables which achieve little, other than to increase the costs ... Judges drawn from the Bar often have little firsthand experience of the practical challenges of preparing cases for trial and they should therefore be slow to order tight timetables against the parties' wishes. They should also be wary of those parties who press for rapid timetables in the hope that this will engender procedural short-cuts, such as less thorough disclosure.

There is a widely held view, recently endorsed by Mr Justice Burton, that parties are trying to use the new rules on disclosure to avoid disclosing harmful documents on the grounds that they are only 'train of enquiry documents'. There is a perceived danger (at least) that they may be allowed to get away with this because orders for further disclosure would upset tight timetables and ultimately threaten trial fixtures. In my view, we should guard against speed being given greater priority than substantive justice.

Robin Knowles: An important aspect of preparing for a CMC is that all the lawyers consider and discuss the issues to which a case gives rise. This can involve a lot of work, but once done, the parties are well equipped to respond to points that the judge may raise without that requiring undue additional work.

Members of the Commercial Bar (including those who have become judges) have direct personal experience of being involved in preparing heavy cases, and of the practical challenges and pressures involved. In my experience, most heavy commercial cases involve a full team effort in which both solicitors and barristers are fully involved. Ted is right to warn that there can be shortcomings in some parties' approach to standard disclosure. To some extent, disclosure depends more than ever on the professional rigour and diligence of the lawyers.

Q: Are costs going up or down?

Ted Greeno: I am concerned that commercial cases are costing more to resolve. It may or may not transpire that some cases will settle earlier than they would have done under the old rules, but it is widely accepted (including by Lord Woolf I understand) that the new rules have introduced additional cost at the pre-action stage (due to the need to follow protocols) and in the early stages of proceedings. A member of the judiciary was recently reported as having said that this was always expected, but that it was thought that it would encourage settlement. If that is right, it does raise concern for access to justice. By making litigation more expensive, people are deterred from pursuing their claims.

In the context of commercial claims, such an assumption would also misunderstand the dynamics which bring about settlement in my experience. Cases do not only settle because they will be expensive to litigate or even because the issues have become clearer. Other factors include changes in business relationships and objectives, as well as changes in management personnel and difficulties with witnesses. Very often, the passage of time is a necessary part of this.

In addition, the parties' views as to when they will have the best negotiating position will play a part. This will often turn on their views as to the evidence to be disclosed during the process (including documents, and witness and expert statements), and this will also dictate the timing of settlements. There is accordingly some real concern that the effect of the new rules has been simply to increase the cost to the parties of reaching a settlement they would have reached anyway under the old rules.

Robin Knowles: There are a number of dynamics in the settlement of commercial cases. But the combination of the CPR and the Commercial Court Guide brings earlier precision to a case: this is a welcome, not an unwelcome, contribution to the dynamics. It allows accuracy to replace uncertainty as a factor. I am not convinced that there is the evidence to say that total costs increase.

I readily accept, however, that costs may often be incurred at an earlier rather than later stage, but it is the greater understanding that those early costs achieve (rather than the costs themselves) that can promote settlement. An early focus on whether and when to use ADR, whether and when to use preliminary issues, how to ensure that the 'cards are on the table' – all these, and more, help reduce the chance of the things that really cost most – the 'door of court' settlement or the trial with more witnesses, documents and issues than are really necessary.

— · — · — · — · — · — · — · — · — · — · — · — · — · — · —

In the next article, Richard Burns, a barrister at the Ropewalk Chambers Nottingham and a Recorder on the Midland & Oxford Circuit, examines the Woolf Reforms from both sides of the Bench.

Richard Burns, 'A view from the ranks' (2000) 151 NLJ 1829

We trained very hard, but it seemed that every time we were beginning to form up into teams we would be reorganised. I was to learn later in life that we tend to meet every new situation by re-organising – and a wonderful method it can be for creating the illusion of progress, while producing confusion, inefficiency and demoralisation. Gaius Petronius (AD 66)

I suspect that very many lawyers grappling with the implications of the Woolf Reforms a couple of years ago looked forward to April 26, 1999 with the same degree of scepticism and cynicism that infected Gaius Petronius. They would have accepted that there were serious deficiencies with the existing system which needed to be addressed urgently, but they would have questioned why we needed a judicial year zero with an entirely new litigation landscape. I had actually read Lord Woolf's final report in order to prepare an *aide memoire* for my chambers and I recall that I was cautiously in favour, although I did wonder whether a more incremental system of reform might not have been better, particularly since very little extra money seemed to be available to the Court Service for increases in judicial manpower and the information technology upgrades Lord Woolf had regarded as central to his reforms.

As a personal injuries practitioner and as a Recorder sitting in the county court, I had a useful double dose of training before the reforms were implemented and I have since had the opportunity to observe how the reforms have worked in practice. These are my impressions seeing it from both sides of the Bench.

Lord Woolf in his *Final Report* identified the following major defects in the existing system of civil justice which he suggested frightened off the average person from litigating and caused litigation to be weighted in favour of the big battalions. Litigation he said was:

- too expensive – with costs frequently exceeding the value of the claim;

- too slow in bringing cases to conclusion;

- unfair – lack of equality between the wealthy and the under-resourced litigant;

- attended with too much uncertainty – as to cost and as to how long a case would last;

- too fragmented – no one with clear responsibility for civil justice;

- too adversarial – parties ran cases – they were taking too long and ignoring rules of court.

The received wisdom, certainly according to the legal press, is that by and large the Civil Justice Reforms have been a quiet success. My view is that the transition has been far smoother than many had anticipated and there have been a number of very worthwhile gains. However, set against the ambitious Woolf aims set out above, I am afraid that the reforms have been a relative failure.

The gains have been in the new Civil Procedure Rules (CPR) the introduction of a unified procedure for all the civil courts, in a greater awareness of the need for the costs of the litigation to bear some passing resemblance to the value of the claim, in vastly improved pro-action cooperation, in more sensible and open pleadings which force the parties to define the key issues at an early stage, in the wider use of jointly instructed and so genuinely impartial experts, and in CPR Part 36, rules cunningly devised to stimulate the parties to settle out of court which by and large are achieving their objective.

However I do not believe that the system as it presently operates has yet realised Lord Woolf's vision.

First, the CPR in the way it is presently being operated, is proving to be more expensive for litigants than the old system. This is because the timetable imposed usually compels the parties to spend time and money progressing claims to trial whether or not they expect to settle. Paradoxically the procedures encouraging as they do the front end loading of expenditure on cases, may lead to more trials – certainly this appears to have been happening in some of the court centres where I appear.

Secondly, the system of case management, which Lord Woolf envisaged would be the engine to drive forward the litigation cheaply and expeditiously, particularly in the county court, is excessively bureaucratic and makes too many demands on the parties. Also, it remains as under-resourced both in terms of court staff, judges and information technology as many feared it would be. There is not even a proper email system and so far, hardly any county courts outside London publish their lists on the Net. This is a disgrace.

It seems to me completely impracticable for judges to manage all cases and counter-productive for them to try. Their burden in the busier courts is so huge that all they can do is skim the surface of the files that cross their desks. It is rare, in my experience, for the same judge to be able to deal with all the interlocutory stages of even the bigger cases and so there is little or no continuity. Moreover, since the majority of cases still settle, many just ahead of trial, most of the time and effort devoted to case management which involves the filling in of allocation questionnaires, the preparation of case summaries and/or skeletons, core bundles draft directions by the parties and often one or more live appearances by the advocates at a case management conference or a pre-trial review, is probably wasted. Judges can, of course, stop the litigation clock at any stage if they want to and they would probably do so if they were told by the parties that a settlement was imminent. But the parties are seldom in a position to declare their intentions in advance.

Thirdly, whilst on the whole cases come on for trial more quickly than they did, I strongly suspect that the overall delay experienced by litigants is much the same as it ever was. This is because solicitors, feeling daunted by the demands made on them by the CPR and lacking the time and resources to manage more than a certain quota of cases through the system, are delaying the issue of proceedings. The delay frequently runs into years.

Fourthly, I cannot see what the CPR in its present form does, or should do, to address the disparity of resources between litigants. The pretence that there can be a level playing field between parties – one employing skilled and experienced lawyers and able to employ the best experts, and one unrepresented and standing alone – is a cruel deception. The system, even stripped of its Latin tags remains as obscure and daunting for the litigant in person as it ever was. The rhetoric of the Overriding Objective (CPR Part 1) simply disguises the fact that with the effective abolition of legal aid for the general run of civil cases (which has been only partially and very inadequately replaced by conditional fees), the gap between rich and poor litigants is wider than ever. Nevertheless, I do not believe that it can be the proper function of the CPR to hobble the party with deeper pockets and insofar as any particular provision may seek to do so (save as regards controlling the amount of expert evidence), it may possibly be incompatible with European Convention rights.

Then there is the summary assessment of costs. The theory seems to be that the degree of transparency introduced by the process will help contain the cost of litigation and ensure that claims remain proportionate. The theory may be sound but in practice, save in the simplest of cases, the system does not work as intended. This is because judges, particularly Circuit Judges and Recorders simply do not have the expertise, information or time to analyse the schedules of costs submitted to them fairly or accurately. The choice therefore is to go through the schedules knocking off bits and pieces in response to off the cuff and sometimes unedifying submissions from the advocates ('I respectfully submit that my Learned Friend cannot possibly justify the 8 hours claimed for his skeleton argument'), which will often result in the successful party having a claim which would have been allowed on a detailed assessment, unfairly disallowed, or in the judge acquiescing in the parties agreeing costs between themselves, which means that the time spent by the parties before the hearing drawing up the schedules will have been wasted, although doubtless it will be charged for.

Lastly, whilst the new rules have introduced a uniform code, because of the wide discretion given to judges and the reluctance of the Court of Appeal to interfere with its exercise, the Lord Chancellor's foot has made a worrying re-appearance with the same rules being interpreted very differently from one area to another. For example, there are marked differences in the way judges interpret CPR r 35 which imposes a duty on them to restrict expert evidence to that which is reasonably required to resolve the proceedings. Some take a liberal view and consider it unjust not to allow the parties to call live expert evidence whenever there is any significant difference between experts. On the other hand, others seem very reluctant to allow any expert at all to be called to give oral evidence unless the differences are glaring and others, particularly those who have taken a dislike to employment consultants, routinely refuse permission to the parties even to adduce the evidence of jointly instructed experts. This variability on the part of the judges can produce some very rough justice and is not satisfactory.

In conclusion therefore, although lawyers and a very dedicated but hopelessly over-burdened and under-resourced court staff, have buckled down and done their best to make the CPR work, I fear that it is only limping along at present and is not fulfilling its promise. There must quickly be an injection of money into the system, ideally to enable the appointment of the extra judges and staff so urgently needed, but certainly for extra IT resources.

Without disturbing unduly the original CPR vision of case management, there are things that can be done to lessen the burden and expense presently borne by litigants. For example, the largely useless and excessively long and complicated allocation questionnaire could be replaced with a simple one page form giving the bare details of the case. If the court want more information they can email or telephone the parties. Then there are the case summaries and the accompanying core bundles which have to be prepared for even routine interlocutory hearings. They should be abolished in most cases. If the judge wants to be informed of the background and the issues he can read the pleadings and ask the advocates at the hearing.

While the courts must still set the framework and it should be fairly tight, the doctrinaire insistence on controlling every aspect of the litigation must cease. By and large the professionals who conduct most of the litigation are reasonable and sensible people who want to do the right thing by their clients and the system. They should be trusted to get on with it and agree things between themselves and not be treated like naughty children, who will backslide if not closely watched.

So, I believe that there needs to be a fundamental shift of emphasis in the CPR to give back to the parties the right, within the overall timetable set by the court, to conduct their litigation at the pace and in the manner which suits them. The court should stop requiring the parties to keep reporting back to it. If after the case has come to trial it emerges that the litigation has been conducted inefficiently and that as a consequence costs have been wasted, the guilty parties, including the lawyers, should be punished in their pockets. This is the best way to obtain an efficient and accountable civil justice system.

_____

The next article is one in which Frances Gibb, the legal editor of *The Times*, analyses the surveys conducted on experiences of the Woolf Reforms after their first year of operation.

Frances Gibb, 'Verdict on Woolf shake-up: it's a qualified success'
(2000) *The Times*, 2 May

Lord Woolf's shake-up of civil justice was a year old last week. To judge from a rash of surveys, the overall verdict is that it is proving a success. Litigation is quicker (some say cheaper) and more likely to lead to early settlement than a courtroom battle. But fears about a lack of resources remain.

Eversheds, the corporate law firm, has conducted an 'access to justice' survey for four years, so its results are telling. Of its respondents, 54 per cent said that the civil litigation process had improved in the past year, a big increase on 1998's 15 per cent. Some 52 per cent of respondents believed that litigation was quicker, but only 22 per cent thought costs were lower.

John Heaps, head of litigation at Eversheds, says: 'The UK legal system historically has been plagued by unsatisfactory delays and expense. The style of dispute resolution is changing as a result of the Woolf reforms; people no longer seek aggressive uncompromising lawyers, but those who look for commercial solutions.'

The survey sought the views of heads of legal departments of UK companies and public sector bodies; 70 per cent of respondents were in the private sector, with 30 per cent in London. From the replies, a change in culture is emerging. Nearly two thirds did not think the reforms would make them less likely to start proceedings but 43 per cent said they were settling cases earlier and almost half said their lawyers were handling disputes differently. Mediation, or alternative dispute resolution (ADR), is also on the rise: 41 per cent have used it, compared with 30 per cent in 1998.

But there is concern that while judges are managing cases more effectively the courts do not have adequate resources. (This was expressed by 50 per cent of respondents.) Only 24 per cent believed that litigants were now getting better justice; 44 per cent said they were not.

Views were also split on costs. Nearly half did not believe costs to have been affected. Arguably more worrying, 19 per cent said costs had risen, particularly in the regions. But a conference on Woolf held by the Centre for Dispute Resolution (CEDR) found that although costs had increased at the start of litigation (front-loading) overall they were down as settlements came sooner.

Conditional or 'no win, no fee' work is attractive in principle but little used: 48 per cent of respondents said they would pay lawyers a higher fee for winning if they could pay a lower fee, or none, if the case was lost. But only 24 per cent had discussed such a deal.

Litigation may be quicker and less likely to go to court, but 52 per cent of respondents expected to have the same number of business disputes next year, with as many being resolved through litigation. One in five was more upbeat and thought fewer disputes would be resolved in court.

Overall the findings are positive, says Heaps. 'Over half the respondents feel the speed of resolving disputes has improved. But there are concerns that the aims and aspirations are not matched by court resources.'

Wragge & Co obtained similar findings. A survey carried out by City Research Group among in-house lawyers from FTSE 1000 companies says lack of resources are 'a major stumbling block'. Some 81 per cent of respondents thought courts did not have the resources to process claims quickly enough, and some complained of 'inconsistent interpretation' between courts. But 89 per cent of respondents backed the changes and said litigation was quicker with fewer 'frivolous claims'. Some 41 per cent thought costs had been cut, and there was strong backing for ADR, with 80 per cent saying it had proved popular. Nine in ten thought clients were more involved in the management of the dispute, but 38 per cent believed that the reforms had compromised justice at the expense of cost-cutting. Like the CEDR survey, the change singled out for the biggest impact is that which allows either party to make a formal settlement offer at any stage – or potentially face cost penalties.

Andrew Manning Cox, senior litigation partner, says the survey mirrored the firm's experiences. Among surprise findings was the low awareness of Woolf among businesses. 'They must look to their lawyers to use the rules to the best tactical advantage,' he says.

Another City law firm, Lovells, found 71 per cent of respondents now treating litigation as a last resort, with 72 per cent willing voluntarily to exchange documents with the other side. Where litigation is unavoidable, it is quicker, with 66 per cent saying that judges now set tighter timetables. Two thirds found the court 'rubber-stamped' joint requests by the parties to move back dates in the timetable, but this flexibility did not extend to trial dates.

The impact of the reforms, though, is patchy. One controversial aspect of Woolf was the ability of courts to appoint a joint expert. But only 7 per cent of respondents were involved in cases with such an expert.

And judges could be more active in managing cases. Only 9 per cent found that the court monitored case progress and chased lawyers to meet deadlines; 42 per cent found the court had sought to narrow the issues as early as it could. The commercial court, Lovells found, was managing cases better than other High Court divisions. And courts did not penalise parties who failed to comply with the new rules.

Asked for the worst aspect of the reforms, respondents chose the rule on summary assessment of costs in preliminary hearings, criticised as a lottery. But Russell Sleigh, head of litigation at Lovells, says the findings were generally encouraging.

—·—·—·—·—·—·—·—·—·—·—·—·—·—·—·—·—·—

A practitioner's point of view was also published in *The Times* on 2 May 2000. The opinion is from Andrew Horrock, litigation partner at Barlow Lyde & Gilbert.

Andrew Horrock (2000) *The Times*, 2 May

This time last year solicitors were worried about the impact of Woolf. The 'overriding objective' was to enable the court to deal with cases justly and in a 'proportionate' way. But what would this mean? One year on, fewer cases are coming to court. Government figures suggest new claims are down 23 per cent. Our experience confirms that more cases are settling, and faster, with fewer preliminary court applications.

The judges' new enthusiasm for immediately quantifying and ordering payment of costs doubtless has something to do with it. Fears have been expressed that judges know little about costs and may make arbitrary decisions. Certainly we have seen examples of judges unfamiliar with London charges and an inconsistency on summary assessment of costs.

With earlier settlements, clients might have hoped for lower bills. That has not always happened. Most pundits predicted that cases would be 'front-loaded', with a higher proportion of costs in the early stages. That has happened. More activity early on means more analysis and advice, so more costs at the outset.

Front-loading and earlier settlements are among the effects of a greater use of the pre-action protocols that govern the conduct of claims before proceedings are issued. In practice these mean the parties think twice before issuing proceedings and are prepared to exchange information. We still exercise our traditional skills of analysis, advice and negotiation but gain a more complete picture earlier on. Once proceedings are issued, cases move faster to trial, so the need for swift tactical and procedural judgment is very much alive.

Mediation is increasing and clients expect advice on whether their dispute should be mediated. Many judges have 'bought into' the Woolf desire for settlement and sometimes will require an attempt to mediate before trial.

Courts differ in the management of cases. We have found masters significantly less interventionist than judges. Routine case-management conferences do not really differ from old-style directions hearings and often proceed by agreement between the parties. By contrast, the new rules restrict parties agreeing to extend court deadlines: the idea is that lawyers and parties should not dictate the pace of litigation. The principle is sound but more flexibility would save bureaucracy and costs.

The reforms have heralded a change on experts. At our recent Woolf seminar, Mr Justice Lightman said experts were already an 'expensive luxury' and their evidence often irrelevant. In our view they will become less common.

Some waters remain to be tested. The procedure on disclosure is thought open to abuse. More reforms are in the pipeline, and the Human Rights Act has yet to take effect. Remodelling the litigation landscape is set to continue.

The Government's keenness to promote the use of electronic services in the civil justice system is evident from the following statement posted on the Court Service website in January 2001.

'Civil courts make a claim for the customer',
www.courtservice.gov.uk/notices/modp.htm (15 January 2001)

Making a claim from your computer or digital TV is just one way that people will be able to get access to justice under plans to improve customer service in the civil and family courts announced today by David Lock, Minister at the Lord Chancellor's Department.

The Court Service consultation paper, *Modernising the Civil Courts*, outlines how technology and new ways of working can be used to improve the range and quality of services available for people who need to use the civil courts. The proposals, which received a £43million funding boost in the Spending Review 2000, are the first major review of the way the civil courts deliver services to the customer. They aim to support the progress made by civil justice reforms launched in April 1999 and create a civil court system fit for the 21st century.

David Lock said:

> This is an unparalleled period in the history of the civil justice system. In the space of less than a decade we have seen significant civil justice reform and the birth of a new era in Human Rights. There have been major changes in the way citizens interact with the state and with each other. Disputes are no longer simply about local problems, and often relate to contracts and agreements made across regional and national boundaries.

> Yet the structure of the civil courts and the way they work has not kept pace with these changes. Most people using the court are still limited to communicating in writing or by attending in person. While this was entirely appropriate for the time of Dickens, it no longer serves modern day society. Nor does the location of county courts best match service to need. While many of the urban and suburban courts are close to each other with good public transport links, rural courts, where public transport is difficult, are thinly spread.

> Developments in technology have given people more direct access to services from their own homes, the library, workplace and even the supermarket. E-mail has become the communication medium of choice for much of business. People are able to see the benefits of technology in other areas of their lives and, rightly, expect better services and modern facilities from the courts.

> These proposals show how the civil courts can, with the help of technology and partnerships with other agencies, provide easier and cheaper access to justice.

The proposals include:

- 'Virtual court' – using the internet, e-mail and digital TV to make small claims and other transactions with the court;

- 'Court on call' – enabling a range of court processes to be available by telephone eg to make a request to enter judgment.

- 'Gateway partnerships' – providing improved access to court services through partnerships with advice agencies and links with the Community Legal Service eg court staff could act as an outpost of the court office, enabling the customer to have access to procedural advice and court services via laptop and similarly advice agencies could be provided with direct access to court services via the web so the advisor can counsel the client and assist in transactions with the court at the same time;

- Easier access to information and advice – providing 24hr information about cases and advice about court procedures via the internet and call centres, kiosks in libraries where people not only get on-screen advice but can link up to a Citizen's Advice Bureau via video-link, partnerships with advice agencies and links with the Community Legal Service to provide people with web-access to court services at the same time as they are getting advice;

- Restructuring the civil court network – providing courts according to regional need, population distribution and transport networks rather than historical accident;
- Improved access to court hearings – through partnerships with magistrates courts, tribunals, use of hired facilities and video-conferencing in addition to the network of primary court hearing centres;
- Improved IT support for the judiciary – development of electronic case filing, electronic presentation of evidence, digital audio recording, video-conferencing and improved electronic communication between the judiciary and court staff and in-court computers to allow access to court files and e-mail.

Ian Magee, Chief Executive of the Court Service said:

> These proposals are about extending court services into the heart of the community. Modern technology allows the court into people's living rooms and offices via personal computers and digital TV, making our services available at times and in ways that suit our customers. But so much of our work involves those who have no access to technology, or who are excluded by language or disability. Through partnerships with advice agencies we hope to reach out into society to those who might otherwise be excluded.
>
> Changes will happen at different speeds. Some ideas are already being tried in the courts, and the report outlines the proposals for more pilot projects. It is important that our customers – those who already use the courts, and those who may have to do so, consider these suggestions and give us their views about the service they want from the civil courts in the 21st century.

Lord Justice Brooke, who represents the judges on the Board that produced the consultation paper, said:

> The Court Service has kept the judges fully informed of these ideas. The judges are keen to see that sensible use is made of modern technology and working methods in the day to day business of the courts, and we will study people's responses to these suggestions with interest.

The pilot projects include:

- On-line applications to the court – This pilot, to be launched on 5 February, will explore the use of e-mail to reduce the need for attendance in court. Parties to cases at Preston County Court will be able to e-mail the judge with their interim applications. See press release 436/00 for further details.
- Kiosk services – This touch screen kiosk, due to be launched shortly, will provide advice, information and court forms from libraries in Telford and nearby Madeley in Shropshire. It includes a video-link to the local Citizens Advice Bureau which will enable customers to dial up on-screen advice on for example filling in a form or what to do next.
- Video-conferencing – This pilot, launched on 28 July 2000, seeks to evaluate the effectiveness, uses, benefits and cost savings of video-conferencing. There are currently three suites installed at the Court of Appeal, Leeds and Cardiff Courts, and the network will be extended to more outlying courts in 2001.

- On-line issue of claims, judgments and warrants – This pilot will provide the citizen and small businesses with a web based claims service in the next financial year.

- Call centres – Still at an early stage, this pilot is seeking ways of extending hours of service to obtain court forms, leaflets and simple procedural advice.

One key feature of the new CPR is the way the appeal system operates. Under the old system, many users and critics complained of procedural complexity and prolixity. In the following article, the new system is evaluated.

Richard Harrison, 'Appealing prospects' (2000) NLJ Practitioner, 4 August, p 1175

Considerations of justice, expedition and proportionality of costs should apply equally to appeals as they do to all other aspects of litigation. It is not surprising that the consequence of Sir Jeffery Bowman's review of the civil appeals system was to meld it into the Lupine landscape. The assumption now is that an appeal should not be an automatic right. The expectation that a higher authority might review your case now only extends to scrutiny for obvious injustice which may or may not lead to 'permission' to appeal. More than one level of an appeal should not be justified save where an important point of principle or practice arises. The principle of proportionality must be applied.

The Access to Justice Act 1999 enabled these reforms to be implemented and the relevant sections are now in force. Section 54 enables Rules of Court to impose a requirement for 'permission' and Section 55 restricts second appeals. Section 56 enables the Lord Chancellor to prescribe the route of appeals from County Courts. Complementing this is a new Part 52 of the Civil Procedure Rules. Detailed procedure is contained in the Practice Direction to Part 52. There is also a specific Court of Appeal Practice Direction, governing administrative matters and the organisation and requirements of that particular court. These new requirements are undoubtedly onerous and require considerable discipline and preparation from practitioners.

The important thing to remember is that the old separate appellate regimes are now harmonised (save for small claims which have special procedures: the Lord Chancellor's Department is currently consulting about bringing them back within the fold). Appeals from masters, registrars, referees and judges had a very tight five-day limit from the date of the making of the order. Appeals to the Court of Appeal had a relatively long four weeks from the date of the sealing of the order. The time limit is now a universal and fairly tight 14 days from the date of decision (not the date of sealing).

There is new terminology: an appellant's notice (N161) must be filed and served in all cases. If you need permission to appeal from the appeal court, it must be sought by this document. There is counter-provision for a respondent's notice and it would go without saying that a respondent's appeal now requires permission to proceed.

You need to be aware of your appeal strategy well before judgment is delivered. The documents which must be filed with the appellant's notice must include or be accompanied by a skeleton argument and, if this is not practicable, one must be lodged and served on all respondents within fourteen days of filing the notice. The sealed copy of the order being appealed must be filed, together with any order giving or refusing permission to appeal. You must also provide a copy of the transcript or an adequate note of the reasons for the judgment of the lower court and of course all other relevant documents.

Judicial guidance: Tanfern

The new regime has been subject to a detailed analysis by the Court of Appeal, including Lord Justice Brooke and Lord Woolf MR in the case of *Tanfern Ltd v Gregor Cameron-Macdonald and Another* [2000] All ER 801.

The case itself decided that under the old regime, an appeal from a district judge sitting in a county court matter should go to a circuit judge, even though the district judge was exercising the jurisdiction of a circuit judge. In future, in the unified multi-track, appeals from a district judge giving a final decision will lie direct to the Court of Appeal. The case specifically did not cover appeals in public law cases or appeals in family proceedings: it confined itself to appeals and civil proceedings in private law matters.

The key points are as follows:

Permission required

Permission is required for an appeal as the general rule. It should be sought from the court to be appealed against immediately following delivery of the judgment. Permission may, however, be granted by the appeal court. If, at an oral hearing, the appeal court refuses permission to appeal, then no further right of appeal exists. Permission to appeal is only given where the court considers that an appeal would have a real prospect of success or that there is some other compelling reason why the appeal should be heard. An order giving permission to appeal may limit the issues to be heard and it may also be made subject to conditions. There are a limited number of specific exceptions.

The appellate approach

All appeals are now a matter of review rather than re-hearing. This has completely changed the assumption that was made from previous appeals from district judges and masters where the application was completely re-heard afresh. Now the appeal court will only interfere if the decision of the lower court was wrong or was unjust because of a serious procedural or other irregularity in the proceedings. 'Wrong' means that the appeal court should only interfere when it considers that the judge at first instance has not merely preferred an imperfect solution which is different from an alternative imperfect solution which the Court of Appeal might or would have adopted, but has exceeded the generous ambit within which a reasonable disagreement is possible. Further, there must be something more than mere procedural irregularity. There is a jurisdiction to strike-out 'appeal notices'.

No second appeal

There is no scope for a second appeal to the Court of Appeal when a first appeal has already been made. No further appeal may be made to the Court of Appeal unless:

(a)   the appeal would raise an important point of principle or practice; or

(b)   there is some other compelling reason for the Court of Appeal to hear it.

As Lord Justice Brooke stated in *Tanfern*: 'The decision of the first appeal court is now to be given primacy ...'

Route to the Court of Appeal

The general rule is that the appeal lies to the next level of judge in the court hierarchy. The exception is that an appeal from a final decision of a district judge or a circuit judge (or of a master or district judge of the High Court) in a multi-track claim is direct to the Court of Appeal ...

Comment

The changes are welcome but getting the benefit requires careful management. The civil justice system does not have unlimited resources and existing resources must be allocated rationally. There can be no automatic right to have two or three levels of appeal and litigants can no longer expect to have all their concerns heard with full consideration by an appellate tribunal. There is now even greater emphasis on the proper use of resources and this means that some cases may now not be included in the appeal system and some unjust decisions will be perpetuated. There is a necessary trade-off for the new benefits of increased access to swift and economic justice. There is greater scope for court control, administrative sanctions and a robust approach. Much emphasis is placed on ensuring that cases are processed promptly and effectively and everything is geared to the administrative convenience of the court. Paradoxically, the effect of transferring case management powers to the courts is to increase case management responsibilities on litigants and their lawyers. The benefits of access to justice will accrue to the well funded and well prepared. Funding and the front-loading of costs remain the biggest issues at all levels of litigation.

––·––·––·––·––·––·––·––·––·––·––·––·––·––

The Human Rights Act 1998 is coming to affect every aspect of the English legal system. In the following piece, Stephen Groz examines some of the ways in which the legislation affects the processes of civil justice.

Stephen Groz, 'Equality of justice' (2000) *Gazette*, 21 September, p 30

It would be unfortunate if case management decisions in this jurisdiction involved the need to refer to the learning of the European Court of Human Rights in order for them to be resolved. In my judgment, cases such as this do not require any consideration of human rights issues, certainly issues under article 6 [the right to a fair trial] ... I hope that judges will be robust in resisting any attempt to introduce those arguments. (*Walker v Daniels*, CA, 2 May 2000.)

Here, Lord Woolf MR is not instructing judges to ignore the Human Rights Act 1998, but simply observing that they have always been in the business of providing fair trials. This may be obvious, but it will inform the judiciary's approach to human rights arguments.

In general, there is no difference between the right to a fair trial and the overriding objective of the Civil Procedure Rules (CPR) of enabling the court to deal with cases 'justly' (part ii), and article 6 does no more than reflect the approach of the common law: *Ebert v Venvil* [1999] 3 WLR 670, CA. Moreover, s 3 of the Act requires that the provisions of the CPR must be read and given effect in a manner which is compatible with Convention rights so far as it is possible to do so.

If this is impossible, the rules will be *ultra vires* unless the incompatibility is required by s 1 and schedule 1 to the Civil Procedure Act 1997: see *mutatis mutandis General Mediterranean Holdings v Patel* [2000] 1 WLR 272, QBD. Further, as public authorities, courts must act in a manner compatible with Convention rights unless incompatible legislation requires otherwise (s 6 of the Act).

Article 6(1) of the Convention applies to the determination of both 'civil rights' and criminal charges. The rest of the article relates to criminal cases only, although the autonomous notion of 'criminal charge' may include civil matters such as committal for contempt. Article 6(1) expressly requires an 'independent and impartial' tribunal, a 'fair' hearing, a public hearing and public pronouncement of judgment, and a determination within a reasonable time. The Strasbourg-based European Court of Human Rights has found the following rights to be inherent in article 6:

- 'equality of arms' – each party must have a reasonable opportunity to present his case under conditions which do not place him at a substantial disadvantage vis-a-vis his opponent: *De Haes & Gijsels v Belgium* (1998) 25 EHRR 1. This principle is echoed in r 1.1(2)(a), the principle of ensuring the parties are on an equal footing;

- access to a court: *Golder v United Kingdom* (1979-80)1 EHRR 524. This right is now familiar to English law: *R v Lord Chancellor, ex parte Witham* [1998] QB 575, DC. It maybe restricted by procedural rules, provided that they do not impair the 'very essence of the right': *Ashingdane v United Kingdom* (1985) 7 EHRR 528; and,

- properly adversarial procedure. This entails the right of a party to have the opportunity to present any evidence needed for his claims to succeed, and to see and comment on all material submitted with a view to influencing the court's decision: *Mantovanelli v France* (1997) 24 EHRR 370. Again, this principle can be derived from r 1.1(2)(a).

One immediate change is that Lord Woolf will probably be unable to sit in any appeal involving the interpretation and application of the CPR, at least where a party seeks to challenge their compliance with a Convention right. He drafted them, and a party might legitimately fear that he would not be open to an argument that the CPR are incompatible with Convention rights.

Other changes may be less dramatic, and judges and lawyers will need to distinguish the good arguments from the bad.

Security for costs

Rule 3.1(5) empowers the court to order a party to pay money into court if that party has, without good reason, failed to comply with a rule, practice direction or protocol. In exercising this power, the court will have to take account of the party's means to ensure it is not thereby imposing a condition with which he cannot comply, since such a bar on access could be disproportionate.

Public hearings and judgments

Most case management decisions 'determine' civil rights, and the courts' power to make them on its own initiative without hearing the parties (CPR 3.3.4) does not violate article 6. Interlocutory orders can be made without a public hearing of the parties, and need not be pronounced in public. Whether article 6(1) requires an oral hearing in other cases is likely to depend on the importance of the proposed order in the context of the overall proceedings, the extent to which the parties can make effective submissions in other ways and the extent to which a party's conduct is directly in issue: *Muylderamys v Belgium* (1993) 15 EHRR 204. CPR 39.2 now provides a general rule that hearings are to be in public, although this does not require the making of special arrangements for accommodating members of the public. The Exceptions in 39.2.3 are broadly in line with those in article 6(1) and must be interpreted compatibly with them. In spite of its wording, article 6(1) does not always require public pronouncement of judgment. Other methods of publicity, for instance depositing judgment in a registry accessible to the public, may be acceptable.

Striking out

Article 6(1) does not prevent the striking out of claims in appropriate cases since it applies only to genuine and serious disputes about civil rights and obligations. However, a claim submitted to a tribunal for determination must be presumed to be genuine and serious unless there are indications to the contrary: *Rolf Gustafson v Sweden* (1998) 25 EHRR 623. See also *Jarvis v Hampshire County Council, The Times,* November 23, 1999, CA.

But courts must be cautious where exercising the r 3.4(2)(a) power would exclude an entire category of claims or confer blanket 'immunities' from civil liability: *Fayed v United Kingdom* (1994) 18 EHRR 393.

Interim orders

The grant of interim remedies under CPR 25.1 may raise issues under article 8 (respect for private life and the home, including professional premises) or Protocol 1 article 1 (peaceful enjoyment of possessions). In most cases interference, for example the grant of a search order, can be justified as necessary 'for the protection of the rights and freedoms of others' (article 8(2)), or as 'in the public interest' (Protocol 1, article 1). Nevertheless the court must have regard to the principle of proportionality inherent in these articles when deciding whether the object of the order can be achieved by less restrictive means.

Section 12 of the Act imposes express restrictions in respect of orders which might affect the right to freedom of expression. Where the respondent is neither present nor represented, no relief is to be granted unless the court is satisfied that all practicable steps have been taken to notify him, or that there are compelling reasons why he should not be notified. Further, no relief is to be given to restrain publication before trial unless the court is satisfied that the applicant is likely to establish that publication should not be allowed.

Disclosure

An order for disclosure is *prima facie* an interference with private life and correspondence, although in most cases it will be justified by the requirements of a fair trial. However, a party may be able to resist the disclosure of confidential information which would involve a breach of a third party's right to respect for private life: *MS v Sweden* (1999) 28 EHRR 313; to protect third party sources (*Gaskin v United Kingdom* (1990) 12 EHRR 36); or journalistic sources (*Goodwin v United Kingdom* (1996) 22 EHRR 123); or for the protection of that party's mental or physical health (*R v Mid-Glamorgan Family Health Services, ex parte Martin* (1995) 1 WLR 110 CA).

A public authority's failure to disclose, or to permit disclosure of, relevant documents which would assist a party to establish its case may breach article 6(1) (*McGinley and Egan v United Kingdom* (1999) 27 EHRR 1). CPR 31.12, relating to specific disclosure, should be applied accordingly. This may be of particular importance in public law proceedings, where disclosure has traditionally been more restrictive.

Experts

Article 6(1) bestows no right to call expert evidence, unless it is necessary to ensure the fairness of the proceedings. The appointment of a single expert is not contrary to article 6(1), although the right to an adversarial procedure may require the parties to be actively involved in the process by which the expert prepares his report, including attending interviews and examining the documents on which the report is based: *Mantovanelli v France* (1997) 24 EHRR 370.

It is not contrary to article 6(1) to allow a party to put additional questions to a joint expert following completion of her report: *Daniels v Walker, The Times*, May 17, 2000, CA.

Proceedings involving the Act and the Convention

Claims alleging that a public authority has breached a Convention right may be brought in 'such court or tribunal as may be determined in accordance with rules': (HRA, s 7(2)). Those rules now appear in the 18th update to the CPR, courtesy of the Civil Procedure (Amendment No 4) Rules 2000 (SI No 2092 (L 16)) [which came into effect on 2 October 2000].

Proceedings may be brought in any court, except that a claim for damages in respect of a judicial act must start in the High Court. A declaration of incompatibility may be made only by the High Court or above, and a case may be transferred from a county court to the High Court 'where there is a real prospect that a declaration of incompatibility will be made' (para 7 of practice direction to CPR part 30).

—— · —— · —— · —— · —— · —— · —— · —— · —— · —— · —— · ——

The next and final piece examines the experience of litigants who act without a lawyer.

Frances Gibb, 'When the quest for justice sours' (2000) *The Times*, 28 November

More than 88,000 people went to court last year to resolve disputes without the aid of a lawyer. The reforms to the civil courts that took effect in April 1999 were meant to encourage more 'do-it-yourself' justice, and there is early evidence that litigants-in-person are indeed on the rise, although there are no firm figures. The experience of most litigants is good, according to research by Professor Hazel Genn of University College London. People are pleased with what they find and often pleasantly surprised.

But when people are not happy with the way their case was handled, an initial dispute can turn into horrendous long-running battles with the justice system itself. That applies equally in the criminal and the civil courts.

The two cases below highlight how a quest for justice can turn sour.

Wendy Morris and her 86-year-old mother became embroiled in a dispute with a builder over the construction of the driveway to her mother's bungalow. The case came up in the small claims court in Chester.

The builder was claiming £500 he said was due; mother and daughter argued that he had not done the work according to the contract. The district judge, who heard the case in his chambers, found in the builder's favour.

Morris, of Little Neston, Cheshire, was appalled at the way the hearing was conducted. The judge took three phone calls during the hearing, which started late and took much longer than it was listed for. The judge also admitted that he had not read the papers.

Morris complained to the Lord Chancellor's Department (LCD), but the answers she received only further exasperated her. In a long reply, the department justified all that had happened and rejected her complaints. It cited the district judge, who said that hearing times could not be guaranteed, although he made the point that litigants should be warned of that in advance.

Over not having read the papers, the judge said he looked through but decided to call the parties in to rehearse the detail of the case rather than waste time reading all the comments in detail.

As for taking three phone calls, the department's letter says that the judge admits to answering the phone. 'If it is a personal call he will not take it unless it is an emergency but will deal briefly with calls about court matters.' The letter adds: 'He says he may well have taken a call regarding his office computer, which needed repairing.' The letter concludes by saying there is nothing more to add. There was no apology, simply a comment that the official was 'sorry (Morris) had felt it necessary to write'. But, she says, if people do not complain, how will the Lord Chancellor become aware of the way judges are behaving? The response, she argues, displayed arrogance and a disregard for users of the court system. 'I am appalled that it is considered acceptable for the judge to take three phone calls during a hearing. Also, I cannot be held responsible for the vagaries of the court listing office. The judge has a duty to be aware of the facts of a case he is to hear, seeking to transfer blame is a dereliction of duty.'

The LCD could not comment, save to say that the case was still 'unresolved'.

In a second case, Joseph Lawrence, of Northwood, Middlesex, is in dispute with the Lord Chancellor over the trial of his case before a circuit judge at Watford County Court in November 1999. The nub of his complaint is that the judge met the solicitors acting for the claimants before giving his judgment. The firm also happened to be the judge's own solicitors and he was seeing them about a will. A letter from Lord Irvine of Lairg's department says that the judge openly declared his visit before its existence emerged in the Court of Appeal.

The letter says the judge did not discuss the case with the solicitors and 'utterly rejects' the notion that he misrepresented the position. Lawrence is not satisfied. 'Until March this year I could not know that the trial judge had visited the claimants' lawyers while considering his judgment. I only found out when I went to the Court of Appeal. I find this all deeply disturbing.'

As with Morris, there is no suggestion that the judge did not reach the right decision. In any case, judges must rightly be independent over their rulings. But in the eyes of the litigant, justice was not seen to be done.

If court officials make mistakes that cause financial loss, people can apply for compensation from the Court Service. In 1996–97, £400,000 was paid out in 1,000 cases; in 1998–99, £380,543 was paid out in 1,143 cases. But if complaints are made about judges' behaviour, little can be done. The new judicial appointments commissioner, to be appointed by Lord Irvine, could do worse than to make introduction of a new complaints system for such cases a priority.

— — · — · — · — · — · — · — · — · — · — · — · — · — · — · —

Under the new CPR, there is a considerable incentive for parties to settle their differences. The rationale for this is that the greater the extent to which many sorts of cases can be compromised rather than thrashed out to a position of one winner and one loser, the better for society. That will not apply to all cases, but it will for many. The court will take into account any pre-action offers to settle when making an order for costs. Thus, a side which has refused a reasonable offer to settle will be treated less generously in the issue of how far the court will order their costs to be paid by the other side. For this to happen, the offer, though, must be one which is made to be open to the other side for at least 21 days after receipt (to stop any undue pressure being put on someone with the phrase 'take it or leave it, it is only open for one day then I shall withdraw the offer'). Also, if the offer is made by the defendant, it must be an offer to pay compensation and to pay the claimant's costs. Several aspects of the new rules encourage litigants to settle rather than take risks in order (as a claimant) to hold out for unreasonably large sums of compensation, or try to get away (as a defendant) with paying nothing rather than some compensation. The system of Pt 36 payments or offers does not apply to small claims but, for other cases, it seems bound to have a significant effect.

At any stage after the commencement of proceedings, the defendant may make a payment into court in satisfaction of the claimant's claim. The claimant may accept the payment or continue the action. If the latter and the damages obtained are not greater than the amount paid in by the defendant, the claimant will be liable for the defendant's taxed (that is, approved by a court official – not 'taxed' in the conventional sense of the word) costs from the time of payment in even though he or she has won the action. When the judge makes an award of damages, he will not know the amount of any payment into court, so he cannot influence the matter of whether the claimant has to suffer under the rule.

CPR Part 36 is set out below.

The Civil Procedure Rules (updated to June 2001)

Part 36

Offers to Settle Payments into Court

Contents of this Part

Scope of this Part

36.1 (1) This Part contains rules about–

    (a)   offers to settle and payments into court; and

    (b)   the consequences where an offer to settle or payment into court is made in accordance with this Part.

  (2) Nothing in this Part prevents a party making an offer to settle in whatever way he chooses, but if that offer is not made in accordance with this Part, it will only have the consequences specified in this Part if the court so orders.

    (Part 36 applies to Part 20 claims by virtue of rule 20.3)

Part 36 Offers and Part 36 Payments – General Provisions

36.2 (1) An offer made in accordance with the requirements of this Part is called–

    (a)   if made by way of a payment into court, 'a Part 36 payment';

    (b)   otherwise 'a Part 36 offer'.

    (Rule 36.3 sets out when an offer has to be made by way of a payment into court)

  (2) The party who makes an offer is the 'offeror'.

  (3) The party to whom an offer is made is the 'offeree'.

  (4) A Part 36 offer or a Part 36 payment–

    (a)   may be made at any time after proceedings have started; and

    (b)   may be made in appeal proceedings.

  (5) A Part 36 offer or a Part 36 payment shall not have the consequences set out in this Part while the claim is being dealt with on the small claims track unless the court orders otherwise.

    (Part 26 deals with allocation to the small claims track)

    (Rule 27.2 provides that Part 36 does not apply to small claims)

A Defendant's Offer to Settle a Money Claim Requires a Part 36 Payment

36.3 (1) Subject to rules 36.5(5) and 36.23, an offer by a defendant to settle a money claim will not have the consequences set out in this Part unless it is made by way of a Part 36 payment.

  (2) A Part 36 payment may only be made after proceedings have started.

    (Rule 36.5(5) permits a Part 36 offer to be made by reference to an interim payment)

    (Rule 36.10 makes provision for an offer to settle a money claim before the commencement of proceedings)

    (Rule 36.23 makes provision for where benefit is recoverable under the Social Security (Recovery of Benefit) Act 1997)

Defendant's Offer to Settle the Whole of a Claim Which Includes Both a Money Claim and a Non-money Claim

36.4 (1) This rule applies where a defendant to a claim which includes both a money claim and a non-money claim wishes–

    (a)   to make an offer to settle the whole claim which will have the consequences set out in this Part; and

    (b)   to make a money offer in respect of the money claim and a non-money offer in respect of the non-money claim.

(2)   The defendant must–

    (a)   make a Part 36 payment in relation to the money claim; and

    (b)   make a Part 36 offer in relation to the non-money claim.

(3)   The Part 36 payment notice must–

    (a)   identify the document which sets out the terms of the Part 36 offer; and

    (b)   state that if the claimant gives notice of acceptance of the Part 36 payment he will be treated as also accepting the Part 36 offer.

    (Rule 36.6 makes provision for a Part 36 payment notice)

(4)   If the claimant gives notice of acceptance of the Part 36 payment, he shall also be taken as giving notice of acceptance of the Part 36 offer in relation to the non-money claim.

Form and Content of a Part 36 Offer

36.5 (1)   A Part 36 offer must be in writing.

(2)   A Part 36 offer may relate to the whole claim or to part of it or to any issue that arises in it.

(3)   A Part 36 offer must–

    (a)   state whether it relates to the whole of the claim or to part of it or to an issue that arises in it and if so to which part or issue;

    (b)   state whether it takes into account any counterclaim; and

    (c)   if it is expressed not to be inclusive of interest, give the details relating to interest set out in rule 36.22(2).

(4)   A defendant may make a Part 36 offer limited to accepting liability up to a specified proportion.

(5)   A Part 36 offer may be made by reference to an interim payment.

    (Part 25 contains provisions relating to interim payments)

(6)   A Part 36 offer made not less than 21 days before the start of the trial must–

    (a)   be expressed to remain open for acceptance for 21 days from the date it is made; and

    (b)   provide that after 21 days the offeree may only accept it if–

        (i)   the parties agree the liability for costs; or

        (ii)   the court gives permission.

(7)   A Part 36 offer made less than 21 days before the start of the trial must state that the offeree may only accept it if–

    (a)   the parties agree the liability for costs; or

    (b)   the court gives permission.

    (Rule 36.8 makes provision for when a Part 36 offer is treated as being made)

(8)   If a Part 36 offer is withdrawn it will not have the consequences set out in this Part.

Notice of a Part 36 Payment

36.6 (1) A Part 36 payment may relate to the whole claim or part of it or to an issue that arises in it.

(2) A defendant who makes a Part 36 payment must file with the court a notice ('Part 36 payment notice') which–

(a) states the amount of the payment;

(b) states whether the payment relates to the whole claim or to part of it or to any issue that arises in it and if so to which part or issue;

(c) states whether it takes into account any counterclaim;

(d) if an interim payment has been made, states that the defendant has taken into account the interim payment; and

(e) if it is expressed not to be inclusive of interest, gives the details relating to interest set out in rule 36.22(2).

(Rule 25.6 makes provision for an interim payment)

(Rule 36.4 provides for further information to be included where a defendant wishes to settle the whole of a claim which includes a money claim and a non-money claim)

(Rule 36.23 makes provision for extra information to be included in the payment notice in a case where benefit is recoverable under the Social Security (Recovery of Benefit) Act 1997)

(3) The court will serve the Part 36 payment notice on the offeree unless the offeror informs the court, when the money is paid into court, that the offeror will serve the notice.

(4) Where the offeror serves the Part 36 payment notice he must file a certificate of service.

(Rule 6.10 specifies what must be contained in a certificate of service)

(5) A Part 36 payment may be withdrawn or reduced only with the permission of the court.

Offer to Settle a Claim for Provisional Damages

36.7 (1) A defendant may make a Part 36 payment in respect of a claim which includes a claim for provisional damages.

(2) Where he does so, the Part 36 payment notice must specify whether or not the defendant is offering to agree to the making of an award of provisional damages.

(3) Where the defendant is offering to agree to the making of an award of provisional damages the payment notice must also state–

(a) that the sum paid into court is in satisfaction of the claim for damages on the assumption that the injured person will not develop the disease or suffer the type of deterioration specified in the notice;

(b) that the offer is subject to the condition that the claimant must make any claim for further damages within a limited period; and

(c) what that period is.

(4) Where a Part 36 payment is–

    (a)   made in accordance with paragraph (3); and

    (b)   accepted within the relevant period in rule 36.11,

the Part 36 payment will have the consequences set out in rule 36.13, unless the court orders otherwise.

(5) If the claimant accepts the Part 36 payment he must, within 7 days of doing so, apply to the court for an order for an award of provisional damages under rule 41.2.

(Rule 41.2 provides for an order for an award of provisional damages)

(6) The money in court may not be paid out until the court has disposed of the application made in accordance with paragraph (5).

Time when a Part 36 Offer or a Part 36 Payment is Made and Accepted

36.8 (1) A Part 36 offer is made when received by the offeree.

(2) A Part 36 payment is made when written notice of the payment into court is served on the offeree.

(3) An improvement to a Part 36 offer will be effective when its details are received by the offeree.

(4) An increase in a Part 36 payment will be effective when notice of the increase is served on the offeree.

(5) A Part 36 offer or Part 36 payment is accepted when notice of its acceptance is received by the offeror.

Clarification of a Part 36 Offer or a Part 36 Payment Notice

36.9 (1) The offeree may, within 7 days of a Part 36 offer or payment being made, request the offeror to clarify the offer or payment notice.

(2) If the offeror does not give the clarification requested under paragraph (1) within 7 days of receiving the request, the offeree may, unless the trial has started, apply for an order that he does so.

(3) If the court makes an order under paragraph (2), it must specify the date when the Part 36 offer or Part 36 payment is to be treated as having been made.

Court to Take into Account Offer to Settle Made Before Commencement of Proceedings

36.10 (1) If a person makes an offer to settle before proceedings are begun which complies with the provisions of this rule, the court will take that offer into account when making any order as to costs.

(2) The offer must–

    (a)   be expressed to be open for at least 21 days after the date it was made;

    (b)   if made by a person who would be a defendant were proceedings commenced, include an offer to pay the costs of the offeree incurred up to the date 21 days after the date it was made; and

    (c)   otherwise comply with this Part.

(3) If the offeror is a defendant to a money claim–

    (a) he must make a Part 36 payment within 14 days of service of the claim form; and

    (b) the amount of the payment must be not less than the sum offered before proceedings began.

(4) An offeree may not, after proceedings have begun, accept–

    (a) an offer made under paragraph (2); or

    (b) a Part 36 payment made under paragraph (3),

without the permission of the court.

(5) An offer under this rule is made when it is received by the offeree.

Time for Acceptance of a Defendant's Part 36 Offer or Part 36 Payment

36.11 (1) A claimant may accept a Part 36 offer or a Part 36 payment made not less than 21 days before the start of the trial without needing the court's permission if he gives the defendant written notice of acceptance not later than 21 days after the offer or payment was made.

(Rule 36.13 sets out the costs consequences of accepting a defendant's offer or payment without needing the permission of the court)

(2) If–

    (a) a defendant's Part 36 offer or Part 36 payment is made less than 21 days before the start of the trial; or

    (b) the claimant does not accept it within the period specified in paragraph (1)–

        (i) if the parties agree the liability for costs, the claimant may accept the offer or payment without needing the permission of the court;

        (ii) if the parties do not agree the liability for costs the claimant may only accept the offer or payment with the permission of the court.

(3) Where the permission of the court is needed under paragraph (2) the court will, if it gives permission, make an order as to costs.

Time for Acceptance of a Claimant's Part 36 Offer

36.12 (1) A defendant may accept a Part 36 offer made not less than 21 days before the start of the trial without needing the court's permission if he gives the claimant written notice of acceptance not later than 21 days after the offer was made.

(Rule 36.14 sets out the costs consequences of accepting a claimant's offer without needing the permission of the court)

(2) If–

    (a) a claimant's Part 36 offer is made less than 21 days before the start of the trial; or

    (b) the defendant does not accept it within the period specified in paragraph (1)–

        (i) if the parties agree the liability for costs, the defendant may accept the offer without needing the permission of the court;

     (ii)   if the parties do not agree the liability for costs the defendant may only accept the offer with the permission of the court.

(3)   Where the permission of the court is needed under paragraph (2) the court will, if it gives permission, make an order as to costs.

Costs Consequences of Acceptance of a Defendant's Part 36 Offer of Part 36 Payment

36.13 (1)   Where a Part 36 offer or a Part 36 payment is accepted without needing the permission of the court the claimant will be entitled to his costs of the proceedings up to the date of serving notice of acceptance.

   (2)   Where–

     (a)   a Part 36 offer or a Part 36 payment relates to part only of the claim; and

     (b)   at the time of serving notice of acceptance the claimant abandons the balance of the claim,

   the claimant will be entitled to his costs of the proceedings up to the date of serving notice of acceptance, unless the court orders otherwise.

   (3)   The claimant's costs include any costs attributable to the defendant's counterclaim if the Part 36 offer or the Part 36 payment notice states that it takes into account the counterclaim.

   (4)   Costs under this rule will be payable on the standard basis if not agreed.

Costs Consequences of Acceptance of a Claimant's Part 36 Offer

36.14   Where a claimant's Part 36 offer is accepted without needing the permission of the court the claimant will be entitled to his costs of the proceedings up to the date upon which the defendant serves notice of acceptance.

The Effect of Acceptance of a Part 36 Offer or Part 36 Payment

36.15 (1)   If a Part 36 offer or Part 36 payment relates to the whole claim and is accepted, the claim will be stayed$^{(GL)}$.

   (2)   In the case of acceptance of a Part 36 offer which relates to the whole claim–

     (a)   the stay$^{(GL)}$ will be upon the terms of the offer; and

     (b)   either party may apply to enforce those terms without the need for a new claim.

   (3)   If a Part 36 offer or a Part 36 payment which relates to part only of the claim is accepted–

     (a)   the claim will be stayed$^{(GL)}$ as to that part; and

     (b)   unless the parties have agreed costs, the liability for costs shall be decided by the court.

   (4)   If the approval of the court is required before a settlement can be binding, any stay$^{(GL)}$ which would otherwise arise on the acceptance of a Part 36 offer or a Part 36 payment will take effect only when that approval has been given.

   (5)   Any stay$^{(GL)}$ arising under this rule will not affect the power of the court–

     (a)   to enforce the terms of a Part 36 offer;

     (b)   to deal with any question of costs (including interest on costs) relating to the proceedings;

(c) to order payment out of court of any sum paid into court.

(6) Where–

 (a) a Part 36 offer has been accepted; and

 (b) a party alleges that–

  (i) the other party has not honoured the terms of the offer; and

  (ii) he is therefore entitled to a remedy for breach of contract,

the party may claim the remedy by applying to the court without the need to start a new claim unless the court orders otherwise.

Payment out of a Sum in Court on Acceptance of a Part 36 Payment

36.16 Where a Part 36 payment is accepted the claimant obtains payment out of the sum in court by making a request for payment in the practice form.

Acceptance of a Part 36 Offer or a Part 36 Payment Made by One or More, but not All, the Defendants

36.17 (1) This rule applies where the claimant wishes to accept a Part 36 offer or a Part 36 payment made by one or more, but not all, of a number of defendants.

 (2) If the defendants are sued jointly or in the alternative, the claimant may accept the offer or payment without needing the permission of the court in accordance with rule 36.11(1) if–

  (a) he discontinues his claim against those defendants who have not made the offer or payment; and

  (b) those defendants give written consent to the acceptance of the offer or payment.

 (3) If the claimant alleges that the defendants have a several liability(GL) to him the claimant may–

  (a) accept the offer or payment in accordance with rule 36.11(1); and

  (b) continue with his claims against the other defendants if he is entitled to do so.

 (4) In all other cases the claimant must apply to the court for–

  (a) an order permitting a payment out to him of any sum in court; and

  (b) such order as to costs as the court considers appropriate.

Other Cases Where a Court Order is Required to Enable Acceptance of a Part 36 Offer or a Part 36 Payment

36.18 (1) Where a Part 36 offer or a Part 36 payment is made in proceedings to which rule 21.10 applies–

  (a) the offer or payment may be accepted only with the permission of the court; and

  (b) no payment out of any sum in court shall be made without a court order.

  (Rule 21.10 deals with compromise etc. by or on behalf of a child or patient)

 (2) Where the court gives a claimant permission to accept a Part 36 offer or payment after the trial has started–

  (a) any money in court may be paid out only with a court order; and

(b)   the court must, in the order, deal with the whole costs of the proceedings.

(3)   Where a claimant accepts a Part 36 payment after a defence of tender before claim$^{(GL)}$ has been put forward by the defendant, the money in court may be paid out only after an order of the court.

(Rule 37.3 requires a defendant who wishes to rely on a defence of tender before claim$^{(GL)}$ to make a payment into court)

Restriction on Disclosure of a Part 36 Offer or a Part 36 Payment

36.19 (1) A Part 36 offer will be treated as 'without prejudice$^{(GL)}$ except as to costs'.

(2)   The fact that a Part 36 payment has been made shall not be communicated to the trial judge until all questions of liability and the amount of money to be awarded have been decided.

(3)   Paragraph (2) does not apply–

(a)   where the defence of tender before claim$^{(GL)}$ has been raised;

(b)   where the proceedings have been stayed$^{(GL)}$ under rule 36.15 following acceptance of a Part 36 offer or Part 36 payment; or

(c)   where–

(i)   the issue of liability has been determined before any assessment of the money claimed; and

(ii)   the fact that there has or has not been a Part 36 payment may be relevant to the question of the costs of the issue of liability.

Costs Consequences Where Claimant Fails to do Better than a Part 36 Offer or a Part 36 Payment

36.20 (1) This rule applies where at trial a claimant–

(a)   fails to better a Part 36 payment; or

(b)   fails to obtain a judgment which is more advantageous than a defendant's Part 36 offer.

(2)   Unless it considers it unjust to do so, the court will order the claimant to pay any costs incurred by the defendant after the latest date on which the payment or offer could have been accepted without needing the permission of the court.

(Rule 36.11 sets out the time for acceptance of a defendant's Part 36 offer or Part 36 payment)

Costs and Other Consequences Where Claimant does Better than He Proposed in his Part 36 Offer

36.21 (1) This rule applies where at trial–

(a)   a defendant is held liable for more; or

(b)   the judgment against a defendant is more advantageous to the claimant, than the proposals contained in a claimant's Part 36 offer.

(2)   The court may order interest on the whole or part of any sum of money (excluding interest) awarded to the claimant at a rate not exceeding 10% above base rate$^{(GL)}$ for some or all of the period starting with the latest date

on which the defendant could have accepted the offer without needing the permission of the court.

(3) The court may also order that the claimant is entitled to–

    (a) his costs on the indemnity basis from the latest date when the defendant could have accepted the offer without needing the permission of the court; and

    (b) interest on those costs at a rate not exceeding 10% above base rate[(GL)].

(4) Where this rule applies, the court will make the orders referred to in paragraphs (2) and (3) unless it considers it unjust to do so.

(Rule 36.12 sets out the latest date when the defendant could have accepted the offer)

(5) In considering whether it would be unjust to make the orders referred to in paragraphs (2) and (3) above, the court will take into account all the circumstances of the case including–

    (a) the terms of any Part 36 offer;

    (b) the stage in the proceedings when any Part 36 offer or Part 36 payment was made;

    (c) the information available to the parties at the time when the Part 36 offer or Part 36 payment was made; and

    (d) the conduct of the parties with regard to the giving or refusing to give information for the purposes of enabling the offer or payment into court to be made or evaluated.

(6) Where the court awards interest under this rule and also awards interest on the same sum and for the same period under any other power, the total rate of interest may not exceed 10% above base rate[(GL)].

Interest

36.22 (1) Unless–

    (a) a claimant's Part 36 offer which offers to accept a sum of money; or

    (b) a Part 36 payment notice,

indicates to the contrary, any such offer or payment will be treated as inclusive of all interest until the last date on which it could be accepted without needing the permission of the court.

(2) Where a claimant's Part 36 offer or Part 36 payment notice is expressed not to be inclusive of interest, the offer or notice must state–

    (a) whether interest is offered; and

    (b) if so, the amount offered, the rate or rates offered and the period or periods for which it is offered.

Deduction of Benefits

36.23 (1) This rule applies where a payment to a claimant following acceptance of a Part 36 offer or Part 36 payment into court would be a compensation payment as defined in section 1 of the Social Security (Recovery of Benefits) Act 1997.

(2) A defendant to a money claim may make an offer to settle the claim which will have the consequences set out in this Part, without making a Part 36 payment if–

    (a)   at the time he makes the offer he has applied for, but not received, a certificate of recoverable benefit; and

    (b)   he makes a Part 36 payment not more than 7 days after he receives the certificate.

(Section 1 of the 1997 Act defines 'recoverable benefit'.)

(3) A Part 36 payment notice must state–

    (a)   the amount of gross compensation;

    (b)   the name and amount of any benefit by which that gross amount is reduced in accordance with section 8 and Schedule 2 to the 1997 Act; and

    (c)   that the sum paid in is the net amount after deduction of the amount of benefit.

(4) For the purposes of rule 36.20, a claimant fails to better a Part 36 payment if he fails to obtain judgment for more than the gross sum specified in the Part 36 payment notice.

(5) Where–

    (a)   a Part 36 payment has been made; and

    (b)   application is made for the money remaining in court to be paid out,

the court may treat the money in court as being reduced by a sum equivalent to any further recoverable benefits paid to the claimant since the date of payment into court and may direct payment out accordingly.

CHAPTER 6

ALTERNATIVE DISPUTE RESOLUTION

It is generally recognised that the very form of law makes it inappropriate to deal adequately with certain areas; family matters being the most obvious example but, equally, disputes between business clients may be exacerbated by recourse to the finality of court action. Equally, it is recognised that the formal and rather intimidatory atmosphere of the ordinary courts is not necessarily the most appropriate one in which to decide such matters, even where the dispute cannot be resolved internally. In recognition of this fact, various alternatives have been developed specifically to avoid the perceived shortcomings of the formal structure of law and court procedure.

Whilst Alternative Dispute Resolution (ADR) is usually regarded as referring to arbitration and mediation, this chapter will extend this meaning to allow an examination of the role of the various administrative tribunals which exercise so much power in contemporary society. Although located within the formal court structure and so, strictly speaking, not a part of ADR, the small claims track will also be considered.

In the first article, the Lord Chancellor Lord Irvine provides a general consideration of the role of ADR.

The Lord Chancellor Lord Irvine of Lairg, Inaugural Lecture to the Faculty of Mediation and Alternative Dispute Resolution, 27 January 1999

Let me begin with a quotation for everyone who still thinks that the concept of alternatives to combative, court-based, Olympian dispute resolution is today's modishness. It is from *The Charitable Arbitrator*, written in 1688, by the so-called 'Prior of St Pierre', who was evidently no fan of litigation. If you are minded to satirise lawyers in print, a pseudonym may have been then, as now, a shrewd move! He wrote:

> ... to be a good mediator you need more than anything patience, common sense, an appropriate manner, and goodwill. You must make yourself liked by both parties, and gain credibility in their minds. To do that, begin by explaining that you are unhappy about the bother, the trouble and the expense that their litigation is causing them. After that, listen patiently to all their complaints. They will not be short, *particularly the first time around*.

The Academy of Experts has worked hard in recent years to improve the standards of dispute resolution in this country. I am delighted to be here today, to deliver the inaugural lecture of this Faculty of Mediation and ADR. I hope that this lecture – like the Faculty itself – will continue to take forward the essential public debate about ADR.

The modern development of ADR has its origins in the United States of America in the 1970s as a reaction against the high cost and long delays of litigating business disputes. ADR has now come to be recognised internationally as an effective alternative to highly expensive and rigid adversarial systems.

ADR has spread primarily through the influence of the institutions. These include the international arbitration organisations, national and regional arbitration and conciliation centres, national arbitration institutions, professional institutions and national courts. Whilst not dependent on government endorsement, this can provide additional impetus. The International Chamber of Commerce, recognising that the conduct of formal arbitration or litigation may be costly, time consuming, and entail considerable disruption for the parties involved, has always had a procedure for conciliation and two thirds of all ICC arbitration cases are resolved through negotiation before the imposition of an award. Other major international arbitration organisations to offer conciliation services include the American Arbitration Association, the London Court of International Arbitration, the World Intellectual Property Organisation and the International Centre for the Settlement of Investment Disputes. Building on this international framework, most national arbitration centres and organisations now actively promote the use of ADR.

In the UK the Centre for Dispute Resolution (CEDR) was launched with the support of the Confederation of British Industry in 1990 to promote ADR in dispute handling. CEDR promotes ADR, trains and accredits mediators and arranges mediations and they claim a 95 per cent success rate in resolving disputes. The Academy of Experts, although its main purpose is to promote the better use of experts, is also at the forefront in the development of ADR processes and was the first UK body to establish a register of qualified mediators. The British Association of Lawyer Mediators was set up in 1995 with the aim of promoting mediation in the UK and of the role of lawyers in mediation and the maintenance of high professional standards. The City Disputes Panel, was founded in 1994 to settle financial disputes in the financial services industry. Its panellists are dedicated to the resolution of financial disputes through mediation, evaluation, determination and arbitration. Also the use of ADR has been established in the UK in resolving family and divorce disputes, employment disputes, environmental disputes, and community or neighbourhood disputes.

The Government freely recognises that ADR has a significant part to play in the delivery of civil justice. In Opposition, we advocated the development of alternatives to litigation, including the use of legal aid to fund access to mediation, arbitration and tribunals. Almost four years ago, at the Labour Party Annual Conference of 1995, we drew attention in our Policy Statement to what we considered to be: 'an imbalance between public provision for traditional litigation on the one hand and mediation services on the other.'

We also made it plain that we proposed to use the existing legal aid budget 'to expand access to alternative forms of dispute resolution such as mediation, arbitration and tribunals'. Last year, I approved the LAB's decision to make legal aid available for mediation.

And in Government we have continued to encourage the use of mediation, most notably in the area of family law, where it is a central tenet of divorce law reform. The importance of mediation and ADR in family law cases can scarcely be understated, given the high incidence of family breakdown and the appalling social consequences which result.

Those of you here who heard me deliver the CEDR conference Keynote Address last November will know that I have no doubt whatsoever of the considerable potential benefits which ADR can deliver, for the system of civil justice, and for the individuals and parties who seek redress through that system. I spoke then of cost-effectiveness; of high approval ratings from those who have used mediation or other alternatives; of the wide endorsement and support that so many experienced judges and senior lawyers have for ADR processes. I wholeheartedly share their enthusiasm, and their desire to develop this potential to its fullest extent.

Equally, I recognise that ADR is not dependent on Government endorsement. It is a thriving, autonomous, profitable industry. In his address to the CEDR Conference, Professor Karl Mackie referred to 'a recognition that ADR is a serious market opportunity for professional firms, a significant management tool for companies'.

Private sector companies and individuals are increasingly choosing to investigate alternatives to the courts and arbitration. Institutions such as CEDR itself, and the City Disputes Panel, are reporting rapidly increasing caseloads. It is also significant that much of this new work is international – an affirmation of London's position as the leading centre for international commercial dispute resolution.

The courts have taken their own steps to ensure that the potential benefits of ADR are, at the very least, given ready consideration by the parties before them. A pilot mediation scheme at the Central London County Courts was set up in 1996. Mediations continue to take place regularly. Those who have participated in them generally express a high degree of satisfaction with the process. I wish to pay tribute tonight to the mediators themselves – some of whom have been provided by the Academy of Experts – for their enthusiasm and support for this pioneering scheme.

I am also pleased to commend the introduction of a mediation initiative in the Technology and Construction Court – a new court which I opened last October. It is well recognised that heavy construction cases in particular are suitable for mediation, and we know from experience both in this country – but particularly in other jurisdictions such as Hong Kong, the United States and Australia – that mediation can be a, if not the, most effective way of resolving such disputes, often within the life time of the contract, and at very considerable cost savings to the parties.

The Court of Appeal continues to support ADR actively. Specialist panels of senior, widely experienced lawyers have been set up, to assist in mediating pending appeals. At the setting down stage, the Master of the Rolls now writes to both parties, urging them to consider ADR. Should they decide not to, they are invited to indicate why. This protocol helps, not only to impress upon appellant and respondent that the Court sees ADR as a serious option, but to gather direct empirical information why it is not entertained by some.

The Commercial Court issued a Practice Direction in 1993, stating that judges of the court wished to encourage parties to consider ADR. This was strengthened in a further direction, in 1996, allowing judges to consider whether a case is suitable for ADR at the interlocutory stage, to invite the parties to try it if appropriate, and to arrange early neutral evaluation.

The active support and participation of the judiciary sends a clear message to litigants and their legal representatives. ADR is not some fashionable quirk – it is a valid avenue of settlement, recognised and even promoted by the courts.

Further a discretionary power for judges will come from the new Rule 26.4, which I have approved, part of that tranche of the civil justice reforms which are due to come into effect this April. The new Rule will enable judges, at their own volition, or if requested by both parties, to stay cases they consider may be amenable to some other, more satisfactory form of resolution, such as mediation. Now, within a process driven by the imperative to keep adjournments and delays to a minimum, this Rule is remarkable in recognising that there may actually be a time benefit in delaying full proceedings, to see if quicker, more satisfactory resolution can be brought about by mediation.

This Government's increased focus on the potential benefit of ADR is, to some extent, a recognition of what the market-place is demonstrating. ADR clearly can succeed – it can deliver great benefits to parties in dispute. Individuals and companies are increasingly willing to pay for the services of mediators and arbitrators because they believe that they can achieve a more satisfactory resolution to their dispute than they are likely to secure through the full process of the court. And for parties who have, or want to leave, 'ongoing' commercial relationships, mediation is of particular value.

Let me make this point clearly. I have no doubt whatsoever that ADR has a role – an expanding role – within the civil justice system. But my Government and my Department's support is neither unconditional, nor is it absolute. There are serious and searching questions to be answered about the use of ADR. I believe that anybody who is genuinely committed to the better development of ADR is not only aware of these concerns, but shares my determination to see them addressed fully. It is in the interests of those who provide ADR to try to ensure that their services are professional, governed by universally-recognised competencies; and, above all, to ensure that they provide a service that people do need.

Professor Mackie referred in his speech to a 'gravy boat' trailing in the wake of current ADR opportunities. It is perhaps an expression that lawyers should avoid. Nobody wants to be accused of lapping at that trough. There may indeed be profits to be made from the provision of alternatives to court-based dispute resolution. But I can assure you that this Government will not be suborned into swelling them.

I want to set out my key concerns to you this evening – because I want you – the practitioners, the interested academics and experts, the experienced lawyers – to help us to find the answers. It is particularly appropriate to use the forum of this inaugural address to put these questions unequivocally on record. And I would ask anyone with views on these questions – based on comparative studies, or with the unique insights borne of experience – to pass your thoughts on to me. Your help in this will be of the greatest value.

The central objective of ADR is to encourage and promote the settlement of disputes without the need to start litigation. If that cannot be achieved, ADR still aims to assist in achieving a negotiated settlement before the trial itself starts. To succeed, ADR settlements must be fair and just, to the satisfaction of both parties in dispute. A settlement achieved without trial must be a sound and valid outcome in itself, not a compromised measure deemed by one or the other party to have short-changed them of something a trial would have achieved.

Some unstinting admirers of ADR assert that all disputes are suitable for ADR, and can benefit from it. I doubt that such unlimited enthusiasm does much to help promote wider use of ADR in the long run. Courts have a vital – indispensable – part to play in the resolution of many categories of dispute. It is, at best, naïve to claim that mediation and its alternatives can adequately equate to this role. An obvious example is the establishment of significant judicial precedent – this can arise in any category of case in dispute. Or consider the issues of cases which set the rights of the individual against those of the State. The experience of the United States suggests this is an extremely sensitive area, which must be approached with extreme care.

I think the use of ADR in administrative cases is of necessity limited. There may be more to be gained from the development of the ombudsman system, though I appreciate that ombudsmen are more concerned with the resolution of grievances, than with the resolution of disputes over conflicting rights.

But this is our current position: we do not have sufficient analytical information about ADR to claim, with certainty, that it can be useful in every category of case. We must undertake a comprehensive process of research and consideration, to answer with certainty the question: what kinds of case are suitable for ADR.

Another key area to be addressed in the development of ADR is, who are the beneficiaries? And how do they benefit? In the broadest sense, our civil and criminal reforms are driven by the need to improve access to justice. Widening the means by which everyone can gain a degree of redress for wrongs done, which lives up to expectations. Providing alternatives to the court-based resolution process must clearly be a step in the right direction.

But each step must be taken with an eye to its effect on all players in the system. Improved access to the courts will inevitably increase the burden of the workload in the courts. The introduction of the small claims arbitration scheme in 1985 was hugely popular and successful. Yet the very success of this measure imposed an unexpectedly significant burden on the county courts and the District Judges charged with administering it.

Consider, for example, the impact on the courts of ADR becoming a significantly more active part of proceedings. We would have to be sure that the Court Service actually had the capacity to deliver this substantive new function. And not at the expense of existing procedures, or other reforms – either in funding or time. Advocates of tangible Government support for ADR have argued that the Court Service will eventually benefit, through a reduction in procedural delays, or a saving of judicial time in court. This may prove to be true. But they, and we, must be able to demonstrate that the wider use of ADR in the courts is economically viable. We will need to measure and evaluate these schemes through widespread monitoring, and through pilots. And those who are active in campaigning for an expansion of ADR will need to co-operate fully in this process of assessment.

The principal argument commonly advanced in support of ADR is the potential for cost savings to the parties themselves. But again, this assumption is not straightforward. When cases do settle through ADR – particularly if this is at an early stage of litigation – very substantial cost savings can be realised. But every case which takes the option of attempting some alternative form of dispute resolution incurs an additional element of cost which does not arise if the conventional route is followed. In doing so, both parties are, in essence, taking a speculative gamble – that the investment of additional money in ADR will be rewarded by a successful pre-trial resolution, or at least a shorter case.

And the simple fact is, that some parties will lose the gamble. And *ex post facto*, they will have wasted time and money on testing the possibility of an alternate resolution – waste which would have been avoided had they chosen to stick to the conventional process of settling their dispute through the courts. The cost of gambling on successful ADR is not borne by the mediators and arbitrators, but by the parties themselves, and by civil justice itself.

Now this is not a matter of trifling costs, or a few days' delay. Those of you with professional or personal experience of ADR will acknowledge that it is often a demanding, skilled and sophisticated process. Proponents of mediation will readily cite statistics relating to saved court time and costs in some of the most complex business disputes. They are perhaps less ready to collate information on the costs arising from failed arbitrations. To ignore these elements – to make no determined attempt to weigh them up against the well-promoted benefits of ADR – is, at best, not balanced.

I don't wish to minimise the less measurable benefits which ADR can bring to parties in dispute. Those who have used it successfully report notably high levels of satisfaction with the actual outcomes achieved, and with the route taken to achieve settlement. ADR can reduce acrimony and aggression which is, regrettably, a common factor in court-based disputes. The benefit of this in mediated family disputes is, I think, very generally accepted.

Last October, speaking at the closing session of the fourth European conference on family law, in Strasbourg, I was pleased to acknowledge the wide international appreciation of the potential of mediation in family cases. I drew attention to the many positive benefits of the family mediation process. In reducing conflict; in encouraging a constructive and forward-looking perspective to the plans and aims of both parties. In securing agreements with a better chance of being adhered to, because they are based on step-by-step decisions reached and accepted by the individuals themselves. In the basic potential for financial savings.

So, we should not ignore the benefit of empowering the parties in less personal, emotional contexts. They too can appreciate a process of settlement which actually leaves them with the conviction that they have received a more truly satisfactory outcome, than that which follows months of stressful, fraught litigation. There is a convincing argument that parties feel more genuine satisfaction from an outcome achieved through a mediated solution.

By definition, practitioners of ADR have the most opportunity to benefit. Those who are able to offer competent and successful ADR and mediation services will find they are part of a burgeoning – and a profitable – new profession.

Lawyers in particular have a great opportunity to increase the range of services they can offer to their clients. That announcement last year from the Legal Aid Board that I referred to – that franchise legal aid will be available for mediation – should also cultivate the interest of many in the legal profession – including perhaps some who have remained sceptical to date.

It is clear that there is much greater awareness and interest in ADR amongst professionals from various disciplines and within the business community than was the case only five years ago or so. One good measure of ADR's growing importance is the number of mediators undergoing institutional training courses, and the fact that the Law Society and other professional bodies are devoting considerable attention to drafting appropriate ethical standards and guidelines for mediators.

New business opportunities will present the legal profession – indeed, all professions whose members are working to develop these alternatives – with considerable challenges. Certainly, compared to the majority of relevant professional organisations, ADR is not governed by any commonly agreed codes of practice, guidelines for training or professional conduct. The degree to which the public – and this Government – will put its faith in ADR, will depend greatly on the level of responsibility which those who wish to practise it can demonstrate.

So I hope that my comments, this evening and elsewhere, have demonstrated my unequivocal support for the better development of ADR. It has already begun to have a significant effect on the overall approach to civil justice. This will continue, and it will expand. My Department has taken active steps in the last year to forge links with leading providers of ADR and mediation services. Their willingness to co-operate with my officials, to offer advice, and to participate in pilot studies in the courts, is greatly appreciated, and augurs well for the future.

It is in our common interest to go forward – but *festina lente* – we must proceed slowly, on the basis of sound analysis and evaluation. This is a lesson which other jurisdictions have learned at a price. America, which often takes the lead in innovative legal practices, is raising serious questions over the claims made for the efficacy of ADR in the courts there. Professor Hazel Genn's thorough scrutiny of the pilot mediation work carried out in the Central London County Court, suggests that much the same challenges may be levelled at ADR in this country.

Perhaps one of the most alarming findings from Professor Genn's Report was that, throughout the time of the pilot exercise, only five per cent of the parties who might have elected to try mediation, actually did so. Only 5%. This was in spite of concerted efforts to encourage take-up.

In part, of course, this can be attributed to a lack of understanding – both of what mediation is, and of how successful and satisfying it can be for those in dispute. In part, it stemmed from concerns over cost. But we must be careful, and certain, that we are promoting and developing a service which meets a genuine – if undiscovered – need. Providers must take particular care that it is not the other way round.

So I want to emphasise this. We need more, detailed, analytical information, answering the specific concerns which I have touched upon tonight, and others. Do people know and understand enough about ADR? Can it really be of benefit to a majority of cases? Under what circumstances is it not the right avenue? Can its benefit be had at a reasonable cost to the system as a whole, and the individual parties? What consideration should we give to an element of compulsion?

This last question is particularly difficult. Many supporters of ADR argue strongly that the current low take-up of pilot schemes comes from lack of knowledge of its potential, and a general resistance to change and the unknown. Only with an element of compulsion, they claim, will those whose reluctance is through ignorance be able to make an informed choice. But to some extent, evidence from America suggests that compulsion does not improve settlement rates. Moreover, there are fundamental constitutional issues about the right of the individual to access of justice in the courts. I have no ready answer for you this evening – the only rational answer at this time is that we must scrutinise, consider and take great care before we act.

Very difficult too is the question of costs sanctions if mediation fails. I suggested earlier that ADR adds an extra layer of costs to the litigation process. How should these costs be dealt with by the trial Judge where mediating has failed? Is it right for the Judge simply to award costs, without making an investigation of what actually happened in the mediation? That would involve the breach of a cardinal principle of ADR, its confidentiality. Is it sufficient – as some have suggested – simply to invite the Judge to exercise his own judgement as to whether this is a case in which ADR ought to have been tried? And if he thinks it should have been but it was not, should he express that opinion in his costs award? Should we ask the mediators, when mediation has failed, to indicate how they think the Judge should exercise his discretion with respect to costs? These questions are increasingly being asked – and they need answers.

I also referred earlier to the responsibility of the professional organisations who want to see greater use of ADR in this country. It is not the habit of the Government to constrain the activities of professional bodies. But if we are to support the expenditure of the justice budget on ADR, we will need to be sure that this industry does not become monopolistic or covert. Practitioners must demonstrate a united approach to developing standards of competence and effective training. A regime of self-regulation measurable by the Government, and by the people whom you will be looking to as clients.

ADR is, I believe, entirely consistent with the principle of the better delivery of justice.

I am optimistic about ADR's future place in the system – but I am required to be a sceptic. As Lord Chancellor, I am charged with the responsibility to ensure that what I endorse can deliver – can make a positive contribution to the justice system in total. It is therefore my duty to ask the difficult questions, and to test the answers to the limit.

ADR has many supporters. But they too have a responsibility to proceed with care. ADR is not a panacea, nor is it cost-free. But I do believe that it can play a vital part in the opening of access to justice. But to do so, it must be properly implemented, properly developed and properly regulated. So let us proceed together, with caution, and in the clear light of experience and consideration. For, if ADR can live up to the hopes of its most passionate advocates, we may together bring about one of the most far-reaching, significant – and universally appreciated – reforms to civil justice.

Now let me end on a more lyric note. It is from *The Lover Arbitrator*, written in 1799. Volnay, a lawyer, is asked to arbitrate a separation between husband and wife. He agrees, with this morally uplifting sentiment:

> Neither accused nor arbitrator, I'll always be a conciliator, Although a lawyer by profession To reconcile is my obsession. And so my business always ends With no more clients, just more friends.

— · — · — · — · — · — · — · — · — · — · — · — · — · — · —

A thorough examination of ADR and its potential role in the legal system was provided in the discussion paper issued by the Lord Chancellor's Department in the course of 1999.

Lord Chancellor's Department, *Alternative Dispute Resolution –*
A Discussion Paper, **1999**

1.1 This Government has embarked on the most radical programme for the modernisation of the civil justice system for 120 years. Encouraging and improving the ways which enable those with legal problems to avoid disputes, or to resolve them outside the court system, have an important part to play in that programme. The Lord Chancellor wishes to shape his thinking on how the Government and the courts can most effectively do that. This paper seeks the views of customers, those who advise them (whether lawyers or not), service providers and judges. Its main questions focus on techniques of alternative dispute resolution (ADR) in non-matrimonial civil areas, but the issues cross some boundaries, and responses may need to as well.

Modernising Justice

1.2 The White Paper on Modernising Justice sets out the aims and objectives of the Government's reform programme. It explains that the civil justice system exists to enable citizens to understand and enforce their rights, and other peoples' duties, under the law. The civil law tends to be accessible only to those who can afford to pay the high and unpredictable costs which accompany litigation; or to those who are so poor they qualify financially for legal aid. A large part of the community feels unable to turn to the law for assistance and remedies. Part of the problem is that the services and remedies sought from the justice system are often disproportionate to the issue at stake.

1.3 The Government aims to bring about a significant increase in access to justice. 'Access to Justice' means that, where people do need help, there are effective solutions that are proportionate to the issues at stake. In some circumstances, this will involve going to court, but in others, that will not be necessary. For most people, most of the time, litigation in the civil courts, and often in tribunals too, should be the method of dispute resolution of last resort.

New Procedure and Rules

1.4 Within the reform programme, new court rules and the Community Legal Service will serve in particular to draw attention to the option of alternative methods of dispute resolution and to increase their use. The new Civil Procedure Rules came into effect on April 26 and established a unified procedural code for the High Court and county courts. Together with the pre-action protocols, they are designed to facilitate the settlement of a dispute at the earliest possible stage. The overriding objective of the rules is to deal with cases justly, and this is being achieved by effective case management, giving the courts powers to control the conduct of litigation. As part of their responsibilities for case management, courts are now under a duty to encourage the use of ADR in appropriate cases.

The Community Legal Service

1.5 The Government aims to improve access to information and help for those with legal problems through the Community Legal Service. The Legal Services Commission (which will succeed the Legal Aid Board) will work in local partnerships with local authorities and other funders and providers of advice services to plan and co-ordinate local networks based on the needs and priorities of local people. The Legal Services Commission will also manage the new Community Legal Service Fund that will replace civil legal aid. Last year the Legal Aid Board decided that work done in mediating a dispute falls within the existing legal aid scheme. In preparation for the establishment of the CLS and the availability, in principle, of public funding for different forms of dispute resolution, the Legal Aid Board consulted earlier this year on the criteria for funding ADR, the best means of providing such funding, and the circumstances in which the availability of ADR should limit entitlement to representation in litigation, as part of the new Funding Code for civil cases. The draft Funding Code is currently the subject of further consultation.

Principles

1.6 In determining the role of ADR, it is important to consider the principles on which the reforms to the civil court procedures were based. In his interim report, Lord Woolf set out the basic principles which should be met by a civil justice system so that it ensures access to justice. These are that the system should be just in the results it delivers, procedures should be fair and, together with cost, proportionate to the nature of the issues involved. The system should deal with cases with reasonable speed, be understandable to those who use it, be responsive to the needs of those who use it, and should provide as much certainty as the nature of particular cases allows. And the system should be effective, ie adequately resourced and organised so as to give effect to the previous principles.

1.7 The Lord Chancellor believes that these principles should also be used in examining ways of dealing with disputes outside the court system.

Alternative Dispute Resolution

1.8 Alternative Dispute Resolution techniques have evolved to meet perceived defects in more formal procedures. They therefore often reflect the principles that civil justice should be proportionate to the problems people have, speedy, and responsive and understandable to users generally, and to particular groups or sections of the community. The supporters of ADR point to real improvements for the customer in some kinds of case, either because ADR processes are simpler, cheaper or quicker than using the court system, or because they are less stressful or less damaging. That is borne out to the extent to which various processes are now used in other common law jurisdictions across the world.

1.9 Here, the last ten years have seen the accelerating development of ADR schemes of widely differing kinds, in different areas, for different purposes. This ranges from the use of arbitration in large commercial and construction disputes, and the development of court-based schemes, to mediation schemes to deal with neighbour disputes, often set up by local authorities as part of an overall strategy to improve estates and areas.

1.10 Increased use of mediation has also been encouraged in family cases. Part III of the Family Law Act 1996 allows for the provision of publicly funded mediation in family proceedings. Over 250 mediation services have concluded contracts with the Legal Aid Board and further contracts will be granted to ensure nationwide coverage by autumn 2000. Section 29 of the Act, which requires those seeking legal aid for representation in family proceedings to attend a meeting with a mediator to consider whether mediation might be suitable in their case, has now been implemented in over 60% of the country and is intended to be in force across England and Wales in 2000.

1.11 The procedure for ancillary relief in divorce cases which has been piloted in 29 courts will, with some modifications, be implemented throughout England and Wales in June next year. It contains provision for a Financial Dispute Resolution hearing, to be conducted by a judge, who will attempt to bring the parties to an agreement, with provision to adjourn the case to allow for mediation out of court, if that would be of benefit.

Aims of this Paper

1.12 Although forms of ADR appear to meet many of the principles for effective civil justice, the proportion of people with legal problems who choose to divert towards them has remained very low, even when there are convenient, and free, schemes available.

1.13 This paper asks why. It is part of a strategy to identify any problems with the current ADR methods and put them right. In line with this Government's commitment to modernising the way it works, we are asking for your views so that we can base the development of policy on the experience of those involved, and ensure that planned action will deliver the right results to meet the needs of users. The paper seeks to find out:

- What methods of alternative dispute resolution are now being used, and by whom

- Who provides them

- What are their advantages for customers, their advisers and the court system

- What are the possible problems for users

- Which cases ADR methods work best for

- How to quantify benefits and savings, and any additional costs

- How we can help people with legal problems, and those who advise them, to find out what forms of ADR may be of use to them

- How the use of ADR techniques can most effectively be encouraged by advisers, the courts, and the Government

- How we can help people and their advisers to be sure that, if they use ADR services, they are of the right quality, and fairly priced

- How the procedures and rules for litigation should take account of ADR

- What role the Government should play

- What more we need to find out to answer these questions

1.14 The paper is primarily concerned with the use of ADR in non-family civil disputes which may be brought before the courts, although it also refers to disputes unlikely to be resolved within the civil justice system. It does not look at the use of mediation in divorce or in disputes about children. Although there are many overlaps, other work is in hand in these areas. The use of mediation in family cases has been steadily increasing in recent years and, where this paper touches on cross cutting issues, current developments in family mediation are referred to for comparison.

There are other classes of dispute which are taken to tribunals and we are aware of tribunals where ADR has an important part to play, most notably the Employment Tribunals with their close association with ACAS. Other forms of dispute resolution, such as some ombudsmen schemes, also make use of ADR. Although the paper does not address these dispute resolution mechanisms to any great extent, if you consider the issues raised relevant in these areas, please include comments on them in your response.

2.1 The phrase Alternative Dispute Resolution now covers a variety of processes which provide an alternative to litigation through the courts, and can be used to resolve disputes where those involved would be unlikely to resort to the courts.

2.2 ADR processes include arbitration, early neutral evaluation, expert determination, mediation, and conciliation. A description of how these processes work is included at Annex A. At least for some, negotiation within the processes of litigation forms part of the ADR repertoire, with important links to existing litigation practice.

2.3 Other more formal mechanisms for resolving disputes such as the private sector ombudsman schemes, utility regulators, trade association arbitration schemes in certain trade sectors, and even tribunals can also provide alternatives to the courts in some circumstances.

2.4 The various processes have very different characteristics. It can, sometimes be unhelpful and confusing to group them together under one heading. A useful distinction is that between processes in which a neutral third party makes a decision and those where the neutral offers an opinion, and/or seeks to bring to the parties to an agreement. In this paper, the term 'alternative adjudication' is used to encompass decision making processes other than litigation through the courts, such as arbitration, and expert determination, ombudsmen and regulators. 'Assisted settlement' is used to encompass processes designed to help the parties come to an agreement, such as mediation, conciliation, and early neutral evaluation. Of course, it is possible to have hybrid processes. 'Med-arb', for example, describes a process where there is an initial agreement to mediate the dispute and, if that fails to achieve settlement, to submit outstanding issues to arbitration. In addition, some ombudsman schemes incorporate mediation into their procedures.

2.5 In this context, the word 'alternative' conveys only that these are methods of dispute resolution which are not those in general use in litigation (which is why, for some, negotiation does not fall within the ADR territory). It does not imply that the use of ADR techniques is in some way second-best to going to court. A case has been made for referring instead to appropriate dispute resolution, to reflect the arguments that some ADR techniques are better suited to the needs of some cases or litigants than court proceedings. The term 'Alternative Dispute Resolution' is, however, probably now so well established that there is little prospect of changing it.

The Benefits of ADR

Simpler, Cheaper, Quicker

4.1 ADR is used for a variety of practical reasons. Procedures may be simpler, and closer to normal business activity. There may be less, or better focused, paperwork. The work done in preparing disputes for the resolution process may be less, or simpler. Parties may choose an arbitrator or mediator for special knowledge or expertise. It may be possible to find earlier or more convenient dates for ADR than court lists permit. These, and other, factors are said to combine to make ADR a less expensive option for many cases.

4.2 There is some evidence to support these claims. Professor Genn's research into the mediation scheme at Central London County Court, although involving only 160 mediated cases, found that mediation is able to promote and speed up settlement. The evidence as to whether mediation saved costs was less clear. Where a form of assisted settlement is used but the parties do not reach an agreement, and then go on to litigate, it is possible for costs to be increased (although Professor Genn also found that court cases where there had been an attempt at ADR were dealt with unusually quickly or cheaply).

4.3 Of course, the court process to which ADR provides an alternative is not static, and has just undergone a thorough reform with the introduction of the new Civil Procedure Rules. The changes to procedure are designed to reduce the cost, delay and complexity of taking a case to court, and more cases will be brought within the scope of the relative informality of the small claims track. It is too early to see how the reforms are working, although their effects will be evaluated in due course. The earliest signs, however, are that the changes have made ADR processes a more, not less, attractive course for some parties (perhaps reacting to judicial signals).

Less Stressful, or Less Damaging

4.4 The other main argument in support of using ADR is different. Many say that being involved in a court case is a stressful experience. In his interviews with people who had been involved in county court litigation leading to a trial in open court, Professor John Baldwin reported that many found the formal court hearing intimidating, and that many of those who funded their own case suffered anxiety about their mounting legal bills and the possibility of having to pay the costs of the other party.

4.5 Typically, a claim for damages proceeds by establishing liability (with any contributory element by the other side), and then determining an award. It is therefore a process focused on finding the fault; not just adversarial, but antagonistic, with an inherent risk of entrenching positions, and encouraging the nursing of grievances. Characteristically, too, in litigation one side wins and one side loses.

4.6 It is strongly argued that some ADR processes reduce or remove these problems. There are several possible factors. Procedures and locations are usually much less formal, and less stressful for that reason alone. Mediations, in particular, often start by giving the parties themselves the chance to tell their own stories, and identify the issues important to them, in their own way. The processes might be considered more constructive: rather than looking for weaknesses in the other side's case, there is a greater concentration on what would constitute a mutually satisfactory solution. Parties therefore review what is really important to them, and what they are prepared to give up. Many ADR processes do not have the stark result of litigation, with one party getting everything and the other nothing; they lead to a settlement with benefits for both sides. Mediated settlements can also include elements which could not form part of a court judgement, such as an apology or an agreed way to handle any future disputes.

4.7 For these, and other, reasons it is argued that ADR techniques may be a better method of dispute resolution, at least for some cases or situations. In particular, it is said their approach – less antagonistic, looking for solutions both sides can accept – has benefits in a dispute between parties who might wish a greater chance than litigation affords of preserving an ongoing relationship, in cases varying from contractual disputes between established business partners, to rows between neighbours (as well as, obviously, matrimonial disputes, particularly where there are children involved). Evidence from the United States shows that litigants are more satisfied with the dispute resolution process where ADR has been used (from *An Evaluation of Mediation and Early Neutral Evaluation under the Civil Justice Reform Act* published by RAND in 1996).

Matching Cases to Dispute Resolution Processes

4.8 There are what appear to be strong arguments for using ADR processes in a wide variety of cases. Yet people do not do so. Even when ADR is available conveniently and very cheaply, very few use it. It is not altogether clear why this is so and this paper seeks to establish some possible reasons. One possibility is that people do not realise that there are alternatives to litigation. It is important to find better ways of helping them judge whether ADR is a good option for their problem.

Indications of Suitability

4.9 Below are set out some circumstances which might indicate that a particular form of ADR is or is not suitable. Factors affecting suitability include the nature and value of the dispute, the attitude and financial resources of the parties, the desired outcome, and the balance of representation.

Both (or all) parties must be willing to submit their dispute to a form of alternative adjudication, or willing to try a form of assisted settlement. (If both parties are not willing, there can be problems in enforcing an apparently contractual agreement to try mediation or conciliation.)

Factors For:

Any form of ADR will be worth considering where the cost of court proceedings is likely to equal or exceed the amount of money at issue.

Where parties wish to preserve an existing relationship, mediation or conciliation may be helpful. Not all neighbour disputes are necessarily suited to mediation, particularly where there are serious issues of harassment or mental health problems. (From 'Neighbour Disputes – comparing the cost-effectiveness of mediation and alternative approaches' by Dignan, Sorsby and

Hibbert, of the Centre for Criminological and Legal Research at the University of Sheffield, October 1996.)

Arbitration may be suitable in cases where there is no relationship to preserve, and a rapid decision is needed.

Where available, trade association arbitration schemes, utility regulators and ombudsmen can provide a cheaper alternative for an individual seeking redress against a company or large organisation, but they may be limited in the redress they can provide.

Early neutral evaluation might be applicable in cases where there is a dispute over a point of law, or where one party appears to have an unrealistic view of their chances of success at trial.

Where there is a technical dispute with a great deal of factual evidence, mediation or determination by an expert in that area might be best.

Parties involved in a commercial dispute may prefer to use a form of ADR to keep sensitive commercial information private.

Mediation has achieved settlement in many apparently intractable multi-party cases.

Factors Against:

In her research into the scheme at Central London County Court, Professor Genn indicated that mediation might not be appropriate in cases where there is a significant imbalance of power.

Litigation is the only option where one party needs to set a legal precedent or obtain an injunction, or where one party is refusing to acknowledge the problem or engage in negotiations.

Cost

4.10 An accurate assessment of how using ADR services will affect the cost of settling a dispute will usually be a major factor. Professor Genn's research shows that the overall cost of mediated cases is significantly less than those which are litigated (and suggests – although only a few cases could be tested – that going through mediation reduces overall costs even in cases which subsequently have to go before the courts).

4.11 The stage at which ADR is tried may have a significant effect on costs. Professor Genn's research looked only at cases where litigation had started. Logic suggests that there would be greater savings if people turn to ADR services earlier in a dispute, and before issuing a claim.

4.12 It may also be important for there to be directly comparable information on the costs of the processes themselves. Court fees are now calculated on a full cost recovery basis, providing an accurate market signal for potential users (as well as to the Court Service in organising its business). Some ADR services are themselves comparatively expensive, because they involve significant amounts of time from highly trained and skilled people. Some ADR schemes are undoubtedly providing services below a realistic commercial rate, for a variety of reasons. An important factor here (and in the United States) may be an element of public service, and commitment to the advantages of ADR.

Developing a Checklist

4.13 From the consideration of the different characteristics of the various ADR processes and such matters as the nature of the dispute, the status of the parties, legal representation, and the attitude of the parties, it might be possible to develop a checklist of questions, which could be used to identify the most suitable form of dispute resolution in each case. Such a checklist could be made available on the Internet to enable people to make informed choices about their own disputes.

The Wider Picture

4.14 An effective civil justice system is important to civil society, not just those actually involved in a dispute. In considering the potential effect on the system as a whole, critics have argued that increased use of ADR, by moving dispute resolution from the public to the private sphere, will prevent the law from developing to meet changing circumstances. Keeping information about the details of settlements out of the public domain prevents their use as comparators and may lead to an increase in the number of claims which are disputed. Private settlements may not take into account the wider implications of the dispute, and may weaken the impact of legislation, for example in the areas of environmental protection or discrimination. It is also necessary to be sure that ADR processes are equally accessible to all sections of the community, and treat all alike.

5.1 Knowing that ADR services may help in resolving a problem is only part of the story. People need to know how to get access to the right kind of ADR – and have confidence in the services they are offered.

Advisers and the Role of ADR

5.2 As ADR develops, it will be particularly important to ensure that those who advise people involved in a dispute understand the range and possible benefits of ADR processes. All those involved in providing advice play a key role in directing people to the most appropriate form of dispute resolution.

5.3 There are many routes through which people seek advice on dispute-related problems, from Citizens Advice Bureaux to Trading Standards Departments, consumer groups and victim support schemes. The advent of the Community Legal Service will bring greater cohesion to many of these services, but the range will always remain wide. The LCD booklet *Resolving Disputes Without Going to Court* was distributed through these services but it was not aimed at advisers.

5.4 At present, many of those contemplating litigation will go first to a solicitor. Professor Genn's research shows widespread misunderstanding about mediation processes amongst solicitors. Many did not know what was involved, or how it differed from traditional practice (like solicitors' negotiations towards settlement). They were therefore not able to advise clients on whether their case was suitable for any form of ADR, or the benefits that might flow from seeking to use it. ADR also may not fit the usual business patterns of litigation, and expected ways of managing and financing cases. It is important to make sure that solicitors have a clear appreciation of the uses of ADR techniques, and are able to advise their clients at appropriate stages about the advantages and disadvantages (including price).

5.5 Legal education is now more likely than before to include courses on ADR. Undertaking training as a mediator contributes towards the continuing professional development of practising solicitors and will count towards the similar scheme planned for barristers. In a recent survey of the top 500 companies in the North West, however, 52% of respondents said that their solicitors had not discussed the possibility of resolving a dispute through mediation (*'North West Mediation Survey'* 1999 by CEDR and Dibb Lupton Alsop).

5.6 Many large corporations, Government departments, local authorities, trades unions, and other organisations have in-house legal advisers. These lawyers are involved in shaping policies on dispute resolution. They may advise on the nature of dispute resolution clauses to be included in the contracts which may later become the subject of disputes and so also have a key role in the development of ADR.

Information about ADR

5.7 Some practical steps may also be necessary. It is not always easy to find information about the different forms of ADR and ADR services. There is no central register of ADR services. Some advice agencies may be aware of local schemes and the types of ADR they provide. Some law firms may have within their practice some people who have been trained as mediators, for example, or may know lawyer mediators in other firms. There are some well established providers of mediation who try to raise the profile of mediation in a number of ways. But there is still a lack of information and understanding about ADR processes and when they might be useful.

Public Awareness

5.8 Surveys into the public awareness of trade association arbitration schemes, utility regulators and ombudsman found that no scheme was known to more than 60% of the population, few schemes could reach 50% awareness, and almost a quarter of the population have not heard of any of the main schemes. It seems likely that levels of awareness of less formal methods of dispute resolution are as low or lower.

5.9 Technology may have an important role to in ensuring that people learn about ADR. The consultation paper *'civil.justice, Resolving and Avoiding Disputes in the Information Age'*, highlighted the ways in which the civil justice system was likely to undergo radical change, in the medium to long term, as a result of a range of new technologies. The paper envisaged that the Internet will increasingly become the first port of call for people who face a legal problem. If there is clear, easily accessible information about ADR services on the Internet, public knowledge, understanding and use of ADR will increase. Links could be developed with the Community Legal Service Gateway website which is to be launched next year.

'Resolving Disputes Without Going to Court'

5.10 In response to Lord Woolf's recommendation in his interim report on Access to Justice that the Lord Chancellor's Department and the Court Service should treat it as one of their responsibilities to make the public aware of the possibilities which ADR offers, LCD published a booklet in 1995 entitled

'Resolving Disputes Without Going to Court'. It is aimed primarily at individuals, although some sections might be of assistance to small businesses. It is designed to help people think about what they want to achieve, and what sort of procedure they are prepared to use, in order to establish what might be the best form of dispute resolution in their case.

5.11 The booklet contains a brief description of some different forms of dispute resolution, sets out the advantages and disadvantages of each, gives some information about the likely costs, and explains what the possible outcomes are. It contains separate sections on direct negotiation, community mediation, commercial mediation, trade association arbitration schemes, non-court based arbitration, and ombudsmen and utility regulators. Although not universally recognised as a form of ADR, direct negotiation was included to help people think about how they might approach the other party in a non-confrontational manner.

5.12 Copies of the booklet have been made available free of charge through county courts, Citizens Advice Bureaux, other advice agencies, Trading Standards Departments, and public libraries. The supply of printed copies has now almost been exhausted, but the text is available, in English and in Welsh, on the LCD website.

Information about ADR services

5.13 The booklet *'Resolving Disputes Without Going to Court'* contains the names and addresses of the leading providers of mediation and arbitration, and the various ombudsmen and utility regulators. However, in recent months there has been a significant increase in the number of independent ADR schemes. There is no comprehensive list of ADR providers in England and Wales.

National Directory

5.14 One of the priorities of the ADR Sub-Committee of the Civil Justice Council is to encourage the provision of information about ADR services at the local level. In addition to this, it might be useful for the Lord Chancellor's Department to develop a directory of organisations providing ADR. Such a directory would complement the one of Community Legal Service providers which is already under development. The CLS directory will supply a comprehensive list of all quality marked providers of legal advice and information and will be available via the CLS website and in the form of a booklet. An ADR directory could similarly be made available via the Internet and through court offices. Keeping the information in electronic form would allow for speedy updating. Such a directory could be organised to show providers operating nationally and locally, as well as by form of ADR. The intention would be to provide basic information about the available services so that prospective users could identify a suitable provider. Categories of information for inclusion might be type(s) of ADR offered, training and qualifications of neutrals, geographical area covered, cost structure, and any area of particular specialism or expertise. (Issues of regulation and accreditation of services is dealt with in section 8 of this paper.)

5.15 Producing an electronic directory of ADR providers would be in line with the key findings emerging from the paper *'civil.justice, Resolving and Avoiding*

Disputes in the Information Age'. The vast majority of those who responded to the consultation paper *civil.justice* supported the idea of a portal site on the World Wide Web which provided information about providers of legal services. In the long term, the existence of an electronic directory would be likely to encourage the development of innovative 'on-line' approaches to ADR, examples of which are already appearing in other jurisdictions.

6.1 In looking at how ADR techniques are currently being used, and how their use can be encouraged in appropriate cases, the Government has to consider whether the existing provision of ADR services is of the right kind; and if not, how provision might be improved – in particular, whether the state itself should take a larger role. This section therefore briefly sets out current arrangements for provision, and then looks at arguments for and against a greater role for Government.

Current ADR Services

6.2 ADR services have developed in response to perceived problems, or new opportunities, in the wide range of dispute resolution mechanisms in a complex society. There is therefore a mixture of:

- services provided for by the state;
- services available from the not-for-profit and commercial sectors but actively supported by the state; and
- purely private ventures.

Government Provision

6.3 It is one of the central functions of the state to ensure that there are effective mechanisms which enable citizens to enforce their rights under the law. Government activity has therefore centred on providing a nationwide network of courts, and on continuing efforts to ensure court procedures are as quick and accessible as possible. The fact that courts provide the formal dispute-resolution mechanism of last resort, however, has not ruled out the development of links between them and the techniques of ADR.

6.4 In particular, district judges use a wide range of procedures when dealing with cases within the small claims jurisdiction, which represents the majority of civil litigation. These regularly contain elements of conciliation and mediation, as well as arbitration (small claims can provide good examples of 'med-arb' – cases which start out in attempts at mediation, and turn into an arbitration if that fails).

6.5 Another way in which the Government has looked for less formal dispute resolution procedures has been the development of specialised fora for handling particular kinds of dispute, such as tribunals, statutory ombudsmen and utility regulators. These are intended to operate more informally than the courts. Moreover, the ombudsmen and regulators can investigate some complaints which could not be brought before the courts.

6.6 Such schemes can make provision for the use of ADR techniques in their own procedures. An example is the regular reference of applications by the employment tribunals to the Advisory, Conciliation and Arbitration Service (ACAS), operating in the sphere of industrial disputes. ACAS is the only national publicly funded service offering arbitration, conciliation and mediation.

Private Provision with Government Support

6.7 Schemes and services have also been developed by the not-for-profit and commercial sectors, some of which have received support from Government in different ways.

6.8 In response to the needs of particular areas of work, or the opportunities offered by particular locations, a number of court based ADR schemes have been established. The enthusiasm of individual judges or practitioners has been a major factor in their development. The principal schemes are described in Annex B.

6.9 Government departments are increasingly considering the use of ADR in the resolution of disputes likely to arise from new legislation. Many community mediation services are supported through local government funding and the national umbrella body for community mediation, Mediation UK, has received grants from central government.

Stand Alone Private Provision

6.10 Most ADR services in this country, however, do not have direct links with the court system or other arm of Government. Some organisations have been established solely as ADR providers, of which some specialise in certain areas of dispute while others deal with a wide range of disputes. Many professional organisations provide a dispute resolution service in their field of expertise. A notable example is the widely used ADR scheme run under the supervision of the Royal Institution of Chartered Surveyors.

6.11 Some commercial sectors have themselves established ombudsman and regulatory schemes to cover their activities. Examples include the Banking Ombudsman (The Financial Services Ombudsman, established by the Financial Services and Markets Bill currently before Parliament, will take over the functions of the Banking Ombudsman and a number of other ombudsman schemes in the financial services sector) and the trade association dispute resolution schemes operated by the Chartered Institute of Arbitrators.

How Government Can Help

6.12 There are many ways in which the Government can help to ensure that the provision of ADR services develops to ensure that those who can benefit from them, do so. It might encourage, commission, or publicise research into ADR's use and benefits (and problems). It can encourage the spread of information to litigants, their advisors and the judiciary. It can look for, and seek to eliminate, barriers to the use of ADR in rules, procedures, and in fee structures.

A Greater Direct Role?

6.13 Some argue that if the use of ADR is to increase substantially the Government should play a greater role in organising the provision of ADR services, either by establishing new ones or by developing additional partnerships with existing service providers.

6.14 In particular, some suggest that if schemes are to develop efficiently, quickly and consistently, there should be a national scheme. Every civil and High Court trial centre should have a mediation scheme, perhaps using court facilities, along the lines of the pilot scheme at the Central London County Court. This would require funding for administration. It would also need agreed arrangements for paying mediators. The evidence suggests that fees in many current schemes are not set at commercial rates, or that work is done *pro bono*. Is it realistic to expect this of any national scheme? If not, what funding and fee arrangement might operate, given the principle that the costs of civil litigation must come from the parties.

6.15 Conversely, there is a case for the Government intervening only where ADR providers are unable to offer sufficiently widespread, uniform services, of guaranteed quality, which met the needs of potential users. Importantly, there is as yet no clear consensus on the benefits and possible problems of particular ADR techniques applied to particular groups of cases, and little quantified information on the savings which may accrue. It is not possible to determine what an adequate level of provision would be. It appears that private sector service providers are already alert to areas where ADR techniques may be of use, and are reacting to fill the gaps. Current arrangements for providing ADR services may not be sufficiently developed to enable rapid progress towards uniform, national schemes.

6.16 For these reasons, it may be that the best course of action is to look, over the next 2–3 years, to encourage the further development of partnerships with existing providers in individual, local schemes dealing with particular areas of work or based in particular locations. This would enable new developments to be properly monitored, allowing the development of comprehensive and quantified information on the best uses of ADR services. Some support for this view may be found in the United States; the use of ADR techniques developed there considerably earlier, and had become more widely used (perhaps because supported by an extensive use of *pro bono* funding), before proceeding to the recent federal legislation.

6.17 New schemes do not necessarily need to be linked to courts. There may be other possibilities, such as developing links with the Community Legal Service. There are arguments that most ADR techniques are very different from the procedures followed in the courts, and that it is therefore desirable to have a clear separation between the two. It is also possible that linking ADR services firmly to the courts may work against their early use, before attitudes and issues become entrenched.

6.18 For high value disputes suited to ADR, which would be allocated to the multi-track if litigated, it makes sense that the parties are able to select an ADR service which meets their needs, or obtain a tailor made service in the private sector. This approach would complement the case management provisions in the multi-track, where directions are tailored to the circumstances of the individual case, and reflects the Commercial Court ADR scheme, where the court's role is confined to identifying suitable cases and providing the parties with a list of organisations offering ADR services. It is left to the parties and the ADR provider to make all the necessary arrangements.

6.19 For cases which would be litigated in the fast track or as small claims, and those unlikely to be pursued through the courts, an off the peg scheme is more likely to be required to keep the costs proportionate to the amount at stake. Such schemes would be more like the one at Central London County Court, where the administrative staff arrange the mediation, the mediators currently provide their services at below cost, and there is a strictly enforced time limit of three hours for the mediation sessions. There have been a number of arbitration schemes established recently, not connected to any court, which offer a fixed fee service.

Delivery

6.20 With the spread of new technology, there is scope for the development of on-line dispute resolution services. Mediation could be conducted by video conferencing, to obviate the need for people to come together in physical space. Paper based arbitration services could be managed with the statements and decision being delivered electronically. Such developments offer the opportunity for quick and cheap dispute resolution processes.

The Civil Procedure Rules

7.1 Following Lord Woolf's Inquiry and his reports on *Access to Justice*, the new Civil Procedure Rules came into effect on 26 April. The Rules establish a unified procedural code for the civil courts.

The Overriding Objective

7.2 Part 1 sets out the overriding objective of the rules, which is to enable the courts to deal with cases justly. Dealing with a case justly includes, so far as is practicable:

- ensuring that the parties are on an equal footing;
- saving expense;
- dealing with cases in ways which are proportionate to the amount involved, the importance, the complexity, and the financial position of each party;
- ensuring that it is dealt with expeditiously and fairly; and
- allotting to it an appropriate share of the court's resources.

7.3 Part 1 goes on to put a duty on the courts to further the overriding objective by actively managing cases, and puts a duty on the parties to help the court. The rule sets out twelve activities which are included in case management. One of these is to encourage the use of ADR if the court considers it appropriate and to facilitate such use.

Stay for Settlement

7.4 Part 26 deals with case management. It provides that, with the allocation questionnaire, a party may request a stay in the timetable while an attempt to settle the case by ADR or other means is made. Further, the court may, of its own initiative, stay the timetable in appropriate cases.

Need for Referral from Court to ADR

7.5 Harnessing the influence of the courts to encourage the use of ADR offers a way of overcoming the reluctance of litigants and lawyers. Moreover, there will often be a need for some relationship between the court system and ADR processes because of the need to protect a right to take legal action before the end of a limitation period, for example, while exploring other means of resolving the dispute.

Need for Guidance

7.6 All full time members of the judiciary have received some awareness training on ADR, in particular, on mediation, and the ADR Sub-Committee of the Civil Justice Council is concerned with monitoring the extent to which opportunities for ADR are being considered in the day-to-day practice of the civil courts. But, as yet there has been no clear guidance on how the courts are to encourage and facilitate the use of ADR and how appropriate cases will be identified. It is desirable that court users should know what approach to ADR the courts will take, and that it will be consistent throughout the court system. This paper will help that process.

Pre-Action Protocols

7.7 The new Civil Procedure Rules are accompanied by two pre-action protocols, which apply to claims about personal injury and clinical negligence. Protocols for other areas of litigation are under development. Protocols are designed to encourage the early exchange of information about a claim, to enable parties to agree a settlement before the issue of proceedings and to ensure that parties will be able to meet the time limits if court proceedings are issued. The court may impose sanctions for non-compliance with the protocols.

7.8 The Protocol for Personal Injury Claims does not refer to ADR, but the notes for guidance remind parties and their representatives that litigation should be a last resort and that claims should not be issued prematurely when a settlement is in reasonable prospect.

7.9 In contrast, the Protocol for the Resolution of Clinical Disputes specifically says that patients and their advisers should consider the full range of dispute resolution options and has a separate section on alternative approaches to settling disputes.

Forms of ADR

7.10 When thinking about the early stages of a dispute and how it could be resolved, it seems appropriate to construe alternative dispute resolution in its widest sense and to encourage disputants to consider all possible processes. Once a party has opted for litigation by issuing proceedings, however, the same consideration might not apply.

7.11 It could be argued that it is not appropriate for cases to move from litigation into a form of alternative adjudication because that is merely moving the decision making process from the public to the private sphere. Forms of assisted settlement can be regarded as complementary to the court process, where the many cases settle before trial through negotiation between the parties. Whereas forms of alternative adjudication are, in a sense, in competition with the courts.

ADR at Allocation

7.12   Although the overriding objective of the Civil Procedure Rules provides that encouraging and facilitating the use of ADR forms part of case management, the only reference to ADR in the general rules is at the allocation stage. Rule 26.4 provides that parties may, when filing the completed allocation questionnaire, make a request for the proceedings to be stayed while the parties try to settle the case by ADR or other means, and that the court may stay the proceedings of its own initiative in appropriate cases.

The Different Tracks

7.13   In small claims cases, allocation provides the only opportunity for the court to consider whether some form of ADR might be appropriate. In cases allocated to the fast track or to the multi-track, there are additional case management events: filing the listing questionnaire, the case management conference, and the pre-trial review. In his report on *Access to Justice*, Lord Woolf recommended that parties should be required to state at the case management conference or pre-trial review whether or not they have discussed ADR. ADR might have been rejected as an option earlier because one or both parties considered they did not have all the information and evidence they required, or because they were already in negotiation, for example, but could prove useful at a later stage.

7.14   While the court has a continuing duty to further the overriding objective and the parties have a duty to support the court in this task, there is no specific requirement for the parties to consider whether some form of ADR might be appropriate at these later stages.

Case Management: Early Neutral Evaluation

ENE in the Commercial Court

7.15   Under the provisions of the 1996 Practice Statement, a judge in the Commercial Court has been able to offer to conduct an early neutral evaluation (ENE) where he thinks it likely to assist in the resolution of the dispute. This involves the judge giving his opinion as to the strengths and weaknesses of each party's case based on a summary of the evidence and argument. The parties can then use this as a basis for settlement or for further negotiation. To preserve his position of neutrality, the judge takes no further part in that case, if it comes back to court, unless the parties agree.

7.16   ENE has only been used in a small number of cases in the Commercial Court. In that forum it would be unusual for parties not to have legal representation, and so they should have already had advice as to their prospects of success in bringing or defending the claim, but ENE may be useful as a 'second opinion', perhaps where a party has been unwilling to accept pessimistic advice.

ENE under the Civil Procedure Rules

7.17   It has been suggested that the powers of case management in the new rules allow judges to give an evaluation in any case. The aims of an ENE are to identify the issues and to enable the parties to hear an independent evaluation of their chances of success. Identifying the issues appears as the second activity listed as part of case management in Part 1 of the Rules, which explains the overriding objective. Another activity is helping the parties to settle the whole or part of the case. So, if a judge considered that an evaluation would help bring about a settlement, he would be able to provide it.

7.18 If a judge thought an evaluation would be helpful in a case allocated to the small claims track, the most suitable option would seem to be for him to order a preliminary hearing under Part 27.6(1)(b) of the Civil Procedure Rules. This states that a preliminary hearing may be held to enable the court to dispose of the case on the basis that one party has no real prospect of success. For cases allocated to the fast track and multi-track, it is arguable that, in a case where it appears that an ENE would be helpful, it is made a explicit separate event, somewhat akin to the court's power to list a case for summary judgement on its own motion under *Part 24*). This would enable the court to make it clear to the parties what was intended and direct them to provide any additional information necessary.

Compulsion

7.19 Although some judges use their powers of persuasion to encourage its use, participation in ADR is essentially voluntary and must be agreed to by both or all parties to a dispute. It has been argued by many that the continued low take up of voluntary schemes stems largely from ignorance and scepticism about forms of ADR, particularly assisted settlement processes. Professor Genn found, when interviewing solicitors in cases where the offer of mediation had been rejected, that suggesting mediation was regarded as a sign of weakness in the context of litigation.

7.20 One way to overcome the lack of knowledge and experience of assisted settlement and to remove the stigma of perceived weakness, would be for a degree of compulsion to be introduced. If the court referred a case to a form of assisted settlement then no appearance of weakness would be involved. If a satisfactory outcome were achieved, this would contribute to the culture change needed to ensure that ADR is used to best effect in the civil justice system.

7.21 When considering any degree of compulsion, care must be taken to ensure that the provisions of Article 6 of the European Convention on Human Rights are complied with. It provides that, in the determination of civil rights and obligations, everyone is entitled to a fair and public hearing by an independent tribunal established by law. Restricting the options of disputants to forms of ADR only and denying access to the courts would not be permissible.

7.22 It may be considered paradoxical to compel the use of processes based on willingness to reach an agreed solution. In addition, there is a danger that introducing a degree of compulsion might result in attempting a form of assisted settlement becoming seen as merely a hurdle in the process of litigation.

7.23 In the Commercial Court, parties are recommended to try ADR and are asked to explain themselves to the judge if they fail to do so. The judge's personal recommendation is only given in a relatively small number of cases, and carries considerable weight with the parties. It may be more difficult for such a personal recommendation to carry as much weight with the greater number and wider variety of cases elsewhere in the High Court or in the county courts, particularly if the process of identifying suitable cases becomes more standardised.

7.24 It could be made compulsory to try a form of assisted settlement or a form of court-annexed non-binding arbitration, such as exists in the United States, where parties have the option of accepting the arbitrator's decision or taking the case back to court. A stronger provision would introduce a presumption that ADR be attempted unless the case was not suitable, and it could be argued that this would merely be an extension of the case management process.

7.25 A balance is needed between increasing the use of ADR in suitable cases and maintaining access to the courts. Requiring parties to opt out of ADR, rather than opt in, but allowing them to do so, could strike such a balance. Such a system might go some way to achieving greater usage of ADR, and would be beneficial in proving additional information from which to evaluate the benefits and drawbacks of the various forms of ADR.

Cost Sanctions

Lord Woolf's Recommendation

7.26 In his final report on *Access to Justice* published in 1996, Lord Woolf recommended that 'where a party has refused unreasonably a proposal by the court that ADR should be attempted, or has acted unco-operatively in the course of ADR, the court should be able to take that into account in deciding what order to make as to costs'.

The Civil Procedure Rules

7.27 This has not been directly incorporated into the new rules on costs. However, Part 44 sets out what the court will take into account when exercising its discretion as to costs. 44.3(4) states that the court must have regard to all the circumstances including the conduct of the parties, which is later expanded to include questions of reasonableness of pursuing an issue and the manner in which a party has conducted his case.

7.28 Attitudes to trying ADR and behaviour during ADR processes could be relevant here. It might be helpful for court users to have some idea of the sort of grounds for refusing to try ADR which the court might consider reasonable, to prevent any sanctions being applied.

Acting Unreasonably

7.29 Acting unreasonably during the course of an alternative adjudication will, no doubt, have been dealt with in that forum when any decision or arrangement as to costs is made. Such conduct may, however, be relevant in cases where a form of assisted settlement fails to bring about a resolution of all the issues. It would not be helpful nor in the spirit of the new rules for one party to agree to mediate, obtain a stay in the timetable, but with no intention of settling and wanting only to draw out the process (A construction barrister claims that ADR helps achieve delay for his clients. From the article '*Survey of construction lawyers' attitudes and practice in the use of ADR in contractors' disputes*' by Dr Penny Brooker in Construction Management and Economics (CME) Volume 17 Issue 6 November 1999). If such a situation could be clearly established, a cost sanction might well be appropriate.

Confidentiality

7.30 It would be difficult for the court to establish that one party had acted unreasonably. One way would be for the court to ask the mediator for a report on the attitude of the parties during the mediation process. One of the features of mediation and other forms of assisted settlement, however, is the confidentiality of the process. This is important, as it encourages the free and open discussion which may be necessary to achieve an effective agreement. If it is thought that the mediator may report back to the court or a judge may attempt to delve into the detail of what was said and done, this may act as a deterrent to try mediation in the first place.

7.31 It has been suggested that a judge could get some idea of the attitude of the parties to a mediation without breaching confidentiality, by posing questions such as 'Did you agree a mediator? How many mediation sessions did you have? How long did they last? Was someone there who had the authority to settle the case? Would you be prepared to try again with a different mediator?'

7.32 Of course, if ordinary negotiations between the parties fail to bring about an agreement, it is open to either party to protect their position as to costs by making an offer to settle or a payment into court under Part 36 of the Civil Procedure Rules. Such an offer or payment could also be made if settlement is not achieved at a mediation or shortly after a neutral evaluation.

8.1 Confidence in the quality of ADR services is needed if they are to be widely used. ADR skills are complex, and the training needs to be good. Effective mediators, in particular, often need highly developed interpersonal skills to be build confidence, and help parties towards solutions. A high degree of trust and probity is also needed, so that the parties can rely on impartiality and confidentiality.

8.2 We need to explore how that confidence can be fostered, whether regulation is required for that purpose, and to safeguard the public. If there is to be regulation, it must be proportionate to the risks. Since ADR services are still developing to meet user needs, it will be particularly important that any forms of supervision or regulation do not stifle innovation and competition.

8.3 This section reviews the position in various areas, and seeks views on the right way forward.

Quality Control of Neutrals

Decision Makers

8.4 Arbitration has a long history in this country. It is a process governed by statute whereby the arbitrator makes a decision according to the law. The safeguards for the parties involved include a right to appeal to the courts on the grounds that the arbitral tribunal did not have substantive jurisdiction, or of serious irregularity affecting the tribunal, the proceedings or the award, the professional standards of the arbitrators in their own fields, such as the General Council of the Bar, and the rigorous series of exams leading to a professional qualification operated by the Chartered Institute of Arbitrators. We see no need to take any steps in this area.

8.5 Neutrals offering facilities such as early neutral evaluation and expert determination are usually either qualified lawyers or qualified in some other profession and so subject to professional standards and codes of conduct.

Mediators

8.6 Some concerns about the need to protect the public have been raised here. Mediation is about bringing people together to an agreement where it is possible that parties could be coerced into a settlement involving a serious abrogation of their legal rights. Mediation is as much or more about good communication skills as about expertise in the law or the subject matter of the dispute, which makes it harder to judge a good mediator by paper qualifications and training. Professor Genn observed a number of mediations at the Central London County Court. She found considerable scope for the exercise of power by the mediators. In effect, they controlled the proceedings by deciding who should speak and when, what evidence was relevant and what could be produced and discussed. She also raised question about the ethics of mediators who were, in some instances, perceived by the participants as pushing parties towards settlement irrespective of the 'rights and wrongs' of the case.

Current Developments

8.7 The private sector is already taking significant steps to develop qualifications and codes of conduct. In the area of training, an NVQ at Level 4 has recently been developed in the core activities for mediators in all disciplines. Several of leading mediation organisations have established training programmes which combine the theory of mediation with role play, and are followed by a pupillage scheme. In addition, various bodies have established codes of conduct. The Law Society, for example, has a Code of Practice for solicitor mediators and is in the process of developing training standards to ensure that solicitors wishing to practise as mediators in civil or commercial cases have the requisite knowledge and skills.

8.8 Leaving regulation to the mediation providers themselves is seen as the way forward in the area of family mediation. The UK College of Family Mediators was established in 1996 as a single professional body. It continues to develop a Code of Practice, standards, a disciplinary code and a complaints procedure.

8.9 Apart from work being done by individual organisations, a Joint Mediation Forum has been established, which includes representatives from CEDR, ADR Group, the Academy of Experts, Mediation UK and others, including mediators specialising in family disputes. It is currently finalising model codes of conduct for mediators as well as training and assessment standards. The Forum is also working towards establishing a new organisation to be an over arching body for the whole profession to set ethical and training standards for community, commercial and family mediators across the country.

8.10 These developments in the private and voluntary sectors towards common standards would seem to render any independent action by Government unnecessary. However, it may be that Government can work in partnership with the private and voluntary sectors to achieve effective procedures for the assurance of good quality mediators.

Approved Schemes

8.11   At present there is no restriction on the establishment of ADR services and no recognised means of controlling the quality of such services. While it would be possible to leave regulation to the operation of the free market, it could be argued that the Government has a responsibility to ensure that services on offer to the general public are of good quality, particularly as the Government actively supports the use of ADR in appropriate cases.

8.12   In Queensland, the Senior Judge Administrator of the Supreme Court operates a panel of mediators who have completed a mediation course run by a recognised provider. However, the community of mediators is much smaller in Queensland than here and such a system may not be appropriate for this jurisdiction on a national scale.

8.13   It would be possible to develop a system for accrediting certain ADR schemes. In the same way that the Quality Task Force has been considering criteria for the adoption of a Community Legal Service Quality Mark for advice services (The results of this work are included in a consultation paper *'The Community Legal Service Quality Mark'* published by the Legal Aid Board in August 1999), a similar mark of quality could be developed for some ADR services. This would provide reassurance to customers about the standards of schemes and may make some form of compulsory referral a more acceptable option. In itself, a recognised form of approval of schemes may encourage increased use of ADR.

EU Measures

8.14   Last year the European Commission issued a Communication on the out of court settlement of consumer disputes, with a Recommendation on the principles applicable to the bodies responsible for such schemes (COM (98) 198 final, 30 March 1998).

The principles include independence, transparency, the right of each party to present its views and hear the other's, procedural effectiveness, the protection of legal rights, liberty (the binding nature of the decision) and the right to representation. The Commission has subsequently proposed, in a draft Directive on Certain Legal Aspects of Electronic Commerce in the Internal Market, that Member States should ensure that ADR bodies apply the principles. This issue is currently under negotiation and the provision may be amended.

Possible Criteria

8.15   Mediation UK, the umbrella organisation for community mediation runs an accreditation scheme for local mediation services which covers the four broad areas of management, service delivery, personnel and premises. The criteria set by the Legal Aid Board for family mediation franchises are similar. Some of this information may not be necessary for private sector commercial schemes, although if public funding is used to support disputants in such schemes under the new arrangements for the Community Service Fund, the Legal Services Commission may wish to impose similar requirements. The Joint Mediation Forum is also looking at setting up standards and benchmark criteria for mediation organisations. However, a system of approved schemes need not be confined to mediation schemes.

8.16 Possible criteria by which schemes could be assessed are listed below:

- training – third party neutrals should have completed adequate training
- quality control – every scheme should have some method of monitoring the performance of its neutrals
- transparency – every scheme should publish its fee structure, details of its procedure, complaints system
- access – every scheme should have a policy for equality of access for all sections of the community and operate its own equal opportunities policy.

8.17 Other criteria which have been suggested include:

- neutrals should hold professional indemnity insurance
- schemes should have in place a clear set of rules or procedure for dealing with cases
- there should be a contact point staffed during normal office hours
- schemes should have a legal identity.

Operation

8.18 If a national system for accreditation or regulation is to be established, there remains open the question as to who should run it. It is arguable that, if the courts are to use the system to recommend certain ADR providers, then the Government should be involved. However, it would make sense for users of ADR to benefit from any steps already taken in this field in the private and voluntary sectors.

9.2 There is still much work to be done to ensure that the full potential of ADR techniques are realised. In addition to this paper, we are considering the scope for further pilot schemes to find out more about the best ways of using and encouraging the use of the various forms of ADR. The Lord Chancellor's Department is commissioning a review of existing research on mediation in both the family and civil fields. The academic consultants conducting the review will consider a number of pertinent questions in the light of the research, such as, the kinds of dispute which can be better addressed through mediation, why has demand been modest to date, and how 'success' could be measured. All this information, together with your responses to this paper, will be used to develop this Government's policy towards ADR.

Annex A – Types of ADR

Arbitration is a procedure whereby both sides to a dispute agree to let a third party, the arbitrator, decide. In some instances, there may be a panel. The arbitrator may be a lawyer, or may be an expert in the field of the dispute. He will make a decision according to the law. The arbitrator's decision, known as an award, is legally binding and can be enforced through the courts.

In the United States, court-annexed non-binding arbitration is widely used. The finding of the arbitrator becomes a binding order of the court if neither party seeks a rehearing by a judge.

Early Neutral Evaluation is a process in which a neutral professional, commonly a lawyer, hears a summary of each party's case and gives a non-binding assessment of the merits. This can then be used as a basis for settlement or for further negotiation.

Expert Determination is a process where an independent third party who is an expert in the subject matter is appointed to decide the dispute. The expert's decision is binding on the parties.

Mediation is a way of settling disputes in which a third party, known as a mediator, helps both sides to come to an agreement which each considers acceptable. Mediation can be 'evaluative', where the mediator gives an assessment of the legal strength of a case, or 'facilitative', where the mediator concentrates on assisting the parties to define the issues. When a mediation is successful and an agreement is reached, it is written down and forms a legally binding contract, unless the parties state otherwise.

Conciliation is a procedure like mediation but where the third party, the conciliator, takes a more interventionist role in bringing the two parties together and in suggesting possible solutions to help achieve an agreed settlement. The term 'conciliation' is gradually falling into disuse and the process is regarded as a form of mediation.

Med-arb is a combination of mediation and arbitration where the parties agree to mediate but if that fails to achieve a settlement the dispute is referred to arbitration. The same person may act as mediator and arbitrator in this type of arrangement.

Neutral fact finding is a non-binding procedure used in cases involving complex technical issues. A neutral expert in the subject matter is appointed to investigate the facts of the dispute and make an evaluation of the merits of the case. This can form the basis of a settlement or a starting point for further negotiation.

Ombudsmen are independent office holders who investigate and rule on complaints from members of the public about maladministration in Government and in particular services in both the public and private sectors. Some ombudsmen use mediation as part of their dispute resolution procedures. The powers of ombudsmen vary. Most ombudsmen are able to make recommendations, only a few can make decisions which are enforceable through the courts.

Utility Regulators are watchdogs appointed to oversee the privatised utilities such as water or gas. They handle complaints from customers who are dissatisfied by the way a complaint has been dealt with by his supplier.

Annex B – Court Based ADR Procedures

The Commercial Court
The first formal scheme to be established was in the Commercial Court, perhaps reflecting the already rapidly developing use of arbitration agreements in contracts in the area in which the court is involved. The scheme was established by a Practice Statement in 1993 ([1994] 1 WLR 14), by which judges could encourage the use of ADR. This was followed by a second Statement in 1996 ([1996] 1 WLR 1024), which allowed the judge to stay the timetable of a case to enable the parties to try ADR. It also provided that a judge could offer to conduct an early neutral evaluation if he thought it would assist settlement.

The same provisions have been carried over in the new Commercial Court Guide introduced to support the new Civil Procedure Rules. In the period from June 1996 to July 1998, ADR orders had been made in at least 67 cases, of which in only 7 cases did the parties fail to attempt ADR or fail to achieve settlement. (In this context ADR must be regarded as meaning assisted settlement.) Judges have conducted early neutral evaluation in only a handful of cases.

The Court of Appeal

An ADR scheme has been set up in the Court of Appeal which primarily offers mediation. Some cases are encouraged to enter the scheme by the personal recommendation of the judge at the stage of seeking leave to appeal or at a leave hearing before a single Lord Justice. Others result from an offer to participate in the scheme which is sent out in all final appeals, except those relating to family and immigration matters and to judicial review. In the period from November 1998 to March 1999, parties in 250 cases were sent information about the scheme and, of these, both sides agreed to mediate in 12 cases.

Central London County Court

The scheme at Central London County Court started in May 1996. Parties to defended cases above the small claims limit to which automatic directions applied were offered mediation. Since the 26 April, the offer has been sent to parties in cases allocated to the fast track and multi-track. Mediation takes place only where both parties agree. This scheme has been evaluated by Professor Hazel Genn of University College, London. During the period of her study, mediation was offered in 4,500 cases, but only 160 mediations took place. She found that 62% of mediated cases reached a settlement at the mediation appointment and that mediation achieved earlier settlement.

Despite repeated exercises in publicising the scheme, only in a small minority of cases have parties opted for mediation. There is some evidence that the numbers are increasing since 26 April, but it is too early to tell whether that is temporary, or an indication of a significant change in attitudes towards ADR.

- -

The Lord Chancellor confirmed his, and the Government's approval, of ADR in the following Press Release from the Lord Chancellor's Department issued on 23 March 2001.

Lord Chancellor's Department, 'Government pledges to settle legal disputes out of court' (2001) Press Release, 23 March

Arbitration, mediation and independent assessments will bring simpler, cheaper, quicker ways of resolving Government legal cases.

Today the Lord Chancellor, Lord Irvine, announced a major new initiative by government to promote Alternative Dispute Resolution (ADR) in place of litigation.

In future, Government Departments will only go to court as a last resort, the Lord Chancellor said. Instead, Government legal disputes will be settled by mediation or arbitration whenever possible. Lord Irvine published a formal pledge committing Government departments and agencies to settle legal cases by ADR techniques whenever the other side agrees to it.

Standard Government procurement contracts will in future include clauses on using ADR to resolve disputes instead of litigation and whenever possible claims for financial compensation will be settled by independent assessment instead of going to court.

ADR techniques include arbitration by an independent third party, mediation to help both sides reach an agreement and evaluation by a neutral professional who gives both sides an assessment intended to settle the issue.

Lord Irvine said,

> The Government wants to lead the way in demonstrating that legal disputes do not have to end up in court. Very often, there will be alternative ways of settling the issues at stake which are simpler, cheaper, quicker and less stressful to all concerned than an adversarial court case. Alternative Dispute Resolution techniques have evolved as an attractive alternative to formal judicial proceedings. They are a valuable way to accessible justice – providing services and remedies and costs which are proportionate to the issues at stake. Where the other side agrees, the Government is now formally pledged to resolve legal disputes by ADR whenever possible.

Lord Irvine said that Government departments will now monitor the effectiveness of ADR techniques in settling legal problems. He acknowledged, however, that there will still be cases which are not suitable for ADR such as those involving intentional wrongdoing, abuse of power, public law, Human Rights and vexatious litigants. There will also be disputes where a legal precedent is needed to clarify the law or where it would not be in the public interest to settle.

TRIBUNALS

A large number of tribunals have been established under various Acts of Parliament to decide issues relating to the operation of the schemes set up under those Acts. Although the members of these tribunals act in a quasi-judicial manner in reaching their decisions, the system of tribunals was specifically created to be outside, although subject to the overview of, the normal judicial/court system. As such, they can be seen as fora for alternative dispute resolution. There are reckoned to be almost 100 distinct types of administrative tribunals and the number of cases/issues decided by them far exceeds cases that are heard by courts and affect far more people. The following lists, provided as a note in the consultation paper on *Review of Tribunals*, indicate the multifarious areas in which tribunals operate.

LCD, *Review of Tribunals,* **Consultation Paper**

(I) Tribunals Under the General Supervision of the Council on Tribunals

Agriculture

Agricultural Land Tribunals (s 73 of the Agriculture Act 1947)

Agricultural Arbitrators (Sch 11 of the Agricultural Holdings Act 1986)

Aircraft and shipbuilding industries

Aircraft and Shipbuilding Industries Arbitration Tribunal (s 42 of the Aircraft and Shipbuilding Industries Act 1977)

Antarctica

Antarctic Act Tribunal (Reg 11 of the Antarctica Regulations 1995)

Aviation

Civil Aviation Authority (s 2 of the Civil Aviation Act 1982)

Banking

Banking Appeal Tribunal (s 28 of the Banking Act 1987)

Betting levy

Betting Levy Appeal Tribunal (s 29 of the Betting, Gaming and Lotteries Act 1963)

Building societies

Building Societies Appeal Tribunal (s 47 of the Building Societies Act 1986)

Chemical weapons

Chemical weapons licensing appeal tribunals (under the Chemical Weapons (Licence Appeal Provisions) Order 1996)

Child support maintenance

Child Support Appeal Tribunals (s 21 of the Child Support Act 1991)

Child Support Commissioners (s 22 of the Child Support Act 1991)

Children's (etc) homes

Registered Homes Tribunals (Part III of the Registered Homes Act 1984)

Commons

Commons Commissioners and Assessors (s 17(2) and (3) of the Commons Registration Act 1965)

Competition

Competition Commission Appeal Tribunals (s 48 of the Competition Act 1998)

Conveyancing

Conveyancing Appeal Tribunal (s 41 of the Courts and Legal Services Act 1990)

Copyright

Copyright Tribunal (s 145 of the Copyright, Designs and Patents Act 1988)

Criminal injuries compensation

Criminal Injuries Compensation Adjudicators (s 5 of the Criminal Injuries Compensation Act 1997)

Dairy produce quota

Dairy Produce Quota Tribunal (Reg 34(1) of the Dairy Produce Quotas Regulations 1997)

Data protection

Data Protection Commissioner (s 6 of the Data Protection Act 1998) (End note 3)

Data Protection Tribunal (s 48 of the Data Protection Act 1998)

Education

Independent Schools Tribunal (s 476 and Sch 34 of the Education Act 1996)

Exclusion appeal panels (under Sch 18 of the School Standards and Framework Act 1998)

Admission appeal panels (under Sch 24 or Sch 25 para 3 of the School Standards and Framework Act 1998)

Special Educational Needs Tribunal (s 333 of the Education Act 1996)

Registered Inspectors of Schools Appeal Tribunal (Sch 2 of the Schools Inspection Act 1996)

School standards adjudicators (s 25 of the School Standards and Framework Act 1998)

Employment

Employment Tribunals (s 1(1) of the Industrial Tribunals Act 1996)

Fair trading

Director General of Fair Trading (functions under the Consumer Credit Act 1974 and Estate Agents Act 1979)

Financial services

Financial Services Tribunal (s 96 of the Financial Services Act 1986)

Food

Meat Hygiene Appeals Tribunal (Part II of the Food Safety Act 1990)

Foreign compensation

Foreign Compensation Commission (Foreign Compensation Act 1950)

Forestry

Forestry Committees (s 16, 17B, 20, 21 or 25 of the Forestry Act 1967)

Friendly societies

Friendly Societies Appeal Tribunal (s 59 of the Friendly Societies Act 1992)

Immigration

Immigration Adjudicators (s 12 of the Immigration Act 1971)

Immigration Appeal Tribunal (s 12 of the Immigration Act 1971)

Indemnification of justices and clerks

Indemnification of justices and clerks (s 54(6) of the Justices of the Peace Act 1997)

Industrial training levy exemption

Industrial Training Levy Exemption Referees (Industrial Training (Levy Exemption References) Regulations 1974)

Industry

Arbitration Tribunal (Sch 3 of the Industry Act 1975)

Insolvency practitioners

Insolvency Practitioners Tribunal (s 396 of the Insolvency Act 1986)

Land

Lands Tribunal (s 1(1)(b) of the Lands Tribunal Act 1949)

Licensing

Persons hearing consumer credit licensing appeals (s 41 of the Consumer Credit Act 1974)

Persons hearing estate agent appeals (s 7 of the Estate Agents Act 1979)

Local taxation

Valuation Tribunals (Sch 11 of the Local Government Finance Act 1988)

London Building Acts

London Building Acts Tribunals (s 109 of the London Building Acts (Amendment) Act 1939)

Mental health

Mental Health Review Tribunals (s 65 of the Mental Health Act 1983)

Mines and quarries

Mines and Quarries Tribunal (s 150 of the Mines and Quarries Act 1954)

Misuse of drugs

Misuse of Drugs Tribunal (Part I of Sch 3 of the Misuse of Drugs Act 1971)

National Health Service

National Health Service Tribunal (s 46 of the National Health Act 1977)

Health Authorities (s 8 of the National Health Act 1977, in respect of functions under the National Health Service (Service Committee and Tribunal) Regulations 1992)

Discipline Committees (Reg 3 of the National Health Service (Service Committees and Tribunal) Regulations 1992)

National Lottery

National Lottery Commissions (functions under s 10, 10A and Sch 3 of the National Lottery Act 1993)

National Savings

National Savings adjudicator (s 84 of the Friendly Societies Act 1992)

Patents, etc

Comptroller-General of Patents, Designs and Trade Marks

Pensions

Pensions Appeal Tribunals (s 8 of the War Pensions (Administrative Provisions) Act 1919 or the Pensions Appeal Tribunals Act 1943)

Fire Service Pensions Appeal Tribunals (scheme under s 26 of the Fire Services Act 1947)

Pensions Compensation Board (s 78 of the Pensions Act 1995)

Occupational Pensions Regulatory Authority (s 1 of the Pensions Act 1995)

Pensions Ombudsman (Part X of the Pensions Schemes Act 1993)

Police Pensions Appeal Tribunals (s 1 of the Police Pensions Act 1976)

Plant varieties

Controller of Plant Variety Rights (functions under para 3 of Sch 1 of the Plant Varieties Act 1997)

Plant Varieties and Seeds Tribunal (s 42 of the Plant Varieties and Seeds Act 1997)

Police discipline

Police appeals tribunals (Sch 6 of the Police Act 1996 and s 38(2) and 82(2) of the Police Act 1997)

Rents

Leasehold Valuation Tribunals (s 142 of the Housing Act 1980)

Rent Tribunals (s 72 of the Housing Act 1980)

Rent Assessment Committees (Sch 10 of the Rent Act 1977, or s 14 or 22 of the Housing Act 1988)

Reserve forces

Reinstatement Committees (para 1 of Sch 2 of the Reserve Forces (Safeguard of Employment) Act 1985)

Reinstatement Umpires (para 5 of Sch 2 to the Reserve Forces (Safeguard of Employment) Act 1985)

Reserve Forces Appeal Tribunals (Part X of the Reserve Forces Act 1996)

Revenue

General Commissioners of Income Tax (s 2 of the Taxes Management Act 1970)

Special Commissioners of Income Tax (s 4 of the Taxes Management Act 1970)

s 706 Tribunal (s 706 of the Income and Corporation Taxes Act 1988)

Road traffic

Traffic Commissioners (Public Passenger Vehicles Act 1981)

Parking Adjudicators (s 73(3) of the Road Traffic Act 1991)

Sea fish conservation

Sea Fish Licence Tribunal (s 4AA of the Sea Fish (Conservation) Act 1967)

Social security

Social Security Appeal Tribunals (s 41 of the Social Security Administration Act 1992)

Disability Appeal Tribunals (s 43 of the Social Security Administration Act 1992)

Medical Appeal Tribunals (s 50 of the Social Security Administration Act 1992)

Unified Appeal Tribunals (Ch 1 of Part I of the Social Security Act 1998)

Social Security Commissioners (s 52 of the Social Security Administration Act 1992)

Transport

Transport Tribunal (Sch 4 of the Transport Act 1985)

Vaccine damage

Vaccine Damage Tribunals (s 4 of the Vaccine Damage Payments Act 1979)

VAT and duties

VAT and duties Tribunals (Sch 12 of the Value Added Tax Act 1994)

Wireless telegraphy

Wireless Telegraphy Appeal Tribunal (s 9 of the Wireless Telegraphy Act 1949)

(II) Tribunals Not Under the Supervision of the Council on Tribunals

Civil liberties

Intelligence Services Tribunal (s 9 of the Intelligence Services Act 1994)

Interception of Communications Tribunal (s 7 of the Interception of Communications Act 1985)

Security Service Tribunal (s 5 of the Security Service Act 1989)

Surveillance Commissioners (s 38 and 82 of the Police Act 1997)

Employment

Employment Appeal Tribunal (s 20(1) of the Industrial Tribunals Act 1996)

Immigration

Special Immigration Appeal Commission (s 1 of the Special Immigration Appeal Commission Act 1997)

Patents etc

Registered Designs Appeal Tribunal (s 28 of the Registered Designs Act 1949)

Trade Marks appointed persons (s 77 of the Trade Marks Act 1994)

(III) Tribunals Proposed by Current Legislation or in Course of Implementation

Civil liberties

Proscribed Organisations Appeal Commission (cl [5] of the Terrorism Bill)

Investigatory Powers tribunal (cl [57] of the Regulation of Investigatory Powers Bill)

Financial Services

Financial Services Authority (cl [1] of the Financial Services and Markets Bill)

Financial Services Ombudsman scheme (cl [220] of the Financial Services and Markets Bill)

Financial Services and Markets Tribunal (cl [129] of the Financial Services and Markets Bill)

Freedom of information

Information Commissioner (cl [16] of the Freedom of Information Bill)

Information Tribunal (cl [16] of the Freedom of Information Bill)

Immigration

Asylum Support Adjudicators (s 102 of the Immigration and Asylum Act 1999)

Immigration Services Commissioner (s 83 of the Immigration and Asylum Act 1999)

Immigration Services Appeal Tribunal (s 87 of the Immigration and Asylum Act 1999)

Local government

Adjudication Panels (cl [69] of the Local Government Bill)

National Health Service

Health Service medicine prices appeal tribunal (under the Health Service Medicines (Price Control Appeals) Regulations 2000)

Protection of Vulnerable Adults

Protection of Vulnerable Adults Tribunal (cl [69] of the Care Standards Bill)

Protection of children

Protection of Children Act Tribunal (s 9 of the Protection of Children Act 1999)

– · – · – · – · – · – · – · – · – · – · – · – · – · – · –

The obviously apparent proliferation of tribunals operating under a variety of powers gave rise to the perceived need to investigate the whole tribunal system. In May 2000 the Lord Chancellor announced a wide ranging, independent review of tribunals in England and Wales. In a speech to the Council of Tribunals conference the Lord Chancellor recognised that there has been a fundamental change in the nature of, and pressures on, tribunals over the last 40 years and said that:

> In his recent report on the Crown Office, Sir Jeffery Bowman pointed to a number of specific issues which need closer examination, including the haphazard growth of tribunals, complex routes of appeal, and the need for mechanisms to ensure coherent development of the law ... The Tribunals system has for too long been ignored. Significant steps have been taken to modernise the civil and criminal justice systems. It is high time that we also looked afresh at the whole system of administrative justice, which has a colossal impact on the lives of well over 470,000 people every year ...

It is astonishing to see the extent to which tribunals have expanded since they were last reviewed in 1957. From the 30 or so tribunals of the 1950s we now have close on 100. Tribunals have been joined by Ombudsmen and many other regulatory bodies, which have similar judicial functions. The administrative justice system now handles more cases than the civil courts ... It is also very diverse: the largest tribunal hears over 300,000 cases a year; some rarely sit. Some are based on a presidential structure, some are regional. Some panels are legally qualified. Some are not. Some are very formal, with legal representation common. Many are not.

The Lord Chancellor appointed Sir Andrew Leggatt to undertake a review of tribunals. Sir Andrew's terms of reference were set out in the *Review of Tribunals* documentation as follows:

To review the delivery of justice through tribunals other than ordinary courts of law, constituted under an Act of Parliament by a Minister of the Crown or for purposes of a Minister's functions; in resolving disputes, whether between citizens and the state, or between other parties, so as to ensure that:

- There are fair, timely, proportionate and effective arrangements for handling those disputes, within an effective framework for decision-making which encourages the systematic development of the area of law concerned, and which forms a coherent structure, together with the superior courts, for the delivery of administrative justice;

- The administrative and practical arrangements for supporting those decision-making procedures meet the requirements of the European Convention on Human Rights for independence and impartiality;

- There are adequate arrangements for improving people's knowledge and understanding of their rights and responsibilities in relation to such disputes, and that tribunals and other bodies function in a way which makes those rights and responsibilities a reality;

- The arrangements for the funding and management of tribunals and other bodies by Government departments are efficient, effective and economical; and pay due regard both to judicial independence, and to ministerial responsibility for the administration of public funds;

- Performance standards for tribunals are coherent, consistent, and public; and effective measures for monitoring and enforcing those standards are established; and

- Tribunals overall constitute a coherent structure for the delivery of administrative justice.

The review may examine, insofar as it considers it necessary, administrative and regulatory bodies which also make judicial decisions as part of their functions.

The first paragraph of the consultation paper concisely set out the need for the review:

The current system of tribunals in the United Kingdom has developed as a pragmatic response to the widened role of the state and its agents in modern society. As the impact of those agents on the lives of the citizens of this country (and in some cases those not yet citizens) has increased, we have developed a large number of separate bodies to resolve a wide range of disputes that can arise when officials make decisions. The list of the bodies which may be affected by the review names 130. Each body deals with a separate area of law, usually with separate membership and separate administrative structures. This approach has obvious strengths. It enables each tribunal to develop procedures and practices which match the particular needs of its area of work, aiming above all for as much accessibility and informality as possible. There are, however, signs, noted most recently in the work of Sir Jeffery Bowman's review of the hearing of administrative cases in the High Court, that the very complexity of the system (if indeed it amounts to a system at all), its diversity, and the separateness within it of most tribunals, may be creating problems for the user and an overall lack of coherence. The purpose of this review is to examine the strengths and weaknesses of the current system and, where relevant and appropriate, to make proposals for reform.

ARBITRATION

Arbitration is governed by the Arbitration Act 1996, although most of the provisions set out in that Act are not compulsory, thus leaving the parties involved a large measure of discretion in the manner in which they resolve their dispute. As the previous articles on ADR have mentioned, arbitration is used extensively in commercial disputes and many contracts contain clauses that require disputes to be resolved by arbitration rather than through the court system. Arbitration also has a significant role in settling consumer disputes where the complaint is passed to a specific trade related arbitration scheme for resolution. Once the arbitrator reaches a decision, it is binding on the parties, subject to limited grounds for appeal under ss 67 and 68 of the Arbitration Act 1996, and can be enforced through the courts if necessary.

If, by and large, tribunals are quicker, cheaper and less formal than courts then arbitration has similar advantages over tribunals. In the field of employment law, employers had accused employment tribunals of being over formal, over complicated, time consuming and expensive. Such complaints led to the setting up of an alternative arbitration procedure to replace the employment tribunal, in relation to straightforward unfair dismissal cases. The new arbitration system operates under the auspices of the Advisory, Conciliation and Arbitration Service (ACAS) and came into force in May 2001. The following material is taken from the booklet explaining the operation of the scheme.

ACAS, *Arbitration Scheme for the Resolution of Unfair Dismissal Disputes*, *May 2001*, www.acas.org.uk

Introduction

1. The ACAS Arbitration Scheme ('the Scheme') has been introduced to provide a voluntary alternative to the employment tribunal for resolution of unfair dismissal disputes. ACAS was given the power to introduce the Scheme by the Employment Rights (Dispute Resolution) Act 1998, which inserted a new section, section 212A, into the Trade Union and Labour Relations (Consolidation) Act 1992, making provision for it. The Scheme has been

designed to initially operate in England and Wales although it is anticipated that a Scheme to cover Scotland will operate from late 2001. This booklet provides guidance on the Scheme itself, on how to make applications under the Scheme, how to prepare for arbitration hearings, and on the procedure which will be adopted by arbitrators at the hearings.

2. The intention is that the resolution of disputes under the Scheme will be confidential, relatively fast and cost efficient. Procedures under the Scheme are non-legalistic and far more informal and flexible than the employment tribunal. The process is inquisitorial rather than adversarial with no formal pleadings or cross examination by parties or representatives. Instead of applying strict law or legal tests (but see paragraphs 12, 85–89) the arbitrator will have regard to general principles of fairness and good conduct in employment relations including, for example, principles referred to in the ACAS Code of Practice Disciplinary and Grievance Procedures and the ACAS Handbook *Discipline at Work* which were current at the time of the dismissal. In addition, as it is only possible to appeal or otherwise challenge an arbitrator's award (decision) in very limited circumstances, the Scheme should also provide quicker finality of outcome for the parties to an unfair dismissal dispute.

3. This Guide outlines how the Scheme caters for both the informality of alternative dispute resolution as well as the constraints and procedural requirements imposed on it as a matter of law.

4. ACAS has established a panel of arbitrators who were recruited through a transparent, accountable and non-discriminatory process. The arbitrators were selected for their knowledge, skills and employment relations experience. They are not employed by ACAS, but are appointed on standard terms of appointment, initially for a period of two years, although this might be renewed by ACAS at its discretion. It is a condition of their appointment that the arbitrators exercise their duties in accordance with the terms of the Scheme. They are appointed by ACAS from the panel on a case by case basis and the parties do not have any choice as to which arbitrator is selected to hear their case. There is however a limited challenge procedure (see paragraphs 122–129). Arbitrators are paid on the basis of time spent in connection with arbitration proceedings. Standard Terms of Appointment are available from ACAS.

5. Although it is called the ACAS Arbitration Scheme, ACAS's role in the Scheme is to recruit the arbitrators, appoint them on a case by case basis and to provide administrative assistance to them. ACAS has no role in any case-related decision making which is undertaken exclusively by the arbitrators.

6. Once the parties to an unfair dismissal dispute have concluded an Arbitration Agreement to have the dispute resolved under the Scheme, the unfair dismissal claim can no longer be heard by an employment tribunal.

What types of cases does the Scheme cover?

7. The Scheme is available as an alternative to going to an employment tribunal hearing only for cases of alleged unfair dismissal, where either an application has been made to the employment tribunal or where an individual claims that circumstances exist in which they could present such an application. The Scheme is intended for straightforward cases of unfair dismissal eg where an employee has been dismissed because of their conduct/capability, which do not involve jurisdictional or complex legal issues nor raise points of EC law.

Inappropriate cases

8. The Scheme excludes from its scope other kinds of claim which are often related to or raised at the same time as a claim of unfair dismissal, for example, sex/race discrimination cases and claims for unpaid wages. If the claim covers alleged breaches of employment rights other than unfair dismissal, and the parties want to have the unfair dismissal claim heard under the Scheme, the other claim(s) will have to be pursued separately before an employment tribunal or settled. If the non-unfair dismissal claims cannot be settled or withdrawn, the parties should consider whether they really want to have two hearings, or whether it would be better to have both the unfair dismissal and other claim(s) dealt with by the employment tribunal at a single hearing.

9. If the parties decide that they want the unfair dismissal dispute resolved by arbitration and the other claim(s) resolved in the employment tribunal the arbitrator may decide, where there is an overlap in the cases or if the evidence or findings in one hearing might have a bearing on the other, to postpone the arbitration proceedings pending the outcome of the claim(s) at the employment tribunal. This, however, is a matter for the arbitrator's discretion.

10. Parties should be aware that the normal time limits apply for applications to the employment tribunal and where they wish the employment tribunal to consider other claims they must ensure that these have been made within the time limits.

    If they have not, although the employment tribunal has discretion to extend time limits in certain circumstances, it is not possible to guarantee in any particular case that it will do so.

11. The Scheme is not intended for cases which raise questions of EC law such as unfair dismissal claims which are based on an EC right. It is strongly recommended that parties who have cases which raise such questions consider applying for their dispute(s) to be heard at the employment tribunal.

    Examples of such cases could include those where an employee is claiming that the reason for their dismissal is sex discrimination; dismissals relating to the transfer of an undertaking; and claims that the dismissal was related to exercising a right under the Working Time Regulations.

12. If cases are referred where EC law is relevant or where such issues are identified during an arbitration hearing, any of the parties may apply to the arbitrator or the arbitrator may decide of his or her own volition, that a legal adviser be appointed by ACAS to report to the arbitrator and the parties on the question of EC law. (See paragraphs 85–89.)

13. Additionally, if the dispute raises complex legal issues, the Scheme should not be used. If parties are unclear as to whether a dispute involves such issues, they should seek advice.

14. Nor should it be used where there is a dispute between the parties over whether or not the employment tribunal has jurisdiction to hear the unfair dismissal case. Examples of jurisdictional disputes include whether the applicant was an employee of the employer; whether the employee had the necessary period of service to bring a claim; whether a dismissal actually took place; or, whether the claim was made within the specified time limits. When agreeing to go to arbitration under the scheme, both parties waive their ability

to have such issues considered and are accepting as a condition of the Scheme that no such jurisdictional issue is in dispute between them. The arbitrator will not therefore deal with such matters and will make the assumption that all jurisdictional issues have been resolved prior to the hearing, even if they are raised by the parties during the arbitration process.

15. ACAS will accept cases of alleged constructive dismissal for hearing under the Scheme where both parties request this but with the following proviso. In such cases, employees are attempting to argue that certain conduct of their employer amounted to a fundamental breach of their contract of employment, and that they were therefore entitled to resign. In such circumstances there will normally be a dispute between the parties as to whether or not a dismissal took place, and an employment tribunal and not arbitration will be the route for having the case heard.

However, if both parties agree that the events which took place amounted to a dismissal, then the case could, if the parties wish, go to arbitration under the Scheme for an arbitrator to decide whether the dismissal was fair or unfair. Indeed, in agreeing to use the Scheme the parties will be taken to have agreed that a dismissal has taken place.

16. Where the parties decide not to use the Scheme, the services of an ACAS conciliator will remain available to the parties if they wish to attempt to reach a settlement which will resolve the matter without the need for an employment tribunal hearing. Where parties or their representatives are in any doubt as to whether to use the Scheme they should contact the Arbitration Section at ACAS Head Office.

When to consider using the Scheme

17. Generally it is better if the parties, or their representatives, can resolve the dispute between them through internal procedures (where these exist), by negotiating directly with each other, or with the help of an ACAS conciliator. When it is clear that none of these ways is likely to resolve an unfair dismissal claim, the parties may wish to consider using arbitration as an alternative to going to an employment tribunal hearing. Each of these methods has different features, and neither one is 'better' than the other. Each party should make themselves aware of the features of each method, so that they can decide which one they would prefer to use. However, as arbitration is voluntary, both parties have to agree to go to arbitration before the Scheme can be used. A comparison of the areas where there are significant differences between the approach adopted by employment tribunals and the one used in arbitration is at Appendix 1.

Legal aid

18. Legal aid might be available for limited initial advice on an employee's case and or preparation for the arbitration hearing. However, legal aid is not available for representation at the hearing.

Entry into the Scheme

Arbitration Agreement

19. Entry to the Scheme is entirely voluntary. Once both parties have concluded an agreement to go to arbitration (the Arbitration Agreement), the unfair

dismissal claim can no longer be pursued in an employment tribunal. It is important therefore that all the parties involved are fully aware of the effect of referring their dispute to arbitration, and that they understand clearly how the arbitration process works. If the agreement to go to arbitration is subsequently not accepted by ACAS because it does not satisfy the requirements set out in the Scheme, the parties will have to resolve their dispute by other means or if available, have recourse to an employment tribunal. Employees will, of course, wish to bear in mind the time limits (normally three months from the effective date of termination) for presenting a claim of unfair dismissal to an employment tribunal.

20. To ensure that parties are fully informed on the implications of referring their dispute to arbitration, an Arbitration Agreement can only be reached either through an ACAS Conciliated Agreement or a Compromise Agreement following advice to the former employee from a relevant independent adviser. Both types of agreement must be in writing, and any Compromise Agreement must conform to the statutory requirements for example at section 203 of the Employment Rights Act 1996.

21. In submitting the dispute to arbitration the parties are accepting that the arbitrator's decision is final and binding. They are also agreeing to do everything necessary for the arbitration process to proceed smoothly, including co-operating in the arrangement of any hearing and complying with any order or direction of the arbitrator. They are accepting the way in which the arbitration process is conducted, as outlined in the Scheme and explained in this Guide, including the procedure at the hearing itself. They will therefore be expected to cooperate fully with the process by fulfilling the duties placed on parties by it (see paragraphs 47–48).

22. The suggested wording for inclusion in Arbitration Agreements is at Appendix 2. However it should be noted that there are other statutory requirements for compromise agreements which must be met. The employee's relevant independent adviser will advise on these requirements.

23. Parties may use their own wording for other parts of a conciliated agreement if they are settling other issues in dispute or reaching agreement on other matters which are outside the scope of the Scheme. However, it is recommended that the agreement to go to arbitration be on a separate document. Although parties can vary the words of the agreement to go to arbitration and not use those suggested in Appendix 2, no provision of the Scheme can be varied.

Waiver

24. Given its informal nature, parties agreeing to refer a dispute to the Scheme are taken to have agreed to waive certain rights that they would otherwise have if the matter had been heard by an employment tribunal. Such rights include; the right to a public hearing; the cross examination of witnesses; compelling the attendance of witnesses; the production of documents to be ordered; the right to a published and fully reasoned decision and the right to have the dispute resolved in accordance with strict law (except in cases involving points of EC Law or issues under the Human Rights Act 1998, other than procedural matters within the Scheme). In order to confirm this waiver, a Waiver Form (a copy is included in this guide) must be completed by each party in all cases

and must accompany either the Conciliated Agreement or Compromise Agreement in order for the Arbitration Agreement to be valid. Employees must personally sign their form although a representative may sign the employer's waiver on their behalf and the signature on the Waiver Form must be witnessed in all cases. The witness can be anyone selected by the party but please note that an ACAS conciliator cannot act in this capacity. Parties are advised to keep a copy of their own waiver form, however, the ACAS Arbitration Section will send a copy of each party's waiver to the other party/ies.

Terms of reference

25. Every Arbitration Agreement under the Scheme will be taken as an agreement that the arbitrator should decide whether the dismissal was fair or unfair and also the appropriate remedy.

26. The terms of reference which will be used by the arbitrator in each case are:

In deciding whether the dismissal was fair or unfair, the arbitrator shall:

have regard to general principles of fairness and good conduct in employment relations (including, for example, principles referred to in any relevant ACAS Disciplinary and Grievance Procedures Code of Practice or *Discipline at Work* Handbook), instead of applying legal tests or rules (eg court decisions or legislation); apply EC law.

The arbitrator shall not decide the case by substituting what he or she would have done for the actions taken by the Employer.

If the arbitrator finds the dismissal unfair, he or she shall determine the appropriate remedy under the terms of this Scheme.

Nothing in these Terms of Reference affects the operation of the Human Rights Act 1998 in so far as this is applicable and relevant and (with respect to procedural matters) has not been waived by virtue of the provisions of the Scheme.

27. Parties are not able to require an arbitrator to hear a case which would require him or her to depart from the provisions of the Scheme. If an Arbitration Agreement seeks to vary any provision of the Scheme, the dispute will not be eligible for arbitration under the Scheme.

Existing dispute

28. The Arbitration Agreement must relate to an existing dispute. There should be no automatic references to the Scheme in an individual's contract of employment or company procedures as this would compromise the voluntary nature of entry to the Scheme.

29. Checklist for a valid Arbitration Agreement

i   the Agreement must be in writing;

ii   the Agreement must concern an existing dispute;

iii   the Agreement must not seek to vary or alter any provision of the Scheme (including the Terms of Reference);

iv   the Agreement must have been reached either with the assistance of an ACAS conciliator (a 'Conciliated Agreement') or through a compromise agreement conforming to the requirements of the Employment Rights Act 1996 (a 'Compromise Agreement');

v the Agreement must be accompanied by completed Waiver Forms (one from each party). There is a copy of the form in this Guide;

vi the Agreement must be received by the ACAS Arbitration Section (address at paragraph 132 of this Guide) within 6 weeks of its conclusion by the parties.

30. In cases where the Arbitration Agreement is reached through a Compromise Agreement it will be the responsibility of the parties' representatives to ensure that a valid Arbitration Agreement for the Scheme is concluded. Where there is any doubt on this issue the ACAS Arbitration Section should be contacted (see paragraph 132). In cases where the Arbitration Agreement is brokered via an ACAS conciliator, the conciliator will inform the parties or their representatives of the requirements of a valid

Notification to ACAS of an agreement to go to arbitration under the Scheme

31. In all cases the concluded Arbitration Agreement should be forwarded to the ACAS Arbitration Section at ACAS Head Office (see paragraph 132) as soon as possible but within the six week time limit after both parties have signed the agreement to go to arbitration and each party has signed a waiver form …

Remedies available under the Scheme

90. In deciding whether a dismissal is fair or unfair in a case which does not involve EC law, the arbitrator will take account of, but not necessarily follow, the provisions for automatic unfairness in Part X (Unfair Dismissal) of the Employment Rights Act 1996. However, where they are deciding a case where EC law applies, the arbitrator must apply the relevant statutory provisions for automatic unfairness.

Re-instatement/re-engagement

91. In all cases where the arbitrator decides that a dismissal is unfair, if the employee so wishes, the arbitrator may order reinstatement or re-engagement. The arbitrator will first consider reinstatement. An order for reinstatement is an order that the employer shall treat the employee in all respects as if he or she had not been dismissed. In deciding whether to make such an order, the arbitrator will take into consideration the employee's wishes; the practicability of complying with an order for reinstatement; and, in cases where the employee was partly to blame for the dismissal, whether or not it would be just to make such an award.

92. If the arbitrator awards re-instatement the order for re-instatement will specify any compensation due to the employee for arrears of pay (or other benefit) for the period between the date of dismissal and the date of reinstatement, any rights such as seniority/pension rights which must be restored to the employee and the date by which these must be complied with. The employee must also benefit from any improvements to their terms and conditions during the period following dismissal eg a pay increase/increased holiday allowance. When assessing the compensation due to the employee the arbitrator will deduct any wages in lieu of notice or *ex gratia* payments received from the

employer, any payments received in respect of employment with another employer since their dismissal and any other benefits which the arbitrator considers appropriate.

93. If the arbitrator decides not to award reinstatement he or she will consider awarding re-engagement and, if so, on what terms this should be. An order for re-engagement, which like any other remedy, must be made in the form of an award, is an order that the employee be re-engaged by the employer, a successor of the employer or an associated employer, in employment comparable to that from which he or she was dismissed (or other suitable employment) ...

Awards of compensation

98. Where reinstatement or re-engagement are not sought by the former employee, or are not considered appropriate by the arbitrator, he or she can award compensation to be paid by the employer to the employee.

99. Where compensation is awarded it will consist of a basic amount, a compensatory amount and, in some circumstances, a supplementary amount. These largely reflect the basic award, compensatory award and supplementary award which employment tribunals may order.

100. The basic amount will be based on the employee's age, length of service and weekly pay. The way in which the arbitrator will make this calculation is set out in the Scheme and summarized in Appendix 4 to the Guide ...

106. The compensatory amount will be calculated to reflect what the arbitrator considers is just and equitable in all the circumstances and will take account of the employee's financial loss insofar as it is attributable to the action taken by the employer. Employees are however, under a duty to reduce this loss by, for example, seeking suitable new employment ...

108. The compensatory amount cannot exceed the employment tribunal statutory limit, which is reviewed from time to time, except in certain Health and Safety cases and in cases where the employee made a protected disclosure (whistleblowers).

109. Where an employee has failed to use an internal appeals procedure provided by the employer to appeal against a dismissal, the Scheme provides for the arbitrator to reduce the compensatory amount by an amount he or she considers just and equitable, up to a maximum of two weeks pay. The Scheme provides for a supplementary amount, which will be an amount the arbitrator considers to be just and equitable up to a maximum of two weeks pay to be payable in certain circumstances where the employer prevented an employee from appealing against dismissal under the organisation's appeals procedure.

— ·— ·— ·— ·— ·— ·— ·— ·— ·— ·— ·— ·— ·—

Even before the ACAS scheme came into operation it came under attack from the Industrial Society, which argued that the new alternative to employment tribunals could well become as rigid, formal and almost as expensive as current tribunal and court processes and claimed that, in any event, the impact on the tribunal system was likely to be slight. The following Press Release provides the gist of the Industrial Society's arguments.

Industrial Society, 'Courts or compromise? Routes to resolving disputes', Press Release, February 2001

Employers hoping that less formal options for resolving employment disputes, such as ACAS's long-awaited voluntary arbitration process, will reduce the time and cost of rising employment litigation, could be disappointed according to a new report from The Industrial Society. *Courts or Compromise? Routes to Resolving Disputes* argues that alternatives to employment tribunals, could well become as rigid, formal and almost as expensive as current tribunal and court processes, and says the impact on the tribunal system is likely to be slight.

Figures show that employment tribunal claims by employees against their companies increased by 25 per cent during 1999–2000. The number of people contacting ACAS enquiry points for advice rose by 40 per cent to 715,000 and employers paid out £2.6million in awards resulting from sex, race and disability discrimination cases. The rise, which is expected to continue, is fuelled by more employment rights, better informed employees and a growing individualism at work. Employers particularly have been intensely frustrated by the cost and time of tribunals. It is against this backdrop that alternative dispute resolution (ADR) schemes – mediation, conciliation and arbitration amongst others – seem so attractive. But alongside the benefits of such schemes – speedier, cheaper, more informal and flexible than tribunals – there are inherent risks. The report argues that ADR does not guarantee fairness or consistency in outcomes. It highlights dangers where there is no appeal process, in lack of precedent and where confidentiality is unjustifiable. It also points to the risk that compensation awarded through ADR may be less than in a tribunal or court. It says that people who opt for ADR need to make sure that they understand the implications – for example where the decision is binding and leaves no route to appeal.

The report concludes that the impact on the tribunal system – one of the central arguments for such schemes – is likely to be small and points out that:

ACAS already has an obligation to encourage settlement of cases before they reach the tribunal stage. It is successful in 76 per cent of cases.

Much of the interest in ADR is based on the supposed existence of increasingly large numbers of 'vexatious' claims and people using the tribunal system simply to extract money from employers. The Society says that this preconception is difficult to support.

Will Hutton, The Industrial Society's chief executive says: 'The real key to reducing workplace conflict is to make recourse to law the last resort. Instead conflict resolution should be embedded in high quality management systems and processes that address the causes of disputes and grievances at their source.'

The Industrial Society recommends that:

The tribunal system is refined and examined to see if the judicial process gets in the way of achieving the quicker settlements that tribunals were originally intended to bring about.

There is better resourcing of ACAS services, so that conciliators can spend more time helping to resolve disputes in the early stages and more of its basic good practice advice can be provided – especially to small organisations. ACAS' resourcing must reflect the increased demand placed on it by the huge increase in claims.

The size of the awards paid out as a result of ADR processes are commensurate with what would be awarded at a tribunal. ADR must not be seen as a way of paying out smaller awards.

Small claims procedure

In light of the lack of formality in the hearings, small claims actions in the County Court used to be known as arbitration. Under the Woolf reforms, such actions are now allocated to the small claims track and are governed by Part 27 of the Civil Procedure Rules. Importantly, the lack of formality, rules as to limited costs and the non-applicability of the normal rules of evidence still operate and judges can now dispose of cases without a formal hearing.

Civil Procedure Rules, Part 27: The Small Claims Track

27.1 (1) This Part–

   (a) sets out the special procedure for dealing with claims which have been allocated to the small claims track under Part 26; and

   (b) limits the amount of costs that can be recovered in respect of a claim which has been allocated to the small claims track.

   (Rule 27.14 deals with costs on the small claims track)

   (2) A claim being dealt with under this Part is called a small claim.

   (Rule 26.6 provides for the scope of the small claims track. A claim for a remedy for harassment or unlawful eviction relating, in either case, to residential premises shall not be allocated to the small claims track whatever the financial value of the claim. Otherwise, the small claims track will be the normal track for–

   • any claim which has a financial value of not more than £5,000 subject to the special provisions about claims for personal injuries and housing disrepair claims;

   • any claim for personal injuries which has a financial value of not more than £5,000 where the claim for damages for personal injuries is not more than £1,000; and

   • any claim which includes a claim by a tenant of residential premises against his landlord for repairs or other work to the premises where the estimated cost of the repairs or other work is not more than £1,000 and the financial value of any other claim for damages is not more than £1,000).

Extent To Which Other Parts Apply

27.2 (1) The following Parts of these Rules do not apply to small claims–

    (a)   Part 25 (interim remedies) except as it relates to interim injunctions$^{(GL)}$;

    (b)   Part 31 (disclosure and inspection);

    (c)   Part 32 (evidence) except rule 32.1 (power of court to control evidence);

    (d)   Part 33 (miscellaneous rules about evidence);

    (e)   Part 35 (experts and assessors) except rules 35.1 (duty to restrict expert evidence), 35.3 (experts – overriding duty to the court), 35.7 (court's power to direct that evidence is to be given by single joint expert) and 35.8 (instructions to a single joint expert);

    (f)   Part 18 (further information);

    (g)   Part 36 (offers to settle and payments into court); and

    (h)   Part 39 (hearings) except rule 39.2 (general rule – hearing to be in public).

    (2)   The other Parts of these Rules apply to small claims except to the extent that a rule limits such application.

Court's Power to Grant a Final Remedy

27.3   The court may grant any final remedy in relation to a small claim which it could grant if the proceedings were on the fast track or the multi-track.

Preparation for the Hearing

27.4 (1) After allocation the court will–

    (a)   give standard directions and fix a date for the final hearing;

    (b)   give special directions and fix a date for the final hearing;

    (c)   give special directions and direct that the court will consider what further directions are to be given no later than 28 days after the date the special directions were given;

    (d)   fix a date for a preliminary hearing under rule 27.6; or

    (e)   give notice that it proposes to deal with the claim without a hearing under rule 27.10 and invite the parties to notify the court by a specified date if they agree the proposal.

    (2)   The court will–

    (a)   give the parties at least 21 days' notice of the date fixed for the final hearing, unless the parties agree to accept less notice; and

    (b)   inform them of the amount of time allowed for the final hearing.

    (3)   In this rule–

    (a)   'standard directions' means–

        (i)   a direction that each party shall, at least 14 days before the date fixed for the final hearing, file and serve on every other party copies of all documents (including any expert's report) on which he intends to rely at the hearing; and

        (ii)   any other standard directions set out in the relevant practice direction; and

(b)   'special directions' means directions given in addition to or instead of the standard directions.

Experts

27.5   No expert may give evidence, whether written or oral, at a hearing without the permission of the court.

(Rule 27.14(3)(d) provides for the payment of an expert's fees)

Preliminary Hearing

27.6 (1)   The court may hold a preliminary hearing for the consideration of the claim, but only–

    (a)   where–

        (i)   it considers that special directions, as defined in rule 27.4, are needed to ensure a fair hearing; and

        (ii)   it appears necessary for a party to attend at court to ensure that he understands what he must do to comply with the special directions; or

    (b)   to enable it to dispose of the claim on the basis that one or other of the parties has no real prospect of success at a final hearing; or

    (c)   to enable it to strike out(GL) a statement of case or part of a statement of case on the basis that the statement of case, or the part to be struck out, discloses no reasonable grounds for bringing or defending the claim.

(2)   When considering whether or not to hold a preliminary hearing, the court must have regard to the desirability of limiting the expense to the parties of attending court.

(3)   Where the court decides to hold a preliminary hearing, it will give the parties at least 14 days' notice of the date of the hearing.

(4)   The court may treat the preliminary hearing as the final hearing of the claim if all the parties agree.

(5)   At or after the preliminary hearing the court will–

    (a)   fix the date of the final hearing (if it has not been fixed already) and give the parties at least 21 days' notice of the date fixed unless the parties agree to accept less notice;

    (b)   inform them of the amount of time allowed for the final hearing; and

    (c)   give any appropriate directions.

Power of Court to Add to, Vary or Revoke Directions

27.7   The court may add to, vary or revoke directions.

Conduct of the Hearing

27.8 (1)   The court may adopt any method of proceeding at a hearing that it considers to be fair.

(2)   Hearings will be informal.

(3)   The strict rules of evidence do not apply.

(4)   The court need not take evidence on oath.

(5)   The court may limit cross-examination CIV.

(6)   The court must give reasons for its decision.

Non-Attendance Of Parties At A Final Hearing

27.9 (1) If a party who does not attend a final hearing–

(a) has given the court written notice at least 7 days before the date of the hearing that he will not attend; and

(b) has, in that notice, requested the court to decide the claim in his absence,

the court will take into account that party's statement of case and any other documents he has filed when it decides the claim.

(2) If a claimant does not–

(a) attend the hearing; and

(b) give the notice referred to in paragraph (1),

the court may strike out$^{(GL)}$ the claim.

(3) If–

(a) a defendant does not–

(i) attend the hearing; or

(ii) give the notice referred to in paragraph (1); and

(b) the claimant either–

(i) does attend the hearing; or

(ii) gives the notice referred to in paragraph (1),

the court may decide the claim on the basis of the evidence of the claimant alone.

(4) If neither party attends or gives the notice referred to in paragraph (1), the court may strike out$^{(GL)}$ the claim and any defence and counterclaim.

Disposal Without a Hearing

27.10 The court may, if all parties agree, deal with the claim without a hearing.

Setting Judgment Aside and Re-hearing

27.11 (1) A party–

(a) who was neither present nor represented at the hearing of the claim; and

(b) who has not given written notice to the court under rule 27.9(1),

may apply for an order that a judgment under this Part shall be set aside$^{(GL)}$ and the claim re-heard.

(2) A party who applies for an order setting aside a judgment under this rule must make the application not more than 14 days after the day on which notice of the judgment was served on him.

(3) The court may grant an application under paragraph (2) only if the applicant–

(a) had a good reason for not attending or being represented at the hearing or giving written notice to the court under rule 27.9(1); and

(b) has a reasonable prospect of success at the hearing.

(4) If a judgment is set aside$^{(GL)}$–

(a) the court must fix a new hearing for the claim; and

(b) the hearing may take place immediately after the hearing of the application to set the judgment aside and may be dealt with by the judge who set aside$^{(GL)}$ the judgment.

(5) A party may not apply to set aside$^{(GL)}$ a judgment under this rule if the court dealt with the claim without a hearing under rule 27.10.

Rules 27.12 and 27.13 are revoked.

Costs on the Small Claims Track

27.14 (1) This rule applies to any case which has been allocated to the small claims track unless paragraph (5) applies.

(Rules 44.9 and 44.11 make provision in relation to orders for costs made before a claim has been allocated to the small claims track.)

(2) The court may not order a party to pay a sum to another party in respect of that other party's costs except–

    (a) the fixed costs attributable to issuing the claim which–

        (i) are payable under Part 45; or

        (ii) would be payable under Part 45 if that Part applied to the claim;

    (b) in proceedings which included a claim for an injunction$^{(GL)}$ or an order for specific performance a sum not exceeding the amount specified in the relevant practice direction for legal advice and assistance relating to that claim;

    (c) costs assessed by the summary procedure in relation to an appeal and

    (d) such further costs as the court may assess by the summary procedure and order to be paid by a party who has behaved unreasonably.

(3) The court may also order a party to pay all or part of–

    (a) any court fees paid by another party;

    (b) expenses which a party or witness has reasonably incurred in travelling to and from a hearing or in staying away from home for the purposes of attending a hearing;

    (c) a sum not exceeding the amount specified in the relevant practice direction for any loss of earnings by a party or witness due to attending a hearing or to staying away from home for the purpose of attending a hearing; and

    (d) a sum not exceeding the amount specified in the relevant practice direction for an expert's fees.

(4) The limits on costs imposed by this rule also apply to any fee or reward for acting on behalf of a party to the proceedings charged by a person exercising a right of audience by virtue of an order under section 11 of the Courts and Legal Services Act 1990 (a lay representative).

(5) Where–

    (a) the financial value of a claim exceeds the limit for the small claims track; but

    (b) the claim has been allocated to the small claims track in accordance with rule 26.7(3),

the claim shall be treated, for the purposes of costs, as if it were proceeding on the fast track except that trial costs shall be in the discretion of the court and shall not exceed the amount set out for the value of the claim in rule 46.2 (amount of fast track trial costs).

(Rule 26.7(3) allows the parties to consent to a claim being allocated to a track where the financial value of the claim exceeds the limit for that track)

Claim Re-allocated from the Small Claims Track to Another Track

27.15   Where a claim is allocated to the small claims track and subsequently re-allocated to another track, rule 27.14 (costs on the small claims track) will cease to apply after the claim has been re-allocated and the fast track or multi-track costs rules will apply from the date of re-allocation.

–‒‒‒‒‒‒‒‒‒‒‒‒‒‒‒‒‒‒‒‒‒‒‒

MEDIATION

The following extract is taken from a brochure entitled *What is Mediation?* produced by the registered charity, MEDIATION UK, which is the umbrella organisation for initiatives and individuals interested in conflict resolution in the UK.

What is mediation?

Mediation is a way of dealing with disputes that aims to enable the people involved to reach an agreement that satisfies everyone. Disagreements can be sorted out quickly and confidentially, without the expense and trouble of going to court.

What can I do if I have a dispute?

The best thing, usually, is to sort it out informally between yourself and the others involved. Look for what you actually want, then pick the right moment to approach the other side or arrange a time to meet. Try, in a calm and friendly way, to look for common ground and a clear solution.

When should I go to mediation?

Sorting things out in this way may not always be possible without help. Going to court may be out of the question for a variety of reasons: the law may not be clear or may not cover your case; you will probably want to keep on good terms with your neighbours; it may be in both your interests to sort things our informally; or you may just be tired of the dispute. This is when mediation can be useful.

Sometimes one or both sides can get caught up in the desire to win the dispute, and to see the other side lose. Often these situations end up with both sides losing. One of the aims of mediation is to create an outcome where both sides benefit.

How is mediation organised?

Local mediation services are most registered charities, although a few are part of another organisation, such as a local authority housing department. Community mediation is usually carried out by volunteers from the community with special training in mediation skills, and is usually available free of charge.

What do mediators do?

Mediators are impartial and won't take sides. They are interested in helping both sides find a solution that suits everyone involved in the dispute. They will not tell anyone else what has been said in the mediation. They will usually:

- Visit the first party to hear their account of what has happened;
- If the first party agrees, ask to visit the other party to get their view of things;
- If both parties are willing, try to arrange a meeting between them in neutral premises.

What happens during a mediation?

Before the mediation process is under way, the mediators (they often work in pairs) will explain the process and ask everyone to agree to some basic rules, such as listening without interrupting, and not making offensive remarks. Each person is then free to talk about the problem as it affects them. The mediators will try to make sure that everyone understands what each person has said, and allow them to respond.

They will then help both parties identify the issues that need to be sorted out, and what each party can do to achieve that. Searching for solutions like this can lead to ideas that no-one had thought of before.

How do I know the agreement will be kept?

If the parties are able to agree, the agreement is usually written down, with both parties signing it.

The mediation service will usually arrange a follow-up to see if the agreement is holding, or if any other disputes have arisen. The agreement cannot be enforced like a court judgment, unless both parties want it to be. But an agreement is usually kept because it is in the best interest of both parties.

An agreement does not affect your legal rights, so you are free to find another way of dealing with the dispute, at any time.

What if no agreement is reached?

There will still be positive results, even if an agreement cannot be reached. You may get a clearer idea of what the real problem is, and you may, at least decide to cease hostilities or come back to try again later.

What sort of disputes can be dealt with by mediation?

The principles can be applied to a variety of situations, such as:

- Neighbour conflicts, which may involve noise, verbal abuse, rubbish, children's behaviour, pets and many other sources of dispute.
- Boundary disputes, especially where the situation is not clear.
- Community conflicts which can go on for a long time if nothing is done.
- Organisations and clubs, where conflict can hamper efficiency or relationships.
- Conflict in schools, to prevent fights and bullying.

All these situations can be helped by mediation, if both sides are willing.

What if I am not satisfied with the service I have received?

Most mediation services have a complaints procedure and ask you to let them know if you are not happy with anything. If you are still not satisfied, you can write to MEDIATION UK, the umbrella organisation to which most mediation services belong.

The 1994/95 annual report of MEDIATION UK contains the following example of mediation in practice:

Reassurance for a victim of burglary

An elderly lady's house was burgled whilst she was away over Christmas. Subsequently the offender admitted the offence and was given a custodial sentence. A major worry for the victim was a fear that her house had been watched, and the offender had seen her leave with her son. She was also anxious to know what had happened to some of the items of jewellery stolen as they were of great sentimental value to her. The offender wrote to the victim through the mediation service, and apologised profusely. In addition, he was able to answer many of her questions. Most importantly, he was able to reassure her that the offence had been a random burglary, the house had not been observed. At the time the offence had been committed, he had been heavily into drug use, but during his period of custody in a Young Offender's Institution he had made a very positive move and examined this problem. He has stated that becoming involved with his victim in this way has had an impact on him, especially when he gained an insight into her fear. The victim has come to terms with the fact that her jewellery will not be returned, but has taken an interest in the offender, and his commitment to change his behaviour.

_ . _ . _ . _ . _ . _ . _ . _ . _ . _ . _ . _ . _ . _

Mediation and the Family Law Act 1996 – a case study

The role of mediation in relation to the Family Law Act 1996 has already been mentioned in paragraph 1.10 of the discussion paper on *Alternative Dispute Resolution* (above) which stated:

> Increased use of mediation has also been encouraged in family cases. Part III of the Family Law Act 1996 allows for the provision of publicly funded mediation in family proceedings. Over 250 mediation services have concluded contracts with the Legal Aid Board and further contracts will be granted to ensure nationwide coverage by autumn 2000. Section 29 of the Act, which requires those seeking legal aid for representation in family proceedings to attend a meeting with a mediator to consider whether mediation might be suitable in their case, has now been implemented in over 60% of the country and is intended to be in force across England and Wales in 2000.

In order to facilitate and, where legal aid was provided require, the use of mediation in divorce, Pt 3 of the Family Law Act 1996 amended the Legal Aid Act 1988 as follows:

Family Law Act 1996, Part III

26.– (1) In the Legal Aid Act 1988 insert, after section 13 –

    13A–(1)   This Part applies to mediation in disputes relating to family matters.

        (2)   'Family matters' means matters which are governed by English law and in relation to which any question has arisen, or may arise–

            (a) under any provision of–

                (i)   the 1973 Act;

                (ii) the Domestic Proceedings and Magistrates' Courts Act 1978;

                (iii) Parts I to V of the Children Act 1989;

                (iv) Parts II and IV of the Family Law Act 1996 ...

27.–   After section 13A of the 1988 Act, insert–

    13B– (1)   The Board may secure the provision of mediation under this Part.

        (2)   If mediation is provided under this Part, it is to be available to any person whose financial resources are such as, under regulations, make him eligible for mediation.

        (3)   A person is not to be granted mediation in relation to any dispute unless mediation appears to the mediator suitable to the dispute and the parties and all the circumstances ...

28.– (1) After section 13B of the 1988 Act, insert–

    13C– (1)   Except as provided by this section, the legally assisted person is not to be required to pay for mediation provided under this Part ...

29.–   In section 15 of the 1988 Act, after subsection (3E) insert–

    (3F) A person shall not be granted representation for the purposes of proceedings relating to family matters, unless he has attended a meeting with a mediator–

        (a)   to determine–

            (i)   whether mediation appears suitable to the dispute and the parties and all the circumstances, and

            (ii) in particular, whether mediation could take place without either party being influenced by fear of violence or other harm; and

        (b)   if mediation does appear suitable, to help the person applying for representation to decide whether instead to apply for mediation ...

In pursuit of its advocacy of mediation, the Lord Chancellor's Department issued the following pamphlet which sought to explain mediation and emphasise the positive role it could play in the context of marital separation and divorce.

Lord Chancellor's Department, *Sorting Things Out Together – How Family Mediation Can Help You,* **January 2001**

Why mediation?

When you divorce or separate, it is generally better if both of you can sort out together the practical arrangements for the future.

The aim of mediation is to help you to find a solution that meets the needs of all of you, especially those of your children, and that you both feel is fair. At the end of mediation, you should feel that there has been no 'winner' or 'loser' but that together you have arrived at sensible, workable arrangements.

Mediation can help to reduce tension, hostility and misunderstandings and so improve communication between you. This is especially important if you have children, as you may need to co-operate over their care and upbringing for some years to come.

Does mediation suit everyone?

You can use mediation whether or not you are married and whether or not you have children.

For mediation to work, it is essential that you both take part and that neither of you feels threatened or pressurised by the other. It is also important that you are prepared to share all relevant information with each other.

Mediators do not take sides with or act for one person or the other. They are trained to act impartially and help each person negotiate fairly and equally.

What can I use mediation for?

You can use mediation to help settle any or all of the issues between you – arrangements for your children, financial arrangements, dividing up your property, or other practical issues connected with your separation or divorce.

If you need to sort out arrangements for your children, the mediator will help you to decide what is best for them, and how and what you should tell them. The mediator will encourage you to concentrate on your children's needs and consider their wishes and feelings when you are making arrangements for their future.

If you need to sort out financial arrangements, the mediator will ask you to fill in a form giving full details of your income and outgoings, your property, loans or other debts, and other relevant information. If you do not give accurate and complete information, a court could overturn any agreement that you make.

When can I use mediation?

You can use mediation at any stage you feel it would help – whether you are still living together, living separately or already divorced.

You can use mediation whether or not you have been to a solicitor, and whether or not you have started court proceedings.

Will I be safe?

Mediators have a duty to make sure that mediation discussions are conducted fairly, and that both of you feel safe. So, the mediator will check before starting mediation, and throughout mediation, that there is not a problem of violence or abuse.

If you are worried about your safety, or that of your children, you should tell the mediator. In that case, the mediator will probably recommend that you see a solicitor and, if necessary, you can apply for a court order to protect you from your partner's behaviour.

If you decide to use mediation but you do not want your partner to know your address or phone number, you should tell the mediator. You can also ask for separate waiting areas when you come to mediation.

What are the alternatives to mediation?

You can negotiate directly with your partner and reach agreement without any outside help.

You can ask a solicitor to negotiate with your partner for you, either directly or through your partner's solicitor. Your solicitor may still suggest that you try mediation to settle a particular issue between you.

You can also apply to the court to settle your dispute for you. However, the court will also encourage you to reach agreement between yourselves if at all possible. If you have not already done so, the court may suggest that you try mediation.

Do I still need a solicitor?

You may find it helpful to talk to a solicitor before you start mediation so that you know where you stand legally, particularly on financial issues.

Mediators can give you general information about the law and the way the legal system works. They cannot give you individual advice about your own legal rights or the best course of action for you. So, you may need to take independent legal advice from a solicitor, both during mediation and at the end, to make sure that the agreement reached is best for you. You may also need a solicitor to draw up an order for the court to make to formalise your agreement.

How is mediation different from counselling?

Counselling is about you and your relationship. It can help you to understand and deal with your feelings and emotions. Sometimes counselling is designed to help couples stay together. Mediation is about the practical and legal arrangements you and your partner make about your children or your property. It is a way of settling disputes over the consequences of your marriage or relationship breaking down.

If the mediator thinks that it would be helpful for you to talk to someone about how you are feeling, or if you and your partner decide to give your relationship another go and need support in doing so, the mediator may suggest that you see a counsellor.

What happens in mediation?

Mediation takes place in a private and informal setting, with usually only the two of you and one, or sometimes two, mediators present.

The mediator is there to help both of you, and to make sure that you both hear what the other has to say; understand each other's needs and concerns; and find a solution. The mediator will not tell you what to do and will not take sides, but they can share ideas with you and help you to explore different solutions.

How long will it take?

This will depend on how complicated your dispute is, but it is usually between two and four sessions. Each mediation session usually lasts about an hour and a half.

How does it end?

At the end of the mediation, you will usually get a written summary of the decisions that you have made together. This document is not legally binding and you have the opportunity to see a solicitor for legal advice before committing yourself to a legal agreement or a court order.

Is mediation confidential?

What you say in mediation is confidential and the mediator will not pass it on to anyone else unless both of you agree. The only exception is if it appears from what is said during mediation that either a child or an adult has suffered significant harm, or is at risk of doing so. The mediator would then have to make sure that the police or social services were told.

What you say in mediation cannot be used in court later if the mediation breaks down. However, this does not apply to the factual information that you provide, such as details of your income, property and so on, which can be used in any later court proceedings and passed to lawyers.

What will it cost?

There is no standard fee for mediation. Different mediators charge different rates, usually by the hour. Some mediators have a sliding scale of fees – this means that you pay according to your income.

If you are on a low income and don't have much in the way of savings or other capital, or you are on benefits, you may be eligible for CLS funding to cover the cost of mediation, as well as the cost of legal advice and help before, during and at the end of mediation.

Public funding for mediation

If you apply for Community Legal Service (CLS) funding (which used to be called Legal Aid) to cover the cost of negotiating through solicitors, or to make or defend an application to the court, you may be required to have your case assessed for its suitability for mediation instead. Your solicitor or mediator will be able to give you details about this.

How do I find a mediator?

If you want to use mediation, you can contact a mediator of your choice and ask for an appointment. Your solicitor will also be able to give you details of local mediators.

If you think that you may be entitled to CLS-funded mediation, you must choose a mediator who can provide it. Mediators who can provide CLS-funded mediation are listed in the Community Legal Service Directory, which you will find at your local Citizens' Advice Bureau or library, or anywhere you see the CLS logo displayed. You can also see the CLS Directory on the Community Legal Service website Just Ask!. You can also call the CLS Directory Helpline on 0845-6081122 (minicom: 0845-609 6677).

Mediation Organisations

There is no overall body that regulates mediation and that all mediators belong to. Many family mediators are members of the UK College of Family Mediators, as well as of other organisations. Solicitor mediators must be members of the Law Society.

— —

Gwyn Bevan, Suzanne Clisby, Zoe Cumming, Gwynn Davis, Robert Dingwall, Paul Fenn, Steven Finch, Rory Fitzgerald, Shelagh Goldie, David Greatbatch, Adrian James, Julia Pearce, *Monitoring Publicly Funded Family Mediation – Summary Report to the Legal Services Commission,* **2000, Legal Services Commission**

The Legal Services Commission funded a detailed study of the operation of the mediation process within the context of the family law area. It was conducted, amongst other things, to assess the relative costs/benefits, both for the assisted person and the taxpayer, of the provision of publicly funded mediation and supporting legal advice. The conclusion of the study was broadly that although those who engaged in the process of mediation were reasonably happy with it, they were even more satisfied with their lawyers and were unlikely to give them and the ordinary legal process up in favour of mediation.

As for the Family Law Act the report concluded that:

> Section 29 as it currently operates is not an effective means of getting those who might benefit from mediation to consider it at what is, for them, the right time. If we are to have mandatory referral to mediation, or mandatory consideration of the mediation option, this needs to be embedded more firmly within legal proceedings. One could certainly defend a system comprising, first, a court assessment which would rule out patently unsuitable cases, followed by mandatory referral to mediation (mandatory in the sense that further legal aid and court resources would not be forthcoming until mediation had been attempted). Section 13 of the Family Law Act 1996 (which has yet to be implemented) confers the necessary powers in that it enables the court to direct the parties to attend a mediation service.

> A second strategy might be to promote mediation as a genuine alternative to litigation. Separating couples might be informed of its existence, and its potential benefits. One could conceive of a number of potential 'information points', without requiring people to attend a special meeting for this purpose.

> Mediation on this level would be judged by its ability to provide a service which people value. Government sponsorship is compatible with this, but it would be unrealistic to expect these services to have much impact upon the demand for lawyer advice, negotiation and representation. Mediation would be supported as a separate, parallel system, with its own distinctive and worthwhile features.'

The full report is available at www.legalservices.gov.uk/misl/news/index.htm but it has to be recognised that the provision of mediation was not the only difficulty facing the Family Law Act. The second part of the Act was to require the divorcing parties to attend 'information meetings' at which they would be instructed about the procedure and of course the possibility of mediation.

However evaluation of pilots of the scheme cast serious doubt on its success or even its viability. Once again the full report is available at www.open.gov.uk/lcd/family/fla/flapt2.htm. Following these reports Lord Irvine announced that Part 2 of the Act would not only not be brought into effect but would be repealed. The following two articles provide consider this situation and summarise the two reports.

—·—·—·—·—·—·—·—·—·—·—·—·—·—·—·—·—·—

The following two articles trace the unfortunate history of the Family Law Act.

ME Rodgers, 'Where now for divorce?' (1999) 28 SLR 50–51

Quietly and without fuss, the government has shelved the planned reforms to divorce law in the Family Law Act 1996 which were anticipated to be brought in to force sometime in 2000.

The statement by Lord Irvine in June 1999 on Pt II of the Family Law Act 1996 is unhelpful in the sense that he has not clearly indicated that the Act will be repealed. It can be suggested that divorce law will change in the future, and also that some of the innovations in the 1996 Act will be retained. But, when and if this will occur is not clear. What is certain is that students will need to consider the Matrimonial Causes Act 1973 in relation to divorce, but also be aware that the divorce process will still remain coloured by some of the changes wrought by the Family Law Act 1996.

Why shelve the reforms?

To talk of 'shelving' is perhaps to adopt too optimistic an approach to the announcement of Lord Irvine with respect to Pt II of the Family Law Act (FLA) 1996. The statement given in Parliament by way of a written answer merely indicated that 'the government did not intend implementing Pt II of the Family Law Act 1996 in 2000' (17 June 1999 – see *Hansard* or Press Releases from Lord Chancellor's Department: www.open.gov.uk). This clearly leaves the door open for full implementation at a later date. The reason given for the delay arises from the results of the initial pilot studies into the effectiveness of the information meetings required under s 8 of the FLA. These meetings start the time clock running for divorce in the sense that one of the couple must attend a meeting and is unable to file a statement of marital breakdown until at least three months have expired since the meeting was held. This three months is seen as a 'cooling off' period and a time during which mediation can be used or counselling services. However, the pilot studies show that:

- only 7% of those attending an information meeting sought mediation;
- 39% were more likely to see a solicitor for legal advice; and
- 'if attendees were uncertain about whether the marriage was over at the time of attending, the meeting was more likely to nudge them into certainty about ending the marriage' (see Information Meetings and Associated Provisions within the Family Law Act 1996 – summary of research in progress 17 June 1999 available via Lord Chancellor's Department: www.open.gov.uk).

Given these findings, it is understandable the government wish to delay the implementation of a regime which relies heavily on the objectives of reducing conflict and the use of lawyers if the starting point is incapable of delivering!

The Family Law Act 1996 – what is in force?

The FLA has been on the statute book for a considerable time and many of its provisions have in fact been brought in to force. Indeed, the provisions regarding divorce are the only ones that had not been implemented – and these are all found in Pt II and the associated Schedules. Those parts of the FLA that are 'up and running' are not insignificant and must be seen to be part of the divorce process under the Matrimonial Causes Act (MCA) 1973. Whether this will result in confusion is not clear since some aspects of the implemented FLA could be argued to complement the MCA rather than pull in the opposite direction.

Part I of the FLA: This part of the FLA, which constitutes one section only, was brought in to force in March 1997. It seeks to establish the key principles to permeate the operation of Pts II and III of the FLA. These principles include:

- the need to support the institution of marriage;
- to assist the saving of marriages through the use of marriage guidance, etc;
- to bring about the end of a marriage that has clearly broken down with minimum distress and with regard to the interests of any children of the family;
- to endeavour to reduce unnecessary expenditure during divorce; and
- to reduce the risk of domestic violence.

Regardless of whether a divorce is to be granted under the MCA or the FLA, these principles should still hold good. It is surely in a couple's best interests to ensure they have considered if the marriage is really at an end, and if it is, to ensure that it is ended with as little trauma as possible. Indeed, the MCA includes a provision whereby a solicitor acting for a client on divorce is required to indicate whether or not they have talked about the prospect of reconciliation (s 6). The MCA itself was also founded on the principle of ending the 'empty shell' of a marriage with a minimum of distress and humiliation for the parties. However, it has to be recognised that under the MCA the focus on reconciliation is weak – it is not a positive duty to discuss the issue, and in any event once parties consult solicitors the time for reconciliation is often passed. Also, the existence of the 'facts' to prove how a marriage has broken down irretrievably within the MCA can be said to exacerbate distress and humiliation (see, for example, the Law Commission Report No 192 – *The Ground for Divorce*). In addition, the MCA does not place emphasis on the needs of children, but, in reality, would divorcing couples not consider their children? Reducing unnecessary expenditure is a novel aim for legislation – this has been seen as evidence that the FLA sought to remove lawyers from the divorce equation and as a push towards mediation. Whilst this provision may be scoffed for this reason alone – it is true to say that many divorcing couples have little or no regard to their costs until all the property they own has been taken to meet costs. It is hard to say whether this disregard is because the couple is unaware of mounting expenditure or because they wish to secure a victory at any cost.

Part III of the FLA: This part of the FLA was also implemented in March 1997 and seeks to amend the Legal Aid Act 1988 to enable legal aid payments towards mediation in divorce and family proceedings. Mediation was seen as a lynch pin of the reforms in the FLA – couples were to be encouraged to use mediation to assist saving marriage – '… I hope and expect that the introduction of mediation will increase the chance of couples choosing to step through the door to reconciliation …', *per* Lord MacKay. The ability to save marriages through the use of mediation is in doubt, given the role that mediators actually undertake and it can be suggested that the then Lord Chancellor was assuming mediation fulfilled the same role as reconciliation. What remains of interest though are the implications of the amendments to the Legal Aid Act 1988 brought about by the FLA and how this will affect the MCA and divorce. Under Pt III, before legal aid can be granted to assist a party in any family matters, the party must attend a meeting with a mediator to assess whether the case is suitable for mediation. Legal aid for legal representation will not be granted unless this meeting has occurred and the mediator has decided that the case is not appropriate for mediation. It should be noted that the definition of family matters includes proceedings under the MCA, and, hence, the above must apply. Consequently, it would appear that the aims of the FLA to reduce costs and encourage mediation are still being achieved, even though the MCA is the legal basis for the actual divorce. The significant issue to remember is that mediation is not covered by Part II of the FLA, and will continue to be provided regardless of whether the divorce reforms are in place.

Part IV of the FLA: This area of the FLA deals with occupation of the matrimonial home and the protection of victims from domestic violence. As such, it can be seen as a very distinct part and will not be influenced by the non-implementation of Pt II.

Where now?

For the foreseeable future, it will be the case that couples who wish to end their marriage will have to resort to the MCA 1973 with its dual system of proof of marital breakdown. This requires the court to be satisfied that the marriage has broken down irretrievably (s 1(1)) and that the petitioner can also prove one or more of the five facts being:

(a) that the respondent has committed adultery and the petitioner finds it intolerable to live with the respondent;

(b) that the respondent has behaved in such a way that the petitioner cannot reasonably be expected to live with the respondent;

(c) that the respondent has deserted the petitioner for a continuous period of at least two years …

(d) that the parties … have lived apart for a continuous period of at least two years … and the respondent consents to a decree being granted;

(e) that the parties … have lived apart for a continuous period of at least five years: s 1(2)).

The divorce will generally be undefended and will proceed by way of the Special Procedure whereby a District Judge will consider the accuracy of the paperwork before granting a decree nisi. Six weeks and one day thereafter the decree absolute may be obtained which will bring the marriage to an end. The proof of the facts is ultimately simple if the divorce is not defended – a District Judge is hardly likely to question whether adultery did or did not take place if the respondent does not contest it. For those more borderline cases, a little ingenuity with words can often make all the difference! Once the divorce has been granted, then the parties will normally enter into what is the nitty-gritty of the procedure – sorting out the financial details and this may take up to two or three years to conclude and this is what costs money. The latter procedure is also the one that generally requires access to the Legal Aid Fund, since undefended divorces will not be covered. And here, as has been shown, the couple will then have to slot in to the FLA and consider mediation – a heady mixture of two conceptually different regimes that in practice may result in unnecessary delay and unwarranted conflict.

The future therefore is unclear – reform is desired by Government but not at the price of failure to meet objectives. Whether we will get reform in the guise of the FLA is not certain, and timing may be crucial. Would a radical divorce law be sufficient to deter voters? Only time will tell.

––·––·––·––·––·––·––·––·––·––·––·––·––·––·––·–

ME Rodgers, 'Part II of the Family Law Act 1996 – goodbye to all that' (2001) 33 SLR 47–48

In the lead up to examinations, many students tend to focus purely on the material covered in their syllabus, and fail to recognise the importance of changes throughout the year. Examiners will give credit for the inclusion of relevant, up to date information and gaining a few extra marks can make a crucial difference to the final classification for the subject.

A major turnround has been the decision to repeal Pt II of the Family Law Act 1996, and this is covered together with a brief note on the new Adoption White Paper.

The Family Law Act 1996

Information meeting research findings
At the start of the academic year, it was clear that all was not well with Pt II of the Family Law Act 1996, which was to implement a new regime for divorce. Interim research commissioned by the Lord Chancellor's Department and conducted at the Centre for Family Studies into the s 8 information meeting pilots had highlighted many problems with this key change in the divorce procedure. As students will know, the information meeting under s 8 is designed to impart information on the divorce process to individuals whose marriage is under stress, and to encourage the parties to the marriage to consider the prospect of saving the marriage via counselling, and to contemplate using mediation to deal with the consequences of divorce if the marriage cannot be saved. The interim research found that many individuals attending the meetings did not go on to marriage counselling, nor mediation, and a considerable number left the meetings more certain to commence divorce proceedings. The final evaluation report into information meetings was presented to the Lord Chancellor in September 2000 and was made available at www.open.gov.uk/lcd/family/fla/flapt2.htm on 16 January 2001.

On the same date, the Lord Chancellor announced that 'the Government intends to ask Parliament to repeal Part II of the Family Law Act 1996' (see press releases at www.open.gov.uk/lcd). The research tested a number of ways to deliver the information required for s 8 but concluded that none of the models were good enough to enable implementation of Pt II on a national scale. Those individuals attending information meeting pilots, whilst valuing the actual process, did not all appreciate the need for information on marriage saving, and would have preferred a meeting that was tailored to their needs rather than those laid out in the statutory provisions. The number of individuals who moved from the information meetings to marriage guidance/counselling was small and the research found that many individuals had already tried to save the marriage before attending an information meeting. The emphasis in the information meetings on mediation in the divorce process did not result in more people using mediation, and the majority of individuals continued to consult a solicitor throughout their divorce. These conclusions cast considerable doubt on the effectiveness of the process within Pt II, and even on their own were inevitably going to affect the successful implementation of a legal regime which had as its focus saving marriage, promoting marriage counselling and limiting the role of lawyers in the process.

Mediation – cost effectiveness

However, the Lord Chancellor's Department has also had to contend with the impact of research carried out by Gwynn Davies *et al* into Publicly Funded Family Mediation (available in full or summary form from www.legalservices. gov.uk/misl/news/index.htm). While this research was commissioned by the Legal Services Commission, its findings are again a sad indictment on the aims of the divorce regime under the Family Law Act 1996. The aim of the study was to evaluate the cost effectiveness of mediation within family justice, not purely, therefore, where couples are divorcing. The study also covered a period prior to the implementation of s 29 of the Family Law Act 1996 and so was able to evaluate the change to mediation that this will have caused. In a lengthy summary, it is clear that mediation was reasonably well received by those who undertook the process, but that their solicitors received higher praise. The extent of mediated agreements was not high, with around one-third of participants reaching agreement when financial matters were the subject of the dispute, but, where children type issues were mediated, a higher agreement rate was achieved. The fact that clients would retain solicitors as well as mediate was highlighted in the context of the assumption that the former would lose 'market share' once mediation became established. The conclusion being that 'there is little prospect of mediation replacing lawyers – or certainly not of its 'replacing them effectively' (Davis, G, 'Mediation and legal services – the client speaks' [2000] Fam Law 110). This is surely a body blow to the Family Law Act 1996.

Unlike the information meeting research, the mediation study will not necessarily result in legislation being repealed. Mediation and compulsory referrals for a mediation assessment are now part of the State Funding regime, under the Legal Services Commission's Funding Code for civil work (available from the Legal Services Commission website). What is happening is a review of the Funding Code itself, with a consultation period ending in March 2001 into family mediation. It is likely that there will be an increase in the exceptions to the mediation requirement where the other party does not wish to engage in mediation – an issue highlighted by Davis *et al* as limiting the success of mediation outcomes. Mediation is battered but not yet down and out.

CHAPTER 7

THE CRIMINAL PROCESS:
THE INVESTIGATION OF CRIME

INTRODUCTION TO THE CRIMINAL PROCESS

The introduction of sweeping new police powers in April 1996, enabling the police to stop and search pedestrians without having to show reasonable grounds for suspicion, was part of a wider and very impassioned debate about the criminal justice system in general. The debate has often been vented in Parliament, in the broadcast media, the print media and in academic and professional journals. Recorded crime has, in recent history, reached very high levels (5.2 m offences during the latest period for which figures are available – Home Office, January, 2001). The number of crimes recorded has risen from around 1 per 100 of the population in the 1950s to 5 per 100 of the population in the 1970s and to 10.6 per 100 of the population in 1992.

In 1999, the Lord Chancellor, Lord Irvine, appointed Lord Justice Auld, a senior judge of the Court of Appeal, to report on the working of the criminal courts by the end of 2000. His terms of reference were to conduct a review:

> ... into the practices and procedures of, and the rules of evidence applied by, the criminal courts at every level, with a view to ensuring that they deliver justice fairly, by streamlining all their processes, increasing their efficiency and strengthening the effectiveness of their relationships with others across the whole of the criminal justice system, and having regard to the interests of all parties including victims and witnesses, thereby promoting public confidence in the rule of law.

The Auld Review, in its *Interim Report 3*, made the following report.

Lord Justice Auld, *Interim Report 3*, **March 2001, www.homeoffice.gov.uk**

Written submissions to the Review have risen to nearly 900, emanating from a wide range of agencies, individuals and organisations involved in the Criminal Justice System, together with a broad cross section of the public. Lord Justice Auld is considering all submissions and has, as yet, reached no final conclusions on any of them.

In addition, Lord Justice Auld has continued his intensive round of consultations begun in January, involving further meetings with groups and individuals. He chaired two special conferences in September, one attended by representatives of the judiciary, magistrates, legal practitioners, the Crown Prosecution Service, the police, academics and senior government officials, and one in Cambridge attended by judges and jurists from a number of other European jurisdictions.

Lord Justice Auld will continue to consult in October and November, and will also visit Northern Ireland and North America. In his consideration of the submissions Lord Justice Auld will keep in mind the civil and family jurisdiction of the courts and the implications of the European Convention of Human Rights. Underlying all his final recommendations will be the need to improve the public perception of, and confidence in, the criminal courts and the criminal justice system as a whole. In particular, Lord Justice Auld is considering how better the public can be educated and informed of the way in which the system and its various parts work, and how to overcome the difficulties in providing for the various and often sharply conflicting interests. Lord Justice Auld has reached the provisional conclusion that the current jurisdiction of lay magistrates should be preserved, for those cases carrying a penalty of up to six months' imprisonment which continue to reach the courts. Lord Justice Auld hopes to submit his final report by the end of the year.

Submissions made to the Review have indicated:

Management of the Criminal Courts within the Criminal Justice System

Recognition of much of the work done within Government to strengthen co-operation between the courts and other criminal justice agencies. But there are questions over the effectiveness of current mechanisms for translating national statements of purpose into local action. Some have suggested there is a need for a simpler and more broadly based line of overall direction at national and local levels.

A widespread view that there is a need to provide the courts and all the agencies with common information and communications technology. Some have suggested that the management of such an integrated information technology system might most effectively be undertaken by a central agency responsible to a strategic body with a membership wide enough to embrace the interests of all those with a stake in the criminal justice system.

Structure of the Court System

Considerable support for unifying and simplifying the management of the Crown Court and Magistrates' Courts. A number of respondents argued for the creation of a single criminal court supported by a unified and nationally funded administration, but within a structure which ensures a significant element of local control and accountability at both the summary and indictable offences level.

Jurisdictional Issues

A widely held view that the criminal courts deal with much work that could be dealt with outside the Criminal Justice System altogether. Examples suggested include television and vehicle excise licence and council tax cases. Other possibilities are the greater use of fixed penalties or the introduction of a form of conditional cautioning in less serious cases in which the defendant is prepared to accept guilt and/or to compensate the victim. Other have suggested that further investigation be undertaken of forms of restorative justice, such as those established in Scotland, Canada, Australia and New Zealand. Some have proposed that some of the present lengthy and expensive cases of fraud and other financial misbehaviour could be removed from the criminal courts to a regulatory process.

At the summary justice level, Lord Justice Auld is satisfied that there is a sound case for retaining both lay and stipendiary magistrates (now District Judges) and their present jurisdiction. A number of respondents have, however, suggested ways in which public confidence in the lay magistracy could be further enhanced, by reforms to the system of appointments and/or the establishment of a national training college.

At the level above summary jurisdiction there has been wide support for the establishment of an intermediate tier of jurisdiction to deal with some of the less serious offences currently categorised as either-way. It has been suggested this might take the form of a District Judge sitting with two lay magistrates and should be combined with the removal of magistrates' power of committal for sentence. Whether or not Lord Justice Auld recommends such an intermediate tier, he is considering proposals as to the defendant's right to opt for jury trial in either-way cases.

For the more serious cases, Lord Justice Auld has provisionally concluded that trial by judge and jury continues to offer the most appropriate means of determining guilt or innocence. Many have, however, suggested that juries should be made more widely representative of the community by reducing the categories of ineligibility and disqualification, and the scope for excusal from jury service.

It has been suggested that there are particular difficulties encountered by juries in complicated cases. There are suggestions that arrangements for jury trial might be modified in cases of fraud, other cases where the exercise for the fact-finder is one of analysis of technical or otherwise complex evidence (rather than assessment of reliability or credibility of witnesses) and cases involving young children as defendants or principal witnesses.

There is recognition of a general need for early identification of the issues at trial, and for tailoring of the evidence accordingly. Some suggest that, in all but the simplest trials, the jury could be provided at the start of the trial with an agreed written statement of the issues and summary of the agreed facts. At the end the judge could direct the jury more concisely, with less reference to the law and evidence than is now conventional, and in a manner that would better assist the jury in reaching a properly structured and logical decision.

There is a widespread view that cases should start and finish in the court or at the jurisdictional level where they are to be tried. It is suggested that if this could be achieved, there would be no need for committals for trial or sentence, or for a higher court to which a case had been allocated referring back parts of it to a lower court.

Case Management

Improvements in case management are regarded by many as a priority, though there is recognition that there are limits to what can be achieved in a process which involves so many agencies and individuals, and which concerns the proof of and response to allegations of criminality. Respondents to the Review have suggested a number of options for change: the effective setting and monitoring of common aims and budgets at national and local levels; a strengthening of the Crown Prosecution Service to enable it to assume a more authoritative and efficient role in the preparation and conduct of trials at all levels, and to protect the interests of victims; a system of incentives and sanctions structured to favour early and proper preparation of defence cases; improvement of mutual advance disclosure by the prosecution and defence so as to achieve early identification of the issues and shorter trials; a more flexible approach to plea and directions and other pre-trial hearings so as to have recourse to them only when necessary; a listing system designed to provide more advance certainty as to trial dates in the interests of avoiding inconvenience and expense to victims and witnesses; A change of culture among legal practitioners, possibly encouraged by their own codes of professional conduct, to achieve earlier and more effective preparation of cases.

Procedure and Evidence

Those who recommend the establishment of a unified criminal court also urge the introduction of a comprehensive and simply expressed procedural code common, so far as appropriate, to all the different jurisdictional levels. There is support for a move away from the technical rules of admissibility of evidence, to a system under which tribunals of fact gave evidence the weight they felt it deserved.

—·—·—·—·—·—·—·—·—·—·—·—·—·—·—·—·—·—·—·—

The following extract from a section of the government website document provides a description of the structures and procedures of the Criminal Justice System (CJS) in England and Wales.

Structures and Procedures of the Criminal Justice System in England and Wales, August 2001, www.homeoffice.gov.uk/rds/cjschap1.html

The Criminal Justice System in England and Wales is comprised of several separate agencies and departments which are responsible for various aspects of the work of maintaining law and order and the administration of justice. The main agencies of the CJS include: The Police Service, The Crown Prosecution Service (CPS), The Court Service, Magistrates' courts, The Crown Court, The Appeal Courts, The Prison Service, The Probation Service, The Serious Fraud Office, The Criminal Defence Service, The Criminal Injuries Compensation Authority, Other victim and witness care services.

The Home Office, Attorney General's Office and Lord Chancellor's Department are the three main government departments with responsibility for the CJS, providing the policy framework, objectives and targets, funding development and support functions. Many of these organisations have a long history and a tradition of autonomy and independence. For example, the judiciary remains independent of political influence in their interpretation of the law and their judgements in a particular case. However, they are expected to work within certain frameworks for sentencing, set by legislation and sentence guideline judgements and other Court of Appeal decisions. Similarly the Crown Prosecution Service remain independent in their decision as to whether to prosecute a particular case or not. This independence acts as a check on the system being used for political purposes. It does not necessarily also facilitate a co-ordinated response to the law and order challenges posed by a diverse and changing society. While many of the various agencies and departments which constitute the CJS do have written aims, unlike many other countries there is no criminal or penal 'code' that sets out the principles on which the justice system operates.

A number of joint working initiatives have recently been set up to achieve a greater degree of communication between the agencies and the development of common strategic and operational frameworks. Restructuring of the various agencies is in progress so that, at a local level, they will share common geographical boundaries.

In addition to the above, the Government has now set aims for the CJS. The two specific aims and associated objectives provide a strategic direction for the CJS as a whole.

Aim A: To reduce crime and the fear of crime and their social and economic costs.

Objectives:

to reduce the level of actual crime and disorder

to reduce the adverse impact of crime and disorder on people's lives

to reduce the economic costs of crime.

Aim B: To dispense justice fairly and efficiently and to promote confidence in the rule of law.

Objectives:

to ensure just processes and just and effective outcomes

to deal with cases throughout the criminal justice process with appropriate speed

to meet the needs of victims, witnesses and jurors within the system

to respect the rights of defendants and to treat them fairly

to promote confidence in the Criminal Justice System.

All the constituent agencies of the CJS have been asked to make sure that their particular aims are integrated with, and complement, these overarching aims. The task is to increase the efficiency and effectiveness of the CJS by encouraging the various participants to work together towards the same aims, while at the same time preserving the autonomy and independence of the various agencies and services. This document provides a brief description of the changes taking place in the CJS and the ways that the various agencies and services perform very specific services and roles.

In order to measure the performance of the system, targets have been set for the aims and objectives of the CJS. These are set out in the *CJS Business Plan 2000/2001*.

Approximately 13 billion pounds will be spent on the CJS in 2000/2001 …

1. Although the majority of prosecutions are handled by the Crown Prosecution Service, other organisations can also bring prosecutions. See section 4.2 for details.

2. A case will be under continued review, and may be discontinued at any stage before the hearing at the magistrates' court or the prosecution may offer no evidence. In addition the charge may be altered up to the final decision of the court.

3. Magistrates may commit to the Crown Court for sentence.

Not guilty pleas result in a contest (hence the term – adversarial) between the two parties arguing over the facts of a case.

In an inquisitorial system a judge is involved in the preparation of evidence by the police and in how the various parties are to present their case at the trial. The judge questions witnesses while prosecution and defence parties can ask supplementary questions. The influence of the judge in the process tends to reduce the level of contest between the two parties. In 1993 a Royal Commission examined the debate over the relative merits of both systems and concluded that, on balance, England and Wales should not move to an inquisitorial system.

Two key tenets of the criminal law in England and Wales are the presumption of innocence, and the standard of proof. The presumption of innocence means that an individual is deemed to be innocent, until proven guilty. The standard of proof required to find a defendant guilty in criminal cases in England and Wales is that the evidence should establish guilt 'beyond reasonable doubt'. This contrasts with the standard of a 'balance of probabilities' used in civil cases, where a person's legal liability is determined if the evidence suggests that the individual is more likely to be guilty than not.

The UK has been a party to the European Convention for Human Rights (ECHR) since 1951. However, in the past any cases where a citizen wanted to lodge an appeal under the ECHR against a particular ruling or decision have had to be dealt with at the European Court in Strasbourg rather than in the UK courts. The Human Rights Act 1998, implemented in October 2000, makes it a legal duty for public authorities (including central and local government bodies, courts and the police) to act compatibly with the ECHR, and for all legislation to be interpreted with the ECHR in mind. This will mean that people are able to take their case to the UK courts if they think a public authority has harmed their human rights. Appeal to the European Court will still be possible if the new domestic routes have failed.

The articles in the convention that are made law by the Act are:

Article 2 – Right to life

Article 3 – Prohibition of torture

Article 4 – Prohibition of slavery and forced labour

Article 5 – Right to liberty and security

Article 6 – Right to a fair trial

Article 7 – No punishment without law – this article states that no person can be punished for an action which did not constitute a criminal offence at the time it was committed

Article 8 – Right to respect for private and family life

Article 9 – Freedom of thought, conscience and religion

Article 10 – Freedom of expression

Article 11 – Freedom of assembly and association

Article 12 – Right to marry

Article 14 – Prohibition of discrimination in the exercise of convention rights

Article 16 – Restrictions on political activity of aliens – this article allows restrictions on the political activities of aliens to be retained

Article 17 – Prohibition of abuse of rights – this article states that nothing in the convention may be used to limit or destroy the freedoms to a greater extent than is provided for in the convention

Article 18 – Limitation on use of restrictions on rights – this article ensures that the restrictions on rights in the convention are not used for any purpose other than those for which they have been prescribed.

First protocol, article 1 – Protection of property

First protocol, article 2 – Right to education

First protocol, article 3 – Right to free elections

Sixth protocol, article 1 – Abolition of the death penalty

Sixth protocol, article 2 – Death penalty in time of war – this allows for the use of the death penalty in times of war.

— · — · — · — · — · — · — · — · — · — · — · — · — · —

The next two articles both concern the impact of the Human Rights Act 1998 on the criminal justice system. The first is by John Wadham and Janet Arkinstall, respectively director of and Research Assistant at Liberty, and the second is by Neil O'May, head of criminal law at Bindman and Partners.

John Wadham and Janet Arkinstall, 'Crime and human rights' (1999) 149 NLJ 381

A defence of 'breach of Convention rights'

The imposition of a criminal conviction may itself breach a Convention right and as such defendants will be able to argue that the Human Rights Act provides them with a defence to the charge. Challenges based on this concept have been argued in Strasbourg with respect to the right to freedom of expression (Art 10), the right to privacy (Art 8) and the right to free assembly and association (Art 11).

In *Steel v UK*[1] it was held that arrest and detention for breaching the peace and refusing to be bound over, in the context of a peaceful political protest, could amount to a disproportionate interference with the Art 10 right to freedom of expression.

Legislation in Northern Ireland which criminalised the sexual behaviour of consenting gay men in private was held to violate Art 8, the right to a private life in *Dudgeon v UK*[2] The Court held that the law was too far-reaching and not proportionate to any possible legitimate governmental aim.

In *Sutherland v UK*[3] the Commission upheld on the merits a complaint in relation to the lower age of consent applicable to sex involving gay men, on the basis that this disclosed discriminatory treatment in the exercise of the applicant's right to respect to private life under Art 8. It would seem that this issue will have a political solution in the not too distant future.

These cases may be contrasted, however, with *Laskey v UK*.[4] A number of men were convicted of consensual sadomasochistic behaviour which constituted the offences of assault occasioning actual bodily harm and wounding. The Court ruled that the State has a legitimate interest in controlling this type of activity on public health grounds, and as such the laws did not unjustifiably interfere with the applicant's right to respect for their private life.

---

1   (1998) *The Times*, 1 October.
2   (1981) 4 EHRR 249.
3   [1998] EHRLR 149.
4   (1997) 24 EHRR 39.

Evidence obtained in violation of the Convention

Surveillance, tapping and bugging

Article 8 guarantees the right to respect for an individual's private life, and allows interference with this right by the state only where it is necessary in a democratic society for certain purposes. In the context of the collection of evidence in criminal matters, these purposes are the interests of national security and public safety, or for the prevention of disorder or crime. In accordance with the principles established by the Court in *Sunday Times v UK*[5] any interference must be prescribed by law – it must have a legal basis which is accessible and precise enough to enable people to know when interference is allowed. The interference must also be necessary and proportionate – in the context of criminal evidence, relevant questions include whether the method of surveillance is the least intrusive, have other methods been tried and found not to be effective, is the offence of sufficient gravity to justify surveillance and the resulting breach of privacy involved? There must be a system of accountability, preferably independent of the police, to authorise and monitor the use of surveillance. Where a person is aggrieved by the use of surveillance there must be a way for them to test whether their rights have been violated, and to provide them with a remedy.

It is clear that some parts of the laws that purport to regulate police surveillance in the UK do not conform to these principles and thus violate the Convention.

The Interception of Communications Act 1985 was enacted as a result of the European Court's decision in *Malone v UK*[6] which held that although the interception of telephone calls by the police in relation to stolen goods was a proportionate and legitimate interference with the right to privacy, the practice of authorising interceptions was not 'in accordance with law' as it was based on administrative guidelines only, that were not sufficiently clear to give citizens an adequate indication of when interception was permitted.

However, the Act leaves a number of significant gaps. It does not apply to private telephone networks, such as internal office systems. In *Halford v UK*[7] the Court held that the interception of a senior police officer's office telephone by a superior amounted to a violation of her right to privacy, and, as the network did not come within the 1985 Act it had no basis in law. It has been held that the Act does not apply to the interception of cordless telephones (*Effick*)[8] or to some international calls (*R v Governor of Belmarsh Prison, ex parte Martin*) and thus there are no statutory controls on this type of surveillance. Where one of the parties to a communication consents to the interception, as will be the case where informers or undercover police are employed to gather evidence, the Act also does not apply.

The Police Act 1997 was introduced to regulate the planting of listening devices, but the police do not require an authorisation under the Act if they have the consent of a person with authority in respect of the property, such as a landlord, hotel owner or employer. The complaints mechanism established by s 102 will not

---

5   (1979) 2 EHRR 245.
6   (1984) 7 EHRR 14.
7   (1997) 24 EHRR 523.
8   [1995] 1 AC 309.

apply to an employee or occupier in such circumstances. As the recent case of *Lambert v France*[9] illustrates this situation violates Art 8 of the Convention due to the absence of any effective remedy available to the subject of an interception made on a third parties' telephone line. Surveillance techniques which do not require the interception of a phone line or entry onto property, such as infra-red cameras and long range microphones, are currently not subject to any statutory regulation.

The Human Rights Act will be invoked in arguments as to the admissibility of evidence gathered where regulatory laws do not conform with the standards set by the Convention and the court. In New Zealand, for instance the courts have held that evidence obtained in violation of their Bill of Rights (on which the Human Rights Act is partially modelled) is *prima facie* inadmissible.

Practitioners would be wise to familiarise themselves with the Strasbourg jurisprudence before the commencement of the Act, because it applies to any proceedings 'brought by or at the instigation of a public authority whenever the act in question took place' s 22(4) HRA. Thus a person who is a defendant in a criminal case will be able to rely on Convention rights if evidence gathered tomorrow were to be used against a suspect in violation of Art 8. Although it would not be open to a defendant to rely upon the Human Rights Act to argue its inadmissibility in a trial in, say, October 1999 (before commencement) it will be if an appeal is heard after October 2000 (assuming this is the date of commencement).

— — — — — — — — — — — — — — — — —

Neil O'May, 'In the dock' (2000) *Gazette*, 13 July, pp 24–28

The European Convention on Human Rights has been primarily associated in the public mind with the criminal justice system. That is not surprising. Of the 500 or so judgments of the European Court of Human Rights since its inception, more than half have been about criminal trials.

It has always been an attractive cry from convicted defendants. With time on their hands, they were able to pursue their human rights' across the Channel, even if there was only a dim prospect of remedy many years down the line.

But it is not just because prisoners complain most assiduously and diligently that this impressive body of case law has dominated the European Court workings. The real reason is that judges in each country (and in the UK in particular) have held the complacent belief that no one else can teach them about freedoms and rights. Against that attitude, complaint after complaint has been made. The European Court has found violations of the articles right at the heart of our criminal process.

The conventional view that the rights and freedoms guaranteed by the Convention could be delivered by our own courts was finally and explicitly condemned in a white paper, the forerunner to the Human Rights Bill. Our common law was criticised as no longer sufficient to safeguard our civil liberties and the European Convention had to be incorporated.

---

9   [1998] HRCD Vol IX, No 10, p 806.

Since the Human Rights Act 1998 received Royal Assent, there has been frenzied training in all parts of the criminal justice system. In those training sessions involving members of the judiciary, there have been two schools of thought. There are those judges who believe that the incorporation of the Convention will have a root-and-branch effect on our law. Others, and perhaps a dwindling minority, still believe that there is nothing that Europe can teach us about fundamental freedoms.

It is true that our common law is in line with many of the decisions in European cases brought against other governments. However, the current thinking is that incorporation of the Convention will impact on every stage of a defendant's progress through the criminal system and much will have to change.

There has been some patronising comment suggesting magistrates will have difficulty in grappling with concepts of human rights in the mundane case list at the local court. In fact, soundings show the contrary. Most of the judiciary is embracing the new concepts and is anxious to implement the new framework of decisions. Here is a whistle-stop tour of the vulnerable areas of our law.

The rights and principles

Article 5 gives everyone a right to liberty and security of person. An individual can only be deprived of his liberty in accordance with a procedure prescribed by law and in the circumstances set out under the article.

Article 6 is the right to a fair trial. Minimum rights are contained within the body of the article, but they are by no means exhaustive. European case law has read in many other requirements for due process and fair trial which are not explicitly set out in the Convention.

Article 7 prohibits retrospective criminal penalties. No one can be convicted of a criminal offence if his act or omission did not constitute a criminal offence at the time of commission.

Article 8 provides a right to respect for private and family life, home and correspondence.

Articles 10 and 11 embody freedom of expression, freedom of assembly and association.

The guarantees of fair trial under article 6 encompass the criminal process from investigation stage to the final appeal court. This is the first stop in assessing whether the Human Rights Act 1998 will have a bearing on the criminal process under scrutiny.

Of these articles, only the rights under article 7 are absolute. The others can be restricted in order to ensure respect for other rights and freedoms under the Convention.

In deciding whether there can be an exception to a right under one of these articles, the European case law has developed several principles.

The Convention is a 'living instrument' and consequently, what might have been an allowable restriction as being 'necessary in a democratic society' a few decades ago might now be inapplicable. The older a case, the less reliable it is.

Where an article speaks of an exception being 'prescribed by law', it means that the law must be explicit and susceptible to challenge with adequate safeguards.

'Proportionality' requires that a fair balance must he struck between the interests of the community and the individual's fundamental rights.

Article 14 provides that all the Convention's rights should be enjoyed by everyone without discrimination.

Finally, there must be effective remedies in place to deal with administrative or legal interference with fundamental rights.

Since Royal Assent, lawyers have been chomping at the bit to test the effect of incorporation. 'This has led to some fascinating pre-emptive litigation through the judicial review process. In *R v Director of Public Prosecutions ex parte Kebilene* [1999] 3 WLR 972, HL, the House of Lords gave some indication of how it saw Human Rights Act litigation taking effect. The Lords deplored any attempt to generate 'satellite litigation'. Challenges under the Human Rights Act should take place within the trial process or on appeal. Only where a person's remedy would effectively be neutralised by delay could a pre-emptive strike be made outside the criminal process.

The Act obliges a court to interpret all legislation to be compatible with the Convention if possible. If the legislation is so much at odds with Convention rights that it cannot be remoulded, the High Court, Court of Appeal or House of Lords can be invited to make a 'declaration of incompatibility'. Although this does not provide an immediate remedy to the defendant, a conviction based upon law that is incompatible with the Convention should not attract any penalty.

Silence and the adverse inference

English common law has made much of the concept of the 'presumption of innocence' and the rule against self-incrimination. Nevertheless, the courts wholeheartedly embraced the changes brought in by the Criminal Evidence and Public Order Act 1994 which allow a court to draw an adverse inference from an accused's silence in the face of questioning in the police station, on charge or at trial.

In *Condron and Another v United Kingdom* (2000) *The Times*, 9 May the European Court applied article 6 to a case in which the jury had been loosely directed on drawing an adverse inference from silence. Their judgment, if it is applied here under the Act, will require far tighter judicial control of a jury's use of the discretion to draw inferences than the Court of Appeal has provided so far. The Judicial Studies Board direction will have to be remodelled so that legal advice to remain silent is given substantial weight. There must be a direction that an adverse inference should only be drawn if a jury is not satisfied with the plausibility of the defendant's explanation.

The recent line of cases from the Court of Appeal has made inroads to a suspect's ability to rely on a solicitor's advice and the privilege that attached to that advice. Convention law suggests that the Court of Appeal has gone too far. What is beyond doubt is that responses to questions obtained by compulsion cannot be used in a criminal trial to secure a conviction. It follows that where an individual is required to answer questions asked by financial regulatory authorities (using powers under s 2 of the Criminal Justice Act 1987, the Companies Act 1985, or the Financial Services Act 1986, for example), the evidence cannot then be used in a trial.

Bail

Article 5 guarantees an individual 'liberty and security' subject to certain exceptions. From the starting point of the presumption of innocence and liberty, the European Court will allow detention if there is a fear of absconding, interference with the course of justice, the prevention of crime or the preservation of public order.

Since these are the only grounds on which bail can be refused, those sections of the Bail Act which reverse the presumption of liberty will fall foul of the European case law. Under our current law, a person convicted previously of the most serious of offences will only be granted bail if there are 'exceptional circumstances which justify it'. Similarly the Bail Act 1976 excludes the right to bail for a serious charge where the defendant allegedly committed the offence on bail for another offence. Suspects arrested on an allegation of breach of bail condition also have bail excluded. In these three cases at least, the courts should find a violation of article 5. Here are examples where the positive rights to liberty under the convention are far more effective than the permissive regime in our law:

The principle of 'equality of arms' will require the prosecution to provide full relevant disclosure of its case and anything that undermines it or assists the defence at the time of the bail application. The CPS will have to institute disclosure of a 'bail information package' for a defendant's first appearance in court.

We are all familiar with the administrative arrangements under which defendants are not produced to the Crown Court for bail appeals or applications to that court. Arguably, where proceedings on such a vital issue are carried on without the defendant present, there would be a violation of the Convention. The prosecution should have to prove an essential fact on which it relies which is at the heart of the bail decision by calling evidence that can be confronted. The regime in the magistrates' court and Crown Court where bail business is done by representations will have to change.

Although the right to a trial within a reasonable time for those denied bail is guaranteed under article 5(3), the European Court has been disappointingly relaxed in deciding what is 'reasonable'. Delays up to two years have proved acceptable.

Right to a lawyer

In the early days of the Police & Criminal Evidence Act 1984, suspects were frequently held 'incommunicado' without access to legal advice on serious offences. The use of that technique by the police has dwindled.

Nevertheless, it might still be used as a weapon in the police armoury of interrogation were it not for the case law from Europe. Recent cases against the UK government held that a defendant is denied a fair trial if he was denied legal advice at crucial moments, including during a police interview. It is now difficult to think of a situation where a suspect would be able to be interviewed without a lawyer being present.

The charge

In European law, a charge is made when the suspect is first 'confronted' with the allegation, and not at the point of the formal charge when the case goes before the court. A suspect has a right to be tried within a reasonable period from the point that the allegation is first put to him. Even in complex fraud cases, delay will violate that right and the European Court has said the finger of suspicion should not point at a suspect for an unconscionable length of time.

The charge itself must not offend against the underlying presumption of innocence. The burden of proof remains with the prosecution and so charges which appear to reverse the onus of proof need to be scrutinised carefully.

The House of Lords has tackled this very point in advance with an eye on the implementation of the Act in October. It suggested that the Convention allows only a shift in the evidential burden to the defence to raise a doubt, provided the legal burden of proof beyond reasonable doubt remains with the prosecution. Unraveling this legal acrobat is not something to go into here but the courts are well aware that charges under the Corruption Act, Financial Services Act and many other statutes will be incompatible with the Convention.

Disclosure

A fair trial under article 6 requires adequate time and facilities for the preparation of a defence. It requires an 'equality of arms', including information. The authorities are under a duty to gather evidence in favour of the accused in advance of the trial, and to disclose all relevant material including information undermining defence witnesses.

While the European Court has considered each case of disclosure on its facts and decided whether non-disclosure led to an unfair trial, there is a very strong presumption in favour of blanket disclosure of relevant information. These cases will now have to be set against the regime in the Criminal Procedure & Investigation Act 1996.

One criticism of the disclosure provisions in that Act is that the disclosure officer is part of the prosecution team. Defence lawyers will be very familiar with the problem of extracting relevant documents from the prosecution. Drawing on the principle of impartiality, that arrangement is likely to be subject to criticism where relevant material is not disclosed to the defence in a trial. Equally, prosecutors will know of the problems created by their reliance on a police officer's view of disclosure. This has to change.

More importantly perhaps, the disclosure under the 1996 Act takes place after committal and, crucially, after the defendant has set out his case. There is nothing in the European cases which suggest that disclosure can be delayed for either reason. In fact, the sense is that full disclosure should take place at an early stage without a mechanism other than the fact of the proceedings themselves. The Director of Public Prosecutions and Home Office have been analysing the operation of disclosure on a practical level in criminal cases. On the back of this, the Human Rights Act should produce a wave of complaint about the practice and procedure for disclosure under the 1996 Act.

The use of public interest immunity (PII) to restrict access to documents has become far more frequent, particularly the use of the *ex-parte* application when the defence has little or no ability to make informed representations. European case law accepts the need to balance the public interest against that of the defendant. However, the scales are tipped firmly in favour of the general right to disclosure, even in cases involving an informer or where the protection of a witness is at stake.

As to the procedure for obtaining a PII order from the court, the European Court has recently sanctioned the *ex-parte* application within the trial procedure. But PII applications can only be determined by the trial judge and not later by the Court of Appeal. If that court rules on PII and the trial court did not, the appellant will not have had a fair trial because the decision to withhold material was not dealt with by the trial judge.

Public order offences

Articles 10 and 11 guarantee the right to freedom of expression and to free assembly. The Convention sets out circumstances in which these rights can be interfered with. Once again the Convention starts off with a positive enforceable right rather than the permissive regime in English law. Free speech will include not only the inoffensive remarks but also the irritating, contentious or heretical provided it does not provoke violence. Freedom of expression also includes demonstrations without using words.

The areas of law that will come under scrutiny with the 1998 Act are those sections in the Criminal Justice and Public Order Act 1994 allowing directions to be made and prosecutions brought where individuals, such as gypsies, refuse to leave land.

Evidence – police tactics

There has been growing use by the police of entrapment techniques. Various ploys have been used to entice individuals to commit offences which have then formed the backbone of a prosecution. Such 'virtue testing' or 'honeypot' cases have been scrutinised by the European Court.

It found that where evidence is obtained without fettering a person's 'free will', there is no prejudice to the fairness of the proceedings, under article 6. However where the police do not confine themselves simply to investigating criminal activity in an essentially passive manner and take steps to incite the commission of an offence, then that evidence, if admitted, will make the trial unfair.

The test is therefore different to English common law. If the suspect has a predisposition to commit the particular act, the channelling of evidence by police ploy would be allowed. However, if the prosecution cannot show there is a predisposition or propensity to commit that act, the entrapment will render any trial unfair.

Examining witnesses

The principle that anyone charged with a criminal offence should be able to confront the witnesses against him means that all evidence should be heard in the presence of the accused; the examination of witnesses should be adversarial; and there should be adequate opportunity to challenge and question the witness either at the time the witness makes a statement or at a later stage.

The European Court will only allow hearsay evidence to be relied on to prove someone's guilt if there are stringent counter-balancing factors which preserve the rights of the defence. Equally, where a witness has claimed a fear of reprisal to avoid giving direct evidence, the court have only sanctioned such arrangements in exceptional cases. Where the witnesses are police officers or government agencies, it is unlikely that they would ever be able to be shielded by screens or given anonymity under Convention law.

Police surveillance

A vast array of technology is available to the police to intercept telephone calls and eavesdrop on conversations. Faxes and e-mails are all open to scrutiny. BT has the ability to eavesdrop on conversations in a room by switching on the telephone handset.

Article 8 guarantees an individual the right to a private life. This can only be interfered with provided the surveillance is 'prescribed by law' and is 'necessary and proportionate'. So, where the surveillance is not regulated by strict controls or judicial scrutiny, it will not be permissible under the article.

The authority to intercept communications must set out clearly all pre-conditions, define the category of citizens to which it will apply and provide adequate safeguards against abuse. It has been held that the use of tape recordings from listening devices introduced into suspects' homes which were only governed by Home Office guidelines issued in 1984 were a breach of article 8.

It does not necessarily follow however that the introduction of such evidence into a trial renders it unfair. However, the government is well aware that all covert surveillance must be operated under a code of law and proposes various pieces of legislation to make these police operations Human Rights Act-compliant.

We shall have to see whether all the regulatory systems do indeed meet the stringent tests under the Convention, and whether mobile phone intercepts are incorporated into a legislative framework.

The principles of due process and proportionality will affect the varied powers of entry, search and seizure contained in criminal statutes. Search and seizure must always be proportionate and have a mechanism to allow challenge.

The authority to search should only be given by a person independent of the enquiry itself. Any issues of legal professional privilege (a concept almost sacrosanct under the Convention) should be decided by an independent tribunal if that privilege might be undermined.

Pre-trial publicity

While the prosecuting authorities can inform the press about a criminal investigation, it requires that they do so 'with all discretion and circumspection necessary if the presumption of innocence is to be respected'.

The modern tendency of the police to give full background briefings to the press, including highly prejudicial material, would undoubtedly lead to a trial being declared unfair if the publicity could be shown to emanate from the prosecuting authorities. Even without briefings by an official, where a campaign has been 'virulent' and a jury is 'likely' to be prejudiced, there would be a breach of article 6. This reinvigorates the applications for abuse of process based on prejudicial press reports before trial.

Court of Appeal

The Court of Appeal will have to look very carefully at its current law and practice when dealing with appeals against conviction. Following the introduction of the single 'safety test' by the Criminal Appeal Act 1995, the court has said that it has to be convinced both that the appellant's trial was unfair and that justice had not been done before questioning a conviction.

In deciding this second question, the Court of Appeal has looked at the evidence as a whole and decided for itself whether it felt that the prosecution had proved its case. Essentially the court takes its own view on whether the appellant is indeed guilty. The Convention cases suggest that this approach is wrong. If there has been a procedural unfairness which renders the trial unfair under article 6, then it follows that the appeal should be allowed. The European Court said that the Court of Appeal does not have sufficient regard for the central role of the jury and that it should not substitute its own views for those of the jury after the trial in deciding what evidence weighed heavily, and why. The Court of Appeal have been interpreting the 'safety' test too broadly and either the case authorities will have to be radically reviewed or primary legislation will bring the Court of Appeal into line with the Human Rights Act.

The European Court took a similar view when considering the application of PII applications in the Court of Appeal. In *Rowe & Davis v United Kingdom* (2000) *The Times*, 1 March, the prosecution had withheld material from the trial judge and defence and only applied for PII certificates in the Court of Appeal. The European Court held that it was unfair for the Court of Appeal to dismiss an appeal while withholding the material on PII grounds when it should be up to the trial judge alone to determine questions of disclosure and PIII.

The proper course was for the Court of Appeal to accept a procedural unfairness by the prosecution withholding the documents from the trial judge and either quash the conviction or return the case for a retrial. Again, the Court of Appeal decided too much on behalf of the jury.

The future

Tony Blair recently proposed a policy of spot-fining hooligan behaviour in the streets. Were he to have had the Human Rights Act in mind, he would have known that a criminal sanction can only be administered after due process in a court. A police officer would just not be able to march a drunken hooligan to a cashpoint machine.

What about the abolition of the right of jury trials for certain defendants? If a person's previous convictions or reputation are a deciding factor in offering a defendant a jury trial, then the law would surely be discriminatory under the Convention. There is everything to play for.

--·--·--·--·--·--·--·--·--·--·--·--·--·--·--·--

A contradiction

In the current debate, there is a friction between two types of policy: policies which are designed to give the police and the courts more powers to stop, search, and interrogate suspects in order to improve the 'fight against crime'; and policies which seek to enhance civil liberties and freedoms by limiting the powers of the police and the State.

One problem, therefore, in this area of the English legal system is that as the growing problems of crime, and the fear of crime, become more important concerns of government, there are emerging two lobbies for change: lobbies which are diametrically opposed.

In this text, the criminal justice system will be examined in two sections. First, the law relating to important pre-trial matters, up to and including the admissibility of confession evidence in court, will be examined and, second, the institutional and procedural aspects of prosecution and matters relating to bail, classification of offences, trials, plea bargaining and the jury will be dealt with. In examining these topics, it is important to keep in mind the various aims of the criminal justice system and the extent to which the existing law serves these aims. Amongst the aims to be borne in mind are the following:

(a) to detect crime and convict those who have committed it;

(b) to have rules relating to arrest, search, questioning, interrogation and admissibility of evidence which do not expose suspects to unfair treatment likely to lead to unjust convictions;

(d) to have rules as above which do not unnecessarily impede the proper investigation of crime;

(e) to ensure that innocent persons are not convicted;

(f) to maintain public order;

(g) to maintain public confidence in the criminal justice system; and

(h) properly to balance considerations of justice and fair procedure with those of efficiency and funding.

In the following article, Frances Gibb, legal editor of *The Times*, examines alarm felt in some quarters of the legal profession by the Home Secretary's approach to the criminal justice system.

Frances Gibb, 'Our legal rights in jeopardy' (2001) *The Times*, 13 March

Is Jack Straw the most dangerous man in Britain? The question once posed by Conservatives of the Prime Minister is now being asked by lawyers of the Home Secretary. He is guilty, they say, of a steady dismantling of the basic tenets of the criminal justice system: the principle of the presumption of innocence is being eroded and the right to a fair trial and legal representation being whittled away so as to bring more criminals to book.

There is no love lost between Straw and members of his former profession. He has accused them, in effect, of 'cosying up' to the criminal fraternity; of driving BMWs in leafy suburbs, unaware of the real impact of crime; of never agreeing except 'about taking money off clients' and of scuppering his antisocial behaviour orders.

The accusations play well with the public. But away from the rhetoric about who can be blamed for failures on crime, there is growing concern about the ways ministers intend to tackle it. Recent initiatives have sought to wrest the balance of the justice system away from the defendant: curbs on jury trial, a prosecution right of appeal, relaxation of the double jeopardy rule, powers to confiscate a suspect's assets and disclosure of defendants' previous convictions to a jury. Add into the mix the Lord Chancellor's squeeze on criminal legal aid pay and the proposed new salaried defender system, and the criminal justice system looks very much under siege.

Malcolm Fowler, secretary of the Law Society's criminal law committee, says the dispute in essence is over the right model of criminal justice system. 'Do you want the business, mechanistic model, where you can measure costs per unit and pull appropriate sentences off the website? Or do you want the justice model, where there is equality of arms between prosecution and defence and people are assumed innocent until found guilty? We are almost into Alice in Wonderland territory – sentence first, trial afterwards.'

Roy Amlot, QC, Chairman of the Bar Council, says he views Straw's proposals and the apparent abandonment of liberal credentials with incredulity. 'I can't believe it. When you think of how Jack Straw behaved in Opposition, it is simply not the same person. It is very worrying and a huge threat. It is quite clear the Government wants to achieve convictions, but justice must be done at the same time. All the time it's kneejerk reactions, trying to find clever ways of making sure people are convicted, when it would be better to concentrate on preventing crime rather than achieving results afterwards.'

John Wadham, director of Liberty, agrees: a plethora of extra police powers are tilting the balance against protesters, suspects and defendants, but with no evident impact on crime. 'It's very hard to challenge this crude populism on law and order. Those fighting for rights are less likely to be met with rational debate than to find themselves caricatured, their concerns belittled and ignored.'

No one could dispute the criminal justice system needs a revamp. It is slow, inefficient, hugely wasteful of resources and user-unfriendly. For that reason Sir Robin Auld was appointed to do a root-and-branch review. When he saw his ideas might be used as election fodder, he seemed to be on a go-slow. His report is now expected shortly, but Tony Blair and Straw went ahead with their ten-year crime plan without him. Yet how far can reform go before safeguards are sacrificed to efficiency? Straw questions the right of 'professional' criminals to exploit the system, opt for costly jury trial to spin things out and plead guilty at the last minute at huge expense. In the same spirit, juries should, he argues, know about previous convictions. James Morton, a former defence solicitor, predicted in the *New Law Journal* last week: 'In a few years there would be no need for evidence after the first conviction or plea of guilty. The successors of Claude Raines's police chief in Casablanca will have a 100 per cent record.'

The test of the system, say lawyers, is not the conviction rate – important though that is. 'This Government must learn to love acquittals,' argues Fowler. Instead of attacking lawyers for doing their job, ministers should put resources into the police and prosecution service.

Another defence lawyer, Mike Mackey, of Burton Copeland, says: 'Straw speaks of aggressive defence lawyers. Would he prefer that we ignore our clients despite the presumption of innocence? Everyone knows the police are underfunded. They don't need any more powers, not for the scales of justice to be weighted in their favour. What they need are resources.' And they maintain the job is not about getting criminals off but about ensuring that no one is convicted if a case is not made out. If some criminals go free as a result, that is the price for a just system. Defence lawyers, and juries, are the bulwark between the citizen against the State, insists Franklin Sinclair, chairman of the Criminal Law Solicitors Association. 'The definition of a civilised society is how it treats uncivilised people. Without a fair system of justice, we are on the road to totalitarian rule.'

Such principles may sound grandiose, but most lawyers believe in them. They feel angry and bitter, therefore, about the simultaneous squeeze on pay – whether through the new contracts for solicitors or fee rates for the Bar. A strike by up to 2,000 firms last week over contracts was averted after intense negotiations. But the modified terms have left them far from content. John Killah, a criminal solicitor in Frome, Somerset, says: 'Like others, I effectively work a seven-day week, helping often-vulnerable clients. We have all been in positions of personal danger. But we do the job because we want to and we believe in the criminal justice system. It is unglamorous and often impinges on family and social life. We can cope with the junk pay and cheap barbs from ministers; but we won't stand for an actual wage cut and an attack on our independence.'

Malcolm Swift, QC, leader of the Bar's North-Eastern Circuit, also warns of the steady lowering of the level of lawyer used – from magistrates' courts to an 80 per cent cut in the use of Queen's Counsel in the Crown Court. He predicts a surge of appeals against convictions. This, in practical terms, could be the upshot of a system pared of its principles. Miscarriages of justice bedevilled the 1970s and 1980s and saw a huge shake-up of criminal justice. Now, lawyers fear, the attack on the present system could see a rerun.

'If,' Fowler says, 'ministers think these miscarriages could not happen now, they are wrong. The problem is that they are obsessed with presentation and showing they are tackling crime, and they think, if we get presentation right and a few principles end up on the cutting-room floor, then so much the better.'

ARREST

Before considering the rights of the citizen and the law governing arrest, detention, what happens in the police station and what evidence is admissible in court, it is appropriate to look first at what the citizen can do if those rights are violated.

Like other areas of law where the liberty of the subject is at stake, the law relating to arrest is founded upon the principle of *justification*. If challenged, the person who has attempted to make an arrest must justify his or her actions and show that the arrest was lawful. Failing this, the arrest will be regarded as unlawful.

There are three possible remedies:

(a) The person, or someone on his or her behalf, can bring proceedings of *habeas corpus*. This ancient prerogative writ used to begin with the words '*habeas corpus*', meaning: 'You must have the body.' It is addressed to the detainer and asks him to bring the detainee in question before the court at a specified date and time.

(b) To use the illegality of the detention to argue that any subsequent prosecution should fail. This type of argument is very rarely successful as illegally obtained evidence is not, *ipso facto*, automatically rendered inadmissible. The House of Lords ruled in *Sang* that no discretion existed to exclude evidence simply because it had been illegally or improperly obtained. A court could only exclude relevant evidence where its effect would be 'unduly prejudicial'.

This is reflected in s 78(1) of the Police and Criminal Evidence Act (PACE) 1984 (below). This perhaps surprising rule was supported by the Royal Commission on Criminal Justice (although the argument there was chiefly focused on the admissibility of confession evidence).

(c) An action for damages for false imprisonment. In some cases the damages for such an action would be likely to be nominal if the violation by the detainer does not have much impact on the detainee. Consider cases under this heading like *Christie v Leachinsky*. Damages can, however, be considerable.

Apart from the question of civil remedies, it is important to remember that, **if the arrest is not lawful, there is the right to use reasonable force to resist it. This is a remedy, however, of doubtful advisability as the legality of the arrest will only be properly tested after the event in a law court.** If a police officer was engaged in what the courts decide was a lawful arrest or conduct, then anyone who uses force against the officer might have been guilty of an offence of assaulting an officer in the execution of his duty contrary to s 51 of the Police Act 1964.

Police Act 1964

Section 51 – Assaults on constables

(1) Any person who assaults a constable in the execution of his duty, or a person assisting a constable in the execution of his duty, shall be guilty of an offence and liable [on summary conviction to imprisonment for a term not exceeding six months or to a fine not exceeding [level 5 on the standard scale] or to both ...].

(3) Any person who wilfully obstructs a constable in the execution of his duty, or a person assisting a constable in the execution of his duty, shall be guilty of an offence and liable on summary conviction to imprisonment for a term not exceeding one month or to a fine not exceeding [level 3 on the standard scale] or to both.

For the purpose of considering the consequences for an unlawfully arrested person faced with prosecution, s 78 of the PACE 1984 states:

78(1) In any proceedings the court may refuse to allow evidence on which the prosecution proposes to rely to be given if it appears to the court that, having regard to all the circumstances, including the circumstances in which the evidence was obtained, the admission of the evidence would have such an adverse effect on the fairness of the proceedings that the court ought not to admit it.

General powers of arrest

In *Spicer v Holt* [1977] AC 987, Lord Dilhorne stated: 'Whether or not a person has been arrested depends not upon the legality of the arrest, but on whether he has been deprived of his liberty to go where he pleases.'

So a person who is detained by the police against his will is arrested. Whether this arrest is lawful will depend on whether the conditions for a lawful arrest have been satisfied. If the arrest is not lawful there is the right to use reasonable force to resist it. This is a remedy, however, of doubtful advisability as the legality of the arrest will only properly be tested after the event in a law court.

Lawful arrests are those: (1) under warrant; (2) without warrant at common law; or (3) without warrant under legislation.

Arrest under warrant

The police lay a written information on oath before a magistrate that a person 'has, or is suspected of having, committed an offence' (Magistrates' Courts Act 1980, s 1). The Criminal Justice Act 1967 provides that warrants should not be issued unless the offence in question is indictable or is punishable with imprisonment.

Common law arrests

The only power to arrest at common law is where a breach of the peace has been committed and there are reasonable grounds for believing that it will be continued or renewed, or where a breach of the peace is reasonably apprehended.

Arrest under legislation

The right to arrest is generally governed by s 24 of PACE (as amended by s 85 of the Criminal Justice and Public Order Act (CJPO) 1994).

PACE 1984

Section 24

(1) The powers of summary arrest conferred by the following subsections shall apply –

    (a) to offences for which the sentence is fixed by law;

    (b) to offences for which a person of 21 years of age or over (not previously convicted) may be sentenced to imprisonment for a term of five years (or might be so sentenced but for the restrictions imposed by section 33 of the Magistrates' Courts Act 1980); and

    (c) to the offences to which subsection (2) below applies,

and in this Act 'arrestable offence' means any such offence.

(2) The offences to which this subsection applies are –

  (a) offences for which a person may be arrested under the customs and excise Acts, as defined in section 1(1) of the Customs and Excise Management Act 1979;

  (b) offences under [the Official Secrets Act 1920] that are not arrestable offences by virtue of the term of imprisonment for which a person may be sentenced in respect of them;

  [(bb)offences under any provision of the Official Secrets Act 1989 except section 8(1), (4) or (5);]

  (c) offences under section ... 22 (causing prostitution of women) or 23 (procuration of girl under 21) of the Sexual Offences Act 1956;

  (d) offences under section 12(1) (taking motor vehicle or other conveyance without authority etc) or 25(1) (going equipped for stealing, etc) of the Theft Act 1968; and

  [(e) any offence under the Football (Offences) Act 1991;]

  [(f) an offence under section 2 of the Obscene Publications Act 1959 (publication of obscene matter);

  (g) an offence under section 1 of the Protection of Children Act 1978 (indecent photographs and pseudo-photographs of children);]

  [(h) an offence under section 166 of the Criminal Justice and Public Order Act 1994 (sale of tickets by unauthorised persons);]

  [(i) an offence under section 19 of the Public Order Act 1986 (publishing, etc material intended or likely to stir up racial hatred);]

  [(j) an offence under section 167 of the Criminal Justice and Public Order Act 1994 (touting for hire car services).]

(3) Without prejudice to section 2 of the Criminal Attempts Act 1981, the powers of summary arrest conferred by the following subsections shall also apply to the offences of –

  (a) conspiring to commit any of the offences mentioned in subsection (2) above;

  (b) attempting to commit any such offence [other than an offence under section 12(1) of the Theft Act 1968];

  (c) inciting, aiding, abetting, counselling or procuring the commission of any such offence;

and such offences are also arrestable offences for the purposes of this Act.

(4) Any person may arrest without a warrant –

  (a) anyone who is in the act of committing an arrestable offence;

  (b) anyone whom he has reasonable grounds for suspecting to be committing such an offence.

(5) Where an arrestable offence has been committed, any person may arrest without a warrant –

  (a) anyone who is guilty of the offence;

  (b) anyone whom he has reasonable grounds for suspecting to be guilty of it.

(6) Where a constable has reasonable grounds for suspecting that an arrestable offence has been committed, he may arrest without a warrant anyone whom he has reasonable grounds for suspecting to be guilty of the offence.

(7) A constable may arrest without a warrant –

    (a) anyone who is about to commit an arrestable offence;

    (b) anyone whom he has reasonable grounds for suspecting to be about to commit an arrestable offence.

_._

A police officer is given additional powers under s 25.

PACE 1984

Section 25

(1) Where a constable has reasonable grounds for suspecting that any offence which is not an arrestable offence has been committed or attempted, or is being committed or attempted, he may arrest the relevant person if it appears to him that service of a summons is impracticable or inappropriate because any of the general arrest conditions is satisfied.

(2) In this section 'the relevant person' means any person whom the constable has reasonable grounds to suspect of having committed or having attempted to commit the offence or of being in the course of committing or attempting to commit it.

(3) The general arrest conditions are–

    (a) that the name of the relevant person is unknown to, and cannot be readily ascertained by, the constable;

    (b) that the constable has reasonable grounds for doubting whether a name furnished by the relevant person as his name is his real name;

    (c) that–

        (i) the relevant person has failed to furnish a satisfactory address for service; or

        (ii) the constable has reasonable grounds for doubting whether an address furnished by the relevant person is a satisfactory address for service;

    (d) that the constable has reasonable grounds for believing that arrest is necessary to prevent the relevant person –

        (i) causing physical injury to himself or any other person;

        (ii) suffering physical injury;

        (iii) causing loss of or damage to property;

        (iv) committing an offence against public decency; or

        (v) causing an unlawful obstruction of the highway;

    (e) that the constable has reasonable grounds for believing that arrest is necessary to protect a child or other vulnerable person from the relevant person.

(4) For the purposes of subsection (3) above an address is a satisfactory address for service if it appears to the constable–

   (a) that the relevant person will be at it for a sufficiently long period for it to be possible to serve him with a summons; or

   (b) that some other person specified by the relevant person will accept service of a summons for the relevant person at it.

(5) Nothing in subsection (3)(d) above authorises the arrest of a person under sub-paragraph (iv) of that paragraph except where members of the public going about their normal business cannot reasonably be expected to avoid the person to be arrested.

(6) This section shall not prejudice any power of arrest conferred apart from this section.

—·—·—·—·—·—·—·—·—·—·—·—·—·—·—·—

Difficulties in practice

In *G v DPP*, the appellant, G, with other juveniles, including a co-accused Gill, went to a police station to complain about being ejected from a public service vehicle. On being asked for their names and addresses by the officer, G the appellant refused to do so; some of the others gave false particulars but Gill gave his real name and address. The officer did not accept that Gill's particulars were correct because, in his experience, people who committed offences did not give correct details (even though the juveniles had only gone to the police station to complain about the way they had been treated on the bus). The juveniles would not accept the officer's advice about their complaint and became threatening and abusive. Gill was arrested for 'disorderly behaviour in a police station' and he struggled and resisted; the appellant joined in, punching the officer and causing him to lose hold of Gill. Both Gill and G were convicted of assaulting a police officer in the execution of his duty. The Divisional Court quashed their convictions. The offence of 'violent behaviour' or 'disorderly behaviour' under the Town Police Causes Act 1847 was not an arrestable offence. The only power the officer therefore had to arrest Gill was under s 25(3) of PACE if there were genuine doubts about Gill's name and address. But the ground given by the officer – about people who commit offences not giving their proper name, etc – was not a proper ground because there was no evidence that the youths had committed any offences; they had gone to the police simply to complain. Therefore, in purporting to arrest Gill, the officer had not been acting in the execution of his duty and the appellant could not, therefore, have been guilty of obstructing him in the performance of such duty.

It should be noted in particular that under s 24(6) no offence need have actually been committed. All that is required is that the police officer reasonably believes that an offence has been committed.

The differences in the powers of arrest in s 24 are based on whether an offence:

(a) is *being* committed: anyone may make the arrest: see s 24(4);

(b) *has been* committed: anyone may make the arrest: see s 24(5) or the *wider* powers of the police, s 24(6), who can arrest where they 'have reasonable grounds for suspecting that an arrestable offence has been committed', whether one has in fact been committed or not;

(c) is *about to be* committed: only a police officer may act here: see s 24(7).

PACE 1984 preserves an old common law distinction in respect of the powers of constables and private individuals when making such arrests. Where an arrest is being made *after* an offence is thought to have been committed then PACE 1984 confers narrower rights upon the private individual than on the police officer.

It is worthy of note that the less prudent arrestor who acts against a suspect when the latter is suspected of being in the act of committing an arrestable offence (s 24(4)) can justify his conduct simply by showing that there were 'reasonable grounds' on which to base the suspicion. They need not show that an offence was in fact being committed. If the arrestor waits until he thinks the crime *has been* committed then, whereas a police officer will only have to show 'reasonable grounds for suspecting than an arrestable has been committed' (s 24(6)), a citizen can only justify his behaviour if an offence 'has been committed' (s 24(5)).

John Lewis & Co v Tims [1952] All ER 1203, 1213

The respondent and her daughter entered the appellant's shop where the daughter stole certain articles. They then left the shop and the daughter placed the stolen articles in a bag carried by the respondent. Two detectives employed by the appellants followed the two women outside the shop and saw them go into another shop where the daughter again stole an article and placed it in the respondent's bag. As they came out into the street, one of the two detectives accosted them, said they had stolen the articles and asked them to come with her. It was a regulation of the appellants that only a managing director or a general manager of the appellants was authorised to institute any prosecution. The respondent and her daughter were taken back to the appellants' shop and detained until the chief store detective and the managing director heard the account of the two detectives, after which the police were sent for and the respondent and her daughter were taken to the police station, charged, and released on bail. Next morning the daughter was tried and convicted, but the charge against the respondent was withdrawn by consent of the court as the appellants were advised that there was insufficient evidence to justify a prosecution.

On a claim by the respondent for damages for false imprisonment: *Held*, where a person in exercise of his common law right arrested a person without warrant, he should take the arrested person before a justice of the peace or a police officer, not necessarily forthwith, but as soon as was reasonably possible; in the circumstances, the taking of the respondent to the appellants' office to obtain authority to prosecute was not an unreasonable delay before handing her over to the police; and, therefore, the appellants were not liable for false imprisonment.

> **Lord Porter**: What the common law requires is that, if a man be arrested on suspicion of felony, he should be taken before a tribunal which can deal with his case expeditiously. The question throughout should be: Has the arrestor brought the arrested person to a place where his alleged offence can be dealt with as speedily as is reasonably possible? But all the circumstances in the case must be taken into consideration in deciding whether this requirement is complied with. A direct route and a rapid progress are, no doubt, matters for consideration, but they are not the only matters. Those who arrest must be persuaded of the guilt of the accused; they cannot bolster up their assurance or the strength of the case by seeking further evidence and detaining the man arrested meanwhile or taking him to some spot where they can or may find further evidence. But there are advantages in refusing to give private detectives a free hand and leaving the determination of whether to prosecute or not to a superior official. Whether there is evidence that the steps taken were unreasonable or the delay too great is a matter for the judge. Whether, if there be such evidence, the delay was in fact too great is for the jury: see *Cave v Mountain* (1840) (1 Man & G 257). In the present case the complaint was, as I have said, not that the detention was too long, but that a direct route from the place of arrest to the magistrate's court had not been taken. In my opinion, that is not the vital question. Rather it is whether, in all the circumstances, the accused person has been brought before a justice of the peace within a reasonable time, it being always remembered that that time should be as short as is reasonably practicable. I would allow the appeal.

What is the meaning of 'reasonable grounds for suspecting'?

Many of the powers of the police in relation to arrest, search and seizure are founded upon the presence of reasonable 'suspicion', 'cause' or 'belief' in a state of affairs, usually that a suspect is involved actually or potentially in a crime.

Castorina v Chief Constable of Surrey (1988) 138 NLJ 180

Detectives reasonably concluded that the burglary of a company's premises was an 'inside job'. The managing director told them that she had recently dismissed someone (the plaintiff) although she did not think it would have been her, and that the documents taken would be useful to someone with a grudge. The detectives interviewed the plaintiff, having found out that she had no criminal record, and arrested her under s 2(4) of the Criminal Law Act (CLA) 1967 (which has now been replaced by s 24(6) of PACE 1984). She was detained at the police station for almost four hours, interrogated and then released without charge. On a claim for damages for wrongful arrest and detention, a jury awarded her £4,500. The trial judge held that the officers had had a *prima facie* case for suspicion, but that the arrest was premature. He had defined 'reasonable cause' (which the officers would have needed to show they had when they arrested the plaintiff) as 'honest belief founded upon reasonable suspicion leading an ordinary cautious man to the conclusion that the person arrested was guilty of the offence'. He said an ordinary man would have sought more information from the suspect, including an explanation for any grudge on her part. In this he relied on the *dicta* of Scott LJ in *Dumbell v Roberts* [1944] 1 All ER 326, p 329, that the principle that every man was presumed innocent until proved guilty also applied to arrests. The Court of Appeal allowed an appeal by the Chief Constable. The court held that the trial judge had used too severe a test in judging the officer's conduct.

Purchas LJ said that the test of 'reasonable cause' was objective and therefore the trial judge was wrong to have focused attention on whether the officers had 'an honest belief'. The question was whether the officer had had reasonable grounds to suspect the woman of the offence. There was sufficient evidence that the officer had had sufficient reason to suspect her.

Woolf LJ thought there were three things to consider in cases where an arrest is alleged to be unlawful:

1. Did the arresting officer suspect that the person who was arrested had committed the offence? This was a matter of fact about the officer's state of mind.

2. If the answer to the first question is yes, then was there reasonable proof of that suspicion? This is a simple objective matter to be determined by the judge.

3. If the answers to the first two questions are both yes, then the officer did have a discretion to arrest and the question then was whether he had exercised his discretion according to Wednesbury principles of reasonableness.

This case hinged on point 2 and, on the facts, the Chief Constable should succeed on the appeal.

Note: The *Wednesbury* principles come from *Associated Provincial Picture Houses Ltd v Wednesbury Corporation* [1948] 1 KB 233. Lord Greene MR laid down principles to determine when the decision made by a public authority could be regarded as so perverse or unreasonable that the courts would be justified in overturning that decision. The case actually concerned whether a condition imposed by a local authority on cinemas operation on Sundays was reasonable. Lord Greene MR said:

> ... a person entrusted with a discretion must, so to speak, direct himself properly in law. He must call his own attention to matters which he is bound to consider. He must exclude from his consideration matters which are irrelevant to what he has to consider. If he does not obey those rules, he may be truly said, and often is said, to be acting 'unreasonably'.

Holgate-Mohammed v Duke [1984] 2 WLR 660

House of Lords: A detective constable, exercising his powers under s 2(4) of the CLA 1967, arrested the plaintiff on suspicion that she had stolen jewellery and took her to a police station where she was questioned. She was not charged with an offence and was released from detention within six hours of her arrest. The plaintiff bought an action in the county court against the Chief Constable for damages for wrongful arrest. The judge found that the detective constable had had reasonable grounds to suspect the plaintiff of having committed an arrestable offence and that the period of detention was not excessive but, because the constable had decided not to interview her under caution but to subject her to the greater pressure of arrest and detention so as to induce a confession, there had been a wrongful exercise of the power of arrest. The plaintiff was awarded £1,000 damages. The Court of Appeal allowed an appeal by the Chief Constable.

On the plaintiff's appeal: *Held* (1) that the *Wednesbury* principles were to be applied in determining, for the purpose of founding an action at common law for false imprisonment, whether the discretion conferred upon a constable by s 2(4) of the CLA 1967 to arrest a person without a warrant had been exercised lawfully, namely whether the discretion had been exercised in good faith and whether all irrelevant matters had been excluded from consideration. *Associated Provincial Picture Houses Ltd v Wednesbury Corp* [1948] 1 KB 223 CA applied. The *dictum* of Lord Devlin in *Hussein v Chong Fook Kam* [1970] AC 942 PC, p 948, was considered. (2) Dismissing the appeal, that since an arrestable offence had been committed and the constable had reasonable cause for suspecting the plaintiff to be guilty of the offence, he was entitled to arrest her under s 2(4) of the Act; that the interrogation of a suspect in order to dispel or confirm a reasonable suspicion was a legitimate cause for arrest, so that the fact that the constable, when exercising his discretion to arrest the plaintiff, took into consideration that she might be more likely to confess her guilt if arrested and questioned at the police station was a relevant matter and, therefore, did not render the exercise of his discretion *ultra vires*; and that, accordingly, the arrest was not unlawful. The decision of the Court of Appeal was affirmed.

> **Lord Diplock**: ... Your Lordships are not concerned with rights of arrest at common law for it is not disputed that an arrestable offence had been committed, and what Detective Constable Offin was purporting to exercise was the statutory power of arrest without warrant conferred upon him by sub-ss (4) and (6) of s 2 of the Criminal Law Act 1967. Subsection (6) confers a right of entry on premises by a constable for the purpose of exercising the power of arrest conferred upon him by sub-s (4) which reads as follows: '(4) Where a constable, with reasonable cause, suspects that an arrestable offence has been committed, he may arrest without warrant anyone whom he, with reasonable cause, suspects to be guilty of the offence.' The word 'arrest' in s 2 is a term of art. First, it should be noted that arrest is a continuing act; it starts with the arrestor taking a persons into his custody [*sic* by action or words restraining him from moving anywhere beyond the arrestor's

control], and it continues until the person so restrained is either released from custody or, having been brought before a magistrate, is remanded in custody by the magistrate's judicial act. In practice since the creation of organised police forces during the course of the 19th century, an arrested person upon being taken into custody by a constable is brought to a police station and it is there that he is detained until he is either brought before a magistrate or released whether unconditionally or upon police bail. In modern conditions any other way of dealing with an arrested person once he has been taken into custody would be impracticable; and s 43 of the Magistrates' Courts Act 1980, providing for grant of bail by the police, is drafted on the assumption that this is what will be done. Strictly speaking, the arrestor may change from time to time during a continuous period of custody since the arrestor is the person who at any particular time is preventing the arrested person from removing himself from custody; but although this may be important in a case where the initial arrest has been made by a person who is not a constable (a 'citizen's arrest'), it is without practical significance in the common case of arrest by a constable and detention in police custody at a police station, since s 48(1) of the Police Act 1964 makes the chief constable of the police area vicariously liable for torts committed by members of the force that he commands in the performance or purported performance of their duties as constables.

Secondly, it should be noted that the mere act of taking a person into custody does not constitute an 'arrest' unless that person knows, either at the time when he is first taken into custody or as soon thereafter as it is reasonably practicable to inform him, upon what charge or on suspicion of what crime he is being arrested: *Christie v Leachinsky* [1947] AC 573. In the instant case, however, there is no suggestion that Mrs Holgate-Mohammed, when she was arrested at her home by Detective Constable Offin, was not fully informed by him of the offence, burglary of jewellery at a house at which she was residing in December 1979, which he suspected her of having committed. Very shortly after the burglary some of the jewellery had been sold to a jeweller in Portsmouth; but it was not until more than four months later, at the end of April 1980, that the victim of the burglary recognised her jewellery in the shop-window and informed the police of this. The jeweller's description of the vendor was thought by the victim to resemble that of her former lodger, Mrs Holgate-Mohammed, and she so informed Detective Constable Offin who had accompanied her to the jeweller's shop. Section 2(4) makes it a condition precedent to a constable's having any power lawfully to arrest a person without warrant, that he should have reasonable cause to suspect that person to be guilty of the arrestable offence in respect of which the arrest is being made. Whether he had reasonable cause is a question of fact for the court to determine. The circuit judge in the county court by whom Mrs Holgate-Mohammed's action for false imprisonment was heard at first instance and who had the advantage of hearing and seeing the witnesses, held that Detective Constable Offin did have reasonable cause for suspecting her to be guilty of the crime of burglary. The Court of Appeal, who had the advantage of examining either a transcript or a note of the oral evidence, came to the same conclusion. Your Lordships have enjoyed neither of these advantages. The only facts that were available to this House are such fragments as can be garnered from the judgments below. Your Lordships are thus faced upon this issue with concurrent findings of fact with which there is no material that could possibly justify interference. There are likewise concurrent findings of fact of the courts below that the duration of Mrs Holgate-Mohammed's detention at Southsea Police Station was, in the circumstances of which your Lordships are not fully apprised, not unreasonable. With the findings on this issue, too, this House in my view is in no position to interfere. So the condition precedent to Detective Constable Offin's power to take the appellant into custody and the power of the other constables at Southsea Police Station to detain her in custody was fulfilled; and, since the wording of the subsection under which he acted is 'may arrest without warrant,' this left him with an executive discretion whether to arrest her or not. Since this is an executive discretion expressly conferred by statute upon a public officer, the constable making the arrest, the lawfulness of the way in which he was exercised it in a particular case cannot be questioned in any court of law except upon those principles laid down by Lord Greene MR in *Associated Provincial Picture Houses Ltd v Wednesbury Corporation* [1948] 1 KB 223, that have become too familiar to call for repetitious citation. The *Wednesbury* principles, as they are usually referred to, are applicable to determining the lawfulness of the exercise of the statutory discretion of a constable under s 2(4) of the Criminal Law Act 1967, not only in proceedings for judicial review but also for the purpose of founding a cause of action at common law for damages for that species of trespass to the person known as false imprisonment, for which the action in the instant case is brought.

The first of the *Wednesbury* principles is that the discretion must be exercised in good faith. The judge in the county court expressly found that Detective Constable Offin in effecting the initial arrest acted in good faith. He thought that he was making a proper use of his power of arrest. So his exercise of that power by arresting Mrs Holgate-Mohammed was lawful, unless it can be shown to have been 'unreasonable' under *Wednesbury* principles, of which the principle that is germane to the instant case is: 'He (*sic* the exerciser of the discretion) must exclude from his consideration matters which are irrelevant to what he has to consider.' As Lord Devlin, speaking for the Judicial Committee of the Privy Council in *Hussein v Chong Fook Kam* [1970] AC 942, 948, said: 'Suspicion in its ordinary meaning is a state of conjecture or surmise where proof is lacking: "I suspect but I cannot prove." Suspicion arises at or near the starting-point of an investigation of which the obtaining of *prima facie* proof is the end. When such proof has been obtained, the police case is complete; it is ready for trial and passes on to its next stage ...' ie bringing the suspect before a magistrates' court upon a charge of a criminal offence. The other side of the same coin is where the investigation, although diligently pursued, fails to produce *prima facie* proof which, as Lord Devlin in the same case also pointed out (p 949), must be in the form of evidence that would be admissible in a court of law. When the police have reached the conclusion that *prima facie* proof of the arrested person's guilt is unlikely to be discovered by further inquiries of him or of other potential witnesses, it is their duty to release him from custody unconditionally: *Wiltshire v Barrett* [1966] 1 QB 312. Detective Constable Offin and, no doubt, those other officers of the Hampshire Police who had been concerned in the inquiries into the burglary that had been committed in December 1979, were well aware that their case against Mrs Holgate-Mohammed depended upon whether the jeweller would be able to identify on an identification parade, a customer whom he had seen only once, and that for a comparatively brief period five months before; and would be able to justify his identification in such a manner as would instil in a jury that high degree of confidence in his not having been mistaken that is called for by the guidance given in *R v Turnbull* [1977] QB 224 … My Lords, there is inevitably the potentiality of conflict between the public interest in preserving the liberty of the individual and the public interest in the detection of crime and the bringing to justice of those who commit it. The members of the organised police forces of the country have, since the mid-19th century, been charged with the duty of taking the first steps to promote the latter public interest by inquiring into suspected offences with a view to identifying the perpetrators of them and of obtaining sufficient evidence admissible in a court of law against the persons they suspect of being the perpetrators as would justify charging them with the relevant offence before a magistrates' court with a view to their committal for trial for it. The compromise which English common and statutory law has evolved for the accommodation of the two rival public interests while these first steps are being taken by the police is two fold:

(1) no person may be arrested without warrant (ie without the intervention of a judicial process) unless the constable arresting him has reasonable cause to suspect him to be guilty of an arrestable offence; and arrest, as is emphasised in the Judges' Rules themselves, is the only means by which a person can be compelled against his will to come to or remain in any police station;

(2) a suspect so arrested and detained in custody must be brought before a magistrates' court as soon as practicable, generally within 24 hours, otherwise, save in a serious case, he must be released on bail (Magistrates' Courts Act 1980, s 43(1) and (4)).

That arrest for the purpose of using the period of detention to dispel or confirm the reasonable suspicion by questioning the suspect or seeking further evidence with his assistance was said by the Royal Commission on Criminal Procedure in England and Wales (1981) (Cmnd 8092) at para 3.66 'to be well established as one of the primary purposes of detention upon arrest.' That is a fact that will be within the knowledge of these of your Lordships with judicial experience of trying criminal cases; even as long ago as I last did so, more than 20 years before the Royal Commission's Report. It is a practice which has been given implicit recognition in rule 1 of successive editions of the Judges' Rules, since they were first issued in 1912. Furthermore, parliamentary recognition that making inquiries of a suspect in order to dispel or confirm the reasonable suspicion is a legitimate cause for arrest and detention at a police station was implicit in s 38(2) of the Magistrates' Courts Act 1952 which is now reproduced in s 43(3) of the Magistrates' Courts Act 1980, with immaterial amendments consequent on the passing of the Bail Act 1976. That subsection, so far as is relevant for present purposes, reads: '(3) Where, on a person's being taken into custody for an offence without a warrant, it appears to any such officer as aforesaid (*sic* a police officer not below the rank of inspector, or the police officer in charge of the police station to which the person is brought) that the inquiry into the case cannot be completed forthwith, he may grant him bail in accordance with the Bail Act 1976 subject to a duty to appear at such a police station and at such a time as the officer appoints unless he previously receives a notice in writing from the officer in charge of that police station that his attendance is not required; …' So whether or not to arrest Mrs Holgate-Mohammed and bring her to the police station in order to facilitate the inquiry into the case of the December burglary was a decision that it lay within the discretion of Detective Constable Offin to take. In my opinion the error of law made by the circuit judge in the instant case was that, having found that Detective

Constable Offin had reasonable cause for suspecting Mrs Holgate-Mohammed to be guilty of the burglary committed in December 1979 to which he rightly applied an objective test of reasonableness, the judge failed to recognise that lawfulness of the arrest and detention based on that suspicion did not depend upon the judge's own view as to whether the arrest was reasonable or not, but upon whether Detective Constable Offin's action in arresting her was an exercise of discretion that was *ultra vires* under *Wednesbury* principles because he took into consideration an irrelevant matter. For the reasons that I have given and in agreement with the Court of Appeal, I do not think that in the circumstances Detective Constable Offin or any other police officers of the Hampshire Police acted unlawfully in the way in which they exercised their discretion. I would dismiss this appeal.

— · — · — · — · — · — · — · — · — · — · — · — · — · — · —

Detention short of arrest

For there to be an arrest, the arrestor must regard his action as an arrest. If he simply detains someone to question him without any thought of arrest, the action will be unlawful. It is often reported in criminal investigations that a person is 'helping police with their inquiries'.

R v Lemsatef [1977] 2 All ER 835

The defendant was detained, together with another man, by customs officers, at about 12.40 am on 28 May 1975, for being concerned in the importation of cannabis. Both men were taken to the Customs House and inquiries proceeded. During the course of the interrogation, at about 4.20 am, the defendant said that he would not answer any more questions until he had seen his solicitor. The customs officers told him that he could not see his solicitor at that time, and that although he was entitled to refuse to answer any more questions they were going to ask him some. At some time before 3.30 am the defendant's house was searched and his wife, having learnt that he was in custody, instructed a solicitor. The solicitor was not allowed to see the defendant until after he had made oral admissions and a written statement, which was completed at 6.18 pm. The defendant was charged with being knowingly concerned in the fraudulent evasion of the prohibition of the importation of cannabis, contrary to s 304(b) of the Customs and Excise Act 1952, as amended. At the trial the judge, in the exercise of his discretion, admitted evidence of the oral admissions and written statement. Evidence was also given by a co-accused that the defendant was dishonest and had made money by dealing in drugs, although he had not put his character in issue. The defendant was convicted.

On the defendant's appeal against conviction on the grounds that the evidence of admissions had been obtained in breach of the Judges' Rules, and the evidence of bad character had been wrongly admitted:

Held, allowing the appeal, that there was nothing to indicate that the judge had exercised his discretion wrongly in admitting the oral and written statements, but that since the defendant had never put his character in issue it was not relevant for evidence of his bad character to be given against him, and when an incident like that happened during that course of a trial the verdict of the jury could not be other than unsatisfactory.

Per curiam: A man in custody is entitled to consult a solicitor at an early stage of the investigation. The only qualification is that he cannot delay the investigation by asking to see a solicitor if the effect would be to cause 'unreasonable delay or hindrance ... to the process of investigation or the administration of justice'. Neither customs officers nor police officers have any right to detain somebody for the purpose of getting them to help with their inquiries: an officer arrests or detains a person because he reasonably suspects him of having committed an offence. While the accused is in detention, the officer is entitled to ask some questions for the purpose of helping his inquiries. It is not a good reason for refusing to allow a suspect to see his solicitor that he has not yet made any admission.

Lawton LJ: ... it must be clearly understood that neither customs officers nor police officers have any right to detain somebody for the purposes of getting them to help with their inquiries. Police officers either arrest for an offence or they do not arrest at all. Customs either detain for an offence or they do not detain at all. The law is clear. Neither arrest nor detention can properly be carried out without the accused person being told the offence for which he is being arrested. There is no such offence as 'helping police with their inquiries'. This is a phrase which has crept into use, largely because of the need for the press to be careful about how they report what has happened when somebody has been arrested but not charged. If the idea is getting around amongst either Customs and Excise officers or police officers that they can arrest or detain people, as the case may be, for this particular purpose, the sooner they disabuse themselves of that idea, the better. What Mr Hinson (a customs officer) should have said, when he was asked these questions by counsel, was that he had detained the defendant because he reasonably suspected him of having committed an offence against the Customs and Excise Act 1952, and that, as he was entitled to do, whilst the accused was in detention he had asked him some questions for the purposes of helping his inquiries.

––·––·––·––·––·––·––·––·––·––·––·––·––·––

There is no police power (except under the Prevention of Terrorism (Temporary Provisions) Act 1989) to detain someone against his or her will in order to make inquiries about that person. This is confirmed by s 29 of PACE 1984.

Section 29

Where for the purpose of assisting with an investigation a person attends voluntarily at a police station or at any other place where a constable is present or accompanies a constable to a police station or any such other place without having been arrested–

(a) he shall be entitled to leave at will unless he is placed under arrest;

(b) he shall be informed at once that he is under arrest if by a constable to prevent him from leaving at will.

Suspects stopped in the street

In *Kenlin v Gardiner* [1967] 1 QB 510 a police officer took hold of the arm of a boy who he wanted to question about the latter's suspicious conduct. The boy did not believe the man was a policeman, despite having been shown a warrant card, and punched the officer in order to escape. The other boy behaved similarly and their convictions for assaulting an officer in the execution of his duty were quashed by the Divisional Court. The court held that the boys were entitled to act as they did in self-defence as the officer's conduct in trying to physically apprehend them had not been legal.

Kenlin v Gardiner [1967] 1 QB 510, pp 518–19

Winn LJ: ... The boys undoubtedly assaulted the police officers: there cannot be any doubt about that, they struck them and kicked them; but the question is whether that was a justifiable or unjustified assault; and that again, as Mr Rogers agreed, depends entirely on whether the answer of self-defence was available to these two boys in the particular circumstances. Of course, in the case of a charge of assault under s 51(1) of the Police Act 1964, as in the case of any charge of assault, the defence or justification – I prefer to call it a justification, because it must always be borne in mind that it is for the prosecution to exclude justification and not for the defendant to establish it – the justification of self-defence is available just as it is in the case of any other assault. That is subject to this, that if the self-defence, in this case self-defence by the two boys against a prior assault such as had been committed, in a technical sense, by the police officers taking hold of an arm of each of these boys, was self-defence against an assault which was justified in law, as, for instance, a lawful arrest, then in law self-defence cannot afford jurisdiction for assault in resistance to justified assault by police officers. So one comes back to the question in the end, in the ultimate analysis: was this officer entitled in law to take hold of the first boy by the arm – of course the same situation arises with the other officer in regard to the second boy a little later – justified in committing that technical assault by the exercise of any power which he as a police constable in the precise circumstances prevailing at that exact moment possessed?

I regret, really, that I feel myself compelled to say that the answer to that question must be in the negative. This officer might or might not in the particular circumstances have possessed a power to arrest these boys. I leave that question open, saying no more than that I feel some doubt whether he would have had a power of arrest: but on the assumption that he had a power to arrest, is to my mind perfectly plain that neither of these officers purported to arrest either of these boys. What was done was not done as an integral step in the process of arresting, but was done in order to secure an opportunity, by detaining the boys from escape, to put to them or to either of them the question which was regarded as the test question to satisfy the officers whether or not it would be right in the circumstances, and having regard to the answer obtained from that question, if any, to arrest them.

I regret to say that I think there was a technical assault by the police officer. From which it follows that the justification of self-defence exerted or exercised by these two boys is not negatived by any justifiable character of the initial assault. It is plain in my own view that it was within the province of the justices to decide whether there was any excess in exercising privilege of self-defence. The court is not asked to send back this case to the justices – that would have given it a quite inflated importance – for them to decide just what was the ambit of the self-defence permissible in the circumstances, what were the reasonable or unreasonable features of the conduct of the boys in seeking to defend themselves. It suffices to say that the self-defence justification was available to these boys, and that it is not shown on the facts found by the justices that there was an excess of that liberty.

--·--·--·--·--·--·--·--·--·--·--·--·--·--·--·--·--·--

In *Mepstead v DPP* [1996] Crim LR 111, it was decided by the Divisional Court that where a constable had taken hold of someone's arm in order to draw his attention to what was being said to him, the officer was acting lawfully and, thus, within the execution of his duty. Police officers were in the course of attaching a 'fixed penalty' notice to a car which was causing an obstruction. The owner returned to the car and behaved abusively to the officers, then he pushed one officer and swore at him. The other officer took hold of the owner's arm and told him to calm down, explaining that the matter was 'only a ticket'.

The owner kicked out at the first officer and then struck the second. He was holding his keys when he struck and the officer was grazed. He was convicted of assaulting an officer in the execution of his duty. Mepstead appealed by way of case stated on the ground that the officer had not been acting in the course of his duty because to have taken hold of his arm was an unlawful use of force. The unlawfulness followed, it was argued, from the factual finding of the magistrate that the taking hold of the arm was done neither to arrest nor detain the car owner. Holding that the taking hold of the arm was lawful in the circumstances described, the court said that the behaviour had to be judged by 'the ordinary standards of everyday life'. If the seizing of the arm had lasted any significant time then it would be open to a court to decide that such an action was intended to detain. If that was so, and there was no power to detain for the misconduct in question, then the officer would be acting unlawfully and, thus, a citizen would be entitled to use force to extricate himself.

There is no legal power of detention short of arrest. As Lawton LJ observed in *R v Lemsatef* (above), the police do not have any powers to detain somebody 'for the purposes of getting them to help with their enquiries'.

It is important, however, to examine the precise circumstances of the detaining officer's conduct because there are cases to suggest that, if what the officer does amounts to only a *de minimis* interference with the citizen's liberty, then forceful 'self-defence' by the citizen will not be justified. In *Donnelly v Jackman*, an officer approached a suspect to ask some questions. The suspect ignored the request and walked away from the officer. The officer followed and made further requests for the suspect to stop and talk. He tapped the suspect on the shoulder and the suspect reciprocated by tapping the officer on the shoulder and saying, 'Now we are even, copper'. The officer tapped the suspect on the shoulder again which was replied to with a forceful punch. Mr Donnelly's conviction was upheld and the decision in *Kenlin v Gardiner* was distinguished, as in the earlier case the officers had actually taken hold of the boys and detained them. The court stated that, '... it is not every trivial interference with a citizen's liberty that amounts to a course of conduct sufficient to take the officer out of the course of his duties'.

Note also that a person may be arrested for being silent or misleading under s 25 of PACE 1984.

Procedure on arrest

In *Christie v Leachinsky*, Viscount Simon said:

> ... a person is *prima facie* entitled to personal freedom [and] should know why for the time being his personal freedom is being interfered with ... No one, I think, would approve of a situation in which when the person arrested asked for the reason, the policeman replied 'that has nothing to do with you: come along with me' ... And there are practical considerations ... If the charge ... is then and there made known to him, he has the opportunity of giving an explanation of any misunderstanding or of calling attention to other persons for whom he may have been mistaken, with the result that further inquiries may save him from the consequences of false accusation ...

PACE 1984

Section 28

(1) Subject to subsection (5) below, where a person is arrested, otherwise than by being informed that he is under arrest, the arrest is not lawful unless the person arrested is informed that he is under arrest as soon as is practicable after his arrest.

(2) Where a person is arrested by a constable, subsection (1) above applies regardless of whether the fact of the arrest is obvious.

(3) Subject to subsection (5) below, no arrest is lawful unless the person arrested is informed of the ground for the arrest at the time of, or as soon as is practicable after, the arrest.

(4) Where a person is arrested by a constable, subsection (3) above applies regardless of whether the ground for the arrest is obvious.

(5) Nothing in this section is to be taken to require a person to be informed –

    (a) that he is under arrest; or

    (b) of the ground for the arrest, if it was not reasonably practicable for him to be so informed by reason of his having escaped from arrest before the information could be given.

—————————————————————————————

An arrest, however, becomes lawful once the ground is given: *Lewis v Chief Constable of the South Wales Constabulary*. Here, the officers had told the plaintiffs of the fact of arrest, but delayed telling them the grounds, for 10 minutes in one case, and 23 minutes in the other. The Court of Appeal said that arrest was not a legal concept, but arose factually from the deprivation of a person's liberty. It was also a continuing act and, therefore, what had begun as an unlawful arrest could become a lawful arrest. The remedy for the plaintiffs was the damages they had been awarded for the 10 minutes and 23 minutes of illegality: £200 each.

In *DPP v Hawkins*, the Divisional Court held that an exception to the rule requiring information to be given to the arrestee exists where the defendant makes it impossible (for example, by his violent conduct) for the officer to communicate the reasons for the arrest to him. In that situation, the arrest is lawful and remains lawful until such a time as the reasons should have been given. The fact that the reasons were not given then does not invalidate the original arrest. The arrest would only become unlawful from the moment when the reasons for it should have been given to the arrested person.

NEW POWERS UNDER THE CRIMINAL JUSTICE AND PUBLIC ORDER ACT 1994

Section 60

Section 60 of the CJPO 1994 provides for a new stop and search power in anticipation of violence and was introduced to deal with violent conduct, especially by groups of young men.

Section 60 ...

(4) This section confers on any constable in uniform power–

    (a)   to stop any pedestrian and search him or anything carried by him for offensive weapons or dangerous instruments;

    (b)   to stop any vehicle and search it, its driver and any passenger for offensive weapons or dangerous instruments.

(5) A constable may, in the exercise of those powers, stop any person or vehicle and make any search he thinks fit whether or not he has any grounds for suspecting that the person or vehicle is carrying any weapons or articles of that kind.

(6) If in the course of such a search under this section a constable discovers a dangerous instrument or an article which he has reasonable grounds for suspecting to be an offensive weapon, he may seize it.

The authorisation required by s 60 must be given by a police officer of, or above, the rank of superintendent (or a chief inspector or inspector where such an officer reasonably believes that incidents involving serious violence are imminent and no superintendent is available). The authorising officer must reasonably believe that:

(a) incidents involving serious violence may take place in any locality in his area; and

(b) it is expedient to grant an authorisation to prevent their occurrence.

Such an authorisation, which must be in writing, will permit the exercise of stop and search powers within that locality for a period of up to 24 hours. The authorisation could conceivably be given in fear of a single incident, even although the CJPO 1994 requires fear of 'incidents'. This is because s 6 of the Interpretation Act 1978 states that the plural includes the singular, unless a contrary intention is shown.

There are several aspects of this section which have been drafted in what appears to be a deliberately vague way. We shall, therefore, have to wait and see how the courts interpret certain words in the CJPO 1994. 'Serious violence' is not defined and this will be very much within the judgment of the senior officer concerned, provided, of course, that his view is based upon reasonable belief. Richard Card and Richard Ward, in a commentary on the Act, have noted that the dictionary includes 'force against property' as within the definition of violence, and this may well become an important matter for decision by the courts.

The word 'locality' is left undefined in the Act. It could be an area outside a particular club or pub, or it might extend to a large estate. The courts have the power to declare an authorisation invalid because of an over-expansive geographical area; they are unlikely to substitute their own view for that of the operational officer.

Other aspects of this section have been defined.

- 'Offensive weapon' (s 60(4), (11)) – means the same as for s 1(9) of PACE 1984. It is (a) any article made or adapted for use for causing injury to persons; or (b) intended by the person having it with him for such use by him or some other person. There is no provision for reasonable excuse for the possession of such weapons.

- 'Dangerous instruments' (s 60(4)) – these will often be caught within the definition of offensive weapons but the definition extends to cover instruments which have a blade or are sharply pointed (s 60(11)).

The authorising officer must reasonably believe that it is 'expedient' to give an authorisation in order to prevent the occurrence of incidents of serious violence. Thus, the authorisation need not be the only way in which such incidents may be prevented. Various policing factors may have to be balanced including the ability of the police force to remain effective and efficient if it were to use other methods.

There is no specification about where the stop and search power may be exercised (unlike s 1 of PACE 1984) but a draft annex to Code of Practice A suggests that the power is exercisable wherever there is public access, even of just a practical (rather than legal) nature.

There is no power to detain especially conferred on officers by s 60 in order to carry out the search, but it does make failure to stop a summary offence. As it stands, there is nothing in s 60 which would permit an officer to use any force to conduct a non-consensual search. It is possible that the courts will imply such a power. When conducting the search the officer must give the suspect his or her name, the police station to which he or she is attached, the authorisation for the search, and the reason for the search. It seems that failure to comply with these conditions will make the search unlawful: *Fennelley*.

R v Edward Fennelley [1989] Crim LR 142

F, a heroin addict, was seen by plain clothes police officers in the street. They believed they had seen him handing something over in exchange for money and suspected that he was selling drugs. F was stopped, questioned and asked what was in his pockets. No drugs were found, but F had with him some jewellery. F was taken to a police station and a strip search authorised. Two small paper packets containing heroin were found in his underpants. F was charged with possession with intent to supply under s 5(3) of the Misuse of Drugs Act 1971.

It was submitted by the defence that evidence of the stop and search and of the strip search at the police station should be excluded by virtue of s 78 of PACE 1984.

On the *voir dire*, the arresting officer, PC Strothers gave evidence that he could not be sure whether F had been told the reason for his arrest, the grounds on which he had been searched in the street or the object of the search. The officer had no note and no specific recollection of doing so. It was submitted that the failure to give F the reason for his arrest made his detention unlawful and that the police had breached the mandatory requirements of s 2(3) of PACE 1984 and had failed to follow the procedure set out in para A:2.4 of the relevant Code of Practice. These breaches affected the fairness of the trial because F had not been given the chance to answer the suspicions of the police at the earliest opportunity. If he had, he might have been able to give an explanation which would have resulted in his being charged with mere possession rather than possession with intent to supply.

The prosecution submitted that the search on the street had been carried out with the permission of F and was therefore a 'consent search' to which the provision of s 2(3) and the Code of Practice did not apply. In any event, no unfairness resulted because it was wholly unrealistic to suggest that F would have offered an alternative explanation to the police on the street, if the reason for his arrest and the object and grounds of the stop and search had been put to him.

Held, the prosecution had not established that F had been told why he was stopped, searched and arrested. There had been a breach of s 2(3) of PACE 1984 and of the Code of Practice. This was not a 'consent search'.

It was a difficult and finely balanced point, but in all the circumstances, including the possibility that F might have provided an explanation which would have scaled down the charge he faced to mere possession, it would be unfair to admit evidence obtained in this way.

The court was not concerned with disciplining the police, but was vigilant in safeguarding the trial of an accused person. This vigilance required the exclusion of evidence obtained, without the kind of explanation that should have been given being given. The evidence of the stop and search in the street and of the search in the police station would be excluded by virtue of s 78 of PACE 1984.

Accountability and s 60 powers

There are dangers that the powers under s 60 could be misused, as no reasonable suspicion is required and the requirements for authorisation are rather nebulous.

The safeguards against misuse include the fact that the admissibility of evidence gained through the use of a dubious stop and search event may be in doubt if there are serious breaches of the revised Code A. Someone charged with obstructing a police officer in the exercise of his duty may raise breaches of the Code in defence. Unlawful search or seizure may also provide a basis for an application for exclusion of evidence thus obtained under s 78 of PACE (above).

As the police have a common law power to take whatever action is necessary in order to prevent an imminent breach of the peace (*Moss v Mclachlan*), then, even if a challenge to the use of a s 60 power is technically successful, the police conduct in question may often be thus justified.

Section 81

Section 81 of the CJPO 1994 creates a new power of stop and search of persons and vehicles where it is expedient to do so to prevent certain acts of terrorism. This was a response to various acts of terrorism involving concealed bombs, and car bombs in 1993. The section inserts a new section (13A) into the Prevention of Terrorism (Temporary Provisions) Act 1989.

Any officer of or above the rank of commander or assistant chief constable may authorise a stop and search where, '... it appears to him to be expedient to do so' in order to prevent acts of terrorism connected with Northern Ireland, or international terrorism. There is no requirement for reasonable suspicion.

If authorisation is granted, the powers of stop and search are exercisable at any place within the area of the senior officer's force, or within a locality.

If authorisation is given, pursuant to s 13A, it confers on any police officer in uniform the power:

(a) to stop any vehicle;

(b) to search any vehicle, its driver or any passenger for articles of any kind which could be used for a purpose connected with the commission, preparation or instigation of acts of terrorism connected with the affairs of Northern Ireland or acts of international terrorism;

(c) to stop any pedestrian and search anything carried by him [but not him] for articles of a kind which could be so used.

This is, thus, a very wide power, and is subject to few restraints. The search could be for virtually anything and it need not be based upon a reasonable suspicion. This power was given in the face of progressively more devastating acts of terrorism and an apparent inability of the State to deal with the threat. Any vehicle may be stopped under the section, whether or not the officer has grounds for suspecting that it contains items to be used in terrorism. It is, thus, unlike the power conferred under s 1 of PACE 1984 which does, to be valid, require a reasonable suspicion that the vehicle contains a proscribed item.

The powers of stop and search can only be exercised for a period specified in the authorisation and this can be as long as 28 days (s 13A(1)). A person failing to stop for such a check, or who wilfully obstructs an officer in the exercise of these powers, is guilty of an offence (s 13A(6)).

The police were granted significant extensions to their powers of stop and search under the Prevention of Terrorism (Additional Powers) Act 1996. This legislation, which amends the Prevention of Terrorism Act, was rushed through Parliament from start to finish within two days. It was promulgated through all House of Commons stages in 11 hours. The Act was introduced in the context of a renewed threat from the terrorist group, the Irish Republican Army (IRA) after the cessation of its 17 month cease fire in Northern Ireland and mainland Britain.

Introducing the Bill, the Home Secretary stated: 'These measures will be of real practical benefit to the police in protecting the public against the threat of terrorism.' (*The Times*, 3 April 1996.)

Opposing the swiftness with which major inroads into civil liberties were being made, one opposition MP, Kevin McNamara, said: 'It is quite outrageous that here we have very serious incursions into people's normal civil liberties and we're only going to have three hours to discuss them.'

The legislation enables the police to search pedestrians in a 'designated area', search listed non-residential premises and freight at ports, cordon off areas and impose temporary parking bans. Anyone who refuses to be searched will be liable to a six month jail sentence and/or a £5,000 fine. Police will have to provide anyone halted under the new stop and search powers with a written statement explaining why they have been searched. Any decision to declare a 'designated area' will have to be taken by an officer of assistant chief constable rank or above. There are no legal restrictions on the size of such an area, but, within 48 hours, the Home Secretary must authorise both the scale and length of time in which the powers operate.

The searches authorised under the revised Act extend to the power to stop and search a pedestrian, including searches of outer clothing and shoes, gloves, hats and outer coats. An officer will be able to make such searches whether or not he has reasonable grounds for believing the pedestrian is carrying a terrorist related device. The officer is given full powers of arrest if he has 'reason to suspect' that a device is secreted on inner clothing, or if illegal drugs are found.

The following view was expressed in a letter to *The Guardian* by Dr CA Gearty.

Dr CA Gearty, 'Stop and search for the motive' (1996) *The Guardian*

A police state is one in which the police determine the content as well as the mode of implementation of the law. [Under the new Act] the police will be able under the authority of a senior officer to stop any pedestrian and search him or her, together with anything they might be carrying, for articles of any kind that could be used for any purpose connected with the commission, preparation or instigation of what [the Act] describes as 'acts of terrorism'.

These powers may specifically be exercised even where the police officer has no suspicion, reasonable or otherwise, about the person he or she is searching. The Act will herald a return to and will fully legitimise the arbitrary stop and search powers that were such a stain on our criminal justice process before the enactment of the Police and Criminal Evidence Act 1984.

This power, and others ... allowing for the search of non-residential premises, the search of unaccompanied goods and the imposition of police cordons, are being smuggled through Parliament at short notice under the catch-all camouflage of the 'terrorist threat'.

They build on the already draconian expansion of the anti-terrorism law that was achieved with the Criminal Justice and Public Order Act, enacted after the Northern Ireland ceasefires were in place in 1994.

The police seem willing to use the fear of terrorism as an intimidatory device with which radically to expand their power over the ordinary citizen. It can now only be a matter of time before Parliament turns the full force of the terrorism laws on mainstream, extra-parliamentary dissent ...

The use of force to effect an arrest

The use of force by a member of the public when arresting someone is governed by the CLA 1967. This states:

   3.   Use of force in making an arrest, etc.

       (1) A person may use such force as is reasonable in the circumstances in the prevention of crime, or in effecting or assisting in the lawful arrest of offenders or suspected offenders or of persons unlawfully at large.

Reasonable force will generally mean the minimum necessary to effect an arrest.

The use of force by police officers is governed by the PACE 1984. This states:

117 Power of constable to use reasonable force
Where any provision of this Act–

(a) confers a power on a constable; and

(b) does not provide that the power may only be exercised with the consent of some person, other than a police officer,

the officer may use reasonable force, if necessary, in the exercise of the power.

Duties after arrest

A person arrested by a constable, or handed over to one, must be taken to a police station as soon as is 'practicable', unless his presence elsewhere is 'necessary in order to carry out such investigations as is reasonable to carry out immediately'.

PACE 1984

Section 30

(1) Subject to the following provisions of this section, where a person–

    (a) is arrested by a constable for an offence; or

    (b) is taken into custody by a constable after being arrested for an offence by a person other than a constable, at any place other than a police station, he shall be taken to a police station by a constable as soon as practicable after the arrest.

(2) Subject to subsections (3) and (5) below, the police station to which an arrested person is taken under subsection (1) above shall be a designated police station.

(3) A constable to whom this subsection applies may take an arrested person to any police station unless it appears to the constable that it may be necessary to keep the arrested person in police detention for more than six hours.

(4) Subsection (3) above applies–

    (a) to a constable who is working in a locality covered by a police station which is not a designated police station; and

    (b) to a constable belonging to a body of constables maintained by an authority other than a police authority.

(5) Any constable may take an arrested person to any police station if–

    (a) either of the following conditions is satisfied–

        (i) the constable has arrested him without the assistance of any other constable and no other constable is available to assist him;

        (ii) the constable has taken him into custody from a person other than a constable without the assistance of any other constable and no other constable is available to assist him; and

    (b) it appears to the constable that he will be unable to take the arrested person to a designated police station without the arrested person injuring himself, the constable or some other person.

(6) If the first police station to which an arrested person is taken after his arrest is not a designated police station, he shall be taken to a designated police station not more than six hours after his arrival at the first police station unless he is released previously.

(7) A person arrested by a constable at a place other than a police station shall be released if a constable is satisfied, before the person arrested reaches a police station, that there are no grounds for keeping him under arrest.

(8) A constable who releases a person under subsection (7) above shall record the fact that he has done so.

(9) The constable shall make the record as soon as is practicable after the release.

(10) Nothing in subsection (1) above shall prevent a constable delaying taking a person who has been arrested to a police station if the presence of that person elsewhere is necessary in order to carry out such investigations as it is reasonable to carry out.

Where a citizen makes an arrest, he '... must, as soon as he reasonably can, hand the man over to a constable or take him to the police station or take him before a magistrate', *per* Lord Denning in *Dallison v Caffery*. There is no requirement, however, that this be carried out immediately, see *John Lewis & Co v Tims* (above).

ENTRY, SEARCH AND SEIZURE

Stop and search

A number of statutes give police officers the power to stop and search people and vehicles where no arrest has been made. See, for example, s 23(2) of the Misuse of Drugs Act 1971. Here we shall concentrate on the powers given under ss 1 and 2 of PACE and Code A, which relate to stolen goods, offensive weapons and articles for use in Theft Act 1968 offences.

Note: PACE 1984 came into force on 1 January 1986. The Act was accompanied by four Codes of Practice (the Codes): Code A on Stop and Search; Code B on Search of Premises; Code C on Detention, Questioning and Treatment of Persons in Custody; and Code D on Identification. A fifth Code E, on Tape-recording of Interviews, was added later. The Codes were produced after consultation with a wide range of interested groups and people and were debated and approved by both Houses of Parliament before being promulgated. Revised versions of these Codes came into force in 1991 and further revisions were made which came into effect in April 1995.

The Codes are not technically law and s 67(10) of PACE 1984 states that a breach of them can lead to neither an action for damages nor a criminal prosecution against police officers. A breach of the Codes is, though, automatically a disciplinary offence (s 67(8)).

The chief significance of a breach of the Codes is that a judge may exclude otherwise relevant evidence if it has been obtained in such a way and an appeal court may quash a conviction where a trial judge has not excluded such evidence (s 67(7)).

In the following article, Roger Ede examines the new Codes of Practice.

Roger Ede, 'New improved PACE' (1995) *Solicitors Journal* 298

Custody record

The most important change for solicitors is to paragraph 2.4 of Code C, which will permit them to consult the custody record on their arrival at the police station. This follows a recommendation of the Royal Commission on Criminal Justice and recognises the stance taken by the Law Society in its *Police station skills for legal advisers* training materials that it is a 'public record' which solicitors should have the right to inspect. This change will remove at a stroke a constant source of confrontation between legal advisers and police officers.

Solicitor's role

At a time when senior police officers regularly accuse solicitors in the media of being obstructive and behaving 'immorally' and 'dishonourably' by advising some suspects not to be co-operative in interview, the change to Note for Guidance 6D in Code C about the solicitor's role, is timely. This accepts representations from the Law Society for an unequivocal statement that 'the solicitor's only role in the police station is to protect and advance the legal rights of his client', pointing out that 'on occasions this may require the solicitor to give advice which has the effect of his client avoiding giving evidence which strengthens the prosecution case'. It also adds seeking 'clarification', to the list of reasons why a solicitor may intervene during an interview.

Consultation in absence of appropriate adult

Some police officers have sought to prevent a solicitor from consulting with a suspect in the absence of an appropriate adult, despite advice from the Law Society that this may be necessary on occasions where there is a risk of the appropriate adult disclosing the details of the consultation to the police. This problem is solved by the new Note for Guidance 1EE in Code C, which will always give a suspect an opportunity to consult privately with a solicitor in the absence of the appropriate adult.

Interrupting or delaying interview

Another area of difficulty has been where the solicitor arrives at the police station only to be told that the client is in an interview which cannot be interrupted. Paragraph 6.15 of Code C will take into account the Law Society's concerns about this and require the police to inform the suspect immediately of the solicitor's arrival, 'whether or not he is being interviewed (and) even if the person concerned has already declined legal advice or having requested it, subsequently agreed to be interviewed without having received advice'.

In addition, when a suspect is reminded of his right to legal advice at the beginning of an interview, paragraph 11.2 of Code C will require the officer to go on to offer to delay the interview so that the suspect can take advantage of this and have the police contact a solicitor.

Access for solicitors and clerks

There have been complaints to the Law Society of police inspectors unreasonably refusing to admit certain clerks to police stations; calling out the duty solicitor when the named solicitor is unavailable but other solicitors in the firm would be willing to attend; and of custody and investigating officers recommending particular firms of solicitors to suspects because the firm is perceived by the police to give 'helpful' advice.

This situation will change as amendments to paragraphs 6.12 and Note for Guidance 6B of Code C will allow automatic access to the police station to trainee solicitors, clerks accredited under the Law Society's Scheme and duty solicitor authorised representatives; the suspect will be offered another solicitor from the firm when the named solicitor is unavailable; police officers will not be allowed to give advice about particular firms of solicitors; and the fact that a clerk may advise a suspect not to answer the officer's questions will not amount to 'hindering the investigation of a crime' so that it is a reason to exclude that clerk from the police station.

Caution

The final version of the new caution, set out in the amended paragraph 10.4 of Code C, takes account of most the Law Society's criticisms of the early draft. But this still leaves the police officer who arrests the suspect with the difficulty of choosing the 'ordinary language' he is required to use to explain the legal consequences of the suspect's failure or refusal to account for objects, substances or marks or his presence at a particular place.

Mental capacity

Other changes which are helpful include the new Note For Guidance 1G in Code C, which requires a custody officer who has 'any doubt as to the mental state or capacity of a person detained' to call an appropriate adult and paragraph 2.0 of Code D which requires the identification officer to provide the solicitor with a copy of the description of the suspect given by a potential witness before an identification procedure takes place.

Room for more improvement

Missing from the new Codes is any requirement for the police to disclose the *prima facie* evidence to the suspect before an interview is conducted. This is despite a recommendation by the Royal Commission on Criminal Justice that there should be an obligation for the police to do this. When the provisions of the Criminal Justice and Public Order Act 1994 which allow an adverse inference to be drawn from a suspect's silence are introduced, the suspect will be placed in the position of being expected to defend himself/herself in the police station without there being any corresponding requirement that the suspect knows the basis for the allegation. The issues of the lack of privacy of telephone consultations between suspects and solicitors is also not dealt with.

—·—·—·—·—·—·—·—·—·—·—·—·—·—·—·—

Non-police station interviews?

Are 'at the scene of the crime' interviews admissible? In the next article, Paul Tain looks at a common misunderstanding of the new law.

Paul Tain, 'Criminal law' (1995) *Solicitors Journal* 299

There seems to be some training on the Criminal Justice and Public Order Act 1994 at the moment which suggests that in certain instances the police will be statutorily permitted to interview away from the police station in circumstances other than those already incorporated into the Police and Criminal Evidence Act Code of Practice before the 1994 Act. The suggestion arises from the interpretation of the provisions relating to persons arrested because they are at a place at or about the time when an offence is committed (s 37) or those who are arrested and have a mark, object or substance (s 36). It also seems to be founded on the belief that this was the intention of parliament in enacting the provisions. It is obviously important that the position is clearly understood because the above would radically change the approach created by PACE in its intention to protect the suspect from the risk of being either deliberately or accidentally misquoted through informal and uncontrolled interviews.

Are intentions of parliament relevant?

The intentions of parliament are only material if the statutory provisions are 'ambiguous or obscure'. In this instance the provisions do not seem to be, nor do they have the effect of leading to 'an absurdity' (*Pepper v Hart* (1992) *Times*, 30 November). The provisions should therefore be construed without reference to parliament and even if the consequence of that were to drive a coach and horses through legislative intention, that would remain the correct interpretive procedure.

Section 37 problem

Under s 37, a man is arrested at a place at or about the time an offence is committed and the arrest is for that offence. There is reasonable belief in the mind of that or another constable that the fact that he is in that place is attributable to his participation in the offence. The arresting constable informs him of that belief having administered the special caution to him. Those are the essential components of s 37. If the man fails to explain why he is there then there is the risk that at trial the court may draw 'such inferences from the failure or refusal as appear proper' (s 37(2d)). Apparently there is a view that the above formula enables that conversation to take place at the time of arrest and presumably at the place where the person is arrested. This cannot be the case.

PACE codes

The Codes of Practice under PACE have now been amended to incorporate the requirements of the new Act but they have not been amended so as to enable roadside interviews in this type of context. Such amendments would have been possible if that had been the intention. The Codes provide as follows:

Code 11.1   Following a decision to arrest he must not be interviewed except at a police station. (NB: The old 'emergency' exceptions to that rule still exist, however.)

Code 11.1.A   An interview is questioning of a suspect which by virtue of Code 10.1.C must be under caution.

Code 10.1   provides that where there are grounds for suspecting that a person has committed an offence he must be cautioned before being questioned.

It is quite clear from reading both the section and the Code together that the s 37 suspect will have been arrested, will have been cautioned and will therefore have to be interviewed at the police station. The only fly in this interpretive ointment is Code 11.2.A which provides that at the police station, the interviewing officer, after cautioning him, shall put to him any significant statement or silence which occurred before the start of the interview. This clearly anticipates something before the police station but does not define precisely what. However, it would simply be the recording of a suspect's uninvited remarks out of interview which occasionally have to be adjudicated on. Perhaps if those remarks are queries at the time they are made and no response is forthcoming to the query, then that silence is the silence referred to. Whatever the intention of Code 11.2.A it cannot be set alongside the other Code provisions so as to overturn them completely, given that they are expressed in clear and unambiguous terms which have been reviewed in the higher courts.

Misplaced suggestion

It might be suggested that there is no need for the provisions in that case because of the existence of s 34 dealing with the consequences which flow from not replying to questions in interview. Such a suggestion would be misplaced. Section 34 does not allow inferences to be drawn from silence but only from the giving of evidence by the accused in due course, which evidence could have been provided in answer form during earlier questioning. Section 34 deals with evidence, whereas ss 37 and 36 deal with silence whether or not the defendant gives evidence.

It is fascinating to juxtapose the intention of parliament, the terms of the sections and the provisions of the Codes. It seems quite clear that any suggestion that 'at the scene' interviews will now become admissible is wrong. It would be contrary to the principles set out in *R v Park* (1994) CLR 285 and other cases. Such interviews will not be admitted by either s 36 or s 37 unless the Court of Appeal reinterprets the revised Codes.

Police and Criminal Evidence Act 1984

1 (1) A constable may exercise any power conferred by this section–

    (a) in any place to which at the time when he proposes to exercise the power the public or any section of the public has access, on payment or otherwise, as of right or by virtue of express or implied permission; or

    (b) in any other place to which people have ready access at the time when he proposes to exercise the power but which is not a dwelling.

(2) Subject to subsection (3) to (5) below, a constable–

    (a) may search–

        (i) any person or vehicle;

        (ii) anything which is in or on a vehicle, for stolen or prohibited articles (or any article to which subsection (8A) below applies); and

    (b) may detain a person or vehicle for the purpose of such a search.

(3) This section does not give a constable power to search a person or vehicle or anything in or on a vehicle unless he has reasonable grounds for suspecting that he will find stolen or prohibited articles (or any article to which subsection (8A) below applies).

(4) If a person is in a garden or yard occupied with and used for the purposes of a dwelling or on other land so occupied and used, a constable may not search him in the exercise of the power conferred by this section unless the constable has reasonable grounds for believing–

(a) that he does not reside in the dwelling; and

(b) that he is not in the place in question with the express or implied permission of a person who resides in the dwelling.

(5) If a vehicle is in a garden or yard occupied with and used for the purposes of a dwelling or on other land so occupied and used, a constable may not search the vehicle or anything in or on it in the exercise of the power conferred by this section unless he has reasonable grounds for believing–

(a) that the person in charge of the vehicle does not reside in the dwelling; and

(b) that the vehicle is not in the place in question with the express or implied permission of a person who resides in the dwelling.

(6) If in the course of such a search a constable discovers an article which he has reasonable grounds for suspecting to be a stolen or prohibited article (or an article to which subsection (8A) below applies), he may seize it.

(7) An article is prohibited for the purposes of this Part of this Act if it is–

(a) an offensive weapon; or

(b) an article–

(i) made or adapted for use in the course of or in connection with an offence to which this sub-paragraph applies; or

(ii) intended by the person having it with him for such use by him or by some other person.

(8) The offences to which subsection (7)(b)(i) above applies are–

(a) burglary;

(b) theft;

(c) offences under section 12 of the Theft Act 1968 (taking motor vehicle or other conveyance without authority); and

(d) offences under section 15 of that Act (obtaining property by deception).

[(8A) This subsection applies to any article in relation to which a person has committed, or is committing or is going to commit an offence under section 139 of the Criminal Justice Act 1988.]

(9) In this Part of this Act 'offensive weapon' means any article–

(a) made or adapted for use for causing injury to persons; or

(b) intended by the person having it with him for such use by him or by some other person.

2 (1) A constable who detains a person or vehicle in the exercise–

(a) of the power conferred by section 1 above; or

(b) of any other power–

(i) to search a person without first arresting him; or

(ii) to search a vehicle without making an arrest, need not conduct a search if it appears to him subsequently–

       (i)   that no search is required; or

       (ii)   that a search is impracticable.

(2) If a constable contemplates a search, other than a search of an unattended vehicle, in the exercise–

    (a)   of the power conferred by section 1 above; or

    (b)   of any other power, except the power conferred by section 6 below and the power conferred by section 27(2) of the Aviation Security Act 1982–

       (i)   to search a person without first arresting him; or

       (ii)   to search a vehicle without making an arrest, it shall be his duty, subject to subsection (4) below, to take reasonable steps before he commences the search to bring to the attention of the appropriate person–

          (i)   if the constable is not in uniform, documentary evidence that he is a constable; and

          (ii) whether he is in uniform or not, the matters specified in subsection (3) below; and the constable shall not commence the search until he has performed that duty.

(3) The matters referred to in subsection (2)(ii) above are–

    (a)   the constable's name and the name of the police station to which he is attached;

    (b)   the object of the proposed search;

    (c)   the constable's grounds for proposing to make it; and

    (d)   the effect of section 3(7) or (8) below, as may be appropriate.

(4) A constable need not bring the effect of section 3(7) or (8) below to the attention of the appropriate person if it appears to the constable that it will not be practicable to make the record in section 3(1) below.

(5) In this section 'the appropriate person' means–

    (a)   if the constable proposes to search a person, that person; and

    (b)   if he proposes to search a vehicle, or anything in or on a vehicle, the person in charge of the vehicle.

(6) On completing a search of an unattended vehicle or anything in or on such a vehicle in the exercise of any such power as is mentioned in subsection (2) above a constable shall leave a notice–

    (a)   stating that he has searched it;

    (b)   giving the name of the police station to which he is attached;

    (c)   stating that an application for compensation for any damage caused by the search may be made to that police station; and

    (d)   stating the effect of section 3(8) below.

(7) The constable shall leave the notice inside the vehicle unless it is not reasonably practicable to do so without damaging the vehicle.

(8) The time for which a person or vehicle may be detained for the purposes of such a search is such time as is reasonably required to permit a search to be carried out either at the place where the person or vehicle was first detained or nearby.

(9) Neither the power conferred by section 1 above nor any other power to detain and search a person without first arresting him or to detain and search a vehicle without making an arrest is to be construed–

    (a) as authorising a constable to require a person to remove any of his clothing in public other than an outer coat, jacket or gloves; or

    (b) as authorising a constable not in uniform to stop a vehicle.

(10) This section and section 1 above apply to vessels, aircraft and hovercraft as they apply to vehicles.

—————————————————————

A failure to give grounds as required by s 2(3)(c) will render the search unlawful: *R v Fennelley*.

The Code of Practice for the Exercise of Statutory Powers of Stop and Search

This revised Code states: 'It is important to ensure that the powers of stop and search are used responsibly and sparingly ... It is also particularly important to ensure that any person searched is treated courteously and considerately.'

A person can be stopped and questioned prior to a search to discover whether the suspicion that a search is required is well founded, but a person cannot be stopped in order to find grounds for a search (Code A, para 2.1). The reasonable suspicion must be based on objective grounds:

> Whether reasonable grounds for suspicion exist will depend on the circumstances in each case, but there must be some objective basis for it. An officer will need to consider the nature of the article suspected of being carried in the context of other factors such as the time and place, and the behaviour of the person concerned or those with him [para 1.6].

The Code goes on to say that reasonable suspicion may exist where information has been received, like a description of an article being carried, or where a person is seen acting 'covertly or warily or attempting to hide something', or where a person is seen carrying something at an unusual time or in a place where a number of burglaries or thefts are known to have taken place recently.

Reasonable suspicion can never be supported on the basis of personal factors alone. For example, 'a person's colour, age, hairstyle or manner of dress, or the fact that he is known to have a previous conviction for possession of an unlawful article' cannot be used alone or in combination with each other as the sole basis on which to search that person (para 1.7).

Search of arrested persons

The power to search after arrest somewhere other than at the police station is governed by s 32 of PACE 1984 (searches of detained persons are dealt with by s 54 and Code C, s 4).

PACE 1984

Section 32

32 (1) A constable may search an arrested person, in any case where the person to be searched has been arrested at a place other than a police station, if the constable has reasonable grounds for believing that the arrested person may present a danger to himself or others.

(2) Subject to subsections (3) to (5) below, a constable shall also have power in any such case–

   (a) to search the arrested person for anything–

      (i) which he might use to assist him to escape from lawful custody; or

      (ii) which might be evidence relating to an offence; and

   (b) to enter and search any premises in which he was when arrested or immediately before he was arrested for evidence relating to the offence for which he has been arrested.

(3) The power to search conferred by subsection (2) above is only a power to search to the extent that is reasonably required for the purpose of discovering any such thing or any such evidence.

(4) The powers conferred by this section to search a person are not to be construed as authorising a constable to require a person to remove any of his clothing in public other than an outer coat, jacket or gloves (but they do authorise a search of a person's mouth).

(5) A constable may not search a person in the exercise of the power conferred by subsection (2)(a) above unless he has reasonable grounds for believing that the person to be searched may have concealed on him anything for which a search is permitted under that paragraph.

(6) A constable may not search premises in the exercise of the power conferred by subsection (2)(b) above unless he has reasonable grounds for believing that there is evidence for which a search is permitted under that paragraph on the premises.

(7) In so far as the power of search conferred by subsection (2)(b) above relates to premises consisting of two or more separate dwellings, it is limited to a power to search–

   (a) any dwelling in which the arrest took place or in which the person arrested was immediately before his arrest; and

   (b) any parts of the premises which the occupier of any such dwelling uses in common with the occupiers of any other dwellings comprised in the premises.

(8) A constable searching a person in the exercise of the power conferred by subsection (1) above may seize and retain anything he finds, if he has

reasonable grounds for believing that the person searched might use it to cause physical injury to himself or to any other person.

(9) A constable searching a person in the exercise of the power conferred by subsection (2)(a) above may seize and retain anything he finds, other than an item subject to legal privilege, if he has reasonable grounds for believing–

(a) that he might use it to assist him to escape from lawful custody; or

(b) that it is evidence of an offence or has been obtained in consequence of the commission of an offence.

(10) Nothing in this section shall be taken to affect the power conferred by (section 15(3), (4) and (5) of the Prevention of Terrorism (Temporary Provisions) Act 1989).

—·—·—·—·—·—·—·—·—·—·—·—·—·—·—·—

Search on detention

Section 54 of PACE 1984 and Code C, para 4.1 require the custody officer (a particular officer with special responsibilities in police stations) to take charge of the process of searching detainees.

PACE 1984

Section 54

Words in square brackets substituted by the Criminal Justice and Public Order Act 1994, s 168(2), Sched 10, para 55.

(1) The custody officer at a police station shall ascertain and record or cause to be recorded everything which a person has with him when he is–

(a) brought to the station after being arrested elsewhere or after being committed to custody by an order or sentence of a court; or

[(b) arrested at the station or detained there as a person falling within section 34(7), under section 37 above).]

(2) In the case of an arrested person the record shall be made as part of his custody record.

(3) Subject to subsection (4) below, a custody officer may seize and retain any such thing or cause any such thing to be seized and retained.

(4) Clothes and personal effects may only be seized if the custody officer–

(a) believes that the person from whom they are seized may use them–

(i) to cause physical injury to himself or any other person;

(ii) to damage property;

(iii) to interfere with evidence; or

(iv) to assist him to escape; or

(b) has reasonable grounds for believing that they may be evidence relating to an offence.

(5) Where anything is seized, the person from whom it is seized shall be told the reason for the seizure unless he is–

    (a)   violent or likely to become violent; or

    (b)   incapable of understanding what is said to him.

(6) Subject to subsection (7) below, a person may be searched if the custody officer considers it necessary to enable him to carry out his duty under subsection (1) above and to the extent that the custody officer considers necessary for that purpose.

[(6A) A person who is in custody at a police station or is in police detention otherwise than at a police station may at any time be searched in order to ascertain whether he has with him anything which he could use for any of the purposes specified in subsection (4)(a) above.

(6B) Subject to subsection (6C) below, a constable may seize and retain, or cause to be seized and retained, anything found on such a search.

(6C) A constable may only seize clothes and personal effects in the circumstances specified in subsection (4) above.]

(7) An intimate search may not be conducted under this section.

(8) A search under this section shall be carried out by a constable.

(9) The constable carrying out a search shall be of the same sex as the person searched.

Premises

Entry by permission

Premises can be searched by consent. Here the constable must get written consent from the occupier of the premises on a special 'Notice of Powers and Rights' form before the search takes place.

Code of Practice B for the Searching of Premises by Police Officers and the Seizure of Property found by Police Officers on Persons or Premises

4.3 An officer cannot enter and search, or continue to search premises under 4.1 [by consent] if the consent is given under duress or is withdrawn before the search is completed.

Consent need not be sought if this would cause disproportionate inconvenience to the occupiers of premises eg where the police wish to briefly check a number of gardens on a suspected escape route.

Entry under the common law

There is a common law right for police officers to enter a building to deal with or prevent a breach of the peace. In *Thomas v Sawkins* [1935] 2 KB 249, the Divisional Court held that police officers were entitled to enter and remain on premises, despite being asked by the occupiers to leave, in circumstances where the officers believed that certain offences (seditious speeches, incitements to violence) would be committed if they were not present. Lord Hewart CJ said:

> I am not at all prepared to accept the doctrine that it is only where an offence has been, or is being, committed, that the police are entitled to enter and remain on premises. On the contrary, it seems to me that a police officer has, *ex virtute officii* full right so to act when he has reasonable grounds for believing that an offence is imminent or is likely to be committed.

Section 17(5)–(6) of PACE 1984 abolishes all common law powers of entry except to deal with or prevent a breach of the peace.

Entry to make an arrest

This is governed by:

PACE 1984

Section 17

17 (1) Subject to the following provisions of this section, and without prejudice to any other enactment, a constable may enter and search any premises for the purpose–

    (a) of executing–

        (i) a warrant of arrest issued in connection with or arising out of criminal proceedings; or

        (ii) a warrant of commitment issued under section 76 of the Magistrates' Courts Act 1980;

    (b) of arresting a person for an arrestable offence;

    (c) of arresting a person for an offence under–

        (i) section 1 (prohibition of uniforms in connection with political objects) ... of the Public Order Act 1936;

        (ii) any enactment contained in sections 6 to 8 or 10 of the Criminal Law Act 1977 (offences relating to entering and remaining on property);

        [(iii) section 4 of the Public Order Act 1986 (fear or provocation of violence);]

        [(iv) section 76 of the Criminal Justice and Public Order Act 1994 (failure to comply with interim possession order);]

    [(ca) of arresting, in pursuance of section 32(1A) of the Children and Young Persons Act 1969, any child or young person who has been remanded or committed to local authority accommodation under section 23(1) of that Act;

    (cb) of recapturing any person who is, or is deemed for any purpose to be, unlawfully at large while liable to be detained–

        (i) in a prison, remand centre, young offender institution or secure training centre, or

> (ii) in pursuance of section 53 of the Children and Young Persons Act 1933 (dealing with children and young persons guilty of grave crimes), in any other place;]

(d) of recapturing (any person whatever) who is unlawfully at large and whom he is pursuing; or

(e) of saving life or limb or preventing serious damage to property.

(2) Except for the purpose specified in paragraph (e) of subsection (1) above, the powers of entry and search conferred by this section–

  (a) are only exercisable if the constable has reasonable grounds for believing that the person whom he is seeking is on the premises; and

  (b) are limited, in relation to premises consisting of two or more separate dwellings, to powers to enter and search–

    (i) any parts of the premises which the occupiers of any dwelling comprised in the premises use in common with the occupiers of any other such dwelling; and

    (ii) any such dwelling in which the constable has reasonable grounds for believing that the person whom he is seeking may be.

(3) The powers of entry and search conferred by this section are only exercisable for the purposes specified in subsection (1)(c)(ii) [or (iv)] above by a constable in uniform.

(4) The power of search conferred by this section is only a power to search to the extent that is reasonably required for the purpose for which the power of entry is exercised.

(5) Subject to subsection (6) below, all the rules of common law under which a constable has power to enter premises without a warrant are hereby abolished.

(6) Nothing in subsection (5) above affects any power of entry to deal with or prevent a breach of the peace.

––·––·––·––·––·––·––·––·––·––·––·––·––·––·––·––

Entry and search of premises in which an arrest was made

The relevant powers here are those discussed above under ss 18 and 32 of PACE 1984. In practice, the police act routinely under s 18 and rarely under s 32.

PACE 1984

Section 18

18 (1) Subject to the following provisions of this section, a constable may enter and search any premises occupied or controlled by a person who is under arrest for an arrestable offence, if he has reasonable grounds for suspecting that there is on the premises evidence, other than items subject to legal privilege, that relates–

(a)   to that offence; or

(b)   to some other arrestable offence which is connected with or similar to that offence.

(2)   A constable may seize and retain anything for which he may search under subsection (1) above.

(3)   The power to search conferred by subsection (1) above is only a power to search to the extent that is reasonably required for the purpose of discovering such evidence.

(4)   Subject to subsection (5) below, the powers conferred by this section may not be exercised unless an officer of the rank of inspector or above has authorised them in writing.

(5)   A constable may conduct a search under subsection (1) above–

(a)   before taking the person to a police station; and

(b)   without obtaining an authorisation under subsection (4) above, if the presence of that person at a place other than a police station is necessary for the effective investigation of the offence.

(6)   If a constable conducts a search by virtue of subsection (5) above, he shall inform an officer of the rank of inspector or above that he has made the search as soon as practicable after he has made it.

(7)   An officer who–

(a)   authorises a search; or

(b)   is informed of a search under subsection (6) above, shall make a record in writing–

(i)   of the grounds for the search; and

(ii)   of the nature of the evidence that was sought.

(8)   If the person who was in occupation or control of the premises at the time of the search is in police detention at the time the record is to be made, the officer shall make the record as part of his custody record.

POLICE POWERS

Inspector's written authority for search and the meaning of PACE 1984, s 18

R v Badham [1987] Crim LR 202

The appellant was convicted at the magistrates' court of obstruction of a police officer in the execution of his duty. The appellant's two sons had been arrested in two separate incidents on the same day at approximately 11 am and 12 pm outside the appellant's house. The sons were taken to the police station. At the police station at about 2 pm the arresting officer obtained authorisation from a police inspector for a search of the appellant's house. The inspector made an entry in his notebook of authorisation having been given. At about 3 pm police officers attempted to search the appellant's premises. The appellant demanded to see the authority for the search and refused the police officers entry. The police officers eventually forcibly entered the appellant's premises. At the magistrates' court the prosecution contended that the entry made in the inspector's notebook was sufficient to satisfy the requirement in s 18(4) of PACE 1984 that the power of entry and search under s 18(1) of the Act must be authorised in writing by an officer of the rank of inspector or above. The prosecution further contended that the police were empowered to enter and search under s 32(2)(b) of the 1984 Act which provides for search upon arrest. The appellant appealed.

Held, allowing the appeal: (1) The police inspector had given his authorisation verbally, and had recorded it in his notebook. 'Authorised in writing' meant more than a mere record of verbal authority. It must be an independent document, that is, a proper authority in writing. Although nothing is said in the Act, such authority should go with the police officers to the premises to be searched. (2) Section 32(2)(b) – this was headed 'Search upon Arrest'. Had the police officers gone into the appellant's home at the time of his sons' arrests, they could have done so. They did not do so until some hours later. Although the Act gave no time limit, this was an immediate power. It would be wrong to have an open ended right to go back to the premises. Had the police wanted to do so, they could only do so under s 18(1).

R v Churchill [1989] Crim LR 226, CA

C was arrested on suspicion of burglary and placed in a police car. The police requested the keys to his car, but C refused to hand them over and, during a struggle, he struck a police officer. At his trial, for assault occasioning actual bodily harm, it was submitted on C's behalf that the police had been acting beyond their powers of search under s 32(2) of PACE 1984 because the keys were not evidence relating to an offence, that is, burglary, and the police, therefore, unlawfully used force which C was entitled to resist. The judge held that since the car might have contained evidence relating to the offence, the keys were in the same category and he ruled against the submission. C was convicted and appealed.

Held, the appeal would be allowed and the conviction quashed. It was not correct to equate the car keys with the car itself; accordingly the prosecution had not established that the police were acting lawfully in requiring the keys.

Per curiam: At the trial, the police evidence had been that it was sought to have the car keys in order to take the car to the police station to be searched, and to have the car in a safe place rather than unlocked in a place where it could have been stolen or damaged. The case could have been argued on the basis of the duty of the police to preserve property and C's obstruction of the police in the execution of that duty: *Rice v Connolly* and *Coffin v Smith*. It also appeared that at the trial the prosecution case had been put on a yet different basis, namely an unexpected and unprovoked blow on the officer by C. However, on the basis of the ruling and the direction to the jury the prosecution case had not been made out and the appeal had to succeed.

Seizure of articles from searches

The scope of the seizure rights is, therefore, quite wide and Professor Zander has argued that the insistence, since *Entick v Carrington* in 1765, that general warrants are unlawful must now be qualified by the knowledge that once the police have entered premises lawfully, it is difficult to hold them to a search restricted to the specific purpose of the search.

Entick v Carrington (1765) 95 ER 807, Court of Common Pleas, Lord Camden CJ

On 6 November 1762, the Earl of Halifax, one of the principal Secretaries of State, issued a warrant to four King's messengers (Nathan Carrington, James Watson, Thomas Adran and Robert Blackmore), '... to make strict and diligent search for John Entick, the author, or one concerned in writing of several weekly very seditious papers, entitled the Monitor, or British Free holder ... and him, having found you are to seize and apprehend, and to bring, together with his books and papers, in safe custody before me to be examined ...'. The messengers entered E's house, the outer door being open, apprehended him, and searched for his books and papers in several rooms and in one bureau, one writing desk and several drawers. Where necessary these were broken open. They seized some books and papers and read others, remaining for about four hours. They then took E and the items seized to Lovel Stanhope, law clerk to the Secretaries of State. E was released on 17 November. He subsequently brought an action in trespass against the messengers. The jury gave a special verdict and assessed the damages at £300. The defendants argued that their acts were done in obedience to a lawful warrant.

> **Lord Camden CJ**: ...[I]f this point should be determined in favour of the jurisdiction, the secret cabinets and bureaus of every subject in this kingdom will be thrown open to the search and inspection of a messenger, whenever the secretary of state shall think fit to charge, or even to suspect; a person to be the author, printer, or publisher of a seditious libel.
>
> This power so assumed by the secretary of state is an execution upon all the party's papers, in the first instance. His house is rifled; his most valuable secrets are taken out of his possession, before the paper for which he is charged is found to be criminal by any competent jurisdiction, and before he is convicted either of writing, publishing, or being concerned in the paper. This power, so claimed by the secretary of state, is not supported by one single citation from any law book extant ...
>
> The arguments, which the defendants' counsel have thought fit to urge in support of this practice, are of this kind.
>
> That such warrants have issued frequently since the Revolution, which practice has been found by the special verdict ...

That the case of the warrants bears a resemblance to the case of search for stolen goods.

They say too, that they have been executed without resistance upon many printers, booksellers, and authors, who have quietly submitted to the authority; that no action hath hitherto been brought to try the right; and that although they have been often read upon the returns of habeas corpus, yet no court of justice has ever declared them illegal.

And it is further insisted, that this power is essential to government, and the only means of quieting clamours and sedition ...

If it is law, it will be found in our books. If it is not to be found there, it is not law.

The great end, for which men entered into society, was to secure their property. That right is preserved sacred and incommunicable in all instances, where it has not been taken away or abridged by some public law for the good of the whole. The cases where this right of property is set aside by positive law, are various. Distresses, executions, forfeitures, taxes, & c are all of this description; wherein every man by common consent gives up that right, for the sake of justice and the general good. By the laws of England, every invasion of private property, be it ever so minute, is a trespass. No man can set his foot upon by ground without my licence, but he is liable to an action, though the damage be nothing; which is proved by every declaration in trespass, where the defendant is called upon to answer for bruising the grass and even treading upon the soil. If he admits the fact, he is bound to shew by way of justification, that some positive law has empowered or excused him. The justification is submitted to the judges, who are to look into the books; and see if such a justification can be maintained by the text of the statute law, or by the principles of common law. If no such excuse can be found or produced, the silence of the books is an authority against the defendant, and the plaintiff must have judgment.

Where is the written law that gives any magistrate such a power? I can safely answer, there is none, and therefore it is too much for us without such authority to pronounce a practice legal, which would be subversive of all the comforts of society.

—·—·—·—·—·—·—·—·—·—·—·—·—·—·—·—

Note: *Entick v Carrington* followed the publication of No 45 of the North Briton, a weekly paper, of which John Wilkes was joint editor and a leading contributor. Its main purpose was to ridicule the recently appointed administration of the Earl of Bute. After No 45 was published, the two Secretaries of State, Lords Egremont and Halifax, issued a general warrant for the arrest of its 'authors, printers and publishers'. Over 45 people were arrested under this warrant, including Wilkes. The warrant was held to be illegal and damages were awarded for trespass.

This case establishes the principle that any public officer must be able to point to lawful authority for actions of his which infringe the rights of others, and not merely some general principle of State necessity. It also shows an unwillingness to invent lawful authority, which has not been a feature of some recent cases.

Today, this area of law is controlled by s 19 and Code B, para 6. The only serious restraint is the requirement in s 16(8) that a search under warrant must be carried out in a manner consistent with the items being looked for and in Code B, para 5.9 which states that 'premises may be searched only to the extent necessary to achieve the object of the search having regard to the size and nature of whatever is sought'.

PACE 1984

Section 19

19 (1) The powers conferred by subsections (2), (3) and (4) below are exercisable by a constable who is lawfully on any premises.

(2) The constable may seize anything which is on the premises if he has reasonable grounds for believing–

   (a) that it has been obtained in consequence of the commission of an offence; and

   (b) that it is necessary to seize it in order to prevent it being concealed, lost, damaged, altered or destroyed.

(3) The constable may seize anything which is on the premises if he has reasonable grounds for believing–

   (a) that it is evidence in relation to an offence which he is investigating or any other offence; and

   (b) that it is necessary to seize it in order to prevent the evidence being concealed, lost, altered or destroyed.

(4) The constable may require any information which is contained in a computer and is accessible from the premises to be produced in a form in which it can be taken away and in which it is visible and legible if he has reasonable grounds for believing–

   (a) that–

      (i) it is evidence in relation to an offence which he is investigating or any other offence; or

      (ii) it has been obtained in consequence of the commission of an offence; and

   (b) that it is necessary to do so in order to prevent it being concealed, lost, tampered with or destroyed.

(5) The powers conferred by this section are in addition to any power otherwise conferred.

(6) No power of seizure conferred on a constable under any enactment (including an enactment contained in an Act passed after this Act) is to be taken to authorise the seizure of an item which the constable exercising the power has reasonable grounds for believing to be subject to legal privilege.

--·--·--·--·--·--·--·--·--·--·--·--·--·--

Search warrants and safeguards

Section 8 of PACE 1984 provides for the issue of warrants by magistrates to enter and search premises for evidence of serious arrestable offences. This gives justices of the peace the power, on written application from a constable, to issue a search warrant where they are satisfied that there are reasonable grounds for believing that a 'serious arrestable offence' has been committed. A 'serious arrestable offence' (as distinct from an 'arrestable offence' defined by s 24) is defined by s 116 and Sched 5 to PACE 1984). The definition divides offences into two categories. One category comprises offences so serious that they are always 'serious arrestable offences'; they are listed in Sched 5 and include treason, murder, manslaughter, rape, kidnapping, incest and possession of firearms with intent to injure, and attempts or conspiracies are treated as if they were completed. Any other arrestable offence is serious only if its commission has led or is likely to lead to any of the consequences specified in s 116(6), namely: (a) serious harm to the security of the State or public order; (b) serious interference with the administration of justice or with the investigation of offences; (c) the death of anyone; (d) serious injury to anyone; (e) substantial financial gain to anyone; (f) serious financial loss to anyone in the sense that having regard to all the circumstances, it is serious for the person suffering loss (the seriousness of the loss is therefore to be measured by the financial position of the potential loser).

The magistrate must also be satisfied that:

(a) there is material on the premises likely to be of substantial value to the investigation (s 8(1)(b));

(b) it is likely to be relevant evidence (s 8(1)(c));

(c) it does not include 'excluded material' (for example, human tissue taken for medical diagnosis and held in confidence; journalistic material held in confidence, see s 11), or 'special procedure material' (for example, confidential business/professional material, see s 14); or material subject to legal privilege (s 10); and

(d) any of the conditions in s 8(3) applies. These are essentially that it is not practicable to gain entry to the premises in question without a search warrant or that the reasons for the search would be frustrated, if the constable did not gain immediate entry upon arrival.

Section 15

One part of s 15 has caused some difficulty for the courts. It relates to the word 'it' in s 15(1) which states that, '... an entry on or search of premises under warrant is unlawful unless it complies with this section and section 16 below'.

What must comply – the warrant or the whole entry and search?

R v Longman [1988] 1 WLR 619

Police officers in plain clothes went to the appellant's premises with a warrant to enter and search the premises for drugs. To gain entry, a woman police constable, pretending to be delivering flowers, knocked on the door and when the appellant opened it, the police officers entered. One of the officers, who had the warrant in his possession and gave evidence that he had it folded in his hand with his warrant card, shouted 'Police, got a warrant'. The appellant reacted by shouting a warning to a man, who was later found in a room with drugs, and then the appellant pulled a knife from the back of the door and lunged at the officer with it. He was arrested and charged with attempted wounding with intent to resist lawful arrest and with obstructing a constable in the execution of his powers under the Misuse of Drugs Act 1971. The recorder ruled that for the entry and search of the appellant's premises and his subsequent detainer to be lawful it was not necessary for the requirements as to identification and production of the warrant imposed by s 16(5) of PACE 1984 to have been complied with before the police entered the premises and, in her summing up to the jury, she defined 'produce' the warrant in s 16(5)(b), as 'available to be seen'. The appellant was convicted.

On appeal against conviction: *Held*, dismissing the appeal: (1) that s 16(5) of PACE 1984 required the constable to identify himself, to produce the search warrant and to provide the occupier with a copy, but it did not require the constable to fulfil those obligations before entering the premises; that where a search warrant was issued under the Misuse of Drugs Act 1971 and the constable had reasonable grounds for believing that delay in entry would frustrate the search, he could, both under s 23(3) of the Act of 1971 and para 5.4 of the Code of Practice, use force or subterfuge to gain entry to the premises before complying with the requirements of s 16(5) of the Act of 1984; and that, accordingly, the police officers' entry into the premises was lawful. (2) That a warrant or warrant card was 'produced' in compliance with s 16(5)(a) and (b) of the Act of 1984 when the occupier was given an opportunity to inspect it; that it was not sufficient that the occupier was merely shown that the officer had a warrant, but the jury could have been in no doubt that before the police officer had time to permit the appellant to inspect the warrant and the warrant card, he had obstructed the police by shouting his warning to the other man in the house and thereby deprived himself of the opportunity to inspect the documents before his arrest.

Lord Lane CJ said, *obiter* (p 623):

Section 15 of the Act of 1984 is not altogether easy to understand. The material parts read: '(1) This section and section 16 below have effect in relation to the issue to constables under any enactment, including an enactment contained in an Act passed after this Act, of warrants to enter and search premises; and' – these are the words it is not easy to interpret – 'an entry on or search of premises under a warrant is unlawful unless it complies with this section and section 16 below.' One asks the question, does that mean that the entry on the premises or the search is unlawful unless the warrant complies with the two sections? Or does it mean that the entry on or search of the premises is unlawful, unless the entry and search comply with the provisions of the Act? It cannot be both, because the word 'it' is used: if it were both, the word 'they' would have to be used. Since it is in section 15, which is headed 'Search warrants – safeguards' and since that section deals with warrants and the way they are to be obtained and treated, one would expect it to be providing that the warrant should comply with the sections. But since the following section, section 16, deals with entry and search, and since section 16 is expressly mentioned in the passage which I have read from section 15, could it mean that the entry and search must comply with the sections? With some hesitation we are inclined to think that it most probably refers to the warrant, but the real probability is that the intention of the framers of the Act of 1984 was to provide that the warrant should comply with the terms of section 15 and the entry and search should comply with section 16. But unhappily that is not what it says. So there we leave that problem unresolved.

INTERROGATION, CONFESSION AND ADMISSIBILITY OF EVIDENCE

It is important to be aware of the general issues in this area of law. Are the rights of suspects being interrogated by the police sufficiently protected by law? Is there scope for abuse of power by the police? Are the police burdened by too many legal requirements when trying to induce a suspect to confess to a crime? What effects are likely to flow from the undermining of the right to silence (see ss 34–37 of the CJPO 1994, above).

Searches of detained persons

Searches of people detained at policed stations are governed by s 54 (above) and Code C of PACE 1984 has been amended by the CJPO 1994 (ss 54–59). The rules governing the taking of intimate and non-intimate body samples have been changed. The new Act also allows 'speculative searches' in which fingerprints, samples, or information in respect thereof, can be checked against other similar data held by the police. The changes follow recommendations of the *Runciman Commission Report* which recommends the establishment of a national DNA database.

A person may only be searched if the custody officer considers this necessary in order to make a complete list of his property (sub-s (6)). There is no automatic right to search all suspects as a matter of routine. The police can, however, search anyone to ascertain whether he has with him anything which he could use to cause physical injury, damage property, interfere with evidence or assist him to escape (s 55, as amended). Section 55 deals with intimate searches. The 1994 Act repeals the old s 118 of PACE 1984 (which defined 'body orifice' – including anus, vagina, mouth, nostrils and ears) and s 54(1) inserts a new definition into s 65 of PACE 1984. Section 65 of PACE 1984 now defines an intimate search as, '...a search which consists of the physical examination of a person's body orifices other than the mouth'.

A physical examination of the mouth is therefore allowed in the circumstances where a non-intimate search of the person may occur, subject to the ordinary safeguards (Code of Practice A, para 3; Code C, para 4). A search of the mouth for drugs is not the taking of a sample as defined by s 65 of PACE 1984, so the restrictions which apply to the taking of samples do not apply here. A search of an arrested person's mouth may, thus, be carried out by a police officer at the station, subject to the safeguards in Code C. The officer carrying out the search must be of the same sex as the arrested person (s 54(9)). Nonetheless, an officer of either sex may search the arrested person's mouth at the time of the arrest, if he has reasonable grounds to believe that the arrested person is concealing therein evidence related to the offence (s 32(2)(b)).

These searches must be authorised by an officer of the rank of superintendent, or above, on the basis of reasonable belief that the arrested person in police detention has concealed on him anything which could be used to cause physical injury to himself or to others and that he might so use it. Intimate searches for weapons can, if a doctor or registered nurse is not available, be carried out by a police officer of the same sex as the suspect. If the search is for drugs, it can only be carried out by a doctor or registered nurse and it cannot be carried out at a police station (s 55(4)). Intimate searches for drugs are limited to those for hard drugs, defined as Class A drugs in Sched 2 to the Misuse of Drugs Act 1971.

The right to have someone informed when arrested

The effect of s 56 and Code C is that when a suspect is under arrest and is being held in custody in a police station he is entitled, if he so requests to have, 'one friend or relative or other person who is known to him or who is likely to take an interest in his welfare,' to be told as soon as practicable that he is under arrest and his whereabouts (s 56(1), Code C 5.1). If such a person cannot be contacted the Code allows for two alternates to be nominated, following which any further alternates can be called at the discretion of the custody officer. Delay is only permissible in the case of a 'serious arrestable offence' (see s 116) and only if authorised by an officer of at least the rank of superintendent. The grounds for delaying appear in Annex B. They are, essentially, that there are reasonable grounds for believing that telling the named person of the arrest will lead to interference with, or harm to, evidence or witnesses, or the alerting of others involved in such an offence; or will hinder the recovery of property obtained as a result of the offence.

Code C, Annex B

Access to a solicitor may not be delayed on the grounds that he might advise the person not to answer any questions or that the solicitor was initially asked to attend the police station by someone else, provided that the person himself then wishes to see the solicitor ...

No one, however, may be prevented from notifying someone outside the police station for longer than 36 hours after 'the relevant time' (s 41(2)), usually the time he arrived at the station. Unless the reasons for a lawful delay (see Annex B) exist, Code C states that the detainee should be allowed to speak on the telephone 'for a reasonable time to one person' (para 5.6) and that this privilege is in addition to the right to phone someone under para 5.1 to inform him or her of the arrest, or, under para 6.1, to obtain legal advice. Children and young persons are afforded additional rights by s 57, the section says that the police should contact a person 'responsible for his welfare' to inform the person about the arrest.

Evidence obtained through prohibited investigation is admissible

In the following case, the House of Lords ruled that, to accord with the words of s.64 of PACE 1984, and 'good sense' evidence obtained through a prohibited investigation could sometimes be admissible.

R v B, AG's Ref (No 3 of 1999)

Law Report (2000) *The Times*, 15 December

Unlawfully retained DNA is usable in court

House of Lords
Before Lord Steyn, Lord Cooke of Thorndon, Lord Clyde, Lord Hutton and Lord Hobhouse of Woodborough
Speeches December 14, 2000

Where a DNA sample taken from an accused on his arrest for an offence had not been destroyed when he was acquitted, as required by section 64(1) of the Police and Criminal Evidence Act 1984, section 64(3B) of that Act, as amended, although prohibiting its use in the investigation of any other offence, did not make evidence obtained as a result of a failure to comply with that prohibition inadmissible but left it to the discretion of the trial judge. The House of Lords so held in reversing a decision by the Court of Appeal (Lord Justice Swinton Thomas, Mr Justice Butterfield and Mrs Justice Rafferty) (*The Times* June 16, 2000; (2000) 3 WLR 1164) on a reference by the Attorney-General, under section 36 of the Criminal Justice Act 1972, following the decision of a trial judge that section 64(3B) required the acquittal of a defendant, B, as a result of the evidence against him having arisen from the wrongful retention of his DNA profile.

Section 64(3B) of the 1984 Act, as amended by the Criminal Justice and Public Order Act 1994, provides:

Where samples are required to be destroyed ... information derived from the sample of any person entitled to its destruction ... shall not be used – (a) in evidence against the person so entitled; or (b) for the purposes of any investigation of an offence.

Mr David Perry and Mr Duncan Penny for the Attorney-General; Mrs Rebecca Poulet, QC and Ms Roxanne Morrell for B.

Lord Steyn said that in 1997 a woman had been assaulted and raped during a burglary at her home. The ordeal of the woman had been horrendous and the offence of rape had been of the utmost gravity. The victim had been medically examined and swabs taken. Semen was found on both swabs and the DNA profile obtained was placed on the national DNA database. In January 1998 B was arrested and charged with an unrelated offence of burglary and a saliva sample was lawfully taken from him without his consent. He was acquitted of the burglary offence and under section 64(1) the sample should have been destroyed. It was not destroyed and information derived from it, namely the DNA profile, remained on the DNA data base. A match was later made between the profile and that obtained from the swabs taken from the victim.

Relying on the match between the two DNA profiles, the police arrested the defendant in October 1998. He denied that he was involved in the offences. The taking of a non-intimate sample of plucked head hair was authorised and a forensic science laboratory confirmed that its DNA profile also matched the DNA profile on the swabs taken from the victim.

The trial

The prosecution case depended solely on DNA evidence. The prosecution did not adduce evidence relating to the January sample but relied solely on the match between the DNA profile of the sample taken in October and that obtained from the swabs taken from the rape victim. It was conceded by the prosecution before the judge that under section 64(1) the January sample should have been destroyed after the defendant's acquittal on the unrelated burglary charge, that such information had been used in the investigation of any offence in contravention of section 64(3B)(b) and that that had led to the arrest of the defendant in October 1998. The judge ruled that section 64(3B)(b) was mandatory and that the evidence tendered by the prosecution was inadmissible. But he also concluded that if section 64(3B)(b) was merely of directory effect he would have exercised his discretion under section 78 of the 1978 Act to exclude the DNA evidence. Given those conclusions the prosecution case collapsed and despite what the Court of Appeal subsequently described as compelling evidence the judge directed a verdict of not guilty.

The Court of Appeal

The Attorney-General referred to the Court of Appeal the following question, which it answered in the negative: 'Where a sample of DNA is lawfully taken from an accused in respect of offence A (of which offence the accused is subsequently acquitted), and information derived from the sample suggests that the accused is guilty of offence B, does a judge have a discretion to permit a prosecution to proceed against the accused for offence B, notwithstanding the terms of section 64(3B)?'

The question before the House

The Court of Appeal referred the very question upon which it had been called to rule to the House. Whatever the opinion of the House on that question the acquittal of the defendant stood. The House had not been asked to consider the correct approach of a judge in dealing with such an issue under section 78 and nothing that his Lordship said was to be taken as an endorsement of the judge's reasoning on that aspect.

Interpretation of section 64(3B)

The difference between parts (a) and (b) of subsection (3B) was striking. Part (a) legislated for the inadmissibility in evidence against the person concerned of the sample that should have been destroyed. By contrast, part (b) contained no language to the effect that evidence obtained as a result of the prohibited investigation should be inadmissible. It did not make provision for the consequences of a breach of the prohibition on investigation. That did not mean that that particular prohibition was toothless. On the contrary, it had to be read with section 78: 'In any proceedings the court may refuse to allow evidence ... if it appears to the court that, having regard to all the circumstances, including the circumstances in which the evidence was obtained, the admission of the evidence would have such an adverse effect on the fairness of the proceedings that the court ought not to admit it.'

In other words, there was in the very same statute a discretionary power in the trial judge, in the face of a breach of subsection (3B)(b), to exclude the evidence if it would be unfair to admit it. Counsel for B had submitted that parts (a) and (b) had to stand together. In other words, because (a) provided for the inadmissibility of evidence (b) had to have a like meaning. That was how the Court of Appeal also reasoned. But, with due respect, that was too simplistic. It did not address the critical difference that part (a) expressly provided for the consequences of a breach but that part (b) did not. It also did not meet the point that no verbal manipulation of (b) was required if it was simply read together with section 78. On the interpretation of the judge and the Court of Appeal a case involving evidence of a very serious rape could never reach the jury. In *R v Weir* (*The Times* June 16, 2000) (heard by the Court of Appeal together with the reference in the instant case) a conviction for a brutal murder was quashed on the ground that the DNA evidence should not have been placed before the jury. It had to be borne in mind that respect for the privacy of defendants was not the only value at stake. The purpose of the criminal law was to permit everyone to go about their daily lives without fear of harm to person or property. And it was in the interests of everyone that serious crime should be effectively investigated and prosecuted. There had to be fairness to all sides. In a criminal case that required the court to consider a triangulation of interests. It involved taking into account the position of the accused, the victim and his or her family, and the public. The austere interpretation which the Court of Appeal had adopted was not only in conflict with the plain words of the statute but produced results which were contrary to good sense. A consideration of the public interest reinforced the interpretation which his Lordship had adopted.

The Human Rights Act 1998

On the supposition that on the ordinary principles of construction section 64(3B)(b) did not provide that the evidence obtained as a result of a prohibited investigation was always inadmissible, counsel for B had argued that the incorporation of the Convention for the Protection of Human Rights and Fundamental Freedoms by the Human Rights Act 1998 compelled the interpretation for which she contended.

Article 8 read: 'Everyone has the right to respect for his private and family life ... There shall be no interference by a public authority with the exercise of this right except such as is in accordance with the law and is necessary in a democratic society ... for the prevention of disorder or crime...' Counsel had submitted that because a sample had to be destroyed after an acquittal it could not ever be 'in accordance with the law' to admit in evidence the results of a prohibited investigation. But if the construction his Lordship had adopted was correct the 'interference' was in accordance with the law, the critical point being that admissibility was governed by judicial discretion under section 78.

And the interference, so qualified, was plainly necessary in a democratic society to ensure the investigation and prosecution of serious crime. In the alternative, counsel had relied in her printed case on article 6 (the right to a fair hearing). In oral argument she had expressly abandoned that argument. That was not surprising. The trial judge had adequate powers to ensure fairness: jurisdiction to stay proceedings as an abuse of the process and discretion to exclude evidence under section 78. If the trial was allowed to proceed, and the evidence was not excluded, the accused would have a full opportunity to contest the reliability of the DNA evidence. In any event, the question of admissibility was a matter for regulation under national law. There was no principle of Convention law that unlawfully obtained evidence was not admissible.

Lord Cooke, Lord Clyde, Lord Hutton and Lord Hobhouse delivered concurring opinions.

— · — · — · — · — · — · — · — · — · — · — · — · — · — ·

Access to legal advice

Section 58(1) of PACE states that: 'A person who is in police detention shall be entitled, if he so requests, to consult a solicitor privately at any time.' The rules relating to persons held under suspicion of terrorist offences are different and will not be covered here. Where the detained person is a juvenile or is mentally handicapped or disordered then 'the appropriate adult' (see Code C, s 3) may exercise the right to ask for legal advice.

Code C, para 6.8

Where the suspect has been permitted to consult a solicitor and the solicitor is available (that is, present at the station or on his way to the station or easily contactable by telephone) at the time the interview begins, or is in progress, the solicitor must be allowed to be present while he is interviewed.

Notifying the suspect of the right to free legal advice

There is clearly the danger that a person's right to legal advice can be effectively curtailed if they are not aware of it. Code C therefore goes to some lengths to ensure the suspect is aware of the right. The custody officer is required (para 3.5) when he authorises a person's detention in the police station to make sure that the suspect signs the custody record signifying whether he wishes to have legal advice at that point. The revised Code adds the following: 'The custody officer is responsible for ensuring that the person signs the custody record in the correct place to give effect to his decision.'

The Code stipulates that police stations must advertise the right to free legal advice in posters 'prominently displayed in the charging area of every police station' (para 6.3). New guidance in the 1995 Code states that (6H): 'In addition to a poster in English advertising the right to legal advice, a poster or posters containing translations into Welsh, the main ethnic minority languages and the principal European languages should be displayed wherever they are likely to be helpful and it is practicable to do so.'

The Code also gives precise rules concerning at what point and in what form a person should be notified of the right to get free legal advice. For example, a person who comes to the station under arrest must be told immediately both orally and in writing (paras 3.1, 3.2). The revised Code para 3.1 states:

> When a person is brought to a police station under arrest or is arrested at the police station having attended there voluntarily, the custody officer must tell him clearly of the following rights [to obtain legal advice] and of the fact that they are continuing rights which may be exercised at any stage during the period in custody.

Duty solicitors

The duty solicitor schemes at police stations and magistrates' courts are run locally, but organised under the auspices of the Legal Aid Commission. At police stations, the duty solicitor is contacted through a special national telephone network provided by a company, Air Call plc. When a suspect asks for a duty solicitor (at any time of the day or night) a call is made to Air Call who then contacts either the rota duty solicitor, or telephones duty solicitors on the panel until, in the latter case, one is found who is able and willing to attend. In rota schemes, there is always (in theory) someone on duty; in panel schemes the panellists are called one after the other on a list beginning with the name after the last solicitor to have come out.

Delaying access to legal advice

The police have no right to delay a suspect's access to legal advice, except in the case of a serious arrestable offence (Annex B to Code C). If the suspect is being held in connection with a serious arrestable offence (s 116), she can be delayed access to legal advice, but the delay must be authorised by an officer of the rank of superintendent and only where he has reasonable grounds for believing that the exercise of the right:

(a) will lead to interference with or harm to evidence connected with a serious arrestable offence or interference with or physical harm to other persons; or

(b) will lead to the alerting of other persons suspected of having committed such an offence but not yet arrested for it; or

(c) will hinder the recovery of any property obtained as a result of such an offence.

If a delay is authorised, the suspect must be told the reason for it and the reason must be recorded in the custody record. The maximum period of delay is 36 hours (Annex B, para 4).

Interviewing before solicitor arrives

The police have a right to start questioning suspects before a solicitor has arrived at the police station, if the situation is an emergency or the solicitor is not likely to arrive for a considerable period. The power is governed by Code C (para 6.6) which states that interviewing may commence without the suspect having had legal advice (where he wants it) provided an officer of the rank of superintendent,or above, has reasonable grounds for believing that:

> ... Annex B [below] applies; or ... (i) delay will involve an immediate risk of harm to persons or serious loss of, or damage to, property; or (ii) where a solicitor, including a duty solicitor, has been contacted and has agreed to attend, awaiting his arrival would cause unreasonable delay to the process of investigation.

The paragraph also applies where a nominated solicitor cannot or will not attend and the suspect has declined a duty solicitor.

Time limits on detention without charges

Under s 42 of PACE 1984, a suspect can be held without being charged for 24 hours before any further authorisation needs to be given. At this point, the situation must be reviewed and further detention must be authorised by an officer of at least the rank of superintendent.

PACE 1984

Section 42

42 (1) Where a police officer of the rank of superintendent or above who is responsible for the police station at which a person is detained has reasonable grounds for believing that–

    (a) the detention of that person without charge is necessary to secure or preserve evidence relating to an offence for which he is under arrest or to obtain such evidence by questioning him;

    (b) an offence for which he is under arrest is a serious arrestable offence; and

(c) the investigation is being conducted diligently and expeditiously, he may authorise the keeping of that person in police detention for a period expiring at or before 36 hours after the relevant time.

(2) Where an officer such as is mentioned in subsection (1) above has authorised the keeping of a person in police detention for a period expiring less than 36 hours after the relevant time, such an officer may authorise the keeping of that person in police detention for a further period expiring not more than 36 hours after that time if the conditions specified in subsection (1) above are still satisfied when he gives the authorisation.

(3) If it is proposed to transfer a person in police detention to another police area, the officer determining whether or not to authorise keeping him in detention under subsection (1) above shall have regard to the distance and the time the journey would take.

(4) No authorisation under subsection (1) above shall be given in respect of any person–

(a) more than 24 hours after the relevant time; or

(b) before the second review of his detention under section 40 above has been carried out.

(5) Where an officer authorises the keeping of a person in police detention under subsection (1) above, it shall be his duty–

(a) to inform that person of the grounds for his continued detention; and

(b) to record the grounds in that person's custody record.

(6) Before determining whether to authorise the keeping of a person in detention under subsection (1) or (2) above, an officer shall give–

(a) that person; or

(b) any solicitor representing him who is available at the time when it falls to the officer to determine whether to give the authorisation, an opportunity to make representations to him about the detention.

(7) Subject to subsection (8) below, the person in detention or his solicitor may make representations under subsection (6) above either orally or in writing.

(8) The officer to whom it falls to determine whether to give the authorisation may refuse to hear oral representations from the person in detention if he considers that he is unfit to make such representations by reason of his condition or behaviour.

(9) Where–

(a) an officer authorises the keeping of a person in detention under subsection (1) above; and

(b) at the time of the authorisation he has not yet exercised a right conferred on him by section 56 or 58 below, the officer–

(i) shall inform him of that right;

(ii) shall decide whether he should be permitted to exercise it;

(iii) shall record the decision in his custody record; and

(iv) if the decision is to refuse to permit the exercise of the right, shall also record the grounds for the decision in that record.

(10) Where an officer has authorised the keeping of a person who has not been charged in detention under subsection (1) or (2) above, he shall be released from detention, either on bail or without bail, not later than 36 hours after the relevant time, unless–

(a) he has been charged with an offence; or

(b) his continued detention is authorised or otherwise permitted in accordance with section 43 below.

(11) A person released under subsection (10) above shall not be re-arrested without a warrant for the offence for which he was previously arrested unless new evidence justifying a further arrest has come to light since his release [; but this subsection does not prevent an arrest under section 46A below].

43 (1) Where, on an application on oath made by a constable and supported by an information, a magistrates' court is satisfied that there are reasonable grounds for believing that the further detention of the person to whom the application relates is justified, it may issue a warrant of further detention authorising the keeping of that person in police detention.

(2) A court may not hear an application for a warrant of further detention unless the person to whom the application relates–

(a) has been furnished with a copy of the information; and

(b) has been brought before the court for the hearing.

(3) The person to whom the application relates shall be entitled to be legally represented at the hearing and, if he is not so represented but wishes to be so represented–

(a) the court shall adjourn the hearing to enable him to obtain representation; and

(b) he may be kept in police detention during the adjournment.

(4) A person's further detention is only justified for the purposes of this section or section 44 below if–

(a) his detention without charge is necessary to secure or preserve evidence relating to an offence for which he is under arrest or to obtain such evidence by questioning him;

(b) an offence for which he is under arrest is a serious arrestable offence; and

(c) the investigation is being conducted diligently and expeditiously.

(5) Subject to subsection (7) below, an application for a warrant of further detention may be made–

(a) at any time before the expiry of 36 hours after the relevant time; or

(b) in a case where–

(i) it is not practicable for the magistrates' court to which the application will be made to sit at the expiry of 36 hours after the relevant time; but

(ii) the court will sit during the six hours following the end of that period, at any time before the expiry of the said six hours.

(6) In a case to which subsection (5)(b) above applies–

(a) the person to whom the application relates may be kept in police detention until the application is heard; and

    (b)   the custody officer shall make a note in that person's custody record–

        (i)   of the fact that he was kept in police detention for more than 36 hours after the relevant time; and

        (ii)   of the reason why he was so kept.

(7) If–

    (a)   an application for a warrant of further detention is made after the expiry of 36 hours after the relevant time; and

    (b)   it appears to the magistrates' court that it would have been reasonable for the police to make it before the expiry of that period, the court shall dismiss the application.

(8) Where on an application such as is mentioned in subsection (1) above a magistrates' court is not satisfied that there are reasonable grounds for believing that the further detention of the person to whom the application relates is justified, it shall be its duty–

    (a)   to refuse the application; or

    (b)   to adjourn the hearing of it until a time not later than 36 hours after the relevant time.

(9) The person to whom the application relates may be kept in police detention during the adjournment.

(10) A warrant of further detention shall–

    (a)   state the time at which it is issued;

    (b)   authorise the keeping in police detention of the person to whom it relates for the period stated in it.

(11) Subject to subsection (12) below, the period stated in a warrant of further detention shall be such period as the magistrates' court thinks fit, having regard to the evidence before it.

(12) The period shall not be longer than 36 hours.

(13) If it is proposed to transfer a person in police detention to a police area other than that in which he is detained when the application for a warrant of further detention is made, the court hearing the application shall have regard to the distance and the time the journey would take.

(14) Any information submitted in support of an application under this section shall state–

    (a)   the nature of the offence for which the person to whom the application relates has been arrested;

    (b)   the general nature of the evidence on which that person was arrested;

    (c)   what inquiries relating to the offence have been made by the police and what further inquiries are proposed by them;

    (d)   the reasons for believing the continued detention of that person to be necessary for the purposes of such further inquiries.

(15) Where an application under this section is refused, the person to whom the application relates shall forthwith be charged or, subject to subsection (16) below, released, either on bail or without bail.

(16) A person need not be released under subsection (15) above–

     (a)   before the expiry of 24 hours after the relevant time; or

     (b)   before the expiry of any longer period for which his continued detention is or has been authorised under section 42 above.

  (17) Where an application under this section is refused, no further application shall be made under this section in respect of the person to whom the refusal relates, unless supported by evidence which has come to light since the refusal.

  (18) Where a warrant of further detention is issued, the person to whom it relates shall be released from police detention, either on bail or without bail, upon or before the expiry of the warrant unless he is charged.

  (19) A person released under subsection (18) above shall not be re-arrested without a warrant for the offence for which he was previously arrested unless new evidence justifying a further arrest has come to light since his release; (but this subsection does not prevent an arrest under section 46A below).

Section 38 states that after being charged, the arrested person must be released, with or without bail, unless:

(a) it is necessary to hold him so that his name and address can be obtained; or

(b) the custody officer reasonably thinks that it is necessary to hold him for his own protection or to prevent him from causing physical injury to anyone or from causing loss of or damage to property; or

(c) the custody officer reasonably thinks that he needs to be held because he would otherwise fail to answer bail or to prevent him from interfering with witnesses or otherwise obstructing the course of justice; or

(d) if he is a juvenile and ought to be held 'in his own interests'.

If the suspect is charged and not released he will have to be brought before a magistrates' court 'as soon as practicable', and not later than the first sitting after being charged (s 46(2)).

Answering police questions and the right to silence

The police are free to ask anyone any questions. The only restriction is that all questioning is supposed to cease once a suspect has been charged.

Code C, para 16.5 states that questions relating to an offence '... may not be put to a person after he has been charged with that offence, or informed that he might be prosecuted for it, unless they are necessary for the purpose of preventing or minimising harm or loss to some other person ...', or where it is in the interests of justice that the person should be given an opportunity to comment on new information which has come to light since he was charged.

There is no obligation on a citizen to answer police questions. A person cannot be charged, for example, with obstructing the police in the execution of their duty simply by failing to answer questions, nor can the judge or prosecutor suggest to the jury that such silence is evidence of guilt.

In *Rice v Connolly*, the appellant was seen by officers in the early hours of the morning behaving suspiciously in an area where house breaking had taken place on the same evening. On being questioned, he refused to say where he was going, or where he had come from. He refused to give his full name and address, though he did give a name and the name of a road which were not untrue. He refused to accompany the officer to a police box for identification purposes saying, 'If you want me you'll have to arrest me'. He was arrested and charged with wilfully obstructing a police officer contrary to s 51(3) of the Police Act 1964.

His appeal against conviction succeeded. Lord Parker CJ noted that the police officer was acting within his duty in inquiring about the appellant and that what the appellant did was obstructive. The critical question, though, was whether the appellant's conduct was 'wilful' within the meaning of s 51. Lord Parker CJ, in the Divisional Court, took that word to mean 'intentional [and] without lawful excuse'. He continued:

> It seems to me quite clear that though every citizen has a moral duty or, if you like, a social duty to assist the police, there is no legal duty to that effect, and indeed the whole basis of the common law is the right of the individual to refuse to answer questions put to him by persons in authority, and to refuse to accompany those in authority to any particular place; short, of course, of arrest.

The court was unanimous although one judge, James J cautioned that he would not go as far as to say that silence coupled with conduct could not amount to obstruction. It would depend on the particular facts of any given case.

In *Ricketts v Cox*, two police officers who were looking for youths responsible for a serious assault, approached the defendant and another man in the early hours of the morning. The justices found that the officers acted in a proper manner in putting questions to the men. The defendant was abusive, unco-operative and possibly hostile to the officers, using obscene language, calculated to provoke and antagonise the officers, and that he tried to walk away. The justices were satisfied that this conduct amounted to an obstruction for the purposes of a charge under s 51(3) of the Police Act 1964. The defendant's appeal was dismissed by the Divisional Court which found that the case raised the point reserved by James J in *Rice v Connolly* – the combination of silence and hostility without lawful excuse. As Zander has observed (1992:131), the state of the law here is now unclear.

Duties to answer

There are certain circumstances where the citizen is under a duty to answer police questions. Where a constable has reasonable grounds for believing that a vehicle has been involved in an accident and he seeks the particulars of the driver, he may arrest that person if the information is not given. With the Home Secretary's consent, and on the authority of a chief constable, coercive questioning (that is, where a suspect's silence can be used in evidence against him or her) can be used in matters under s 11 (as amended) of the Official Secrets Act 1911. There are also wide powers under the Companies Act 1985 to require officers and agents of companies to assist inspectors appointed to investigate the company. Refusal to answer questions can be sanctioned as a contempt of court (s 431) and as a criminal offence (s 447). A person can also be required to answer questions put to him or her by a liquidator of a company: *Bishopsgate Management Ltd v Maxwell Mirror Group Newspapers*.

Other powers to compel answers on pain of penalties for refusal exist under the Prevention of Terrorism (Temporary Provisions) Act 1989, and refusal to answer certain allegations from the prosecutor can be treated as acceptances of them under the Drug Trafficking Offences Act 1986.

The closest English law comes to creating a duty to give one's name and address is the power given to the police under s 25(3) of PACE 1984 (above).

Effective abolition of the right to silence

The Government ignored the recommendations of the Runciman Commission and, in ss 34–37 of the CJPO 1994, effectively abolished the right to silence. 'Abolished' may be too strong a word because everyone still has the right to remain silent in the same circumstances as they did before the 1994 Act; what has changed is the entitlement of a judge or prosecuting counsel to make adverse comment on such a silence.

The issue has now been addressed by the European Court of Human Rights (ECtHR). The leading case is *Condron v UK* [2000] Crim LR 679. In 2000, two convicted drug dealers won a landmark ruling in Europe that the UK Government's curbs on the right to silence denied them a fair trial. The ECtHR in Strasbourg stated that, where juries are allowed to draw adverse inferences from silence under police questioning, they must be properly directed by the judge.

In a key finding, it ruled that the Court of Appeal should look not just at whether a conviction was 'safe', but also at whether a defendant received a fair trial. The ruling will be likely to lead to other appeals.

The case, backed by Liberty, the human rights group, was brought by William and Karen Condron, who were convicted of supplying drugs in 1995. The pair, who did not answer police questions, were jailed for four years.

The ECtHR said that the jury had not been properly directed. As a result, the couple's right to a fair trial, as guaranteed by Art 6 of the European Convention on Human Rights, was breached. It awarded each defendant £15,000.

Silence could not be regarded as 'an absolute right', the court said, and drawing inferences was not itself in breach of the right to a fair trial, but caution was needed. The jury should have been directed that, '... if it was satisfied that the applicants' silence ... could not sensibly be attributed to their having no answer, or none that would stand up to cross-examination, it should not draw an adverse inference'. The law report from *The Times* appears below.

Condron and Another v United Kingdom (Application No 35718/97)
(2000) *The Times*, ECtHR

Breach over direction on silence of accused Before J-P Costa, President, and Judges Sir Nicolas Bratza, L Loucaides, P Kuris, W Fuhrmann, HS Greve and K Traja. Section Registrar: S Dollé [Judgment May 2, 2000]

The European Court of Human Rights held unanimously that a trial judge had not properly directed the jury on the issue of the applicants' silence during police interview and as a consequence the applicants did not receive a fair trial within the meaning of article 6.1 of the European Convention on Human Rights.

Article 6 of the Convention provides: '1 In the determination of ... any criminal charge against him, everyone is entitled to a fair ... hearing ...'. The applicants, William Condron, an Irish citizen, and Karen Condron, a British citizen, were born respectively in 1965 and 1963 and were living in London at the time of the events giving rise to their application.

They stood trial at Kingston upon Thames Crown Court (Judge Thomas and a jury) between October 16, 1995 and November 2, 1995 on charges of supplying heroin and possession of heroin with intent to supply. The prosecution case relied, among other things, on the fact that a police surveillance team had observed the applicants passing various items to their neighbour and co-accused from the balcony of their flat. At the time of their interview with the police, the applicants' solicitor considered that they were not fit to be questioned since they were suffering from heroin withdrawal symptoms; the doctor who examined them at the police station disagreed with their solicitor's assessment.

Before the start of their interview the applicants were cautioned. During the interview the applicants remained silent and did not reply to questions concerning the above-mentioned items. The applicants gave evidence at their trial and offered an explanation as to why certain items were seen to be exchanged over their balcony. The applicants also declared that they had not answered police questions because their solicitor had advised that they were not in a fit condition to be interviewed.

With reference to section 34 of the Criminal Justice and Public Order Act 1994, the trial judge gave the jury the option of drawing an adverse inference from the applicants' silence during interview. The applicants were found guilty.

Although the Court of Appeal (Lord Justice Stuart-Smith, Mr Justice Mantell and Mr Justice Moses) found the trial judge's direction to the jury on the question of the applicants' silence deficient, it was satisfied that the convictions were safe (*The Times* November 4, 1996). The application was lodged with the European Commission of Human Rights on November 13, 1996. On November 1, 1998 the case was transmitted to the Court, which declared the application admissible on September 7, 1999.

In its judgment the European Court of Human Rights held:

I Alleged violation of article 6.1
The applicants contended that their right to a fair trial, guaranteed by article 6 of the European Convention of Human Rights, was violated on account of the decision of the trial judge to leave the jury with the option of drawing an adverse inference from their silence when interviewed by the police.

The Court's assessment

The Court observed with reference to its earlier judgment in *Murray v United Kingdom* (*The Times* February 9, 1996) that the right to silence could not be considered an absolute right. Whether the drawing of inferences from an accused's silence during police interview infringed article 6 was a matter to be determined in the light of all the circumstances of the case. For the Court, the fact that the question of an accused's silence was left to the jury could not, of itself, be considered incompatible with article 6.

However, given that the right to silence lay at the heart of the notion of a fair procedure guaranteed by that article, the Court stressed, in line with its *Murray* judgment, [*Murray v UK* (1996) 22 EHRR 29] that particular caution was required before a domestic court could invoke an accused's silence against him. It reiterated in that connection that it would be incompatible with the right to silence to base a conviction solely or mainly on the accused's silence or on a refusal to answer questions or to give evidence himself. That being said, it was obvious that right could not and should not prevent that the accused's silence, in situations which clearly called for an explanation from him, be taken into account in assessing the persuasiveness of the evidence adduced by the prosecution. The Court noted that the domestic law of the respondent state provided a number of safeguards in order to ensure that a proper balance was struck between an accused's exercise of his right to silence and the drawing of an adverse inference from that fact at a jury trial. It observed that the applicants in the instant case were not exposed to any penal sanction on account of their decision to remain silent and were cautioned in clear terms about the possible consequences of their decision.

Notwithstanding the presence of those safeguards, the Court found fault with the manner in which the trial judge directed the jury on the issue of the applicants' silence. In its opinion, the terms of the direction could not be said to reflect the balance which the Court in its *Murray* judgment sought to strike between the right to silence and the circumstances in which an adverse inference could be drawn from silence. It noted that the applicants put forward an explanation at their trial for their failure to mention during the police interview why certain items were exchanged between them and their co-accused. They testified that they remained silent on their solicitor's advice. Although the trial judge drew the jury's attention to the applicants' explanation for their silence, the Court considered that he did so in terms which left the jury at liberty to draw an adverse inference notwithstanding that it might have been satisfied as to the plausibility of the explanation. In the Court's opinion, as a matter of fairness, the jury should have been directed that if it was satisfied that the applicants' silence at the police interview could not sensibly be attributed to their having no answer or none that would stand up to cross-examination, it should not draw an adverse inference. The Court considered that a direction to that effect was more than merely 'desirable', as found by the Court of Appeal. It noted that the responsibility for deciding whether or not to draw an inference rested with the jury and it was impossible to ascertain what weight, if any, was given to the applicants' silence since a jury did not provide reasons for its decisions. The Court did not accept the Government's submission that the fairness of the applicants' trial was secured in view of the appeal proceedings. It stated in that connection that the Court of Appeal had no means of ascertaining whether or not the applicants' silence played a significant role in the jury's decision to convict.

It noted that the Court of Appeal was concerned with the safety of the applicants' conviction, not whether they had in the circumstances received a fair trial. Since the jury was not properly directed the imperfection in the direction could not be remedied on appeal. In view of the above considerations the Court concluded that the applicants were denied a fair hearing, in violation of article 6.1.

II Alleged violation of article 6.2
The Court held that the applicants' complaint under article 6.2 gave rise to no separate issue.

III Alleged violation of article 6.3(b) and (c)
Having regard to its finding on the applicants' complaint under article 6.1, the Court considered that it was not necessary to examine their complaints from the standpoint of article 6.3(b) and (c).

IV Application of article 41
The Court held that the respondent state was to pay the applicants, within three months from the date on which the judgment became final according to article 44.2 of the Convention, for costs and expenses, £15,000, in addition to any value-added tax that might be chargeable.

CHAPTER 8

THE CRIMINAL PROCESS: THE PROSECUTION

Until 1986, England was one of only a few countries which allowed the police to prosecute rather than handing the task over to a State agency, like the district attorney in the USA. The Crown Prosecution Service (CPS) was established by the Prosecution of Offences Act 1985 and the police now technically play no part in prosecutions beyond the stage of charging the suspect.

The move to establish a CPS was precipitated by a report from Justice (British Section of the International Commission of Jurists) in 1970. It argued that the police were not best suited to be prosecutors because they would often have a commitment to winning a case, even where the evidence was weak. They were also not best placed to consider the public policy aspects of the discretion not to prosecute. The police were firmly opposed to such a change. They argued that statistics showed that the police were not given to pursuing cases in a way which led to a high rate of acquittal. They also showed that, in cases involving miscarriages of justice, the decision to prosecute had been taken by a lawyer.

THE CPS AND THE POLICE

A recent move to integrate the work of the CPS and the police can be seen, in some ways, as taking the prosecution system back to the model operating in 1985 when the CPS was established.

One of the most prominent reasons for the establishment of the CPS was the perceived need to separate the investigative and prosecutorial roles, historically both performed by the police. It was thought that the old system raised too great a danger that police officers, who had investigated a crime and charged a suspected culprit, might, in many cases, not have sufficient detachment to form a balanced view of the weight of the evidence.

The police were also not best placed, it was argued, to consider any public policy aspects inherent in the discretion to prosecute. However, after 15 years of the CPS, lack of communication between the police and CPS prosecutors was seen by many (especially some police officers who, distressed at the number of case files they submit which are not prosecuted, have dubbed the CPS the 'Criminal Protection Society') as problematic. In an attempt to improve liaison between the police investigating a case and the CPS, a pilot scheme, launched in several police stations in 1996, put a CPS officer with a desk in the police station. The Government then resolved to introduce such 'Criminal Justice Units' on a national basis.

Now the CPS has launched what it terms the start of a 'revolution' in prosecuting crime. In June 2000, Lord Williams of Mostyn, the Attorney General, opened the first of many new justice units to be rolled out over the following two years across England and Wales (http://tap.ccta.gov.uk/cps/infoupdate3). The units were a key recommendation of Sir Iain Glidewell in his report on the CPS in 1998. For the first time since the service was established in 1986, Crown prosecutors and the police will work together on cases in the same office.

The reforms will see a return to the principle of police and lawyers working on a case together. The first units will be set up in Avon and Somerset: a trials unit, to handle serious crimes, is being set up at the CPS offices in Bristol and a criminal justice unit, based in police accommodation, will handle the magistrates' courts cases. In place of duplicate police/CPS files for 30,000 magistrates' court cases, will be one single file on which both lawyer and police officer will work.

The trials unit will be staffed by 41 CPS and 10 police staff, and will handle 3,000 serious Crown Court cases a year. The Director of Public Prosecutions (DPP), David Calvert-Smith QC has stated that the new system will see: '... police detectives and senior prosecution lawyers working more closely on serious casework such as rape, armed robbery and murder. CPS lawyers will be on hand at the outset of police inquiries to advise senior officers on legal aspects of investigations and subsequently prepare cases for Crown Court.'

Under the old system, the police would build a file, then copy it to the CPS – a process repeated in 30,000 cases a year. All the evidence and witness statements were similarly copied and sent off to the CPS under separate cover. Notifying witnesses would also be done on paper, through the post. Technology will now enable instant updating of files with investigating officers and CPS lawyers communicating about cases via email.

Under the new system, the police still retain the decision to charge. Even so, the architects of the innovation hope that the police will more readily ask prosecutors for legal advice before charge and, thereby, reduce the likelihood of cases being discontinued at a later stage.

Neil Addison, a barrister and former prosecutor, has acknowledged that closer links will cut costs. 'Administration between CPS and the police has been the major weakness in the way the CPS was set up. I've always taken the view that they do have to work together ... it is unrealistic to think they can work in self-contained cocoons.' (*The Times*, 27 June 2000.) There are, however, still serious misgivings in some quarters about such close liaison between police and prosecuting lawyers. Some defence lawyers and prosecutors are worried about a return to the 'bad old days' before the CPS when, during the 1970s and 1980s, many suspects were wrongly convicted because strong evidence proving their innocence was deliberately disregarded. There is concern that, under the new system, with lawyers and police officers working in the same office the police could pressurise prosecution lawyers into taking flawed cases to court. Malcolm Fowler, chairman of the Law Society's criminal law committee has suggested that '... the problem is when the police develop a case theory for the crime and then only present evidence which fits that theory' (*The Independent*, 26 June 2000).

THE DPP

The DPP, David Calvert-Smith QC, was interviewed by Frances Gibb, the legal editor of *The Times*, in January 2001, and the following article illustrates the past and future challenges to the CPS.

Frances Gibb, 'Whipping boy moves to lead the field' (2001) *The Times*, 9 January

David Calvert-Smith, QC, is looking like the proverbial cat after the cream – with good reason. The Director of Public Prosecutions is poised to enjoy the biggest cash boost for the Crown Prosecution Service (CPS) in its 14-year history.

First it secured an extra £70 million on top of next year's £338.7 million budget in the spending review in July; now just over £30 million is on its way. 'This year funding has been exceptionally tight and so we've been accustomed to cutting our coat to suit our cloth. Next year the position will be much better ... and I would hope that overall, we are able to increase our spending on running costs – that is, the people we employ,' he says.

Once upon a time, the CPS was the whipping boy of criminal justice. Set up with inadequate resources, it got off to a bad start. A critical staff shortage led to missing files, delays and adjournments – and, no doubt, lost cases. Sir Iain Glidewell, in his 1998 report, found a service riddled with low morale and swamped with bureaucracy. But it now seems to have turned a corner.

CPS prosecutors, once derided as the no-hopers who could not make it in private practice, will, from next April, see their pay rise to the same levels as defence lawyers. A big programme to push CPS advocates in the Crown Court is under way: by the end of next March, the aim is to have taken 2,900 Crown Court sessions compared with just 750 from April to June this year. Plans are afoot to enable CPS lawyers to move in and out of private practice – even become judges. And within the CPS areas in England and Wales, prosecutors are no longer bogged down with paperwork and have gone back to lawyering.

What of the users of the system? The DPP, like ministers, is keen to see more done for victims of crime. The new rules on disclosure of evidence should cut miscarriages of justice, he says; but will equally ensure that offenders are brought to book.

> Obviously, the worst thing is for someone to be locked up when innocent. But victims and some witnesses have sometimes felt not enough has been done to catch and deal with the perpetrators. We have to watch that the criminal justice system is not turned into a benevolent lynch mob.

The Human Rights Act has put the CPS, as other public bodies, on notice: a series of challenges are under way over bail, self-incrimination and the burden of proof. The Act gives people the right to a fair trial within a reasonable time by an independent tribunal. 'We must provide access to relevant material and do our best to protect the rights of victims. So far none of the human rights challenges has had wide impact, but it is still early days.'

Meanwhile, Calvert-Smith wants a more effective system. The parts of the criminal justice system could work together more closely; this distinctly on-message theory of 'joined-up' justice is already being practised by the three ministers responsible for justice. Secondly, he wants an end to the culture that revolves around the judge, a move to a system 'which serves the parties rather than the parties being there to serve the courts. The courts are there to provide a service. Management of judicial time has been too important for too long, sometimes to the exclusion of the time of victims, witnesses, defendants and lawyers'.

He favours other reforms likely to come out of the current review under Sir Robin Auld, such as a new hybrid court of lay and professional magistrates. This, he believes, would be 'better equipped' to tackle cases, particularly in cities. With magistrates now needing to give reasons for decisions, cases may take longer. 'And I feel the presence of a professional is bound to speed up the process.' A comprehensive code on criminal law and procedure would also help lawyers and the public.

Controversial areas remain, in particular the prosecution of rape cases and, internally, the CPS's own record on race relations. Calvert-Smith favours looking at granting defendants in rape cases anonymity until conviction. He defends the CPS's record on rape prosecutions: 'We prosecute more cases than are justified by results ... the conviction rate is not high. But we will continue to bring cases where we believe a reasonable jury is more likely to convict than acquit.' But there is room, he says, to improve the ways rape victims and other vulnerable or disabled witnesses give evidence.

Within the CPS, measures, including a black prosecutors' association, are on stream after allegations of racism. Meanwhile, the Commission for Racial Equality (CRE) is investigating the CPS's race record at its Croydon branch. But a nationwide inquiry seems unlikely. Instead, the CPS is working with the CRE to promote good practice including a new statutory duty to promote equality. The service, the DPP believes, will move to being a 'leader in this field, rather than a follower'. Calvert-Smith has been lucky. He has benefited from the Glidewell reforms – not least the split in his own role which has seen Mark Addison, as chief executive, do the organisational side. More than that, the CPS – and its minister the Attorney-General – have had Tony Blair's ear. But Calvert-Smith has also brought a new, lower-key style of leadership. His predecessor, Dame Barbara Mills, was abrasive and forceful; but her job was harder. Calvert-Smith, a lawyer rather than administrator, does not stand up above the parapet. But he is quietly getting his troops in very good shape.

Prosecution of Offences Act 1985

Guidelines for Crown Prosecutors

10 (1) The Director shall issue a Code for Crown Prosecutors giving guidance on general principles to be applied by them–

    (a) in determining, in any case–

        (i) whether proceedings for an offence should be instituted or, where proceedings have been instituted, whether they should be discontinued; or

        (ii) what charges should be preferred; and

    (b) in considering, in any case, representations to be made by them to any magistrates' court about the mode of trial suitable for that case.

(2) The Director may from time to time make alterations in the Code.

THE CODE FOR CROWN PROSECUTORS

The Code for Crown Prosecutors issued in 1985 and revised in 1994 was revised again in 2000. In the following piece, the DPP explains the rationale of the changes. There then follows the new Code.

'The Code for Crown Prosecutors' (2000) 150 NLJ 1494

'If it's not broken, don't fix it.' Those are the words that entered the minds of most Crown Prosecutors on hearing that their Code was to be the subject of a comprehensive review. The Code for Crown Prosecutors, issued under s 10 of the Prosecution of Offences Act 1985, is of fundamental importance to the core business of the Crown Prosecution Service. It provides guidance on the general principles to be applied in all cases, from offences of murder to minor traffic matters.

The Code's main purpose is to ensure that decisions are fair and consistent, particularly when deciding whether or not cases started by the police can and should proceed. In order to achieve this, the Code states that a prosecution can only take place where there is sufficient evidence to provide a realistic prospect of conviction, and a prosecution is in the public interest. The Code does, however, have a second purpose: one that has always been recognised and valued by the Crown Prosecution Service, but which is growing in importance in the current political climate of openness. It serves as a public statement of principles which enables our criminal justice system colleagues and the general public to see for themselves the factors that govern our decisions and, if appropriate, to challenge those decisions.

There is no doubt that the Code as originally drafted in 1986 and revised in 1994. has served the Crown Prosecution Service well. Although the application of the Code by prosecutors has, at times, been the subject of judicial review by the High Court, the principles set out in it have not. So, why change what is generally held to be a successful and effective document?

The answer lies with the fact that the criminal justice system of England and Wales is constantly evolving. In order to keep pace with this process, the Crown Prosecution Service must ensure that the principles according to which it works remain appropriate and in line with major legislative and procedural changes.

In the six years since the Code was last comprehensively revised, there has been a number of such important developments. These include changes to the way in which youths are dealt with under the Crime and Disorder Act 1998; a greater emphasis on issues of disclosure with the Criminal Procedure and Investigations Act 1996; and, of course, the Human Rights Act 1998, which came fully into force on October 2. The recommendations made by Sir Iain Glidewell following his review of the Crown Prosecution Service, led to its adoption of a more decentralised, 42 Area structure. *The Narey Report* on tackling delays in the criminal justice system has led to the introduction of Designated Caseworkers for the fast-track prosecution of certain cases. Both the Glidewell review and the Macpherson inquiry into the death of Stephen Lawrence have increased awareness of the interests of victims and witnesses. The Macpherson inquiry also highlighted the importance of racial equality issues. The list could go on.

Clearly, the last six years have been busy ones for the Crown Prosecution Service and the criminal justice system as a whole. The decision to review the Code was made in order to reflect internal structural changes and to take account of important social, legislative and procedural developments. It was not motivated by any perceived flaw in its principles, or by any external criticism.

The consultation process

As the Code makes clear the Crown Prosecution Service prosecutes in the public interest. It is also an enthusiastic participant in the 'joined up' criminal justice system, which promotes inter-agency cooperation. With this in mind, it was decided to open up the review to public consultation, and this was announced by the Solicitor General, on March 23, 2000.

A programme of written consultation was carried out during March and April at both national and local level, with the judiciary, the police, the legal profession, other domestic and foreign government departments, and a wide selection of interest groups. The views of the general public as well as those of Crown Prosecution Service staff were also sought. In addition, a seminar was held in May under the chairmanship of the Director, to explore the opinions of eminent academics and criminal justice system commentators.

As expected, the consultation process produced varied, and at times completely polarised opinions and suggestions. The experiences of defendants accused and ultimately acquitted of serious offences made thought-provoking reading. Equally disturbing were the harrowing accounts of victims whose lives had been devastated by crime. Accommodating all the suggestions made was a formidable and at times impossible task. It is inevitable that many of those who responded to the consultation process will be disappointed that the revised Code does not reflect their own priorities. However, the exercise was a valuable one. Almost every aspect of the Code was commented upon, which meant in turn that every detail of the Code was scrutinised and reconsidered.

It was decided early in the review process that the length, format and language of the Code should be retained, and that only general principles should be included. Information on operational matters or legal points is covered by internal guidance. There was also a clear need for caution when considering every potential change. The Code had been generally acknowledged during the consultation process as familiar, effective and easily understood. It was apparent that any significant changes made to such a successful document should be clearly justifiable. Even changes in vocabulary could be misconstrued by some as signalling a significant change in approach where none was intended. Instead, the review process returned again and again to the original purpose of the project: to ensure the Code remains in line with major structural, legislative and procedural changes.

As a result, much of the Code has remained unchanged. In particular, the Code tests of evidential sufficiency and public interest have not been altered. Although this conceals the amount and rigour of the analysis that has underpinned the review project, we are satisfied that our basic principles have stood the test of time.

An overview of the main changes

What, then, are the changes that have been made and how will those changes affect the application of the Code?

The first new feature is the section located on the front flyleaf of the Code booklet. This does not form part of the body of the Code itself, but gives a brief account of the status, role and structure of the Crown Prosecution Service, and emphasises from the outset our independence from the police. It also establishes that the term 'Crown Prosecutor' is being used, for the purpose of the Code, to include Designated Caseworkers where appropriate, thereby recognising this significant procedural development within the Service.

Reordering and redrafting the paragraphs in s 2, which deal with general principles, has helped to emphasise that fairness is the most important principle espoused by the Code. It also highlights in express terms, the prosecutor's duty to act in the interests of justice, and not solely for the purpose of obtaining a conviction. This is a principle that has always been adhered to and does not, in any way, detract from our aim to prosecute rigorously and effectively.

Two new paragraphs have also been introduced to this section. The first sets out the role of the prosecutor in very brief form, in terms of our duty to review, advise on, and prosecute cases in the courts. It also emphasises the importance of complying with disclosure obligations. The second new paragraph makes reference to the Human Rights Act 1998. It acknowledges simply and concisely both our legal status and our general obligations under the legislation. The brevity of this reference to the Act belies the enormous amount of work and training of staff carried out by the Crown Prosecution Service in anticipation of its coming fully into force. Its potential impact upon the day to day work of prosecutors is fully appreciated and analysed elsewhere.

As already mentioned, the evidential test has not been changed. However, it has now been set in the context of the criminal standard of proof required by the courts, in order to emphasise the difference between the two. Although this distinction is clear to prosecutors and legal practitioners who are familiar with both tests, members of the public often find the difference confusing. It is hoped that this change will clarify the position. In addition, there has been some redrafting of the section that deals with the reliability of evidence and two new points have been introduced. These changes deal in particular with witness credibility and the reliability of confessions, stressing the need for prosecutors to be pro-active in seeking further evidence where appropriate.

The basis of the public interest test has not been changed. The recommendation in the Glidewell report to exclude from it the words 'in cases of any seriousness', has already been included as an amendment to the existing Code. This creates a general presumption in favour of prosecution for all cases in which there is sufficient evidence, unless there are public interest factors that clearly outweigh those in favour of prosecution.

The lists of public interest factors for and against prosecution remain largely unchanged. The factor in favour of prosecution where an offence involves racial, sexual, or any other form of discrimination, has, however, been extended. It now covers offences where the suspect may not have been specifically motivated by such discrimination but nevertheless demonstrates hostility towards a victim based on his membership of a particular section of society.

The review also introduced one new public interest factor against prosecution. This covers cases where the defendant has already been made the subject of a substantial sentence in relation to another separate offence and is unlikely to face any extra penalty if convicted of further offences. This factor is, however, expressly subject to the particular circumstances of the case which may nevertheless require a prosecution to be conducted.

The section of the Code that deals with our relationship with victims has received particular attention. It continues to emphasise that the Crown Prosecution Service prosecutes on behalf of the general public. However, it also acknowledges the importance of taking into account both the effect upon victims of prosecutors' decisions, and any views expressed to prosecutors by victims or their families, when making public interest decisions. A new paragraph has also been added to reflect the importance attached to the principle of keeping victims informed about decisions that make a significant difference to the case in which they are involved. This issue is the subject of an on-going pilot project, the final outcome of which is as yet unknown.

The section on youths has been substantially changed to incorporate the new system of reprimands and final warnings, whilst preserving the Crown Prosecution Service's public interest discretion. A new paragraph on police cautioning reflects the fact that these now relate only to adults. It also clarifies that where the prosecutor has recommended disposal by way of a caution but this has not taken place, either because the suspect refuses to accept it or the police refuse to administer one, the prosecutor retains the choice to proceed with the case or to discontinue it, on public interest grounds.

Finally, there has been some redrafting of the section dealing with accepting guilty pleas. Two new paragraphs highlight the prosecutor's role in relation to Newton hearings, mandatory minimum sentences and ancillary orders. This section also stresses the need for caution when accepting pleas to lesser offences where the original charge involved aggravating features. One example of such a situation would be where a plea is offered to a simple offence of common assault, rather than to the racially aggravated offence initially charged.

The Code will be more accessible to ethnic minority communities. It will be produced in 12 languages in addition to English and Welsh, and all of these will be available on the Internet. Translation into any other language required will also be provided on request. In addition, the Code is being published in Braille and an audio-taped version will be available on request.

This Code review has been carried out with the assistance of Crown Prosecution Service staff, external consultees from the criminal justice system, legal academic world, and the general public. Their contribution was enormous and was greatly appreciated.

This wide consultation process has allowed every aspect of the Code to be reconsidered. A significant number of important amendments and additions have been made to keep it abreast of legislative, procedural and internal structural developments. However, it has not been necessary to make wholesale changes. This is testimony to the effectiveness of the Code for Crown Prosecutors as a successful working document. We believe that the changes made will enhance that success.

The Code for Crown Prosecutors, 2000

1. Introduction

1.1 The decision to prosecute an individual is a serious step. Fair and effective prosecution is essential to the maintenance of law and order.

Even in a small case a prosecution has serious implications for all involved – victims, witnesses and defendants. The Crown Prosecution Service applies the Code for Crown Prosecutors so that it can make fair and consistent decisions about prosecutions.

1.2 The Code helps the Crown Prosecution Service to play its part in making sure that justice is done. It contains information that is important to police officers and others who work in the criminal justice system and to the general public. Police officers should take account of the Code when they are deciding whether to charge a person with an offence.

1.3 The Code is also designed to make sure that everyone knows the principles that the Crown Prosecution Service applies when carrying out its work. By applying the same principles, everyone involved in the system is helping to treat victims fairly and to prosecute fairly but effectively.

2. General Principles

2.1 Each case is unique and must be considered on its own facts and merits. However, there are general principles that apply to the way in which Crown Prosecutors must approach every case.

2.2 Crown Prosecutors must be fair, independent and objective. They must not let any personal views about ethnic or national origin, sex, religious beliefs, political views or the sexual orientation of the suspect, victim or witness influence their decisions. They must not be affected by improper or undue pressure from any source.

2.3 It is the duty of Crown Prosecutors to make sure that the right person is prosecuted for the right offence. In doing so, Crown Prosecutors must always act in the interests of justice and not solely for the purpose of obtaining a conviction.

2.4 It is the duty of Crown Prosecutors to review, advise on and prosecute cases, ensuring that the law is properly applied, that all relevant evidence is put before the court and that obligations of disclosure are complied with, in accordance with the principles set out in this Code.

2.5 The CPS is a public authority for the purposes of the Human Rights Act 1998. Crown Prosecutors must apply the principles of the European Convention on Human Rights in accordance with the Act.

3. Review

3.1 Proceedings are usually started by the police. Sometimes they may consult the Crown Prosecution Service before starting a prosecution. Each case that the Crown Prosecution Service receives from the police is reviewed to make sure it meets the evidential and public interest tests set out in this Code. Crown Prosecutors may decide to continue with the original charges, to change the charges, or sometimes to stop the case.

3.2 Review is a continuing process and Crown Prosecutors must take account of any change in circumstances. Wherever possible, they talk to the police first if they are thinking about changing the charges or stopping the case. This gives the police the chance to provide more information that may affect the decision. The Crown Prosecution Service and the police work closely together to reach the right decision, but the final responsibility for the decision rests with the Crown Prosecution Service.

4. Code Tests

4.1 There are two stages in the decision to prosecute. The first stage is the evidential test. If the case does not pass the evidential test, it must not go ahead, no matter how important or serious it may be. If the case does meet the evidential test, Crown Prosecutors must decide if a prosecution is needed in the public interest.

4.2 This second stage is the public interest test. The Crown Prosecution Service will only start or continue with a prosecution when the case has passed both tests. The evidential test is explained in section 5 and the public interest test is explained in section 6.

5. The Evidential Test

5.1 Crown Prosecutors must be satisfied that there is enough evidence to provide a 'realistic prospect of conviction' against each defendant on each charge. They must consider what the defence case may be, and how that is likely to affect the prosecution case.

5.2 A realistic prospect of conviction is an objective test. It means that a jury or bench of magistrates, properly directed in accordance with the law, is more likely than not to convict the defendant of the charge alleged. This is a separate test from the one that the criminal courts themselves must apply. A jury or magistrates' court should only convict if satisfied so that it is sure of a defendant's guilt.

5.3 When deciding whether there is enough evidence to prosecute, Crown Prosecutors must consider whether the evidence can be used and is reliable. There will be many cases in which the evidence does not give any cause for concern. But there will also be cases in which the evidence may not be as strong as it first appears. Crown Prosecutors must ask themselves the following questions:

Can the evidence be used in court?

a   Is it likely that the evidence will be excluded by the court? There are certain legal rules which might mean that evidence which seems relevant cannot be given at a trial. For example, is it likely that the evidence will be excluded because of the way in which it was gathered or because of the rule against using hearsay as evidence? If so, is there enough other evidence for a realistic prospect of conviction?

Is the evidence reliable?

b   Is there evidence which might support or detract from the reliability of a confession? Is the reliability affected by factors such as the defendant's age, intelligence or level of understanding?

c   What explanation has the defendant given? Is a court likely to find it credible in the light of the evidence as a whole? Does it support an innocent explanation?

d   If the identity of the defendant is likely to be questioned, is the evidence about this strong enough?

e   Is the witness's background likely to weaken the prosecution case? For example, does the witness have any motive that may affect his or her attitude to the case, or a relevant previous conviction?

f   Are there concerns over the accuracy or credibility of a witness? Are these concerns based on evidence or simply information with nothing to support it? Is there further evidence which the police should be asked to seek out which may support or detract from the account of the witness?

5.4 Crown Prosecutors should not ignore evidence because they are not sure that it can be used or is reliable. But they should look closely at it when deciding if there is a realistic prospect of conviction.

6. The Public Interest Test

6.1 In 1951, Lord Shawcross, who was Attorney General, made the classic statement on public interest, which has been supported by Attorneys General ever since: 'It has never been the rule in this country – I hope it never will be – that suspected criminal offences must automatically be the subject of prosecution'. (House of Commons Debates, volume 483, column 681, 29 January 1951.)

6.2 The public interest must be considered in each case where there is enough evidence to provide a realistic prospect of conviction. A prosecution will usually take place unless there are public interest factors tending against prosecution which clearly outweigh those tending in favour. Although there may be public interest factors against prosecution in a particular case, often the prosecution should go ahead and those factors should be put to the court for consideration when sentence is being passed.

6.3 Crown Prosecutors must balance factors for and against prosecution carefully and fairly. Public interest factors that can affect the decision to prosecute usually depend on the seriousness of the offence or the circumstances of the suspect. Some factors may increase the need to prosecute but others may suggest that another course of action would be better.

The following lists of some common public interest factors, both for and against prosecution, are not exhaustive. The factors that apply will depend on the facts in each case.

Some common public interest factors in favour of prosecution.

6.4 The more serious the offence, the more likely it is that a prosecution will be needed in the public interest. A prosecution is likely to be needed if:

a   a conviction is likely to result in a significant sentence;

b   a weapon was used or violence was threatened during the commission of the offence;

c   the offence was committed against a person serving the public (for example, a police or prison officer, or a nurse);

d   the defendant was in a position of authority or trust;

e   the evidence shows that the defendant was a ringleader or an organiser of the offence;

f   there is evidence that the offence was premeditated;

g   there is evidence that the offence was carried out by a group;

h   the victim of the offence was vulnerable, has been put in considerable fear, or suffered personal attack, damage or disturbance;

i   the offence was motivated by any form of discrimination against the victim's ethnic or national origin, sex, religious beliefs, political views or sexual orientation, or the suspect demonstrated hostility towards the victim based on any of those characteristics;

j   there is a marked difference between the actual or mental ages of the defendant and the victim, or if there is any element of corruption;

k   the defendant's previous convictions or cautions are relevant to the present offence;

l   the defendant is alleged to have committed the offence whilst under an order of the court;

m   there are grounds for believing that the offence is likely to be continued or repeated, for example, by a history of recurring conduct; or

n   the offence, although not serious in itself, is widespread in the area where it was committed.

Some common public interest factors against prosecution

6.5 A prosecution is less likely to be needed if:

a   the court is likely to impose a nominal penalty;

b   the defendant has already been made the subject of a sentence and any further conviction would be unlikely to result in the imposition of an additional sentence or order, unless the nature of the particular offence requires a prosecution;

c   the offence was committed as a result of a genuine mistake or misunderstanding (these factors must be balanced against the seriousness of the offence);

d   the loss or harm can be described as minor and was the result of a single incident, particularly if it was caused by a misjudgement;

e   there has been a long delay between the offence taking place and the date of the trial, unless: the offence is serious; the delay has been caused in part by the defendant; the offence has only recently come to light; or the complexity of the offence has meant that there has been a long investigation;

f   a prosecution is likely to have a bad effect on the victim's physical or mental health, always bearing in mind the seriousness of the offence;

g   the defendant is elderly or is, or was at the time of the offence, suffering from significant mental or physical ill health, unless the offence is serious or there is a real possibility that it may be repeated. The Crown Prosecution Service, where necessary, applies Home Office guidelines about how to deal with mentally disordered offenders. Crown Prosecutors must balance the desirability of diverting a defendant who is suffering from significant mental or physical ill health with the need to safeguard the general public;

h   the defendant has put right the loss or harm that was caused (but defendants must not avoid prosecution solely because they pay compensation); or

i   details may be made public that could harm sources of information, international relations or national security;

6.6 Deciding on the public interest is not simply a matter of adding up the number of factors on each side. Crown Prosecutors must decide how important each factor is in the circumstances of each case and go on to make an overall assessment.

The relationship between the victim and the public interest

6.7 The Crown Prosecution Service prosecutes cases on behalf of the public at large and not just in the interests of any particular individual. However, when considering the public interest test Crown Prosecutors should always take into account the consequences for the victim of the decision whether or not to prosecute, and any views expressed by the victim or the victim's family.

6.8 It is important that a victim is told about a decision which makes a significant difference to the case in which he or she is involved. Crown Prosecutors should ensure that they follow any agreed procedures.

Youths

6.9 Crown Prosecutors must consider the interests of a youth when deciding whether it is in the public interest to prosecute. However Crown Prosecutors should not avoid prosecuting simply because of the defendant's age. The seriousness of the offence or the youth's past behaviour is very important.

6.10 Cases involving youths are usually only referred to the Crown Prosecution Service for prosecution if the youth has already received a reprimand and final warning, unless the offence is so serious that neither of these were appropriate. Reprimands and final warnings are intended to prevent re-offending and the fact that a further offence has occurred indicates that attempts to divert the youth from the court system have not been effective. So the public interest will usually require a prosecution in such cases, unless there are clear public interest factors against prosecution.

Police Cautions

6.11 These are only for adults. The police make the decision to caution an offender in accordance with Home Office guidelines.

6.12 When deciding whether a case should be prosecuted in the courts, Crown Prosecutors should consider the alternatives to prosecution. This will include a police caution. Again the Home Office guidelines should be applied. Where it is felt that a caution is appropriate, Crown Prosecutors must inform the police so that they can caution the suspect. If the caution is not administered because the suspect refuses to accept it or the police do not wish to offer it, then the Crown Prosecutor may review the case again.

7 Charges

7.1 Crown Prosecutors should select charges which:

    a   reflect the seriousness of the offending;

    b   give the court adequate sentencing powers; and

    c   enable the case to be presented in a clear and simple way. This means that Crown Prosecutors may not always continue with the most serious charge where there is a choice. Further, Crown Prosecutors should not continue with more charges than are necessary.

7.2 Crown Prosecutors should never go ahead with more charges than are necessary just to encourage a defendant to plead guilty to a few. In the same way, they should never go ahead with a more serious charge just to encourage a defendant to plead guilty to a less serious one.

7.3 Crown Prosecutors should not change the charge simply because of the decision made by the court or the defendant about where the case will be heard.

8 Mode of Trial

8.1 The Crown Prosecution Service applies the current guidelines for magistrates who have to decide whether cases should be tried in the Crown Court when the offence gives the option and the defendant does not indicate a guilty plea. (See the 'National Mode of Trial Guidelines' issued by the Lord Chief Justice.) Crown Prosecutors should recommend Crown Court trial when they are satisfied that the guidelines require them to do so.

8.2 Speed must never be the only reason for asking for a case to stay in the magistrates' courts. But Crown Prosecutors should consider the effect of any likely delay if they send a case to the Crown Court, and any possible stress on victims and witnesses if the case is delayed.

9 Accepting Guilty Pleas

9.1 Defendants may want to plead guilty to some, but not all, of the charges. Alternatively, they may want to plead guilty to a different, possibly less serious, charge because they are admitting only part of the crime. Crown Prosecutors should only accept the defendant's plea if they think the court is able to pass a sentence that matches the seriousness of the offending, particularly where there are aggravating features. Crown Prosecutors must never accept a guilty plea just because it is convenient.

9.2 Particular care must be taken when considering pleas which would enable the defendant to avoid the imposition of a mandatory minimum sentence. When pleas are offered, Crown Prosecutors must bear in mind the fact that ancillary orders can be made with some offences but not with others.

9.3 In cases where a defendant pleads guilty to the charges but on the basis of facts that are different from the prosecution case, and where this may significantly affect sentence, the court should be invited to hear evidence to determine what happened, and then sentence on that basis.

10 Re-starting a Prosecution

10.1 People should be able to rely on decisions taken by the Crown Prosecution Service. Normally, if the Crown Prosecution Service tells a suspect or defendant that there will not be a prosecution, or that the prosecution has been stopped, that is the end of the matter and the case will not start again. But occasionally there are special reasons why the Crown Prosecution Service will re-start the prosecution, particularly if the case is serious.

10.2 These reasons include:

a rare cases where a new look at the original decision shows that it was clearly wrong and should not be allowed to stand;

b cases which are stopped so that more evidence which is likely to become available in the fairly near future can be collected and prepared. In these cases, the Crown Prosecutor will tell the defendant that the prosecution may well start again; and

c cases which are stopped because of a lack of evidence but where more significant evidence is discovered later.

—·—·—·—·—·—·—·—·—·—·—·—·—·—·—·—

PLEA BARGAINING

In his excellent survey of the crisis in the criminal justice system (*In the Name of the Law: The Collapse of Criminal Justice*, 1996, London: Jonathan Cape), David Rose observes that:

> English criminal justice is in a crisis without precedent, its solutions uncertain and its effects deeply damaging. At a time when the crime rate has reached an all time high, the system often fails to identify offenders: it locks up the innocent while the guilty go free. Often they are not prosecuted at all.

In this context, the debate about 'plea bargaining' has assumed a particular significance. The practice has been defined as 'the practice whereby the accused enters a plea of guilty in return for which he will be given some consideration that results in a sentence concession' (Baldwin and McConville, *Negotiated Justice: Pressures on Defendants to Plead Guilty*, 1977, London: Martin Robertson). In practice, this can refer to either:

(a) a situation either where there has been a plea arrangement for the accused to plead guilty to a lesser charge than the one with which s/he is charged (for example, charged with murder, agrees to plead guilty to manslaughter). This is sometimes called 'charge bargaining'; or

(b) where there is simply a sentencing discount available on a plea of guilty by the accused. This is sometimes called a sentence bargain.

Andrew Sanders and Richard Young are leading authorities in this area. An extract from their book *Criminal Justice* sets the theoretical context of the judge's role in the Crown Court.

Andrew Sanders and Richard Young, *Criminal Justice*, 2nd edn, 2000, London: Butterworths

(iv) Judicial supervision of charge bargaining in the Crown Court

If anyone could be expected to monitor the propriety of charge bargains it would surely be the judge. The judiciary's role as professional dispensers of justice would seem to mark them out as especially fitted for this task. According to McCabe and Purves, 'every one of the charge bargains they identified had been expressly endorsed by the judge.' Zander too argues that judicial supervision provides a safeguard in this area, citing in support the *Yorkshire Ripper*'s case in 1981. Here, the trial judge refused to endorse the prosecution's acceptance of Peter Sutcliffe's plea of guilty to manslaughter, insisting that the original murder charge be proceeded with. At one time, the appellate courts required that the charge brought should correspond to the facts alleged. In *Coe*, for instance, the court deprecated charge reduction in the interests of convenience and ruled that the overriding consideration must always be the proper administration of justice. This attitude has since been replaced by a recognition of the advantages of charge bargaining and the dangers of judicial involvement. We have already seen that in *Herbert* the Court of Appeal accepted that it was proper for prosecuting counsel to take into account the savings in public expenditure that a charge bargain could achieve.

The Court of Appeal in *Grafton,* subsequently decided that the trial judge is powerless to prevent Counsel dropping or reducing any charges except where the latter seeks the seal of judicial approval for a proposed deal. This rule (and its exception) is an incentive for counsel to keep judges out of charge bargaining altogether. Thus, if a case similar to that of Peter Sutcliffe were to go before the courts today, prosecuting counsel would be free to accept a plea of guilty to manslaughter so long as no express sanction was sought from the judge.

Should one classify *Grafton* as laying down a crime control *enabling* rule – encouraging counsel to pursue charge bargaining free of judicial interference? Or is it merely a rule which *legitimises* a long-established practice? The answer depends on how far trial judges had previously ensured that charge bargains were based, as far as they can be, on considerations of justice rather than merely convenience and efficiency. What is the evidence on this point? The *Peter Sutcliffe* case provides an example of due process inspired judicial control (no doubt prompted by the high profile of that case) but there are many other cases which tend to show that trial judges are just as likely to encourage as restrict the practice of charge bargaining, and that the appellate judiciary welcome this. In *Winterflood,* the judge had sent for counsel after four days of the trial and asked if the defendant would plead guilty to handling stolen property if a robbery charge was dropped. The defendant agreed to this but appealed against the sentence imposed. In dismissing the appeal, the Court of Appeal stressed that private discussions before or during a trial were undesirable but that there was no reason why the discussion in this case should not have taken place, in the absence of the jury, in open court. Similarly, in *Llewellyn*, the Court of Appeal emphasised that trial judges should not feel inhibited from taking part in pre-trial reviews to discuss such matters as the correct way of proceeding with the charges brought.

The great majority of Crown Court judges are recruited from the ranks of the practising Bar. Many hold part-time appointments only, spending most of their time as barristers rather than judges. Prosecution and defence counsel have little to fear in seeking the approval of a judge for a charge bargain since all of the parties involved share a common outlook, all stand to gain from short-circuiting the formal trial process, and all are encouraged to enter into negotiations by the Court of Appeal. Sometimes judges, by indicating their desire for a speedy resolution of the case, exert much indirect pressure on their fellow lawyers to cut a deal. In an example given by McConville *et al*, defence counsel had been called to see the judge privately just before a trial listed for three days was due to begin. The judge said he wanted the jury to be able to retire to consider their verdict by 11 am the following morning because he was going on 'his holidays' in the afternoon of that day. This led counsel to try to persuade the client that it would be tactically astute to agree to the trial being truncated because the judge 'is a fast judge ..., he likes the bare bones of a case ...' (The judge's desire to pack his case and rest his bones in the sun was not conveyed to the client.) The client resisted, which prompted counsel to depict the preference for a full trial as 'complete madness' and 'bloody crazy!'. The client responded: 'You're not the one who might go away [to prison] at the end of the day. I've lost my family and now I might lose my liberty. I want to do it properly, it *must* be done right; I don't want to rush it now.' It is a pity that more of those working in the criminal courts do not share this freedom perspective or this concern for procedural propriety. The appellate courts proclaim that charge bargains should represent a proper, not merely an inexpensive, outcome to a case, but is this mere lip-service to the interests of justice? The point, after all, of these bargains is to circumvent the very safeguards and procedural protections designed to discover the truth and to produce justice. To take just one example, the rationale for the rule that a jury should not be told of an accused's previous convictions is that the prejudicial effect of this knowledge would outweigh any probative value. Yet barristers engaged in charge bargaining act in full knowledge of any previous record that an accused might have. It is easy to see how a presumption of guilt might arise in these circumstances. The judge, whose independence is supposed to protect defendants against improper pressure, is merely an interested spectator (and potential dealer) at the market place of justice.

A more open system of plea bargaining was advocated by the Runciman Royal Commission on Criminal Justice (para 156). The report argues that this would do much to alleviate the problem of 'cracked trials' in which defendants do not plead guilty until the last moment, wasting the time of witness, the police, the CPS and the court. In a system where the vast majority of cases in the Crown Court and magistrates' courts result in guilty pleas (79% and 81.5%, respectively) the operation of the plea bargain becomes very important.

The Commission research indicated that 'cracked trials' accounted for more than a quarter of all cases. The Commission also noted that sentence discounts of between 25% and 30% for guilty pleas have been long established practice in the crown court. The Commission suggested that higher discounts should be available for those who plead guilty earlier in the process. The report states:

> The most common reason for defendants delaying a plea of guilty until the last minute is a reluctance to face the facts until they are at the door of the court. It is often said too that a defendant has a considerable incentive to behave in this way. The longer the delay, the more the likelihood of witnesses becoming intimidated or forgetting to turn up or disappearing.

It recommends (para 157): 'At the request of defence counsel on instructions from the defendant, judges should be able to indicate the highest sentence that they would impose at that point on the basis of the facts as put to them.'

On the issue of charges, it recommends (para 161): 'Discussions on the level of charge (charge bargaining) should take place as early as possible in order to minimise the need for cases to be listed as contested trials.'

Requests made to the judge could be made at a preparatory hearing, at a hearing called specially for the purpose, or at the trial itself.

Richard Young and Andrew Sanders, 'Plea Bargaining and the Next Criminal Justice Bill' (1994) 144 NLJ 1200

> The party conference season is almost upon us once more and those who are committed to the ideals of an adversarial criminal justice system have good cause to feel uneasy. The parliamentary passage of the Criminal Justice and Public Order Bill and the Police and Magistrates' Courts Bill has seen a number of reverses for the Government. The Home Secretary is certain to reassert his 'tough on crime' credentials at this year's Tory party conference. What, then, can we expect in the next Criminal Justice Bill? The Government will probably look once again for measures that can be presented as increasing the effectiveness of the system in convicting the guilty. There is plenty of material among the 352 recommendations of the Royal Commission on Criminal Justice from which to fashion such a legislative programme, since effectiveness was one of its central concerns. (See Field, S and Thomas, P, 'Justice and Efficiency? The Royal Commission on Criminal Justice', 21 *Journal of Law and Society* 1.) In particular, the Royal Commission was much exercised by the large numbers of defendants who change their plea to guilty at a late stage in criminal proceedings, thus causing trials to 'crack'. What is the problem here? Is it that people who want to plead not guilty are persuaded to change their minds? Or is it that people who want to plead guilty 'play the system' by not declaring this initially? The Royal Commission clearly

took the second approach. It recommended a number of procedural changes to increase the incentives to defendants to plead guilty at an early stage. The key proposals (see *Royal Commission on Criminal Justice Report*, Cmnd 2263 (HMSO 1993) at 111–44) were that:

- There should be clearer articulation of the sentencing principle that the earlier in the proceedings a guilty plea was entered, the greater the sentencing discount should be.

- Defendants should have the right to initiate a 'sentence canvass' whereby defence counsel would be able to ask the trial judge what the maximum sentence would be if a plea of guilty was entered at that stage (sentence bargaining).

- Negotiations between defence and prosecution concerning a reduction in the level of charge in return for a plea of guilty (charge bargaining) should be encouraged to take place as early as possible.

These proposals were widely reported in the press as heralding the introduction of an American-style system of plea bargaining. (For example, when the Attorney General declared his support for the 'sentence canvass' proposal, the *Guardian* (8 October 1993) reported this as paving the way for 'the introduction of formal 'plea bargaining' into British courts for the first time'.) But in a book published last month (Sanders, A and Young, R, *Criminal Justice*, 1994, Butterworths) we argue that plea-bargaining is already an integral part of the criminal justice system. We also show that the reasoning of the Royal Commission on this topic is deeply flawed, flowing as it does from an inadequate understanding of the operation of criminal justice. In this article we will summarise our argument on these points and go on to question the principles on which plea bargaining rests.

Sentence discounts and sentence bargaining

It is a well established principle of sentencing that a discount should generally be given to those pleading guilty. As Lord Widgery CJ put it in *Cain* ([1976] Crim LR 464) 'Everyone knows that it is so and there is no doubt about it. Any accused person who does not know about it should know about it. The sooner he knows the better.' This statement implies, and subsequent cases have expressly confirmed (see, for example, *Hollington and Emmens* (1986) 82 Cr App R 281 and *Buffrey* (1993) 14 Cr App R(S) 511) that the sooner the guilty plea is entered, the larger the discount which may be obtained. In *Turner* ([1970] 2 WLR 1093 at 1097) it was emphasised that defence counsel are under a duty to give accused persons best advice, and this will often include advice 'in strong terms ... that a plea of guilty, showing an element of remorse, is a mitigating factor which may well enable the court to give a lesser sentence than would otherwise be the case'. There is no reason to believe that barristers are neglecting their duty. In a recent study of defendants convicted in the Crown Court conducted by Hedderman and Moxon, 65 per cent of those pleading guilty said that their decision had been influenced by the prospect of receiving a discount (Hedderman, C and Moxon, D, 'Magistrates' Court or Crown Court? Mode of Trial Decisions and Sentencing' (Home Office Research Study, No 125) (HMSO 1992)) and research has shown that barristers frequently use the sentence discount principle to pressurise defendants into pleading guilty. For example, one defendant told Baldwin and McConville that: 'The barrister then said, "If you're found guilty you will get about 10 or 15 years but if you plead guilty you will get 4 or 5 years." I was really shocked. I was so scared, sweating and nervous and he frightened me with this 10–15 years stuff and saying I had no chance ... I agreed to plead guilty but it wasn't my decision; I had no choice about it.' There scarcely needs to be any clearer articulation of the sentence discount principle than this.

Though the principle is clear, there are no rules. (The complexities of the case law are discussed in Sanders and Young, above, pp 318–26.) The appellate courts argue that sentencing is a subjective exercise which must be tailored to all the circumstances of each individual case. There is some evidence to suggest that it is conventional to 'knock off' (the language used in *Boyd* (1980) 2 Cr App R(S) 234) a quarter or a third of the sentence that would have been passed following an unsuccessful not guilty plea (see *Williams* [1983] Crim LR 693 and the accompanying commentary at 694) or even more in special circumstances. (See *Buffrey* above.) On the other hand, the Court of Appeal has ruled that there are circumstances in which the judge can properly give no discount for a plea of guilty (see especially Costen (1989) 11 Cr App R(S) 182) and Crown Court judges vary in their willingness to reward such a plea. (See Baldwin, J, and McConville, M, 'The Influence of the Sentencing Discount in Inducing Guilty Pleas' in Baldwin, J and Bottomley, A (eds), *Criminal Justice: Selected Readings*, 1978, p 119, Martin Robertson.)

Further uncertainty is introduced by the absence of standard sentences for specific offences. There is thus no starting point from which to calculate the length of a discounted sentence. Research suggests that trial judges are not even aware of their own (inconsistent) pattern of sentencing, never mind those established by their colleagues or prescribed by appellate judges. (Ashworth, A, Genders, E, Mansfield, G, Peay, J, and Player, E, 'Sentencing in the Crown Court' (Occasional Paper No 10) (Oxford Centre for Criminological Research, 1984, p 49.)

The upshot is that there is a strong incentive for counsel to approach the judge on a case-by-case basis to enquire what discount would be offered in return for a guilty plea. The *Turner* (above) rules prohibit trial judges from revealing this information, but expressly preserve freedom of access between themselves and counsel. One reason for doing this was so that the latter could indicate that, whatever the defendant's plea, a particular form of sentence (for example probation) would be passed. But many of those operating in the criminal courts have concluded that it is artificial and unrealistic for the law to encourage guilty pleas through the sentence discount whilst simultaneously denying the defence the opportunity to discover exactly what, if anything, is on offer in the case at hand. (The vast majority of barristers and two-thirds of trial judges want the law changed to allow sentence bargaining: Zander, M, and Henderson, P, 'The Crown Court Study' (Royal Commission on Criminal Justice Research Study No 19) 145 (HMSO 1993).) In practice, both defence counsel and judges have abused their right to meet in private and have put two fingers up to the Court of Appeal by engaging in sentence bargaining on a wide scale. (See the sharp criticism expressed in *Smith* [1990] 1 WLR 1311 at 1314 by Russell LJ that 'despite frequent observations made in this Court discouraging unnecessary visits to the judge's room, they appear to continue up and down the country'. See also *Pitman* [1991] 1 All ER 468: 'No amount of criticism and no amount of warnings and no amount of exhortation seems to be able to prevent this happening' (*per* Lord Lane CJ at 470). Research confirms this picture of widespread abuse. See especially *Negotiated Justice* (above) and Morison, J, and Leith, P, *The Barrister's World*, 1992, p 135, OUP. Sentence canvassing is already common and the Royal Commission proposals would simply legitimise and encourage the practice.

Charge bargaining

This too is already an entrenched feature of the system. That defence counsel are obliged to advise defendants as to the advantages that may be secured by agreeing to plead guilty to a lesser charge than that originally brought was stressed in *Hall*: 'it is the clear duty of any counsel representing a client to assist the client to make up his mind by putting forward the pros and cons, if need be in strong language, to impress upon the client what the likely results are of certain courses of conduct' ((1968) 52 Cr App R 528 *per* Lord Parker CJ). Similarly, according to the Court of Appeal in *Herbert* ((1991) 94 Cr App R 230) the practice whereby counsel indicated that the Crown would be prepared to accept pleas of guilty to lesser offences than those charged, or to certain only of the charges, has long been accepted as properly part of counsel's duty. The Court of Appeal also accepts that it is permissible for trial judges to promote charge bargains so long as this is done openly. (See *Winterflood* [1979] Crim LR 263 and *Llewellyn* (1978) 67 Cr App R 149.) And so the law provides defendants with a double incentive to plead guilty. It encourages some charges to be dropped in exchange for guilty pleas to others, thus reducing the probable sentence in itself. And then it provides for the sentences on those remaining charges to be discounted (and the earlier the bargain is struck, the greater should be the discount). Nearly a third of the Hedderman and Moxon sample claimed to have pleaded guilty as a direct result of a charge bargain (above. And see *Standing Accused*, above, pp 252–63.) The obvious question this raises is whether all these defendants really were guilty.

Faulty reasoning

The Royal Commission accepted that 'it would be naive to suppose that innocent persons never plead guilty because of the prospect of the sentence discount' but conveniently rejected the notion that its proposal for clearer articulation of this sentencing principle would lead to more miscarriages of justice. (See Report, above, at pp 110–12.) We have criticised elsewhere this idealistic notion that one can improve the effectiveness of the system in convicting the guilty without also increasing its effectiveness in convicting the innocent. (See Young, R, and Sanders, A, 'The Royal Commission on Criminal Justice: A Confidence Trick?' (*Oxford Journal of Legal Studies*).) One simply has to make a value choice about the weight to be given to protecting the innocent relative to other important values such as repressing crime and economy in the use of scarce resources. The Royal Commission was unwilling to come clean and admit that it favoured more crime control and less due process. Similarly dishonest was the reasoning employed in supporting a 'sentence canvass'.

The Royal Commission declared that 'to face defendants with a choice between what they might get on an immediate plea of guilty and what they might get if found guilty by the jury does amount to unacceptable pressure'. (Report above, p 113.) Yet a few sentences further on it recommended that judges should be able to tell defence lawyers what sentence would be imposed on a plea of guilty being entered. Since the defence will be able to calculate the likely sentence on a not guilty plea by adding a third or a quarter to this maximum, the defendant will be faced with exactly that form of pressure that the Commission itself regarded as 'unacceptable'. As for charge bargaining, the Royal Commission dealt with the subject in a single sentence, stating that it saw 'no objection to such discussions'. (*Ibid*, p 114.) It ignored the enormous critical literature in academic journals (a useful starting point is McConville, M, and Mirsky, C, 'Looking Through the Guilty Plea Glass: The Structural Framework of English and American State Courts', (1993) 2 *Social and Legal Studies* 173). It marshalled no arguments to justify its stance, and not one of its 22 research studies focused on plea bargaining.

Objections to plea bargaining

Based on nothing more than prejudice (and misrepresentation of the Seabrook report) (see on this Bridges, L, 'Normalizing Injustice: The Royal Commission on Criminal Justice', 21 *Journal of Law and Society* 20 at 30) the Royal Commission paints a picture in which inconvenience and waste occur 'because the defendant has decided to plead guilty at the last minute'. (Report, above, p 111.) It envisages that the sentence canvass 'would be initiated solely by, and for the benefit of, defendants who wish to exercise a right to be told the consequence of a decision which is theirs alone'. (*Ibid*, p 113.) This is all to assume that plea bargaining benefits defendants and that last minute plea changing is the product of their 'reluctance to face the facts until they are at the door of the court'. (*Ibid*, p 112.) The research evidence, however, indicates that these negotiations generally benefit, and are initiated by, lawyers. (See Bottoms, A, and McClean, J, *Defendants in the Criminal Process*, 1976, Routledge and Kegan Paul, 1976) 130; *Negotiated Justice*, above, 31; Bredar, J, 'Moving up the day of reckoning: Strategies for Attacking the 'Cracked Trials' Problem' [1992] Crim LR 153 at 155 and *Standing Accused*, above.) Most defence advisers are pre-disposed to settle cases, even where this is not in the interests of the client (as where the prosecution evidence is known to be weak). Clients are managed so effectively by their lawyers that they have decisions taken for them. Further, the timing of pleas has as much to do with the prosecution as with the defence. The idea that the plea is a matter for the defendant alone is an utter nonsense in reality. Introducing a sentence canvass will simply provide the lawyers on both sides with a new tool with which to batter defendants into submission. The inevitable consequence will be a fresh stream of miscarriages.

As we argue in *Criminal Justice* (above, Chapter 7) defendants do not commonly play the system; the system plays with them, their rights and their freedom. The Royal Commission lacked any insight into the function of the adversarial system as an integral part of constitutionalism. Thus it remarks that, 'Provided that the defendant is in fact guilty and has received competent legal advice about his or her position, there can be no serious objection to a system of inducements designed to encourage him or her so to plead.' (Report, above, p 110.)

In fact, the objections are absolutely fundamental. The adversarial system does not merely aim at producing accurate determinations of guilt and innocence. Rather it seeks to strike an appropriate balance in the relationship between the state and the individual. (See McConville, M, and Mirsky, C, 'To plea or not to plea', *Legal Action* February 1993, 6.) Only if the state has acted within the bounds of constitutional propriety in collecting and presenting evidence against the defendant can the imposition of punishment be justified. The high burden of proof which the state must satisfy in open court is intended, in part, as a protection against abuses of police and prosecutorial power. The factually guilty are as much entitled to that protection as anyone else. Similarly, the House of Lords recently refused to 'countenance behaviour that threatens either basic human rights or the Rule of Law', regardless of the actual evidence of guilt or innocence in the case. (*Bennett v Horseferry Road Magistrates' Court* [1993] 3 WLR 90.)

A system of plea bargaining fatally undermines these principles since it allows the state to secure convictions based on vague and unsubstantiated allegations. Even within the parameters of the Royal Commission's limited view of the purpose of the criminal justice system, its expression of support for inducements to plead guilty is objectionable. First, as alluded to above, there is simply no way of ensuring that only the factually guilty will be persuaded by such inducements to plead guilty. Second, as a recent research monograph virtually screams from the rooftops (*Standing Accused*, above.) the great mass of defendants do not receive competent legal advice. All too often defendants' stories and protestations of innocence are simply brushed aside by their defence advisers who, like most police, prosecutors and judges, operate with a presumption of guilt. That the Royal Commission was oblivious to this is unsurprising. It failed to fund any research on the adequacy of defence lawyering and while its report has a chapter on 'The Prosecution' there is none on 'The Defence'. Some would argue that the Royal Commission's proposals on plea bargaining at least have the virtue of openly acknowledging the practice, thus allowing for its easier regulation and the transmission of more accurate information to the defendant. But this response is defeatist. If the practice is wrong in principle, as we argue it is, then steps should be taken to secure its eradication. Failing that, the status quo is to be preferred to the Royal Commission's recommendations for change. Covertly to tolerate plea bargaining is hypocritical; but to approve its legality smacks of totalitarianism. (See Packer, H, *The Limits of the Criminal Sanction*, 1969, p 179, Stanford University Press.) It is already the case that much plea bargaining in this country is perfectly lawful and any further moves in this direction should be resisted fiercely. The Court of Appeal's dogged efforts to keep judges out of sentence bargaining (whatever its true motive might be) (see *Criminal Justice*, above, 330–31 and 336) should not now lightly be thrown away.

BAIL

Bail is the release from custody, pending a criminal trial, of an accused on the promise that money will be paid if he absconds. All decisions on whether to grant bail, therefore, involve delicate questions of balancing interests. A person is presumed innocent of a criminal charge unless he or she is proved guilty of it; this implies that no one should ever be detained unless he or she has been found guilty. For several reasons, however, it can be regarded as undesirable to allow some accused people to go back to society before the case against them is tried in a criminal court. To refuse bail to an accused might involve depriving liberty to someone who is subsequently found not guilty, or convicted but given a non-custodial sentence. Such a person will probably have been kept in a police cell or in a prison cell for 23 hours per day. Unlike the jurisdictions in Holland,

Germany and France, no compensation is payable in these circumstances. On the other hand, to allow liberty to the accused pending trial might be to allow him or her to abscond, commit further offences, interfere with witnesses and obstruct the course of justice. The introduction of human rights law in the UK has had a substantial effect on all aspects of the bail process, and a good overview of the challenges for the courts is provided in the excellent article by John Burrows, a barrister at Goldsmith Chambers, at the end of this section.

Bail Act 1976 (c 63)

3.– General provisions

(1) A person granted bail in criminal proceedings shall be under a duty to surrender to custody, and that duty is enforceable in accordance with section 6 of this Act.

(2) No recognizance for his surrender to custody shall be taken from him.

(3) Except as provided by this section–

   (a) no security for his surrender to custody shall be taken from him;

   (b) he shall not be required to provide a surety or sureties for his surrender to custody; and

   (c) no other requirement shall be imposed on him as a condition of bail.

(4) He may be required, before release on bail, to provide a surety or sureties to secure his surrender to custody.

(5) If it appears that he is unlikely to remain in Great Britain until the time appointed for him to surrender to custody, he may be required, before release on bail, to give security for his surrender to custody.

   The security may be given by him or on his behalf.

(6) He may be required ... to comply, before release on bail or later, with such requirements as appear to the court to be necessary to secure that–

   (a) he surrenders to custody;

   (b) he does not commit an offence while on bail;

   (c) he does not interfere with witnesses or otherwise obstruct the course of justice whether in relation to himself or any other person;

   (d) he makes himself available for the purpose of enabling inquiries or a report to be made to assist the court in dealing with him for the offence [and, in any Act, 'the normal powers to impose conditions of bail' means the powers to impose conditions under paragraph (a), (b) or (c) above].

[(6ZA) Where he is required under subsection (6) above to reside in a bail hostel or probation hostel, he may also be required to comply with the rules of the hostel.]

[(6A) In the case of a person accused of murder the court granting bail shall, unless it considers that satisfactory reports on his mental condition have already been obtained, impose as conditions of bail–

   (a) a requirement that the accused shall undergo examination by two medical practitioners for the purpose of enabling such reports to be prepared; and

   (b) a requirement that he shall for that purpose attend such an institution or place as the court directs and comply with any other directions which may be given to him for that purpose by either of those practitioners.

(6B) Of the medical practitioners referred to in subsection (6A) above at least one shall be a practitioner approved for the purposes of [section 12 of the Mental Health Act 1983].]

(7) If a parent or guardian of a child or young person consents to be surety for the child or young person for the purposes of this subsection, the parent or guardian may be required to secure that the child or young person complies with any requirement imposed on him by virtue of [subsection (6) or (6A) above] but–

(a) no requirement shall be imposed on the parent or the guardian of a young person by virtue of this subsection where it appears that the young person will attain the age of seventeen before the time to be appointed for him to surrender to custody; and

(b) the parent or guardian shall not be required to secure compliance with any requirement to which his consent does not extend and shall not, in respect of those requirements to which his consent does extend, be bound in a sum greater than £50.

(8) Where a court has granted bail in criminal proceedings [that court or, where that court has committed a person on bail to the Crown Court for trial or [released a person on bail on transferring proceedings against him to the Crown Court for trial or has committed him on bail to the Crown Court] to be sentenced or otherwise dealt with, that court or the Crown Court may] on application–

(a) by or on behalf of the person to whom [bail was] granted; or

(b) by the prosecutor or a constable, vary the conditions of bail or impose conditions in respect of bail which [has been] granted unconditionally.

[(8A) Where a notice of transfer is given under [a relevant transfer provision], subsection (8) above shall have effect in relation to a person in relation to whose case the notice is given as if he had been committed on bail [released on bail on the transfer of proceedings against him] to the Crown Court for trial].

(9) This section is subject to [sub-section (2) of section 30 of the Magistrates' Courts Act 1980] (conditions of bail on remand for medical examination).

3A.– [Conditions of bail in case of police bail]

[(1) Section 3 of this Act applies, in relation to bail granted by a custody officer under Part IV of the Police and Criminal Evidence Act 1984 in cases where the normal powers to impose conditions of bail are available to him subject to the following modifications.

(2) Subsection (6) does not authorise the imposition of a requirement to reside in a bail hostel or any requirement under paragraph (d).

(3) Subsections (6ZA), (6A) and (6B) shall be omitted.

(4) For subsection (8), substitute the following–

(8) Where a custody officer has granted bail in criminal proceedings he or another custody officer serving at the same police station may, at the request of the person to whom it was granted, vary the conditions of bail; and in doing so he may impose conditions or more onerous conditions.

(5) Where a constable grants bail to a person no conditions shall be imposed under subsections (4), (5), (6) or (7) of section 3 of this Act unless it appears to the

constable that it is necessary to do so for the purpose of preventing that person from–

(a) failing to surrender to custody, or

(b) committing an offence while on bail, or

(c) interfering with witnesses or otherwise obstructing the course of justice, whether in relation to himself or any other person.

(6) Subsection (5) above also applies on any request to a custody officer under subsection (8) of section 3 of this Act to vary the conditions of bail.]

This section (above) was added by the Criminal Justice and Public Order Act 1994, s 27(3).

– . – . – . – . – . – . – . – . – . – . – . – . – . – . – . – . –

4. – *General right to bail of accused persons and others*

(1) A person to whom this section applies shall be granted bail except as provided in Schedule 1 to this Act.

(2) This section applies to a person who is accused of an offence when–

(a) he appears or is brought before a magistrates' court or the Crown Court in the course of or in connection with proceedings for the offence; or

(b) he applies to a court for bail [or for a variation of the conditions of bail] in connection with the proceedings.

This subsection does not apply as respects proceedings on or after a person's conviction of the offence or proceedings against a fugitive offender for the offence.

(3) This section also applies to a person who, having been convicted of an offence, appears or is brought before a magistrates' court to be dealt with under [Part II of Schedule 2 to the Criminal Justice Act 1991 (breach of requirement of probation, community service, combination or curfew order)].

(4) This section also applies to a person who has been convicted of an offence and whose case is adjourned by the court for the purpose of enabling inquiries or a report to be made to assist the court in dealing with him for the offence.

(5) Schedule 1 to this Act also has effect as respects conditions of bail for a person to whom this section applies.

(6) In Schedule 1 to this Act 'the defendant' means a person to whom this section applies and any reference to a defendant whose case is adjourned for inquiries or a report is a reference to a person to whom this section applies by virtue of subsection (4) above.

(7) This section is subject to [section 41 of the Magistrates' Courts Act 1980] (restriction of bail by magistrates court in cases of treason).

[(8) This section is subject to section 25 of the Criminal Justice and Public Order Act 1994 (exclusion of bail in cases of homicide and rape).]

8.– Bail with sureties

(1) This section applies where a person is granted bail in criminal proceedings on condition that he provides one or more surety or sureties for the purpose of securing that he surrenders to custody.

(2) In considering the suitability for that purpose of a proposed surety, regard may be had (amongst other things) to–

    (a) the surety's financial resources;

    (b) his character and any previous convictions of his; and

    (c) his proximity (whether in point of kinship, place of residence or otherwise) to the person for whom he is to be surety.

(3) Where a court grants a person bail in criminal proceedings on such a condition but is unable to release him because no surety or no suitable surety is available, the court shall fix the amount in which the surety is to be bound and subsections (4) and (5) below, or in a case where the proposed surety resides in Scotland subsection (6) below, shall apply for the purpose of enabling the recognizance of the surety to be entered into subsequently.

(4) Where this subsection applies the recognizance of the surety may be entered into before such of the following persons or descriptions of persons as the court may by order specify or, if it makes no such order, before any of the following persons, that is to say–

    (a) where the decision is taken by a magistrates' court, before a justice of the peace, a justices' clerk or a police officer who either is of the rank of inspector or above or is in charge of a police station or, if magistrates' courts rules so provide, by a person of such other description as is specified in the rules;

    (b) where the decision is taken by the Crown Court, before any of the persons specified in paragraph (a) above or, if Crown Court rules so provide, by a person of such other description as is specified in the rules;

    (c) where the decision is taken by the High Court or the Court of Appeal, before any of the persons specified in paragraph (a) above or, if Supreme Court rules so provide, by a person of such other description as is specified in the rules ...

(5) Where a surety seeks to enter into his recognizance before any person in accordance with subsection (4) above but that person declines to take his recognizance because he is not satisfied of the surety's suitability, the surety may apply to–

    (a) the court which fixed the amount of the recognizance in which the surety was to be bound; or

    (b) a magistrates' court for the petty sessions area in which he resides, for that court to take his recognizance and that court shall, if satisfied of his suitability, take his recognizance.

(6) Where this subsection applies, the court, if satisfied of the suitability of the proposed surety, may direct that arrangements be made for the recognizance of the surety to be entered into in Scotland before any constable, within the meaning of the Police (Scotland) Act 1967, having charge at any police office or station in like manner as the recognizance would be entered into in England or Wales ...

Bail (Amendment) Act 1993

1.– *Prosecution right of appeal*

1. (1) Where a magistrates' court grants bail to a person who is charged with or convicted of–

(a) an offence punishable by a term of imprisonment of 5 years or more; or

(b) an offence under section 12 (taking a conveyance without authority) or 12A (aggravated vehicle taking) of the Theft Act 1968, the prosecution may appeal to a judge of the Crown Court against the granting of bail.

(2) Subsection (1) above applies only where the prosecution is conducted–

(a) by or on behalf of the Director of Public Prosecutions; or

(b) by a person who falls within such class or description of person as may be prescribed for the purposes of this section by order made by the Secretary of State.

(3) Such an appeal may be made only if-

(a) the prosecution made representations that bail should not be granted; and

(b) the representations were made before it was granted.

(4) In the event of the prosecution wishing to exercise the right of appeal set out in subsection (1) above, oral notice of appeal shall be given to the magistrates' court at the conclusion of the proceedings in which such bail has been granted and before the release from custody of the person concerned.

(5) Written notice of appeal shall thereafter be served on the magistrates' court and the person concerned within two hours of the conclusion of such proceedings.

(6) Upon receipt from the prosecution of oral notice of appeal from its decision to grant bail the magistrates' court shall remand in custody the person concerned, until the appeal is determined or otherwise disposed of.

(7) Where the prosecution fails, within the period of two hours mentioned in subsection (5) above, to serve one or both of the notices required by that subsection, the appeal shall be deemed to have been disposed of.

(8) The hearing of an appeal under subsection (1) above against a decision of the magistrates' court to grant bail shall be commenced within forty-eight hours, excluding weekends and any public holiday (that is to say, Christmas Day, Good Friday or a bank holiday), from the date on which oral notice of appeal is given.

(9) At the hearing of any appeal by the prosecution under this section, such appeal shall be by way of re-hearing, and the judge hearing any such appeal may remand the person concerned in custody or may grant bail subject to such conditions (if any) as he thinks fit.

(10) In relation to a child or young person (within the meaning of the Children and Young Persons Act 1969) –

(a) the reference in subsection (1) above to an offence punishable by a term of imprisonment is to be read as a reference to an offence which would be so punishable in the case of an adult; and

(b) the reference in subsection (5) above to remand in custody is to be read subject to the provisions of section 23 of the Act of 1969 (remands to local authority accommodation).

(11) The power to make an order under subsection (2) above shall be exercisable by statutory instrument and any instrument shall be subject to annulment in pursuance of a resolution of either House of Parliament.

_ . _ . _ . _ . _ . _ . _ . _ . _ . _ . _ . _ . _ . _ . _ . _ . _

Criminal Justice and Public Order Act 1994

Sections 25–30

Bail

25.– No bail for defendants charged with or convicted of homicide or rape after previous conviction of such offences

(1) A person who in any proceedings has been charged with or convicted of an offence to which this section applies in circumstances to which it applies shall not be granted bail in those proceedings.

(2) This section applies, subject to subsection (3) below, to the following offences, that is to say:

   (a) murder;

   (b) attempted murder;

   (c) manslaughter;

   (d) rape; or

   (e) attempted rape.

(3) This section applies to a person charged with or convicted of any such offence only if he has been previously convicted by or before a court in any part of the United Kingdom of any such offence or of culpable homicide and, in the case of a previous conviction of manslaughter or of culpable homicide, if he was then sentenced to imprisonment or, if he was then a child or young person, to long-term detention under any of the relevant enactments.

(4) This section applies whether or not an appeal is pending against conviction or sentence.

(5) In this section: 'conviction' includes:

   (a) a finding that a person is not guilty by reason of insanity;

   (b) a finding under section 4A(3) of the Criminal Procedure (Insanity) Act 1964 (cases of unfitness to plead) that a person did the act or made the omission charged against him; and

   (c) a conviction of an offence for which an order is made placing the offender on probation or discharging him absolutely or conditionally;

   and 'convicted' shall be construed accordingly; and

   'the relevant enactments' means:

   (a) as respects England and Wales, section 53(2) of the Children and Young Persons Act 1933;

   (b) as respects Scotland, sections 205 and 206 of the Criminal Procedure (Scotland) Act 1975;

(c) as respects Northern Ireland, section 73(2) of the Children and Young Persons Act (Northern Ireland) 1968.

(6) This section does not apply in relation to proceedings instituted before its commencement.

26.– No right to bail for persons accused or convicted of committing offence while on bail

In Part I of Schedule 1 to the Bail Act 1976 (exceptions to right to bail for imprisonable offences):

(a) after paragraph 2, there shall be inserted the following paragraph: '2A. The defendant need not be granted bail if:

(a) the offence is an indictable offence or an offence triable either way; and

(b) it appears to the court that he was on bail in criminal proceedings on the date of the offence'; and

(b) in paragraph 9, after the words 'paragraph 2' there shall be inserted the words 'or 2A'.

27.– Power for police to grant conditional bail to persons charged

(1) Part IV of the Police and Criminal Evidence Act 1984 (detention of persons, including powers of police to grant bail) shall have effect with the following amendments, that is to say, in section 47 (bail after arrest):

(a) in subsection (1), for the words after 'in accordance with' there shall be substituted the words 'section 3, 3A, 5 and 5A of the Bail Act 1976 as they apply to bail granted by a constable'; and

(b) after subsection (1) there shall be inserted the following subsection:

'(1A) The normal powers to impose conditions of bail shall be available to him where a custody officer releases a person on bail under section 38(1) above (including that subsection as applied by section 40(10) above) but not in any other cases.

In this subsection, 'the normal powers to impose conditions of bail' has the meaning given in section 3(6) of the Bail Act 1976'.

(2) Section 3 of the Bail Act 1976 (incidents including conditions of bail in criminal proceedings) shall be amended as follows:

(a) in subsection (6), the words '(but only by a court)' shall be omitted;

(b) at the end of subsection (6) there shall be inserted:

'and, in any Act, "the normal powers to impose conditions of bail" means the powers to impose conditions under paragraph (a), (b) or (c) above';

(c) after subsection (9), there shall be inserted the following subsection:

'(10) This section is subject, in its application to bail granted by a constable, to section 3A of this Act.'

(3) After section 3 of the Bail Act 1976 there shall be inserted the following section:

3A.– Conditions of bail in case of police bail [see above]

28.– Police detention after charge

(1) Section 38 of the Police and Criminal Evidence Act 1984 (which requires an arrested person charged with an offence to be released except in specified circumstances) shall be amended as follows.

(2) In subsection (1) (a), for sub-paragraphs (ii) and (iii) there shall be substituted the following sub-paragraphs:

'(ii) the custody officer has reasonable grounds for believing that the person arrested will fail to appear in court to answer to bail;

(iii) in the case of a person arrested for an imprisonable offence, the custody officer has reasonable grounds for believing that the detention of the person arrested is necessary to prevent him from committing an offence;

(iv) in the case of a person arrested for an offence which is not an imprisonable offence, the custody officer has reasonable grounds for believing that the detention of the person arrested is necessary to prevent him from causing physical injury to any other person or from causing loss of or damage to property;

(v) the custody officer has reasonable grounds for believing that the detention of the person arrested is necessary to prevent him from interfering with the administration of justice or with the investigation of offences or of a particular offence; or

(vi) the custody officer has reasonable grounds for believing that the detention of the person arrested is necessary for his own protection;'.

(3) After subsection (2), there shall be inserted the following subsection:

'(2A) The custody officer, in taking the decisions required by subsection (1)(a) and (b) above (except (a)(i) and (vi) and (b)(ii)), shall have regard to the same considerations at those which a court is required to have regard to in taking the corresponding decisions under paragraph 2 of Part I of Schedule 1 to the Bail Act 1976.'

(4) After subsection (7), there shall be inserted the following subsection:

'(7A) In this section "imprisonable offence" has the same meaning as in Schedule 1 to the Bail Act 1976.'

29. – Power for police to arrest for failure to answer to police bail

(1) Part IV of the Police and Criminal Evidence Act 1984 (detention of persons, including powers of police to grant bail) shall be amended as follows.

(2) After section 46 there shall be inserted the following section:

'46A.– Power of arrest for failure to answer to police bail

(1) A constable may arrest without a warrant any person who, having been released on bail under this Part of this Act subject to a duty to attend at a police station, fails to attend at that police station at the time appointed for him to do so.

(2) A person who is arrested under this section shall be taken to the police station appointed as the place at which he is to surrender to custody as soon as practicable after the arrest.

(3) For the purpose of:

(a) section 30 above (subject to the obligation in subsection (2) above); and

(b) section 31 above,

an arrest under this section shall be treated as an arrest for an offence.'

(3) In section 34 after subsection (6), there shall be inserted the following subsection:

'(7) For the purposes of this Part of this Act a person who returns to a police station to answer to bail or is arrested under section 46A below shall be treated as arrested for an offence and the offence in connection with which he was granted bail shall be deemed to be that offence.'

(4) In consequence of the foregoing amendments:

(a) in section 37(1), paragraph (b) shall be omitted;

(b) in sections 41(9), 42(11) and 43(19), at the end, there shall be inserted the words; 'but this subsection does not prevent an arrest under section 46A below.';

(c) in section 47, subsection (5) shall be omitted;

(d) in section 47(6), for the words 'is detained under subsection (5) above' there shall be substituted the words 'who has been granted bail and either has attended at the police station in accordance with the grant of bail or has been arrested under section 46A above is detained at a police station'; and

(e) in section 47(7), at the end, there shall be inserted the words; 'but this subsection does not apply to a person who is arrested under section 46A above or has attended a police station in accordance with the grant of bail (and who accordingly is deemed by section 34(7) above to have been arrested for an offence).'

(5) This section applies whether the person released on bail was granted bail before or after the commencement of this section.

30.– Reconsideration of decisions granting bail

After the section 5A of the Bail Act 1976 inserted by Schedule 3 to this Act there shall be inserted the following section:

'5B Reconsideration of decisions granting bail

(1) Where a magistrates' court has granted bail in criminal proceedings in connection with an offence, or proceedings for an offence, to which this section applies or a constable has granted bail in criminal proceedings in connection with proceedings for such an offence, that court or the appropriate court in relation to the constable may, on application by the prosecutor for the decision to be reconsidered:

(a) vary the conditions of bail;

(b) impose conditions in respect of bail which has been granted unconditionally; or

(c) withhold bail.

(2) The offences to which this section applies are offences triable on indictment and offences triable either way.

(3) No application for the reconsideration of a decision under this section shall be made unless it is based on information which was not available to the court or constable when the decision was taken.

(4) Whether or not the person to whom the application relates appears before it, the magistrates' court shall take the decision in accordance with section 4(1) (and Schedule 1) of this Act.

(5) Where the decision of the court on a reconsideration under this section is to withhold bail from the person to whom it was originally granted the court shall:

    (a) if that person is before the court, remand him in custody; and

    (b) if that person is not before the court, order him to surrender himself forthwith into the custody of the court.

(6) Where a person surrenders himself into the custody of the court in compliance with an order under subsection (5) above, the court shall remand him in custody.

(7) A person who has been ordered to surrender to custody under subsection (5) above may be arrested without warrant by a constable if he fails without reasonable cause to surrender to custody in accordance with the order.

(8) A person arrested in pursuance of subsection (7) above shall be brought as soon as practicable, and in any event within 24 hours after his arrest, before a justice of the peace for the petty sessions area in which he was arrested and the justice shall remand him in custody.

In reckoning for the purposes of this subsection any period of 24 hours, no account shall be taken of Christmas Day, Good Friday or any Sunday.

(9) Magistrates' court rules shall include provision:

    (a) requiring notice of an application under this section and of the grounds for it to be given to the person affected, including notice of the powers available to the court under it;

    (b) for securing that any representations made by the person affected (whether in writing or orally) are considered by the court before making its decision; and

    (c) designating the court which is the appropriate court in relation to the decision of any constable to grant bail.'.

How these powers will operate has been addressed by Clifford Williams in the following article.

Clifford Williams, 'New bail powers for custody officers' (1995) 145 NLJ 685

Sections 25 to 30 of the Criminal Justice and Public Order Act (CJPO) 1994 make substantial changes to bail provisions and provide police custody officers with much the same authority as the courts in imposing conditions on bail. These changes came into effect on April 10, 1995 along with other sections of the CJPO and the revised (2nd revision) Police and Criminal Evidence Act (PACE) Codes of Practice. Custody officers now need to go through a series of decision making steps in order to determine whether to bail with or without conditions, or keep detained persons in custody for court. Furthermore, persons released on bail by the police with conditions can request, after they have been bailed, that their conditions be altered. This request can be made to a custody officer at the police station from which they were bailed, or to the court to which they are due to surrender (Sched 3(3) CJPO).

Police forces have been busily preparing for the changes and, in particular, training custody officers in their new responsibilities. In order to understand the series of decision making steps brought about by the new legislation, please refer to the flow chart 'Bail Provisions for Police Officers' (see p 686).

Following a charge, s 38 of PACE 1984 requires the custody officer to release a person from detention unless certain criteria apply. These are listed in s 38(1) PACE and this list is altered by s 28 of the CJPO. On April 10, 1995 the criteria were widened. Added to the list is 'the case of a person arrested for an imprisonable offence' where the 'custody officer has reasonable grounds for believing that the detention of the person arrested is necessary to prevent him from committing an offence'. This is much wider than the previous 'to prevent him from causing physical injury to any other person or from causing loss or damage to property'. Indeed, the new criteria state 'committing an offence', which could be driving with no vehicle excise licence, failing to keep a dog on a lead, etc, and although the person needs to have been arrested for an imprisonable offence, he could have been charged with a non-imprisonable or minor offence. The previous criteria 'to prevent him from causing physical injury'/'loss of or damage to property' are retained but in reference to persons arrested for non-imprisonable offences. The custody officer will consider if any of the criteria in s 38(1) apply. If none of the criteria apply he should release on unconditional bail. He cannot impose conditions unless first the criteria for refusing bail are met. (Bail Act 1976, s 3A(5), as amended by s 27(3) CJPO.) If the custody officer decides that the charged person's detention is necessary for his own protection, or additionally, in the case of a juvenile, in his own interests, he can refuse bail. In these circumstances the Bail Act 1976 does not allow conditions to be imposed and the detained person will be kept in detention for the next court. Juveniles will be transferred to local authority accommodation in accordance with s 38(6) PACE 1984. If the custody officer doubts whether a name or address given by the person charged is their real name or address, or their name or address cannot be ascertained, then bail can be refused and no conditional bail is available. Whereas it is clear that in this situation granting conditional bail would not solve the problem of identity, in the case of detaining for a person's own protection or interests, conditional bail might ensure they reside at a safe location, for example. This might seem fairer than keeping them in detention; however, conditional bail is not allowed in such circumstances. Section 25 CJPO adds a further set of criteria where bail shall be refused. No bail shall be given where a person has been charged with murder, rape or manslaughter (or attempted murder or rape) and that person has previously been convicted of such an offence or of culpable homicide. Having examined those cases where no bail is granted and no conditional bail is possible, let us go on to look at the other cases where s 38 PACE allows the custody officer to refuse bail. Where the custody officer has reasonable grounds for believing that:

(i) a person will fail to appear in court to answer bail; or detention is necessary to prevent:

(ii) the commission of a further offence on bail;

(iii) causing injury to another or loss of or damage to property;

(iv) interference with the administration of justice or with the investigation of an offence/s; the custody officer will then have to consider, in a like manner to the courts, the considerations in Sched 1, Part 1, para 2 of the Bail Act 1976.

That is, are there substantial (not just reasonable) grounds for believing that if the person charged was released on bail (with or without conditions) they would:

(i) fail to surrender to custody; or

(ii) commit an offence on bail; or

(iii) interfere with witnesses or otherwise obstruct the course of justice.

If there are, then bail can be refused. If, however, the imposition of conditions would secure surrender to custody, that an offence is not committed, or that there is no interference with witnesses or obstruction of the course of justice, then conditions which are necessary to secure such aims can be imposed by the custody officer (s 27(3) CJPO). No conditions can be imposed other than to secure such aims (Bail Act 1976, s 3A(5) (as amended)). A security may be required if 'it appears that the "person charged" is unlikely to remain in Great Britain until the time appointed for him to surrender to custody' (Bail Act 1976, s 3(5)). A security may take any form. This is not a change in legislation as the police had the power to require a security prior to the changes.

In addition, the requirement to provide a surety or sureties (Bail Act 1976, s 3(4)) is not a change in legislation. Now conditions may be in addition to or instead of a security or surety. There are few restrictions on the conditions custody officers can impose. They are not able to make a condition requiring a person to reside in a bail hostel or probation hostel. Any conditions that are imposed need to be enforceable. Home Office Circular 206/1977 provided courts with guidance on imposing conditions. These guidelines are still of value. If bail is granted with conditions the reasons for those conditions shall be recorded in the custody record and the person bailed provided with a copy of the reasons. This will normally be made out on a bail condition form similar to those in use throughout the courts. Once bailed with conditions from the police station, a person can request either of the police or the court that his bail conditions be varied. If this request is to the police it shall be to a custody officer serving at the same police station where bail was granted. It is not clear whether the application needs to be in person. If such a request is made, the custody officer may impose varied or more onerous conditions or cancel the conditions. He cannot, however, alter the court date or venue. If the person bailed with conditions applies to the court (under s 43B Magistrates' Courts Act 1980 (as amended by Sched 3 CJPO)) or a person is bailed by the court, he cannot then make a request to the police for any change to those conditions. As well as the person charged applying for reconsideration of bail conditions, the prosecution can apply for a variation of conditions or to withhold bail or impose conditions on persons granted unconditional bail. Section 30 CJPO allows this for offences which are indictable and where information was 'not available to the court or constable when the decision (to bail) was taken'. Section 26 CJPO allows the court to deny bail where the offence is indictable and 'it appears to the court that he was on bail in criminal proceedings on the date of the offence'. Aimed at the 'bail bandits', use of this section could substantially increase the remand prisoner population. It is interesting to note, however, that s 26 CJPO does not extend to a custody officer's right to refuse bail, although the commission of an offence whilst on bail could be reasonable grounds for believing detention is necessary to prevent someone committing an offence.

Finally, s 29 CJPO grants the police a power to arrest persons who fail to answer police bail (those under a duty to attend at a police station). The proviso contained in s 29(4)(d) CJPO means, however, that anyone so arrested will have included in their detention period any time spent in police detention prior to being granted the 'original' bail. As the person arrested for failing to answer bail 'shall be taken to the police station appointed as the place to which he is to surrender to custody as soon as practicable after the arrest' this would seem to preclude the person being dealt with at a place other than that to which they were to surrender. Complications may arise, especially in larger police force areas, especially where the time spent in custody prior to release on police bail will bring the person near to the limit of detention (s 41 PACE). For example, a person arrested in Exeter for failing to answer police bail was due to surrender to Penzance Police Station (same police area). He is taken to the police station at Exeter, his custody time clock restarts and he still has the journey to Penzance to go (120 miles). Police officers could 'save on the clock' by taking him directly to Penzance. The legislation would seem to preclude the person being dealt with at Exeter. These substantial changes come at a time of great change in the procedure and administration of justice. Custody officers and courts will require up-to-date details of pending cases and convictions when reaching decisions in relation to bail. This up-to-date information should be available through the enhanced Police National Computer Phoenix System due to come into operation some time this summer. With the conditional bail provisions available to the police, one might anticipate fewer 'overnight' prisoners appearing at courts after charge, but with the overall targeting of 'bail bandits' (eg s 26 CJPO) one would rather anticipate more remands into custody.

Bail after the Human Rights Act 1998

In the following piece John Burrow considers the extent to which the Human Rights Act (HRA) 1998, the European Convention on the Protection of Human Rights and Fundamental Freedoms (the Convention) and the precedents from the European Court of Human Rights (ECtHR) will affect bail decisions in this country.

The UK has been a signatory to the Convention since 1950. But it is the advent of the HRA 1998, which came into force in October 2000, which has brought its provisions directly into UK law.

John Burrow, Bail and the Human Rights Act 1998 (2000) 150 NLJ 677

Under the HRA, primary and subordinate legislation must be read and given effect as far as it is possible to do so, in a way that is compatible with the Convention (ss 2 and 3). It will be unlawful for public authorities, (which include courts of law) to act in a way which is incompatible with the Convention (s 6). Under the HRA an individual can rely on a Convention right in any legal proceedings (s 7(1)(b)).

In bail proceedings, therefore, courts will have a duty to interpret the Bail Act 1976 as far as possible in a way that is compatible with the Convention, and their decisions to grant or withhold hail must accord with Convention rights. Individual defendants can of course rely upon their Convention rights in bail proceedings.

The relevant Convention rights are contained in Art(s) 3(1)(c), 5(3), 5(4) and 6(2). Article 5(l)(c) provides:

1 Everyone has the right to liberty and security of person. No one shall be deprived of his liberty save in the following cases and in accordance with a procedure prescribed by law.

   (c) the lawful arrest or detention of a person effected for the purpose of bringing him before the competent legal authority on reasonable suspicion of having committed an offence or when it is reasonably considered necessary to prevent his committing an offence or fleeing after having done so.

Article 5(3) provides:

3 Everyone arrested or detained in accordance with the provisions of paragraph 1(c) of this Article shall be brought promptly before a judge or other officer authorised by law to exercise judicial power and shall be entitled to trial within a reasonable time or to release pending trial. Release may be conditioned by guarantees to appear for trial.

Article 5(4) provides:

1 Everyone who is deprived of his liberty by arrest or detention shall be entitled to take proceedings by which the lawfulness of his detention shall be decided speedily by a court and his release ordered if the detention is not lawful.

Article 6(2) provides:

2 Everyone charged with a criminal offence shall be presumed innocent until proven guilty.

These basic rights have been considered and interpreted by the ECtHR in an extensive body of jurisprudence. Over the years principles have emerged which have been applied vigorously and consistently by the Court. By s 2 of the 1998 Act, a UK court must take these decisions into account in any judgment or decision.

General principles

The purpose of Art 5 is to protect the individual from arbitrariness.

Judicial control of interferences by the executive with the individual's right to liberty is an essential feature of the guarantee embodied in Art 5(3), which is intended to minimise the risk of arbitrariness. *Brogan v UK* 11 EHRR 117.

In the first instance arbitrariness is to be safeguarded by domestic 'procedure prescribed by law' (Art 5(1)), but the ECtHR adopts a supervisory jurisdiction and will consider first whether the domestic court has complied with its own legal provisions *and* whether those provisions are compatible with the Convention. Frequently the ECtHR affords little or no 'margin of appreciation' in their decisions on bail matters.

The Court always adopted a strict approach to reviewing compliance with Art 5, tending to limit the length of pre-trial detention: *W v Switzerland* A/254 (1993) 17 EHRR 60. Dissenting judgment of Judge Pettiti.

The question which the ECtHR considers is the 'reasonableness' of the decision to arrest and detention.

The reasonableness of the suspicion on which an arrest must be based forms an essential part of the safeguard against arbitrary arrest and detention which is laid down in Art 5(3): *Fox, Campbell and Hartley v UK* A182 (1990), 13 EHRR 157.

A defendant must not he held for more than a 'reasonable time'. The ECtHR declines to specify what a reasonable time is in terms of weeks, months or years. The Court will look at the reasonableness of the grounds advanced by the prosecuting authority. These must be set out by the domestic court: *Stogmuller v Germany* A/9 (1969) 1 EHRR 155.

What is reasonable will, of course, depend to some extent on the facts of the case, but there are a number of clear principles which the court will follow in assessing reasonableness

(a) Presumption of innocence

The first and most important of these and, the starting point for all pre-trial remand decisions, is the presumption of innocence. Set out in the Convention itself at Art 6(2), it is difficult to over-emphasise the importance which the ECtHR attaches to this principle. The principle pervades all aspects of the Court's review of the decision to remand in custody.

Article 5(3) enshrines the right to liberty pending trial. The presumption of innocence which is demanded by Art 6 is no empty formula. It is a very real thing and not simply a procedural rule taking effect only at the trial: *W v Switzerland* A/254 (1993) 17 EHRR 60. Dissenting judgments of Judges Walsh and Loizou.

Article 5 is an article which protects personal freedom and limits pre-trial detention. Article 5 in combination with Art 6 is an important provision of the convention for protecting the presumption of innocence. In interpreting Art 5 and the nature of pre-trial detention it must he born in mind that liberty is the rule, detention is the exception. Provisional or pre-trial detention must not damage the presumption of innocence: *W v Switzerland* A/254 (1993) 17 EHRR 60. Dissenting judgment of Judge Pettiti.

It falls in the first place to the national judicial authorities to ensure that, in a given case, the detention if an accused person pending trial does not exceed a year's time. To this end they must examine all the facts arguing for or against the existence of a genuine requirement of public interest justifying, with due regard to the principle of presumption of innocence, a departure from the rule of respect for individual liberty: *Mansur v Turkey* A/319-B (1995) 20 EHRR 505.

(b) Relevant and sufficient

The second principle is that 'reasonableness' will be judged according to whether there were 'relevant' and 'sufficient' reasons to remand in custody. 'There must be "relevant and sufficient" reasons to justify his continued detention. The detention on remand must not be prolonged beyond a reasonable time': *Wemhoff v Germany* (1968) 1 EHRR 55.

Relevance

The ECtHR has identified a number of factors which may be relevant in justifying detention, at least for a period of time. These include:

- absconding;
- interference with witnesses;

- committing further offences;
- a need for further investigation;
- disturbance to public order and
- defendant's own protection.

These factors are considered further in Part II of this article. The ECtHR has held that a number of other factors are or should be irrelevant to the bail decision, particularly when taken alone. These include:

- the strength of the evidence alone, particularly after some lapse of time;
- the seriousness of the offence alone.

Further offending cannot automatically be assumed from previous convictions.

The ECtHR's concern is to ensure there is no automatic refusal of bail merely because, for instance the offence is a serious one. The primacy (if the presumption (if innocence dictates that bail should only be refused after careful consideration of all relevant factors.

Sufficiency

Not every relevant factor will justify detention. The Court will also consider whether the relevant factor is sufficient in its weight to justify the remand in custody. For example, the risk of absconding is a matter which can properly be taken into account, but in many cases this has been held not to carry sufficient weight to justify a remand in custody. Frequently, a relevant factor may carry sufficient weight to justify a remand in custody in the early stages, but later may become insufficient.

(c) Evidence

The consideration of pre-trial custody must be carried out on *proper evidence*. That is to say there must be proper and sufficient evidence before a remand in custody can occur. If there is no *evidence* then there can be no remand in custody. There can be no substitution for objective evidence by judicial speculation or intuition.

> Judges deciding applications for provisional release from custody are expected to decide on evidence the issues raised. There should be no place for judicial speculation or judicial intuition as a substitute for objective evidence. The issues involved should be judged by the same objective standard which is the basis of all other justiciable controversies: *W v Switzerland* A/254 (1993) 17 EHRR 60. Dissenting judgment of Judges Walsh and Loizou.

(d) The burden of proof

The burden of establishing one of the permissible grounds for refusing bail lies firmly on the prosecution. It is for the prosecution to show, for example, that an accused will abscond, it is not for the accused to show he will not.

> In interpreting Art 5 and the nature of pre-trial detention it must be born in mind that liberty is the rule, detention is the exception. *W v Switzerland* A/254 (1993) 17 EHRR 60. Judge Pettiti.

> One cannot reverse the burden of proof and require the detainee to prove that he will not abscond, a negative which is virtually impossible to prove: *W v Switzerland* A/254 (1993) 17 EHRR 60. Judge Pettiti.

(e) The standard of proof

The ECtHR has never directly stated what the standard of proof is in a criminal matter. This is true not just for the matter of pre-trial detention, but in criminal proceedings generally. In several cases the Court has spoken of a principle that: 'any doubt should benefit the accused', and in others there has been an indirect suggestion that the standard is 'beyond reasonable doubt'.

Whether the burden should be any less for pre-trial bail decisions remains presently unclear. It seems right that the same principle should apply throughout the proceedings. On the other hand, in respect of bail decisions the fact finder is dealing with future predictions rather than past fact, and for that reason a lesser burden might be appropriate. The Court's insistence on the supremacy of the presumption of innocence, on objective evidence and the rejection of judicial speculation suggests a high standard is required. And if the standard is not to be beyond reasonable doubt what is it to be – the balance of probabilities? This seems too low in view of the factors mentioned above. In the case of *Stogmuller v Germany* A/9 (1969) 1 EHRR 155, the ECtHR rejected a test which amounted to the balance of probabilities in respect of a fear of absconding, requiring a higher degree of evidence embracing a number of different factors. In respect of another ground – disturbance of the peace – the ECtHR has clearly sought a high standard:

> It must be based on facts capable of showing the accused release would actually disturb public order: *Kemmache v France* A/218 (1991) 14 EHRR 520.

The Law Commission Consultation Paper No 157, November 15, 1999 (the Law Commission) has suggested (para 3.22) that different standards of proof may be necessary in respect (if different grounds – higher for the defendant's own protection and disturbance to public order and lower for absconding. However, often the grounds are not considered individually but overlap one with the other, and differing standards of proof would create confusion and uncertainty.

(f) The dynamics of bail

Consideration of reasonableness includes both an assessment of whether it was reasonable to remand in custody *at all, and* whether it was necessary to remand the accused in custody for as long as he was in fact remanded. This is an important principle. What may be reasonable at the start of an investigation may, (and in the ECtHR decisions frequently does) become unreasonable after a period of time.

> A defendant must not be held for more than a 'reasonable time': *Stogmullerr v Germany* A/9 (1969) 1 EHRR 155.

> Until conviction an accused person must be presumed innocent and the purpose of Art 5(3) was essentially to require his provisional release once his continuing detention ceased to he reasonable: *Neumeister v Austria (No 71)* A/8 (1968) 1 EHRR 91.

For the ECtHR the issue of bail is never finally decided at any one point in the remand. What may be a correct decision at one point may be incorrect a week or two later. In the UK it will be necessary for both representatives and courts to keep bail under constant review in order to comply with the Convention.

> In the court's opinion the nature of detention on remand calls for reviews at short intervals: *Bezicheri v Italy* (1989) 12 EHRR 210.

For the ECtHR the mere passage of time can make continued detention unreasonable. For instance a number of cases talk of the likelihood of absconding decreasing with the passage of time, as time served in remand eats into any eventual prison sentence and removes the fear of imprisonment.

It is questionable therefore whether the restriction under s 154 of the Criminal Justice Act 1988 (inserting Part A into Sch I to the Bail Act 1976) meets the letter or the spirit of Art 5(3). Section 154 absolves magistrates' courts from hearing repeat arguments in bail applications unless there is a fresh argument as to fact or law. Few magistrates' courts accept that the mere passage of time can constitute a fresh argument as to fact.

The ECtHR does not accept that the need for continual monitoring of the bail position can be compromised because of the workload or inconvenience it entails.

> The Court notes that the Convention requires the Contracting States to organise their legal systems so as to enable the courts to comply with its various requirements: *Bezicheri v Italy* All 64 (1989) 12 EHRR 210.

Yet it was precisely this argument concerning the inconvenience of repeated bail applications which was the main justification for the Nottingham Justices decision and the later enactment of s 154.

The Law Commission (para 12.19) says that a refusal by a court to hear arguments put forward at a previous hearing may well infringe a defendant's rights under Art 5(4). They advise that courts should be given guidance that lapse of time itself should be treated as a fresh argument.

(g) Early disclosure

Frequently in the UK only limited disclosure is made in the earliest stages of a case. The defence advocate often knows only the barest facts of the allegation while the prosecution have access to the full file, often making bail applications ineffective. The ECtHR have established two important principles in this area. First, they have held that the principle of 'equality of arms' applies as much at the early pretrial stage of proceedings as it does to the trial itself, and secondly they have held that in order to comply with this principle there must be full disclosure even in the earliest stage of the case. Disclosure must be full and it must be made even if it is inconvenient to the prosecution to do so.

In the case of *Lamy v Belgium* 11 EFIRR 529 neither L nor his lawyer were allowed access to the investigation file during the first 30 days of custody. This prevented L from challenging during the first appearance before the *chambre de conseil* the confirmation of the arrest warrant. In effect this procedure decides whether a defendant is to be released or remanded in custody. After the first 30 days his lawyer, (but not him), was allowed access for 48 hours before each remand hearing. It is to be noted that even during the first 30 days Mr Lamy had:

- a copy of the arrest warrant which 'set out at length' the reasons for the arrest;
- been informed of the content of some if the police reports;
- heard the investigating judge's report read out at the first hearing;
- had filed two sets of pleadings during the early hearings.

The prosecution claimed that:

- under an inquisitorial system the investigation file was ongoing and was and should be secret;
- there were logistical difficulties in disclosing the investigating file to the defence while it was being worked on;
- photocopying all the documents was impossible in practice.

None of the prosecution arguments prevailed. The court held that the failure to disclose or grant access to the file in the first 30 days – in particular for the first appearance when the confirmation of the arrest warrant was considered – effectively prevented the defendant from challenging the reasons relied on to remand in custody. The procedure failed to ensure equality of arms, it was not truly adversarial, and breached Art 5(4).

If courts ... are to meet their duties under the Convention in this respect, new procedures must be put in place to ensure that the defence have all relevant papers from a much

(h) Written record of reasons

The fifth principle is that there must be a full court record made of the bail decision. Despite the requirements of ss 5(3) and 5(4) of the Bail Act 1976, magistrates seldom give fully reasoned bail decisions. Still less is the recorded decision fully set out in the court record. Indeed s 5(4) only requires a 'note' to be made. Instead there is commonly a proforma decision sheet which is ticked in the various decision boxes. This practice is not acceptable to the ECtHR. The reason for this is that the ECtHR has to form a judgment as to whether an accused has been held in custody for more than a 'reasonable time'. To form this judgment the court will look first and foremost at the reasons given by the domestic court for the remand in custody. If these reasons are mere stereotyped phrases repeated time and time again on successive hearings they are highly likely to be struck down as unreasonable. United Kingdom courts will therefore be expected to record fully argued reasons for the refusal of hail. Furthermore, these reasons must take into account arguments put forward by the defendant. This approach has been adopted by the Law Commission (para 4.25) where it has said that decisions should be recorded in such a way as to clearly indicate how a decision has been reached.

> It was for the national judicial authorities to seek all the facts arguing for or against the existence of a genuine requirement of public interest justifying a departure from the rule of respect for individual liberty. It was essentially on the basis of the reasons given in the decisions on the applications for release pending trial, and of the true facts mentioned by the applicant in his appeals, that the court was called upon to decide whether or not there had been a violation of the convention: *Neumeister v Austria* (No) A/8 (1968)1 1771 IRR V 91.

It is essentially on the basis of the reasons given in these decisions and of the true facts mentioned by the applicant in his appeals, that the ECtHR is called upon to decide whether or not there has been a violation of Art 5(3). Here the decisions were expressed in stereotyped form and gave no reasons – 'the nature of the offence' and 'the state of the evidence': *Mansur v Turkey* A/319-B (1995) 20 ECtHR 535.

In the case of *Clouth v Belgium* A225 (1991) 14 ECtHR 198-C was charged with murder. He gave 11 different accounts of where he was on the day of the killing.

There was a very extensive police investigation. The domestic court had used a stereotyped formula 'the requirements of the investigation' to justify the refusal of bail. The ECtHR said 'where the needs of the investigation are invoked in such a general and abstract fashion they do not suffice to justify the continuation of detention'.

It is likely that the current pro-forma forms are inadequate to meet the ECtHR requirements. The Law Commission says (para 4.21) that a refusal of bail recorded in standard form is in danger of being held to violate Art 5 and, (para 4.25) that magistrates and judges should be given training on making and recording their decision-making in such a way as to clearly indicate how their decisions have been reached.

Conclusion

UK courts, therefore, considering bail applications under the HRA, will have to adopt a new approach. It will not just be a matter of considering whether there are 'substantial grounds' for believing one of the exceptions to bail is made out. Courts will have to consider and give weight to the principle of the presumption of innocence. They will have to ensure the presumption informs their entire hail decision. They will have to consider whether there really is relevant and sufficient objective evidence which justifies a departure from the right to liberty. There must be no judicial speculation. And judges and magistrates will have to show a greater willingness to keep the situation under review by allowing applications at regular intervals covering all aspects of the case throughout the period of remand, accepting that the passage of time is a relevant consideration. Fully argued decisions will have to be given, which must incorporate the defendants own arguments and these decisions will have to be fully recorded.

CHAPTER 9

LEGAL SERVICES

This chapter covers the services provided through the Legal Services Commission, the Community Legal Service, the public defender service, the key themes surrounding the work of solicitors and barristers, conditional fee arrangements (no win, no fee arrangements), the future of the legal professions, rights of advocacy and the liability of advocates.

Legal services have undergone very significant change in recent times. Expanded rights of advocacy for solicitors and others (including patent agents) have changed the traditional picture of the courts as the domain of barristers. The introduction of the Legal Services Commission and the Community Legal Service marks a sea-change in the delivery of publicly funded law, and the move to a public defender system carries the potential for far reaching change for both the legal system and for the public as consumers of its services. The chapter is divided into five sections:

- publicly funded legal services;
- solicitors;
- conditional fee arrangements;
- barristers;
- liability of advocates.

PUBLICLY FUNDED LEGAL SERVICES

The first extract below sets out briefly the main institutions of the new legal scenery. The extract is followed by part of an article which explains why and how the old legal aid system was replaced.

From the Legal Services Commission website: www.legalservices.gov.uk, July 2001

The Legal Services Commission is an executive non-departmental public body created under the Access to Justice Act 1999 to replace the Legal Aid Board. It is responsible for the development and administration of two schemes in England and Wales:

The Community Legal Service, which from 1st April 2000 replaced the old civil scheme of legal aid, bringing together networks of funders (eg Local Authorities) and suppliers into partnerships to provide the widest possible access to information and advice.

The Criminal Defence Service which from 2nd April 2001 replaced the old system of criminal legal aid and provides criminal services to people accused of crimes.

eBusiness. The Legal Services Commission is committed to embracing the benefits e-Business offers. These benefits include improved levels of service and faster response times to our customers and suppliers. A pilot e-mail service has been introduced to explore the possibilities of using this type of communication. Our online reporting scheme for civil contracting is also being expanded. A pilot scheme for criminal contracted suppliers (SPOCC online) will begin in summer 2001. Updates and more information will continue to be published in Focus and on this site ...

What are Community Legal Service Partnerships?

To make it easier for you to get legal help and advice, the Community Legal Service is establishing Community Legal Service Partnerships (CLSPs). These Partnerships bring together organisations offering legal and advice services – such as solicitors in private practice, Citizens' Advice Bureaux, Law Centres, local authority in-house services and a host of other organisations. The Partnerships also include representatives of the Legal Services Commission, local authorities and other funders, and users, of legal and advice services. All the Partners act together to improve access to, and delivery of, legal and advice services in their local community. One of the ways they achieve this is by setting up and running referral networks. Effective referral is also one of the requirements of the CLS Quality Mark. The eventual aim is to have a Community Legal Service Partnership for every part of England and Wales, although in some areas they are not yet established. At the end of January 2001 there were 124 Community Legal Service Partnerships already active. Details of these CLSPs are available, and regularly updated, on the 'Just Ask!' website (www.justask.org.uk). Many more Community Legal Service Partnerships are planned and are at various stages of formation.

If you would like any information about Community Legal Services Partnerships in your area or would like to get involved, you should contact the Planning and Partnership teams in your nearest Legal Services Commission regional office. For general information, you can also contact the Planning & Partnership Development team at head office ...

The Criminal Defence Service

From 2nd April 2001 the Legal Services Commission will be responsible for administering the Criminal Defence Service, which will replace the old system of criminal legal aid. This section of the website has been created to enable you to locate information relating to criminal work easily throughout the site ...

Duty Solicitor Manual

A draft copy of this Manual has been issued for consultation and is available for review on the LSC website. This Manual is intended to provide guidance to the Commission's CDS staff on duty solicitor issues from 2nd April 2001. The Manual is available in the Consultation (criminal) section of the website.

Criminal Bills

Guidance in the form of a Costs Assessment Manual for Criminal Bills and a Criminal Bills update is available in the 'Guidance' section. The guidance applies to work done prior to the launch of the CDS on 2 April 2001 ...

Very High Cost Cases

Under the Legal Aid (Notification of Very High Cost Cases) Regulations 2000 firms are under an obligation to notify the Very High Cost Case unit of all new cases falling within the VHCC definition. From April 2001, the VHCC unit will have authority to contract for any new criminal cases where the trial is likely to last 25 days or more, or total defence costs are likely to be in excess of £150,000. Individual case contracts will become the only method of VHCC management in April 2002 when all VHCC cases will be managed this way.

—·—·—·—·—·—·—·—·—·—·—·—·—·—·—·—·—

The first government legal website offering legal help over the internet was launched in April 2000. The website, 'Justask!', accessible through digital television, games consoles such as Dreamcast, in supermarkets and on kiosks in railway stations, is the linchpin of the new Community Legal Service. This replaced the £800 m civil legal aid scheme in an overhaul that saw legal aid abolished for cases including some personal injury claims, neighbour disputes, conveyancing and wills.

The money saved instead finances the new Service, which consists of more than 6,000 solicitors' offices and advice centres working to contracts. People whose claims no longer qualify for public funds will pursue cases on a no win, no fee basis which can increase their fees by double if they win. Other reforms will ensure that winners recoup these extra fees from their opponent. The background to these innovations is dealt with in the following piece.

Gary Slapper, 'Modernising justice' [1999] SLRYB 81

The government's White Paper *Modernising Justice: the Government's plans for reforming legal services and the courts* was published at the end of last year. It proposes what would be, in effect, the most fundamental changes in the English legal system for over forty years.

The paper says:

> A fair and efficient justice system is a vital part of a free society. The criminal justice system exists to help protect us from crime, and to ensure that criminals are punished. The civil justice system is there to help people resolve their disputes fairly and peacefully. This Government has a radical programme of reform for the whole country. The justice system cannot be left out. We want a clearer, fairer, better system, that will make justice available to all the people.

The paper states that many people are put off getting help with legal problems, because the legal system is slow, expensive and difficult to understand. It proposes a new Community Legal Service that will ensure that 'people's needs are properly assessed, and that public money is targeted on the cases that need help most.'

Providing value for money in law is identified as a key aim of reform. The paper argues that taxpayers have, year on year been paying heavily legal aid, while fewer people have been helped. By introducing contracting for legal services (the franchise system) and abolishing restrictive practices, the government aims to increase competition among lawyers and help keep costs down. It says it will create new avenues to justice by extending conditional fees, and modernising court procedures.

The Community Legal Service

About £800 million a year is spent on lawyers' fees under the civil legal aid system. Another £150 million a year from local government, central government, charities and businesses is spent on the voluntary advice sector, including Citizens' Advice Bureaux, law centres and other advice centres. The government intends to set up a Legal Services Commission to take the lead in establishing a Community Legal Service to co-ordinate the provision of legal services in every region. The plan is to achieve control over the legal aid budget and to gradually change over to a system in which the governmental spending on legal aid and voluntary sector advice is managed from one fund.

The Legal Services Commission will manage the Community Legal Service fund, which will replace legal aid in civil and family cases.

Why replace civil legal aid?

The government argues as follows. Taxpayers spend £800 million a year through the civil legal aid system on buying legal services from lawyers for those who cannot afford to pay for themselves, and this system now needs radical change.

–   It is too heavily biased towards expensive court-based solutions to people's problems.

–   Despite a merits test, legal aid is sometimes used to fund cases that appear to be undeserving.

–   It is not possible to control spending effectively. From 1992–93 to 1997–98 spending on civil and family legal aid grew by 35% from £586 million to £793 million; but at the same time, the number of cases funded actually fell by 31% from 419,861 to 319,432.

–   Lawyers are paid according to the amount of work claimed for, so there is no incentive to handle cases quickly or work efficiently.

Who will do the work and who will qualify for help?

The Legal Services Commission will buy services for the public under contracts. Only lawyers and other providers with contracts will be able to work under the new scheme. This will enable budgets to be strictly controlled, will help to ensure quality of service, and will provide a basis for competition between different providers. The fund will be targeted on those people who are most in need of help, and on high-priority cases. There will be no absolute entitlement to help, and the fund will not be spent on cases which could be financed by other means, such as conditional fees. The Government does, however, intend to increase the number of people potentially eligible for advice and assistance under the scheme, to bring this into line with eligibility for representation. At the same time those who can afford to contribute towards their legal expenses will be required to do so.

How will the Government help people who do not qualify for help from the Community Legal Service fund?

It is clear that not everyone will benefit under the new scheme. In this context, the government states that it will work with the insurance industry to widen cover (it says that 17 million people are already covered by one sort of legal insurance or another, although this figure includes people entitled to legal services in respect of only one type of situation like a traffic accident or holiday disasters). It is also intended to widen the scope of the conditional fee system.

The Civil Courts

The Government is concerned to modernise and simplify court procedures wherever possible, and to reduce delay. The White Paper promises the production of a unified code of procedural rules, written in plain English, to replace the separate High Court and county court rules. There are to be 'pre-action protocols' setting standards and timetables for the initial stages of cases before they reach court. Judges will be expected to enforce the protocols strictly and to punish those who breach them. We shall also have a 3 track system for dealing with civil cases in court according to the value and complexity of the case.

- Most cases worth less than £5,000 will be dealt with informally by a district judge in the small claims procedure.

- Cases worth from £5,000 to £15,000 will be dealt with under a fixed timetable in the fast track procedure.

- Cases worth over £15,000, or which are unusually complex will be dealt with under a multi-track procedure, closely supervised by a judge and tailored to each case.

Appeals in civil cases will be reformed (to ensure that the appeal process is not clogged up with weak cases) by requiring parties to seek leave to appeal, and by allowing only one appeal to take place in normal circumstances.

Criminal Defence Service

The Government states that it will maintain the fundamental principle that those facing a criminal trial should not be afraid that lack of resources and proper representation might lead to their wrongful conviction. However, serious weaknesses in the current criminal legal aid system are identified:

> The cost has risen from £507 million in 1992–93 to £733 million in 1997–98 – an increase of 44%. At the same time the number of cases dealt with has increased by only 10%. Although standard fees are now paid in many cases, the most expensive cases are paid in the traditional way by calculating the bill after the event. This gives lawyers an incentive to boost their fees by dragging cases out, and these cases take up a disproportionate amount of money. The system for means testing defendants to see whether they should contribute to the costs of their case is a waste of time and money. The test has not stopped some apparently wealthy defendants from receiving free legal aid, and 94% of defendants in the Crown Court pay no contribution.

The Government intends to replace the current criminal legal aid scheme with a new Criminal Defence Service (CDS). To begin with, the CDS will be run, by the Legal Services Commission, but it will be an entirely separate scheme from the Community Legal Service, with a separate budget. The Commission will develop contracts for different types of criminal defence services and implement them following pilot schemes. All contracts for criminal defence services will include quality requirements, and wherever possible prices for the contracts will be fixed in advance. Fixed prices create an incentive to avoid delay, and reward efficient practice. Eventually, contracts with solicitors firms will cover the full range of defence services, from advice at the police station to representation in court. If a case requires the services of a specialist advocate in the Crown Court, this is likely to be covered by a separate contract. Opponents of this move argue that fixed-price work is not conducive to justice as such a system of payment encourages corner-cutting and work of an inferior standard.

Very complex and expensive cases – where the trial is expected to last 25 days or more – will not be covered by ordinary contracts. A defendant's choice of solicitor will be limited to firms on a specialist panel, and a separate contract will be agreed in each case.

Pressing questions here are whether the Government will introduce a salaried defender service, and, if so, whether client choice will be limited? The Government has stated that it believes that the CDS should be free in principle to employ lawyers directly to offer services to the public, as well as contracting with lawyers in private practice. The CDS will be expected to take account of the current pilot scheme involving public defence solicitors in Scotland. The government has also said that 'In most cases', suspects and defendants will be able to choose any lawyer who has a current contract with the CDS. The fact that lawyers have a contract will also be a guarantee that they have met the relevant quality standards. In very expensive cases, where special skills and experience are often needed, the defendant's choice will be limited to those lawyers who are on a special CDS panel and have demonstrated their ability to handle cases of this type.

Lawyers however have expressed fear at this proposal. The Law Society has said that famous campaigning lawyers such as Gareth Peirce (who helped release the Guildford Four and the Birmingham Six) and Jim Nicol (who represented the appellants in the Carl Bridgewater case) might be shunned by the CDS.

Who will decide whether to grant criminal representation, and how? As now, it will be for the court to decide whether to grant a defendant representation at public expense, according to the interests of justice. But the current requirement for a means test will be abolished. Instead, after a case is over, a judge in the Crown Court will have the power to order a convicted defendant to pay some or all of the costs of his defence. This will mean that assets frozen during criminal proceedings, and any assets which only come to light during proceedings, will be taken into account, so some wealthy criminals will pay much more than they do now.

— · — · — · — · — · — · — · — · — · — · — · — · — · — · — · —

The following two articles seek to evaluate the work of the Community Legal Service after it had been operating for one year. The first is from David Lock MP, Parliamentary Secretary to the Lord Chancellor's Department; the second is from Karen Mackay, Director of the Legal Action Group.

David Locke MP, 'The Community Legal Service one year on' (from a speech to the Society of Labour Lawyers) (2001) 151 NLJ 613

The idea for a Community Legal Service was first floated as long ago as 1968 when the Society of Labour Lawyers published a pamphlet about the need to develop Community Legal Services. Some 35 years on, the CLS is coming to the end of its first year; and more and more people are starting to realise just how radical the CLS is, and how it is transforming access to legal and advice services.

The Lord Chancellor's Department believes the CLS has a vital part to play in tackling social exclusion, as many of the problems faced by socially excluded communities and individuals eventually involve the legal process. The CLS will make it far easier for people to understand their rights and responsibilities, and enable them to resolve disputes, enforce their rights, or if necessary, seek the protection of the courts.

The CLS is challenging the traditional public perception of the legal world and lawyers and is introducing concepts such as quality marking, best value and priorities into the world of some private practice lawyers. It is a key part of the CLS that the concept of legal services is redefined so that they are relevant to all who believe in the importance of public services. The word 'community' in CLS must not be forgotten: these are services for the community – not just for an individual client who is being served with public money.

This year the Government expects to spend something in the order of £810 million on the Community Legal Service Fund. Over the next three years it will spend an average of £700 million each year-of which, around £232 million per year will be spent on Legal Help. This lower average expenditure over the next three years reflects the fact that personal injury is no longer within scope and substantial funds will flow into the legal aid coffers from settled personal injury cases. Until April 2000 about 64,000 legal aid certificates were granted each year (98/99 and 99/00) for personal injury cases. The legal services market has responded rapidly to the introduction of conditional fee agreements. The lack of legal aid has not affected claims going in to the insurers; and there is anecdotal evidence that general insurance premiums are taking the strain of an increased number of claims.

In addition, since April last year, the expenditure on national and local priorities has been refocused, through the letting of contracts and the introduction of the Funding Code. This has enabled more money to be released to support advice work within the CLS. With the increased money being spent on Legal Help, disputes can be resolved at an earlier stage without involving the courts – and, of course, thereby avoiding higher costs.

Through targeted funding and expansion packages – as well as the continued development of new and innovative methods of service delivery – we believe there are now sufficient contractors in almost all categories of law to ensure access to quality assured services across the country. A number of incentives have been introduced since April 2000 to encourage firms to expand their services in areas of law which have been targeted as priority areas for funding within the CLS – the first of which came when the Lord Chancellor announced details of the additional £46 million Legal Help package.

Eligibility is also a core issue in access to justice. Eligibility for public funding under the CLA is being reformed, and Legal Help eligibility limits will be increased to bring around five million more people into scope, and we've taken the decision not to introduce Legal Help contributions.

This means that these people will be able to receive advice entirely free of charge. We believe that it will also make the scheme easier for solicitors and advice agencies to administer – a further step towards cutting the mountain of bureaucracy associated with later legal aid. Legal Help limits will be increased to the same as those for Legal Representation, bringing a further two million people into scope.

A simplified means test has also been introduced, so that applicants need only supply a relatively small amount of information. This will make the means testing process more transparent and easier to understand. In addition, to avoid people on low incomes being deterred from applying for publicly funded legal services, it has been decided not to introduce contributions from equity.

The effect of these changes is that the package will cost an additional £30 million over the next three years. But the money can be released because of the spending controls in the system. These important changes will be implemented from October 1, 2001.

The CLS has developed strong local links in the past year with the community it serves, which are absolutely crucial if it is going to address the legal needs of each different local community. The Access to Justice Act placed a statutory duty on the LSC to establish, maintain and develop the CLS. This has meant that the LSC has had to actively engage with a wide range of people and organisations to make it a reality, and is why the new Community Legal Service Partnerships (CLSPs) are at the heart of what we are trying to achieve.

The CLSPs bring together all the local funders and providers of services so they can plan local provision on the basis of meeting local needs and priorities. The different partners come together to gain the benefits of pooling expertise and knowledge in order to do those things which are of mutual interest and concern. In a CLSP, funders get much better value for the money they spend on legal and advice services, and it will involve providers in the decision-making process, enabling much better informed decisions to be taken when allocating funding.

During the course of 1999, the concept of CLSPs was developed in a number of pioneer areas, which provided a solid evidential base to take forward the partnerships. By the time of the official launch in April 2000, there were already 70 CLSPs. Since then, the number of CLSPs has continued to grow in leaps and bounds; there are now 170 CLSPs covering 80% of the population of England and Wales.

Over the coming years CLSPs will become increasing influential as: they take on a greater role in funding decisions; increasingly help deliver the objectives of other Government Departments, such as the consumer advice initiative, neighbourhood renewal, and Connexions; and they take on a wider role through embracing family legal services.

It is important that the CLS is a policy with a strong empirical base. Professor Hazel Genn's research 'Paths to Justice', and the conclusions she reached in respect of legal needs and access to legal advice, have played a large part in the thinking on the CLS. The Legal Services Research Centre have, therefore, been commissioned to undertake a long-term research project to measure and characterise levels of legal need in England and Wales. The project will be known as the National Periodic Survey, and will be based on a detailed survey of 4,500 households. It should provide a rich source of data on justiciable problems, and help future development of policy. It is vital that the systems put in place in the CLS develop the capacity to collect and test information, and improve the evidence base for the future.

The CLS should also lead to innovation, and in many areas, it is already doing so. The new relationships formed through the CLS have unleashed new ideas and energy. This is to be encouraged – especially in the partnerships – and so at the end of 2000, the Lord Chancellor announced the setting up of a Partnership Innovation Budget (worth £15 million over the next three years). This money will produce new initiatives to help those communities that have been badly served by existing services, such as the socially excluded groups, and provide essential 'seedcorn' funding for new initiatives by the local partnerships.

Innovation is also essential if the fundamental problem of 'Advice Deserts' is to be successfully tackled. The local CLS Partnerships and the introduction of contracts in new methods of delivery by the LSC should help address this. The CLS encourages new ways of reaching clients who are put off by the traditional forms of service delivery or frightened to exercise their rights through pilots in telephone services, outreach services, and advice desks on county court possession days.

Of course, an essential part of encouraging new methods of delivery, through expansion of under-supplied services or providing new services, is remuneration. In addition to the increases made last year, and in order to safeguard the good range of quality assured legal firms in the CLS, a package of remuneration increases for family law and social welfare solicitors have been put forward. The increased rates are aimed at solicitors working in areas such as domestic violence, cases involving children's welfare and cases which are about helping people escape from social exclusion.

The package, which was implemented on April 2, 2001, includes increases of around 10% in legal help rates in most priority categories of law and the introduction of payments for file review. In order to encourage greater specialisation and expertise within publicly funded work, a further guaranteed minimum 15% enhancement for legal representation for solicitors who have achieved accreditation to either the Solicitor's Family Law Association Panel or the Law Society Children's Panel have been introduced.

New minimum levels of standards through the development of the CLS Quality Mark have also been agreed. By the end of the year, the public should have access to over 10,000 quality-assured organisations providing legal information and advice. The Quality Mark is also being developed to support the new and innovative methods of service delivery, and standards for telephone advice, websites and outreach services are now being designed. In addition, other organisations are being encouraged to adopt the Quality Mark – such as the Office of the Immigration Services Commissioner.

The CLS is also making excellent use of the Internet. The Just Ask! website makes use of information technology to disseminate information and advice and aims to support legal services on the ground by being available 24 hours a day. In doing so, it forms part of the Lord Chancellor's Department's commitment to using the opportunities presented by IT to deliver better and cheaper services which are responsive to customers' needs.

In summary, there has been a great deal of progress in the last year, and I am confident the Community Legal Service will go from strength to strength to strength in the future.

- - - - - - - - - - - - - - - - - - - -

Karen Mackay, 'Evaluating the Community Legal Service'
(2001) NLJ 615

On March 6, 2001, at a recent meeting of the Society of Labour Lawyers, David Lock, parliamentary secretary at the Lord Chancellor's Department, gave a comprehensive overview of the activities and future plans of the Community Legal Service (see NLJ pp 163–64). It is a year since the CLS was officially launched by the Lord Chancellor, with a new logo, a website, CLS directories covering the country and a new quality mark that covered for the first time services that were funded by local authorities or charities rather than just those funded by the Legal Aid Board. The Board itself was reinvented as the Legal Services Commission. At the time these changes seemed largely cosmetic: new names, new logos – a very New Labour project – but it was not clear what those changes would deliver.

One of the problems with the CLS has been its definition. It has been difficult to summarise exactly what it is and its purpose. One of the first appearances of the concept of a Community Legal Service was in the Labour party manifesto before the 1997 General Election, where there was simply a bald commitment to establish a 'community legal service' without any further elaboration. The Access to Justice Act, when it was published in December 1998, gave a broad outline of the CLS – including the rather circular description of the CLS – as a 'service ... for the purpose of promoting the availability to individuals of services ...'. The subsequent consultation paper on the CLS in May 1999 did not give any overall description of the CLS or its purpose. The CLS seems to defy a neat description because it is a hybrid being: it exists to fund services and to manage contracts and so has a direct role in ensuring services are available, but it also has the more nebulous role of promoting access to publicly funded legal services.

At its core, the CLS is still about civil legal aid. Under the new regime, the lion's share of money goes towards funding representation through lawyers in private practice, and the Legal Services Commission administration is concerned with processing more than one million acts of assistance, including civil certificates and legal help. Some 5,000 solicitors offices and not-for-profit agencies were issued with CLS contracts at the beginning of January 2000 and those numbers have not significantly reduced at the beginning of the second year of contracting. Around 300 of those contracts are with not-for-profit agencies. In the coming year, the size of the CLS fund will be more than £700 million. This level of funding still far outstrips that from charities, local authorities and other central government departments for advice services in the not-for-profit sector and local government.

However, the legal services system the CLS inherited was unco-ordinated, with no overall control or rationale. Funded by a variety of sources from local authorities, government departments and charities and made up of public sector, voluntary and private organisations, it had developed from a mix of market forces and the decisions of funders, rather than on the basis of any objective assessment of what was needed in the local community. This led to inconsistency in services, with some areas having generous provision while others had nothing. One of the primary objectives, therefore, of the CLS, in its role of promoting access to justice, is to bring together funders and providers to better co-ordinate local services, to identify legal needs and to meet gaps in services.

It is difficult to assess the extent to which this objective is being met. In New Labour terms, a more joined up way of working should operate to the advantage of clients, as well as service providers. Clients should be more readily referred to an appropriate service and the work should be done at the right level. That, at least, is the theory. However, there are problems with this. In a cash-limited environment, the incentives are different from those in the old demand led system. Like diary cows, clients may be assessed on their 'yield' for the practitioner. Private practice will not want to use up valuable case starts on cases that will not translate into higher paying work or on difficult, time consuming clients. Cherry picking will be inevitable, and where there are shortages of advisers, as there are in most areas of civil law, many clients may find it difficult to find an adviser or representative to take their case.

Funders will also find it easier to cherry pick. Anecdotal evidence suggests that some hard pushed local authorities are already seeing the advent of contracts from the Legal Services Commission as an opportunity to cut their funding to the not-for-profit sector, often despite the existence of a local CLS Partnership (CLSP). The Commission are then faced with a choice of increasing their funding to make up the shortfall – and running the risk that further cuts could be made – or maintaining their funding, which in effect becomes replacement funding for local authority money and no new resources are created. The lack of control that the CLS has over other funders in the system has the potential to blow large holes in the planning process, and the market forces which dominated the development of legal services under the old regime could be exchanged for the whims of other non-CLS funders. If the Government is serious about planning services, it needs to create a duty on local authorities to fund services in the CLS, at least to match the money put in by the Legal Services Commission.

Estimates vary, but there are probably around 2,500 non-CLS funded agencies in England and Wales, many of which provide services which are similar to or complement legal aid services. The CLS does not yet give us any real information about how those services are filling the gaps in CLS funded services. Nor do we have any information about the level of service those agencies are providing. Monitoring and evaluation remain problematic within the CLS. The CLSPs, together with the regional legal services committees, are pulling together information about likely legal need and priorities for legal services in their respective areas. However, this information is gathered to plan services, not to evaluate them. The Legal Services Commission intends to refine its tools for assessing local legal need, but there are no plans to monitor what the service is actually delivering and to whom.

As the CLS enters its second year it is vital that there is some monitoring and evaluation of what the CLS is delivering. Currently, we do not know what happens to those people who need publicly funded legal services. Case starts and numbers of certificates issued can be counted, but there are no means to register those who fail to access services. Unlike the NHS, there are no waiting lists of those who need legal help, but have not yet received it. As Hazel Genn pointed out in her study of how people access legal services, (Hazel Genn, *Paths to Justice: What People Do and Think About Going to Law* (1999)) many people with a legal problem who do not get help at an early stage frequently take no further steps, with the subsequent risk that their problem gets worse. It should be an aim of the CLS to reach those who fall outside the net of legal help, but without any means of finding out who those people are, it is difficult to devise any strategies to reach them.

In many areas of the country, certain areas of law have been designated 'low priority' because significant numbers of people are unlikely to have a problem in that area of law. Contracts, generally, are not let for these low priority areas, but this prioritisation has nothing to do with an assessment of the seriousness of the problem to the individual, who may not be able to access the services they need. Nor can the predictive needs models, used by the Commission to assess legal need, help to evaluate competing priorities. There is no information about how money from areas identified as low priority by the regional planning process may have been reallocated to those areas designated as high priority, nor about whether local authorities are funding new services to meet identified gaps. Without this kind of information it is difficult to assess how the CLS is performing and the extent to which it is meeting needs for legal services and filling the advice gaps identified by the planning and assessment process.

It is also difficult to see behind the figures for the CLS. Expenditure on the CLS was generous for its first year: an estimated £810 million. However, we are now told that next year, in 2001/02, expenditure will be reduced by around £100 million. This, David Lock explained, is because in future years there will be better reconciliation of monthly payments against bills submitted and the Commission will continue to recoup payments for settled personal injury cases, while not taking on any funding for new personal injury cases. There is a lack of transparency in the figures which make it difficult to assess where the money is actually going in the CLS. We have headline figures; but it is not clear where the additional funds to pay for increased remuneration and eligibility will be coming from, or whether there will be any more money for new case starts or more contracts.

Some evaluation of whether the CLS is achieving its basic targets is needed. There is a lack of clear and understandable information about the impact and performance of the CLS. In the field of criminal contracting, the Commission have offered to establish a contract monitoring body in conjunction with the Law Society and practitioner groups. Clearly there is a need for this kind of oversight for criminal contracts, where the failure to let sufficient contracts in a particular area could result in a breach of Art 6 of the Human Rights Convention. However, there is no proposal for a similar oversight of civil contracts and the operation of the CLS.

The lack of an independent means of scrutinising the operation of the CLS is disturbing. Although the CLS is based on local partnerships, those only operate at a local level, and have a very limited view of the CLS. They do not go outside their own geographic area, nor can they look at other issues, such as the operation of new services or the administration of legal aid. Arguably there should be an independent inspectorate for the Legal Services Commission overall, given the scope and range of its responsibilities for both criminal and civil legal aid, but, failing that, at the very least there should be an independent monitoring body made up of the national organisations which have an interest in the progress of the CLS, which can evaluate whether the CLS is delivering the services it should.

—·—·—·—·—·—·—·—·—·—·—·—·—·—·—·—·—

Another branch of publicly-funded law is the Salaried Defence Service. The following extract explains the background to recent developments.

Gary Slapper, 'The Salaried Defence Service' (2001) 32 SLR 29

Plans for the new Salaried Defence Service (SDS) are now more than under way. The easiest way to comprehend this new institution is to see it as a counterpart to the Crown Prosecution Service, in other words an organisation of lawyers who are paid a salary by the state in order to defend defendants – whereas the CPS is the same thing but with the purpose of prosecuting defendants. Adverts recently appeared in the legal press seeking six lawyers to be the 'pioneers of a radical far reaching initiative', and the Legal Services Commission (LSC) is now interviewing candidates selected from more than 100 applicants.

The Service in its pilot stage will comprise six offices with at least three opening in April 2001. The proposals are causing some concern in the solicitors' branch of the legal profession, especially among those smaller firms, which currently pay their lawyers in private practice to do criminal defence work. The worry is that if the SDS became established nationally then criminal defence lawyers in private practice would be lured into the large institution – which looks like paying more than private practice. The SDS salaries are set to go up to £50,000 and in practice many people currently on £25,000 in a private firm look like being able to make a £10,000 leap in their salary by joining the SDS. Peter Binning, a former Crown Prosecutor, has identified a problem in this area – that of working for public organisations such as the CPS. He says that 'the professional integrity of the individual lawyer is subsumed to the organisation's priorities.' (*Gazette*, 16 November, 2000, p 29) There are other objections in principle to the Public Defenders Scheme. The State arrests, prosecutes and sentences individuals involved in the criminal justice system. For the state to purport to defend that individual will allow a breeding ground for miscarriages of justice, according to the Criminal Courts Solicitors Association. Some solicitors have been wary about the development of a 'canteen culture' where deals are struck between Crown Prosecutors and Public Defenders over a coffee in the morning. Both lawyers would be on a salary and a pension and neither would want to rock the boat.

--- · --- · --- · --- · --- · --- · --- · --- · --- · --- · --- · ---

One potential difficulty in this area was squaring: (i) the right of a defendant under human rights legislation to be represented by a lawyer of his or her choice; and (ii) the concern of the Government that defendants should not be able to try always to choose the most expensive and experienced lawyers, irrespective of the type of case against them. The following extract from a Government paper explains the way it aims to proceed.

Lord Chancellor's Department, 'Criminal Defence Service: choice of representative consultation paper, the Government's conclusions', February 2001, www.open.gov.uk/lcd/consult/saldef/chrepresp.htm

General Background

6. The Government is committed to ensuring that the criminal justice system is fair and efficient and commands people's confidence. It should be sensitive to the needs of victims and witnesses, and to the public interest in the speedy and effective administration of justice. For a criminal justice system to be fair, people suspected of a criminal offence or facing criminal proceedings must receive legal advice and assistance in preparation of a case before a court, when the 'interests of justice' criteria require.

7. Defence lawyers play an essential part in this process. They have the role of protecting the interests of the suspect or defendant, ensuring that the prosecution proves its case and advising the defendant on the appropriate course of action. The provision of legal advice and assistance should help the defendant secure his rights and ensure that the process is effective and reduces unnecessary delay.

8. Under the Access to Justice Act 1999 the Legal Services Commission (the Commission) is required to secure the services of advice, assistance and representation through lawyers in private practice, or by providing them itself through salaried defenders employed by the Commission, or by organisations it sets up for that purpose. Therefore, from 2 April 2001, when the Criminal Defence Service comes into being and salaried defence schemes are established, solicitors under contract and salaried defenders will carry out all criminal work funded by the Commission. [Salaried defender schemes will be established in April 2001.]

9. The Government is committed to ensuring that legal representation through contracts for those suspected or accused of a criminal offence is of good quality. All lawyers working under contracts will be expected to meet quality assurance standards and will, where possible, cover the full range of services from arrest until the case is completed. It follows from this that choice of legal representative must be limited to those lawyers who pass the Commission's quality assurance audit. In more specialist cases (e.g. serious fraud) those firms which have the expertise to do that type of work may be few in number and the defendant's choice will be limited to those firms. These are referred to as 'Very High Cost Criminal Cases', because their defining feature is the length of trial and associated cost. Only firms that are members of a specialist panel will be able to undertake this work. The Government believes that the limitation in choice in this area is more than outweighed by the advantage to the suspect or defendant in having a representative capable of dealing effectively with the complexities of the case.

10. There must also be some restriction of choice to ensure that suspects and defendants do not change their representative without good cause. Unnecessary change is not in the interest of the suspect or defendant or other defendants in the case or the system of justice. Changes create delay and additional cost. But suspects and defendants must also be able to make a proper informed choice of representative; a proper balance has to be struck.

11. This document deals with the question of choice in 3 areas:

   * Advice and assistance and work done by solicitors in the magistrates' courts.

* Representation in the Crown Court and above.

* Very high cost criminal cases.

12. Article 6(3)(c) of the European Convention on Human Rights states that everyone charged with a criminal offence has the minimum right to defend himself in person or through legal assistance of his own choosing or, if he has not sufficient means to pay for legal assistance, to be given it free when the interests of justice so require. A number of countries working under the ECHR do not allow an accused person to choose his lawyer if he is benefiting from the appointment of a publicly funded defender. The Government does not intend, in general, to adopt that policy and believes that giving the defendant a lawyer in whom he or she has confidence is important. The Government also believes that its proposals in this paper are ECHR compliant.

Executive Summary

13. In the light of the responses to the consultation paper, the Government will introduce new regulations for choice of representative. A more detailed explanation of the policy decisions are set out in the following pages but in summary, the Government proposes that:

> In the majority of cases, the suspect or defendant will be able to choose any defence lawyer who has a contract with the Legal Services Commission or a salaried defender.

* In certain special and limited circumstances, choice will be restricted to those particularly qualified to undertake the work e.g. for serious fraud trials.

* The decision to allow a change of representative should remain with the judge and not be transferred to the Commission

* No period of reflection should be allowed. The solicitor's firm or salaried defender named in the application for funded representation will be considered the defendant's choice of legal representative unless and until it is changed in one of the ways set out below:

  * There is a conflict of interest for the lawyer who represents more than one defendant in the same case, so that it would not be professionally appropriate for the lawyer to continue to act for that defendant;

  * There is a breakdown of the professional relationship between the lawyer and the defendant (this would have to be certified by the lawyer who had been providing the representation);

  * The lawyer is professionally embarrassed so that it would not be professionally appropriate for the lawyer to continue to act for that defendant;

  * Through circumstances beyond their control the firm or salaried defender can no longer provide assistance;

  * There is a another reason which makes a change of solicitor reasonable in all the circumstances.

Reasonable change should be allowed at any time in the process. Regulations will define the circumstances that will be considered reasonable to allow a change of representation.

The public defender system has drawn heated exchanges from lawyers who have argued passionately for and against the provision of such a publicly funded legal service. The merits and demerits of the public defender system are examined in the following article by Jon Robins.

Jon Robins, 'What is the real price of justice?' (2001) *The Independent*, 9 January

'Defence lawyers stand between state and the citizen. They serve a vital interest in democracy under the rule of law.' So declared the Lord Chancellor, Lord Irvine in a parliamentary debate only a couple of years ago.

Just how that interest will remain defended under a Salaried Defender Service (SDS) as envisaged by the Government is a moot point. Presently, the Legal Service Commission is sifting through over 100 CVs in search of six 'pioneers' – as they would have it – to lead a public defender service.

One thing is clear – lawyers are not impressed. In the recent round of responses to the government's consultation exercise, the Bar Council reprimanded the policy makers, claiming that the plans were 'not properly thought-through', were 'costly and inefficient' and would ultimately lead to injustice. The Criminal Law Solicitors Association (CLSA) were even more dismissive. 'Unnecessarily and grossly expensive' and 'a waste of valuable resources' was their frank assessment.

The SDS in its pilot stage will comprise six offices, and at least three will be up and running by next April. The Government hopes that after four years the project will go nationwide, with many more offices throughout the land. Much of the opposition to a public defence revolves around a steadfast refusal to believe that it will be funded properly. But there are also fundamental fears about cases falling under the control of the state. 'The state arrests, prosecutes and sentences individuals involved the criminal justice system,' the CLSA argued. 'For the state to purport to defend that individual will allow a breeding ground for miscarriages of justice.'

Many commentators look despairingly at the experience across the Atlantic, where US public defender offices are run on shoe-string budgets and plea bargaining is rife. Bruce Houlder QC, vice chairman of the Bar Council's criminal law committee, sees such decline as inevitable under the new system. 'The trouble is that in a statistic-based civil service, one department tends to measure its results in the case of a prosecution service upon the number of successful prosecutions and, no doubt in the case of the SDS, the number of successful defences,' he says. There is an evident 'costs savings interest' in striking a bargain and claiming a victory for a department. 'And there is no justice in that,' he adds.

It is hardly likely that the Government is shocked by the outbreak of hostility to the new service, as it comes at a time when relations between criminal defence lawyers and the state have plummeted to an all-time low. This month sees the prospect of duty solicitors taking industrial action – or 'a day of rest' – as a response to legal aid rates not being upped for the best part of decade.

The backdrop for these fraught times is the new contracting regime which comes into being – along with the SDS – in April. The Law Society is already taking legal advice from City firm Kingsley Napley to see whether the new contracting arrangements are fair.

Rodney Warren, chairman of the Society's access to justice working party, is bemused to see a Government hell-bent on unpopular privatisations, such as National Air Traffic Services, whilst at the same time taking criminal defence work back under state control.

Like many, he doubts that a nationalised service will be able to deliver any great cost savings. So what is it all about, then? He puts it down to 'simple political dogma'. 'It is difficult to understand and extremely difficult to justify,' he says. 'It is the clearest indication that they do not understand the crisis that criminal law firms are now in, when they can't even afford to pay their staff.'

He illustrates the point by recounting the experience of a duty solicitor colleague, who had recently locked himself out of the house at nine o'clock in the evening and called out a locksmith. 'It took 10 minutes to get him into the house and he was charged £70,' he says. 'The duty solicitor worked out that he would have to go out to a police station and work for well over an hour to earn anything like that.'

Many suspect that the sole reason for a SDS is to further tighten the screws on defence lawyers. 'It is a backstop, so if in future we don't play ball and want more money, they'll say that the public defender is there and you can get lost,' says Franklin Sinclair, chair of the CLSA.

It is an argument that Richard Collins, head of the Criminal Defence Service, has heard many times. 'What surprises me is the extent to which people have linked the issues of contracting and the SDS,' he says, adding that practitioners have been too eager to construct 'some vast conspiracy theory' of 'some Machiavellian plot' by Government to drive lawyers into the arms of the SDS by making life hell in private practice through contracting.

But isn't the purpose of the SDS a way of keeping the lid on legal aid? Unsurprisingly, Collins does not see it like that. 'What it will give us is much better information as to what it costs to undertakes work. I would have thought from their point of view that would be a good thing,' he says.

North of the border, the Public Defence Solicitors Office is two years into its own pilot project, employing five solicitors. Leaks from the pilot do not augur well. According to one press report, the average cost of a case fought by the PSDO costs £360, compared to £290 to use a high street lawyer.

Alastair Watson, director of the office, says that such figures should be taken with a pinch of salt. But he adds that any commentator who expects an office of five lawyers to make significant savings is living in 'cloud cuckoo-land'.

Watson is an advocate for a public defender system, and believes that public and private lawyers co-existing is the way forward. 'The inherent dangers of either system are potentially counter-balanced in a mixed economy of the two,' he says. 'Most of the problems with either system tend to come from the fact that they operate in a monopoly.'

The Scottish project got off to a bad start, because it relied upon suspects born in two particular months being compelled to be represented by the office. Baroness Kennedy memorably damned the scheme as 'justice by star sign', and the Scottish Law Society have opposed the scheme from the start. Alastair Watson is the first to admit that compulsory referrals overshadowed the office, but adds that life has improved immeasurably since it was scrapped in July.

John Scott, the secretary of the Edinburgh Bar Association, reports that the direction had a substantial effect on his own practice in terms of lost business (amounting to 'a five-figure sum') and forced at least a couple of practitioners to leave criminal law. 'I wouldn't say that anyone is happy with the idea, but it is a lot easier to live with now,' he says. He has no major criticisms of the PSDO, but he adds: 'It is going to be well funded and properly backed up now, but it's easy to turn the tap of funding off once it is properly established.'

It is a theme that Rodney Warren picks up on. 'Look at the railway, the health service and the schools,' he says. 'Why should defending unpopular criminals be a priority for any Government? It's going to be the most vulnerable public service I could imagine.'

Of course, many are mindful of another, less than glorious nationalisation of the criminal justice system – the Crown Prosecution Service. 'It failed us for 15 years and it proved an unwieldy and expensive bureaucracy,' Bruce Houlder says, adding that there was already a national infrastructure of prosecution offices for the CPS, whereas the SDS is 'starting from scratch'. He fears that it could become a black hole for public money. 'We don't want another Dome, do we?'

--- --- --- --- --- --- --- --- --- --- --- --- --- ---

SOLICITORS

The solicitors' branch of the legal profession has undergone much change in the last 10 years. It has lost the exclusive right to conduct conveyancing, and has had to cope with the advent of new technologies, European and human rights law, the new challenges of the community legal service and, at times, a superfluity of would-be entrants to the profession. In the following piece, Michael Napier (Law Society president in 2001) gives a good overview of the challenges facing solicitors. That is followed by an extract from an article by Anne Mizzi about the rise of the civil law solicitor-advocate.

Michael Napier, 'Wind of change' (2000) *Gazette*, 9 November, p 20

Solicitors play a major part in moving the legal process forward on behalf of their clients, preparing cases, and increasingly appealing as solicitor advocates; increasingly, too, as solicitors who apply to join the bench. Even if progress is (apparently) being made in the system of judicial appointments, the Law Society still urges the Lord Chancellor, Lord Irvine, to go the whole hog by setting up a judicial appointments commission to ensure diverse selection on the surface of a level playing-field that is visible for all to see.

Information superhighway

My greatest challenge is to be president at a time when the Law Society is on the cusp of significant change. I want to see the Law Society re-established both internally and externally as a formidable presence on the legal landscape, valued by our members for the full range of our activities, advocating effectively their interests, and respected by stakeholders as a model regulator, maintaining our leading voice on law reform, on best practice of law, and on client care.

In pursuing this aim, we must recognise that the dual responsibilities of regulation and representation are not mutually exclusive, but a mixture that is reconcilable provided that both functions are performed well – and if we cannot perform both well we should be ashamed of ourselves.

We have a special responsibility to the young and new solicitors to fulfil their high hopes in the age of the Internet economy.

Today, the click of a mouse can bring up the Law Society's new Web site (solicitors-online.com) which has just hit no 2 in the charts of busiest legal Web sites – 2.82 million hits last month. It is now the authoritative source for the public to find a solicitor, the specialist firm, the nearest firm, even the virtual solicitor's office.

With true modernising spirit, government policy includes widening IT access for the public to give better access to justice through the community legal service.

Excellent though that concept may be, the fact remains that much of the time there is still no substitute for direct advice. Access to justice cannot always be dematerialised from screen to screen. Direct representation when the clients' questions are answered and minds put at rest cannot always be found at the end of a modem.

Lawyers in the community

Nowhere is compassion and understanding more evident than in the excellent daily work of the family law solicitor, emphatically confirmed by research from the Nuffield Foundation into the role and task that family lawyers perform. The authors of the study explode the myth that there is anything fundamentally flawed in the way lawyers deal with family breakdown. They found that:

- Solicitors discourage clients from making unreasonable claims;
- When children are involved, solicitors routinely 'encourage the parties to agree between themselves rather than using lawyers unnecessarily';
- Solicitors actively 'discourage tit for-tat attitudes in family disputes.

The survey found much more to confirm the invaluable role of family lawyers, whose pivotal position in the community legal service must quickly be recognised by the incentive of a long overdue increase in hourly rates. Frankly, unless the government and the Legal Services Commission provide proper incentives for firms to continue doing this crucial public work these 'thin cat' – to quote *The Guardian* – community lawyers will vote with their feet. It will then be too late for the Lord Chancellor to remember what he said to the North Yorkshire Business Forum on 16 June 2000: 'I would like to correct one myth. On the whole, lawyers working on legal-aid rates are not the fat cats of the legal system. Many are dedicated, efficient, caring individuals, providing important services to the poor and disadvantaged.'

I agree. But those words must he followed up with more resources, otherwise the watershed moment that I have warned the Lord Chancellor about will become a reality. It cannot be in the public interest to play the brinkmanship of seeing how far community lawyers (often in small firms) can be pushed – and that includes the not-for-profit sector, which employs many poorly-paid and highly committed solicitors.

Even worse is the current plight of criminal practitioners contemplating the proposed terms of the criminal defence service contracts and the salaried defence service pilots. Throughout, the Law Society has insisted that if there is to be a

Salaried Defence Service, it must include equality of arms between prosecution and defence, guaranteed freedom of choice for clients, and a level playing-field between private practice firms and the Salaried Defence Service firm.

How can goodwill for this policy be engendered by the seductive language of the Legal Service Commission's advertisement for the salaried defence service, which says 'we would also he interested to hear from applicants who would bring an existing base of clients or an established criminal defence team'? At a salary of £50,000 plus benefits, when their current practices are hanging on by a thin financial thread because of no meaningful increase in rates for eight years, it will be a strong temptation to jump ship.

What will the competition lawyers have to say? Is this a level playing field, particularly when the contract is completely silent about money? There is plenty in it about more administrative work, about no additional payment for being on duty for up to 24 hours at a time, about greater restrictions on how much work can be done or paid for but nothing about rates of pay. How can the commission expect firms to embrace, or even to consider the contract details and make their business plans if they don't know what rates of payment to expect? Rates have increased since 1992 by only 5% – against an increase in overheads of 3%. Is it any wonder that overdraft limits, redundancies and recruitment problems are the daily talk of criminal lawyers?

Reach out and reform

The Law Society's office holder team has adopted the approach of doing what Basil Fawlty described as 'the bleeding obvious' – talking to the leaders, the groups, the associations, the City, the senior partners and the opinion formers, and above all making the effort to get out of Chancery Lane and listen to firms of all sizes. This is all timely because we have a serious agenda to discuss – the radical, even revolutionary, reform programme set out in the consultation paper that every solicitor received as a pull-out supplement to the 19 October issue of the *Gazette*. The proposals recognise that only five years ago the profession voted a ballot to maintain the dual roles f regulation and representation, a view that has been confirmed by qualitative focus group research, and reaffirmed by the council several times. The need to do better all areas of the Society's activities at the forefront of the council's are fully thought through and concerted reform programme which is designed to strengthen the profession's customer-focused stance and its own standing in the eyes of government and stakeholders, who are all quick to remind us that self-regulation is a privilege that can be taken away rid not a right to be taken for ranted.

Another plank of the reform process is to produce a body that is relevant to solicitors as a streamlined and efficient decision-making organisation based on a corporate model, consistent with the way that any small plc would expect to run its business. The reform process is not a leap in the dark. Many people have worked hard to get this far. If the mood of the profession says we have got it right, the framework can be put in place at a special general meeting in February, with a larger council that is more representative of our membership, acting as a platform for stronger links with the profession. The standards focus of the reforms will soon be delivered by a new and simplified modern rulebook during 2001.

Yes minister?

We have designed a fresh Law Society. One that will allow us when appropriate to show welcome agreement with the Lord Chancellor, who said last February in the *Financial Times* that he 'wanted to see a strong, independent and articulate Law Society because it was in the public interest that a great and important profession consisting of 90,000 solicitors should give a good account of itself in the public interest'.

There are many areas where, despite a robust relationship on some issues, we can enjoy a mutually beneficial relationship with the government. I welcome, for example, the efforts of the Lord Chancellor's Department to open new areas for English and Welsh lawyers abroad. The Law Society's international expert help on those missions is invaluable and it helps to bring home the bacon – about £720 million annually in overseas invisible earnings. I also welcome the letter that arrived from the parliamentary secretary, David Lock, announcing an initiative to reduce the paperwork bureaucracy for firms dealing with the Legal Services Commission. I also have confidence in a fair and sensible outcome of the advanced negotiations with the Lord Chancellor on the content of the compulsory elements of the practising certificate fee.

However, I fear the government may have to think again about its rules and regulations on conditional fees where recoverability of the success fee and the insurance premium was offered as the plug to fill the gap of removal of legal aid in personal injury cases. The news that defendant insurers will, as they are entitled to do, challenge premium recovery in all cases where there are no proceedings could scupper the whole process, simultaneously sabotaging Lord Woolf's civil justice reforms that encourage early settlement with litigation as the last resort. It will be ludicrous if, in a claim which would otherwise settle, the claimant has to issue proceedings to recover the insurance premium. We warned the LCD about this problem and raised it during the passage of the access to justice bill, asking for clarity that recoverability would apply regardless of the issue of proceedings, but to no avail – and it now looks as if we are heading for high volumes of satellite litigation.

Client care

For the umpteenth time I want to stress that treating clients well, so that they do not complain – or, if they do, handling the complaint properly – does not require a PhD in rocket science. By putting our clients first, as we are required to do, and by marketing our self-regulated status we can distinguish solicitors from the growing band of unqualified competitors, who are offering legal services today with their aggressive techniques.

By excellent practice management standards such as Lexcel, by being transparent about fees, by being available and affordable and by giving value for money we can easily distinguish ourselves from the competition and readily cope with the understandable tendency of clients to complain if their reasonable expectations are not met – sometimes even if their unreasonable expectations are not met. When that happens we should be prepared if necessary to say that small but important word 'sorry' and to do our utmost to put right what may have gone wrong or, just as likely, what is thought to have gone wrong but is often more perceived than real.

In August and September this year in 1,500 telephone interviews, independent researchers asked clients what they thought about their solicitors. The Law Society commissioned the research. The findings are encouraging. But while we should celebrate these findings we cannot ease up on improving the client care culture.

The small percentage of time when we don't quite satisfy the client has a high reputation cost and a high business cost. Solicitors must be affordable, efficient, approachable and fair– sensitive to the fact that like any other business the customer is king. Moreover, the Law Society's drive to promote practice excellence will help those firms which have a poor complaints record.

Polluter pays

To square the circle, I make no apology for introducing the polluter pays principle as part of the Law Society reform agenda. It is included in the consultation paper and I shall be surprised if the profession does not support the idea that those who do not cause complaints should not be expected to bear all the financial burden of handling the complaints of those who do.

We now stand more than a fighting chance of meeting the December numbers target at the Office for the Supervision of Solicitors – where there is no longer a backlog of files waiting for caseworker allocation.

Polluter pays will reduce the flow of complaints because it will encourage firms to deal with them at source. And, if the reform proposals for a lay commissioner-led redress scheme are supported, the OSS will achieve quicker resolution of service complaints through a conciliatory approach, complaints that currently make up 60% of the OSS workload. One final thing is clear – in adjudicating complaints the OSS is totally independent. But the responsibility for ensuring that there is an efficient complaints handling system rests squarely on the shoulders of the Society on behalf of the profession and the public.

I am confident that we can deliver a new Law Society to help our members serve their clients. We can make a difference and we can all share in the success. That excites me as president and, consistent with my favourite aphorism that 'the less we worry about who takes the credit the more we get things done'. I wrote in *The Times* a couple of weeks ago that 'I want all solicitors to share in the buzz of making it happen'. It is crucial that you do and I hope you will.

─ ─ · ─ · ─ · ─ · ─ · ─ · ─ · ─ · ─ · ─ · ─ · ─ · ─ · ─ · ─ ·

Rights of audience for solicitors in the higher courts became technically possible in 1990 with the Courts and Legal Services Act of that year.

Anne Mizzi, 'Solicitors on trial' (2000) *Gazette*, 31 August, p 30

From 1 October, trainee solicitors can begin working for their advocacy qualification even before they emerge from their training contracts. And when they are admitted, they will only need six more months' advocacy experience.

This is good news for City law firms, with their massive litigation departments and international clients who fail to see why they should pay twice for legal advice if their case ends up in court.

But that is not the only reason why the City firms have welcomed the new regulations. Ever since the then Lord Chancellor, Lord Mackay of Clashfern, and a team of judges broke the Bar's monopoly on higher courts appearance rights in 1993, City solicitors have struggled find the right kind of work to give their lawyers the 'flying hours' in court they need. The top City firms say they have been taking on chargeable and *pro bono* work in the hope that the cases will end up in the lower courts.

The old regulations were based on training and tests geared towards solicitors who were already regular lower court advocates. They needed two years' advocacy experience prior to their application, had to pass a written test on law and procedure, and had to complete a six-day residential course.

From October, there will be three routes to qualification. The transitional 'accreditation' and 'exemption' routes will be phased out in five years. After that, the only route available will be the radical 'development' route of training and assessment in higher court procedure, evidence, ethics and advocacy skills, plus a year's litigation and advocacy experience.

Trainee solicitors can already get the training and assessment and up to six months' experience under their belts during the training contract.

The new fast track for novice lawyers is perhaps the most controversial element of the new package, as it leaves the Law Society open to criticism of dumbing down standards by unleashing inexperienced trial lawyers.

Mark Humphries, chairman of the Solicitors Association of Higher Court Advocates and head of advocacy at City giant Linklaters, says this will not happen: 'The qualification regulators require a standard of advocacy which is much higher than the expertise of a pupil barrister. There is going to be no flood of inexperienced advocates going into the higher courts without the necessary competence.'

But Clifford Chance's managing partner for litigation, John Potts, says he is concerned about standards: 'The standards at the moment are not demanding and I do worry about it. I would like to see the standards of training kept high. The Bar and our side of the profession have got to work together sensibly on this, because even though the Bar will hold up for so long, we are going to end up with one profession.'

Allen & Overy litigation partner David St John Sutton is also cautious. 'It shouldn't lead to a lowering of standards if the necessary training takes place,' he says.

Just to be sure, Allen & Overy has established a team to examine the implications of the new regulations. Allen & Overy already encourages its litigators and arbitrators to attend National Institute of Trial Advocacy' (NITA) courses, run by the US advocacy trainers in association with Nottingham Law School and the College of Law.

Aspirant advocates from the top eight City firms – Clifford Chance, Slaughter and May, Linklaters, Allen & Overy, Freshfields, Herbert Smith, Lovells and Norton Rose – already mingle on the NITA courses. But in their struggle to create a competitive advantage, firms like Linklaters and Allen & Overy are examining the basic training their lawyers are receiving on these courses and looking at how they can improve their qualifications later down the line.

Linklaters recently announced plans to introduce its own branded advanced advocacy qualification, and is asking law schools to hid for the contract (see [2000] *Gazette* 17) ...

— · — · — · — · — · — · — · — · — · — · — · — · — · —

CONDITIONAL FEE ARRANGEMENTS

In the first versions of Conditional Fee Arrangements (CFAs, that is, 'no win, no fee' agreements between a lawyer and client) in the 1990s, only people who expected to win money from their case could benefit from conditional fees. This was the only way that most people could afford to pay the success fee. This meant that a successful litigant would not receive all the money he or she had been awarded. So in 2000, the Government used its power under the Access to Justice Act 1999 to make it possible for the winning party to recover the success fee, and any insurance premium, from the losing party. This will ensure that it is the person or organisation that has committed the legal wrong who pays, and it will allow defendants and claimants (other than in family law cases) whose case is not about money to use CFAs.

The workings of CFAs in England and Wales have been of particular concern to those looking at how the English legal system is managing to provide access to legal services to those (perhaps 60% of the adult population) who are too rich to pay full legal fees, but too poor to get State funded services from the CLS. The latest development in this is a set of Regulations (www.open.gov.uk/lcd) enabling the bulk purchase and provision of legal services through collective conditional fee agreements (CFA) which came into effect on 30 November 2000.

Since 1 April 2000, successful individuals bringing cases using CFAs, or who are covered by insurance policies, have been able to recover the success fee or insurance premium from their losing opponents. However, those measures were primarily designed for the High Street solicitor. The collective CFAs are designed specifically for mass providers and purchasers of legal services – such as trade unions, insurers or commercial organisations. A collective CFA will enable a trade union to enter into a single agreement with solicitors to govern the way in which cases for its members will be run and paid for; by simplifying the process it will reduce the cost of pursuing separate individual cases. The scheme will also benefit commercial organisations who will be able to enter collective CFAs to pursue or defend claims arising in the course of business.

The following two articles examine the current status of the CFA, identify problems with the system and suggest possible solutions.

The first is from Richard Moorhead, a Senior Research Fellow at the Institute of Advanced Legal Studies and the erstwhile Convenor of the Society of

Advanced Legal Studies Working Party Report on the *Ethics of Conditional Fee Agreements*, and Avrom Sherr, Woolf Professor of Legal Education at the Institute of Advanced Legal Studies. The second extract is from Richard Harrison, a partner at Laytons.

Richard Moorhead and Avrom Sherr, 'Midnight in the garden of the CFA people' (2001) 151 NLJ 274

There is a lot riding on the success of conditional fee agreements (CFAs). They are a central plank in the Government's legal services policy and, for many in the profession, they offer the opportunity to reclaim practices damaged by the erosion and removal of legal aid. The Law Society has endorsed a CFA referral scheme backed by insurance and there are numerous insurance companies selling CFA related policies. More fundamentally, CFAs currently represent the best hope for the general public of gaining access to justice. Little surprise then that a report, produced by a working group of the Society of Advanced Legal Studies (SALS). *The Ethics of Conditional Fee Arrangements*, should provoke a strong reaction from CFA lawyers (see 'Conditional Fee Agreements', NLJ February 9, 2001, pp 156–159.

As the SALS report states all fee arrangements can lead to conflicts of interest, and that these problems must be kept in mind in assessing the pros and cons of CFAs. Similarly, the working party was well aware of the changes introduced by the Access to Justice Act 1999; changes fully described in Chapter 2 of the report. It is understandable that the Government and some practitioners – with so much invested in the success of the scheme – would claim that the 1999 Act provides an answer to all of the problems raised by CFAs. Unfortunately, whilst CFAs should open up access to justice for some clients, it is clear that CFAs raise ethical and consumer protection issues, quite apart from the sustainability, desirability and cost of having a justice system in symbiotic union with the insurance industry.

A principal problem with CFAs is the mismatch of the rhetoric of 'no win no fee' and the claim that, 'the public love CFAs because they take the risk away from the public and put it on solicitors, where it belongs.' The truth is that these agreements are enormously complex, and at times loaded against the interests of the clients. Research indicates how difficult these complexities are for clients.

The 'no win no fee' rhetoric, and the claim that all the risk falls on the lawyer can be judged initially by looking at the definition of 'win'. The Law Society's standard CFA defines a 'win' as: 'Your claim for damages is finally decided in your favour, whether by a court decision or an agreement to pay you damages.' Win does not mean the payment of damages. So clients need to understand that if damages are not recovered, they have still 'won' and a fee is payable. As a result, clients – not lawyers – bear the risk of non-recovery of a damages agreement/award. It would be a simple matter to make the definition of 'win' accord with what clients think it means and CFAs would become less complex. For that reason, the report recommended that for CFAs aimed wholly or mainly at recovering damages for the client, 'success' should be defined in terms of damages recovered rather than damages awarded, with provisions for solicitors to derogate from this approach where they can demonstrate fully informed consent from the client (to assume the risk of non-recovery).

There are other areas where the simple appeal of 'no win win no fee' masks its complexities from clients. Where a client wants to pull out of a CFA case they do not 'win', yet they are liable for a fee. Similarly, the notion of 'fee' is confined only to the claimant lawyers' profit costs, a distinction which needs to be made absolutely clear to clients who will not immediately understand what it means when they are told they can be asked to pay for disbursements and unrecovered insurance premiums. The Working Party did not think that lawyers should be prevented from charging clients in these circumstances but suggested that this be dealt with by giving clients a short 'cooling off period' to think about the implications of the CFA (particularly as pulling out of a CFA is likely to be difficult) and the production of a video to explain the intricacies of CFAs in a palatable form.

A final area which needs some examination is the role of cost caps in CFAs. One of the myths surrounding the 1999 Act is that it now protects clients from paying their own lawyers for success fees which are not recoverable from the opposition. This is not true. Success fees are split into two parts: the part based on risk (which should only be recoverable from the opposition) and the part based on the cost of borrowing. Lawyers can only recover this bit of the success fee from clients (and from their damages). Early indications are that the most scrupulous lawyers will either not claim any cost of borrowing uplift or will only claim a minor sum. About others, or less profitable firms, we can be less sure. Defendant lawyers (and their insurer clients) are itching to reduce the amounts that claimant lawyers receive under CFA success fees. If they succeed, even in part, there is a real concern that some lawyers will cover themselves by claiming increasing amounts under the cost of borrowing element of a success fee. This type of success fee is not only applicable in 'very limited circumstances'; it is possible in every single CFA case. This is one of the areas where there is almost no protection for the client, and is one reason why the Working Party recommended a cap on the total costs recovered from the client's damages. Similarly, the report addresses the question of a cap on costs breaching the indemnity principle directly on p 53 ('an issue which is not addressed in the report' according to the NLJ article): the report's proposals on a cap are contingent on abolition of the indemnity principle.

Proponents of CFAs have a good case on the need for CFAs (or something like them) to protect access to justice in the absence of legal aid, but CFAs and the 1999 Act have not yet struck a deal which is genuinely in the interests of the consumer or which will promote the good repute of the profession. It will be a shame if the loopholes and snags in the CFA scheme begin to loom larger in the public consciousness when more members of the general public are caught out. These problems need to be dealt with quickly to prevent lawyers, CFAs, and the justice system, being tinged with disrepute.

Richard Harrison, 'Dealing with conditional fee arrangements: practical steps' (2000) NLJ Practitioner, 16 June, p 895

Lawyers who wish to enter into risk and reward sharing agreements with litigation clients will feel as though they are walking a tightrope across a minefield. Any conditional fee agreement signed after April 1, 2000 must comply with the Conditional Fee Agreements Regulations 2000 (SI 2000 No 692) ('the regulations'). However, the detailed costs rules and practice directions governing how those agreements will operate under the amended Civil Procedure Rules ('the rules') so as to permit the recovery of percentage uplifts and insurance premiums are still being discussed. At least we now have the very helpful article by John O'Hare (*New Law Journal*, May 26) to provide some guidance on the new regime and he has made the latest 90 page draft available for review and comment on the web site run by Laurie West-Knights QC.

There follows a review of the practical steps involved in running conditional fee agreements in the light of these radical changes. What is certain is that, once we progress beyond a tested field of hulk litigation, any reasonably substantial conditional fee agreement is an undertaking of immense complexity. There are going to be many pitfalls, hoops and hurdles. Drafting the agreement is the relatively straightforward part. However, the most important aspects are the project planning and the management of the client relationship before, during and after the litigation.

The way the law works

Revisiting some of the legislative background might be helpful. The fundamental provision is the amended s 58 of the Courts and Legal Services Act, which was substituted by relevant sections of the Access to Justice Act 1999. The previous s 58 provided that a conditional fee agreement that complied with the regulations was not unenforceable merely by reason of its being a conditional fee agreement. The Court of Appeal in *Awwad v Geraghty & Co* [2000] 1 All ER 608 decided that what have become known as Thai Trading agreements, under which lawyers' fees and expenses are only payable in specified circumstances ('conditional normal fees' or 'contingent fees'), were unenforceable at common law.

Under the new s 58, Thai Trading agreements are now included within the definition of 'conditional fee agreements' and the new section is starkly clear: all conditional fee agreements are unenforceable unless they comply with all the relevant requirements. However, the requirements differ depending on the type of conditional fee agreement. If a party seeks to recover a success fee element or an insurance premium from an unsuccessful opponent (as now permitted by the Access to Justice Act), the necessary agreement will be subject to even more rigorous regulation. Such an agreement will (in Part 43 of the rules) be defined as a 'funding arrangement' and the newly recoverable amounts will be defined as 'additional liabilities'. A conditional normal fee agreement is not a 'funding arrangement' and the requirements are consequently somewhat less strict. This may have an effect on how you structure your negotiations with a client.

To be enforceable, every conditional fee agreement must be in writing and must comply with the regulations. Agreements that provide for a success fee must state the percentage increase and, the percentage increase must not exceed the prescribed maximum. The Conditional Fee Agreements Order (SI 200 No 823) made on March 20, 2000 came into force on April 1, 2000. It permits all proceedings to he the subject of conditional fee agreements, save for specified family proceedings and criminal proceedings other than those under s 82 of the Environmental Protection Act 1990. And, contrary to expectations, the Order retains the limit on uplift at 100%, even in the most difficult commercial cases.

The new rules

Recovery of the fees, uplift and insurance premiums from the other side and from your client will depend on compliance both with the regulations and with the revised rules. As mentioned by John O'Hare, the rules will be changed and supplemented by the proposed Civil Procedure (Amendment) (No 3) Rules 2000 (SI 2000 No 1317) and these will rely heavily on the new Costs Practice Direction, discussed in John O'Hare's article, and its accompanying forms. The new provisions are expected to be in force by early July and will, thankfully, provide a period of grace of 28 days for parties to ensure that agreements entered into since April 1 are compliant.

You should note, however, that if you have already been running an action under a conditional fee agreement (including a Thai Trading agreement), you will he unable to create a new 'funding arrangement' to make your client's 'additional liabilities' recoverable. This is because the order bringing the relevant sections into force (SI 2000 No 900) provides that they do not apply to proceedings where there has been a conditional fee agreement before April 1, 2000. Further, you will find that you cannot discontinue old proceedings and launch a new action with a fresh conditional fee agreement.

So, assuming you want to enter into a conditional fee agreement, in particular one providing for a success fee uplift, how do you best go about it? The following points might help focus your preparation but they are only suggestions.

Step 1: risk assessment

The first task involves detailed research and risk assessment and discussion with the client. It may be impracticable to do this under any sort of formal conditional fee agreement. Either the client pays on a normal basis, or the work is retrospectively brought into the eventual conditional fee agreement (with no guarantee of it being recovered from the opponent), or the lawyers do it as part of the cost of doing business. Risk analysis is a topic in itself but you should aim to end up with something in writing, which identifies the various weak points in the case and justifies an additional payment for sharing the risk of lack of success. It is far too simplistic to decide that a client has a 'strong case' and that you should put your money where your mouth is; it is equally simplistic to add 100% because 'it all depends on the evidence'. In fact, it may come down to this in the end but you will need to explain it in a more sophisticated way. Success in litigation, strangely and frustratingly, rarely arises exclusively from the efforts and abilities of the lawyers involved. It depends far more often on the evidence and support provided by clients. So, possibly, you will want to get some contractual commitment from your client.

Step 2: talk to the client

Having done the risk assessment exercise on a preliminary basis, you must have a personal meeting with your client to explain everything. This is going to be required by the regulations and the agreement into which you will enter must provide for it to have taken place. You must explain to the client the various matters set out in reg 4. You must outline to the client the circumstances under which the client is liable to pay costs under the proposed agreement (presumably in accordance with the definition of 'success'). You must look at insurance issues, in particular existing policies and alternative methods of financing liability for costs. This is, of course, a topic in itself.

You must explain orally the circumstances under which the client may seek assessment of your fees and expenses, and the procedure involved. You can either do this briefly ('there are court procedures ...') or in full. If so, there may be no alternative but to show the client the relevant costs rules and practice directions and let him make head or tail of them. You must also explain whether you consider that any particular financing method is appropriate and set out your reasons for recommending a contract of insurance or any particular such contract and whether you have an interest in that recommendation.

Step 3: negotiate the conditional fee agreement

There will certainly be a considerable overlap between explaining the conditional fee agreement and negotiating it. In cases with any degree of complexity, the client should assume obligations and responsibilities as well as the solicitor. Detailed drafting will come later.

Step 4: write to the client

You must confirm in writing the oral explanation concerning the effect of the proposed conditional fee agreement and about the availability of insurance and the basis of your recommendation.

If the conditional fee agreement is going to provide for a success fee, you must be prepared to annex to it a summary of the risk assessment justifying the percentage increase (and the client must agree to waive any privilege in the document). You must also specify how much of the percentage increase relates to your own financing cost of postponing payment.

You will not recover this part, so it may be in your interests to ensure that the means of calculation brings it out as low as possible. Given the new draft practice direction's 15 factors to be taken into account on assessment of an insurance premium, you might find it helpful to do a detailed note of the reasons for agreeing the premium.

Step 5: draft the conditional fee agreement, (re-negotiate it) and sign it

Having done all this preparatory work, you can enter into the conditional fee agreement, making sure that it does indeed comply with the regulations in all its formal aspects. As mentioned, drafting is a relatively easy part of the exercise. I would recommend starting with the Law Society's 'running repairs' version of its revised model agreement but there are bound to be changes required for particular circumstances. There may well be overlap with other stages as part of the negotiating process: a sophisticated conditional fee agreement must be seen as a commercial transaction between solicitor and client, subject to a clear conflict of interest and possibly calling for independent legal advice on both sides. The regulations require that the agreement should contain various provisions. These include a summary of the risk assessment, a provision waiving legal professional privilege in the risk assessment in certain circumstances and a provision waiving the shortfall in recovered (or agreed) costs as between solicitor and client unless the court is satisfied that it should continue to be payable. You may want to retain the right to ensure that the client cannot instruct you to agree a lower uplift in a settlement offer from the other side than would satisfy you, simply because the client will recover all his damages and thus retain no interest in seeing his solicitor properly rewarded.

Ensuring proportionality

Additional liabilities will be subject to either summary assessment or detailed assessment (but only after trial). The court can split the process: making a summary assessment of basic costs and ordering detailed assessment of additional costs. The discretion given to costs judges will provide great scope for satellite litigation. As mentioned, there are at present 15 factors which the court will take into account in assessing the reasonableness of any insurance premium and dealing with them will not be easy or predictable. One of them, for instance is: 'the manner in which the case was conducted' and yet the court is required to have regard to the circumstances as they reasonably appeared to the solicitor at the time when the funding arrangement was entered into.

There is considerable debate over the court's power on assessment to make a reduction on the basis of 'proportionality'. It can he argued that this should not apply to additional liabilities. In any event, the parties should not expect the court to award the full amount claimed, even though it appeared reasonable to do so at the time. The more the court applies 'proportionality' (in reality, unfettered discretion) to the uplift and insurance premium, the greater the risk of shortfall.

—·—·—·—·—·—·—·—·—·—·—·—·—·—·—·—

BARRISTERS

The Bar has recently undergone a period of considerable change and challenge. In the following piece, Lord Justice Sedley sets out some of the issues facing the barristers and their professional institutions. It is an extract from a lecture delivered as part of the Cardiff Law School Public Lecture series.

Sir Stephen Sedley, 'The future of advocacy', the Lord Morris Memorial Lecture, Cardiff University, 28 September 1999, published in Philip Thomas (ed), *Discriminating Lawyers*, 2000, London: Cavendish Publishing

... [W]hy should a trainee lawyer have to opt for advocacy before he or she or anyone else knows whether they will be any good at it? In New Zealand, for example, you qualify and embark upon practice as a member of a single profession. Within a law firm you may try your hand at advocacy, and if, in due course, your aptitude takes you that way, you may hang up your shingle as barrister sole and make advocacy your career. It has repeatedly struck me as wasteful of time and talent that law students in this country have to opt for or against advocacy as the mainstream of their future work before they or anyone else know whether it's the right choice for them. The result can be seen daily: some young barristers, often of great intellectual ability, for whom every hearing in court is an ordeal which eats holes in their lives, but who are now on a career treadmill which they cannot get off; and other lawyers who, lacking confidence at 21, chose to become solicitors and have since found that they have a talent for advocacy which is painfully frustrated every time they have to sit mutely behind counsel less able than themselves. The anomaly is enhanced by the fact that there are practising barristers – conveyancing counsel, for example – who barely ever go into court, and solicitors – magistrates' court advocates, for example – who rarely go anywhere else.

I will return to the spin-offs of this problem when I look later at rights of audience, but for the moment let me return to the new graduate who has decided to become an advocate and who needs, therefore, to be called to the Bar. She or he will have first to join an Inn of Court[1] – one of the four ancient collegiate institutions through whose doors all intending barristers must pass, but whose modern and future role is still undetermined. As disciplinary bodies, they have passed on their summary functions to the Bar Council – a necessity if consistent standards are to be applied – though they retain the ultimate powers delegated to them by the judges. As educational bodies, which for centuries they were in a haphazard but indispensable way, their core work has now been handed on to the professional providers of a modern Bar Vocational Course (BVC) which the Inns themselves could not have hoped to provide. The dinners at which trainee barristers for centuries somewhat casually absorbed the culture and some of the learning of the profession have correspondingly lost much of their point, and the Inns have accordingly, if at first reluctantly, substituted optional collegiate activities for the slightly ridiculous process of eating your way to the Bar. They are turning their attention to the provision of advocacy training and wider forms of legal education than the BVC needs to provide. They continue to provide major law libraries and are, in any event, established entities of very considerable wealth, principally through the land they own and occupy. Their future existence is, therefore, not in question: it is their role in an already complex professional structure, weighed down with its own history and culture, which – as I think they all accept – needs to be addressed and modernised.

Meanwhile, what matters for the intending Bar student is that the Inns hold and distribute considerable sums by way of scholarships to their student members – not nearly enough to fund them all through the Bar Vocational Course, but enough to help a proportion of them through a worrying and expensive period of their lives.[2] Even so, it is plain that the money distributed to their student members by the Inns of Court cannot meet anything like the full extent of need.

Joining an Inn is unproblematical, provided you have the fee and do not have a criminal record. Nor is it too difficult, if you can get on to it,[3] to complete the Bar Vocational Course and be called to the Bar in due course by your Inn of Court. The result, however, is a throughput of qualified students, many of whom are then unable to find a pupillage; without having done a pupillage, they cannot practise. These students find themselves in a situation in which, after years of study and the acquisition very often of a crippling burden of debt, they are denied the opportunity to seek work in a profession which welcomed them as newcomers, but is now turning its back on them. This is an unhappy situation which the Bar collectively, in spite of the real concern of its representative body, tolerates by inertia.

---

1 Gray's Inn, Lincoln's Inn, the Inner Temple or the Middle Temple. It will be apparent that, from here on, I am dealing only with England and Wales.

2 Last year, a sum approaching £2 m was distributed among 321 students, the majority of them on the Bar Vocational Course but about a fifth of them non-law graduates taking the Common Professional Examination to qualify them for professional training as lawyers. As a non-law graduate myself, I strongly favour this route into the profession: it enlarges and humanises a culture which can easily become dry and inward-looking.

3 The Bar Council's 1997–98 figures show that the uniform criteria used to select candidates for the BVC admitted a somewhat higher proportion of white applicants (62%) than of ethnic minority applicants (53%), suggesting some initial educational disparity. The failure rate in 1998 was 28%.

There has been a conscious, if modest, expansion of the number of students taking the Bar Vocational Course. To replace the monopoly of the Inns of Court School of Law, the Bar has since 1997 validated professional training courses in seven other academic institutions. Together, acting through a central clearing house, the providers now offer a total of 1,442 full time and 100 part time places on the BVC, all of them oversubscribed and permitting the better qualified candidates to be chosen.[4] The new syllabus is a much-needed departure from the old Bar Final Examinations: it recognises, for the first time, that interpersonal and advocacy skills are something barristers don't just possess and need to learn. But the result – allowing for failure and dropout – is an annual output of about 1,000 aspiring barristers, academically fully qualified after either four or five expensive years' study, called to the Bar by their respective Inns at a glittering ceremony, but still unable to practise until they have served out a full year's pupillage. Their numbers are swelled – currently almost doubled[5] – by the residue of previous years' students who are still trying to find a pupillage. They face a distressing and, in places, anarchic situation. We know that fewer than half of them will succeed in getting a pupillage.[6] Some – perhaps as many as half – will now give up and move on to desk jobs in the employed sector or leave the law altogether. Of those who do find a first pupillage, perhaps six out of 10 will eventually obtain tenancies.

In these circumstances it is necessary, first of all, to be clear about where the Bar's obligations begin and end. No profession can guarantee work to everyone who qualifies for it unless entrant numbers are limited, with legal underpinning, to those it knows it can absorb. In earlier years, this was done by the simple expedient of limiting to eight the number of students each Inn would call to the Bar in any one term: an annual total of 128 students.[7] But the Bar has proved a poor forecaster of its own prospects. Early in the decade which has now come to a close, the Bar Council, in its then customary mood of defensive pessimism, predicted that the profession would shrink by one-third by the end of the century. Instead it has grown by more than a half: today, there are 10,847 barristers in practice.[8] To have allowed the Bar in this period formally to limit its intake to its self-predicted needs would have robbed advocacy of its seed-corn. But to accept this is not to reject the case for a limit on numbers: it is to point to the need for cautious and objective forecasting. Instead, trapped by the Office of Fair Trading's

4   See Watson, 1997, p 82, for a description of the new system and its syllabus. The ICSL, before it diversified provision, offered up to 1,400 places, so the expansion has not been great. About 2,500 students apply each year for places. The Bar Council's brochure Steps to the Bar describes the qualification process well. Both it and the Inns' brochures warn intending applicants of the serious obstacles to success. It also lists some of the main attributes needed by a barrister: 'intellectual ability; presentation and advocacy skills – that is, the ability to put across a point of view convincingly in public; personal coping skills – that is, the ability to digest large volumes of information in a short time and to handle the stress of long hours, tight deadlines and great responsibility; motivation.' I would have liked to see integrity in the list.

5   In 1998–99, PACH had 1,967 applicants seeking pupillage placements.

6   In 1997, 840 out of 1,870 applicants obtained a pupillage; in 1998, 747 out of 1,826; in 1998–99 there were 1,967 applicants.

7   Odgers, 1901, p 31.

8   Ie, from a 1990 base of 6,645 – a process which, curiously enough, after the postwar doldrums which, by 1960, had reduced the Bar's numbers to under 2,000, has restored the Bar to the size it had at the beginning of the 20th century. ('In 1800 there were only 598 men at the Bar; now there are no less than 9,457': Odgers, 1901, p 30.)

view that a limit on numbers would be unacceptably anti-competitive,[9] the Bar has left it to a process of natural selection – as cruel and arbitrary as anything observed by Darwin – to whittle down the numbers to those the Bar finally wants. I do not suggest that the Bar's numbers can be forcibly expanded: only individual chambers can decide what room they have for new tenants. But without a completed pupillage, the opportunity to seek a tenancy does not exist.

Even in the present situation there is no moral or practical reason why every student who requires a pupillage should not have one, and a welter of reasons why they should. The Bar, through its collegiate bodies and through the Bar Council, has invited them to invest a crucial year of their lives and money which most of them do not have in the first stage of vocational training. It does not, and cannot, promise them eventual work; but it has an inescapable moral obligation not to arbitrarily deny any of them the second stage of a barrister's vocational training, pupillage, without which none of them can ever seek work at the Bar. There are enough qualified junior counsel to take the BVC's annual throughput, yet probably fewer than 800 of them in this year will take on a pupil,[10] a large proportion of them unfunded or underfunded.

It was not always like this. In the days (which lasted into the 1970s) when pupils paid a hundred guineas for a pupillage, there was no shortage of juniors willing to take them.[11] Today, for good organisational reasons, the acceptance and allocation of pupils is a function of chambers rather than of individual practitioners; but, for economic reasons, chambers are now typically many times the size that they were, and some of them, including many of the most prosperous, recruit pupils not with any sense of obligation to train the profession's next generation but simply in order to maintain their own establishment. The consequence is that a set of 60 barristers who in past years might have composed three separate sets of chambers with half a dozen pupils in each, may now take on a single pupil or at best a handful. This process of attrition, in different proportions, is widely replicated across the Bar.

As a consequence of the want of a fair and uniform system, the selection of pupils is in many instances arbitrary and possibly discriminatory. The Bar in this respect has shown a depressing nonconformity between what it says and what it does. What it says is exemplary. The Bar Council supported the extension to the legal profession of the race and sex discrimination legislation.[12] It has adopted an advanced Equality Code, setting out detailed practices and principles for ensuring that pupillages and tenancies go to the best applicants, not simply the best-

---

9   This was in response to the recommendation of the Taylor Report, 1991.

10   The Inns' registers of qualified juniors, now being pruned, till recently carried over 3,000 names. PACH statistics show that in 1997, 840 out of 1,870 qualified applicants obtained pupillages; in 1998, 747 out of 1,826 – 161 of them unfunded. I do not accept the argument that, since this is not far above the number of new tenants taken on in those years (viz 613 in 1996–97, 502 in 1997–98 and 446 in 1998–99), the Bar is giving the right number of pupillages. What it is doing in effect (I do not suggest that it is planned) is preserving a seller's market in advocacy, expanding the size of existing chambers where the surplus of work justifies it, but ensuring that there is no pool of qualified young non-tenant barristers such as in past years have set up their own new chambers and enlarged the market.

11   There are many accounts of juniors with small armies of pupils, some within living memory. Campbell, the future Chief Justice, was one of 12 pupils simultaneously under the aegis of Tidd (Odgers, 1901, pp 31–32).

12   Courts and Legal Services Act 1990, s 64.

connected ones, and has made observance of the Code a rule of professional conduct.[13] It has set up a clearing house for pupillage applications, PACH, which depends upon chambers observing common standards and which in return assumes the initial burden of sifting and ordering applications. And it has recommended that all pupils be paid a modest salary by their chambers, giving credit against it for anything they earn in their second six months,[14] when they are allowed to take briefs. The reality, by contrast, is a reproach to the profession. Some chambers – a creditable number – sift and interview the applicants forwarded by PACH who have indicated a preference for those chambers; they take on a number of them as pupils, warning them that there is unlikely to be room for many, or any, of them as tenants, but recognising the obligation to give all of them the chance they have worked so hard for; and they pay them, out of the chambers' income, a decent salary, often well above the Bar Council's recommended figure.[15] But these chambers, and the Bar as a whole, are let down by those who buck the system. These are the chambers which refuse to participate in PACH and, instead, go headhunting at universities of their choice among the second year students, looking for a star student who will be paid perhaps £25,000 as a prospective tenant; or chambers which participate in PACH but refuse to take any candidate but their own first choice (who, in the nature of things, may well have been the first choice of other sets too); or chambers which take on pupils but pay them little or nothing.[16]

It is not simply that the end product is an inadequate and unfair allocation of pupillages, though it is both of those things. In some ways the most serious consequence of the present situation is that the Bar's intake risks reverting to what it was at the beginning of the century: a social, economic and racial elite. It does the Bar credit that its ethnic minority component at present exceeds that in the UK population generally.[17] Statistical evidence of racial disadvantage in the progression from BVC to pupillage to tenancy is worrying, but, at present, inconclusive.[18] What may matter more for now is the risk that some of the Bar's present practices may unwittingly be lending themselves to such a process.

---

13 See the Bar's Equality Code and the brief account given by Anthony Thornton QC, 'The professional responsibility and ethics of the English Bar', in Cranston, 1995, pp 95–96.

14 The figure, £6,000 a year, was adopted in 1990 upon the recommendation of Sir Nicholas Phillips' Report, which envisaged 450 funded pupillages a year. The target has never been met and the figure has never been increased. See Bowley, 1999.

15 See the Bar Council's annual Pupillages and Awards handbook for the range and terms of pupillages on offer through or outside the Bar Council's Pupillage Applications Clearing House (PACH).

16 Thus, in 1998, of 671 pupillages offered through PACH, only 586 were allocated; and, of these, not more than 226 were funded, in many cases at token figures of £1,500 or less.

17 Of the known ethnicity of the current membership of the practising Bar, pupils and squatters included, almost 10% is ethnic minority (Bar Council records).

18 The Bar has different recording systems for the successive career stages, making it impossible at present to track an ethnically or gender–differentiated cohort though the stages. The static picture available for 1996–97 shows overall about a quarter fewer candidates obtaining tenancies than obtained an initial pupillage. Broken down by gender and ethnicity, the proportionate drop is about 20% for men against 30% for women; but, importantly, there is no drop at all for white candidates against about 24% for ethnic minorities. If this turns out to be replicated over time for a single cohort, it will be serious cause for concern.

Take, for example, the apparently innocuous question of the university where pupillage applicants took their degrees. It is right, of course, that individual chambers should set their own criteria of selection. But little attention seems to be given to the indirectly discriminatory effect of the preference which is in many cases accorded to particular universities, or to first class degrees. A student's chance, up to the age of 24, of being offered a pupillage ranges from nearly nine out of 10 for an 'Oxbridge' first to one out of 20 for a 2.2 from a former polytechnic; for older students, the disparity gets worse. But doesn't this reflect the class of degree, rather than the institution? Unfortunately not: even with a 2.2, an 'Oxbridge' graduate has almost a 38% chance of a pupillage – one percentage point higher than a student from a former polytechnic with a first.[19] The possible social, economic and racial implications of this can be glimpsed in the comparison, first of all, between the ethnic make-up of the law schools in the older universities and those in the former polytechnics. Leaving out overseas students, the Oxbridge law schools are 85% white; but some former polytechnics – Nottingham Trent, Glamorgan, and Derby, for example – are not far off that figure. Moreover, all these institutions have, for known and creditable reasons, a higher ethnic minority component than in the population as a whole. But if you compare the ethnic minority component in the law schools of a city's old university with that in its former polytechnic City neighbour – Oxford, Birmingham, Leicester, Leeds, Liverpool, Manchester, and Nottingham, for instance – in each of these cities there is a higher concentration of ethnic minority students in the former polytechnic than in the old university. Of the working sample of 25 universities which I have used, only Bristol's two universities invert the pattern.[20] Averaging the sample, rather more than a fifth of the UK law students in the established universities are from ethnic minorities – a creditable figure; but in the former polytechnics, this proportion is almost doubled.[21] It is possible, then, that chambers which give preference to graduates of the established universities are unwittingly making it harder for ethnic minority students, taken as a group, to obtain pupillages.[22]

Such skewing, if it exists, is troubling not only because all English and Welsh degrees are, and have for a long time, been validated to the same national standard, but because there seems also to be an element of localised grade inflation which may exaggerate the differentials I have mentioned. A law student at Cambridge has a chance of almost one in five of getting a first; at Oxford, of better than one in six; at Cardiff, however, less than one in 100; and on average outside Oxbridge, little better than one in 50. There are, no doubt, reasons for this: the tendency of many schools to steer the brightest of their students towards

19 Figures published by PACH.
20 Figures from a sample of 25 universities' 1998 returns, published in full by the Higher Education Statistics Agency. Ethnicity figures relate to UK-domiciled students; overseas students are excluded from these statistics.
21 Figures *ibid*: the law schools of the established universities in the sample average 77.7% white; those of the ex-polytechnics 61.4%.
22 If this is right, the recently proposed change to a sandwich-course system, slotting pupillage into the BVC, will make things worse: if students without a pupillage cannot get on to the BVC, any racial differential in access will be brought forward in time and perhaps seen more sharply. The proposal is set out in a Bar Council discussion paper, 'Restructuring vocational training for the Bar' (June 1999): in essence, it suggests 20 weeks' BVC; six months' pupillage; 10 more weeks' BVC; assessment and call to the Bar with a provisional practising certificate; and a full practising certificate after a second six month pupillage.

Oxbridge; the supervision system there, which offers personalised tuition; and, possibly, a more catholic approach to the syllabus. There is certainly no direct racial correlation: Cardiff Law School, 91% white, gave only two firsts last year. But when one observes the relatively low ethnic minority representation in the Oxbridge law schools, the potential racial implication of reliance on a combination of degree class and university begins to be seen.

Women now form almost half the annual intake to the Bar Vocational Course, and they succeed at a rate pretty close to that of male students.[23] If the Equality Code is taken seriously by chambers, the marked under-representation of women at the practising Bar (less than a quarter were women in 1995) will be redressed in the course of the next generation.[24] There is already encouraging evidence of a significant drop in sexual harassment at the Bar since it was first highlighted.[25] But there are also incipient grounds for concern. I have mentioned an apparent gender gap in obtaining tenancies. Added to these is another less-noticed problem: age discrimination. The Bar historically has benefited greatly from late entrants; but current figures show that, from the age of 25, candidates are finding it increasingly difficult to obtain a pupillage.[26] This may well now be aggravated – though for reasons which I am going to suggest are not respectable – by the High Court's ruling that pupils rank as apprentices for the purposes of the minimum wage legislation, since it is from the age of 26 that apprentices benefit from it.[27]

I will not spend time on the knock-on effects of this situation. It is well known that, among other things, it constricts the flow of capable female and ethnic minority candidates for silk and for the bench. The Lord Chancellor's Department takes seriously the need for non-discriminatory criteria for appointments, to the extent that the complaint now most frequently heard – and equally mistaken – is that women and ethnic minorities do better than they deserve to. What does, I think, deserve mention is the odd way in which talent and discrimination interact. There are a number of women, and a smaller number of ethnic minority barristers, who have shone and prospered at the Bar and (mainly in the case of the former) on the bench. Most of these will tell you that they have encountered no discrimination in their careers; and their success confirms what they say. There is no doubt that the Bar is a profession in which a real star can shine regardless of gender or race –

---

23   In 1998, 795 men and 728 women were called to the Bar. In 1922, the first year when women were admitted, 10 out of the 387 called were women. The steep climb in recent years is traced in *Without Prejudice?*, the report on sex equality at the Bar and in the judiciary, prepared in 1992 for the Lord Chancellor's Department and the Bar Council by TMS Consultants.

24   Bar Council figures – an excellent example of the value of ethnic and gender audits – for 1996–97 show fall-offs of 7% and then 20% for men, compared with 10% and then 30% for women. Choices in relation to child care are likely to account for some continuing disparity, however. For ethnic minority pupils, there was a rise (from 93 to 106) from first to second six month pupillages, but then a dramatic fall (to 71) for tenancies.

25   The Shapland and Sorsby Report on *Work and Training at the Junior Bar*, 1994, found that 40% of women had encountered sexual harassment, about one-eighth of it serious. The same authors' follow-up in 1997 found that the incidence had dropped by about a quarter, and by more for serious cases. This was almost certainly an example of an enforced and beneficial change in the Bar's sense of acceptable behaviour.

26   In 1998–99, the best chance of pupillage (31.2%) was for men aged under 25; for women under 25 it was 26%. Aged 35 or over, the chance for both fell to around 10%. See, generally, Bowley, 1998.

27   Since overset on appeal: *Edmonds v Lawson* (2000) unreported, 10 March, CA.

though we have no way of knowing that it is always so. The worry is not the outstanding but the average practitioner. A woman barrister, or a black barrister, who is no better than average may well find in the dismissiveness of some colleagues and the paucity of good work a handicap which the average –sometimes very average – white male barrister does not experience.[28] It is here that the potential for indirect discrimination begins; and it is why it is to the Bar that the public ought principally to look when it asks – as it rightly and repeatedly does – why there are so few female and black QCs and even fewer judges.

I have spoken about racial, sexual and age differentials. There are also serious social and economic ones, which the present system may be tending to promote. It starts most obviously with the near-abolition of local authority grants and the introduction of student loans. It continues with the need for more borrowing during the BVC year. In spite of Inn scholarships[29] and favourable bank loans,[30] it is not uncommon for a student without private or family means to embark on pupillage with a burden of debt of £25,000 or more. It is not surprising that a substantial proportion of such students go from the BVC into employment because they cannot face the further risk and stress of seeking a pupillage and then, if they manage to get one, seeking a tenancy. Nor is it surprising that between a quarter and a third of students rely on parental support to see them through the BVC year.[31] But it is plain that any group which can fall back on parental means in sums running to many thousands of pounds is a socially and economically advantaged group, and where that group makes up over a quarter of the BVC intake it is equally plain that a privileged cohort is making its way through the system. We should not be surprised, if this pattern persists, if in the years to come the Bar returns towards the narrow stereotype from which, in the last two decades, it has been escaping.

But the means of escape are still there. They require, first and foremost, that the Bar acknowledge the straits it is in. While the leadership of the Bar Council has shown a far less defensive face to government in the drafting and passage of the Access to Justice Act 1999 than it has in the past shown to measures which threatened the Bar's prosperity, it still has to grasp the nettle of access to pupillage. This has two aspects: the first is equitable consideration of candidates, which I have now considered in some detail; the second is relief from economic hardship while pupillage is completed. Until pupillage is reached, students may have to continue to find funding where they can. After it is completed, they must expect to compete for work without cushioning. But the Bar has a clear moral obligation, once it has accepted them on its vocational course, to enable them at least to complete their vocational training. First, then, the Bar has to make it a breach of professional etiquette to refuse without good cause to take a pupil. Good cause may be as personal as a personality clash or as impersonal as the physical or organisational capacity of chambers; but the ground rule for chambers admission

---

28 See *Without Prejudice?*. In 1991, the proportion of women barristers in the bottom earnings bracket was twice that of men; in the top bracket, half that of men.

29 About 27% of BVC students rely on Inn awards for their fees, but only 10% for their living expenses: Goldsmith Report, 1998.

30 See the Tuckey Report, 1999.

31 *Ibid*, Goldsmith Report. A further 29% depend on loans; 7% on LEA grants, but for fees only; 20% live on savings or earnings; and 11% on 'other' sources, including, presumably, private incomes.

procedures has to be that a qualified junior barrister has an obligation to help to train the next generation of the Bar, not merely the next tenant in his or her own chambers. In turn this means that PACH, at present in a parlous state for want of full support, may have to be restored by rule, so that every BVC student who wants a pupillage has an equal chance of getting one – indeed, is guaranteed one.

Then there is funding. At present, perhaps the greatest disincentive to taking on more pupils than is absolutely necessary is the expectation that chambers will pay them a salary. To abandon payment would simply exaggerate the privilege differentials.[32] The answer is not to withhold pupillages: it is to spread the cost of supporting pupils equally across the Bar. Until this year, any such proposal was a pipe-dream, because there was no way of making the Bar pay and every prospect of a legal challenge to a levy. But at a late stage of the passage of the Access to Justice Bill the government introduced what is now s 46(2)(b), authorising the Bar Council to raise funds, by way of fees for practising certificates, sufficient to pay for the training of pupils. The Bar's total gross income in the last complete financial year will probably be between £1.2 and £1.4 bn.[33] A levy of, say, 1% (deductible from taxable income, but spread, I would hope, unevenly so as to spare the often unacknowledged 'thin cats' at the Bar who work hard on unglamorous cases for very little reward)[34] would raise enough to guarantee 1,500 trainee barristers an income, when earnings are taken into account, of perhaps £10,000 in their pupillage year – a sum corresponding well with the national minimum wage for a 60 hour week.[35] It would be for the Bar to decide whether to means-test the grants. The important thing is that, in combination with an allocation policy which recognises every BVC student's moral entitlement to a pupillage, it will go some way to equalising opportunity in a profession which will eventually die if it fails both to attract and to accommodate the brightest students, whatever their means or their origins.[36] It is fair treatment of pupils across the board, not trying to compete with the big solicitors' firms by expensively headhunting individuals, which will set and keep such a process in motion.

But there is one corollary which government, in its turn, must be prepared to accept. A well ordered but small profession cannot hold its door perpetually open. A point will have to come, indeed has probably been reached, at which the numbers admitted to the BVC have to correspond with what the Bar can realistically absorb. To pour unsustainable numbers into the Bar, once the obligation to provide all qualified applicants with a pupillage is recognised, would

---

32   The Bar Council has been advised by specialist leading and junior counsel that pupils are 'workers' for the purposes of the Working Time Regulations 1998.

33   BDO Stoy Hayward, 1999, para 5.1. This projection corresponds reasonably well with the total of just under £1 bn recorded by Bar Mutual Assurance for the year 1997–98.

34   See Carr, 1999.

35   At £3.60 an hour, a 60 hour week for 48 weeks a year carries a minimum wage of £10,368.

36   I have not touched on the case made in the report to the Bar Council of the committee under Sir John Collyear (*Blueprint for the Future*, May 1999) for the non-practising first part of a pupillage to be served in employment. The proposal may well be viable in certain areas of work – the Government Legal Service, for example – but any idea that it can bail out the Bar by absorbing all the hundreds who want a practising pupillage is to be treated with great caution, not least because employers, who do not necessarily share the interests of the practising Bar, may not want them.

inexorably put the profession once again in breach of faith with its students.[37] Anti-competitive or not, sanction will need to be given to a negotiated[38] cut-off of numbers at the point of entry into – not, as at present, exit from – the BVC; not so as to regenerate a seller's market in advocacy, but so as to prevent continuing waste, disappointment and the eventual slide of standards.[39] So long, however, as the Bar recognises no general obligation to see trainees through their pupillage, it has no basis on which to seek authority to restrict student numbers: the answer will always be to go on relying on 'natural' wastage with all that that implies for the many who finally lose out ...

— ·· — ·· — ·· — ·· — ·· — ·· — ·· — ·· — ·· — ·· — ·· — ·· — ·· —

In the following piece, in a Question and Answer session, Frances Gibb, legal editor of *The Times*, critically considers the alleged advantages of the Queen's Counsel system for the legal profession and for consumers.

Frances Gibb, 'The future of the legal profession – QCs' (2001) *The Times*, 8 March

What are the advantages of the Queen's Counsel system for both the consumer and the legal world? The QC system is a badge of seniority and achievement for the Bar. Senior barristers who attain a certain level of experience get this as a hallmark of accomplishment. It marks them out as the top of the profession – only 10 per cent have it – and they can charge significantly higher fees when they attain that rank.

Consumers don't brief barristers directly. They don't have any bargaining or purchasing power over barristers. Barristers are chosen by solicitors under the regulations at the moment. The Office of Fair Trading has said that if this is the case then what do solicitors need this kitemark of quality for? They should know who the best in the field are.

What the QCs would argue is that every profession has its senior ranks. You have a hospital consultant for example. The reason this raises concerns is that the rank of QC is appointed upon the recommendation of the Lord Chancellor who is a member of the Government. In medicine there isn't that direct power of patronage. What are the advantages of briefing a barrister without going to a solicitor first?

---

37 The Taylor Report, 1991, concluded that numbers should be limited at the point of entry to training, but the Director General of Fair Trading took the view that to do so would be anti-competitive. It is the throughput of the consequent validated courses which now determines the number seeking entry.

38 By 'negotiated', I mean agreed between the Bar and government, as well as other interested professions and bodies, such as the Consumers' Association. Much is going to depend in the immediate future on the effect of the radical reordering of legal aid under the Access to Justice Act 1999 on the volume of work available, in particular, to young barristers. Even more will depend on the uptake and impact of the extension of rights of audience under the Act to non-practising barristers, solicitors and, in due course, other professions.

39 For the reasons I have given, the superficially attractive expedient of limiting numbers on the BVC by requiring entrants to have obtained a pupillage first would accentuate any racial and other disadvantage in the present state of pupillage allocation. In a better-ordered system, no doubt, it would work well, though the accredited providers would have reason to feel let down as their student numbers fell.

What the profession would argue is that the Bar operates as a group of self-employed people who don't deal with clients' money as solicitors do. They act as a referral service. The advantage of this means that anywhere in the country people can brief the expert in his field. You can go to a solicitor in Macclesfield and brief the top tax QC in the land. In a way that is also like the medical profession – you go to a GP and they refer you to a hospital consultant.

What the OFT and the solicitors say is that it is very expensive to have to brief two lawyers. They ask, 'why can't the first lawyer that you go to do the whole case?' That is the argument for solicitors now taking cases in court which they can now do. To some extent that argument has already been won as solicitors can now do what previously only barristers could have done, and actually take trials.

Is the idea of 'one-stop' shops, in which lawyers, accountants and other professions set up a mixed partnership a feasible proposal?

Yes. There's a lot of support for this now. It's an argument that has gone on for a long time now and the legal profession has shifted its ground. A lot of big city law firms are quite keen to be able to set up joint partnerships. They might want an accountancy department or some other group of professionals in their offices. Not just the big firms either, small firms of solicitors might want a patent expert or forensic pathologist on their team, but at the moment they can only employ them and can't have them in joint partnership. Thus a lot of people would favour that.

Would there be a risk of lowering standards if banks and building societies offered conveyancing, probate and wills?

There will be worries about them offering conveyancing to their customers. While they may be able to offer a cut price service due to the sheer bulk they are turning over. The argument that the legal profession will raise is that the borrower won't be able to say 'No, I don't want my conveyancing done by you, I want it done by a solicitor down the road'. The banks and building societies will have a lot of muscle power and a conflict of interest will arise.

Indeed it could be argued as being anti-competitive. What are the disadvantages of lifting restrictions so that barristers can advertise success rates and cold-calling clients? The argument about success rates is rather like doctors publishing their death and complication figures. To take the medical analogy you might be in an area of work where most of your patients are likely to survive, or you might be in an area where all your patients have terminal cancer. Lawyers would argue that the fact you don't win all your cases is not a comment on your ability. I've heard QCs say that the cases win or lose themselves to a degree and thus aren't an accurate comment on your ability. Will the proposed changes ultimately be implemented by the the legal profession?

The proposal to look at the QC system will at the very least be handed to the profession itself. If the Bar wants senior ranks within its body then the Bar itself should award it. There are only historical reasons why the Government should be involved in it at all. The multi-disciplinary partnership is inevitably going to come about because the professions themselves are moving towards it.

Advertising restrictions and conveyancing proposals will be argued out but I don't think there will be huge changes. It is an incremental change, the legal profession has been through a lot of change in the last ten years. Ultimately what we are probably looking towards is a fused profession in which the two branches –

barristers and solicitors – won't be separate in quite the same way, although I am sure there will always be specialist advocates who take work on referral from solicitors.

— · — · — · — · — · — · — · — · — · — · — · — · — · —

LOSS OF NEGLIGENCE IMMUNITY FOR ADVOCATES

The liability of advocates for negligence in the court room was established as a legal possibility by the House of Lords in *Arthur JS Hall & Co (A Firm) v Melvyn Keith Simons: Barratt v Ansell and Others (T/A Woolf Seddon (A Firm)): Harris v Scholfield Roberts & Hill (A Firm)* [2000] 3 All ER 673; [2000] 3 WLR 543. Below is a digest of the case, followed by a commentary.

Those pieces are followed by the full opinion of Lord Millett.

Arthur JS Hall & Co v Simons and Other Appeals [2000] TLR, 21 July, House of Lords, www.parliament.the-stationery-office.co.uk/pa/ld199900/ldjudgmt

Background

Lawyers are, for the general public, the most central and prominent part of the English legal system. They are, arguably, to the legal system what doctors are to the health system. For many decades a debate has grown about why a patient injured by the negligence of a surgeon in the operating theatre can sue for damages, whereas a litigant whose case is lost because of the negligence of his advocate cannot sue. It all seemed very unfair. Even the most glaringly obvious courtroom negligence was protected against legal action by a special advocates' immunity. The claim that this protection was made by lawyers (and judges who were lawyers) for lawyers was difficult to refute. In this House of Lords' decision the historic immunity has been abolished in respect of both barristers and solicitor-advocates (of whom there are now over 1000 with higher courts rights of audience) and for both civil and criminal proceedings.

Facts

In three cases, all conjoined on appeal, a claimant raised a claim of negligence against a firm of solicitors, and in each case the firms relied on the immunity attaching to barristers and other advocates from actions in negligence. At first instance, all the claims were struck out. Then, on appeal, the Court of Appeal said that claims could have proceeded. The solicitors appealed to the Lords and two key questions were raised: should the old immunity rule be maintained and, in a criminal case, what was the proper scope of the principle against 'collateral attack'? A collateral attack is when someone convicted in a criminal court tries to invalidate that conviction outside the criminal appeals process by suing his trial defence lawyer in a civil court. The purpose of such a collateral attack is to win in the civil case, proving negligence against the criminal trial lawyer and, thus, by implication, show that the conviction in the criminal case was unfair.

Findings

Held: the House of Lords held (Lord Hope, Lord Hutton and Lord Hobhouse dissenting in part) that, in the light of modern conditions, it was now clear that it was no longer in the public interest in the administration of justice that advocates should have immunity from suit for negligence for acts concerned with the conduct of either civil or criminal litigation.

Lord Hoffmann (with Lord Steyn, Lord Browne-Wilkinson and Lord Millett delivering concurring opinions) said that over 30 years had passed since the House had last considered the rationale for the immunity of the advocate from suit, in *Rondel v Worsley* [1969] 1 AC 191. Public policy was not immutable and there had been great changes in the law of negligence, the functioning of the legal profession, the administration of justice and public perceptions. It was once again time to re-examine the whole matter. Interestingly, Lord Hoffmann chose to formulate his opinion in a creative mode to reflect public policy rather than in the tradition of what can be seen as slavish obedience to the details of precedent:

> I hope that I will not be thought ungrateful if I do not encumber this speech with citations. The question of what the public interest now requires depends upon the strength of the arguments rather than the weight of authority.

The point of departure was that in general English law provided a remedy in damages for a person who had suffered injury as a result of professional negligence. It followed that any exception which denied such a remedy required a sound justification. The arguments relied on by the court in *Rondel v Worsley* as justifying the immunity had to be considered. One by one these arguments are evaluated and rejected.

Advocate's divided loyalty

There were two distinct versions of the divided loyalty argument. The first was that the possibility of being sued for negligence would actually inhibit the lawyer, consciously or unconsciously, from giving his duty to the court priority to his duty to his client. The second was that the divided loyalty was a special factor that made the conduct of litigation a very difficult art and could lead to the advocate being exposed to vexatious claims by difficult clients. The argument was pressed most strongly in connection with advocacy in criminal proceedings, where the clients were said to be more than usually likely to be vexatious.

There had been recent developments in the civil justice system designed to reduce the incidence of vexatious litigation. The first was r 24.2 of the new Civil Procedure Rules which provided that a court could give summary judgment in favour of a defendant if it considered that '... the claimant had no real prospect of succeeding on the claim'. The second was the changes to the funding of civil litigation introduced by the Access to Justice Act 1999 which would make it much more difficult than it had been in the past to obtain legal help for negligence actions which had little prospect of success.

There was no doubt that the advocate's duty to the court was extremely important in the English justice system. The question was whether removing the immunity would have a significantly adverse effect. If the possibility of being held liable in negligence was calculated to have an adverse effect on the behaviour of advocates in court, one might have expected that to have followed, at least in some degree, from the introduction of wasted costs orders (where a court disallows a lawyer from being able to claim part of a fee for work which is regarded as unnecessary and wasteful). Although the liability of a negligent advocate to a wasted costs order was not the same as a liability to pay general damages, the experience of the wasted costs jurisdiction was the only empirical evidence available in England to test the proposition that such liability would have an adverse effect upon the way advocates performed their duty to the court and there was no suggestion that it had changed standards of advocacy for the worse.

The 'cab rank'

The cab rank rule provided that a barrister could not refuse to act for a client on the ground that he disapproved of him or his case. The argument was that a barrister, who was obliged to accept any client, would be unfairly exposed to vexatious actions by clients whom any sensible lawyer with freedom of action would have refused to act for. Such a claim however was, in the nature of things, intuitive, incapable of empirical verification, and did not have any real substance.

The witness analogy

The argument started from the well established rule that a witness was absolutely immune from liability for anything that he said in court. So were the judge, counsel and the parties. They could not be sued for libel, malicious falsehood or conspiring to give false evidence. The policy of the rule was to encourage persons who took part in court proceedings to express themselves freely. However, a witness owed no duty of care to anyone in respect of the evidence he gave to the court. His only duty was to tell the truth. There was no analogy with the position of a lawyer who owed a duty of care to his client. The fact that the advocate was the only person involved in the trial process who was liable to be sued for negligence was because he was the only person who had undertaken such a duty of care to his client.

Collateral attack

The most substantial argument was that it might be contrary to the public interest for a court to retry a case which had been decided by another court. However, actions for negligence against lawyers were not the only cases that gave rise to a possibility of the same issue being tried twice. The law had to deal with the problem in numerous other contexts. So, before examining the strength of the collateral challenge argument as a reason for maintaining the immunity of lawyers, it was necessary to consider how the law dealt with collateral challenge in general.

The law discouraged relitigation of the same issues except by means of an appeal. The Latin maxims often quoted were *nemo debet bis vexari pro una et eadem causa* and *interest rei publicae ut finis sit litium*. The first was concerned with the interests of the defendant: a person should not be troubled twice for the same reason. That policy had generated the rules which prevented relitigation when the parties were the same: *autrefois acquit* (someone acquitted of a crime cannot be tried again for that crime), *res judicata* (a particular dispute decided by a civil court cannot be re-tried) and issue estoppel (a person cannot deny the fact of a judgment previously decided against him).

The second policy was wider: it was concerned with the interests of the State. There was a general public interest in the same issue not being litigated over again. The second policy could be used to justify the extension of the rules of issue estoppel to cases in which the parties were not the same but the circumstances were such as to bring the case within the spirit of the rules. Criminal proceedings were in a special category because, although they were technically litigation between the Crown and the defendant, the Crown prosecuted on behalf of society as a whole. So a conviction had some of the quality of a judgement in rem, which should be binding in favour of everyone.

Not all re-litigation of the same issue, however, would be manifestly unfair to a party or bring the administration of justice into disrepute. Sometimes, there were valid reasons for re-hearing a dispute. It was, therefore, unnecessary to try to stop any re-litigation by forbidding anyone from suing their lawyer. It was 'burning down the house to roast the pig; using a broad-spectrum remedy without side-effects could handle the problem equally well'.

The scope for re-examination of issues in criminal proceedings was much wider than in civil cases. Fresh evidence was more readily admitted. A conviction could be set aside as unsafe and unsatisfactory when the accused appeared to have been prejudiced by 'flagrantly incompetent advocacy': see *R v Clinton* [1993] 1 WLR 1181. After conviction, the case could be referred to the Court of Appeal, if the conviction was on indictment, or to the crown court, if the trial was summary, by the Criminal Cases Review Commission.

It followed that it would ordinarily be an abuse of process for a civil court to be asked to decide that a subsisting conviction was wrong. That applied to a conviction on a plea of guilty as well as after a trial. The resulting conflict of judgments was likely to bring the administration of justice into disrepute. The proper procedure was to appeal, or, if the right of appeal had been exhausted, to apply to the Criminal Cases Review Commission. It would ordinarily be an abuse, because there were bound to be exceptional cases in which the issue could be tried without a risk that the conflict of judgments would bring the administration of justice into disrepute.

Once the conviction has been set aside, there could be no public policy objection to an action for negligence against the legal advisers. There could be no conflict of judgments. On the other hand, in civil, including matrimonial, cases, it would seldom be possible to say that an action for negligence against a legal adviser or representative would bring the administration of justice into disrepute. Whether the original decision was right or wrong was usually a matter of concern only to the parties and had no wider implications. There was no public interest objection to a subsequent finding that, but for the negligence of his lawyers, the losing party would have won.

But again there might be exceptions. The action for negligence might be an abuse of process on the ground that it was manifestly unfair to someone else. Take, for example, the case of a defendant who published a serious defamation which he attempted unsuccessfully to justify. Should he be able to sue his lawyers and claim that if the case had been conducted differently, the allegation would have been proved to be true? It seemed unfair to the plaintiff in the defamation action that any court should be allowed to come to such a conclusion in proceedings to which he was not a party. On the other hand, it was equally unfair that he should have to join as a party and rebut the allegation for a second time. A man's reputation was not only a matter between him and the other party. It represented his relationship with the world. So it might be that in such circumstances, an action for negligence would be an abuse of the process of the court.

Having regard to the power of the court to strike out actions which had no real prospect of success, the doctrine was unlikely in that context to be invoked very often. The first step in any application to strike out an action alleging negligence in the conduct of a previous action had to be to ask whether it had a real prospect of success.

Lord Hope, Lord Hutton and Lord Hobhouse delivered judgments in which they agreed that the immunity from suit was no longer required in relation to civil proceedings but dissented to the extent of saying that the immunity was still required in the public interest in the administration of justice in relation to criminal proceedings.

Comment

This decision is of major and historic importance in the English legal system for several reasons. It can be seen as a bold attempt by the senior judiciary to drag the legal profession (often a metonymy for the whole legal system) into the 21st century world of accountability and fair business practice. In his judgment, Lord Steyn makes this dramatic observation:

> ... public confidence in the legal system is not enhanced by the existence of the immunity. The appearance is created that the law singles out its own for protection no matter how flagrant the breach of the barrister. The world has changed since 1967. The practice of law has become more commercialised: barristers may now advertise. They may now enter into contracts for legal services with their professional clients. They are now obliged to carry insurance. On the other hand,

today we live in a consumerist society in which people have a much greater awareness of their rights. If they have suffered a wrong as the result of the provision of negligent professional services, they expect to have the right to claim redress. It tends to erode confidence in the legal system if advocates, alone among professional men, are immune from liability for negligence.

The case raises and explores many key issues of the legal system including the proper relationship between lawyers and the courts, the proper relationship between lawyers and clients, the differences between criminal and civil actions, professional ethics, the nature of dispute resolution, and the circumstances under which the courts should make new law. Above all, however, the case has one simple significance: '... it will,' in the words of Jonathan Hirst QC, Chairman of the Bar Council, 'mean that a claimant who can prove loss, as the result of an advocate's negligence, will no longer be prevented from making a claim. We cannot really say that is wrong' ((2000) *Bar News*, August, p 3).

> **Lord Millett**: My Lords, I have had the advantage of reading in draft the speeches of my noble and learned friends Lord Steyn and Lord Hoffmann, with which I am in full agreement.
>
> I understand that all your Lordships would abolish the advocate's immunity in civil proceedings, but that some of you would retain it in criminal cases. I readily acknowledge that the case for abolition is stronger in civil litigation, and given my lack of experience of the criminal justice system I have given anxious consideration to the views of those of your Lordships who would retain the immunity in criminal proceedings. I have, however, come to the conclusion that such a partial retention of the immunity should not be supported.
>
> My reasons for this conclusion are twofold. In the first place, I think that to make the existence of the immunity depend on whether the proceedings in question are civil or criminal would be to draw the line in the wrong place. There is a wide variety of cases tried before the magistrates which are for all practical purposes civil in character, and in which the retention of the immunity would be anomalous, but which are commenced by information or summons and which are classified as criminal proceedings. Conversely disciplinary proceedings before professional bodies are classified as civil proceedings but are criminal or quasi-criminal in character. Here the abolition of the immunity would be anomalous but its retention difficult to justify.
>
> In the second place, even if the immunity were retained only in criminal cases tried on indictment, in which the liberty of the subject is at stake (and which is probably the kind of case your Lordships primarily have in mind), it is difficult to believe that the distinction would commend itself to the public. It would mean that a party would have a remedy if the incompetence of his counsel deprived him of compensation for (say) breach of contract or unfair dismissal, but not if it led to his imprisonment for a crime he did not commit and the consequent and uncompensated loss of his job. I think that the public would at best regard such a result as incomprehensible and at worst greet it with derision. The more thoughtful members of the public might well consider that we had got it the wrong way round.

These considerations persuade me that we ought not to retain the immunity in criminal proceedings in the absence of compelling reasons to do so. I acknowledge that there is a particularly high public interest in the efficient administration of criminal justice, that the need to ensure that the accused has a fair trial makes it difficult for the judge to intervene, and that both judge and defence counsel are likely to err on the side of caution. But that is the position today, despite the existence of the immunity. I have some scepticism in accepting the proposition that its removal will make matters significantly worse, and I observe that two of your Lordships with experience of criminal trials do not think that it will.

In my opinion the defending advocate in a criminal trial will retain formidable safeguards against vexatious attack even if he no longer enjoys a formal immunity from suit. His former client will not be allowed to challenge the correctness of the conviction unless and until it is set aside, and a claim which does not challenge the correctness of the conviction, like that in *Rondel v Worsley* [1969] 1 AC 191 itself, should normally be struck out as an abuse of the process of the court. The withdrawal of legal aid combined with the new powers of the court to strike out hopeless claims even though they plead a good cause of action should make the great majority of unmeritorious claims still-born. But if the immunity from suit is retained for the moment in criminal cases alone, then sooner or later a case is bound to arise in which the House will be called on to reconsider the question. It will be a bad case involving a clear miscarriage of justice, for otherwise the immunity will not be engaged. It will be a case in which the accused was plainly innocent but was wrongly convicted and served a term of imprisonment as a result of the gross incompetence of his counsel. The conviction will have been quashed on appeal, perhaps accompanied by severe criticism from the court of the conduct of the counsel who was responsible. And by the time the civil claim reaches the House, the public will have become accustomed to read of cases where advocates have been successfully sued for incompetence in the course of civil proceedings even though far less than their client's liberty was at stake. Moreover, the Human Rights Act 1998 will be in force, and the House will have to reconsider the question in terms of article 6 of the European Convention of Human Rights.

I would grasp the nettle now. I believe that the general public would find the proposed distinction indefensible. In the absence of compelling reasons to support it based on more than instinct or intuition, of which I can find none, I find it hard to disagree. I also think that it is difficult to defend a blanket professional immunity in terms of the European Convention on Human Rights. I would dismiss these appeals and declare that the advocate has no immunity from suit in relation to his conduct of proceedings whether civil or criminal.

CHAPTER 10

THE JURY

THE ROLE OF THE JURY

It is generally accepted that the jury of '12 good men and true' lies at the heart of the British legal system. The implicit assumption is that the presence of 12 ordinary lay persons, randomly introduced into the trial procedure to be the arbiters of the facts of the case, strengthens the legitimacy of the legal system by introducing a democratic, humanising element into the abstract, impersonal trial process. The function of the jury is to decide on matters of fact. Matters of law are the province of the judge. Judges have the power to direct juries to acquit the accused where there is insufficient evidence to convict them, and this is the main safeguard against juries finding defendants guilty in spite of insufficiency of evidence. There is, however, no corresponding judicial power to instruct juries to convict and juries have, in the past, failed to convict accused who would have appeared to have had no defence against the charges levied at them. This occurrence is understood to represent the exercise of what is known as the 'jury's equity'.

In her article below, Penny Darbyshire questions the traditional justifications used in praise and defence of the jury, suggesting that some of them are conceptually unsound.

Penny Darbyshire, 'The lamp that shows that freedom lives – is it worth the candle?'
[1991] Crim LR 740–52

In this paper I hope to examine some of the commonly held beliefs and assumptions which underline traditional and oft-repeated adulation of jury trial. I take as my starting point Ashworth's 1979 plea on the criminal justice system that we 'should devote some time to reflection on the theory behind it all'. Theory, says Ashworth, 'is essential, because social and legal arrangements – especially in so sensitive an area as criminal justice – need to be *justified* if they are to be acceptable'. Ashworth suggests, and I accept for the purposes of this paper, that the general justifying aim of the administration of criminal justice is that the guilty should be detected, convicted and duly sentenced, which he calls, for convenience, 'crime control'.

The jury has probably provoked more comment and research than any other component of the criminal justice system. It seems to attract the most praise and least theoretical analysis. There is a wealth of material on the common law jury, predominantly American, English and Australian, and defenders of the jury seem to outnumber its opponents by about a hundred to one. There are a few notable works which make a serious attempt to analyse the basis of the jury: Bankowski and Mungham; Freeman; Duff and Findlay; and Bankowski.

Everyone seems to have an opinion on the jury and few are indifferent. It is as much the territory of the journalist, the politician, the pressure group and the lay person as it is of the lawyer or the academic. This is as it should be and hardly surprising, considering its very essence as a powerfully symbolic lay element in the criminal justice system. Juries, as Baldwin and McConville observe, provoke comments which are little short of hysterical. The academic owes it to the rest, however, to be a little more analytical and to justify her or his assertions.

The English legal system has traditionally been characterised by smug complacency amongst lawyers, politicians and lay people alike. We seldom feel the need to justify our institutions, in the way required by Answorth. Knowing that our legal system has been copied by newer anglophone countries, we assume that it must be a sound model. We have heard propaganda, since childhood, that our legal system is the best in the world, the epitome of the due process model.

Such complacency has allowed our legal system to remain virtually static between the Judicature Acts of the 1870s and the sweeping reforms of the 1980s and 1990s, with minor disturbances such as the introduction of juvenile courts and the CPS. When we do examine our legal system, via Royal Commissions, review boards, working parties and the like, we tend to focus on existing institutions and to examine the part and not the whole. Most proposals for change, this century, have been shelved or rejected. The Civil Justice Review was quite revolutionary in its breadth, its depth and its success rate. Moreover, it was shockingly heretical in asking whether we really need two levels of trial court and on what basis we can justify dividing the work between them. One can only hope that this pattern is repeated by the new Royal Commission on Criminal Justice.

The Commission must ask the parallel questions of why we have two levels of criminal trial court and whether we are justified, in the sense Ashworth demands, in retaining three sets of decision makers within them: lay magistrates, advised mostly by non-lawyers; stipendiary magistrates, advised mostly by lawyers; and the judge and jury. There is little legal logic or design in the division of their jurisdictions. They have simply evolved through the last 10 centuries or more.

If the jury is such a 'palladium' of English justice (Blackstone), why is it reserved for such a small number of cases, most defendants being treated to the quicker, cheaper, less flamboyant 'trivial' justice of the magistrates' court? If the jury is such a guardian of our liberties and of justice, are we implying that magistrates dispense some lesser form of justice? Are we implying, since we invest so much cash and rhetoric in the jury system, that it is more likely to do justice and get the verdict right, whatever that means, than the magistrates? If so, why do we, in this, the fairest of legal systems, allow most of our defendants to be processed by the magistrates' courts? And, this being the case, why have academics invested so much argument and research into the jury?

There is one obvious answer to my questions here. The symbolic function of the jury far outweighs its principal significance. I shall argue in this paper that this sentimental attachment to the symbol of the jury is dangerous. Adulation of the jury is based on no justification or spurious justification. It has fed public complacency with the English legal system and distracted attention from its evils: a systematic lack of due process pre-trial and post-trial and certain deficiencies in the trial process itself. It has distorted the truth. The truth is that for most people who pass through the criminal justice system this palladium is simply not available and for those who can and do submit themselves to its verdict, it will not necessarily safeguard their civil liberties.

A 'constitutional right' to jury trial

This justification for the jury is perhaps the best known and the most often served up without explanation, as a self-evident truth. Three problems arise under this heading:

a   the supposed guarantee of a right to jury trial in *Magna Carta*;

b   what is meant by a constitutional right to jury trial in the English legal system? and

c   what is meant, in jurisprudential terms, by asserting that there is a right to jury trial?

(a) Magna Carta

Many writers claim that jury trial was enshrined as a constitutional right in *Magna Carta*, 1215, clause 39, which provided for a 'trial by peers'. Later authors undoubtedly derived this myth from Devlin, who perpetuated it in 1956, having taken it from Blackstone's *Commentaries*.

Whilst Blackstone's grandiloquent account of the English legal system in the 18th century is of great entertainment value, few later legal historians or constitutional lawyers would accept it as historically accurate. Some of his assertions have been used to quite an alarming extent, however, in establishing the constitutional foundations of newer common law jurisdictions.

The famous clause 39 of *Magna Carta* reads:

> *Nullus liber homo capiatur vel imprisonetur, aut disseisiatur aut utlagetur, aut exuletur, aut aliquo modo destruatur, nec super eum ibimus nec super eum mittemus, nisi per legale judicium parium vel per legum terrae.*

which Holdsworth translates as:

> No freeman shall be taken or/and imprisoned, or disseised, or exiled, or outlawed, or in any way destroyed, nor will we go upon him nor will we send upon him, except by the lawful judgment of his peers or/and by the law of the land.

Legal historians have been at pains to point out that clause 39 has nothing to do with trial by jury and, as Cornish said, 'It has always been bad history to trace the system back to *Magna Carta*'. Holdsworth acknowledges that the misinterpretation of clause 39 has had sweeping effects on English constitutional history but explains:

> ... it is also clear that the words *judicium parium* do not refer to trial by jury. A trial by a royal judge and a body of recognitors was exactly what the barons did not want. What they did want was firstly a tribunal of the old type in which all the suitors were judges of both law and fact, and secondly a tribunal in which they would not be judged by their inferiors. Some of them did not consider that the royal judge, none of them would have considered that a body of recognitors, were their peers.

Earlier, in his *History of Trial by Jury*, Forsyth had said that it was a common but erroneous opinion that *judicium parium* or trial by one's peers had reference to the jury and had misled many, including Blackstone. He explains that *judicium* implies the decision of a judge, not a jury verdict. I would add that it is crucial to remember that, in 1215, the jury was still a group of oathswearing witnesses, or compurgators. They did not pronounce judgment. The *pares*, suggests Forsyth, were:

members of the county and other courts, who discharged the function of judges, and who were the peers or fellows of the parties before them.

As these and other historians have pointed out, by *Magna Carta* the barons simply sought to secure a deal from King John, within which they safeguarded their right to be judged by judges of no lesser rank than themselves. *Liber homo* has been translated as either 'freeman' or 'freeholder' and 'freeman' did not mean what it does today. As we should remember from school history, freemen were a limited class in the feudal system.

(b) A constitutional right?

Even if one were to concede that it has become a constitutional convention, since the 14th century, when statute prescribed that jurors be independent, that juries be used in certain criminal trials, I balk at the concept of trial by jury's being 'more than one wheel of the constitution'. Devlin and others speak as if there were an entrenched right to jury trial, as there is in the United States Constitution or the Canadian Bill or Rights. The concept of a 'constitutional right' has, historically, been so alien to British constitutional lawyers, that the phrase seldom appeared in textbooks before the 1980s and now it only appears in the context of the debate over the need for a Bill of Rights. Indeed, the call for a Bill of Rights has arisen for this very reason: the sovereignty of parliament dictates that we do not have any entrenched rights, especially in issues beyond the grasp of EU or international law. This is manifest in relation to jury trial. Parliament has almost rendered the civil jury extinct and has continually eroded the use and availability of the jury in the criminal trial.

(c) A right?

There is also a jurisprudential problem with those who justify the use of jury trial as a right. The term 'right', at least to 'will' theorists, implies a choice. When we speak of procedural rights in the criminal justice system, we imply a choice. For example, I do not have to exercise my right of silence. Similarly, if I am charged with an offence which is triable either way, I can choose to be tried by judge and jury or magistrates. This choice can properly be called a 'right' to jury trial. What of indictable offences? Here, I must appear before the Crown Court, where my only choice is as to plea. My only right is as to trial. I cannot choose to be tried by judge alone, as I could in the United States. Thus, it is correct to speak of a 'right', in general terms, in the English legal system, as so many defenders of the jury are wont to do.

By reasoning thus, I am accepting that the essence of a right must be a power of waiver. MacCormick would take issue with this and argue that restricting my power of waiver does not negate my right. To this, I would repeat Simmonds's reply: 'It is doubtful if paternalism of this kind is best interpreted as a protection of the party's rights.'

Not only does the concept of a right to jury trial in indictable offences fail to accord with 'will' theories of rights, it also fails to satisfy classical 'interest' theories of rights and I would extend my argument here to include triable either way offences. According to interest theories, as I would apply them here, jury trial can only be described as a 'right' if the intended beneficiary of the court's duty to provide that right is the defendant. If the purpose of jury trial is primarily ideological, as I argue here, as a symbol to legitimate the criminal justice system, then the defendant is the unintended beneficiary and thus cannot be said to have real right to jury trial.

'Trial by peers': random or representative or selected by 'Voir Dire'?

My next objection is to the jury protagonists' lack of clarity over what virtues they are celebrating in the composition of 'trial by peers'. A similar point has been raised before, by Marshall and Duff and Findlay, but bears repeating, since it seems to have been ignored. Frequently, randomness is treated as a synonym for representativeness and some even fail to recognise that any form of *voir dire* is incompatible with the other two concepts. This problem is faced by Enright and Morton and Gobert and touched on but not tackled by Bankowski. While I will accept that a random jury can be said to represent the community in the most abstract sense, many writers assume random selection will, magically, throw up a representative cross section of the population, reflecting the views of the community at large. For example, Frieberg, says:

> The legitimacy of the jury's role depends upon a strict adherence to some basic tenets of jury selection procedures, principally random selection and impartiality. A key factor in ensuring the jury's impartiality is its representativeness. The aim of jury selection is to create a jury of one's peers.

The conceptual confusion here is quite breathtaking. Indeed, Frieberg cites the Departmental Committee on Jury Service (1965), making the same mistake: 'A jury should represent a cross-section drawn at random from the community ...'

Random selection from the community is unlikely to produce a cross-section, unless some form of stratified sampling is used, which is not the case in summoning a jury. Random selection may throw up juries which are all male, all Conservative, all white.

As to my second point, many civil libertarians hail the right to a randomly selected jury as part of our constitutional heritage and in this notion ground their objections to vetting by the prosecution. Many of these see nothing incompatible in also arguing for defence rights of challenge to be strengthened.

Apart from these problems, civil libertarian claims to a right to trial by random jury is historically and factually inaccurate. Property qualifications were only abolished in 1972, before which jurors were all householders, mostly male. Many assert that 'the law' prescribes random selection. For instance, Thompson: 'That is the common understanding of the common law of this land.' There is no case authority for this notion. Many rely on the Lord Chief Justice's 1973 Practice Direction, declaring 'A jury consists of 12 individuals chosen at random ...' but Practice Directions are not 'the law'. Indeed, the key statute on jury composition is the Juries Act 1974, which makes no mention of randomness and provides for its very antithesis, its schedules excluding long lists of the ineligible, the disqualified and the excusable.

Furthermore, different practices of local summoning officers in excusing summoned jurors further distorts jury randomness or representativeness, as Baldwin and McConville found. Moreover, 'self-deselection' of unwilling jurors from the panel exacerbates this distortion. The truth is that juries are far from being either a random or a representative section of the population.

An injection of democracy into the legal system

'Each jury is a little parliament', says Devlin and cites Blackstone in support. He celebrates and justifies the jury, along with so many others, as a symbol of participatory democracy. This symbolism has been analysed and defended most carefully by Bankowski and Mungham; Freeman and Bankowski.

One element of this notion is that lay involvement in the legal system gives people confidence in its fairness, especially if they are personally involved. As Cornish said:

> ... the system has the intrinsic advantage that in drawing upon a steady stream of ordinary citizens it is not only educating them in the work of the courts, but also, since they are generally satisfied with their own performance, sending them back to their ordinary lives with a sense of the fairness and propriety of the judicial process in this country.

And McEldowney goes as far as to claim: 'jury service has now become a citizen's right as well as his duty'. This kind of romanticism is quite devoid of constitutional or jurisprudential support. The power of the symbolism of participatory democracy is, however, highly significant. It underlies most pro-jury polemic produced by lawyers, academics, civil libertarians, politicians and public alike. As Cornish says:

> It would certainly be foolish to dismiss too hastily the obvious fact that a great many people simply believe in the jury system.

If jurors' personal accounts are to be believed, however, many people strain to avoid jury service and, of those who do not, many are bored, resentful and generally disillusioned by their experience.

Most of those who justify the jury as the quintessence of lay participation in a lawyers' paradise ignore the massive involvement of lay people in decision making in the English legal system. Devlin and Blackstone argue as if democracy would collapse into tyranny if we were to abolish 'this sacred bulwark of our nation' (Blackstone) and 'the lamp that shows that freedom lives' (Devlin). Modern repetition of these sentiments either ignores the part played by over 28,000 lay justices in our criminal justice system, or disregards them as part of the legal establishment. Blackstone clearly viewed them as such, in the 18th century. While I would concede that the 20th century lay justices are not representative of the community as a whole, I would point out that neither is the jury, as I have argued above.

I couple these objections with the observation that the jury's symbolic significance is magnified beyond its practical significance by the media, as well as academics, thus unwittingly misleading the public. Of criminal cases, about five per cent are dealt with by the Crown Court. Of those cases, over two-thirds are resolved in a guilty plea, leaving just under two per cent to be tried by jury.

Yet, so powerful is the symbol of jury trial that the public image of a criminal trial is surely a Crown Court trial, complete with wigs, gowns, a red judge and Rumpole in defence; a democratic portrayal repeated on news items which so often focus on the swing doors of the Old Bailey. In contrast, the 'trivial' activities of the magistrates' courts seldom make the national news, yet it is to the justice of the magistrates that most people will, or must, submit, should they be charged with a criminal offence.

Jury equity: our defence against state power

Justifications for the jury under this heading are so often recited that their sources are too many to mention, but among them are Blackstone, Devlin, Thompson, Harman and Griffith, Bankowski and Mungham and most writers in Findlay and Duff. There are several ideas here:

(a) that in 'State' trials, the jury will acquit where it sees the defendant has been prosecuted unfairly;

(b) that the jury will acquit in ordinary cases, where it considers the prosecution unfair or the law to be unpopular, or sympathises with the defendant;

(c) that in doing either of these things, it may disobey the law and apply its own equity, thus acting as a democratic brake on the State.

Much of the pro-jury polemic eulogises the jury for departing from the law. For instance, Kalven and Zeisel said:

> It represents also an impressive way of building discretion, equity and flexibility into a legal system. Not the least of the advantages is that the jury, relieved of the burdens of creating precedent, can bend the law without breaking it.

> Whether or not one comes to admire the jury system as much as we have, it must rank as a daring effort in human arrangement to work out a solution to the tensions between law and equity and anarchy.

Presented with this image of the plucky little jury battling it out on our behalf against the all powerful State, who can fail to share the civil libertarian outrage when the jury is vetted or statute removes more offences from the ambit of jury trial? This imagery does not, however, bear close scrutiny.

(a) 'State' trials

This justification has been examined and found waiting by Williams and Cornish, who cited many such trials where the jury convicted. For all those who now cite the acquittal of Clive Ponting, I would remind them of the so called Winchester Three, the Guildford Four, the Maguires and the Birmingham Six. In these last three, the police were clearly over-anxious to secure convictions, to be seen to be satisfying the clamour for crime control from an outraged British public. They appear to have ignored many of the (weak) safeguards of due process provided for the defendants at the pre-trial stage, and to have fabricated evidence and extracted false confessions. The juries were not to be blamed for these wrongful convictions but they failed to remedy the lack of due process at the pre-trial stage and thus did not provide the break on oppressive State activity claimed for the jury by its defendants. Devlin's 'lamp that shows that freedom lives' did not offer a glimmer of hope to these defendants.

(b) Unfair laws/oppressive prosecutions

Defences of the jury under this heading usually emphasise the examples of juries re-writing the law to suit the defence. Writers conveniently disregard or underrate the fact that jury equity is a double-edged sword which may also convict the innocent. For instance, Freeman and Bankowski cite McCabe and Purves' example of a hot-dog salesman, acquitted of wounding on the illegitimate grounds of provocation, presumably by a sympathetic jury. Freeman concludes:

What they were saying was that provocation ought to be a defence not merely to charges of murder and in saying this they would have the support of the bulk of the population.

I have two objections to this. First, in the absence of a reasoned decision, how do we know whether juries acquit out of sympathy or for some extraneous reason? Secondly, the argument ignores the potential for wrongful convictions in allowing the jury to re-write the law.

Baldwin and McConville found little evidence of this romantic notion of jury equity. Unexpected verdicts apparently occurred at random. Personal accounts of ex-jurors indicate that they will sometimes acquit or convict, for a variety of extraneous reasons which have nothing to do with replacing the law with their own sense of fairness or equity. They include the pressure of incarceration in the jury room and the replacement of the high standard of proof 'beyond reasonable doubt' with a lesser standard of proof 'on the balance of probabilities'.

Jurors also sometimes base their decisions on sympathy or hostility towards other trial participants, notably counsel and witnesses, as indicated by the accounts in Barber and Gordon's book and elsewhere. To illustrate this, I will counter the story of the hot-dog salesman with a story of my own. I sent my new first year law students out to watch courts of their own choice. They were asked to report back to tutorials but to no set structure. Several groups gave me different accounts of the same case which had taken their fancy because of the dramatic content and the surprising result.

A shop assistant was charged with theft of 20 items of clothing from her employers. She did not deny that she had ripped off the price labels, hidden the clothes in a bag in a cupboard and then taken them home and gone abroad for a fortnight's holiday. Her defence was that she had taken the bag home by accident and had meant to pay for the clothes. When she discovered her error, she had panicked and gone away on holiday. The students thought defence counsel's performance was 'brilliant' and they had noted (and some had learned) some of his tear-jerking lines. By contrast, prosecuting counsel was portrayed as a 'wimp' who was a little disorganised. The defendant was acquitted.

By great good luck, I met one of the jurors, the following week, socially. When I asked her why they had acquitted, the main reason that she gave was that prosecuting counsel had 'put the jury's backs up'. 'The judge even had to send us out to give him a ticking-off,' she explained. As my students had already told me, the judge had indeed sent out the jury, in order to conduct a trial within a trial on the admissibility of evidence, which my students had observed from the gallery. The juror then went on to recount the performance of defence counsel, whose impressive lines she had also learned.

Even the most avid jury defenders would find it hard to justify this sort of jury behaviour in terms which are theoretically warrantable. It certainly does not bear out the notion of Bankowski and Mungham and others that the jury helps to 'cultivate alternative realities in the courtroom'.

What jury defenders must also face is the research finding of Baldwin and McConville of a disturbingly high number of doubtful convictions, showing that odd decisions by the jury may convict the innocent as well as acquit the guilty. This has serious implications for what Ashworth has termed principles of fairness and weighting in the criminal justice system. As Baldwin and McConville said:

But the performance of the jury did not always appear to accord with the principle underlying the trial system in England that it is better to acquit those who are probably guilty than to convict any who are possibly innocent. On the contrary, the jury appeared on occasion to be over-ready to acquit those who were probably guilty and insufficiently prepared to protect the possibly innocent.

This finding has important bearings on the principle upon which our criminal justice system seeks to strike a balance between convicting the innocent and acquitting the guilty and the margins of error we are prepared to allow from the unattainable ideal line of convicting all the guilty and acquitting all the innocent.

Ashworth has examined this principle and pointed out that the two margins are not the same:

> Indeed it has traditionally been said that, far from there being any such equivalence, it is better that 10 guilty men should go free that one innocent man should be convicted. This proposition clearly indicates a weighting of the rules towards protection of the defendant: what are its credentials? Its main strength is said to lie in its valuation of individual rights and individual suffering. Thus it insists that the liberty of an innocent individual should not be sacrificed in order to increase the efficiency of crime control.

Ashworth, Williams and Allen have all examined this 10 to one ratio, acknowledging that it has been variously expressed as 20 to one, five to one and 100 to one. They all point to the great importance of the ratio. As Ashworth says:

> If the maxim is really meant to say something about the balance of the criminal justice system, the ratio it expresses cannot be a matter of indifference.

This ratio is often discussed in the context of procedural rules designed to protect the defendant, as it is by Ashworth and Williams, but I would suggest that, theoretically, the entire functioning and structure of our criminal justice system should be geared towards satisfying the ratio. Baldwin and McConville's findings that 36 per cent of their sample of acquittals and five per cent of their convictions were questionable clearly indicates that the 10 to one ratio may not always be fulfilled by jury trial.

Furthermore, wrongful convictions are a double failure or abstract justice in a system aimed at crime control tempered by due process. Not only do the real culprits go free, as in a wrongful acquittal, defeating crime control, but there is an overwhelming loss of due process to the innocents convicted.

(c) The jury replacing the law with their own equity

My next objection is to the support given to the jury as a re-drafter of the law in the example of the hot-dog salesman. What business have the jury to be re-writing the law? Arguments along this line are not novel. Weber objected to the misfit of jury equity in an otherwise rational legal system and the point has been well expanded by Frank, Duff and Findlay and McHugh, amongst others. The jury is an anti-democratic, irrational and haphazard legislator, whose erratic and secret decisions run counter to the rule of law. Freeman asserts, on the acquittal of the hot-dog salesman, that the jury were saying that the defence of provocation ought to have been available 'and in saying this they would have the support of the bulk of the population'. How, I would ask, does the jury, or Freeman, know what the bulk of the population want? We have elected the House of Commons and selected the

Law Lords to re-write the law for us. As Duff and Findlay argue, far from being Devlin's 'little parliament', the jury is the very antithesis, 'unaccountable and its decision is designed to permit no argument'. They continue, in a point pertinent to Freeman's hot-dog salesman:

> ... The jury, so irrationally selected, would appear to be a crude engine for the job of checking unpopular laws ... The jury then may be counter-productive in such situations, as the legislature may not feel constrained to intervene if they know that harsh or outdated laws are not being strictly applied.

Finally, I would add, in respect of those instances where the jury base their decision on something extraneous, as in my theft example, that we do have a legitimate expectation, surely, that the jury will at least address the issue before them. There is little point in the Court of Appeal and House of Lords, as well as countless academics, agonising over the definitions of the components of the Theft Act, such as appropriation and dishonesty, if the jury are to accord their verdict as a reward for the good looks and charm of the best barrister.

Freeman and Bankowski and Mungham have attempted to defend jury irrationality in an otherwise supposedly rational adversarial system. I would argue that this is anomalous. Lay justices and judges are frequently criticised for their irrational and inconsistent sentencing patterns and gratuitous remarks, as are civil juries criticised for irrational awards of damages. Why, then, is it theoretically warrantable and praiseworthy behaviour in this tiny element of decision making in our criminal justice system that they act irrationally?

The sacrosanctity of the verdict

One more undesirable aspect of the sacrosanctity of the jury is the sheer impenetrability of its verdict. The consequences of this have been discussed by Williams; Baldwin and McConville; Duff and Findlay; McHugh and others. There are two important results: first, the reluctance of the Court of Appeal to overturn a jury's verdict, which has been criticised repeatedly, especially by Justice and the Home Affairs Select Committee (1981–1982) as being almost a brick wall in the path of access to justice at the post-trial stage. This point has been explored at length before, so I would only add that Lord Lane CJ used the excuse of non-interference with the jury's verdict, for disallowing the 1987 appeal of the Birmingham Six.

The second major result of jury sacrosanctity is s 8 of the Contempt of Court Act 1981, which precludes discussion and observation of a real jury verdict and thus renders much of the debate on the jury's function purely speculative.

Conclusion

Too often, eulogies are heaped upon the jury by its defendants who blindly follow their predecessors' mistakes (on *Magna Carta*) or atheoretical assertions (on jury trial as a constitutional right). They confuse randomness with representativeness and justify the jury as a democratic guardian of civil liberties re-writing the law on our behalf.

In heaping unquestioning praise on the jury, the commentators deceive themselves and the public into thinking jury trial is the 'centrepiece' (Blake) of the criminal justice system. A mass of research on pre-trial decision-making and plea-bargaining has taught us that this is simply not the case. As Ashworth reminded us in 1988: 'There are few who would now propound the view that the centrepiece of the English criminal process is the trial', but the jury defenders are still doing just this.

In reality, only a tiny fraction of cases find their way to the Crown Court, with many defendants 'opting' for summary trial simply because they do not know or understand or care about their 'right' to jury trial or because they want to 'get it over with' in the magistrates' court. Most people pass through the court simply to be sentenced for a guilty plea, which may be the result of a bargain struck by a calculating and persuasive lawyer, who may leave his client protesting his innocence years later.

Of the minority of cases where a trial does take place, its usual forum is the unromantic and unseen magistrates' court, where McBarnet's 'ideology of triviality' is daily acted out and upon which the majority of defendants must rely for the benefit of 'participatory democracy' and the safeguarding of their civil liberties.

There is not space in this article to explore alternative decision-makers. Existing ones such as magistrates and judge-only courts are fraught with problems of their own, but it should be remembered that existing models are not the only ones. In an atmosphere of reform and argument surrounding the Royal Commission on Criminal Justice, there has never been a better time to question the *status quo* and the traditional justifications which have underpinned it and to see if there is not some better, new, alternative.

JURY CHALLENGE

The defence has the power to challenge any number of potential jurors for cause, that is to say, where there is a substantial reason why a particular person should not serve on the jury to decide a particular defendant's case. A simple example would be where the potential juror has had previous dealings with the defendant or has been involved in the case in some way (see *R v Gough*, below).

The prosecution has more scope to challenge jurors. It has the same right as the defence to challenge for cause. In addition, however, the prosecution has the option of excluding potential jury members by simply asking them to 'stand by' until a jury has been empanelled. The Attorney General issued a Practice Note in 1988 providing that the Crown should only exercise its power to stand by potential jurors in particular circumstances.

Attorney General's Guidelines on the Exercise by the Crown of its Right of Stand By [1988] 3 All ER 1086

The Attorney General has issued the following guidelines on the exercise by the Crown in England and Wales of its right to stand by. The guidelines are to have effect from 5 January 1989 to coincide with the implementation of s 118 of the Criminal Justice Act 1988, which abolishes the right of peremptory challenge. The Attorney General has also reissued his guidelines on jury checks. These incorporate amendments made in 1986, together with a new amendment to para 9 whereby the Attorney General's personal authority is required before the right to stand by can be exercised on the basis of information obtained as a result of an authorised check.

1. Although the law has long recognised the right of the Crown to exclude a member of a jury panel from sitting as a juror by the exercise in open court of the right to request a stand by or, if necessary, by challenge for cause, it has been customary for those instructed to prosecute on behalf of the Crown to assert that right only sparingly and in exceptional circumstances. It is generally accepted that the prosecution should not use its right in order to influence the overall composition of a jury or with a view to tactical advantage.

2. The approach outlined above is founded on the principles that (a) the members of a jury should be selected at random from the panel subject to any rule of law as to right of challenge by the defence, and (b) the Juries Act 1974 together with the Juries (Disqualification) Act 1984 identified those classes of persons who alone are disqualified from or ineligible for service on a jury. No other class of person may be treated as disqualified or ineligible.

3. The enactment by Parliament of s 118 of the Criminal Justice Act 1988 abolishing the right of defendants to remove jurors by means of peremptory challenge makes it appropriate that the Crown should assert its right to stand by only on the basis of clearly defined and restrictive criteria. Derogation from the principle that members of a jury should be selected at random should be permitted only where it is essential.

4. Primary responsibility for ensuring that an individual does not serve on a jury if he is not competent to discharge properly the duties of a juror rests with the appropriate court officer and, ultimately, the trial judge. Current legislation provides, in ss 9 and 10 of the Juries Act 1974, fairly wide discretions to excuse or discharge jurors either at the person's own request, where he offers 'good reason why he should be excused', or where the judge determines that 'on account of physical disability or insufficient understanding of English there is doubt as to his capacity to act effectively as a juror'.

5. The circumstances in which it would be proper for the Crown to exercise its right to stand by a member of a jury panel are: (a) where a jury check authorised in accordance with the Attorney General's Guidelines on Jury Checks (see below) reveals information justifying exercise of the right to stand by in accordance with para 9 of the guidelines and the Attorney General personally authorises the exercise of the right to stand by or (b) where a person is about to be sworn as a juror who is manifestly unsuitable and the defence agree that, accordingly, the exercise by the prosecution of the right to stand by would be appropriate. An example of the sort of exceptional circumstances which might justify stand by is where it becomes apparent that, despite the provisions mentioned in para 4 above, a juror selected for service to try a complex case is in fact illiterate.

—·—·—·—·—·—·—·—·—·—·—·—·—·—·—·—

JURY VETTING

This is the process in which the Crown checks the background of potential jurors to assess their suitability to decide particular cases. The procedure is clearly contrary to the ideal of the jury being based on a random selection of people; but it is justified on the basis that it is necessary to ensure that jury members are not likely to divulge any secrets made open to them in the course of a sensitive trial, or alternatively on the ground that jurors with extreme political views should not be permitted the opportunity to express those views in a situation where they might influence the outcome of a case.

The most recent guidelines were published in 1988.

Attorney General's Guidelines on Jury Checks [1988] 3 All ER 1086

1. The principles which are generally to be observed are (a) that members of a jury should be selected at random from the panel, (b) the Juries Act 1974 together with the Juries (Disqualification) Act 1984 identified those classes of persons who alone are either disqualified from or ineligible for service on a jury; no other class of person may be treated as disqualified or ineligible, and (c) the correct way for the Crown to seek to exclude a member of the panel from sitting as a juror is by the exercise in open court of the right to request a stand by or, if necessary, to challenge for cause.

2. Parliament has provided safeguards against jurors who may be corrupt or biased. In addition to the provision for majority verdicts, there is the sanction of a criminal offence for a disqualified person to serve on a jury. The omission of a disqualified person from the panel is a matter for court officials but any search of criminal records for the purpose of ascertaining whether or not a jury panel includes any disqualified person is a matter for the police as the only authority able to carry out such a search and as part of their usual function of preventing the commission of offences. The recommendations of the Association of Chief Police Officers respecting checks on criminal records for disqualified persons are annexed to these guidelines.

3. There are, however, certain exceptional types of case of public importance for which the provisions as to majority verdicts and the disqualification of jurors may not be sufficient to ensure the proper administration of justice. In such cases it is in the interests of both justice and the public that there should be further safeguards against the possibility of bias and in such cases checks which go beyond the investigation of criminal records may be necessary.

4. These classes of case may be defined broadly as (a) cases in which national security is involved and part of the evidence is likely to be heard in camera, and (b) terrorist cases.

5. The particular aspects of these cases which may make it desirable to seek extra precautions are (a) in security cases a danger that a juror, either voluntarily or under pressure, may make an improper use of evidence which, because of its sensitivity, has been given in camera, (b) in both security and terrorist cases the danger that a juror's political beliefs are so biased as to go beyond normally reflecting the broad spectrum of views and interests in the community to reflect the extreme views of sectarian interest or pressure group to a degree

which might interfere with his fair assessment of the facts of the case or lead him to exert improper pressure on his fellow jurors.

6. In order to ascertain whether in exceptional circumstances of the above nature either of these factors might seriously influence a potential juror's impartial performance of his duties or his respecting the secrecy of evidence given in camera, it may be necessary to conduct a limited investigation of the panel. In general, such further investigation beyond one of criminal records made for disqualifications may only be made with the records of police Special Branches. However, in cases falling under para 4(a) above (security cases), the investigation may, additionally, involve the security services. No checks other than on these sources and no general inquiries are to be made save to the limited extent that they may be needed to confirm the identity of a juror about whom the initial check has raised serious doubts.

7. No further investigation, as described in para 6 above, should be made save with the personal authority of the Attorney General on the application of the Director of Public Prosecutions and such checks are hereafter referred to as 'authorised checks'. When a chief officer of police has reason to believe that it is likely that an authorised check may be desirable and proper in accordance with these guidelines he should refer the matter to the Director of Public Prosecutions with a view to his having the conduct of the prosecution from an early stage. The Director will make any appropriate application to the Attorney General.

8. The result of any authorised check will be sent to the Director of Public Prosecutions. The Director will then decide, having regard to the matters set out in para 5 above, what information ought to be brought to the attention of prosecuting counsel.

9. No right of stand by should be exercised by counsel for the Crown on the basis of information obtained as a result of an authorised check save with the personal authority of the Attorney General and unless the information is such as, having regard to the facts of the case and the offences charged, to afford strong reason for believing that a particular juror might be a security risk, be susceptible to improper approaches or be influenced in arriving at a verdict for the reasons given above.

10. Where a potential juror is asked to stand by for the Crown, there is no duty to disclose to the defence the information on which it was founded but counsel may use his discretion to disclose it if its nature and source permit it.

11. When information revealed in the course of an authorised check is not such as to cause counsel for the Crown to ask for a juror to stand by but does give reason to believe that he may be biased against the accused, the defence should be given, at least, an indication of why that potential juror may be inimical to their interests but because of its nature and source it may not be possible to give the defence more than a general indication.

12. A record is to be kept by the Director of Public Prosecutions of the use made by counsel of the information passed to him and of the jurors stood by or challenged by the parties to the proceedings. A copy of this record is to be forwarded to the Attorney General for the sole purpose of enabling him to monitor the operation of these guidelines.

13. No use of the information obtained as a result of an authorised check is to be made except as may be necessary in direct relation to or arising out of the trial for which the check was authorised.

Annex to the Attorney General's Guidelines on Jury Checks
Recommendations of the Association of Chief Police Officers

1. The Association of Chief Police Officers recommends that in the light of observations made in *R v Mason* [1980] 3 All ER 777, [1981] QB 881, the police should undertake a check of the names of potential jurors against records of previous convictions in any case when the Director of Public Prosecutions or a chief constable considers that in all the circumstances it would be in the interests of justice so to do, namely (i) in any case in which there is reason to believe that attempts are being made to circumvent the statutory provisions excluding disqualified persons from service on a jury, including any case when there is reason to believe that a particular juror may be disqualified, (ii) in any case in which it is believed that in a previous related abortive trial an attempt was made to interfere with a juror or jurors, and (iii) in any other case in which in the opinion of the Director of Public Prosecutions or the chief constable it is particularly important to ensure that no disqualified person serves on the jury.

2. The association also recommends that no further checks should be made unless authorised by the Attorney General under his guidelines and no inquiries carried out save to the limited extent that they may be needed to confirm the identity of a juror about whom the initial check has raised serious doubts.

3. The association further recommends that chief constables should agree to undertake checks of jurors on behalf of the defence only if requested to do so by the Director of Public Prosecutions acting on behalf of the Attorney General. Accordingly if the police are approached directly with such a request they will refer it to the Director.

4. When, as a result of any checks of criminal records, information is obtained which suggests that, although not disqualified under the terms of the Juries Act 1974, a person may be unsuitable to sit as a member of a particular jury the police or the Director may pass the relevant information to prosecuting counsel, who will decide what use to make of it.

JURY COMPETENCE

The ability of juries actually to follow what goes on in court has been repeatedly questioned. The accusation of lack of understanding tends to arise with particular regularity in relation to extremely complex company law and fraud trials. A useful report of the difficulties facing juries in such trials was produced by Michael Gillard in *The Observer*.

Michael Gillard, 'Why fraud juries need help' (1994) *The Observer*, 30 October, www.guardian.co.uk

'Thank God for the jury. It would be madness to lose the jury system,' declared a grateful and much-relieved George Walker, the former Brent Walker chief executive who was acquitted last week of 'orchestrating' a £19 million 'false profits' fraud.

Wilfred Aquilina, his loyal ex-finance director, is unlikely to share his boss's enthusiasm. He was convicted of false accounting on a majority verdict.

This contradictory outcome to the 75-day £5m trial again brought into question the way that complex fraud trials are handled. Days before the verdict, Lord Justice Henry – who presided over the Guinness trials – warned 'Serious fraud is near the limit of criminal jurisprudence. There is a risk that a system designed for very different trials may be tested to destruction'.

That view was echoed by Richard Ferguson QC, the chairman of the Criminal Bar Association who defended Guinness boss Ernest Saunders. 'There is a growing recognition that marathon cases cannot be tolerated. A creeping malaise will strangle the system.'

Former Scotland Yard Fraud Squad chief Tony McStravick is more direct. 'It's grinding to a halt. There is no longer a search for the truth. Lawyers take every step to obstruct and delay.'

The unanimous verdict of judges, barristers, prosecutors, jurors, police officers and fraud experts interviewed by *The Observer* is that the system of handling major fraud trials is far too costly and must be changed if justice is to be delivered by design, not accident.

What is needed, say those involved in the process, is not to replace the jury with a tribunal – although a minority of judges now strongly support this step, according to a senior judge – but to make the existing system more effective, quicker and cheaper.

And that means addressing the inter-related questions of jury selection and the length of trials. As Lord Justice Henry declared two years ago: 'The jury needs help and we must see that they get it.'

The Brent Walker trial – though shorter than Blue Arrow (12 months), Guinness 1 and Barlow Clowes (both seven months) – was a microcosm of the problem.

The only qualification for a juror is to be over 18 and not among the wide category of those automatically excluded – doctors, dentists, nurses, clergymen, lawyers, servicemen, even MPs. There is no educational or even literacy qualification.

Certainly the large numbers excused as jurors on the grounds that they cannot afford the time for their civic duty often render juries wholly unrepresentative. 'The professional people run for the hills,' admits one judge. So the accused City suit is rarely judged by his business peers.

The demand that a juror should serve for several months was anyway admitted to be 'unfair' by one Law Lord. So the likelihood is that the fraud trial jury will be dominated by the unemployed, the retired, those who do not work or those who have jobs they will not miss or be missed from plus a smattering of those who can take the time and are interested in the crime.

'Something has to be done so that the jury is really democratic,' argues Edna Wijeratna, a counsellor at a London college who sat on the Guinness 2 jury.

The Brent Walker jury was made up of 10 men and two women. Six men and one woman were in their 20s or 30s. The remainder were middle aged. That is all that is known – even by the court.

The jury, as is the norm, was confronted by reams of financial documents about complicated transactions concerning the £19m that was allegedly used over several years via a number of phoney film deals to generate false profits.

Every day the jury peered over several ring binders of documents, containing up to 300 pages and seven flow charts detailing a maze of financial transfers between banks and companies in Britain, the United States, the Bahamas, Monaco, Hong Kong and Liechtenstein.

At times it was like a Turkish audience hearing Britain's entry in the Eurovision Song Contest. The words were strange and the tune hard to follow. *Nil points.* The jury also listened to 82 witnesses – including Walker, but not Aquilina. However, there were several vital witnesses that they did not hear.

The jury entered the courtroom in mid-summer. By the time they returned their verdicts British summer time had ended. But in between how much light had been thrown on Brent Walker and what the judge tried to insist was not 'a world apart'?

'Juries are able to handle the issue of dishonesty,' declares Richard Ferguson, 'but I have very considerable doubt that they can handle technical matters.' Yet that is what fraud trials today are all about. 'It is like addressing an audience of people enrolled at the tech on quantum physics,' says Michael Levi, the criminologist and leading fraud expert.

'They do not understand the mischief and are led by the nose', fears Lord Alexander, former Bar Council chairman.

But Mrs Wijeratna denies that 'little people' are unable to understand City ways. 'Trials depend on the abilities of the judge and the main legal characters to translate to the jury who should be treated as responsible people.'

After four months of evidence, the Brent Walker jury faced Mr Justice Rivlin's detailed summing up spread over seven days. At times some jurors seemed less than attentive. One last seen with head in hands was shortly afterwards discharged on health grounds.

'You will remember document C126 ... E286 ... D207,' intoned Mr Justice Rivlin confidently, 'Document 201A, I am sure that you remember it ... That document that you remember so well.'

Jurors reached for their bundles. Some made notes, others showed expressions suggesting disinterest to exasperation or exhaustion.

Anyway by the seventh day even the judge was confused about which was the right document, which – as they all recalled so well – was E150. Hardly surprising then that just before Mr Justice Rivlin sent them out to start what turned into six days of deliberations, he acknowledged their request for 'a long rest'.

Despite constant calls for change since the Roskill committee on fraud trials reported in 1986, the Brent Walker trial suggests that while all involved talk the talk (endlessly), no one is prepared to walk the walk.

Lord Justice Henry's verdict on fraud trials says it all: 'They take too long. They are open-ended as to time and cost. They are insufficiently focused on the real issue. They cost too much. They happen too late.'

Many judges agree that after four months jury concentration and comprehension decreases. 'They are not used to sitting still trying to absorb a mass of detail,' declared one experienced fraud judge. 'A 50 minute lecture is difficult enough to listen to,' says academic Michael Levi.

Many judges now support time limits on speeches and evidence. Other suggestions include reducing the number of charges, limiting documentation and forcing defendants to admit more uncontested facts and reveal their defence.

Although defence lawyers argue that this would undermine their clients' rights, Richard Ferguson agrees that there 'should be a firm time-scale and no messing about' in the pre-trial period. However, he believes that most answers rest with the trial judge. 'He should have the courage of his convictions and be prepared to intervene.'

Lord Justice Henry too has called for judges to be more 'interventionist' with a legal yellow card waved at time-wasting and verbose counsel. But a senior Law Lord responds: 'The modern judge is too frightened of a possible appeal to intervene. They are not wholly in control.'

Edna Wijeratna, who endured the aborted 68-day trial of merchant bankers Roger Seelig and Lord Spens, agrees that trials take too long and are too slow. 'The same matter is gone over several times with different witnesses.'

While there may not be support for the Monty Python colonel who interrupted sketches with orders to 'get on with it', senior judges believe that judges must take charge of their courts.

If trials were reduced then more representative juries could be chosen because more people would be prepared to give up their time.

But there is one enormous *lacuna* – hole in lawyerspeak – in the debate: the Contempt of Court Act prevents us knowing how juries reach their verdicts. How often is the ouija board brought out?

And while the judges and lawyers repeat, at least in public, the mantra 'Juries rule OK', the evidence from the United States, where jurors can be interviewed, is hardly reassuring.

A study of the jury that acquitted Imelda Marcos and Adnan Khashoggi of plundering the Philippines revealed that jurors are all too often swayed by irrational or emotional issues or prejudice and can be hopelessly confused by financial complexity.

Yet here, the Government has still to decide whether to accept a recent Royal Commission recommendation in favour of probing the secrets of the jury room.

Twelve Angry Men may be the ideal but it is far from the reality in Manhattan or at the Old Bailey. All too often in fraud trials the jury is consigned by what a Canadian judge called 'a judicial never-never land' and one that fails to produce a fairy-tale ending.

In a consultation paper produced jointly by the Home Office in conjunction with the Lord Chancellor's Department in February 1998, a number of alternatives were canvassed which retain the jury, but ensure that it would be better equipped to fulfil its role.

Home Office/Lord Chancellor's Department, *Juries in Serious Fraud Trials:* *A Consultation Document,* **1988**

Chapter 4: Special Juries

Preamble

4.1 The public can only be expected to retain confidence in the criminal justice system if the tribunals which judge defendants are both competent to fulfil their duties and just in discharging them. Over the years, the competence of jurors in long and complex fraud trials has been questioned. It has been suggested that no jury could do a good job in the given circumstances. Other commentators, however, have suggested that jurors could do a good job in complex fraud trials if they were selected in a special way. These suggestions are discussed in this chapter under the broad heading of 'special juries'.

Jury selection: the present law

4.2 Most of the present law in relation to juries is to be found in the Juries Act 1974. The basic qualifications for jury service are

   (1) being registered to vote,

   (2) being aged 18–70 inclusive and

   (3) being ordinarily resident in the UK.

   Judges, lawyers and police officers, clergy and those with a mental disability are ineligible. Persons with serious or recent convictions are disqualified. Those over 65, parliamentarians, service personnel and health professionals are excusable as of right. The court has power to excuse jurors with personal knowledge of a case, or 'on grounds of personal hardship or conscientious objection'. The principle is that a jury should be comprised of members of the public randomly selected from those in eligible groups who live in the area local to the Crown Court.

4.3 Illiteracy is not in itself a ground for excluding a person from a jury. The Juries Act does specifically provide that where 'on account of physical disability or insufficient understanding of English there is doubt as to capacity to act effectively as a juror' the judge may discharge the summons. It is hard to see, however, that the word 'understanding' in the 1974 Act can be interpreted to mean 'ability to read and write'. In many Crown Court cases all the evidence is presented orally and it would be inappropriate to require jurors to be able to read and write. In practice, potential jurors with literacy problems are often identified (and, as a result, discharged) when they experience difficulty reading the juror oath on the card but this is hardly reliable. It is much more likely to identify jurors who are called to take the oath early in the empanelling process. Those called later will have heard the oath taken by their predecessors and are less likely to stumble over the words.

4.4 In some recent fraud trials, prosecution and defence counsel have devised a questionnaire for potential jurors to fill in. These questionnaires are designed (1) to enable jurors to put forward any personal hardship grounds for excusal and (2) to ensure that no jurors are biased against, or have personal knowledge of, the defendants. It is clear from the transcripts of the Maxwell trial that the questionnaires were also used by the court to identify and excuse jurors with obvious and serious literacy problems. This, however, was incidental.

Numbers

4.5 All the options for special juries discussed below raise, in varying degrees, the potential difficulty of finding sufficient numbers of 'special' jurors to serve. It is often argued that any such difficulty can be resolved by introducing a smaller jury, of perhaps seven or eight members. While there are examples of both smaller and larger juries in other jurisdictions, we are not aware of any jurisdiction where jury size can vary depending on the nature of the case. Any such proposal would raise arguments of principle, for example the fairness of providing that a smaller number of jurors need to be convinced of the guilt of a particular defendant merely because the criminal offence is of some specified nature. Smaller juries would also be more vulnerable to illness or interference. For the purposes of the special jury options considered below, the absolute minimum acceptable size for a jury is taken to be six members (with a verdict coming from a majority of at least five).

Special juries: historical background

4.6 Special juries were once available in civil and criminal cases. They were the same size as common juries, but special jurors had to have the status of 'banker, merchant or esquire' and had to occupy property with a higher rateable value than was laid down for qualification as a common juror. The original justification was to identify people of higher social standing and intelligence. By the early 20th century, however, it was said that the criteria resulted in there being little difference between a common and special jury 'merchant' included many small shopkeepers and excluded many newer professionals such as accountants and brokers. Special juries in criminal cases were abolished in the Juries Act 1949. The possibility of a special jury from the City of London was retained for some civil commercial cases (but little used) until abolished in the Courts Act 1971. 'Special' status based on the value of one's property is obviously not acceptable in modern conditions. Identifying those whose profession and qualifications testify to their having certain skills and abilities might, if workable, be more acceptable.

Options for reform of the present juror selection process

4.7 The purpose of reforming the juror selection process would be to increase public confidence in the competence of juries in serious fraud cases. Whilst it may be that many jurors with literacy problems are identified and excused under the present arrangements, new procedures might more successfully target the particular abilities which are sought in serious fraud jurors and also allow any selection process to be conducted in private. 'Selection' is a contentious topic and it would be important for any approach to minimise the possibility of offence and embarrassment to potential jurors.

4.8 The first option is to apply some sort of screening procedure to jurors summoned in the normal way to a court where a serious fraud trial is about to begin. The second, more radical and much more difficult, option is to introduce an entirely separate pool of jurors to be summoned exclusively to sit on serious fraud trials.

Jury Option 1: Screening of summoned jurors

4.9 All jurors in serious fraud trials need to be able to 'deal with' the type of evidence which will be presented. This may go beyond 'reading and writing' since the vocabulary and structures which appear in a typical serious fraud case jury bundle set a fairly high standard. (There are established techniques for assessing the 'reading difficulty' of particular sorts of document.) An ability to negotiate tabular information is also required, as is an appreciation of the significance of numerical information (rather than 'numeracy' itself). It has also been suggested that a colour-blind juror might be at a disadvantage in dealing with flow-charts and computer-aided information displays.

4.10 There are two sub-sets of the screening option. Both have the major advantage of developing out of the normal principle of random selection, and the normal procedure of summoning from the electoral roll. The first sub-option is screening for qualifications. The second is screening by way of an aptitude test. In either case, the screening would be a form-filling exercise which could be linked in with the increasingly common use of questionnaires about personal hardship and bias in serious fraud trials.

Jury Option 1A: Screening for qualifications

4.11 The first way of 'screening' would be to ask potential jurors some standard questions about their educational attainments or professional qualifications. These questions could be included with the standard summoning form wherever it is known that a relevant serious fraud case is to commence on the day of the juror's first attendance. Alternatively, a form requesting the information could be dispensed when the potential juror arrives at court.

Potential advantages

4.12 Potential advantages of this option are:

i. Increased juror competence: public confidence in the trial process might be increased if it was known that jurors had a certain level of education or training.

ii. Trial process changes: the parties might amend their case presentation if they were confident of the skills and abilities of the jurors. This could lead to shorter and more focused trials.

Potential Disadvantages

4.13 Potential disadvantages of this option are:

i. Missing the target: the public will not have confidence in a screening system which selects people with irrelevant qualifications, while deselecting unqualified people with relevant skills. The great difficulty would be to identify the qualifications most likely to match the skills needed. Suggestions have ranged from A-Levels in both English and Maths to primary-school level literacy but whatever baseline is chosen its validity may be challenged.

ii. Discrimination: access to qualifications can depend on age, social class, race and sex. This might lead the public, with justification, to perceive a juror selection system based on paper qualifications as unfair and discriminatory.

iii. Verification: some people might claim qualifications they do not have, while some might hide qualifications they do have, out of unwillingness to serve on a serious fraud jury.

iv. No change to the trial process: if the qualification required were anything other than highly restrictive, jurors would still be unlikely to have any expertise in complex financial transactions. The established trial process may therefore not change at all as a result of jurors having qualifications.

v. Numbers: depending on the standard set and the numbers of trials affected, there might be difficulties in finding sufficient jurors to serve.

Cost implications

4.14 Details of costs associated with different components of court proceedings are provided at Annex A. Elements of cost increases or savings for this option are:

- Additional costs: summoning an increased number of jurors to cater for the deselection of some; devising and administering the form to be filled in; verifying the qualifications claimed.

- Costs savings: there seem unlikely to be any costs savings associated with this option, unless (which is unlikely) the nature of the jury so affects the way the evidence is presented that trials become shorter. There would be savings in jury payments if the size of the jury was reduced, unless each juror was, on average, paid more than jurors on traditional juries.

Jury Option 1B: Aptitude screening

4.15 An alternative way of 'screening' jurors would be to devise a short aptitude test designed to test whether they had the skills necessary to comprehend the evidence to be presented. (The principle behind this approach is not entirely novel – in the Maxwell trial, for example, questionnaires were used by the court to identify and excuse jurors with obvious and serious literacy problems, although this was incidental to their main purpose.) The test could either be general in nature so that those who passed it were qualified to sit on any fraud case to which the alternative method of trial applied; or tailored tests could be devised for each trial so that the particular competencies needed by jurors to understand the details of that specific case were identified. Either form of test would be administered at the court of trial under supervised conditions.

Potential advantages

4.16 The potential advantages of this option are:

i. Increased juror competence: public confidence in the trial process might be increased if it was known that jurors had been screened for their ability to deal with the evidence.

ii. Trial process changes: the parties might amend their case presentation if they were confident of the skills and abilities of the jurors. This could lead to shorter and more focused trials.

iii. Targeting: the test could be specifically designed by relevant experts in applied psychology and linguistics to look for the skills needed to deal with the evidence in a serious fraud case.

Potential disadvantages

4.17 The potential disadvantages of this option are:

i. Public resistance: depending on the length and nature of the test, there might be strong public objection to having to complete a test, especially for one particular sort of case.

ii. Verification: there is a significant danger that once the purpose of the test becomes known, people will answer the questions with the intention of 'failing'. For many people, there are few incentives to sitting on a serious fraud jury.

iii. No change to the trial process: jurors would still be unlikely to have any expertise in complex financial transactions, especially if a standardised aptitude test was used to cover all fraud cases tried by this method.The established trial process may therefore not change at all as a result of an aptitude test – the length of the trial would probably not be reduced and the jury's capacity to understand the material presented may not be much greater than a jury selected in the existing, random way.

iv. Numbers: depending on the standard set and the numbers of trials affected, there might be difficulties in finding sufficient jurors to serve, especially if tailored aptitude tests were designed which sought out specific – and very rare – knowledge.

v. Scope for disputes: especially where case-specific aptitude tests were employed there is likely to be considerable scope for disputes about the validity of the competencies and knowledge sought by that test. There might well be appeals against the decision of the tribunal of fact arising out of the selection process that was adopted.

Cost implications

4.18 Details of costs associated with different components of court proceedings are provided at Annex A. Elements of cost increases or savings for this option are:

- Additional costs: summoning an increased number of jurors to cater for the deselection of some; devising and administering the form to be filled in.

- Costs savings: there seem unlikely to be any costs savings associated with this option, unless (which is unlikely) the nature of the jury so affects the way the evidence is presented that trials become shorter. There would be savings in jury payments if the size of the jury was reduced, unless each juror was, on average, paid more than jurors on traditional juries.

Jury Option 2: Creating a special pool of 'serious fraud' jurors

4.19   The alternative to screening potential jurors once they have been summoned to attend court is to maintain a separate pool of jurors who would be summoned to attend serious fraud trials. This option involves a significant departure from the principle that jurors are randomly selected from the population local to the Crown Court in question. It also goes beyond the argument which could justify the screening options, namely that the jury needs to be able to 'deal with' the type of evidence which will be presented.

4.20   In procedural terms, this option would constitute a much more radical disruption to the present system of jury selection, based on the electoral register. Crown Court summoning officers would have to be provided with separate lists of potential 'serious fraud' jurors. Somebody, such as the Lord Chancellor's Department, would have to be responsible for compiling and updating such lists for 36 Crown Court centres currently designated to deal with cases transferred under section 4 of the 1987 Act and any other centres which might handle section 7 cases that were not so transferred. It would seem to follow from the principles of jury service that inclusion on the list would be mandatory and not voluntary. The special pool would consist of jurors with specialist background knowledge of trade or finance. The prime difficulty would be identifying those to be included in the pool. Once the pool was established, the Crown Court would summon potential jurors at random from the special list.

Potential advantages

4.21   Potential advantages of this option are:

   i.   Increased juror competence: public confidence in the trial process might be increased if it was known that jurors had specialist knowledge about financial or business matters (although different serious fraud trials can involve very different background issues).

   ii.   Trial process changes: this option might lead to some significant changes in case presentation, since counsel would have to assume that all jurors were familiar with business and financial matters. This could lead to shorter and more focused trials. Much of the evidence, and especially the expert accountancy evidence, could be dealt with more quickly because the jury would be well able to absorb it.

Potential disadvantages

4.22   Potential disadvantages of this option are:

   i.   Lack of independence: financial expert jurors might find it hard to judge the case exclusively on the basis of the evidence. The public might lack confidence in a jury composed exclusively of those who work or move in circles very like those of the defendant.

   ii.   Administrative complexity: procedures to identify these new pools of jurors would have to be initiated. Membership of certain recognised professional bodies or institutes could be taken to indicate the necessary level of expertise. Examples would be the Institute of Chartered Accountants, the Chartered Association of Certified Accountants, the Insurance Brokers Registration Council and the Institute of Actuaries. The existing regulatory framework might make it possible to identify those who work in the financial services sector, since the FSA self-regulatory organisations (PIA, SFA and IMRO) all register individual practitioners. In addition, certain paper qualifications, especially an MBA, could be taken to indicate the necessary expertise. If people are to be included on a mandatory rather than a voluntary basis, however, reliance on membership of, or registration with, some established body seems the only way to proceed.

iii. Missing the target: there seems to be no workable way of identifying all those who might have the financial or business expertise which could assist in understanding the background to a serious fraud. Many people work in 'trade' or business without holding professional qualifications or being members of professional bodies. Conversely, some of those with relevant qualifications might have decided to work in some quite different sector.

iv. Availability: financial experts might be more likely to claim that they would suffer personal (professional) hardship if they had to serve on a particularly long trial.

v. Remuneration: many who work in the financial sector earn much more than is presently allowed as maximum loss of earnings for jurors. Criticism could be expected if certain sorts of juror were to be remunerated at a higher rate than others.

vi. Personal knowledge: because of the restricted nature of the pool, potential jurors would be more likely to have personal knowledge of the defendants, victims and witnesses and to be unable to serve for that reason.

vii. Limited changes to the trial process: the jurors would be without legal training, and would remain obliged to listen to the trial, rather than participating actively in it. The traditional reliance on oral evidence would be likely to continue.

viii. Numbers: depending on the standard set and the numbers of trials affected, there might be difficulties in finding sufficient jurors to serve.

Cost implications

4.23 Details of costs associated with different components of court proceedings are provided at Annex A. Elements of cost increases or savings for this option are:

Additional costs: there would be significant new costs involved in selecting and maintaining a pool of people with specified skills for each of the Crown Court areas which might hear these trials. If many potential jurors were excused for hardship or bias, the costs of maintaining the pool would be wasted. There would be additional costs in jury payments if the financial loss rules were to be relaxed.

Costs savings: it is possible, with this option, that the nature of the jury might so affect the way the evidence is presented that trials become shorter (bringing savings in court, prosecution and defence costs as estimated in Annex A). There would be savings in jury payments if the size of the jury was reduced, unless each juror was, on average, paid more than jurors on traditional juries.

A further option

4.24 Another option which has been suggested would be to have a professional assessor from a highly qualified panel, such as an accountant, stockbroker or banker depending on the nature of the fraud, sitting as the twelfth juror. He or she would have the same rights as the remaining 11 but would be able to guide them through the technicalities of the evidence. The expert juror would effectively be offering expert evidence to the other jurors in the absence of both prosecution and defence; his or her opinion may therefore weigh heavily with the other jurors. The option would not, however, address the problems of trial length.

- -

JURY BIAS

Article 6 of the European Convention on Human Rights provides:

Right to a fair trial

In the determination of his civil rights and obligations or of any criminal charge against him, everyone is entitled to a fair and public hearing within a reasonable time by an independent and impartial tribunal established by law ...

It naturally follows that any prejudice against an accused harboured by a jury member cannot but vitiate the impartiality of the tribunal determining the guilt or innocence of the accused. The English legal system has developed its own rules relating to bias amongst jury members but, consequent upon the implementation of the Human Rights Act 1998, these rules are now subject to the jurisprudence of the European Court of Human Rights (ECtHR). The following material specifically deals with bias within the jury but the principles involved can, and in the following chapter will, be extended to cover judicial bias.

The test for establishing jury bias

The question of bias in jurors was considered, and the appropriate test for questioning a decision on such grounds stated, by the House of Lords in *R v Gough*.

R v Gough [1993] AC 646; [1993] 2 All ER 724

The appellant and his brother were charged with robbery. At the committal proceedings the brother was discharged and the appellant was indicted on a single count that he had conspired with his brother to commit robbery. At his trial, the brother was frequently referred to by name, and a photograph of him and the appellant was shown to the jury and his address was contained in a statement read to the jury. One of the jurors was a next door neighbour of the brother, but she did not recognise him or connect him with the man referred to in court until he started shouting in court after the appellant had been convicted and sentenced to 15 years' imprisonment. The appellant appealed on the ground that, applying the test of whether a reasonable and fair-minded person sitting in the court and knowing all the relevant facts would have had a reasonable suspicion that a fair trial of the appellant had not been possible, the presence of the juror on the jury constituted a serious irregularity in the conduct of the trial.

The Court of Appeal held that the proper test for determining whether a conviction obtained on a trial on indictment should be quashed on the grounds of possible bias on the part of a juror was whether there was a real danger that the accused might not have had a fair trial and not whether a reasonable and fair-minded person sitting in court and knowing all the relevant facts would have had a reasonable suspicion that a fair trial of the defendant had not been possible. The court held that, applying that test, the circumstances of the case were such that there was no danger that the appellant might not have had a fair trial, and it dismissed the appeal. The appellant appealed to the House of Lords.

Lord Goff of Chieveley: ... The Court of Appeal identified ... two strands of authority, revealing that differing criteria have been applied in the past when considering the question of bias. The two tests have, as will appear, themselves been variously described. The Court of Appeal identified them as being (1) whether there was a real danger of bias on the part of the person concerned or (2) whether a reasonable person might reasonably suspect bias on his part. In the end, the court concluded that the former test was to be applied in cases concerned with jurors, and the latter in those concerned with magistrates or other inferior tribunals. The court therefore applied the real danger test in the present case and, on that basis, held that the appeal must fail, as indeed had been accepted by counsel for the appellant ... A layman might well wonder why the function of a court in cases such as these should not simply be to conduct an inquiry into the question whether the tribunal was in fact biased. After all it is alleged that, for example, a justice or a juryman was biased, ie that he was motivated by a desire unfairly to favour one side or to disfavour the other. Why does the court not simply decide whether that was in fact the case? The answer, as always, is that it is more complicated than that. First of all, there are difficulties about exploring the actual state of mind of a justice or juryman. In the case of both, such an inquiry has been thought to be undesirable; and, in the case of the juryman in particular, there has long been an inhibition against, so to speak, entering the jury room and finding out what any particular juryman actually thought at the time of decision. But there is also the simple fact that bias is such an insidious thing that, even though a person may in good faith believe that he was acting impartially, his mind may unconsciously be affected by bias ...

My initial reaction to the conclusion of the Court of Appeal in the present case was one of surprise that it should be necessary to draw a distinction between cases concerned with justices and those concerned with jurymen, and to conclude that different criteria fell to be applied in investigating allegations of bias in the two categories of case ... In conclusion I wish to express my understanding of the law as follows. I think it possible, and desirable, that the same test should be applicable in all cases of apparent bias, whether concerned with justices or members of other inferior tribunals, or with jurors, or with arbitrators. Likewise, I consider that, in cases concerned with jurors, the same test should be applied by a judge to whose attention the possibility of bias on the part of a juror has been drawn in the course of a trial, and by the Court of Appeal when it considers such a question on appeal. Furthermore, I think it unnecessary, in formulating the appropriate test, to require that the court should look at the matter through the eyes of a reasonable man, because the court has first to ascertain the relevant circumstances from the available evidence, knowledge of which would not necessarily be available to an observer in court at the relevant time. Finally, for the avoidance of doubt, I prefer to state the test in terms of real danger rather than real likelihood, to ensure that the court is thinking in terms of possibility rather than probability of bias. Accordingly, *having ascertained the relevant circumstances, the court should ask itself whether, having regard to those circumstances, there was a real danger of bias on the part of the relevant member of the tribunal in question, in the sense that he might unfairly regard (or have unfairly regarded) with favour, or disfavour, the case of a party to the issue under consideration by him;* though, in a case concerned with bias on the part of a magistrates' clerk, the court should go on to consider whether the clerk has been invited to give the magistrates advice and, if so, whether it should infer that there was a real danger of the clerk's bias having infected the views of the magistrates adversely to the applicant.

The test for bias stated in *R v Gough* was subsequently amended in *Director General of Fair Trading v Proprietary Association of Great Britain* (2000 1 WLR 700) which will be reconsidered in relation to judicial prejudice in Chapter 11.

Racial prejudice

Given the conclusion of the *McPherson Report* on the killing of the young black man Stephen Lawrence, and the implications that findings of 'institutional racism' have for every aspect of the justice system, it is significant that the ECtHR distinguished its previous decision in *Gregory v United Kingdom* (1995) in relation to claims of racial prejudice within juries.

Sander v The United Kingdom (Application No 34129/96), ECtHR, 9 May 2000

The circumstances of the case

In March 1995 the applicant, an Asian, appeared ,together with JB and GC, before the Birmingham Crown Court, composed of a judge and a jury, to be tried for conspiracy to defraud. After the defence had stated its case, the judge started his summing up, which he had almost completed by Friday evening when he adjourned. On Monday morning a juror arrived at the court and handed an envelope to the court usher containing the following complaint:

> I have decided I cannot remain silent any longer. For some time during the trial I have been concerned that fellow jurors are not taking their duties seriously. At least two have been making openly racist remarks and jokes and I

fear are going to convict the defendants not on the evidence but because they are Asian. My concern is the defendants will not therefore receive a fair verdict. Please could you advise me what I can do in this situation.

The juror who had written the complaint was asked not to join the other jurors. The judge discussed the complaint with counsel in chambers and then adjourned and listened to submissions in open court. The defence asked the judge to dismiss the jury on the ground that there was a real danger of bias. The judge, however, decided to call the jury back into court, at which stage the juror who had written the complaint joined the others. The judge read out the complaint to them and told them the following:

> Members of the jury, this morning I received a note from one of your number expressing extreme concern that some of your number are not taking your duties seriously, are making openly racist remarks and jokes about Asians and may not reach your verdicts upon the evidence but because of some racial prejudice.

> I am not able to conduct an inquiry into the validity of those contentions and I do not propose to do so. This case has cost an enormous amount of money and I am not anxious to halt it at the moment, but I shall have no compunction in doing so if the situation demands.

> When you took the oath or affirmed as jurors it was, you will remember, to bring in true verdicts according to the evidence. That is solemn and binding and means what it says.

> I am going to adjourn now and I am going to ask you all to search your conscience overnight and if you feel that you are not able to try this case solely on the evidence and find that you cannot put aside any prejudices you may have will you please indicate that fact by writing a personal note to that effect and giving it to the jury bailiff on your arrival at court tomorrow morning. I will then review the position. Thank you very much.

The next morning the judge received two letters from the jury. The first letter, which was signed by all the jurors including the juror who had sent the complaint, stated the following:

> We, the undersigned members of the jury, wish to put on record to the Court our response to yesterday's note from a juror implying possible racial bias.

> 1. We utterly refute the allegation.

> 2. We are deeply offended by the allegation.

> 3. We assure the Court that we intend to reach a verdict solely according to the evidence and without racial bias.

The second letter, which the judge commended, was written by a juror who appeared to have thought himself to have been the one who had been making the jokes. The juror in question explained at length that he might have done so, that he was sorry if he had given any offence, that he was somebody who had many connections with people from ethnic minorities and that he was in no way racially biased.

The judge decided that he would not discharge the jury and told them the following:

> Ladies and gentlemen, the events of yesterday afternoon were clearly distressing for you, but I am sure you will see and realise that when a judge receives a note from one of your number raising those sort of issues it is the judge's duty to bring it to the attention of the whole jury.
>
> Whether the suggestions were well or ill-founded is not something I or any judge can decide, nor is it something that can be investigated by the judge. It would be an improper activity. I took the course I did in the exercise of my discretion and I am sorry you were offended and upset.
>
> However, all twelve of you have this morning utterly refuted the allegation, expressed your deep offence at it and assured the Court that you intend to reach a verdict or verdicts solely according to the evidence and without racial bias. One of your number has also written at length a most cogent and balanced letter, and it is quite clear to me that each and every one of you are conscious of the oath or affirmation that you have taken and are dutifully prepared to abide by.

On 8 March 1995 the jury found the applicant guilty, but acquitted GC, who was also Asian. On 20 April 1995 the judge imposed on the applicant a sentence of five years' imprisonment.

The applicant was given leave to appeal against conviction. In his appeal he raised, *inter alia*, the following ground: the judge should have reacted to the juror's complaint by dismissing the jury; in any event, the juror who had written the complaint should not have been segregated from the other members of the jury in the early stages and the judge should not have disclosed to the jurors the contents of the complaint.

On 1 March 1996 the Court of Appeal dismissed the applicant's appeal. As regards the above-mentioned ground, it considered the following: the court had regard to the letter signed by all the members of the jury, and the letter of the juror who was probably responsible for the remarks that had given offence, and found that the trial judge did not err in reaching the conclusion that there was no real risk of bias. Moreover, the judge was right to confront the jury with the problem and ask them to consider it. It was perhaps unfortunate that the juror who had written the complaint was for a time segregated from the other members of the jury, as this led to his identification. However, it would be unrealistic to suppose that the jury would not have wanted to know who the author of the complaint was and the judge dealt with the possibility of tensions among the jurors perfectly sensibly in the direction he gave to them.

The Law

The applicant complained that he was not tried by an impartial tribunal, contrary to Article 6, s 1 of the European Convention on Human Rights, which provides:

> In the determination ... of any criminal charge against him, everyone is entitled to a fair hearing ... by an ... impartial tribunal ...

The Court recalls that it is of fundamental importance in a democratic society that the courts inspire confidence in the public and above all, as far as criminal proceedings are concerned, in the accused. To that end it has constantly stressed that a tribunal, including a jury, must be impartial from a subjective as well as an objective point of view (see *Gregory v UK* 1995).

The Court also recalls that the present case concerns clear and precise allegations that racist comments had been made by jurors called upon to try an Asian accused. The Court considers this to be a very serious matter given that, in today's multicultural European societies, the eradication of racism has become a common priority goal for all Contracting States (see, *inter alia*, Declarations of the Vienna and Strasbourg Summits of the Council of Europe).

The Court notes that the allegations in question led the applicant to the conclusion that he was tried by a racially prejudiced jury. The applicant's complaint is, therefore, that there was subjective bias on the part of some jurors.

The Court recalls that the personal impartiality of a judge must be presumed until there is proof to the contrary (see the *Piersack v Belgium* judgment of 1 October 1982, Series A no 53, pp 14–15, § 30). The same holds true in respect of jurors.

In the circumstances of the applicant's case, a member of the jury submitted a note alleging that two fellow jurors '[had] been making openly racist remarks and jokes' and stating that he feared that 'they [were] going to convict the defendants not on the evidence but because they were Asian'. Another juror, being confronted with these allegations, accepted that 'he might have done so' and stated that 'he was sorry if he had given any offence'. The Court, therefore, considers that it was established that at least one juror had made comments that could be understood as jokes about Asians. In the Court's view, this does not on its own amount to evidence that the juror in question was actually biased against the applicant. Moreover, the Court notes that it was not possible for the trial judge to question the jurors about the true nature of these comments and the exact context in which they had been made. It follows that it has not been established that the court that tried the applicant was lacking in impartiality from a subjective point of view.

This is not, however, the end of the Court's examination of the applicant's complaint. The Court must also examine whether the court was impartial from an objective point of view, ie whether in the circumstances there were sufficient guarantees to exclude any objectively justified or legitimate doubts as to the impartiality of the court. Although the standpoint of the accused is important in this connection, it cannot be decisive The Government submitted that there existed such guarantees. They referred in principle to the redirection of the jury by the judge and to the unequivocally positive assurance of impartiality that the judge sought and received from the jurors.

As regards the latter, the Court recalls that, the morning after the submission of the note about the racist jokes, all the jurors signed a letter to the effect that the allegations in question were unfounded. However, the Court considers that this letter cannot on its own discredit the allegations contained in the original note, for the following reasons.

First, one of the jurors wrote a separate letter indirectly admitting that he had been making racist jokes. The Court considers that this is a matter that cannot be taken lightly since jokes of this nature, when made by jurors in the context of judicial proceedings, take on a different hue and assume a different significance from jokes made in the context of a more intimate and informal atmosphere.

Secondly, the collective letter was also signed by the juror who had submitted the note. In the Court's view, this in itself casts some doubt on the credibility of the letter. The note, which was the product of a genuine, spontaneous reaction, the honesty of which has not been questioned, expressed fear that the defendants could be convicted because they were Asian. The letter, which reflected the common position of a number of persons with not necessarily the same interests in mind, denied any possible racial bias. The two cannot be reconciled and the Court considers the note more reliable. In addition, the Court notes that the juror who had submitted the note had been treated in such a way that it had become obvious to the other jurors that he was the one who had made the allegations. It is obvious that this must have compromised his position *vis-à-vis* his fellow jurors.

Thirdly, the Court considers that the collective letter does not discredit the allegations contained in the original note because openly admitting to racism is something which the average person would have a natural tendency to avoid. *A fortiori*, an open admission of racism cannot be easily expected from a person in jury service, the latter being generally regarded an important civic duty.

Given all the above, the Court finds that the collective denial of the allegations contained in the note could not in itself provide a satisfactory solution to the problem.

Moreover, in the present case the Court is not prepared to attach very much weight to the judge's redirection of the jury. The Court considers that, generally speaking, an admonition or direction by a judge, however clear, detailed and forceful, would not change racist views overnight. Although in the present case it cannot be assumed that such views were indeed held by one or more jurors, it has been established that at least one juror had been making racist comments. In these circumstances, the Court considers that the direction given by the judge to the jury could not dispel the reasonable impression and fear of a lack of impartiality, which were based on the original note.

As for the rest, the Court is not prepared to attach much weight to the fact that the judge had direct contact with the jurors either. The Court has already noted that, under domestic law, the judge could not question the jurors on the allegations contained in the note. Nor can GC's acquittal be of decisive importance, since there is nothing to indicate that the two cases were comparable. Finally, the fact that the Court of Appeal rejected the applicant's appeal applying principles that corresponded to the Convention case-law can offer only limited assistance to the Court in the present case.

The Court, therefore, considers that the allegations contained in the note were capable of causing the applicant and any objective observer legitimate doubts as to the impartiality of the court, which neither the collective letter nor the redirection of the jury by the judge could have dispelled.

In this connection, the Court observes that the facts of the applicant's case can be distinguished from the above-mentioned *Gregory* judgment, in which the Court found no violation of the Convention. In the latter case there was no admission by a juror that he had made racist comments, in the form of a joke or otherwise; there was no indication as to who had made the complaint and the complaint was vague and imprecise. Moreover, as opposed to *Gregory v United Kingdom*, in the present case the applicant's counsel insisted throughout the proceedings that dismissing the jury was the only viable course of action.

The Court has accepted that, although discharging the jury may not always be the only means to achieve a fair trial, there are certain circumstances where this is required by Article 6 s 1 of the Convention (see the above-mentioned *Gregory* judgment, p 310, § 48). In the present case the judge was faced with a serious allegation that the applicant risked being condemned because of his ethnic origin. Moreover, one of the jurors indirectly admitted to making racist comments. Given the importance attached by all Contracting States to the need to combat racism (see paragraph 23 above), the Court considers that the judge should have reacted in a more robust manner than merely seeking vague assurances that the jurors could set aside their prejudices and try the case solely on the evidence. By failing to do so, the judge did not provide sufficient guarantees to exclude any objectively justified or legitimate doubts as to the impartiality of the court. It follows that the court that condemned the applicant was not impartial from an objective point of view.

There was, therefore, a violation of Article 6 s 1 of the Convention.

Application of Article 41 of the Convention

36. Article 41 of the Convention provides:

> If the Court finds that there has been a violation of the Convention or the Protocols thereto, and if the internal law of the High Contracting Party concerned allows only partial reparation to be made, the Court shall, if necessary, afford just satisfaction to the injured party.

Damage

The applicant claimed 458,000 pounds sterling in respect of the earnings he lost and the property he had to sell during his imprisonment. He also considered that he should be compensated for the future loss of earnings resulting from the damage to his reputation caused by his conviction and for his divorce. Finally, he demanded compensation for the three years he spent in prison.

38. The Government have not made any comments on the applicant's claims.

39. The Court considers that no causal link has been established between the violation found and the claimed damage. It therefore dismisses the claim.

For These Reasons, The Court

1. *Holds* by four votes to three that there has been a violation of Article 6 s 1 of the Convention;

2. *Dismisses* unanimously the applicant's claims for just satisfaction.

Dissenting Opinion Of Judge Sir Nicolas Bratza joined by judges Costa and Fuhrmann

I regret that I am unable to agree with the majority of the Court that there has been a violation of Article 6 s 1 of the Convention in the present case ...

The majority of the Court in the present case have, correctly in my view, rejected the complaint that the jury lacked impartiality from a subjective standpoint. As in the *Gregory* case, it was not possible for the trial judge to inquire into the precise nature of the comments made or the exact context in which they had been made. Nor is such information available to the Court. In the absence of such information, the fact that a juror made comments that could be understood as jokes about Asians cannot of itself amount to evidence that the particular juror was actually biased against the applicant; still less can it amount to evidence establishing actual bias on the part of the jury as a whole.

However, in contrast to the decision of the Court in the *Gregory* case, the majority have concluded that the fact that a juror made racist jokes in the present case gave rise to justified and legitimate doubts as to the impartiality of the trial court and that sufficient guarantees did not exist to exclude or dispel these doubts.

I cannot agree. While I readily accept that the making of racial jokes is unacceptable in any circumstances, and particularly in the context of a jury trial, such comments as may have been made cannot in my view be seen in isolation and without regard to the steps subsequently taken by the trial judge to dispel any risk of bias.

The majority of the Court attach little weight to the letter signed by each member of the jury, or to the judge's redirection of the jury on two occasions or to the fact that the judge had direct contact with the members of the jury and thus was arguably in a better position to assess what measures were called for.

I do not share this view. The collective letter was written in response to an express reminder to the jury of their oath or affirmation as jurors and to the instructions by the trial judge that they were to indicate if, after reflection, they felt they were unable to try the case solely on the evidence or to put aside any prejudices they might have. The letter contained an explicit assurance that the jury intended to reach a verdict solely according to the evidence and without racial bias, thus responding both to the fears and concerns expressed in the note and to the judge's admonition.

Unlike the majority, I find no inconsistency between the note and the letter. Nor can I accept that the reliability or credibility of the letter is undermined by the fact that it was signed by the juror who had written the note. There is no evidence to suggest that the fact that his identity must have been known to the other jurymen might have compromised his position or subjected him to pressure to drop his allegations. His signing of the letter seems to me to be at least equally consistent with his acknowledgment that his fears and concerns that certain jurymen would reach a verdict on a racial basis were dispelled. That this was the true position seems to me to be borne out by the fact that the jury acquitted one of the applicant's co-defendants, a matter to which I, like the Court of Appeal, attach some, if not decisive, importance.

Again, unlike the majority of the Court, I place considerable weight on the fact that a highly experienced trial judge, having presided over the trial for several days and having been able to observe the jurors as the trial progressed, considered that it was inappropriate to discharge the jury immediately on receiving the note but chose rather to resolve the matter by giving a firm direction and admonition to the jury. I attach weight, also, to the fact that having reviewed the position, as he indicated he would, in the light of the collective letter and separate letter from one juryman, he took the view that the case could be safely left to the jury without any danger of bias causing injustice to the defendants – a view which was fully endorsed by the Court of Appeal.

The majority of the Court, while acknowledging that their conclusion is at variance with that of the Court in the *Gregory* case, seek to distinguish the two cases on their facts. Two such grounds of distinction are suggested. In the first place, it is pointed out that the complaint of bias in the *Gregory* case was vague and imprecise while, in the present case, there was an admission by a juror that he might have made racist jokes. While this is true, it is not to my mind a material point of distinction, the important question in each case being whether sufficient steps were taken to dispel any objectively justified fears that a verdict would be reached on grounds of racial prejudice. Secondly, it is said that in the present case, unlike in *Gregory*, the applicant's counsel insisted throughout the proceedings that the discharge of the jury was the only proper course. I do not find this point compelling either. It was certainly the recollection of defence counsel in the *Gregory* case that he had asked the judge to discharge the jury. More importantly, the fact that the trial judge, having consulted counsel for all parties, did not accept the view of the defence but chose a different course does not mean that a fair trial was not guaranteed. As the Court noted in its *Gregory* judgment, safeguards other than the discharge of a jury, including a carefully worded redirection to the jury, may be sufficient. In my view, it was sufficient in the present case.

In conclusion, I fully endorse the importance to be attached to the need to combat racism. What I cannot accept is that this consideration should have caused the trial judge in the present case to have reacted 'in a more robust manner' or that only the discharge of the jury could have satisfied the requirements of Article 6 s 1.

----·----·----·----·----·----·----·----·----·----·----·----·----·----·----

INVESTIGATIONS INTO JURY ACTIVITY

Section 8 of the Contempt of Court Act 1981 makes it an offence for any person to obtain, disclose or solicit any particulars of statements made, opinions expressed, arguments advanced or votes cast by members of a jury in the course of their deliberations. This section has prevented any real objective investigation into the ways in which juries actually work in practice, so it is not at all clear whether the anecdotal reports on the way in which juries reach their decisions, and some of these are extremely worrying, are accurate or not.

The scope of s 8 was determined in *AG v Associated Newspapers Ltd and Others*.

AG v Associated Newspapers Ltd and Others [1994] 2 AC 238; [1994] 1 All ER 556

The appellants, the publishers and editor of a national newspaper and a journalist employed on the paper, published an article in the paper referring to statements, opinions and arguments made by some members of the jury as they discussed their verdicts in a well publicised fraud trial. The appellants had not obtained the information directly from the jurors concerned, but from transcripts of interviews with the jurors, conducted supposedly for the purpose of *bona fide* research by persons who had placed an advertisement in another newspaper offering a reward to jurors who had taken part in the trial if they contacted a box number. The Attorney General brought proceedings for contempt under s 8(1) of the Contempt of Court Act 1981 (see Lord Lowry's judgment below for details) against the appellants for publishing the information. The appellants contended that the prohibition against disclosure of the deliberations of a jury was confined to disclosure by jurors themselves and did not apply to publication of information about the jury's deliberations which had been obtained indirectly from another source.

Lord Lowry: My Lords, this appeal is concerned with the meaning of s 8(1) of the Contempt of Court Act 1981, which reads:

> Subject to subsection (2) below, it is a contempt of court to obtain, disclose or solicit any particulars of statements made, opinions expressed, arguments advanced or votes cast by members of a jury in the course of their deliberations in any legal proceedings.

The question is whether the word 'disclose', as used in the subsection, refers exclusively to disclosure of information by a juror or signifies disclosure generally, including both disclosure by a juror and (where the facts published were not already well known) publication by a newspaper.

As your Lordships have seen, this subsection is expressed to be subject to s 8(2):

> This section does not apply to any disclosure of any particulars – (a) in the proceedings in question for the purpose of enabling the jury to arrive at their verdict, or in connection with the delivery of that verdict, or (b) in evidence in any subsequent proceedings for an offence alleged to have been committed in relation to the jury in the first mentioned proceedings, or to the publication of any particulars so disclosed.

The only relevance, however, of sub-s (2) for present purposes is that the words in the last line are consistent with the argument that the publication (in a newspaper, for example) of particulars already disclosed by a juror would itself be regarded as a disclosure if it had not been expressly excluded by the words referred to.

Mr Pannick QC, who appeared with Miss Rose for the appellants, accepted, as he had done before the Divisional Court, that, if the word 'disclose' in s 8 was to be given the unrestricted meaning contended for by the Attorney General, a contempt was proved. But he submitted that the scope of s 8(1) could be either widely or narrowly interpreted and that in context the word 'disclose' applied only to a revelation by a juror to another person and not to a further revelation by that person or by another person in his turn. While conceding, frankly but also unavoidably, that what the appellants did amounted to disclosure in the ordinary sense of that word, he contrasted publication with disclosure and contended that the word 'disclose' must here be given a restricted meaning.

The cardinal rule, as stated in the textbooks on interpretation, for example in *Maxwell on the Interpretation of Statutes* (12th edn, 1969) pp 28–29, is that words in a statute *prima facie* bear their plain and ordinary meaning. If that rule is applied without modification, then the appellants disclosed the relevant particulars. There is no conflict or contrast between publication and disclosure. The latter activity has many manifestations and publication is one of them. To disclose is to expose to view, make known or reveal and in its ordinary meaning the word aptly describes both the revelation by jurors of their deliberations and further disclosure by publication in a newspaper of the same deliberations, provided always – and this will raise a question of fact – that the publication amounts to disclosure and is not a mere republication of already known facts.

I have looked in vain, first in s 8 and then in the other provisions of the 1981 Act, for a clue which might justify the imposing of a restriction on the natural meaning and effect of the word 'disclose'. Indeed, as I have observed, the concluding words of s 8(2) seem to me to point away from the restriction and I can find no principle which lays down that something which has been disclosed by A to B cannot be further disclosed by B to C and by C, in his turn, to the public at large.

--- --- --- --- --- --- --- --- --- --- --- --- ---

The functioning of the jury was one of the major areas, and almost certainly the most controversial one, considered by the Runciman Committee.

THREAT TO THE JURY SYSTEM

During the term of the last Parliament, the Government made two separate attempts to reduce defendants' right to elect for jury trial in relation to either way offences by transferring the decision on the mode of trial to the magistrates' courts. Both Bills were defeated in the House of Lords, but the right to elect for jury trials in such cases remains under threat as it has for some time. The following briefing note gives an indication of where the last Government thought it was most likely to be questioned on its proposals and what it considered to be the most appropriate responses.

Criminal Justice (Mode of Trial) Bill Briefing Note

Frequently Asked Questions

What is the background to the Bill?

The Bill is part of the Government programme to modernise the criminal justice system including its aims to reduce delay, help victims and witnesses and to ensure that the system best punishes the guilty and protects the innocent.

The Royal Commission on Criminal Justice in 1993 recommended that defendants should not be able to elect to be tried by a jury in cases which magistrates have indicated that they would be content to hear. In 1997, the Narey *Review of Delay in the Criminal Justice System* came to the same conclusion.

What does the term 'election for jury trial' mean?

Some offences can be tried only in the Crown Court by judge and jury; others can be tried only in magistrates' courts. But there is a range of offences (termed 'either-way' offences) which may be tried either by the magistrates or by jury. At present, where the magistrates would be willing to deal with a case involving an either-way offence, they can do so only with the defendant's consent. By withholding his consent, the defendant may choose ('elect') to be tried in the Crown Court.

What is the purpose of the Bill?

The Criminal Justice (Mode of Trial) Bill would remove the requirement for consent, so that the decision where these cases are heard would rest with the magistrates. There would however be a new right of appeal for defendants to the Crown Court against the magistrates' decision to try the case themselves.

Will the Bill prevent certain offences from being tried by jury?

No. Offences which are triable either way would still be capable of being tried in either court. The difference is that, under the Bill, defendants would no longer be able to choose (or 'elect') to be tried by a jury in cases which magistrates had indicated that they were content to hear.

What type of cases are tried in different types of courts?

The venue for a criminal trial is determined by the seriousness of the offence which is charged. The most serious offences, such as murder, rape and robbery, can only be tried in the Crown Court. Then there are offences which can only be tried by the magistrates. These include common assault, taking without consent and criminal damage to property worth less than £2,000. Some summary offences can have consequences for an offender if convicted, just as serious as for many convictions for either-way offences, for example, drink-driving, assault on a police officer and taking without consent are all summary only offences. Finally, there are offences which can be tried either in the magistrates' courts or the Crown Court, for example theft and burglary. In these cases, the defendant must currently give his or her consent to be tried by the magistrates and by not consenting may elect to be tried by a jury in the Crown Court.

Won't the Government's proposals result in magistrates' courts dealing with cases which are too serious for them?

No. The cases in question are cases which the magistrates have already determined are suitable for them to try. They will continue to direct serious cases to the Crown Court; there is nothing in the Bill which will cause magistrates to seek to deal with such cases themselves. There is also an appeal to the Crown Court against the magistrates' decision to try a case.

Isn't the main reason that either-way cases go the Crown Court that they are directed there?

Yes. 47,000 either-way cases were directed by the magistrates to the Crown Court in 1998. But there is nevertheless a substantial number of cases where defendants elect.

Won't the introduction of a new right of appeal lead to delays?

No. This is an interlocutory appeal to a single Crown Court judge – similar to the procedure for Crown Court bail applications. We envisage that most cases will be dealt with very quickly.

Why do defendants elect Crown Court trial?

There are many possible reasons. Defendants who plead not guilty may believe that they stand a greater chance of acquittal with a jury. For many defendants the motive is to delay the proceedings. They may hope that prosecution witnesses will fail to turn up or that their memory will have faded with the passage of time.

What estimate has the Government made of the costs of the new appeals?

If there is an interlocutory appeal in 25% of the formerly elected cases which the magistrates decide to try themselves, it will cost less than £500,000. The resource savings from the Bill are over £100 million.

How will the Bill ensure that defendants will be treated fairly if the ability to elect is removed?

The Bill includes an interlocutory right of appeal to the Crown Court against the magistrates' decision on mode of trial.

Justification

What empirical evidence does the Government have to support these proposals?

18,500 defendants elected for jury trial even though the magistrates were content to try the case. In a sample of nearly 1000 cases in the six Narey pilot areas in 1998, about 60% of those who elected Crown Court trial pleaded guilty before the trial started. Only 15% of those who elected were acquitted by a jury.

Separate Home Office research conducted in 1989–90 suggested that nearly 90% of those who elected jury trial and were convicted had previous convictions.

Is this just the pursuit of efficiency at the expense of the individual's rights?

The Government believes that it is important to balance the rights of defendants against the rights of all those involved, including victims and witnesses. Moreover, a person who elects jury trial and is convicted faces more serious penalties. The majority of the resource savings which are expected from the Bill – £66 million out of £105 million – would occur in the Prison Service simply because the magistrates' courts impose shorter sentences.

What is 'plea before venue'?

Plea before venue is a procedure, implemented in October 1997, whereby a defendant charged with an either-way offence indicates a plea before the magistrates' court makes its decision on mode of trial. If he pleads guilty, he is convicted by the magistrates' court and is either sentenced by that court or committed to the Crown Court for sentence, as appropriate. Where a not guilty plea (or no plea) is indicated, the magistrates' court considers where the case should be tried, in the usual way. The arrangement helps to retain business in the magistrates' courts and allows for the early disposal of appropriate cases.

Are these changes really necessary, given that 'plea before venue' is already reducing the number of elections?

Yes. The benefit of 'Plea before Venue' is that it allows those who wish to plead guilty to do so in the magistrates' court, which was not possible in directed cases prior to its implementation. No doubt this earlier opportunity to plead, together with the prospect of maximum sentence discount, will have had some impact on some of those who might previously have delayed a guilty plea. But there is a substantial number of cases – 18,500 in 1998 – where the defendant does not indicate a guilty plea and elects Crown Court trial.

Are the Government's proposals purely about saving money?

There are important arguments of principle here. As the Lord Chief Justice recently said, it is wrong for the defendant 'on whose list of priorities the reaching of a just and expeditious decision may not rank very highly' to have the ability to choose the mode of trial. But the Government also took into account in considering these reforms the estimated savings of over £100 million to the cost of running the criminal justice system.

Other Points

Why interfere with the age-old right to jury trial?

The right of election was provided by the 1855 Criminal Justice Act, not by *Magna Carta*. The measure was designed to ensure that the magistrates dealt with the bulk of such cases. It is only right that the arrangements for jury trial are kept under review. Every time any change has been proposed, there have been strong objections which have proved to be unfounded. For example, the 1967 reform to allow majority verdicts was opposed by critics who argued that it would lead to injustice; few would make that claim today. Removing the defendant's peremptory right to challenge jurors was also the subject of controversy. Again, there is no evidence to suggest that this has led to unfair trials.

Scotland

How is mode of trial determined in Scotland?

In Scotland the decision on which court an either way case will be tried in is taken by the Procurator Fiscal (the Prosecutor).

Will the Government follow the Scottish model which does not allow a case which has been tried summarily to be committed to the higher courts for sentencing?

No. In Scotland the decision is taken by the Prosecutor, who has access to information – especially about previous convictions – which a magistrates' court will not have.

What about the concerns that defendants have to elect in order to get the CPS to agree on correct charges?

Over-charging is wrong. But concerns about the appropriateness of charges can be dealt with in the magistrates' courts. It should not be necessary for cases to go to the Crown Court just because the defence believes that charges are set too high. The consequences for the defendant in electing this route may outweigh anything gained in getting the charges reduced.

Reputation

Does the Government recognise that, for people of good character, a conviction may have very serious consequences?

The Government has acknowledged that there are some circumstances where a conviction might have more serious consequences for one defendant than for another. The Bill will require the courts to take account of the effect of a conviction upon the accused's reputation and livelihood.

Will the Bill create two-tier justice?

No. Most cases in England and Wales are currently tried in the magistrates' courts. Under the Magistrates' Courts Act 1980 the court is already required to have regard to the nature of the case and whether the circumstances make the offence one of serious character. It is right that the court should also be required to consider the seriousness of the case from the defendant's perspective.

Isn't it unfair?

No. This is not a new phenomenon in criminal law. Similar provision already exists in the Legal Aid Act 1988 as a factor to be taken into account by the court in determining whether it is in the interests of justice that representation be granted.

Are the Government's proposals compatible with the ECHR?

Yes. The European Convention on Human Rights guarantees the right to a fair trial, not trial by jury. Over 90% of all criminal cases in England and Wales are dealt with in the magistrates' courts. Many Convention countries, for example the Netherlands, do not have jury trial at all.

CHAPTER 11

THE JUDICIARY

Central to the general idea of the Rule of Law is the specific proposition that it involves the rule of *law* rather than the rule of *people*. Judges hold a position of central importance in relation to the concept of the Rule of Law. They are expected to deliver judgment in a completely impartial manner through a strict application of the law, without allowing their personal preference, or fear or favour of any of the parties to the action, to affect their decision in any way.

This desire for impartiality is reflected in the constitutional position of the judges. In line with Montesquieu's classical exposition of the separation of powers, the judiciary occupy a situation apart from the legislative and executive arms of the State; and operate independently of them. Yet, increasingly, judges are being involved in deciding essentially socio-political questions that have been formulated in legal terms. Such occurrences require an analysis both of the role of the judiciary and of the terms on which they determine such socio-political issues as come before them. It also inevitably raises questions as to representative nature and competence of judges to take such decisions.

In a speech to the delegates to the worldwide Common Law Conference, the Lord Chancellor, Lord Irvine, addressed a number of current key issues, including judicial independence and constitutional reform, but perhaps of most interest is his understanding of the role of the office of Lord Chancellor.

Lord Irvine of Lairg, Speech to the Third Worldwide Common Law Judiciary Conference, University of Edinburgh Conference Centre, 5 July 1999

Fellow judges, on behalf of all the judiciary of the United Kingdom, I welcome you to Edinburgh. We are grateful to you for coming to this conference. It is an honour for us to welcome you here. We British judges are proud that this small island was the birthplace of the common law. We are, however, also very conscious that the common law is not our exclusive property. We share it with many other countries, who have developed and improved it with distinction.

You have a wide-ranging and challenging agenda for discussion over the next four days. I am sorry that I cannot be present for more of it. As I cannot hope to cover all the topics that you will be discussing, I will focus in this introduction on the cornerstone issue of judicial independence and, in particular, on some aspects of our own experience here in the United Kingdom, especially in relation to the balance between judicial independence and accountability.

We in this country are in the midst of a major programme of constitutional reform, launched by the Government of which I am a member. Our reforms will have important consequences for the judges, and there is public debate, as there should be, about those consequences. I would like to offer you my own thoughts. First, to set the scene, I will summarise how judicial independence is secured in the United Kingdom, and especially in England and Wales. Secondly, in the light of the forthcoming reforms, I will speak about the position of our senior judges, the Law Lords. And finally I will touch on my own, ancient but still highly functional, office of Lord Chancellor, and how it serves both independence and accountability.

Judicial Independence

The need for an independent judiciary is recognised throughout the free world. It is a cornerstone of Britain's constitutional arrangements, as it is of yours, for without judicial independence, there can be no rule of law. In this country, our constitution does not embody a full separation of powers. Our Parliamentary democracy makes for a considerable fusion of the executive and legislative branches. Unlike, for example, the position in the United States, every Cabinet Minister is a member of one or other House of Parliament. Taken with our doctrine of Parliamentary sovereignty and the powerful influence of the executive upon the legislature, the judicial arm is not as strong, yet it must ensure that the executive is kept subject to the rule of the law.

We have, therefore, to take especial care to guarantee judicial independence. We do so by various means, the first of which is law and convention. The security of tenure of our senior judges has been guaranteed by statute ever since the Act of Settlement of 1701. A senior judge can only be removed on the joint address of both Houses of Parliament, and this has never happened to an English judge. Our judges are also given security of remuneration. Their salaries cannot be reduced by Government action. The judges are also granted high official rank and the legal immunities necessary to perform their judicial duties. But judicial independence does not depend only on the law. It is also nourished by a political and professional culture. With us, this derives from the free and self-confident legal profession from which our judges are drawn. This enables every judge to look the Government, his fellow judges, or anybody else in the eye and do his duty, in the words of the judicial oath, 'without fear or favour, affection or ill-will'.

Yet another important bulwark of judicial independence in our system is the office of Lord Chancellor, to which I will return. In return for the independence we guarantee to our judges, the trust we place in them is that they will carry out their duties impartially. I define impartiality as the absolute recognition and application by judges of an obligation of fidelity to law.

Against this background, concern has been voiced in some quarters that this Government's programme of constitutional reform will 'politicise' the judiciary and threaten their judicial independence. The aim of our constitutional reforms has been to decentralise power in the United Kingdom, and to enhance the citizen's power to enforce his human rights, within a more open society. We have already carried the devolution and Human Rights Acts into law. We have recently published a draft Freedom of Information Bill. And we are now engaged on House of Lords reform – unfinished business of a century ago.

However, the new legislation has been carefully framed to preserve the traditional constitutional restraints on judicial interpretation of the law, particularly the sovereignty of Parliament. The Human Rights Act, for example, will lead the courts to exercise a more intensive form of scrutiny over Government and public authorities. The judges will have to deploy such concepts as proportionality and necessity, permitting the Government to cut down human rights only if it does so in response to a pressing social need.

The courts *will* be drawn into a greater number of politically controversial issues. But they will not as a result be enabled to strike down Parliamentary legislation, although they will be able to declare it incompatible with the European Human Rights Convention. Whilst changing the nature of the interpretative process, the Act does not confer on the courts a licence to construe legislation in a way which arrogates to the judges a power completely to rewrite existing law: that is a task for Parliament and the executive. In my view, the advent of the Human Rights Act makes no material difference to the position of the judiciary. The judges in this country are used to interpreting the law in controversial cases in a way which may bring them into conflict with the executive, but which respects our constitutional settlement. Judges in the House of Lords, and below, have traditionally made decisions, under the law, which were highly controversial – in landmark cases on civil liberties; on trade union immunities; on citizens' rights in time of war; on natural justice; on freedom of expression and freedom of the press; on contempt of court; and on the whole modern development of judicial review under which the judges have struck down executive decisions as contrary to law. The most that our reforms will do is to make a difference of degree, not kind; and one which will rightly enhance the role and standing of the judiciary.

The Law Lords

The vital role of interpreting the new legislation will fall above all to our most senior judges, the Law Lords. Our highest appellate court is unusual in western democracies, in that it is an organic part of our legislature. This is an example of our flexible approach to the separation of powers. The appellate function of the House of Lords goes back many centuries, but in its modern form, it dates from 1876. And it is important of course to appreciate that this function is not exercised by the peers at large, but by a small and highly professional court. Although this court sits in our Parliament building, it consists only of the Law Lords.

The Law Lords are full members of the House of Lords. They may take part in the House's legislative activities, under certain conventions. They are 'cross-benchers' who have no connection with any political party. In particular, they avoid making any comment in the House on any issue that is, or may come, before them judicially. Within these conventions, the Law Lords make a distinctive contribution to the work of the House of Lords in debates on the administration of justice, and in the valuable specialist contributions they make to many Select Committees. Their knowledge in these areas is unequalled and the House would be the loser without them. Therefore, to the question whether the House of Lords in its legislative capacity must lose the benefits the Law Lords confer because of the doctrine of the separation of powers, I say 'no' for two reasons: first, because we do not apply the doctrine strictly; and, secondly, provided their role in the legislature does not prejudice their primary role as our final appellate judges, there is no need to change a beneficial system.

Some suggest that Article 6 of the European Convention, which is entitled 'right to a fair trial', requires Britain, by a side wind from the guarantee of that right, to change our long-settled constitutional arrangements. But Article 6 requires a fair and impartial hearing, not a strict separation of powers. Provided a Law Lord hearing a case in the House of Lords has abstained from expressing a concluded view in the legislative chamber, on an issue coming before him judicially, then there will be no breach of Article 6 if he sits.

The reform of the House of Lords is the next plank of the Government's reform programme. A Bill is currently passing through Parliament to remove the rights of hereditary peers to sit and vote in the House of Lords. A Royal Commission has been appointed to make recommendations on the role and functions of a reformed second chamber, and on the composition required to meet those needs. The Royal Commission has been asked to report by the end of this year. Some commentators suggest that the time has come for legislation to remove our highest appellate court from the House of Lords, and to establish a separate Supreme Court. The Government will of course give careful consideration to any recommendations which the Royal Commission may make, but at present it does not regard the case for this legislative change as made out.

The Lord Chancellor

As Lord Chancellor, I am a senior member of the Cabinet and a Minister of Justice. But I am also, like my predecessors over many centuries, a judge. In this capacity, I am the president of the appellate committee of the House of Lords, as I am of the other superior courts in England and Wales. This role is a significant part of our constitutional arrangements to protect the independence of the judiciary. Let me explain why.

I have already said that the fusion of executive and legislative power in this country, coupled with legislative supremacy, leaves the judicial branch correspondingly weak. The judicial branch as a whole must also shoulder a degree of accountability. This does not mean that the judges can be made answerable for their judicial decisions, duly made, although these may of course be subject to review in the appeal courts. Judicial accountability requires that the public must be able to see that justice is being done. Just as judicial impartiality is the other side of the coin of judicial independence, so open justice as witnessed by an attentive media is a strong spur to judicial impartiality in practice. This was recognised by the authors of the European Convention on Human Rights, which guarantees a hearing which is not only fair, but also normally takes place in public. However, a modern democracy also demands accountability to Parliament and public for the overall efficiency and effectiveness of the system of justice. This includes the good conduct of the judges and the proper use of public resources. We also need to have procedures for selecting the judges which ensure appointment strictly on merit. Proper accountability must never be allowed to develop into improper pressure, which could encourage the judiciary to make decisions with a view to public or Parliamentary popularity. That would turn judicial independence into a sham.

Striking the balance between accountability and independence is never easy. The problem is universal, and different countries have different solutions. The office of Lord Chancellor has evolved as the English solution to this problem. The office dates back at least to the eleventh century, and probably earlier. It is older than our parliament, older than our democratic system. The Lord Chancellor is the head of the judiciary and President of the highest courts in the country. In this capacity, he is a serving judge. He is also a member of the executive, as a senior Cabinet Minister, and he presides over the upper house of the legislature. The office carries significant authority within all three branches of Government. This position makes the Lord Chancellor uniquely well-qualified to protect the independence of the judiciary in this country.

Lord Chancellors always come to the office after a long career in the law, whether as judges or as senior advocates. Their profession puts independent individual judgment above all else. They come to the office imbued with the values that underpin our democracy: the rule of law; the independence of the judiciary from any executive interference; the duty of the courts to stand between citizen and state; and to confine public authorities within the law. The public and the judges can have a well-founded confidence that, for any Lord Chancellor, these values, together with the authority of his office, would be armour against executive pressure.

The value of a Lord Chancellor is that he upholds judicial independence and can mediate between the executive and judiciary when need be. The judiciary has a representative in the Cabinet, and the Cabinet in the judiciary. The Lord Chancellor can also speak to the public on behalf of the judges, in a way that professional judges themselves cannot. The office of Lord Chancellor is the guarantor of judicial independence in our constitution. It holds the different parts together, and withstands pressure from all sides. Let me give you two examples of how the office of Lord Chancellor protects the independence of the judiciary. I spoke earlier about the importance of an appointments system which ensures that judicial appointments are made on merit. With us, as in the majority of countries, judicial appointments are made by the executive. It is thus important that there are checks within the system, which prevent candidates from being appointed on the ground of their political beliefs or on any other grounds which seem convenient to the executive, but are not justified on merit. In this country, the appointment or recommendation for appointment of judges is one of the Lord Chancellor's most important responsibilities. He provides executive involvement in the appointments process, without compromising judicial independence, because of his dual role, and because he exercises these important functions away from the fierce party political controversies in the House of Commons.

Like my predecessors, I make judicial appointments strictly on merit, and I have effective systems and resources to do so. My central policy is to appoint, or recommend for appointment, those candidates who satisfy the statutory qualifications and who best meet the criteria for appointment. This is without regard to factors such as gender, ethnic origin, marital status or disability. I believe strongly in equal opportunities and encourage applications from any individual who meets the criteria for appointment. However, I am resolutely opposed to any proposition that our courts should be sculpted to conform to any notion of social, political, gender or any other balance.

No one appointments system has a monopoly on delivering appointments based solely on merit. Methods of appointment vary, and different systems must reflect the different traditions, cultures and conventions of individual states. But it is vital that judicial appointments command the respect and confidence of the legal community, and of Parliament and public. I firmly believe that in this country they do, and I am content to be judged by the quality of the product.

My second example relates to judicial accountability. The position of the Lord Chancellor enables him to be responsible, as a Minister, through Parliament to the public for the overall efficiency of the justice system, in a way in which the judiciary cannot. The Lord Chancellor is accountable for the overall quality of the Bench; for the good conduct and discipline of the judges; and the proper deployment of the substantial resources voted by Parliament for the administration of justice. If these are not delivered to the satisfaction of Government or Parliament, the Lord Chancellor is responsible to the Prime Minister – as no other judge can be, or should be. In exercising his responsibility for the administration of justice, the Lord Chancellor must work in close co-operation with the judiciary. The Lord Chancellor is in an ideal position to mediate between the interests of the executive and the interests of the judiciary on difficult issues, such as the resourcing of the courts.

The role exercised by the Lord Chancellor depends on his position as head of the judiciary. Without it, he could not command the same respect and confidence of the judges, which is essential since he is responsible for their good conduct and discipline. In this capacity, it is important that he sits as a judge. Until the middle of this century, Lord Chancellors sat judicially for most of their time. Although the demands of the Lord Chancellor's responsibilities in Cabinet and in the legislative chamber now make it impossible for me to sit frequently, all my recent predecessors in this office have sat judicially, except one who was Lord Chancellor for only a few months. Like my predecessors, I exercise my discretion not to sit where I consider it would be improper to do so. I have no doubt that any future Lord Chancellor would do likewise. Provided that the Lord Chancellor has abstained from expressing concluded views on an issue coming before him judicially; and he does not sit in any case where the interests of the executive are directly engaged; there is no reason at all why he should not sit and preside judicially.

There are those who think that the time has come to dismantle the office of Lord Chancellor. They base themselves in part on a purist view of the separation of powers – which if pursued with purity would lead them to drive every Cabinet Minister from the House of Commons or the House of Lords. In part they also argue that the Government's programme of constitutional change will produce more politically controversial cases and make it impossible for the Lord Chancellor to sit judicially.

I am not persuaded this view is correct and I am re-enforced by my experience in office. The role of the Lord Chancellor is to compensate for the fusion of powers elsewhere. The new constitutional settlement gives the judges greater powers to settle *vires* disputes between the Scottish Parliament, the various Assemblies and Westminster. It gives them powers under the Human Rights Act to declare Westminster legislation incompatible with the Convention. I accept that these responsibilities will increase the potential for controversy between the executive and the judiciary. But I draw the opposite conclusion from the critics. I am clear that the only effect these changes will have on the office of Lord Chancellor is to make it more valuable and necessary than ever, as a buffer between executive and judiciary; and as a bulwark of our constitution.

I conclude, in summary, by saying that judicial independence in principle and practice is fundamental to the functioning of a parliamentary democracy and to freedom under the law. And that our constitutional settlement, including the Law Lords, and the office of Lord Chancellor, provides for both independence and accountability. And that these features of our constitution have as relevant and useful a part to play in the future as they have in the past. You have now heard enough from me about how we deal with the balance of judicial independence and accountability in this country. I look forward to benefiting from the experience and thoughts of others; and I wish you every success with your discussions.

—··—··—··—··—··—··—··—··—··—··—··—··—

In the above speech Lord Irvine makes reference to the fact that the office of Lord Chancellor 'carries significant authority within all three branches of Government'. Such diverse authority raises questions as to its appropriateness within a contemporary constitution and, indeed, its legality under the European Convention on Human Rights (ECHR). In a case which many saw as concerning a surrogate of the Lord Chancellor, the European Court of Human Rights (ECtHR) did not have to decide the issue as to the various roles assumed by the Bailiff of Guernsey, but it still remains open to argument in the future that the Lord Chancellor's multi-functional role within the constitution is contrary to the ECHR. The additional judgment of Sir John Laws in the case is quite apparently designed to support the position of the Lord Chancellor. The Lord Chancellor's department has insisted that the decision in the present case has no relevance for the Lord Chancellor, but he has declined to act as a judge in several 'political' cases.

McGonnell v United Kingdom (2000) (Application No 28488/95), ECtHR

I.   The Circumstances Of The Case

...

7. The applicant bought the Calais Vinery, Calais Lane, St. Martin's in 1982. A number of planning applications were made to permit residential use of the land in the ensuing years. The applications were all refused, an appeal being dismissed by the Royal Court in July 1984. In 1986 or 1987 the applicant moved into a converted packing shed on his land.

8. In 1988 the applicant, through an advocate, made representations to a planning inquiry which was considering the draft Detailed Development Plan No. 6 (DDP6). In his report to the President of the Island Development Committee (IDC), the inspector set out the arguments led by the applicant's advocate and by the advocate for the IDC, and concluded that a dwelling on the applicant's site would be an intrusion into the agricultural/horticultural hinterland. He supported the IDC's proposed zoning of the land as an area reserved for agricultural purposes and in which development was generally prohibited.

9. The President of the IDC submitted DDP6, in draft, to the President of the States of Deliberation on 22 May 1990.

10. The States of Deliberation, presided over by Mr Graham Dorey, the Deputy Bailiff, debated and adopted DDP6 on 27 and 28 June 1990. The zoning of the applicant's land was not changed.

11. A retrospective application for planning permission to convert the packing shed into a dwelling was rejected by the IDC on 11 July 1991 as the IDC was bound to take into account DDP6 on which the site was zoned as a Developed Glasshouse Area where residential development was not allowed.

12. On 27 March 1992 the applicant was convicted by the Magistrate's Court on his guilty plea of changing the use of the shed without permission, contrary to Section 14 (1) (a) of the Island Development (Guernsey) Law 1966 ('the 1966 Law'). He was fined GBP 100, with 10 days' imprisonment in default.

13. On 15 February 1993 the IDC applied for permission under Section 37 (1)(h) of the 1966 Law itself to carry out the necessary works to remedy the breach of the planning legislation. The application was adjourned in Ordinary Court by the Deputy Bailiff on 25 February 1993 for a date to be fixed. The Deputy Bailiff was also unwilling to hear the matter on the grounds of having dealt with the applicant when he was Her Majesty's Procureur.

14. A further application on the applicant's behalf for permission to continue living in the shed was dismissed by the IDC on 18 May 1993, and a request for the Section 37 (1) (h) proceedings to be adjourned was dismissed by the Bailiff on 20 May 1993. On 25 June 1993 the Royal Court comprising the Bailiff and three Jurats granted the IDC's application under Section 37(1)(h) …

16. On 6 June 1995 the Royal Court, comprising the Bailiff, by then Sir Graham Dorey, and seven Jurats, heard the applicant's appeal. The applicant's representative accepted that the written statement provided for no development other than Developed Glasshouse of the area, but submitted that there were nevertheless reasons in the case to permit the change of use: the external appearance of the building would not change and there would be no future prejudice to the horticultural use of the land, such that it was unreasonable for the IDC to take an unduly narrow view of what it allowed under the DDP. The Bailiff then summed up the applicant's complaints to the Jurats, instructing them that the ultimate burden of proof was on the IDC, to satisfy the Jurats that the IDC's decision was reasonable. The appeal was dismissed unanimously. The decision recites the grounds of appeal, but gives no reasons.

II. Relevant Domestic Law And Practice

17. The Court has been referred to one recent official document relating to the constitution of Guernsey generally … The Bailiff is appointed by the Sovereign by Letters Patent under the Great Seal of the Realm and holds office during Her Majesty's Pleasure subject to a retiring age of seventy years. He is President of the States of Election, President of the States of deliberation, President of the Royal Court, President of the Court of Appeal and head of the Administration.

The Bailiff, as President of the States of Deliberation, is entitled to speak on any matter and has no original vote but he has a casting vote if the Members are equally divided. In general, the Bailiff uses his voice to ensure a further investigation of questions on which the States are in doubt. He places measures before the States at the request of the States Committees but he can also on his own initiative place any matter before the assembly.

He is, with the Lieutenant-Governor, a channel of communication between the Privy Council and the Secretary of State for the Home Department on the one hand and on the other, the Island authorities; and in a number of questions, as the head of the Administration of the Island, would be expected to guide the Island authorities.

He has been relieved of some of his administrative responsibilities by the appointment of the States Advisory and Finance Committee which is in the nature of a co-ordinating committee with advisory powers but the Bailiff may, in his own discretion, lay before the States any matter which he has previously referred to the Committee providing that he gives the Committee an opportunity to acquaint the States with its views.

While the Bailiff is responsible for arranging the business to come before the States, he is not in a position to refuse to place before the States any question of business if so requested by Members or committees of the States. The assembly looks to the Bailiff for advice on matters affecting the Constitution of the Island.

In the course of insular legislation or in discussions arising from communications from the Privy Council or the Home Department, it is the duty of the Bailiff to represent the views of the Island in constitutional matters.

In the event of differences between the Crown and the States it is the historical duty of the Bailiff to represent the views of the people of the Island.

18. The Bailiff is the senior judge of the Royal Court. In the modern era, he has usually occupied the offices of Her Majesty's Comptroller, Her Majesty's Procureur (Solicitor-General/Attorney-General respectively) and, since 1970, Deputy Bailiff, before finally becoming Bailiff. In his judicial capacity, the Bailiff is the professional judge (with the lay Jurats) in the Royal Court, and is *ex officio* President of the Guernsey Court of Appeal. In his non-judicial capacity, the Bailiff is President of the States of Election, of the States of Deliberation, of four States Committees (the Appointments Board, the Emergency Council, the Legislation Committee and the Rules of Procedure Committee), and he plays a role in communications between the Island Authorities and the Government of the United Kingdom and the Privy Council. Where the Bailiff presides in his non-judicial capacity, he has a casting, but not an original, vote ...

36. The applicant claimed that he did not have the benefit of the guarantees of Article 6 § 1 of the Convention at the hearing of his case before the Royal Court of Guernsey on 6 June 1995. The relevant parts of Article 6 provide:

    1. In the determination of his civil rights and obligations or of any criminal charge against him, everyone is entitled to a fair and public hearing within a reasonable time by an independent and impartial tribunal established by law ...

46. The applicant pointed to the non-judicial functions of the Bailiff, contending that they gave rise to such close connections between the Bailiff as a judicial officer and the legislative and executive functions of government that the Bailiff no longer had the independence and impartiality required by Article 6. As specific examples, the applicant pointed to three matters which were not referred to before the Commission. They are the facts that the Bailiff is invariably appointed from the office of the Attorney General, that he acts as Lieutenant Governor of the island when that office is vacant, and that the Bailiff who sat in the present case had also presided over the States of Deliberation when DDP6, the very act which was at issue in the applicant's later case, was adopted. He also claimed that the Royal Court gave inadequate reasons for its judgment.

47. The Government recalled that the Convention does not require compliance with any particular doctrine of separation of powers. They maintained that whilst the Bailiff has a number of positions on the island, they cannot give rise to any legitimate fear in a reasonably well informed inhabitant of Guernsey of a lack of independence or impartiality because the positions do not involve any real involvement in legislative or executive functions. In particular, they underlined that when the Bailiff presides over the States of Deliberations or one of the four States Committees in which he is involved, his involvement is not that of an active member, but rather he is an independent umpire, who ensures that the proceedings run smoothly without taking part or expressing approval or disapproval of the matters under discussion. In connection with the reasons for the Royal Court's judgment, the Government considered that the Bailiff's summing up, taken together with the decision of the Jurats, gave sufficient reasons to comply with Article 6 of the Convention.

48. The Court recalls that it found in its *Findlay v United Kingdom* judgment (judgment of 25 February 1997, Reports 1997-I, p 198, § 73) that:

> in order to establish whether a tribunal can be considered as 'independent', regard must be had, *inter alia*, to the manner of appointment of its members and their term of office, the existence of guarantees against outside pressures and the question whether the body presents an appearance of independence ...

> As to the question of 'impartiality', there are two aspects to this requirement. First, the tribunal must be subjectively free of personal prejudice or bias. Secondly, it must also be impartial from an objective viewpoint, that is, it must offer sufficient guarantees to exclude any legitimate doubt in this respect ... The concepts of independence and objective impartiality are closely linked ...

49. In the present case, too, the concepts of independence and objective impartiality are closely linked, and the Court will consider them together.

50. The Court first observes that there is no suggestion in the present case that the Bailiff was subjectively prejudiced or biased when he heard the applicant's planning appeal in June 1995. It has not been alleged that the Bailiff's participation as Deputy Bailiff in the adoption of DDP6 in 1990 gives rise to actual bias on his part: the applicant states that it is not possible to ascertain whether there was actual bias because of the Bailiff's various functions, but he does not contend that the Bailiff was subjectively biased or prejudiced.

51. The Court can agree with the Government that neither Article 6 nor any other provision of the Convention requires States to comply with any theoretical constitutional concepts as such. *The question is always whether, in a given case, the requirements of the Convention are met. The present case does not, therefore, require the application of any particular doctrine of constitutional law to the position in Guernsey: the Court is faced solely with questions of whether the Bailiff had the required 'appearance' of independence, or the required 'objective' impartiality* [emphasis added].

52. In this connection, the Court notes that the Bailiff's functions are not limited to judicial matters, but that he is also actively involved in non-judicial functions on the island. The Court does not accept the Government's analysis that when the Bailiff acts in a non-judicial capacity he merely occupies positions rather

than exercising functions: even a purely ceremonial constitutional role must be classified as a 'function'. The Court must determine whether the Bailiff's functions in his non-judicial capacity were, or were not, compatible with the requirements of Article 6 as to independence and impartiality.

53. The Court observes that the Bailiff in the present case had personal involvement with the planning matters at the heart of the applicant's case on two occasions. The first occasion was in 1990, when, as Deputy Bailiff, he presided over the States of Deliberation at the adoption of DDP6. The second occasion was on 6 June 1995, when he presided over the Royal Court in the determination of the applicant's planning appeal.

54. The Court recalls that in the case of *Procola v Luxembourg*, four of the five members of the Conseil d'Etat had carried out both advisory and judicial functions in the same case (judgment of 28 September 1995, Series A no 326, p 16, § 45).

55. The participation of the Bailiff in the present case shows certain similarities with the position of the members of the Conseil d'Etat in the case of *Procola*. First, in neither case was any doubt expressed in the domestic proceedings as to the role of the impugned organ. Secondly, and more particularly, in both cases a member, or members, of the deciding tribunal had been actively and formally involved in the preparatory stages of the regulation at issue. As the Court has noted above, the Bailiff's non-judicial constitutional functions cannot be accepted as being merely ceremonial. *With particular respect to his presiding, as Deputy Bailiff, over the States of Deliberation in 1990, the Court considers that any direct involvement in the passage of legislation, or of executive rules, is likely to be sufficient to cast doubt on the judicial impartiality of a person subsequently called on to determine a dispute over whether reasons exist to permit a variation from the wording of the legislation or rules at issue* [emphasis added]. In the present case, in addition to the chairing role as such, the Deputy Bailiff could exercise a casting vote in the event of even voting and, as the Bailiff stated in the *Bordeaux Vineries* case, there was no obligation on him to exercise his casting vote against a proposition before the States where that vote impinged on his conscience. Moreover, the States of Deliberation in Guernsey was the body which passed the regulations at issue. It can thus be seen to have had a more direct involvement with them than had the advisory panel of the Conseil d'Etat in the case of *Procola* with the regulations in that case (above-mentioned judgment, p 12, § 25)

56. The Court also notes that in the case of *De Haan*, the judge who presided over the Appeals Tribunal was called upon to decide upon an objection for which he himself was responsible. In that case, notwithstanding an absence of prejudice or bias in the part of the judge, the Court found that the applicant's fears as to the judge's participation were objectively justified (*De Haan v Netherlands* judgment of 26 August 1997, Reports 1997-IV, pp 1392, 1393, §§ 50, 51).

57. The Court thus considers that the mere fact that the Deputy Bailiff presided over the States of Deliberation when DDP6 *was adopted in 1990 is capable of casting doubt on his impartiality when he subsequently determined, as the sole judge of the law in the case, the applicant's planning appeal* [emphasis added]. The applicant therefore had legitimate grounds for fearing that the Bailiff may have

been influenced by his prior participation in the adoption of DDP6. That doubt in itself, however slight its justification, is sufficient to vitiate the impartiality of the Royal Court, and it is therefore unnecessary for the Court to look into the other aspects of the complaint.

58. It follows that there has been a breach of Article 6 § 1.

Concurring opinion of Sir John Laws (who sat as an additional judge in the ECtHR)

I add a few words of my own merely to emphasise that the only objective basis upon which, on the facts of this case, a violation of Article 6 § 1 may properly be found depends in my view entirely upon the fact that the Bailiff who presided over the Royal Court in the legal proceedings giving rise to this case presided also (as Deputy Bailiff) over the States of Deliberation in 1990 when DDP6 was adopted. That is the thrust of the reasoning in paragraph 57 of the principal judgment, with whose terms I entirely agree.

If it were thought arguable (perhaps by reference to the reasoning in paragraph 52) that a violation might be shown on any wider basis, having regard to the Bailiff's multiple roles, I would express my firm dissent from any such view. Where there is no question of actual bias, our task under Article 6 s 1 must be to determine whether the reasonable bystander – a fully informed layman who has no axe to grind – would on objective grounds fear that the Royal Court lacks independence and impartiality. I am clear that but for the coincidence of the Bailiff's presidency over the States in 1990, and over the Royal Court in 1995, there are no such objective grounds whatever.

COMPOSITION OF THE JUDICIARY

In a speech delivered to the Association of Women Barristers, the Lord Chancellor encouraged more women to apply for positions in the judicial structure whilst maintaining a firm commitment to appointing on the sole criterion of merit. Progress is evidently being made, but is it as fast as it should/could be?

Lord Irvine Of Lairg, Speech to the Association of Women Barristers Annual Dinner, February 1998

I am wholly committed to equal opportunities. Everybody should be given an equal chance to fulfil his or her personal potential. Negative discrimination on the grounds of sex; race; religion; sexual orientation; class; or any other factor should never be tolerated. One of my wins at the Bar, which I look back on with most pleasure, was when I was instructed by the Commission for Racial Equality and had a unanimous House of Lords reverse a unanimous Court of Appeal, presided over by Lord Denning, and hold that a Sikh boy was discriminated against if he was not allowed to wear his turban at school. I am sure you will remember the case *Mandla and Another v Dowell Lee and Another* [1983] 1 All ER. I am the opponent of discrimination – both negative and positive. I have said it before, but it bears saying again: judicial appointments must always be made on merit. Vacancies must be filled by the best person available.

There are two parts to this equation. First, able people must put themselves forward for appointment.

I say to you: 'Don't be shy! Apply!'

And, second, the judicial appointments system must be flexible enough to take account of career patterns, experience and achievements which may be untypical. I have some control over the second – but the first is up to you, the members of the legal profession.

None who meet the eligibility requirements should exclude himself or herself from the competition for appointment because of a private fear that his or her background or personal profile does not match up to the stereotype of a judge. Yes, it is true that many judges today are white, Oxbridge educated men. But it is also true that they were appointed on merit, from the then available pool, at the time the vacancies arose. They are the people who have shown the necessary merit in the past but from a limited field of candidates, from a limited pool.

It does not mean that the social composition of the judiciary is immutably fixed. For too long barristers were drawn from a narrow social background. As this changes over time, I would expect the composition of the Bench to change too. That is inherent in the merit principle.

Though it is more than 70 years since women were first called to the Bar, it is only recently that there have been a significant number with over 15 years call – a level of experience when people begin to feel able and ready to put themselves forward for judicial appointment. Today, 14% of barristers with over 15 years call are women. But look elsewhere and we see a changing scene. 43% of new recruits to the Bar in 1997 were women.

Against that background, while it comes as no real surprise that the number of women in the judiciary has historically been low, we can expect the male dominated image of the judiciary to change significantly over time.

In fact, things are already on the move. In December 1994, 7.6% of the main tiers of the judiciary – by which I mean the Lords Justices of Appeal, High Court, Circuit Bench, Recorders, Assistant Recorders and District Judges – I repeat, 7.6% were women. It is now a little over 9%. Not a meteoric rise, true, but a steady one. It is a rise which, I hope, will encourage more of you to think of seeking a move from the Bar to the Bench. There will never be significantly more women judges unless more women lawyers put themselves forward for appointment.

I know that many women lawyers struggle to maintain their careers during the years they are having and caring for their children. They may face prejudice – perhaps a belief among their seniors, or among their clerks, that women with family responsibilities are not really committed to their work. They may not be considered for more challenging or high profile cases. They may lose ground in the competition to keep up with their male peers. But none of this is a reflection on their intellectual abilities or legal skills. Many women lawyers find themselves disadvantaged in their careers simply by circumstances. The effects of career breaks, or other factors which may make career histories appear untypical, may be robbing me of excellent women candidates for judicial appointment. I am determined to find ways to establish a level playing field between those who have followed a standard career path and those who have not.

Josephine Hayes and Susan Ward (who are, I understand, here this evening) are closely involved in the Equal Opportunities Joint Working Group. I know the Group will be making recommendations for possible changes to the judicial appointments system in the near future. I will consider these recommendations with the care they deserve and I will respond. But I would not want to give the impression that I have been sitting back complacently in the nine months since I became Lord Chancellor. I have ideas of my own, some of which I have already announced. I will not go into them in detail now – I hope many of you will be at the Woman Lawyer Conference in April, when I plan to say much more about my proposals.

But I would like just to mention three which you may find of particular interest.

First, I am ending the system of appointments to the High Court Bench by invitation only. My intention is to advertise for eligible lawyers to put themselves forward for consideration. That way I can be sure that I am aware of all the potential candidates. Applicants for an openly advertised selection procedure have a fair and equal chance to explain how their experience and achievements fulfil the criteria for appointment. I intend to retain the power to offer appointments to those who have not applied. I must have a way of reaching those who are able but are unwilling to press their own claims.

But open competition, on the basis of applications, is the way forward. It can only strengthen the principle of appointment on merit. The first advertisements for the High Court will appear soon.

Second, I am looking at ways of making part-time sitting arrangements more flexible. I am particularly anxious to cater for those who have taken time out of their practice for family reasons.

I have therefore made a decision which I believe will be welcome to you. It is to enable those who have taken career breaks and are appointed to part-time judicial office to undertake their sittings in more concentrated blocks wherever possible – if they wish to do so. For instance, sittings that would normally be spread over a period of, say, three years may be undertaken in the first year of appointment. Where such arrangements apply, it will help to make up for the time effectively lost.

There has been flexibility in sittings arrangements in a number of Tribunals and in the Stipendiary Magistracy for some time. I now wish to build on and extend these arrangements for this purpose, to meet the circumstances of those who have taken a career break. For example, I am keen to apply these arrangements to the District Bench. In addition, the forthcoming Assistant Recorder competition will, for the first time, give successful applicants at this level an opportunity to use this facility. I hope that these arrangements will be of particular help to women and encourage them to apply for appointment.

And, third, I am increasing the upper age limit for appointment as an Assistant Recorder from 50 to 53 in the next competition. This will help everyone – not just women – who entered the legal profession later in life. And it will be fair to those who have lost a few years of their career because they have devoted themselves to their family responsibilities. It is also one expression of my opposition to all forms of discrimination, in this case age-ism. Let me mention another. At the Bar Council Conference in 1996, I said that homosexuality should be no bar to judicial appointment. As soon as I became Lord Chancellor, I ensured the guidance notes which accompany application forms were changed to make this clear, so that it is made clear that there is no obligation to disclose a gay orientation or permanent gay relationship.

So you will see that I am playing my part in changing the system to make it more open to women and others who are disadvantaged by an unnecessarily rigid approach. But I must call on you to play your part – to consider putting yourselves forward for appointment. The success rate for women lawyers who do compares favourably with the number of women in the profession as a whole. In the last competition for Assistant Recordership, 16% of the applicants were women. This in itself is an encouraging figure – as I have already mentioned, they make up only 14% of barristers over 15 years call. But, even more interestingly, 22% of the successful applicants were women. So I repeat my sound-bite: don't be shy! Apply!

And that is not the only contribution you can make. Chambers are the gardens in which many future judges grow. You have a right to enjoy an equal opportunity to become a judge, but you also have a responsibility to create an environment in which other women lawyers have the chance to develop their careers. The Association plays an important role in this. Judging from this evening's attendance, the Association is thriving!

Too often in the past, women were channelled into what were thought of as 'appropriate' areas of the law, for example family and matrimonial work. Some of you may feel this is still the case. Of course, these areas are concerned with important human issues; and some women may feel they have a particular flair for them.

But women are just as capable as men of handling the whole range of problems and challenges which the law can pose. I am glad that women lawyers today are increasingly establishing themselves in areas which have traditionally been the preserve of men. This must be a healthy development for the legal profession and for the justice system. I would like to think that everyone in the profession shares that view.

My point is this. All lawyers, whether men or women, must be encouraged to develop their interests and talents, wherever they may lie. All must have an equal chance to take on the most demanding cases. All must have the chance to be stretched and to achieve. I ask the profession to keep its own practices and values under constant critical review – to make sure that all its members are given real opportunities to fulfil their potential. In return, I will do my utmost to ensure the judicial appointments process treats everyone fairly and equally; and I ask you to judge me over time, and by deeds, not words.

––––––––––––––––––––––––––––––––

The actual numbers of both women and members of ethnic minorities can be seen in the following statistical breakdown produced by the Lord Chancellor's Office.

Lord Chancellor's Department: Ethnic Minority Appointments, May 2001

Note: The database of the ethnic origin of the judiciary may be incomplete as (a) candidates are asked to provide the information on a voluntary basis and (b) such details have only been collected since October 1991. Correct as at 1 May 2001.

		Black	Asian	Other	total ethnic minority	total in post	% ethnic minority
Lords of	Men	0	0	0	0	12	0%
Appeal	Women	0	0	0	0	0	0%
in Ordinary	Total	0	0	0	0	12	0%
Heads	Men	0	0	0	0	4	0%
of Division	Women	0	0	0	0	1	0%
	Total	0	0	0	0	5	0%
Lord Justices	Men	0	0	0	0	33	0%
of Appeal	Women	0	0	0	0	2	0%
	Total	0	0	0	0	35	0%
High Court	Men	0	0	0	0	99	0%
Judges	Women	0	0	0	0	8	0%
	Total	0	0	0	0	107	0%
Circuit Judges	Men	0	2	2	4	521	0.8%
(inc judges	Women	1	1	0	2	44	4.5%
of the Court of	Total	1	3	2	6	565	1.1%
Technology &							
Construction)							
Recorders	Men	13	11	6	30	1204	2.5%
	Women	4	3	1	8	170	4.7%
	Total	17	14	7	38	1374	2.8%
Recorders	Men	0	1	0	1	51	2%
in Training	Women	0	0	0	0	12	0.0%
	Total	0	1	0	1	63	1.6%
District	Men	0	4	2	6	350	1.7%
Judges (inc	Women	0	1	1	2	67	3%
Fam Division)	Total	0	5	3	8	417	1.9%
Deputy	Men	3	2	4	9	612	1.5%
District	Women	1	2	0	3	152	2%
Judges (inc	Total	4	4	4	12	764	1.6%
Fam Division)							
District Judges	Men	0	1	0	1	83	1.2%
(Magistrates'	Women	0	1	0	1	15	6.7%
Courts)	Total	0	2	0	2	98	2%

MAGISTRATES

Given the proposals to extend further powers to magistrates' courts in relation to modes of trial (see Chapter 10 above) it is important to consider the way in which such courts are operate. The results of a particularly thorough research project comparing lay magistrates and professional District Judges (magistrates' courts), the former stipendiary magistrates, were reported in December 2000 and will no doubt inform the outcome of Lord Justice Auld's current review of the criminal courts.

The following is merely the summary of a very extensive research project by Rod Morgan (University of Bristol) and Neil Russell (RSGB). The full report is available on the internet. at

Rod Morgan and Neil Russell, *Judiciary in the Magistrates' Courts*, 2000, prepared for Home Office and Lord Chancellor's Department: www/homeoffice.gov.uk/rds

Summary

This research was jointly commissioned by the Lord Chancellor's Department and the Home Office. The study was undertaken during the first nine months of 2000 by a research team comprising the University of Bristol and two commercial companies, RSGB (a division of Taylor Nelson Sofres plc) and CRG, Cardiff, specialists in market research and cost benefit analysis respectively.

Lay magistrates sit part time and are not paid for their services. They are selected for appointment on the basis of six key qualities: good character, understanding and communication, social awareness, maturity and sound temperament, sound judgement and commitment. They deal with criminal matters in the adult and youth courts and with civil matters, particularly family matters in the Family Court. Magistrates who are members of specialist committees are responsible for the administration of the liquor licensing system and for the grant or refusal of applications for licences or permits relating to betting and the registration of gaming clubs. Lay magistrates are advised on legal points by a professionally qualified legal advisor.

Stipendiary magistrates sit full time and are legally qualified members of the professional judiciary (they must be solicitors or barristers). They undertake the same range of criminal and civil work as lay magistrates but are often assigned to deal with cases which are likely to be lengthy or particularly complex. There are also part time or acting stipendiary magistrates who are similarly legally qualified. Since August 2000 stipendiary magistrates have borne the title District Judge (Magistrates' Courts), in recognition of their membership of the professional judiciary, but in this report they are referred to by the more familiar title.

Purposes of the research

The research was commissioned to:

- investigate the present balance of lay and stipendiary magistrates and the arguments
- supporting this balance
- test the weight and validity of these arguments

- consider whether each type of magistrate is deployed in the most effective way.

Existing arguments for and against lay and stipendiary magistrates can be summarized as:

- participatory democracy and justice versus consistency and the rule of law
- local justice versus national consistency
- open versus case-hardened minds
- symbolic legitimacy versus effectiveness and efficiency
- cost – high or low.

Methodology

The research comprised seven types of data collection:

- baseline information on the budgets, buildings, court staff and magistrates' characteristics. Data were gathered both nationally and locally, and included information on ten magistrates' courts in London and the provinces, with and without stipendiaries
- 2,019 self-completed magistrates' diaries, spanning three-week sessions, covering activities, timings etc from the ten courts
- 1,120 self-completed magistrates' questionnaires addressing issues of sitting arrangements, their views on balance between lay and stipendiaries etc from the ten courts
- observations of 535 court sessions at the ten courts
- 400 telephone interviews with regular court users from the ten courts
- public opinion survey: conducted with a nationally representative sample of 1,753 members of public
- 23 responses to a letter to representatives of the Council of Europe member states.

Composition and working practices of the magistracy

Composition

At the time of the research the magistracy comprised:

- approximately 30,400 lay magistrates
- 96 full-time stipendiaries
- 146 part-time stipendiaries.

The lay magistracy:

- is gender balanced
- is ethnically representative of the population at a national level
- is overwhelmingly drawn from professional and managerial ranks
- comprises a high proportion (two-fifths) who have retired from full-time employment.

In comparison, stipendiaries:

- are mostly male and white
- tend to be younger.

Sitting patterns

Lay magistrates:

- sit in court an average 41.4 occasions annually (although many sit a good deal more frequently)

- devote (taking holidays into account) an extended morning or afternoon to the post once a week

- additionally spend the equivalent, on average, of a full working week on training and other duties.

The contracts of full-time stipendiaries require them to perform judicial duties five days a week, 44 weeks of the year. However there is some ambiguity as to what this means in terms of court sittings. Provincial stipendiaries sit more often than their colleagues do in London, but both groups sit in court closer to four days per week.

Lay magistrates usually sit in panels of three, but sometimes of two (16% of observed panels). Stipendiaries nearly always sit alone but on rare occasions sit together with lay magistrates.

Caseload allocation

While stipendiaries take on more or less the full range of cases and appearances, they tend to be allocated more complex, prolonged and sensitive cases. Unlike lay magistrates, their time is concentrated on triable-either-way rather than summary cases.

Working methods and decision-making

Speed

Stipendiary magistrates deal with all categories of cases and appearances more quickly than their lay colleagues because they retire from court sessions less often and more briefly (0.2 compared to 1.2 occasions per session, for only 3 compared to 16 minutes). They also deal with cases more quickly on average (9 minutes compared to 10 minutes). This means:

- stipendiaries hear 22 per cent more appearances than lay magistrates per standardised court session (12.2 compared to 10)

- if stipendiaries were allocated an identical caseload to lay magistrates, it is estimated that they would deal with 30 per cent more appearances.

The greater speed of stipendiaries is not achieved at the expense of inquisition and challenge; on the contrary, hearings before stipendiaries typically involve more questions being asked and more challenges being made.

Manner of working: adjournments and bail

Both lay and stipendiary magistrates are invariably judged to meet high standards in dealing with court business (attentiveness, clarity of pronouncements, courtesy, and so on). However, stipendiaries are considered to perform better in relation to those criteria that suggest greater confidence – showing command over the proceedings and challenging parties responsible for delay.

Fewer appearances before stipendiaries lead to adjournments (45% compared to 52%). This is partly because fewer applications are made to stipendiaries but also because they are more likely to resist applications for adjournments (97% compared to 93%). It is therefore likely that the employment of additional stipendiaries would lead to fewer court appearances overall.

Lay magistrates are less likely to:

- refuse defendants bail in cases where the prosecution seeks custody and the defence applies for bail (19% compared to 37%)

- make use of immediate custody as a sentence (12% of triable-either-way cases compared to 25%).

The employment of additional stipendiaries might therefore significantly increase the prison population.

Stipendiaries tend to run their courts themselves and rely very little on their court legal advisors when it comes to making and explaining decisions and announcements. This calls into question whether they need legally qualified court advisors.

The views of regular court practitioners

A sample of 400 court practitioners (court advisors, solicitors, CPS personnel, probation officers) were surveyed by telephone.

Very few court users expressed 'no' or only 'a little' confidence in either type of magistrate, but stipendiaries were more likely to inspire a 'great deal' or a 'lot' of confidence. Users found it harder to generalise about lay magistrates, indicating a greater range in their performance.

The court users expressed very similar views to the court observers when asked to rate dimensions of behaviour. Stipendiaries were widely seen as:

- more efficient, more consistent and more confident in their decision-making

- questioning defence lawyers appropriately

- giving clear reasons for decisions

- showing command over proceedings.

Lay magistrates were more often judged better at:

- showing courtesy to defendants and other court members

- using simple language

- showing concern to distressed victims.

But the majority of respondents did not think lay and stipendiary magistrates differed on these criteria.

Regular court practitioners, particularly lawyers and CPS personnel, said that they and their colleagues behave differently when appearing before lay and stipendiary magistrates. They:

- prepare better for stipendiaries

- try to be more precise and concise in their statements to them

- anticipate that they will be questioned and challenged more.

Court legal advisors on the other hand said that they prepare more for lay magistrates, because they anticipate the need to give legal advice to them.

Public opinions of the magistracy

A nationally representative sample of 1,753 members of the public were interviewed regarding their views on, and knowledge of the magistracy. Whereas the overwhelming majority of the public is aware of the terms 'magistrate' and 'magistrates' court', only a minority have heard of 'lay' as opposed to 'stipendiary' magistrates.

When the difference between them is explained, almost three-quarters (73%) say that they were not aware of this difference.

Only a bare majority of respondents correctly identify that most criminal cases are dealt with in the magistrates' courts, and that juries do not make decisions there. Knowledge about the qualifications and sitting practices of lay magistrates is even less accurate. Respondents who are more knowledgeable about the system tend to have greater confidence in it.

Having had the differences explained to them, most of the public thinks that:

- lay magistrates represent the views of the community better than stipendiaries (63% compared to 9% – the remaining 28% see no difference or don't know)

- lay magistrates are more likely to be sympathetic to defendants' circumstances (41% compared to 12%)

- stipendiaries are better at making correct judgements of guilt or innocence (36% compared to 11%) and managing court business effectively (48% compared to 9%)

- there is no difference between lay and stipendiaries in awareness of the effect of crimes on victims and approaching each case afresh.

In addition, when comparing single magistrates with panels:

- a small majority of respondents (53%) consider that motoring offences are suitable to be heard by a single magistrate

- a large majority think that the more serious decisions of guilty/not guilty (74%) and sending to prison (76%) should be decided by panels of magistrates.

Most respondents think that the work of the magistrates' courts should be divided equally between the two types of magistrates, or that the type of magistrate does not matter.

The direct and indirect costs of lay and stipendiary magistrates

If only directly attributable costs (salaries, expenses, training) are considered, lay magistrates are much cheaper because they are not paid directly and many do not claim loss of earnings. A sizeable minority does not even claim their allowable travelling expenses. A lay magistrate costs on average £495 per annum compared to the £90,000 per annum total employment costs of a stipendiary. These translate into a cost per appearance before lay and stipendiary magistrates of £3.59 and £20.96 respectively (Table 1). When indirect costs (premises, administration staff, etc) are brought into the equation the gap between the two groups narrows, to £52.10 and £61.78.

Table 1 The cost of appearing before lay and stipendiary magistrates (per appearance)

	Lay magistrates £	Stipendiary magistrates £
Direct costs (salary, expenses, training)	3.59	20.96
Indirect costs (premises, administration staff etc)	48.51	40.82
Direct & indirect costs	52.10	61.78

The effect upon costs of substituting stipendiary for lay magistrates

There would have to be a significant increase in the use of the more productive stipendiaries to enable administrative staff and courtroom reductions to be made on any scale.

If blocks of work currently undertaken by lay magistrates were transferred to stipendiaries:

- one stipendiary would be needed for every 30 magistrates, if all lay tribunals comprised three justices

- one for every 28, if the present proportion of tribunals comprising only two lay justices were to continue.

Stipendiaries' greater tendency to resist adjournments and their greater use of custody at the pre-trial and sentencing stages means that if the number of stipendiaries were doubled (assuming present patterns were retained):

- there would be a reduction of 10,270 appearances in connection with indictable offences, giving an additional cost of £0.88 million per annum (a net increase because the reduced rates of adjournments do not overcome the higher attributable costs of stipendiaries)

- the number of remands in custody would increase by 6,200 per annum. Assuming an average remand period of 46 days, this has an associated cost of around £24 million (essentially falling on the Prison Service)

- the number of custodial sentences would increase by 2,760 per annum, costing £13.6 million. Set against this is the cost of the type of sentence that the offender would have received in the place of a prison sentence. If this is taken as some form of community penalty then the overall additional cost of this increase in custodial sentences would be around £8.5 million.

The effect upon costs of substituting lay for stipendiary magistrates

Alternatively if there were no stipendiaries, then there would be an increase in the number of appearances of 10,270, the number of remands in custody would decrease by 6,200, and the number of custodial sentences would decrease by 2,760 – with each of the consequent cost savings.

Other jurisdictions

Drawing on the 23 responses from the Council of Europe member states and enquiries to other (mostly Common Law) jurisdictions, it can be seen that there are three principal models of adjudication:

- the *professional*
- the *lay*
- the *hybrid* (mixed lay and professional).

Each of these can be refined in terms of whether decision-making is by single persons or panels, and the number of tiers into which criminal cases and courts are divided.

However there is no straightforward relationship between the degree to which democracy is embedded and lay involvement in judicial decision-making. Many longstanding democracies involve lay persons while others do not. The re-establishment of democracy in a country does not necessarily stimulate the introduction of lay involvement in judicial decision-making, sometimes the reverse occurs, depending on the cultural and political tradition.The most common arrangements for lay involvement comprise lay persons making decisions in the lowest tier, or sitting alongside professional judges in the middle or higher tiers. However, it is also common that their decisions are restricted to minor non-imprisonable offences. More serious decisions are invariably made by professionals or hybrid panels.

England and Wales is the only jurisdiction identified in this research where such a high proportion of criminal cases, including serious cases, are decided by lay persons. In addition, the allocation of cases to either lay or stipendiary magistrates by chance, rather than by policy, is unique to this jurisdiction.

Conclusion

Though the research does not point in a particular policy direction, the findings do indicate how the public and court users are likely to react to certain proposals for change. Although the public do not have strong feelings about the precise role of magistrates, they think that summary offences, particularly if not contested, can be dealt with by a single magistrate but that panels should make the more serious judicial decisions. Cost considerations suggest that this could only be achieved (in the short-term at least) by continuing to make extensive use of lay magistrates.

Criminal justice practitioners, while appreciative of the quality of service given by lay magistrates, have greater confidence in professional judges (stipendiaries). Furthermore governmental pressure to make the criminal courts more efficient, and to reduce the time that cases take to complete, will also tend to favour the greater efficiency of stipendiary magistrates. However, this has to be balanced against the potential increase in cost to the Prison Service. The nature and balance of contributions made by lay and stipendiary magistrates could be altered to better satisfy these wider considerations, but should not prejudice the integrity and support of a system founded on strong traditions. Not only is the office of Justice of the Peace ancient and in an important tradition of voluntary public service, it is also a direct manifestation of government policy which encourages *active citizens in an active community*. In no other jurisdiction does the criminal court system depend so heavily on such voluntary unpaid effort. At no stage during the study was it suggested that in most respects the magistrates' courts do not work well or fail to command general confidence. It is our view, therefore, that eliminating or greatly diminishing the role of lay magistrates would not be widely understood or supported.

JUDICIAL BIAS

In the previous chapter attention was focused on the possibility of bias within the jury. In this section, the concept of bias is extended to cover the judge and, as will be seen, the previous common law rules covering the area have been extended to cover new areas and to bring them into conformity with the ECHR.

The recent activity in this area was initially generated by the extraordinary case involving the former dictator of Chile, General Augusto Pinochet.

G Slapper and D Kelly, *The English Legal System*, 5th edn, 2001, London: Cavendish Publishing, Chapter 6, para 1.3

No consideration of the operation of the judiciary generally, and the House of Lords in particular, can be complete without a detailed consideration of what can only be called the *Pinochet* case (the various cases are actually cited as *R v Bow Street Metropolitan Magistrates ex p Pinochet Ugarte (No 1)* (1998) (House of Lords, first hearing); *(No 2)* (1999) (House of Lords, appeal against Lord Hoffman); *(No 3)* (1999) (final House of Lords decision). These cases established that Pinochet's office as Head of State gave him no general immunity to extradition for offences against the United Nations Convention Against Torture, since the date it was incorporated into UK law by the Criminal Justice Act 1988.

In September 1973, the democratically elected government of Chile was overthrown in a violent army coup led by the then General Augusto Pinochet Ugarte; the President Salvador Allende, and many others were killed in the fighting. Subsequently, in the words of Lord Browne-Wilkinson, in the final House of Lords hearing:

> There is no doubt that, during the period of the Senator Pinochet regime, appalling acts of barbarism were committed in Chile and elsewhere in the world: torture, murder and the unexplained disappearance of individuals on a large scale.

Although it was not suggested that Pinochet had committed these acts personally, it was claimed that he was fully aware of them and conspired to have them undertaken.

In 1998, General Pinochet, by now Senator for life and recipient of a Chilean amnesty for his actions (extracted as the price for his returning his country to democracy), came to England for medical treatment. Although he was initially welcomed, he was subsequently arrested, on an extradition warrant issued in Spain, for the crimes of torture, murder and conspiracy to murder allegedly orchestrated by him in Chile during the 1970s. Spain issued the international warrants, but Pinochet was actually arrested on warrants issued by the metropolitan stipendiary magistrate under s 8(1)(b) of the Extradition Act 1989.

The legal question for the English courts was whether General Pinochet, as Head of State at the time when the crimes were committed, enjoyed diplomatic immunity. In November 1998, the House of Lords rejected Pinochet's claim by a three to two majority, Lord Hoffman voting with the majority but declining to submit a reasoned judgment.

Prior to the hearing in the House of Lords, Amnesty International, which campaigns against such things as State mass murder, torture and political imprisonment, and in favour of general civil and political liberties, had been granted leave to intervene in the proceedings, and had made representations through its counsel, Geoffrey Bindman QC. After the *Pinochet* decision, it was revealed, although it was hardly a secret, that Lord Hoffman was an unpaid director of the Amnesty International Charitable Trust, and that his wife also worked for Amnesty. On that basis, Pinochet's lawyers initiated a very peculiar action: they petitioned the House of Lords, about a House of Lords decision: for the first time, the highest court in the land was to be subject to review, but to itself; only itself differently constituted. So, in January 1999, another panel of Law Lords set aside the decision of the earlier hearing on the basis that Lord Hoffman's involvement had invalidated the previous hearing. The decision as to whether Pinochet had immunity or not would have to be heard by a new, and differently constituted, committee of Law Lords.

It has to be stated in favour of this decision that the English legal system is famously rigorous in controlling conflicts of interest which might be seen to affect what should be a neutral decision making process. The rule, which applies across the board to trustees, company directors and other fiduciaries as well as judges, is so strict that the mere possibility of a conflict of interest is sufficient to invalidate any decision so made, even if in reality the individual concerned was completely unaffected by their own interest in coming to the decision. In the words of the famous *dictum* of Lord Hewart, it is of fundamental importance that justice must not only be done but should manifestly and undoubtedly be seen to be done (*R v Sussex Justices ex p McCarthy* (1924)). With regard to the judicial process, it has been a long established rule that no one may be a judge in his or her own cause, that is, they cannot judge a case in which they have an interest. This is sometimes known by the phrase *nemo judex in causa sua*. Thus, for example, judges who are shareholders in a company appearing before the court as a litigant must decline to hear the case (*Dimes v Grand Junction Canal* (1852)). It is, therefore, astonishing that Lord Hoffman did not withdraw from the case, or at least declare his interest in Amnesty when it was joined to the proceedings. The only possible justification is that Hoffman assumed that all of those involved in the case, including the Pinochet team of lawyers, were aware of the connection. Alternatively, he might have thought that his support for a charitable body aimed at promoting civil and political liberties was so worthy in itself as to be unimpeachable: could not, and indeed should not, every English judge subscribe, for example, to cl 3(c) of the Amnesty International Charitable Trust memorandum, which provides that one of its objects is to procure the abolition of torture, extra-judicial execution and disappearance?

In either case, Lord Hoffman was wrong. Once it was shown that Lord Hoffman had a relevant interest in its subject matter, he was disqualified without any investigation into whether there was a likelihood or suspicion of bias. The mere fact of his interest was sufficient to disqualify him unless he had made sufficient disclosure. Hitherto, only pecuniary or proprietary interests had led to automatic disqualification. But, as Lord Browne-Wilkinson stated, Amnesty, and hence Lord Hoffman, plainly had a non-pecuniary interest, sufficient to give rise to an automatic disqualification for those involved with it.

It is important not to overstate what was decided in *Re Pinochet*. The facts of that case were exceptional and it is unlikely that it will lead to a mass withdrawal of judges from cases; however, there might well be other cases in which the judge would be well advised to disclose a possible interest.

R v Bow Street Metropolitan Magistrates ex p Pinochet Ugarte (No 3) (1999), [2000] 1 AC 147

In the course of the leading judgment in the case Lord Browne-Wilkinson considered the question of bias as follows.

Apparent bias

As I have said, Senator Pinochet does not allege that Lord Hoffmann was in fact biased. The contention is that there was a real danger or reasonable apprehension or suspicion that Lord Hoffmann might have been biased, that is to say, it is alleged that there is an appearance of bias not actual bias. The fundamental principle is that a man may not be a judge in his own cause. This principle, as developed by the courts, has two very similar but not identical implications. First it may be applied literally: if a judge is in fact a party to the litigation or has a financial or proprietary interest in its outcome then he is indeed sitting as a judge in his own cause. In that case, the mere fact that he is a party to the action or has a financial or proprietary interest in its outcome is sufficient to cause his automatic disqualification. The second application of the principle is where a judge is not a party to the suit and does not have a financial interest in its outcome, but in some other way his conduct or behaviour may give rise to a suspicion that he is not impartial, for example because of his friendship with a party. This second type of case is not strictly speaking an application of the principle that a man must not be judge in his own cause, since the judge will not normally be himself benefiting, but providing a benefit for another by failing to be impartial.

In my judgment, this case falls within the first category of case, viz where the judge is disqualified because he is a judge in his own cause. In such a case, once it is shown that the judge is himself a party to the cause, or has a relevant interest in its subject matter, he is disqualified without any investigation into whether there was a likelihood or suspicion of bias. The mere fact of his interest is sufficient to disqualify him unless he has made sufficient disclosure: see Shetreet, *Judges on Trial*, 1976, p 303; De Smith, Woolf and Jowell, *Judicial Review of Administrative Action*, 5th edn, 1995, p 525. I will call this 'automatic disqualification'.

In *Dimes v Proprietors of Grand Junction Canal* (1852) 3 HL Cas 759, the then Lord Chancellor, Lord Cottenham, owned a substantial shareholding in the defendant canal which was an incorporated body. In the action the Lord Chancellor sat on appeal from the Vice-Chancellor, whose judgment in favour of the company he affirmed. There was an appeal to your Lordships' House on the grounds that the Lord Chancellor was disqualified. Their Lordships consulted the judges who advised, at p 786, that Lord Cottenham was disqualified from sitting as a judge in the case because he had an interest in the suit. This advice was unanimously accepted by their lordships. There was no inquiry by the court as to whether a reasonable man would consider Lord Cottenham to be biased and no inquiry as to the circumstances which led to Lord Cottenham sitting. Lord Campbell said, at p 793:

> No one can suppose that Lord Cottenham could be, in the remotest degree, influenced by the interest he had in this concern; but, my Lords, it is of the last importance that the maxim that no man is to be a judge in his own cause should be held sacred. And that is not to be confined to a cause *in which he is a party*, but applies to a cause in which he has an interest. [Emphasis added.]

On occasion, this proposition is elided so as to omit all references to the disqualification of a judge who is a party to the suit: see, for example, *R v Rand* (1866) LR 1 QB 230; *R v Gough* [1993] AC 646, 661. This does not mean that a judge who is a party to a suit is not disqualified just because the suit does not involve a financial interest. The authorities cited in the *Dimes* case show how the principle developed. The starting-point was the case in which a judge was indeed purporting to decide a case in which he was a party. This was held to be absolutely prohibited. That absolute prohibition was then extended to cases where, although not nominally a party, the judge had an interest in the outcome.

The importance of this point in the present case is this. Neither AI, nor AICL, have any financial interest in the outcome of this litigation. We are here confronted, as was Lord Hoffmann, with a novel situation where the outcome of the litigation did not lead to financial benefit to anyone.

The interest of AI in the litigation was not financial; it was its interest in achieving the trial and possible conviction of Senator Pinochet for crimes against humanity.

By seeking to intervene in this appeal and being allowed so to intervene, in practice AI became a party to the appeal. Therefore if, in the circumstances, it is right to treat Lord Hoffmann as being the *alter ego* of AI and therefore a judge in his own cause, then he must have been automatically disqualified on the grounds that he was a party to the appeal. Alternatively, even if it be not right to say that Lord Hoffmann was a party to the appeal as such, the question then arises whether, in non-financial litigation, anything other than a financial or proprietary interest in the outcome is sufficient automatically to disqualify a man from sitting as judge in the cause.

Are the facts such as to require Lord Hoffmann to be treated as being himself a party to this appeal? The facts are striking and unusual. One of the parties to the appeal is an unincorporated association, AI. One of the constituent parts of that unincorporated association is AICL. AICL was established, for tax purposes, to carry out part of the functions of AI those parts which were charitable which had previously been carried on either by AI itself or by AIL. Lord Hoffmann is a director and chairman of AICL, which is wholly controlled by AI, since its members (who ultimately control it) are all the members of the international executive committee of AI. A large part of the work of AI is, as a matter of strict law, carried on by AICL which instructs AIL to do the work on its behalf. In reality, AI, AICL and AIL are a close-knit group carrying on the work of AI.

However, close as these links are, I do not think it would be right to identify Lord Hoffmann personally as being a party to the appeal. He is closely linked to AI but he is not in fact AI. Although this is an area in which legal technicality is particularly to be avoided, it cannot be ignored that Lord Hoffmann took no part in running AI. Lord Hoffmann, AICL and the executive committee of AI are in law separate people.

Then is this a case in which it can be said that Lord Hoffmann had an 'interest' which must lead to his automatic disqualification? Hitherto only pecuniary and proprietary interests have led to automatic disqualification. But, as I have indicated, this litigation is most unusual. It is not civil litigation but criminal litigation. Most unusually, by allowing AI to intervene, there is a party to a criminal cause or matter who is neither prosecutor nor accused. That party, AI, shares with the government of Spain and the CPS, not a financial interest but an interest to establish that there is no immunity for ex-heads of state in relation to crimes against humanity. The interest of these parties is to procure Senator Pinochet's extradition and trial a non-pecuniary interest. So far as AICL is concerned, clause 3(c) of its memorandum provides that one of its objects is 'to procure the abolition of torture, extra-judicial execution and disappearance'. AI has, amongst other objects, the same objects. Although AICL, as a charity, cannot campaign to change the law, it is concerned by other means to procure the abolition of these crimes against humanity. In my opinion, therefore, AICL plainly had a non-pecuniary interest, to establish that Senator Pinochet was not immune.

That being the case, the question is whether in the very unusual circumstances of this case a non-pecuniary interest to achieve a particular result is sufficient to give rise to automatic disqualification and, if so, whether the fact that AICL had such an interest necessarily leads to the conclusion that Lord Hoffmann, as a director of AICL, was automatically disqualified from sitting on the appeal? My Lords, in my judgment, although the cases have all dealt with automatic disqualification on the grounds of pecuniary interest, there is no good reason in principle for so limiting automatic disqualification. The rationale of the whole rule is that a man cannot be a judge in his own cause. In civil litigation the matters in issue will normally have an economic impact; therefore a judge is automatically disqualified if he stands to make a financial gain as a consequence of his own decision of the case. But if, as in the present case, the matter at issue does not relate to money or economic advantage but is concerned with the promotion of the cause, the rationale disqualifying a judge applies just as much if the judge's decision will lead to the promotion of a cause in which the judge is involved together with one of the parties. Thus in my opinion if Lord Hoffmann had been a member of AI he would have been automatically disqualified because of his non-pecuniary interest in establishing that Senator Pinochet was not entitled to immunity. Indeed, so much I understood to have been conceded by Mr Duffy.

Can it make any difference that, instead of being a direct member of AI, Lord Hoffmann is a director of AICL, that is of a company which is wholly controlled by AI and is carrying on much of its work? Surely not. The substance of the matter is that AI, AIL and AICL are all various parts of an entity or movement working in different fields towards the same goals. If the absolute impartiality of the judiciary is to be maintained, there must be a rule which automatically disqualifies a judge who is involved, whether personally or as a director of a company, in promoting the same causes in the same organisation as is a party to the suit. There is no room for fine distinctions if Lord Hewart CJ's famous *dictum* is to be observed:

> ... it is 'of fundamental importance that justice should not only be done, but should manifestly and undoubtedly be seen to be done': see *R v Sussex Justices ex p McCarthy* [1924] 1 KB 256, 259 ...

I do, however, wish to make it clear (if I have not already done so) that my decision is not that Lord Hoffmann has been guilty of bias of any kind: he was disqualified as a matter of law automatically by reason of his directorship of AICL, a company controlled by a party, AI.

— — · — · — · — · — · — · — · — · — · — · — · — · — · — · — · —

In the above extract from *The English Legal System*, we suggested that the *Pinochet* decision would not lead to a mass withdrawal of judges from cases. That prediction has been borne out, although there have been some cases where judges have withdrawn. There was, however, a significant increase in allegations of judicial bias after the decision. These cases came to a head in Court of Appeal in November 1999, as explained in the following article from the *Student Law Review*.

Gary Slapper, 'Rights of advocacy, human rights, publicly funded law, court delays, and impartial judges' (2000) 29 SLR 31

Expansions and contractions in advocacy

This year will see further changes to the composition of those who act as advocates. Fewer Queen's Counsel (QCs) will be acting as defence and prosecution advocates in criminal cases and patent agents will be given rights of audience in the civil courts.

Both these changes can be set in the context of a governmental concern to sweep away restrictive rules which, it argues, promote inefficient and uneconomic conduct of cases.

The government intends to change the Criminal Legal Aid Regulations on the use of advocates in the Crown Court. It is proposing to tighten the criteria relating to the assignment of QCs and also to the use of more than one advocate. The assignment of QCs and more than one advocate in the Crown Court is currently governed by reg 48 of the Legal Aid in Criminal and Care Proceedings (General) Regulations 1989.

It is proposed that, before an application to increase or alter the number or seniority of advocates is made to the Crown Court, the case must meet specified criteria designed to ensure it actually warrants the assignment of a QC or more than one advocate. Government departments with responsibility for bringing criminal prosecutions will also be asked to ensure that a QC or more than one advocate are only instructed by the prosecution when necessary. There are nine such departments, including the Crown Prosecution Service, the Department of Environment, Transport and the Regions, the Department of Social Security and the Department of Trade and Industry.

Over the last two years, barristers have already compromised over legal aid defence work remuneration. They now work for fixed fees, instead of hourly rates, in 90% of such cases. Rates of pay for such work have fallen by 15% over the last four years. One significant danger here is that many able defence lawyers will be alienated from this vitally important area of advocacy by levels of pay notably lower than that which their qualifications could command in other areas of law.

While QCs might be getting less criminal court work, patent agents will be joining the ranks of advocates in the civil courts. The Chartered Institute of Patent Agents (CIPA) has been designated an 'authorised body' for the purposes of the Courts and Legal Services Act 1990. The application for 'authorised' status had previously been approved by the Lord Chancellor and the designated judges under the Courts and Legal Services Act 1990, and by both Houses of Parliament. The Courts and Legal Services Act 1990 established a framework for the granting of rights to conduct litigation and rights of audience. The CIPA is the second new authorised body to come into existence under the 1990 Act. The Institute of Legal Executives was the first in April 1998, which was successful in its application to be able to grant rights of audience to its Fellows.

The application will allow CIPA to grant rights to conduct litigation and rights of audience to suitably qualified Fellows in restricted proceedings. The rights include:

- the right to conduct litigation in the Chancery Division of the High Court, including the Patents Court, and in the county court, and to conduct appeals from the Patents County Court, the county court and the Chancery Division of the High Court, in respect of any matter relating to the protection of any invention, design, technical information or trade mark, or as to any matter involving passing off;

- the right of audience in hearings in the judge's room and on preliminary matters ancillary to Intellectual Property litigation.

Announcing the change, the Lord Chancellor, Lord Irvine, said:

> This will lead to a small but important increase in the number of people qualified to appear before the courts. Patent agents work in a small, highly specialised field and it is right that the public are given every opportunity to draw on the expertise within the profession. The CIPA now joins the Bar Council, The Law Society and the Institute of Legal Executives, both as an authorised body in its own right and as a fully fledged part of the legal profession.

It is of great significance that the Lord Chancellor refers to patent agents as part of 'the legal profession'. This is in line with governmental plans to greatly widen the variety of specialist legal practitioners, and move beyond the simple solicitor-barrister dichotomy which, during the last century, became so embedded in public consciousness. It is worthy of note that, in fact, all changes to the structure of the legal profession have, over the centuries, been greeted with grave doubt by the old guard. There was a time when solicitors were not regarded as proper lawyers. The attorney, the forerunner of the solicitor, was originally an officer of the court whose task was to help the client in the preparatory stages of a case. Attorneys were not admitted to the Inns of Court.

The assumption that a specialist practitioner must have qualified as a barrister or solicitor is coming under sharper public scrutiny. Provided that he or she has a good knowledge of court procedure, the law of evidence and some parts of related law, a highly specialist patents agent would, for many litigants, be just as desirable as their court advocate as a qualified barrister. The Bar, naturally, takes a different view, and argues that in the court environment there is no adequate substitute for a dedicated court advocate.

Human rights

The Human Rights Act 1998, due to come into effect this year, is set to cause major reverberations throughout the English legal system. The recent case of *Z and Others v UK* (European Court of Human Rights) illustrates several points of legal significance.

On 10 September 1999, the European Commission on Human Rights in Strasbourg ruled unanimously that the United Kingdom was in breach of its obligations to protect children from inhuman and degrading treatment under Art 3 of the Convention. The case arose from litigation brought by adults who had been abused while children in the care of social services. The Official Solicitor was first appointed in April 1993 as litigation friend for these children. In this capacity, he brought proceedings in the domestic courts to obtain compensation for the damage suffered by them. When the children's claim failed in the House of Lords, where it was held that social services departments had immunity from claims by children in these circumstances, the Official Solicitor pursued the matter on the children's behalf to Strasbourg.

The Commission also ruled unanimously that the House of Lords' decision of 29 June 1995 amounted to a breach of the children's right to pursue a remedy in the civil courts under Art 6. The case will now be considered by the European Court of Human Rights. This case was brought under the old rules which required the Commission to give a preliminary view before a case went to the full court. From this year, cases will go direct to the Human Rights court in Strasbourg and the average waiting time of five years and six months it took for a case to come to the court will be reduced to about one-fifth of the time.

The case also illustrates the way in which major areas of apparently domestic law can be dramatically affected by human rights considerations. Another recent example concerns Scotland where the 1998 Act came into force last year. A sign of struggles ahead was given by a decision from Scotland's most senior appeal court. The court decided that the legal basis on which 129 Scottish judges have been appointed means that people they have tried might not have received an 'independent and impartial' trial.

The reason is that the judges, part-time temporary sheriffs, had been appointed by the Lord Advocate, Lord Hardie, who is also Scotland's chief prosecutor. This seems to violate Art 6 of the European Convention on Human Rights (ECHR) which enshrines the right to a fair and impartial trial. The judges could be seen as having their impartiality compromised because the Lord Advocate, a member of Scotland's executive, also had the power to offer them a full-time appointment and a salary of £90,000. Lord Cullen said: 'I consider that there is a real risk that a well informed observer would think that a temporary sheriff might be influenced by his hopes and fears as to his prospective advancement.' Since the decision, all cases involving temporary sheriffs have been suspended.

A society recognising and enforcing human rights law is, in this writer's view, indisputably better for the majority of people than one that does not recognise such rights. Anyone in doubt about that can contact Amnesty International and consider the evidence of what occurs in some of the world's more rigorous regimes. Some countries' leaders, however, take the view that legal human rights are an impediment to stable society and economic prosperity. Nonetheless, even in their most positive setting, human rights in themselves are not the universal panacea they are sometimes held out to be.

Legally enforceable human rights exclude any guarantee of social or economic benefits, and many people in ECHR signatory countries end up in such a wretched condition that all notions of legal rights are remote and irrelevant to their lives. For example, several charity organisations now estimate that there are over 200,000 young homeless people in the UK. It is eminently possible that none of these people sleeping on the streets or drifting through society has any valid legal claim that their human rights, as expressed in the ECHR has been violated. Thus, however good they are at improving life for one segment of the population (albeit perhaps a large segment), they are useless at protecting the interests of other sections of the community. Consider another case, one in which a child suffering from leukaemia was deprived of possibly life saving treatment because the local health authority had calculated that the treatment would not be financially justified in view of a low success rate for the treatment. Such a decision deprives a person of the chance of life. Article 2 of the ECHR guarantees the right 'to the legal protection of life' but there would be no legal basis for declaring a health authority to have violated Art 2 even if treatment was deliberately refused on the basis of cold cost benefit calculation.

In the view of the 19th century legal writer Jeremy Bentham, 'natural' rights were simple nonsense and 'natural and imprescriptible rights' (that is, inalienable rights) were rhetorical nonsense. He called them 'nonsense upon stilts' (see Waldron, J (ed), *Nonsense upon Stilts*, 1987, Methuen, p 53). Beneficiaries of human rights law will clearly reject this cynical view but it might well re-surface if ever an expected right is nullified by political fudge.

New era of publicly funded law

Over 5,000 contracts have now been awarded to law firms and advice agencies in the first key stage of the reforms which will eventually see the almost complete replacement of the legal aid system as it was previously known.

From 1 January 2000, only contract holders have been allowed to provide publicly funded advice and assistance, and only providers with proven expertise and experience will be able to hold such contracts.

The Legal Aid Board has awarded around 5,000 general civil contracts to solicitors' firms and a further 330 to not-for-profit agencies (such as Citizens' Advice Bureaux) for civil advice and assistance work (the old Green Form scheme).

The government has argued that these contracting arrangements will improve the quality of legal services and achieve two other key objectives: control costs and target priority needs.

The contracting system sets a range of controls, such as specifying the number of new advice and assistance cases a solicitor can undertake in a year, although a flexible approach is being adopted so the number of cases could be increased if demand warranted. The Legal Aid Board will be retaining a reserve fund for such cases. By the same token, the number of cases funded could be reduced if a firm's average case costs are exceeding their budget terms. Further contracts for other types of legal assistance – such as legal representation in civil cases and criminal legal aid will be phased in until everything covered by the current legal aid fund will be subject to contracting from April 2001.

The Legal Services Commission (LSC) will replace the Legal Aid Board in April 2000, which is also the date for the launch of the Community Legal Service. The LSC and its Regional Committees will establish priorities (in many respects locally set) for publicly funded legal advice and assistance. From April, ordinary personal injury claims will not normally be publicly funded as the government believes that such cases are best conducted by way of conditional fee (no-win, no-fee) agreements. The quality of such agreements has, however, been called into question. Michael Gould, a solicitor and legal academic, wrote to *The Times* on this issue last year ((1999) *The Times*, 23 November). He noted:

> I was recently asked for advice by a student on behalf of a friend who was being asked to enter into [a no-win, no-fee] agreement. The friend had been injured in an accident while a passenger in a car. The agreement provided for a charging rate of £165 per hour, whatever level of fee earner handled the case, and that the client would be responsible for payment of the fees if he ended the agreement early. It authorised the solicitors to retain one quarter of the damages recovered.

> The implications of these provisions appeared to me to be that if the client became dissatisfied with the way the office cleaner was handling his claim and took his business elsewhere he would pay at the rate referred to above. If he waited until damages were recovered (as they almost inevitably would be in these circumstances), he would hand over a quarter of his damages to his solicitors in addition to the costs they would recover from the defendant.

> If this sort of arrangement is common (and that is difficult to tell), then it is clear that many clients are clearly not getting a fair deal.

The cost of court delay

Delay and adjournments are an enormous cause of frustration to citizens who have to use the courts. A new report from the National Audit Office (Lord Chancellor's Department, Crown Prosecution Service, Home Office, *Criminal Justice: Working Together*, HC 29 1999/2000, 1 December 1999, ISBN: 0105566179 Price: £16.70) reveals some alarming facts about the extent of this problem.

It costs about £9 billion each year to process some two million defendants through the criminal courts. Efficient and effective progression of cases depends on the police, the Crown Prosecution Service, the courts and other agencies working closely with each other as well as with victims, defendants, witnesses and others.

The report contains 63 recommendations designed to deepen collaboration and improve performance.

The report's key findings, conclusions and recommendations include the following:

- The limited information currently collected suggests there are considerable variations in the time taken locally to progress cases through the magistrates' courts. For the more serious cases, it takes between 60 and 100 days on average to complete a case depending on the local area in which the case is heard.

- The number and length of adjournments are key factors in the time taken to complete a case, but there is no single national source of data on the reasons for adjournments.

- National Audit Office survey data suggest that nearly three quarters of a million magistrates' court hearings each year have to be adjourned because of errors or omissions on the part of one or more of the participants, including defence. They may result in wasted expenditure of over £40 million each year and an average additional delay of more than two weeks in the progress of each case. Ineffective trials in the Crown Court may result in waste of an estimated £15 million each year.

Clearly, there is much room here for organisational improvement.

Impartial judges

In what circumstances should a judge excuse him or herself from presiding in a case because of a possible partiality? The law in this area was, until recently, quite meagre. Judges related to parties before them, or judges with a pecuniary interest in one side of a case were clearly required to stand down. Beyond that, however, in the areas of social interest, things were much less clear. In 1999, the House of Lords set aside one of its earlier decisions (in the *General Pinochet* case) on the grounds that one of the Lords who delivered an opinion in the first case had a connection with Amnesty International – a body which had issued an opinion on the case (see (1999) 27 SLR 28).

Following a number of other cases in which lawyers sought to challenge a judgment on the grounds that, through a social interest or remote financial connection, the judge was potentially biased, the Court of Appeal has now given authoritative guidance on this area. The extraordinary judgment was delivered by Lord Bingham of Cornhill, Lord Chief Justice, Lord Woolf, Master of the Rolls and Sir Richard Scott, Vice Chancellor.

Locabail (UK) Ltd v Bayfield Properties Ltd and Another (1999) The Times, 17 November, CA

In respect of five decisions in which the judge's impartiality was questioned, the Court of Appeal ruled on general principles as follows:

(1) A judge who allowed his judicial decision to be influenced by partiality or prejudice deprived a litigant of the right to a fair trial by an impartial tribunal and violated a most fundamental principle on which the administration of justice rested.

(2) The most effective protection of his right was, in practice, afforded by disqualification and setting aside a decision where real danger of bias was established. Every such case depended on its particular facts, real doubt being

resolved in favour of disqualification. It would, however, be as wrong for a judge to accede to a tenuous objection as it would be for him to ignore one of substance.

(3) In determination of their rights and liabilities, civil or criminal, everyone was entitled to a fair hearing by an impartial tribunal. That right, guaranteed by the European Convention for the Protection of Human Rights and Fundamental Freedoms (1953, Cmd 8969), was properly described as fundamental.

The reason was obvious. The Court of Appeal ruled that all legal arbiters were bound to apply the law as they understood it to the facts of individual cases as they found them without fear or favour, affection or ill will: that is, without partiality or prejudice.

Any judge (that term embracing every judicial decision maker whether judge, lay justice or juror) who allowed any judicial decision to be influenced by partiality or prejudice deprived the litigant of his important right and violated one of the most fundamental principles underlying the administration of justice.

There was one situation where, on proof of the requisite facts, the existence of bias was effectively presumed and in such cases it gave rise to automatic disqualification: namely, where the judge was shown to have an interest in the outcome of the case which he was to decide or had decided: see *Dimes v Proprietors of the Grand Junction Canal* ((1852) 3 HL Cas 759); *R v Rand* ((1866) LR 1 QB 230); and *R v Camborne Justices ex p Pearce* ((1955) 1 QB 41).

In any case where the judge's interest was said to derive from the interest of a spouse, partner, or other family member, the link had to be so close and direct as to render the interest of that other person for all practical purposes indistinguishable from an interest of the judge.

The automatic disqualification rule until recently, had widely, if wrongly, been thought to apply only in cases of a judge's pecuniary or proprietary interest in the outcome of the litigation. However, *R v Bow Street Metropolitan Stipendiary Magistrate ex p Pinochet Ugarte (No 2)* ((1999) *The Times*, 18 January; [1999] 2 WLR 272, pp 283, 284 and 293) made it plain that the rule extended to a limited class of non-financial interests, such as an interest in the subject matter in issue arising from the judge's promotion of some particular cause.

The law was settled in England and Wales by the House of Lords in *R v Gough* ([1993] AC 658, pp 668, 670) and, in consequence, the relevant test was whether there was in relation to any given judge a real danger or possibility of bias.

When applying the real danger test, it would often be appropriate to inquire whether the judge knew of the matter relied on as appearing to undermine his impartiality. If it were shown that he did not, the danger of its having influenced his judgement was eliminated and the appearance of possible bias dispelled.

It was for the reviewing court, not the judge concerned, to assess the risk that some illegitimate extraneous consideration might have influenced his decision. The position of solicitors was somewhat different, for a solicitor who was a partner in a firm of solicitors was legally responsible for the professional acts of his partners and did, as a partner, owe a duty to clients of the firm for whom he personally might never had acted and of whose affairs he personally might know nothing.

While it was vital to safeguard the integrity of court proceedings, it was also important to ensure that the rules were not applied in such a way as to inhibit the increasingly valuable contribution which solicitors were making to the discharge of judicial functions.

Problems were more likely to arise where a solicitor was sitting in a part time capacity, and in civil rather than criminal proceedings. But, such problems could usually be overcome if, before embarking on the trial of any assigned civil case the solicitor conducted a careful 'conflict search' within his firm, even though such a search, however careful, was unlikely to be omission proof.

While it would be dangerous and futile to attempt to define or list factors which might or might not give rise to a real danger of bias, since everything would depend on the particular facts, the court could not conceive of circumstances in which an objection could be soundly based on the religion, ethnic or national origin, gender, age, class, means or sexual orientation of the judge.

Nor, at any rate ordinarily, could an objection be soundly based on his social or educational or service or employment background or history, nor that of any member of his family; nor previous political associations, membership of social, sporting or charitable bodies; nor Masonic associations; nor previous judicial decisions; nor extra-curricular utterances, whether in textbooks, lectures, speeches, articles, interviews, reports, responses to consultation papers; nor previous receipt of instructions to act for or against any party, solicitor or advocate engaged in a case before him; nor membership of the same Inn, circuit, local Law Society or chambers.

By contrast, a real danger of bias might well be thought to arise if there were personal friendship or animosity between the judge and any member of the public involved in the case; or if the judge were closely acquainted with any such member of the public, particularly if that individual's credibility could be significant in the decision of the case; or if, in a case where the credibility of any individual were an issue to be decided by the judge, he had in a previous case rejected that person's evidence in such outspoken terms as to throw doubt on his ability to approach such a person's evidence with an open mind on any later occasion.

Comment

In one way, the Court of Appeal was bound to come to this conclusion. Had it ruled that membership of certain societies, or a particular social background, or the previous political associations of a trial judge were grounds for appeal, two consequences would follow. First, there would be a rapid expansion of the use by law firms of special units that monitor and keep files on all aspects of judges' lives. Secondly, there would be a proliferation of appeals in all departments of the court structure at the very time when there is such a concerted effort to reduce the backlog of appeals.

What this decision leaves us with is a question of profound jurisprudential importance: how far can judges judge in an entirely neutral and socially-detached manner? Under the new Court of Appeal guidelines, a judge who was a keen hunter and member of the pro-hunting Countryside Alliance would not be required to stand down from presiding in a case involving anti-hunt protesters. It is difficult, however, to see a practicable alternative way to operate a judiciary.

In his judgment in *Locabail*, Lord Bingham of Cornhill C.J stated that...

When applying the test of real danger or possibility (as opposed to the test of automatic disqualification under the *Dimes* case, 3 HL Cas 759 and *Ex parte Pinochet (No 2)* [2000] 1 AC 119) it will very often be appropriate to inquire whether the judge knew of the matter relied on as appearing to undermine his impartiality, because if it is shown that he did not know of it the danger of its having influenced his judgment is eliminated and the appearance of possible bias is dispelled ... In any case giving rise to automatic disqualification on the authority of the *Dimes* case, 3 HL Cas 759 and *Ex parte Pinochet (No. 2)* [2000] 1 AC 119, the judge should recuse himself from the case before any objection is raised ...

It would be dangerous and futile to attempt to define or list the factors which may or may not give rise to a real danger of bias. Everything will depend on the facts, which may include the nature of the issue to be decided. We cannot, however, conceive of circumstances in which an objection could be soundly based on the religion, ethnic or national origin, gender, age, class, means or sexual orientation of the judge. Nor, at any rate ordinarily, could an objection be soundly based on the judge's social or educational or service or employment background or history, nor that of any member of the judge's family; or previous political associations; or membership of social or sporting or charitable bodies; or Masonic associations; or previous judicial decisions; or extra-curricular utterances (whether in textbooks, lectures, speeches, articles, interviews, reports or responses to consultation papers); or previous receipt of instructions to act for or against any party, solicitor or advocate engaged in a case before him; or membership of the same Inn, circuit, local Law Society or chambers ... By contrast, a real danger of bias might well be thought to arise if there were personal friendship or animosity between the judge and any member of the public involved in the case; or if the judge were closely acquainted with any member of the public involved in the case, particularly if the credibility of that individual could be significant in the decision of the case; or if, in a case where the credibility of any individual were an issue to be decided by the judge, he had in a previous case rejected the evidence of that person in such outspoken terms as to throw doubt on his ability to approach such person's evidence with an open mind on any later occasion; or if on any question at issue in the proceedings before him the judge had expressed views, particularly in the course of the hearing, in such extreme and unbalanced terms as to throw doubt on his ability to try the issue with an objective judicial mind (see *Vakauta v Kelly* (1989) 167 CLR 568); or if, for any other reason, there were real ground for doubting the ability of the judge to ignore extraneous considerations, prejudices and predilections and bring an objective judgment to bear on the issues before him. The mere fact that a judge, earlier in the same case or in a previous case, had commented adversely on a party or witness, or found the evidence of a party or witness to be unreliable, would not without more found a sustainable objection. In most cases, we think, the answer, one way or the other, will be obvious. But if in any case there is real ground for doubt, that doubt should be resolved in favour of recusal. We repeat: every application must be decided on the facts and circumstances of the individual case. The greater the passage of time between the event relied on as showing a danger of bias and the case in which the objection is raised, the weaker (other things being equal) the objection will be.

Although following the precedent established in *R v Gough*, the Appeal Court in *Locabail* recognised that it was not totally in accord with the jurisprudence of the European Court of Justice. Once the Human Rights Act 1998 came into force in October 2000 it was open to and, indeed, required of the court to consider and refine the test in *Gough* in the light of the ECtHR's decisions.

Director General of Fair Trading v Proprietary Association of Great Britain [2000] 1 WLR 700

Lord Phillips MR:

The law in relation to bias

Article 6 of the European Convention on Human Rights provides:

Right to a fair trial

In the determination of his civil rights and obligations or of any criminal charge against him, everyone is entitled to a fair and public hearing within a reasonable time by an independent and impartial tribunal established by law ...

Since October 2, 2000 English courts have been obliged under the Human Rights Act 1998 to give effect to the right to a fair trial as embodied in Article 6. The requirement that the tribunal should be independent and impartial is one that has long been recognised by English common law. An appellate or reviewing court will set aside a decision affected by bias. The precise test to be applied when determining whether a decision should be set aside on account of bias has, however, given rise to difficulty, reflected in judicial formulations that have appeared in conflict. The House of Lords in *R v Gough* [1993] AC 646 attempted to resolve that conflict. In *Locabail (UK) Ltd v Bayfield Properties Ltd* [2000] QB 451 at 476 this court observed that the test in *Gough* had not commanded universal approval outside this jurisdiction and that Scotland and some Commonwealth countries preferred an alternative test which might be 'more clearly in harmony with the jurisprudence of the European Court of Human Rights'. Since October 2 the English courts have been required to take that jurisprudence into account. This then is an occasion to review *Gough* to see whether the test it lays down is, indeed, in conflict with Strasbourg jurisprudence ...

Bias is an attitude of mind which prevents the judge from making an objective determination of the issues that he has to resolve. A judge may be biased because he has reason to prefer one outcome of the case to another. He may be biased because he has reason to favour one party rather than another. He may be biased not in favour of one outcome of the dispute but because of a prejudice in favour of or against a particular witness which prevents an impartial assessment of the evidence of that witness. Bias can come in many forms. It may consist of irrational prejudice or it may arise from particular circumstances which, for logical reasons, predispose a Judge towards a particular view of the evidence or issues before him.

The decided cases draw a distinction between 'actual bias' and 'apparent bias'. The phrase 'actual bias' has not been used with great precision and has been applied to the situation

(i) where a judge has been influenced by partiality or prejudice in reaching his decision and

(ii) where it has been demonstrated that a judge is actually prejudiced in favour of or against a party.

'Apparent bias' describes the situation where circumstances exist which give rise to a reasonable apprehension that the judge may have been, or may be, biased.

Findings of actual bias on the part of a judge are rare. The more usual issue is whether, having regard to all the material circumstances, a case of apparent bias is made out. We do not propose to refer to more than a few of the many cases that were reviewed in *Gough* and *Locabail*. We believe that two critical and interrelated questions are raised by the authorities, and we propose to focus on the cases which exemplify those questions. The questions are:

(i) Must the reasonable apprehension of bias be that of the reviewing Court itself, or that which the reviewing Court would attribute to an informed onlooker?

(ii) What are the circumstances that fall to be taken into account when applying the test of bias and how are those circumstances to be determined? ...

After examining cases decided by the ECtHR, Lord Phillips continued:

We would summarise the principles to be derived from this line of cases as follows:

(1) If a judge is shown to have been influenced by actual bias, his decision must be set aside.

(2) Where actual bias has not been established the personal impartiality of the judge is to be presumed.

(3) The court then has to decide whether, on an objective appraisal, the material facts give rise to a legitimate fear that the judge might not have been impartial. If they do the decision of the judge must be set aside.

(4) The material facts are not limited to those which were apparent to the applicant. They are those which are ascertained upon investigation by the court.

An important consideration in making an objective appraisal of the facts is the desirability that the public should remain confident in the administration of justice.

This approach comes close to that in *Gough*. The difference is that when the Strasbourg court considers whether the material circumstances give rise to a reasonable apprehension of bias, it makes it plain that it is applying an objective test to the circumstances, not passing judgment on the likelihood that the particular tribunal under review was in fact biased.

When the Strasbourg jurisprudence is taken into account, we believe that a modest adjustment of the test in *Gough* is called for, which makes it plain that it is, in effect, no different from the test applied in most of the Commonwealth and in Scotland. The court must first ascertain all the circumstances which have a bearing on the suggestion that the judge was biased. It must then ask whether those circumstances would lead a fair-minded and informed observer to conclude that there was a real possibility, or a real danger, the two being the same, that the tribunal was biased.

The material circumstances will include any explanation given by the judge under review as to his knowledge or appreciation of those circumstances. Where that explanation is accepted by the applicant for review it can be treated as accurate. Where it is not accepted, it becomes one further matter to be considered from the viewpoint of the fair-minded observer. The court does not have to rule whether the explanation should be accepted or rejected. Rather it has to decide whether or not the fair-minded observer would consider that there was a real danger of bias notwithstanding the explanation advanced. Thus in Gough, had the truth of the juror's explanation not been accepted by the defendant, the Court of Appeal would correctly have approached the question of bias on the premise that the fair-minded onlooker would not necessarily find the juror's explanation credible ...

THE CHANGING ROLE OF JUDGES

This content of this book has changed much since its first edition, reflecting the considerable, perhaps even revolutionary, changes that have taken place in the legal system it attempts to examine. Of these changes the most significant are the introduction of the new Civil Procedure Rules following the Woolf report on the Civil Justice System and the introduction of the ECHR into the United Kingdom constitution in the form of the Human Rights Act 1998. Both of these measures will require significant changes in the role of judges not just within the legal system itself, but also within the wider social context. Canada introduced a rights based constitution some time ago and in the final article, a Canadian judge, Justice McLachlin, considers the consequences of such a change for the role of judges. It is surely unarguable that her conclusions will not apply equally within the contemporary United Kingdom.

Beverley McLachlin, 'The role of judges in modern commonwealth society' (1994) 10 LQR

We all possess a certain image of a judge. He is old, male, and wears pin-striped trousers. He decides only what is necessary, says only what is necessary, and on no account ever talks to the press. He is respected and revered. His word is, literally and figuratively, the law, eternal, majestic. Even those of us who do not fit naturally into the traditional image tend to grow into it. The truth cannot be avoided. We judges like the old image. We cling to it. And why not? It brings comfort, that of knowing one is right, at least pending the verdict of the Court of Appeal, although most of us have learned to rationalise that as well. It brings security, the security of knowing what to do and when to do it. And it brings gratification, the gratification of knowing we are important and appreciated. As Lord Hewart is said to have put it to the guests at the Lord Mayor of London's banquet in 1936:

His Majesty's judges are satisfied with the almost universal admiration in which they are held.

In similar vein Lord Devlin suggested in 1979 that:

The English judiciary is popularly treated as a national institution ... and tends to be admired to excess.

In similar vein also can be cited the story of Sir George Jessel MR, who upon learning that Lord Selborne LC proposed to begin an address to the Queen with the words 'We, Your Majesty's judges, conscious as we are of our manifold defects,' is said to have objected strongly, saying 'I am not conscious of manifold defects, and if I were I should not be fit to sit on the bench.'

But wait a minute. What is this I'm hearing? What is this I'm reading? Is this the world I thought I knew? Not too long ago I picked up a copy of *The Spectator*, and was shocked to stumble on an article entitled 'The Judge is a Bastard', followed closely by a second entitled 'The Era of the Blabbing Judge'. In my own country, Canada, journalists have declared open season on judges. Not a week goes by, it seems, that one does not read some commentary critical of the judiciary. And the criticism is not confined to the journalists. While for the most part they prove unsubstantiated, public complaints about the judiciary are on the increase. This is not the world we judges thought we knew, comfortable and secure. What, we are driven to ask, is happening?

The prolific English lawyer and writer, John Mortimer, speaks of 'a general decrease in the awe and wonder with which the population looks at its established institutions', an attitude from which the courts are not exempted. He puts it this way:

> Many years ago, when I first took up the law, proceedings in court were shrouded in myth. In those days the country at large believed that trials invariably came to the right conclusion, that police officers told nothing but the truth, and that judges were miraculously conceived and were born unencumbered with the usual human luggage of preconceived ideas, kneejerk reactions, prejudice, failures of the imagination, inability to admit mistakes or pure bloody-mindedness. These myths have now, no doubt to the regret of many members of the legal profession, gone the way of witchcraft and the Flat Earth Society. Trials have, despite energetic whitewashing by appeal tribunals, been shown to have gone horribly wrong. Police evidence is now taken by juries with large helpings of salt. And the pronouncements of some judges, before and since retirement, have gone beyond endearing eccentricity to give some cause for alarm.

We arrive, then, at an appropriate paradox. Judges in the Commonwealth are more and more the subjects of critical scrutiny. But at the same time the truth is that the public has never held the judiciary in higher esteem. This is demonstrated by the fact that it turns to the judiciary more and more for the resolution of its problems ...

I believe that the combination of these two phenomena – increasing critical scrutiny of judges and increasingly reliance on judges to sort out society's problems – is not, on closer scrutiny, a paradox at all, but the other result of a radical alteration in the public perception of the role of judges in modern Commonwealth society. The old role of the judge as a symbol of authority, sometimes scrutable, sometimes not, whose edicts from on high must be uncritically accepted as just and fitting, has gone the way that absolutist-classist government went in the nineteenth century. The judges in modern society are not potentates: they are rather servants, servants of the people in the highest and most honourable sense of that term. The judge has a task, a more important task than ever before. It is precisely because of the importance of this task that the judge is expected to perform it well and efficiently, to be responsive and responsible.

This new view of the judge involves changes on every front. Changes in the task and duties of the judge. Changes in the way they discharge those duties. Changes in the process through which the duties are discharged: the administration of justice. Changes in the terms of office of judges: how they get their jobs and how they are disciplined and removed. And finally, changes in the way judges relate to the public. I would like to discuss each of these areas of change in a little more detail.

Changes in the work of judges

There was a time, not so long ago, when the main job of judges was to resolve disputes. The whole common law is predicated on this notion. Two parties find themselves in a disagreement. They cannot resolve it. So they go to a judge for a decision. Parliament made the laws. The judge applied them to the case. That was the entire story, or almost.

Resolving disputes is still the primary and most fundamental task of the judiciary. But for some time now, it has been recognised that the matter is not so simple. In the course of resolving disputes, common law judges interpreted and inevitably, incrementally, with the aid of the doctrine of precedent or *stare decisis*, changed the law. The common law thus came to recognise that while dispute resolution was the primary task of the judge, the judge played a secondary role of lawmaker, or at least, law-developer. In the latter part of the twentieth century, the lawmaking role of the judge in Commonwealth countries has dramatically expanded. Judicial lawmaking is no longer always confined to small, incremental changes. Increasingly, it is invading the domain of social policy, formerly the exclusive right of Parliament and the legislatures.

This expansion can be attributed to a number of factors. One is the trend to the constitutionalisation of rights. The new perspective of social policy which confronts modern courts is fuelled in large part by a heightened collective awareness of human rights. It is this feature, perhaps more than any other, which characterises legal thinking as we approach the twenty-first century. In Canada, a series of human rights statutes has culminated in a constitutional bill of rights, the Charter. In the European Community, similar documents shape policy for hundreds of millions of people. And the trend continues. Israel, for example, not in the Commonwealth but whose legal system, like ours, is grounded in the British tradition, is working toward passage of a comprehensive Basic Law of fundamental rights and freedoms. This trend has its effect even in countries which themselves do not possess a constitutional bill of rights, like England and Australia. Wherever we live, the legal dialogue increasingly centres on individual rights and liberties: the political liberties of democratic participation; liberty of religion and expression; the guarantee of equality regardless of gender, race or age. The trend to the constitutionalisation of human rights increasingly implicates the courts in a broad range of social policy issues. The bills of rights guarantee to each person certain fundamental rights. When legislation or governmental action offend these guaranteed rights, people go to the courts for a ruling that the law or conduct is unconstitutional. And the courts, which were formerly compelled to accept Parliament's decree as the last word, now are obliged, if it violates the constitutional code of rights, to declare the law or action illegal. The nature of these guarantees, most particularly guarantees of equality, freedom of speech and freedom of religion, is such that the courts are, whether they like it or not, required to give judgements on matters of social policy.

Another factor in the new social policy role of judges cited by scholars is the perceived inability or unwillingness of legislative bodies to deal with pressing social issues. Much has been written of this in the United States, where the division of powers between the legislative bodies and the executive has at times led to legislative paralysis. In Canada, we have encountered the same problem: some issues, like abortion and euthanasia, are too controversial for Parliament to take on. The result has been that the courts are asked to resolve these issues. Whatever the reasons, it seems clear that, as Lamer CJ recently put it, the agenda of courts in the years to come is going to take on an increasingly social face. Gone are the days when judges could spend their days musing on the principles of contract, tort and criminal law. Their field includes these, but much more as well.

The necessary concomitant of the increasing insistence on human rights and the new social face of the law is an independent judiciary, ready and able to review a wide range of government action. While the legislative and executive branches of government have an important role to play in supporting human rights, the difficult burden of interpreting the rights and maintaining them even in the face of governmental intransigence if need be rests on the shoulders of the courts.

The new task which judges have been assigned is not easy. There is a very real question whether courts, which lack the resources for gathering and collating information and opinion available to the legislatures, are the best institutions to decide complex social policy questions. But that question is increasingly moot ... In the final analysis, courts charged with responsibility for deciding difficult social questions must acquire, to quote Lamer CJ yet again, 'a whole new range of skills.' We must learn to deal intelligently with questions of social policy, to identify the kinds of social fact evidence and expert evidence which the particular problem requires, and to use it wisely. All this, of course, must be premised on 'a deep understanding of the most fundamental principles of the law; and understanding which is broad enough to relate to a wide variety of disciplines.'

Changes in the way judges discharge their duties

The changing role of judges, and in particular their greater involvement with social policy, will have an important effect on the way judges work. The simple fact is that judicial decisions on such questions matter more, and to more people. A contract action matters, but mainly to the parties involved. A criminal conviction has broader scope, particularly where the crime is one affecting the security of the public, but still, the person mainly interested is likely to be the accused. Decisions on social policy issues may affect thousands if not millions of people who may have had nothing to do with the lawsuit. This results in an expectation, indeed a demand, from the public as a whole or from important interest groups within the public, that the judge has properly considered all the factors relevant to his decision and its consequences. It leads to the attitude of critical scrutiny of the judiciary mentioned earlier.

The nature of the questions they decide, and the public expectation that they will decide them fairly and well, place new demands on judges. It no longer suffices to be a competent legal scholar and a fair arbiter. To perform their modern role well, judges must be sensitive to a broad range of social concerns. They must possess a keen appreciation of the importance of individual and group interests and rights. And they must be in touch with the society in which they work, understanding its values and its tensions. The ivory tower no longer suffices as the residence of choice for judges. The new role of judges in social policy also demands new efforts of objectivity. Often the judge will have strong personal views on the questions which a judge is asked to decide: questions like abortion, capital punishment or euthanasia. But the task of judging is not accomplished simply by plugging one's personal views into the legal equation. The judge must strive for objectivity. This requires an act of imagination. And it requires an attitude of 'active humility', which enables the judge to set aside preconceptions and prejudices and look at the issue afresh in the light of the evidence and submissions. The judge must seek to see and appreciate the point of view of each of the protagonists. She must struggle to enunciate the values at issue. Then she must attempt to strike the balance between the conflicting values which most closely conforms to justice as society, taken as a whole, sees it. It is impossible to eliminate the judge's personal views. But by a conscious act of considering the other side of the matter, the judge can attain a level of detachment which enables him or her to make decisions which are in the broader interests of society. In the end, the judge can know no other master than the law, in its most objective sense. As Sir Robert Megarry put it:

> The judge's duty is one of obedience to the law and to his judicial conscience. He must do not what he wants to do but what he ought to do.

Changes in the process: the administration of justice

The new demands on judges in the modern Commonwealth will bring changes in the processes by which cases are heard and judicial decisions are rendered. Not only is the scope of the issues which courts are being asked to decide expanding rapidly, but more and more people are coming to court. Moreover, they are demanding justice which is not only right, but justice which is prompt and efficient.

This places great pressure on the process. Finding dates for trials and appeals is becoming more difficult all over the world. There never seem to be enough judges. And after a case is heard, courts sometimes find themselves ill-equipped, in terms of staff and recourses, to produce the judgement in a prompt and efficient manner ...

Terms of office: appointment, discipline and removal of judges

As a consequence of their changing role and the increasing importance of the matters which they decide, the appointment and governance of judges is coming under increasing scrutiny. The appointment of judges has always been of great interest to lawyers, who enjoy or suffer directly, as the case may be, the effects of a good or bad judicial appointment. But lately, the public has become involved in the debate. The appointment of judges has become a matter of some controversy in Canada. This applies particularly to appointments to the highest court, the Supreme Court of Canada. The concern arises from the fact that the judges of this court are called upon to decide matters of great importance, not only to the litigants, but to the country as a whole. Democratic government, it is said, requires at a minimum that the appointment of judges deciding these questions be subject to review by a commission or Parliamentary committee. Such a process, it is suggested, would ensure that the judges appointed are not only competent legal scholars, but that they are sensitive to the values and tensions at work in society. Additionally, it is widely accepted that the court should be representative of a cross-section of Canadian society. This means that it should include women and people from varied social and ethnic backgrounds. It is no longer acceptable to have a bench composed entirely of ageing white males.

The same sorts of pressure may in the future lead to changes in judicial discipline and removal. We in Canada have established a system in which complaints are reviewed by a committee of judges under the aegis of the Canadian Judicial Council. If the matter is found to warrant further consideration, it may be referred to Council and ultimately to a hearing which has the power to recommend impeachment proceedings. Some people think the public should be represented in the process. Everyone agrees that we must ensure that the judges who sit on the courts of the modern Commonwealth must be persons of the highest competence and integrity. Nothing less will do, given the gravity of their role. On the methods by which this goal may be attained, there is less unanimity. For example, Parliamentary hearings on nominations to the Supreme Court, akin to the Senate hearings on nominations to the Supreme Court of the United States, risk the politicisation of the appointment process, something which has largely been avoided in Canada up till now, and, some suggest, might deter qualified candidates who prize their privacy from standing for office. At the same time, it is questionable if the well-rehearsed questions and answers really shed much light on the suitability of the candidate to sit as a judge. Another possibility is a commission system, such as that used in Israel. The commission, made up of nominees from the legislature, the bar, and the judiciary selects new judges. This has the advantage of allowing a wide spectrum of input as well as depoliticising the process. Whatever the process chosen, one thing seems clear. The demand for some democratisation of the judicial appointment process and some share in the judicial disciplinary process is unlikely to abate in the near future. The task of finding mechanisms which will accomplish this end while preserving the independence of the judiciary and the ability to attract and maintain the best candidates is not an easy one.

The relationship of judges to the public

The new role of judges in modern Commonwealth society will change the traditional relationship between judges and the public. Judges have traditionally held themselves aloof from the public. They have lived in quiet isolation. They have deliberately severed ties with old friends and acquaintances, the better to assure their independence. Save for exceptional circumstances, they have refused to talk to the press. And they have generally declined to speak out in public on anything other than the dull business of the legal process, and then only with great circumspection.

In the modern era, judges face new expectations. The public that pays the judges and takes its cases before them, increasingly takes the view that it is entitled to know who these people are. The result is a debate in my country on the subject of judges speaking in public. It is accepted by all that judges should not comment on matters which may come before them. There also seems to be general acceptance that it wold be unseemly for a judge to respond publicly to criticism. But there the consensus stops. Some judges, particularly Chief Justices responsible for the administration of the courts, find it necessary from time to time to speak out on matters of concern to the justice system. Others would advocate freedom to speak out even where there is no necessity, arguing that there is much to gain from improving public understanding of the task judges face and how they go about it, and little danger, provided the judge stays away from controversial litigable issues. Still others think it unwise to speak other than through their judgements, save for special occasions, as when a judge is newly appointed or elevated. Different judges situate themselves in different places on the spectrum of opinion on the subject of judges pronouncing in public. What seems clear is that wherever a judge places himself, the entire spectrum has shifted significantly toward some degree of intercourse between the judiciary and the public as a consequence of the new and more important role courts play in our society.

Conclusion

Judging is not what it used to be. Judges are more important now: judges are more criticised. And judges face more difficult tasks than they ever have before faced in the history of the Commonwealth. If judges are to meet these challenges they must be educated, competent and engaged. They must be prepared to work hard. But all this will be to little avail if the one quality which has always been required of a judge, independence, is forgotten. In discharging its new role, the modern judiciary must fall back on the source of strength it has drawn upon over the centuries – its institutional and individual independence. It is this independence, coupled with integrity, which has made the judiciary the important institution that it is. And on the broader political plain, it is this independence that guarantees respect for human rights and the rule of law in the countries which we ask judges to serve, and hence the advancement of all our peoples. The task facing judges in the modern Commonwealth is not an easy one. But it is one of critical importance. If we fail, the rule of law will fail. It is as simple as that.

INDEX